Server Architectures

Server Architectures
Multiprocessors, Clusters, Parallel Systems, Web Servers, and Storage Solutions

René J. Chevance

ELSEVIER
DIGITAL
PRESS

Amsterdam · Boston · Heidelberg · London · New York · Oxford
Paris · San Diego· San Francisco · Singapore · Sydney · Tokyo

Elsevier Digital Press
30 Corporate Drive, Suite 400, Burlington, MA 01803, USA
Linacre House, Jordan Hill, Oxford OX2 8DP, UK

∞ Recognizing the importance of preserving what has been written, Elsevier prints its books on acid-free paper whenever possible.

Library of Congress Cataloging-in-Publication Data
Application submitted.

British Library Cataloguing-in-Publication Data
A catalogue record for this book is available from the British Library.

ISBN: 1-55558-333-4

For information on all Elsevier Digital Press publications
visit our Web site at www.books.elsevier.com

For this work which treats industrial products and technological projects, many sources of information were used. These sources of information are referred at the time of their use. It is obvious that all the inaccuracies or omissions are the fact of the author and do not engage the companies, organizations or people having produced information being used as source. The comments and opinions presented in this work engage only the author.

Trademarks cited herein are the property of their respective owners.

04 05 06 07 08 09   10 9 8 7 6 5 4 3 2 1

Printed in the United States of America

To Josiane, Cyrille and Maxime

Acknowledgements

Creating a book and preparing it for publication is, for its author, a rather private effort but one which is fed and nourished through many discussions and exchanges of opinion. I must therefore start by thanking my colleagues at Bull along with the industry representatives and researchers with all of whom I have had many fruitful exchanges and discussions.

But I must go further and single out some colleagues for special thanks: Jean Papadopoulo, Jean-Jacques Pairault, Michel Pontacq and Pierre Roux of Bull for their comments and suggestions for the preliminary version; Lazzaro Pejsachowicz for his help with the section on security; my collegaues at CNAM—and in particular Jean-Pierre Meinadier, a full professor and Systems Integration Chair there—for the many exchanges and discussions.

I added a new chapter on storage for the English language version, which benefitted greatly from input from Jean Papadopoulo and Michel Pontaq (Bull) and Jacques Péping (StorageAcademy).

Finally, the translation into English was done to my complete satisfaction by Pete Wilson (also ex-Bull), who brought an excellent spirit of cooperation to the task along with his understanding of the subject matter to allow us to bring the work to a successful conclusion. Thank you to Tim Donar who reviewed and performed the technical edits for the American printing.

About the Author

René Chevance has an engineering degree from Conservatoire National des Arts et Métiers (CNAM) and a Doctorat d'Etat Es-Sciences from Université Paris 6.

He joined CII in 1968, a Company which later merged with Groupe Bull. In his role of system architect and later as Chief Scientist, he has initiated a large number of projects.

He has also a wide teaching experience for 20 years at Université Paris 6 (Compiler Construction, Software Engineering) and for more than 10 years, as an Associate Professor, at CNAM (System Architecture and System Integration).

He wrote several papers and a book on server architectures "Serveurs Multiprocesseurs, clusters et architectures parallèles" Eyrolles (Paris april 2000).

He left Groupe Bull in 1999 to become an independent consultant.

He can be reached at rjc@chevance.com or through his Web site www.chevance.com.

Contents

Preface

Objective of the Book

The ambition of this work is to present and compare various options regarding server architecture from two separate points of view: firstly, that of the information technology decision-maker who must choose a solution matching his or her company's business requirements, and secondly, that of the systems architect who finds him- or herself between the rock of changes in hardware and software technologies and the hard place of changing business needs.

This book presents different aspects of server architecture are presented, from databases designed for parallel architectures to high-availability systems, and *en route* touches on often-neglected performance aspects.

A Changing Industry Based on Changing Technology

Technology is constantly evolving, resulting in profound changes to the computer industry. Our discussion of these changes should be interpreted in the context of the time when these words were written (from 2002 through 2004). While we offer glimpses into possible futures, such forward-looking exercises must—to be useful over time—be supported by an ongoing "technology watch," along with critical observation of the changing structure of the industry and its marketplaces.

At Whom is the Book Aimed?

The book is intended to be useful for a number of different people:

- IT managers, decision makers and project leaders who want to better understand the implications of server architecture and to acquire knowledge sufficient to understand the choices made in, and capabilities of, systems offered by various vendors

- Engineers specializing in data processing who need to balance the characteristics of their applications against the capabilities and nature of various architectural choices

- Students interested in data processing, to whom we offer an integrated view of the concepts in server architecture, a view accompanied by discussion about these concepts' effects on the evolution of the data processing industry

- Professionals embarked on technology comparisons or competitive analysis, to whom we offer a historical perspective and some indications of likely future developments

Structure of the book

The book is divided into three major parts:

- The first part concentrates, after a short presentation of the options available in server architecture, on hardware technology, covering processor, memory, magnetic devices, peripherals, and I/O in general. This section concludes with a summary and an initial look at what the future could hold.

- In the second part, we outline the various architectural options for servers, and then comment on and compare them, covering symmetrical multiprocessors, clusters, and parallel machines. Then we cover the architectures of database systems aimed at parallel architectures, followed by a presentation and discussion of solutions to high-availability requirements. Again, we conclude the section with a summary and an initial look at what the future could hold.

- In the third part, we discuss aspects of performance and the selection criteria appropriate for choosing between offerings; in addition, we touch on the concept of total cost of ownership.

We end the book with a final review, reflecting on the issues and possibilities discussed.

Origin of the Book

This book was first published in French by Eyrolles in April 2000. The contents have undergone a complete revision for this first edition in English, with the dual goals of ensuring that the information was up-to-date and extending the book's coverage through the addition of a new chapter on data storage.

Server FAQs

Given the shift to widespread use of Intel microprocessors, is the importance of hardware architecture—once the province of systems manufacturers—tending to decrease?

Standardization at the hardware level, as well as increasing integration of systems functions into standard hardware, reduces the potential value-add of a systems manufacturer. This effect is particularly marked for entry-level and mid-range systems. Microprocessor suppliers—especially Intel, given its market volumes—are in the best position to produce (or to have produced):

- Chipsets (the auxiliary components surrounding the processor)
- Add-in electronic cards aimed at entry-level and mid-range servers
- Complete sets of components for a server platform

In very large volume and therefore at very competitive prices. Further, since these parts can all be designed concurrently in the same advanced technology as the processor itself, microprocessor vendors can bring the collection to market more quickly than anyone else could manage (in the same technology).

These facts sharply reduce the degrees of freedom of any independent systems manufacturer operating in these market segments, in terms of both the economic impact and the time-to-market effects. Such vendors are faced with the following alternatives: either become distributors of platforms supplied by the microprocessor vendor, or continue to develop their own platforms (if their market share is large enough to amortize their development costs). Systems vendors still can profit from adding value to the hardware platforms through provision of systems solutions and associated services.

The high-end server market neatly avoids this dilemma because of its very low volume.

Systems manufacturers, because of their long experience, are well placed to meet the needs of the high-end systems, whether in terms of performance, storage, communications or high availability. As technology advances, the boundary between mid-range and high-end tends to move. As an example, at the time of writing, a four-processor server is a commodity; sometime soon, that role will move to the eight-processor systems. To this technology-based effect we must add one based in economics: the necessary attempt to amortize the R & D costs associated with high-end systems across a market segment that is only a small fraction of the server market. The result of these two effects is consolidation in the server industry.

Given that they are extremely complex to implement, will MPP architectures be confined to scientific and technical markets?

To take advantage of a massively parallel architecture, one must have applications written for it. The cost of developing such applications—or of adapting other applications for MPP use—restricts the number of applications. For applications needing intense numerical computation, companies computed the ROI (Return On Investment) and decided that the investment was worthwhile.

MPP architectures force the development of applications using the message-passing paradigm. For a long time, the major barrier was the lack of interface standards and development environments. Some candidate standards have appeared (such as PVM, MPI, or OpenMP), and there is a steadily-increasing number of applications built on these.

We should note here that the efficiency of such applications is usually dependent on the performance (in particular, the latency) of message-passing (including all relevant hardware and software times). Not unreasonably, the first MPP applications to appear were those that could straightforwardly be decomposed into more or less independent subtasks, which needed only a small number of synchronizations to interwork effectively. Thus, mainly scientific and technical applications (in fields like hydrodynamics, thermo-dynamics, and seismology) were first to appear for MPP.

There is another brake on the flourishing of this class of machine—the lack of low-level standards providing access to the interconnect. This lack means that there is substantial difficulty in adapting higher-level libraries to the various hardware (and interconnect) platforms; effecting such a port requires high technical knowledge and skills, so moving between one manufacturer and another is difficult. Various industry initiatives, such as VIA or Infiniband, could bring sufficient standardization that MPP could spread.

MPP products are challenged in yet another direction: the appearance of peer- to-peer systems, grid computing, and clusters of PCs. A key factor of such solutions is low cost, driving the development of applications that can quickly turn into industry standards. The rise of these approaches could condemn the MPP proper to an early grave.

To finish this discussion, recall that in 1984 Teradata brought to market what were probably the first MPP systems. These systems, deploying Teradata's own proprietary DBMS, were used in decision support, needing the processing of very large volumes of data (several terabytes). With the advent of large clusters and MPP systems from other manufacturers, the major database vendors subsequently produced versions of their software to run on this class of machine.

Are RISC processors dead, killed by Intel?

What drives the market to settle on an architecture is, almost certainly, the availability of applications; IA-32 (Intel Architecture 32-bit, once known as x86) has clearly benefited from this effect since the introduction of the PC. This architecture, because of its complexity, is not positioned to offer the best performance potential; but its extremely large sales volumes allowed Intel to make substantial investments in research and development (R&D), allowing its processors to match the best RISC processors (except for floating point).

Development of IA-32 has not stopped, and RISC processors will have an increasingly difficult time competing with the architecture for entry-level and mid-range systems.

With the new IA-64 architecture, Intel squarely faces RISC machines on their own ground—high performance (both integer and floating point) together with 64-bit addressing. Itanium, the first implementation of this architecture, hardly met expectations in terms of integer performance or availability date. Itanium 2 and its successors are likely to remedy this situation. In looking at the situation, recall that IA-64 performance has two interrelated components: compilers, which must extract and express the internal parallelism in programs; and the performance of the processor itself. HP's contribution, especially for the compiler, is invaluable to Intel, to whom this is a new field.

We should not forget that there is constant progress in IA-32 implementations (and in IA-32 compatibles), a factor that delays the penetration of IA-64, a new architecture lacking the large applications catalogue of IA-32.

Our comment on the Itanium catalogue refers to the IA-64 native catalogue; Intel has provided IA-64 with the ability to execute IA-32 applications, thereby getting Intel the support of the key vendors of applications, databases, middleware, and operating systems—albeit not at the same performance as could be obtained with native Itanium applications.

Because the investment needed to develop new implementations of an architecture keeps growing faster than the market, the tendency will be for the number of RISC architectures to reduce. The survivors will be those with either sufficient market volume, or very strong compatibility reasons. We have already seen a number of RISC architectures fall by the wayside; we can reasonably suppose that just a few years in the future we will see a maximum of two RISC architectures (plus IA-64) surviving. Of course, IA-32 will continue to exist, too.

The real challenge for IA-64 in the area of IA-32 support arises with AMD's introduction of a straightforward extension of IA-32 to 64-bit architecture, allowing a smooth coexistence and migration between the two architectures. This will be particulary interesting to watch in the next few years.

What should we think of manufacturers who claim 99.999% availability for their hardware?

Hardware availability is just one, albeit important, factor in server availability. Over the past few years, hardware availability has increased because of technology improvements. Key factors in this are the increasing level of integration (which reduces the component count necessary to implement a system, as well as the number of connectors needed), improvements in data integrity, and the use of formal methods during the design of hardware components.

Systems based around standard technologies increasingly integrate functionality—such as system partitioning or the ability to swap subsystems "online," i.e., without requiring that the system be brought down—that was until very recently the prerogative of mainframe systems and of "Fault Tolerant" systems. As a result of such advancements, it is possible to reach very high levels of hardware availability without entering the domain of specialized, expensive machinery.

On the other hand, it must be realized that software failures are more frequent than hardware failures. This trend is increasing. Hardware reliability keeps improving, but the amount of software in a system keeps increasing while its quality (as measured, for example, by the number of defects per thousand lines of code) shows little sign of improving. What matters, for a system, is total availability—a combination of hardware quality, the quality of software written or provided by the manufacturer, the quality of third-party software, and finally the quality of any application and/or operating procedures developed within the company. This last factor requires special attention—only too often, underestimating the importance of the quality of the in-house applications and/or operating procedures has its effect on the failure rate of the system.

It is appropriate to be very precise in any calculation concerning availability. To illustrate this point, consider a system that works 24 hours a day, 7 days a week, with an availability of 99.999%. This figure implies that the system is down no more than five minutes a year. Whether planned downtime is included in this budget makes a big difference in the difficulty of achieving this objective. Finally, we must not forget that any use of redundancy to improve availability tends to have an effect on performance.

How much longer will system performance continue to increase?

A number of factors contribute to system performance: the performance of the processor(s), memory, I/O, network, and disks, as well as that of various software components (including OS, middleware, and applications), all have an effect. However, the largest effects have been seen—and will continue to be seen—in the area of processor performance and memory capacity. And as far as microprocessor performance and memory capacity is concerned, there seems little reason to suppose that the technology improvement curve will slow before 2010 or thereabouts; thus, microprocessor suppliers will have enough transistors and frequency capability on hand to keep processor performance on track for quite a while (although if it is not constrained, the increase in thermal dissipation associated with the higher frequencies could be a roadblock to achieving the desired level of performance). Memory capacity increases will make it possible to track the growth in software size and in the amount of data handled; this growth in memory size will make it possible (through the use of cache technologies) to compensate in large part for the lack of equivalent improvements in disk and network access times. But the possibility of a breakdown in the smooth progression of system performance remains, if memory access times and bandwidths get too far out of step with the demands of processor performance.

This drive for growth is driven by software's insatiable appetite for storage capacity and processing power. And there are no objective reasons to suppose that the appetite or growth will stop. The open questions, however, are the growth rate and the effect that these phenomena will have on the industry.

One could observe, across several information-processing domains, that the industry goes through successive phases: a phase of stability, followed by a phase of disruption. A stability phase is characterized by a continuity in architectural concepts and incremental improvements. During such an equilibrium phase, we can observe intense technological developments, often far afield from the mainstream. A disruption is characterized by a sudden questioning of established verities, together with a flood of new ideas coming to a head. New architectural concepts, approaches and products appear; the market makes its choice (not always in favor of the new), and the structure of the industry moves on. A new phase of stability then commences.

Compare and contrast the three major multiprocessor architectures: SMP, massively parallel and cluster.

An SMP (for *Symmetrical Multiprocessor*) is a system in which several processors share the same memory and function under the control of just one executing operating system. An SMP generally provides—within its configurability limits—the best scalability and the best price/performance ratio. SMPs are tending to become commodities at the entry level, although there are some problems in extending SMP to support a very large number of processors—at the time of writing, somewhere around 100 processors seems the upper boundary. While this amount will increase over time, for applications that call for extreme processing capabilities (intensive numerical operations or decision support across very large databases), one turns to cluster or MPP systems.

A cluster is a collection of otherwise independent systems ("nodes") connected by a fast interconnect. Each node runs under the control of its own copy of the operating system, although cluster software gives the user the illusion that it is a single, extremely powerful, high-capacity system. Clusters support high availability in a very natural way: any applications running on a failing node can be retried on the surviving nodes. While clusters can provide high performance, they do require that applications be written to support the programming model provided by the cluster. Both DBMSs and integrated management packages (for Enterprise Resource Planning) have been ported to cluster systems. While it can be hard for a cluster to deliver on the promise of its performance for transaction processing, it is much more straightforward for decision support.

From an architectural point of view, the only difference between a cluster and an MPP is the maximum number of processors supported—several hundreds for the MPP, instead of tens—together with a very high- performance interconnect. Key applications for MPP are intensive scientific workloads and decision support. To leverage the available raw performance, applications must be carefully written to match the platform architecture, with extreme attention being paid to extracting and exposing the maximum parallelism. Peer-to-peer networks, grid computing and clusters of PCs can offer an economic alternative to an MPP system.

Machine costs decrease every year; how long can this go on?

Hardware cost reductions should continue. At least in the entry level, we can distinguish two pricing models: constant performance with reducing price, and constant price with increasing performance. It is better to make comparisons using the price/performance ratio. It should be noted that the increasing investment necessary to build such systems will reduce the number of vendors, and that such a reduction in competitors could diminish the rate of cost reduction.

As to software, the logic of a volume market works as well as for hardware. And phenomenon of free software will tend to stabilize or even reduce the cost of commercial offerings.

Does high availability mean that a fault-tolerant machine is needed?

Traditionally, fault tolerant machines were based around hardware redundancy, and able to survive hardware failures without any break in service.

High availability no longer requires such fault-tolerant machines. There are many solutions based on cluster architectures that are able to satisfy the majority of high availability needs.

It should be noted that the reliability and maintainability capabilities of the platforms used to construct a cluster system are of primary importance in obtaining a system able to meet extreme availability needs.

Fault-tolerant systems are used in situations when the time between a failure and complete resumption of services must be very short. Hardware reliability continues to improve (a trend that will continue for technology reasons), while software reliability marks time at best (granted, the quality of a given piece of software will improve over time—given appropriate management—but there always seems to be *more* software). Failures attributable to software substantially exceed failures due to hardware. Cluster-based solutions provide some protection against software failures, while purely hardware-based fault-tolerant machines can cope only with hardware failure.

When considering the whole system (hardware, software, network and applications) isn't the cost of the hardware negligible?

Hardware cost is just a fraction of total system cost, although it must be noted that the cost of storage is an increasing porting of hardware cost. This has given rise to some new storage approaches (SAN for Storage Area Network and NAS for Network-Attached Storage). And hardware cost is far from being negligible for high-end systems.

Just because hardware cost is reducing does not mean that choice of hardware is irrelevant. Indeed, the choice of a platform sets compatibility constraints within which the company will have to live for many years; migrating to another platform brings costs and risks. As indicated in some earlier FAQs, hardware costs and, even more, price/performance continually decrease. Software prices have also dropped significantly, although not to the same degree, because of the volume effects (compare the price of proprietary operating systems to those of UNIX and NT).

The price reduction in software has been less than for hardware because standardization of software is much less than for hardware. It is worth noting that well standardized fields generally show very low prices (operating systems, for example), while more fragmented domains see much higher prices, offering comfortable margins to their vendors (as with cluster-based systems).

It seems likely that current software trends (such as free software, Java, software components, etc.) will drive software cost erosion faster than in the past. This will drive the major portions of IT expenditure towards exploitation: integration, operation, administration, safety, performance tuning, and so on.

Why were parallel databases a limited success?

As with any new technology, time is needed for development and experience in tuning for good performance and acceptable stability. Recall, again, that Teradata has been providing massively parallel systems running a proprietary DBMS since 1984. The major DBMS vendors embarked on their versions towards the end of the 80s.

When used for decision support, parallel databases provide excellent results. On the other hand, their use for transaction processing has been less satisfactory.

The difficulty in obtaining a suitable scalability in transaction processing (a much larger portion of the market than decision support) explains their limited success. This is a real-world example of the difficulties faced in writing software for massively parallel architectures.

Will UNIX-based clusters continue to offer a comfortable advantage over Windows 2003-based equivalents?

The concept of a cluster has been known for a long time - since the end of the 70s for Tandem and since 1983 for Digital. UNIX clusters appeared at the very start of the 90s, while Windows 2000 clusters did not arrive until the late 90's. UNIX clusters not only offer excellent functionality, but extremely good stability, which they acquired after years of experience. For Microsoft, this experience is still in its very early stages, so one may judge that UNIX clusters have a solid advantage today.

The problems faced by the UNIX clusters are due to their diversity; each cluster solution is specific to a UNIX vendor, each of which offers its own software interfaces. Each UNIX cluster vendor therefore has to support the development of its own cluster extensions and, at the same time, any third-party software vendor who wants to take advantage of the high availability and the scalability of the various cluster solutions must somehow handle this wide range of diversity.

Converging on some smaller number of UNIX versions, perhaps triggered by the introduction of IA-64, could effect a remedy to these diversity problems—unless the systems vendors decide to reserve the cluster extensions for use just on their own systems. Because Microsoft's cluster solution is an integration of proprietary interfaces and of implementation, it answers just one part of the problem. The key problem remains unanswered: that qualification of application software on a given system platform is a necessity.

Finally, we should note that Linux-based cluster solutions could offer a threat to Windows-based systems similar to the threat they offer to the fragmented and divided UNIX market.

Introduction

Before we can do any analysis of the various components of a server, we must first look at some of the application areas that servers handle. These include several different types of applications, such as:

- Web server
- Database access
- Transaction processing systems
- Decision-support systems
- Distributed file services
- High-performance computing

Transaction processing and decision-support applications, along with Web-serving, merit special attention. The nature of transaction-processing and decision-support applications allows us to draw parallels and comparisons between them, but Web servers are of a different nature entirely. So we will first review transaction processing and decision support applications, and then later look at the characteristics of Web servers.

We will then provide a quick review of the criteria for choosing server hardware; these criteria are further detailed and discussed in Chapter 11.

Transaction Processing and Decision Support

Transaction processing applications cover a significant market, being found more or less everywhere in the various branches of industry, not just in the area of business applications.[1] Decision support is a growing field: intense competition between companies means they need to better know their customers and their needs. Therefore, to anticipate their customers' needs, companies mine historical data to better make their decisions.

From the point of view of server architecture, transaction-processing and decision-support applications have characteristics that will be worthy of comments in the conclusions of this book, after different architectural options have been presented (in Chapter 12).

Table 1 (after [GRA92]) compares and contrasts the characteristics of decision support and transaction processing applications.

Table 1.1   *A comparison of the characteristics of transaction processing and decision-support.*

Characteristic	Transaction processing	Decision Support
Sharing of information	Both read and write, by the collection of users. Must obey ACID properties	Mostly read. Specialized database (different from database used in production).
Workflow	Irregular	Irregular
Complexity of functions	Not very complex - typically 10^5 to 10^7 instructions, plus 10 I/Os	Frequently, complex requests making use of very large amounts of data
Batch Processing	Batch processing can be used as long as the ACID properties are maintained	Used for particularly long requests
Number of users	A very large number (several thousand, or several tens of thousands)	Relatively small number of workstations
Type of users	Intelligent clients—workstations, other systems (servers, network terminals)	Intelligent clients—workstations
High availability	Typical requirement. Recovery relies on ACID properties	Not normally a requirement. Rather, the time to create or recreate the database is an important parameter
Database size	Proportional to the amount of business the company does	Proportional to the amount of time the company has been in business

Table 1.1   *A comparison of the characteristics of transaction processing and decision-support.*

Characteristic	Transaction processing	Decision Support
Amount of data manipulated by one request	Very little data "touched" in any one transaction	A great deal of data "touched" by any one request
Load balancing	Automatic	No load balancing
Performance	Short response time and throughput guarantee (achieved through interrequest parallelism)	Shorter response time is better (achieved through intrarequest parallelism)
Scalability	Typical requirement	Typical requirement

There is a major difference between transaction processing and decision-support in the area of sharing data. In transaction processing, the data is shared between all the users, and is updated during their use of it. A transaction comprises a start event, a set of operations on the data, and an end event. All operations on the data must be implemented in such a way that they obey a set of properties known as ACID: Atomicity, Consistency, Isolation, and Durability.

Atomicity

For a transaction to respect the atomicity property, the collection of operations in the transaction must either be carried out in their totality or not at all; that is, either all the actions are carried out, or none are. A transaction is delimited by the existence of two events: transaction start and transaction end. There are two types of transaction end events: *commit* or *abort*. The commit event ensures that the set of actions carried out within the transaction of the framework are made valid and their effects are made visible. In an abort, the actions carried out are canceled.

Consistency

For a transaction to respect the consistency requirement, it must effect a correct transformation of the system state. The operations carried out within the transaction, taken as a whole, must not break any of the integrity constraints associated with the system state.[2]

Isolation

During the transaction, the data involved is manipulated. The modified values of the data will be visible to other transactions only when the transaction is completed by a commit action. In other words, any intermediate values of the data created during the course of the transaction are invisible to other transactions; only the final values are visible, and those only when the transaction is committed.

Durability

When a transaction completes with a commit, the modifications produced by the transaction must not be lost. If the system crashes, the changes must not be lost. In other words, restarting the system after a crash must result in all the data modifications caused by transactions committed before the crash being visible.

The ACID properties impose very stringent requirements. To illustrate their implications, let us consider a deliberately simplified banking example, which handles a transaction between two accounts in the same bank. A transfer transaction comprises two separate elementary operations: withdrawal of a certain amount from one account, and deposit of that amount in another. The transaction is effective only when both operations succeed: the **atomicity** requirement. The database managing the accounts must reflect the withdrawal from the transmitting account and the deposit in the receiving account to show **coherence**. Since the operations are internal to the one bank, we can see that the sum of the funds managed by the bank remains constant. While the transaction is proceeding, the intermediate states of the transmitter and receiver accounts are not visible to other transactions, demonstrating **insulation**.

A withdrawal logically begins by checking that the transmitting account has sufficient funds for the transaction. If the insulation property is not properly respected, a withdrawal transaction on the receiving account could be refused because the crediting transaction had not yet been committed. Once that transaction has been committed, it cannot be cancelled out; it produces a lasting, **durable** change. Of course, when it is necessary to cancel a transaction, that can be done—a bank officer needs to effect a new transaction to move the funds back, and this new transaction must itself respect the ACID properties.

As we shall see, solutions for several systems problems, such as guaranteeing continuity of service, can be based upon these properties.

In the case of decision support, it is possible for data to be shared, but generally just shared for reading. Any modification of the data is preferably done on a specific copy of the database tailored to the application. This might occur, for example, in the simulation of a scenario in which data must change to reflect the effects of the decisions made (i.e., a "what-if" simulation); there will be then as many copies of the database as there are users simulating scenarios simultaneously.

Database technology allows, in principle, the simultaneous support of both transaction-processing and decision-support applications on the same database. In practice, however, separate databases are used, with the decision-support versions being created by extracting data from the production transaction-processing databases; being able to do this automatically is a much-valued capability. Quite often, decision support systems and their databases are dedicated systems. When such systems are used for specific dedicated tasks, such as general management or market analysis, it is usual to call them "Datamarts" or specialized data warehouses.

The **arrival rate of transactions** in a transaction-processing system is irregular, since it reflects the company's ordinary activities, which vary on a daily, weekly and yearly basis (although if electronic commerce becomes truly global, it is possible that the fluctuations might decrease in amplitude). For decision support, the request rate seen by a system is also irregular, because typical usage has pauses while data and the experiment are prepared, interspersed with actual experimental runs and then analysis of the results.

In transaction processing, the **type of work** is repetitive; the system only offers a limited set of functions to its users, all rigidly defined ahead of time. To extend the repertoire of functions requires a development team to write new code, or to set new parameters in the software package deployed. In contrast, decision support generally does not provide a fixed repertoire of functions; rather, the user guides progress depending on the results of prior requests and consideration and analysis of these results.

Transaction requests generally call up **functions of limited complexity**, since each transaction generally touches some small amount of data. Transactions of the general flavor of those used in the TPC-C benchmark (see Chapter 7, which discusses performance) require the execution of just a few million machine instructions per transaction (including instructions executed in the application, the DBMS, and the OS) together with round 10 input/output operations. Again, decision support is different—each function is generally complex and can require access to a very large amount of data (for example, looking at every item in a database).

In transaction processing systems, some operations can be carried out "offline" in a **batch-processing** mode; this is generally done at times of low usage of the system (e.g., when the company is closed for the weekend). Obviously, such batch operations must themselves respect the ACID properties. Decision support can also make use of delayed actions, typically to handle extremely long requests.

The **number of users** supported in a transaction-processing system is essentially the number of customers active at any one time; with the increase in electronic commerce, these numbers may be expected to increase considerably. A decision-support system, however, is likely to have a relatively small number of users, and that number is not likely to increase much over time.

Increasingly, transaction-processing **users** make use of workstations, or are actually software running on other systems. A common characteristic is local processing capability.

Typically, transaction-processing systems require **high availability**. The company's ability to do business often depends on the information-processing system, and so its unavailability reflects immediately into lost business. It is therefore important for such systems to minimize the likelihood of the system being unavailable. When the system does fail for some reason, the ACID properties ensure that the system can be restarted in a coherent state—some transactions may have been lost, but the data reflects all the committed transactions. Decision-support systems do not usually require high availability, but it can be needed in some fields: for example, systems used in a stock exchange, or to provide support to military operations, must always work. In such applications, it is wise to equip the systems with recovery points, so that in the case of failure the operation may be rolled back to the most recent recovery point.

It is worth noting that a key parameter for a decision-support system is the amount of time it takes to create or regenerate the database.

As regards **the size of the databases**, rules of thumb are:

- In transaction processing, the size of the database reflects the activity of the company

- In decision support, the size of the database reflects the history of the company

Given that the size of the company's business reflects the number of customers, we can see that the size of the database is a function of the number of customers (and the number of orders, and the number of items offered for sale, etc.). Reflecting this, as we will see in Chapter 7 (which discusses performance), the definition of the TPC-C benchmark (used industry-wide as an indicator of transaction processing performance) stipulates that the size of the database to be used in the benchmark is proportional to the system performance, which itself directly reflects the number of simultaneous users of the system.

On the other hand, the size of a decision-support system more typically reflects the amount of data accumulated during the life of the company (rather than its current activity rate). As examples of decision support, one might use historical data to analyze the effect of store placement on the sales of a particular product, or the effect of promotional campaigns, or the geographical distribution of customers. In these fairly typical situations, the size of the decision-support database is a function of the company's history. We note in passing that while the TPC-D benchmark—used to indicate performance for decision support (again, see Chapter 7)—expresses decision-support performance as a function of database size, it does so (contrary to TPC-C) without any indication of any relationship between database size and system performance.

As noted above, in general the **amount of data manipulated** in a transaction processing environment is rather small, while that amount tends to be quite large for decision support—perhaps even the whole database.

Since a key characteristic of transaction-processing systems is the handling of many simultaneous requests, the system must, of necessity, be able to provide some automatic **load-balancing** to give each user roughly the same performance. In decision support, the very large amount of data, the varying characteristics of each request, and the small number of users means that such load-balancing is not required.

As regards system **performance**, transaction processing requires a high data bandwidth to ensure the maximum number of transactions completed per unit of time, along with the guaranteed response time. In fact, a key figure of merit for a transaction-processing system is a combination of a low response time (below two seconds is preferred) and, even more, the repeatability of that low response time. Response time is particularly important for Internet-accessed applications (although the variability of the network response time tends to dominate). Good response time is achieved through *intra-request parallelism*—that is, simultaneous execution of the components of a transaction.

In decision support, bandwidth is not the key property; rather, we seek to minimize the response time. This is accomplished by *inter-request parallelism*, that is, the execution of multiple transactions simultaneously. Chapter 8 examines the techniques used inside the DBMS to satisfy this need.

Scalability is the ability of the system to be adapted to meet the size of the problem. We have to look at the scalability of a server in each of the dimensions of a system: processing capability (the number of processors one can install), address space (which means, in practice, 64-bit address space), physical memory capacity, how many storage systems or subsystems may be attached, and communications capacity (how many lines, and aggregate bandwidth).

When a server does not display good scalability, the practical result is that when new needs (e.g., computational performance, main memory capacity, storage capacity, connectivity, or bandwidth) arise, the server cannot adapt to the new needs and must be swapped out for a new one. Replacing one server with another incurs costs beyond the price of the new machine and its installation; in addition, one must usually pay for the costs of an interruption in service.

It is precisely to meet this scalability requirement that multiprocessor architectures, in all their various forms (as described in this book), were created towards the end of the 60s.

It's worth noting that, more often than not, a change in needs translates into a growth in needs. But one should also look at the case where for one reason or another a reduction in capability is called for. As an example, consider a system to be installed on many sites across a company, each site having needs which vary in the various dimensions noted above. Given a scalable platform, there is a possibility of equipping each site with a machine form the same family. If the machine is not scalable, then different products will be needed across the company with concomitant costs in application porting and with increased support costs.

Web Servers

There are many uses of the Web, and several attempts to characterize these uses have been made. We will summarize and comment on some of the results which seem to us most interesting.

One can distinguish two (non-exclusive) main categories of Web user:

- Document servers providing research and navigation capabilities (for example, search engines)
- Transaction-processing server handling commerce orders (e-commerce: order, follow-up, invoice)

The categories are not exclusive, because a user who wants to place an e-commerce order will likely first do a search for available bargains. An initial reference study, [ARL96], looked at six sites to sort out the fundamentals. [PIT98] collects the various results published in 1998.

[MEN00] looked at two electronic commerce sites (one selling books, the other managing auctions for Internet domain names) and identified some key characteristics of electronic trade. Unfortunately, since Web traffic and habits keep changing, such studies must be repeated. Rather than being repetitive, we simply summarize the key points found by these studies.

Although the [ARL96] study is now somewhat dated, it does contain interesting data:

- The hit rate for a server is about 88%
- The average size of transfers is less than 21 KB
- The distribution of file sizes accessed has a Pareto distribution (that is, the probability of a file being accessed decreases as its size increases)
- There is a locality of reference: 10% of references account for 90% of data transferred
- There is locality in the source of requests: while a site can receive requests coming from thousands of domains, 10% of domains account for 75% of the utilization

Among the extra insights afforded by [PIT98] are:

- File accesses have a Zipf distribution - that is, the file most frequently accessed is twice as likely to be accessed as the next most likely.
- About half the files are requested more than once by any one customer
- 25% of the sites represent 85% of the traffic

- The average life of a document is 50 days, with HTML files being modified more often than other types

And among the statistics offered by [MEN00] for e-commerce sites, we should note:

- The majority of the sessions last less than 1000 seconds
- The major part of the session is devoted to choosing products
- File accesses have a Zipf distribution
- 16% of the accesses are generated by Web robots
- 88% of the sessions comprise fewer than 10 requests
- The distribution of number of requests per session is "long-tailed"— that is, even if the average number is low, there is a non-zero probability of there being a large number of requests in a session

As is clear from these observations, characterizing Web traffic is not as straightforward as characterizing transaction processing or decision support. We will return to these issues in Chapter 7, when we discuss benchmarks developed for the Web.

Selection Criteria

Below we list—non-exhaustively—selection criteria appropriate for an IT professional to use in choosing a server, following the list by a discussion of each criterion in turn:

- Availability of applications and development tools
- System availability
- Data integrity
- Security
- Performance
- Scalability
- Price
- Support for the client/server model
- Architectural maturity
- Investment risk

Note that the list is given in no particular order; when selecting a server, the individual needs of the business will drive the relative weighting of the criteria.

The **availability** of a vast catalogue of **applications** and **development tools** eases the construction of business solutions and is an indication that the server family under consideration has a strong and active marketplace. Such an active market has beneficial indirect effects: reduced prices because of volume and competitive effects; enhanced confidence in the continuity of the vendor and platform; widespread availability of experts in the applications and the tools. We should note in passing that the success of a platform is rarely an effect of the intrinsic merits of its technology (whether hardware or software); it is the marketplace that decides.

Since business activities rely more and more on their data processing resources, three criteria of increasing importance are **availability**, **data integrity**, and **security**. By *availability*, we mean the ability of the system to perform its function every time that it is requested; *integrity* corresponds to the system's ability to manage its data without damage to the data; and *security* is the ability to ensure that there is no unauthorized access to that data.

The **performance** of a system is an important characteristic, as we shall see later in the book, but it is difficult to characterize with a single number. The best way of capturing performance is to identify what the system must do to fulfill its mission and then identify the values that allow one to characterize performance for that mission. If the analysis of the workload shows that one or more standard benchmarks is a close approximation to the workload, then one may use the relative performance of different systems on the relevant benchmark(s) to provide a good predictor of performance on the company's workload. If no benchmarks fit well, then one can compare performance only by running tests on the real workload. Since systems needs often change over time, it is generally a good idea to leave some "headroom" in available performance when choosing a system.

We have already presented (and shown the importance of) the concept of **scalability** in this chapter. Scalability—the ability of a system to match the dimensions of the problem it has to manage—is closely related to performance. But given the choice of two systems, one may prefer a less powerful system with good scalability over a more powerful system with less growth potential.

Over the course of time, the ways of comparing **price** have changed, shifting from a simple price comparison of the systems under consideration (both hardware and software) with support and maintenance costs added in, to a "Total Cost of Ownership" approach, which also integrates internal costs, such as the staff needed to operate the system, system management and user support costs, the economic impact on the company were the system to become unavailable, etc.

Support for the **client/server** model depends on the availability of appropriate middleware; some platforms are better served than others in this area. For example, standard[3] systems present a significant potential market, and so attract the attention of middleware publishers.

Although the various concepts used in server architectures are widely known, the development of a new architecture often takes longer than originally expected by its developers. As we will see again and again in this book, the various aspects of **maturity** are very powerful forces; one such effect is the difficulties innovative architectures often meet while going to market.

Installing a server and the necessary applications represents a major investment, in terms of both immediate expenditure (acquisition costs of hardware and software) and associated costs (training, implementing new applications, etc.). Given the usual size of these costs, the **investment risk** is an important criterion. It is particularly important that a server vendor stay in existence for as long as its customers are using its products, and so this issue presents a particular problem to start-ups, since so many collapse while young. This difficulty can be less severe for suppliers of products like storage subsystems, since these have extremely well defined interfaces with their host systems—so, if the supplier collapses, all is not lost—alternative products from other vendors can be deployed in the same way and with the same connections as the products from the ill-fated start-up. In general, however, the subsystems purchased from the defunct vendor must be replaced, since such subsystems will, in general, only run software provided by their vendor.

Endnotes

1. For a real-time system controlling (for example) some industrial process, the handling of a command (which can involve updating one or more databases) may also be looked upon as an atomic operation: it is either done completely or not at all.

2. Respecting this property assumes that not only the hardware, operating system, and the database itself are working properly, but that the application itself is correct. Inconsistencies in the

data may often be the fault of the application. In practice, therefore, it is particularly important to test the application rigorously.

3.   Some nomenclature: By a standard system we mean one that is widespread, and for which tools and skills are widely available—that is, one that the industry has adopted. An open system is one that is owned in common by none or by more than one company (whether hardware or software). Windows and its spawn are standard systems, since they are widespread but the intellectual property is owned solely by Microsoft. UNIX is both open and standard. In the point made in the text, we wish not to exclude Windows and its derivatives, and so we use the term standard.

Part 1: Architectural Options and Technology Evolution

This first portion of the book reviews hardware technologies that have an effect on server performance and architecture. The hardware analysis is broken up into two parts, first looking at processors and memory and then at I/O and peripheral subsystems.

The evolution of software technologies are then examined.

First of all, we present the key elements of systems architecture which must be understood before analyzing the evolution of server architecture.

P.1   Systems Architecture Basics

As we shall see, a server's processing performance is limited by, among other things, microprocessor performance. In the search for high performance and to satisfy the goal of scalability, systems vendors have turned (since the end of the 60s) to multiprocessor systems. Multiprocessor servers fall into one of two major classes:

- *Tightly-coupled, or Symmetrical Multiprocessor (SMP)*, in which all the processors can see and use all systems resources (memory, I/O devices). An SMP operates under the control of just one copy of the operating system, which manages all the system resources.

- *Loosely-coupled*, in which a system is constructed by interconnecting (using a fast local area network technology) some number of independent systems, each having its own resources (processors, memory, I/O) and running under the control of its own copy of the operating system. Each such system is called a node.

Clusters and Massively Parallel (MPP) systems both fall into the loosely-coupled classification. The term loose-coupling refers to that fact there is no shared hardware in such systems (except for the interconnect and, in some systems, the storage subsystems).

Figure Part 1.1 and Figure Part 1.2 outline the two architectural approaches.

In a *tightly coupled processor* (or SMP), the processors share memory and I/O devices. The system operates under the control of a single copy of the OS. To increase processing capability, one adds a processor (up to the limits supported by the system). It is thus an economic solution to meeting a need for increased performance.

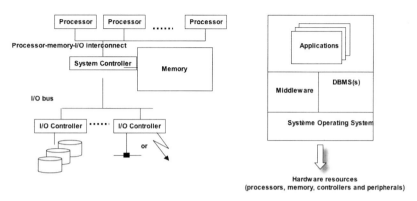

Figure Part 1.1
Tightly-coupled architecture.

a) Hardware view of a Symmetrical Mutiprocessor   b) Software View of a Symmetrical Multiprocessor

The term *symmetrical* refers to the fact that all the processors are equal in the system—anything that one can do, any can do—unlike some other *asymmetric* systems in which the processors were specialized. In an asymmetric system, for example, one processor might be given the job of running the OS and I/O, with other processors limited to running applications.

The components making up a multiprocessor system are as follows

■ A collection of processors

■ Interconnect between the processors and the rest of the system (shown here as a bus connecting the processors to a memory controller and to an I/O bus)

■ I/O controllers connected on a specialized bus (the I/O bus)

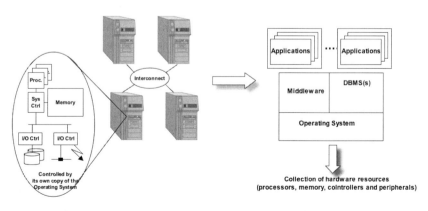

Figure Part 1.2
Loosely-coupled architecture.

a) Loosely-coupled Architecture   b) Idealized View of a Loosely-Coupled Architecture

Figure Part 1.3
Software execution model for an SMP.

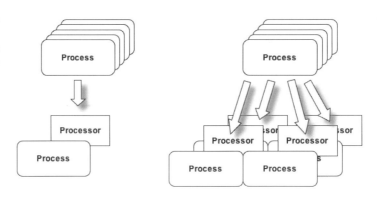

a) - Uniprocessor   b) - Tightly-Coupled Multprocessor/SMP

All of these hardware resources are managed by a single copy of the operating system. The various software components (DBMS, middleware and applications) function under the control of the OS. For the software to take advantage of the multiprocessor configuration, it must be structured as a collection of units able to be executed in parallel—that is, as multiple processes. Communication between processors and between applications may be done through shared memory; this implies a synchronization mechanism.

Figure Part 1.3 illustrates the model of software execution on a symmetrical multiprocessor.

In a uniprocessor, there is a single process queue. An operating system module, the *scheduler,* chooses the process to run on the processor. At any given moment, just one process is running.

In the case of an SMP, there is still just one process queue, but there can be as many processes executing at one time as there are processors. In an SMP, it is still the scheduler that chooses which processes should run, and where.

If we assume that each application is implemented as exactly one process, then an SMP with N processors is capable of executing N processes simultaneously, and thus to have throughput (expressed as processes executed per unit time) higher than that of a uniprocessor. On the other hand, because of resource contention introduced by the SMP architecture, each process will take just as long to execute—or longer—on an SMP than on a uniprocessor. To avoid this restriction, it is best to structure each application not as one process, but as several processes, or lightweight processes, called *threads*. As we will see in Chapter 4, threads allow performance optimization. Communication between processes making up an application is done through shared memory; as we will see later, this is the most efficient interprocess communication mechanism.

As an aside, it should be clear that an application structured to work well on an SMP will also run correctly on a uniprocessor.

In a loosely-coupled multiprocessor, the system is made up of a collection of local systems. These systems, called *nodes*, maintain all the capabilities that would allow them to operate as completely independent systems—they have their own processors, memory, I/O, and, above all, *their own copy of the operating system*. A means of high-speed communication (perhaps a fast local area network such as Gigabit Ethernet, or Fibre Channel, or even a proprietary interconnect)—which we shall refer to as the interconnect network—ties the nodes together into one system. By means of software (primarily the operating system and DBMS), such a collection presents itself to its users as a single system with substantial processing power (potentially, the sum of the processing capabilities of its nodes).

The differences between a distributed system and a loosely-coupled system are:

- In a loosely-coupled system, the nodes are homogeneous.

- In a loosely-coupled system, the nodes are close together; a cluster or an MPP is a means of creating a powerful server from smaller ones. To ease physical management of the servers that make up the cluster, it is convenient to have them in geographical proximity—a choice emphasized by constraints imposed by some peripherals which must be shared.

- In a loosely-coupled system, the resources are, in general, pooled (e.g., one File System for the cluster, a single IP address for the cluster), which makes the collection look like a single system to its users. This is referred to as a "Single System Image."

Figure Part 1.4 illustrates the model of execution on a multiprocessor with loose coupling.

Each node supports some number of applications. On a given node, assuming that it is an SMP, the application can take advantage of the multiple processors as described above. On the other hand, as there is no sharing of memory between the nodes (while there are exceptions, this is the general case for such architectures, a subject to which we will return), applica-

Figure Part 1.4
Loosely-coupled execution model.

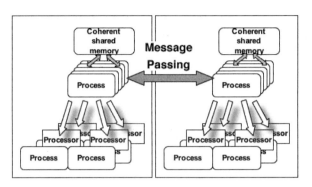

c) - Loosely-Coupled Processor

tions running on different nodes that need to communicate with each other must resort to "message passing." This communication style requires specific programming, and can suffer from lower performance than shared-memory communications.

As hinted previously, there are two major classes of loosely-coupled machines:

A *cluster* is characterized by:

- The use of some standard interconnection network (such as a fast local area network, or Fibre Channel)

- Some reasonably-constrained number of nodes (perhaps of the order of ten, although there are larger clusters than this)

An *MPP* (Massively Parallel Processing) machine is characterized by:

- The use of specific nonstandard interconnect intended to optimize inter-node communication—that is, it is aimed both at minimizing latency (the amount of time it takes for a message to get between nodes) and increasing inter node bandwidth

- Packaging designed to allow increasing the size of the system in a straightforward manner

- An upper limit on the number of nodes of the order of a few hundred

After this general introduction to the two major architectural options, we will be able to examine how technologies have changed (and will change) over time. We will reexamine these architectures in greater detail in Chapters 4, 5, and 6.

As has been seen, the two options are by no means exclusive; the nodes of a cluster or MPP can beneficially be constructed from SMPs (without requiring the nodes all to have the same number of processors). The search for scalability can be exercised in two dimensions (possibly simultaneously):

- The addition of processors to nodes (in the SMP dimension)
- The addition of nodes (in the cluster/MPP dimension)

These two approaches are sometimes referred to under the following terms:

- *Scale-up*, or vertical growth for addition of processors to the SMPs
- *Scale-out*, or horizontal growth for the addition of nodes

Growing in the Cluster/MPP dimension can allow specialization of the node designs, as is shown in Figure Part 1.5.

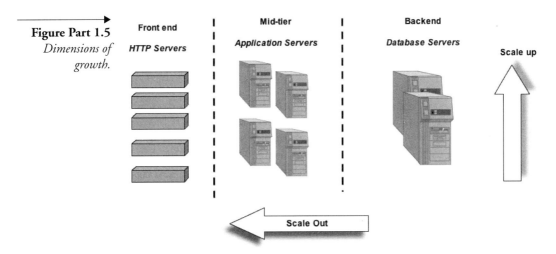

Figure Part 1.5
Dimensions of growth.

This example shows a Web site in which service was divided into three levels:

- The front end, with HTTP servers
- The mid-tier, with applications servers
- The backend, with database servers

The component nodes of these levels are organized as a cluster and can have specialized hardware and software configurations—for example, "blade" servers as the HTTP servers; SMPs with limited disk capacity as application servers; and SMPs with extremely large disk capacity as the database servers.

Load balancing between the machines in any level can be managed either by special equipment or by software.

We will return to the characteristics of this sort of approach later in the book.

P.2   Historical Notes about System Architecture

A forward-looking prospect is shaped by history, so we will begin this discussion by recalling key milestones in systems architecture.

Figure Part 1.6 illustrates some outstanding milestones in systems architecture from the past 40 years. We are most interested in the first implementations of novel, important concepts; or in their first commercial appearance. As with all historical analysis, there is some arbitrariness in our choices; we hope those omitted will forgive us.

IBM's System/360 not only introduced a new 32-bit architecture, but also the key concept of a compatible family of machines spanning a broad range of performance. In developing the 360 family, IBM exploited con-

Figure Part 1.6
Key system architecture milestones.

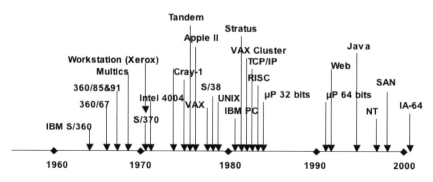

cepts that were already understood, and in some cases had already been implemented: the concept of virtual memory with the 360/67; the concept of memory caches with the 360/85; and a number of innovations improving processor performance with the 360/91. As noted, neither virtual memory nor cache were concepts novel to the 360 family, but it was the 360 that popularized the approaches (although the models incorporating the new technology were sold in relatively low volumes).

The MULTICS time-sharing system [ORG72], developed at MIT on a GE 645 system (whose modern descendants are the hardware supporting the Bull GCOS 8 operating system) is the inspiration for the majority of modern operating systems, notably Windows 2000 and UNIX. MULTICS introduced two key notions:

- The concept of *dynamic linking*, where the links between program units—programs and subroutines—can be made during program execution rather than at an earlier, obligatory stage (an approach called static linking). Dynamic linking provides great flexibility in how programs can be constructed, and allows, for example, for programs that call for the same subroutines to be given different versions of the subroutines, depending on the context in which the program or programs are executed. This concept spread, and has been integrated into UNIX and Windows 2000.

- The concept of *mapping* a file into virtual address space: in this approach, the files contents are copied into virtual address space, where a program can access them directly without any I/O operations, and with any necessary movement of data between memory and disk being accomplished by the OS's demand-paging mechanisms. This concept was included in UNIX (initially in the BSD variants from the University of California at Berkeley) and later in Windows 2000. Its usage, however, is still rather limited, although one imagines this will change with a move to 64-bit address spaces.

IBM's introduction of virtual memory and their cache innovations were done on systems that may be regarded as experimental (the 360/67 and 360/85), but that formed the basis of the 370 Series introduced at the beginning of the 70s. The architectural processor performance improvements embodied in the 360/91 are now widely employed by high-performance microprocessors.

The first microprocessor, Intel's 4004, was a 4-bit machine and the starting point of a phenomenon that was to deeply transform the computing industry.

Xerox developed the first workstations at Xerox PARC (Palo Alto Research Center). These machines had a graphical user interface supporting multiple windows and the use of a mouse for interaction. Although they were never successfully commecialized by Xerox, they are viewed as the basis of today's personal computers and graphical user interfaces.

Seymour Cray founded his own company after leaving Control Data and developed the eponymous CRAY-1, the first in a line of vector supercomputers.

Tandem introduced fault-tolerant systems for transactional systems that also exhibited the ability for modular growth; these systems inspired today's cluster solutions.

Apple's Apple II made microcomputers real. The rapid spread of these systems resulted, a few years later, in IBM's reactive introduction of the IBM PC, which was to have enormous success.

Digital's VAX 11/780 changed the world's view of minicomputers; rather than being a breed apart from "real" computers, they were thereafter seen to be equally capable, but available at much more affordable prices. The VAX architecture was also a source of inspiration to the standard microprocessors that became the basis of UNIX platforms and started becoming available in the 80s.

IBM's System/38 [SOL95] (known later as AS/400 and now as iSeries) generalized the concept of mapping files into virtual memory by simply removing any distinction between memory and disks, calling the concept *One Level Store*. This necessitates a large address space, of course; it is noteworthy that the S38, introduced in 1978, had a virtual address space size of 2^{64} bytes (in fact 2^{48} for the first implementation), still large by modern standards.

UNIX was developed in the 70s by Ken Thompson and Dennis Ritchie, two Bell Laboratories researchers [THO74]. It took as a starting point many of the concepts of MULTICs and its implementation aimed at ensuring the portability of the operating system across architectures.

In 1981, IBM introduced its PC. The repercussions of this moment are still occuring, and we have still not finished understanding the consequences across multiple fields.

Stratus introduced a family of fault-tolerant products based on hardware-level redundancy.

Digital introduced the VAX Cluster in 1983, very likely to attempt to mitigate performance shortfalls in their offering occasioned by delays in the development of their high-end machines. VAX Cluster inspired the various cluster solutions available in both the UNIX and Windows worlds.

The beginning of the 80s saw the emergence of the TCP/IP communications protocols, driven particularly by the spread of UNIX. The key factors in TCP/IP's success were its simplicity and broad availability, and it constitutes an excellent example of a *de facto* standard—one adopted by the market and by the near-totality of market players.

The first RISC systems hit the market in 1984, and inspired a new generation of microprocessors.

This was also the moment when the first servers based on 32-bit microprocessors made their appearance. The characteristics of these systems (performance, virtual memory, etc.) positioned them as direct competitors to the extant minicomputers.

In turn, 64-bit microprocessors began supplanting the 32-bit machines, putting these systems in direct competition with mainframes to support business-critical applications.

The rather fantastic rise of the Web drove deep changes in user practices, and gave rise to new requirements placed on servers. As much for TCP/IP as the Web, we can comment that it was not so much a single event with a precise date as a continuous phenomenon leading to general adoption of the technology and associated solutions.

About the middle of the 90s, Sun introduced Java. More than just another programming language, Java and the environment accompanying it support a new paradigm allowing program portability at the level of object code. This paradigm introduced the possibility of mobile code, and code that, moreover, could be personalized on the fly and was capable of executing on any platform having a Java environment. Java represents an attempt, perhaps the strongest-led we have encountered, to be free of the specifics of any particular platform (processor, OS, etc.) while preserving security. However, so far the results do not completely match the hopes.

With Windows 2000, Microsoft hoped to address the requirements met by UNIX workstations, and by proprietary or UNIX servers.

The problem of I/O, at least as far as storage devices and subsystems within enterprise systems are concerned, should start to get a solution with the emergence of the SAN (*Storage Area Network*).

IA-64 marks a break in Intel's long tradition of binary compatibility since the 8086 (although IA-64 can execute IA-32 binaries). The IA 64 architecture also—in its search for performance— explores a new balance between hardware and software.

One may get the impression from Figure Part 1.6 that the pace of innovation slowed somewhat in the 90s, but this is simply because the figure relates only to system architectures and does not show many interesting innovations such as distributed object environments like CORBA or DCOM/COM+; N-tier applications architectures, Java, Enterprise Java Beans, and so on. And one should also bear in mind that identifying significant milestones tends to benefit from a certain distance between observer and event; instant acclamations tend not to last.

Processors and Memory

This chapter looks at the technologies used for processors and memories from a historical point of view. We examine the mechanisms behind memory hierarchy (caches), techniques for parallelism and problems arising from the implementation of tightly coupled multiprocessors. In this chapter, we discuss binary compatibility, architecture retargeting, and interpreted languages, concentrating on Java. We conclude this chapter with a discussion on microprocessor and memory evolution.

1.1 Semiconductors and Microprocessors

At the hardware level, several factors have contributed to the improvement of server performance:

- Improvements in the intrinsic performance of processors

- Increases in system memory capacity

- Increases in the throughput of the connections between subsystems (i.e., throughput on the system bus or the input-output subsystem)

- Increases in the performance of magnetic peripherals

- Increases in network throughput, etc.

The various technologies relevant to each factor do not improve at the same rate. Without question, it is processor performance and memory capacity which have seen (and will continue to see) the strongest growth rates. Moore's Law (also known as "Moore's First Law," proposed by Gordon Moore, one of the founders of INTEL) suggests that the density of integrated circuits doubles every 18 months.

Figure 1.1
*Evolution of
processor
performance.*

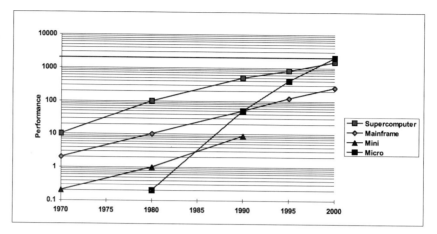

Figure 1.1, inspired by [HEN02], shows the evolution of processor performance.

The performance numbers in the chart are given as multiples of the processing capability of a minicomputer of the end of the 1970s. As can be seen on this chart, the growth of microprocessor performance far outpaces that of the other types of processor. It should be noted that the chart plots raw performance, a measure of the intrinsic power of the processors, rather than reflecting the processing capability available to actual applications.

Microprocessors and Performance

Certain authorities consider that microprocessor computing power also doubles every 18 months, thereby extending Moore's Law to cover performance as well as density. In fact, by observing the progression of integer computational performance (using the SPECint benchmark, which is presented in Chapter 7) and by looking at only the best microprocessors, it appears that the performance doubles about every 24 months. When we look at performance forecasts provided by the microprocessor suppliers and again considering only the highest-performance microprocessors, we see that they predict that performance will double every 19 months!

This is probably an illustration of the fact that it is easier to publish plans (the infamous Microprocessor Road Maps) than to actually *develop* microprocessors.

The gain in terms of microprocessor performance is of course due to the increase in technology capabilities (see later), but it is important to understand that it is also a side effect of the increase in market size for microprocessor-based systems. The advent of the PC is at the root of this phenomenon; the commoditization of technology leads to a fall in prices (both as an effect of the competition between the suppliers and as an effect of volume), and the availability of software eases the adoption of systems by users. In return, the volume of systems sold generates increased opportunities for investment on the part of the vendors (of microprocessors, systems, and software). The economic model which results from this makes the tendency irreversible. We must note that the suppliers of proprietary systems such as IBM, Unisys, and Bull, had for some time been using the same technology as that employed in standard microprocessors for their own custom designs—that is, using CMOS to build air-cooled single-chip processors. Earlier, such machines were generally built using bipolar technology and needed liquid cooling. Bull was a pioneer in the move to CMOS, bringing its DPS 7000 system to market in 1987.

The easily-observed difference in raw computational capability between standard and proprietary processors—the standard microprocessors generally are faster—is a side effect of the economic model mentioned above. Standard microprocessors are produced by the millions, while the proprietary machines are built only in the thousands; this much larger volume allows the builder of a standard microprocessor to spend much more money on its development than the proprietary vendor can afford, and also funds the development of architectural innovations. The R&D necessary to provide high performance is expensive, and the marketplace addressed by the machines must pay for this. Thus, an architecture with weak intrinsic capabilities but with extremely large sales volumes can see vastly improved performance thanks to the money available from the sales volumes, while other architectures with greater intrinsic merit and greater potential but much lower volumes can see their performance marking time; as a result, they eventually disappear.

In the field of scientific computing, requiring intensive numerical computations, the reign of the classic supercomputer began to be challenged in the second half of the 1990s by the appearance of microprocessor-based systems. The problems this caused for the established supercomputer manufacturers is illustrated by SGI's purchase of Cray.

Figure 1.2 shows the change in the number of transistors per microprocessor, projected up to 2011; the curve shows the numbers for successive Intel processors from the 4004 to the Pentium 4.

As shown by the graph, the number of transistors per processor from the first machine—the 4004, in 1971—up to the Pentium 4 follows a growth

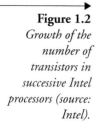

Figure 1.2
Growth of the number of transistors in successive Intel processors (source: Intel).

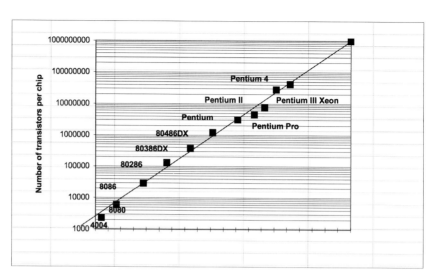

in accordance with that predicted by Moore. Repeating the exercise for microprocessors from other vendors would show a similar pattern.

If the growth rates shown continue into the future, they would lead to a chip with 100 billion transistors in 2011, a transistor count 100 times larger than today. Achieving this target requires significant manufacturing investment; each new generation of technology requires the construction of new manufacturing facilities ("fabs", for fabrication facilities). The cost for each new generation of fabs also follows an exponential law, Moore's Second Law, illustrated in Figure 1.3.

It costs billions of dollars to build a new fab.[1] To these costs, one must add the development costs for the new generation of processors, an amount of the order of a hundred million dollars or more. This is for a new genera-

Figure 1.3
Semiconductor fab cost trends (Moore's Second Law).

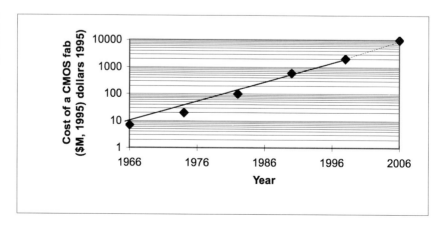

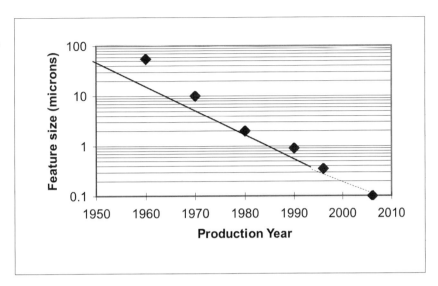

Figure 1.4
Evolution of lithographic feature size.

tion of an established architecture; creating a new architecture along with a new processor implementation—such as Intel's IA-64—increases the costs considerably.

This makes it clear that only very high volumes of sales of the resulting processors can pay for the investment necessary to bring them to market. This means that the industry concentrates around a small number of architectures, making the introduction of new architectures—however worthy— problematic. We will tackle microprocessor economic issues in the next sec-

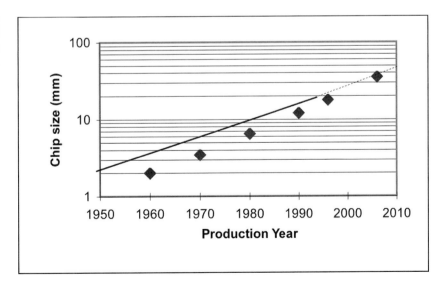

Figure 1.5
Evolution of chip area.

tion. Figures 1.4 and 1.5 illustrate the progression of semiconductor technology in terms of lithographic feature size and chip area.

The feature size[2]—roughly, the smallest feature which may be safely formed on the chip—controls the number of active devices per unit area as well as the maximum frequency of operation of the chip. If n is the minimum feature size, maximum frequency of operation varies as $1/n$ and the number of devices per unit area as $1/n^2$. Thus improvement in lithography has a potential for an $1/n^3$ improvement in microprocessor capability.

Making use of this trend of an ever-increasing number of transistors in a design is a major problem for processor designers. Several options are available to handle the problem: try an increased level of parallelism within the instruction stream; integrate ever-larger caches onto the chip; or even integrate several processors onto the same chip.

Exploiting parallelism within an instruction stream

There are several approaches to exploiting the intrinsic parallelism of an instruction stream. Among them are superscalar techniques, architectures with very long instruction words (VLIW) and most recently the for Explicitly Parallel Instruction Computing (EPIC) concept behind the IA-64 architecture from Intel and HP.

In EPIC, the parallelism is intended to be detected by the compiler once the parallelism is detected, it is presented to the hardware in instructions which make it straightforward for the hardware to exploit it. The VLIW concept was introduced in the 1980s, primarily by Multiflow, which has since disappeared. Other companies, including HP, also worked on the approach, which relies on compiler techniques to detect parallelism within the program and to generate groups of instructions that may be executed together. A VLIW processor is thus a machine which can, each clock cycle, execute a large number of instructions simultaneously—Multiflow's implementations were intended to variously execute 7, 14, or 21 instructions per cycle. Unlike a superscalar machine, in which the microprocessor itself detects parallelism as it executes the instructions and avoids any possible conflicts between concurrently-executed instructions, in a VLIW machine it is the compiler's job to schedule (organize) the instructions in such a manner that there are no conflicts. The VLIW approach has not met with commercial success. The EPIC approach builds on VLIW concepts in that the burden of detecting concurrency rests on the compiler. We examine the architectural evolution which led to EPIC at the end of this chapter.

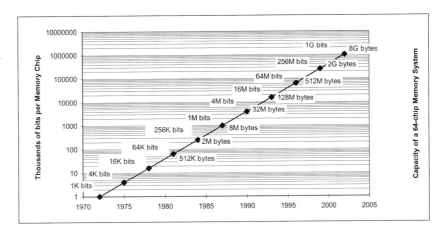

Figure 1.6
Evolution of the capacity of DRAM chips and a 64-chip memory system.

Another effect of increasing integration is the increase in system reliability. This is caused by:

- A reduction in the number of chips needed to build a system
- A reduction in the number of connections needed within a system

Chapter 9 looks at this increase in reliability, backed with numbers.

Figure 1.6 shows two things. First, it charts the evolution of the capacity of the DRAM (*Dynamic Random Access Memory*) memory chips, which are used to construct computer memory systems. And second, it charts the evolution of the capacity of a memory system constructed from 64 such chips (that is, using a constant number of chips regardless of their capacity).

We make here the assumption that 64 chips are used for data storage, thereby excluding any extra chips used to ensure data integrity. Given the size of server memory systems and the need for data integrity, an error correcting code (ECC) is essential. Typically, an ECC makes it possible to correct a single error (i.e., an erroneous bit) and to detect a double error (i.e., two erroneous bits). To do this, for example, requires 72 bits (64 bits of data and 8 bits of error-correcting code) to represent each 64 bits of information, or 288 bits (256 bits of data and 32 bits of ECC).

Given the assumptions, it can be seen that a memory system's natural size has grown one thousandfold in just 15 years—between 1985 and the end of the 1990s, the example memory system grows from 2 MB to 2 GB.

There is a large and growing gap between processor speed and memory speed, and between memory speed and the speed of magnetic disks. To handle the problems arising from these differences, system architects have, since the 1960s, deployed *caches* within their systems. We examine how these work in section 1.5, "Memory Hierarchy."

1.2   Semiconductor Technology Projections

Here we summarize the information in the 2003 edition of "The International Roadmap for Semiconductors", an annual publication of the ITRS representing the work of industry experts from across the world.

1.2.1   DRAM Memory

Figure 1.7 shows projections for DRAM capacity over the coming years. Two sorts of dates are considered by the ITRS—the introduction date and production date. The introduction dates is when the most-advanced vendor is able to make small numbers of chips, delivering small quantities—perhaps just thousands. The production date is the date when the major manufacturers are able to start real production, at rates of perhaps 10,000 per month. In general, one may expect to see about 12 months between introduction and production for a DRAM chip.

Since our interest is in usable technology for our server systems, we show just production dates.

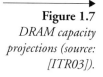

Figure 1.7
*DRAM capacity
projections (source:
[ITR03]).*

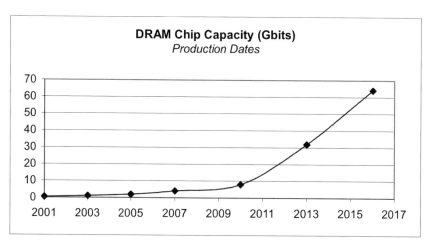

As shown in the figure, it is expected that 2-Gbit chips will be in production in 2005. The figure also shows a projected slowing of the rate of growth: up until 2018, capacity is projected to double about every three years.

1.2.2   Microprocessors

Table 1.1   *Microprocessor characteristics projection (source [ITR03])*

	2004	2006	2008	2010	2012	2016	2018
Transistors (millions)	553	878	1393	2212	3511	8848	14405
Total number of pins	1600	1936	2354	2782	3338	4702	5426
Thermal dissipation (W)	158	180	200	218	240	288	300
On-chip frequency (Mhz)	4171	3906	10972	15079	20065	39683	53207

Derived from the same source material, Table 1.1 gives projections for a number of key microprocessor characteristics. The ITRS characterizes several different classes of microprocessor for different applications and expected volumes; given what is of interest for servers, we show only the projections for the high performance (and relatively low volume) machines.

As noted above, making use of the increasing numbers of transistors is a challenge to microprocessor architects.

The thermal dissipation figures given assume a separate heat sink.

The frequency numbers given are those for the internal functioning of the chip; the ITRS expects that some external signals will be clocked at the same rate as the internal signals, while some will be at a lower frequency.

Without going into the details of the technology, it can be seen that substantial headroom is available in future microprocessor performance, although designers are faced with ever more difficult problems in designing the interfaces, a key area. We will return to this subject several times over the course of the book.

1.3   Economic Aspects of Microprocessors

In this section we look at some economic aspects of microprocessors. In the preceding section, we saw Moore's Second Law, which predicts the cost of an integrated circuit fab. At the beginning of the twenty-first century, that cost was a few billion dollars; paying for that requires very high volume sales of the resulting products.

Figure 1.8 shows what Gartner Group's 2003 predictions for the shares of the currently existing microprocessor architectures in the server market.

This chart shows a slight increase in the market share of PowerPC and a relative decrease in SPARC architectures, while Alpha (HP/Digital/Compaq), MIPS (Silicon Graphics, or SGI), and PA (HP's Precision Architecture) have disappeared. Alpha has had some difficulties maintaining credibility, and the announcement in October 1999 that NT for Alpha was being abandoned cannot have helped. A portion of Alpha's market represents a continuation of the VAX family (which, starting with the 11/780 introduced in 1978, was the architecture which made DEC a success). Eventually discontinued as a distinct line, its life was prolonged through "architecture retargeting" onto the Alpha family (see section 1.12, "Architectural Retargeting"). The agreement between Digital/Compaq and Intel on Alpha technology signaled the end for the Alpha architecture; although it was expected that Alpha architecture would be replaced by IA-64 in the

Figure 1.8
Evolution of the server market share for various architectures (source data: Gartner Group 2003).

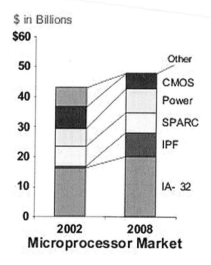

mid-term, HP's purchase of Compaq in 2002 precipitated Alpha's inevitable end.

As for MIPS, the systems vendors who had chosen this architecture (NEC and Siemens in particular) decided to change direction in favor of IA-64. SGI, which acquired MIPS (the company) in 1996, develops MIPS architecture chips for its own use; however, since it too has chosen IA-64 for some of its systems, it may gradually retreat from the MIPS architecture.

As regards PA, HP has partnered with Intel in the creation of IA-64 and has announced its intention to migrate to this new architecture. Intel's announcements of delays in the availability of Itanium, the first implementation of the IA-64 architecture (code name Merced), led HP (as it had SGI) to refocus on their own architectures—to improve their implementations and even to develop a new generation of machines.

IA-32 is expected to maintain its leadership, while IPF (Itanium Processor Family or IA-64) will grow, but slowly. In other words, IA-64 is not expected to displace IA-32 by 2008.

The server market portions marked "CMOS" and "others" in the figure are that served by the proprietary architectures (IBM and the vendors of compatible products, Bull and NEC, Unisys for the mainframes) implemented in CMOS or in other technologies. It is expected that, by 2008, all proprietary architectures will have either been migrated to standard microprocessors (retargeted) or be in the process of implementation using CMOS technology. However, a strong decrease in the market portion served by proprietary architectures is expected.

It is worth noting that these figures are for servers, which account for only a small portion of shipped microprocessors. The figures for sales of servers and PCs are:

- 4.5 million servers by 2002
- More than 163 million PCs sold in 2004

In April 2003, according to Intel, one billion X86 processors have been sold (25 years after the debut of 8086 on June, 8 1978). It is expected that about two billion PCs will have been sold by 2008.

It should also be mentioned that some derivatives of the MIPS architecture have had considerable success in embedded applications (games consoles, for example, with several tens of millions of delivered units).

1.4   Embedded Systems

Before the advent of Java, the capabilities of an embedded system would have been set by software built-in during manufacture, changeable only by system replacement or by some appropriate maintenance activity—such as replacing the read-only memory containing the software (PROM, for Programmable Read Only Memory) or by rewriting that memory (when EEPROM, for Electrically Erasable Programmable Read Only Memory, was used) using special write cycles unavailable during normal operation.

With Java, it is possible to download new application versions (*applets* and *servlets*) as needed. It is worth noting that the market for reprogrammable systems, like PCs and servers, is very different from that for embedded systems; success in one does not guarantee success in the other. Desirable characteristics for an embedded processor include low cost, low electrical power consumption (and therefore low heat dissipation, removing any need for fans), and the ability to integrate with the processor specialized hardware (e.g., input/output controllers). Further, the pressure to be backwards-compatible with prior generations is less strong than for mainstream computing, since the amount of software involved is (usually) not very large. Thus, if a new processor family can offer material reductions in system cost, the volume of systems made can justify the cost of porting or rewriting the software. IBM and Motorola have each developed PowerPC microprocessors aimed at the embedded market, and these have had reasonable success in some markets—automobiles, set top boxes and games consoles, for example.

In the embedded systems market, the ARM architecture is the volume leader and accounts for about two-thirds of the dollars. Other major architectures in embedded include MIPS, ARC, and PowerPC. PowerPC is projected to have the largest percentage revenue growth through 2006. The embedded market for processors is expected to reach $8.6 billion by 2006 (source: IN-Stat MDR 2002).

Here are indicative figures relating to the cost of developing a new microprocessor implementation:

- A few hundreds of million dollars for a new implementation of a high end microprocessor
- A few tens of million dollars for an improvement of an existing implementation

MDR[3] developed a manufacturing cost model for microprocessors which indicates, for example, that the manufacturing cost of Pentium III (including its module) would be about 75 dollars, while its selling price is about 700 dollars (at the time of its commercial introduction). According to MDR, the manufacturing cost of a microprocessor varies by few tens of dollars between 200—300 dollars. Taking into account the lifespan of a microprocessor generation and about 18 to 24 months before its first technological "refresh" and about three to four years between each new generation,[4] it is obvious that, for microprocessors would be used only in servers (families of microprocessors share a market only of some five million systems a year), the dominating factor in the cost of a server microprocessor would be recovering the development cost. To cover the costs of microprocessor development, it is clearly necessary to reach a volume market.

This is certainly the case for Intel's X86 with the PC, and, to a lesser extent, for PowerPC with Apple's Macintosh. One could observe over the past few years that the implementations became somewhat specialized to meet the perceived needs of the various markets. For example, add multimedia extensions (like Intel's MMX and now SSE for IA-32) and omitting multiprocessor support when targeting workstations; on the other hand implementations aimed at servers support multiprocessing and provide very large caches. However, this differentiation is more the effect of marketing strategies and a desire for higher margins than a reliable indication of fundamental technical differences between the markets. The evolution of multiprocessor workstations will begin to eliminate this artificial differentiation, starting at the high end.

At the end of this chapter, we will look at how microprocessor architecture and implementation have evolved together over time; some of the changes seen are intended to address problems raised here.

1.5   Memory Hierarchy

Over the years, the difference between processor performance and that of traditional DRAM memory and of disks has kept growing. In practice, the result is that without specific means to handle the problem, processors spend the majority of their time waiting for the memory system to provide them with the data they need for computation, while memory also waits on the delivery of data from the disks.

The performance gulf between processors, memory and disks is not only expressed in terms of latency (elapsed time), but also in terms of throughput, since processors are increasingly demanding in this area.

We now introduce the concept of *memory hierarchy*, initially from the angle of managing memory access time. We will then consider throughput issues and look at ways of solving the problems which arise from technology limitations.

Following this train of thought, in Chapter 2 we will present methods of organizing a collection of disks to increase throughput through parallel transfers.

1.5.1　Characteristics of the Various Levels in a Memory System

Figure 1.9 illustrates the performance gap between processor cycle time and the access time of the DRAM chips used to build the memory system.

It must be noted that the access time of a memory system is greater than the access time of the memory chips comprising it. To compute system memory access time, one must add to the chip's access time the time needed to get a request from the processor through the system interconnect (for example, a bus), plus the time needed by the error-correction hardware,

Figure 1.9
Evolution of the ratio of memory chip access time to microprocessor cycle time.

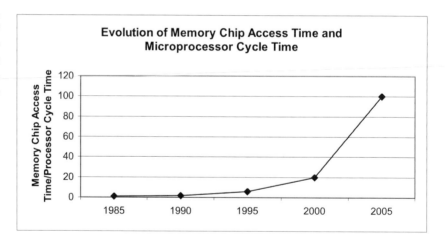

plus the time to get the data back to the processor. Figure 1.10 shows the composition of the total (average) system memory access time (for a read operation) in a system where a bus is used to connect the processor(s) to the memory. The times shown are merely indicative—they can change not only with the technology deployed and memory organization, but also with the load on the system. The memory system shown here has several chips, with a larger access time than a single-chip memory. The diagram wraps in an

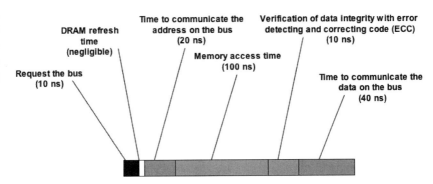

Figure 1.10
Components of the total time of access for a Memory read operation.

average time for memory refresh into access time—for DRAM chips to retain data, it is necessary to periodically rewrite ("refresh") the data.

It should be noted that the fields are not drawn to scale. In this example, the total access time is 180 nanoseconds (ns).

Few studies have been published on the components of the total access time for memory, especially for servers. Access time depends on both memory chip technology and memory system organization; [CUP99] has compared memory organizations, although for a workstation rather than a server.

As for disks, while their densities are increasing, their access times have hardly improved at all. We should note in passing that the mass market for the PC has driven disk prices down sharply; this has led the data-processing industry to align itself with the PC industry and to use the same disks.

So there are obvious parallels between disks and microprocessors; servers are now based on standard microprocessors—the same machines used in as workstations and PCs, or perhaps straightforward derivatives thereof—together with exactly the same disks. Only proprietary systems use non-standard processors, because they need to maintain binary compatibility.

In Chapter 2, we will discuss Disk Arrays, an arrangement of disks frequently found on servers.

To mask these memory latency effects, system architects have long had recourse to the technique of *caches*. The concept of a cache, or memory hierarchy, is to provide the effect of a very large, very fast memory by combining a large-capacity, cheap memory with a much smaller and faster, but more expensive, memory. The behavior of the combination is statistically similar to a large, fast memory, but its cost is very close to that of the large, slow memory.

Figure 1.11
*Levels of memory
in a system.*

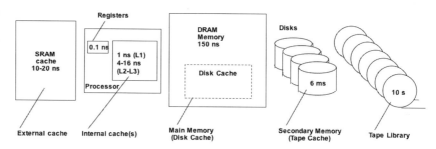

Figure 1.11 illustrates the various levels of memory in a system, giving access times for each level. In the diagram, we generalize the concept of memory hierarchy: each level is a cache for the next higher level, except for the last level, which in this example is a tape library.

Table 1.2   *Illustration of the differences in access time for the various levels of the memory hierarchy.*

Technology	Typical Access Time	Human Scale	Approximate Capacity	Approximate Price ($/MB)
Processor Register	100ps	0.1 s	64 × 64 bits	(part of microprocessor)
Integrated Cache	L1: ~1ns L2-L3: 4-16 ns (depending on cache size)	16 s	fraction of a MB up to several MB	(part of microprocessor)
External cache	10-20 ns	~10-20 s	4-8 MB	~$10
Main memory	~150 ns	~25 min	>= 1GB	$0.125
Disk	~6 ms	~700 days	> 70 GB/disk	~$0.005
Tape (in a robot)	~10 s	~3200 years	~100GB/tape	<$0.001

Table 1.2 illustrates the differences between access times for various memory technologies found in a system, and maps their differences into a human scale—assuming that a human takes about one tenth of a second to access something from his or her memory. We also indicate a cost for each technology, shown as cost per megabyte.

The microprocessor's registers constitute the first level of the hierarchy. Unlike the other levels of the hierarchy, in which complete transparency is desirable (see hereafter), the registers are explicitly manipulated by program.

Looking at the times in this table shows the significant improvements that a cache can offer to access time. As one example, a disk cache implemented in main memory allows one to trade an access time of around 700 days (in human scale) for one of about 25 minutes with no significant increase in system price.

1.5.2   Space-Time Locality Properties

Caches exploit the locality properties of programs. When we observe programs executing, we can see *locality* behaviors:

- If a piece of information is accessed, there is a high probability that it will be accessed again in the near future (*temporal* locality)

- If a piece of information is accessed, there is a high probability that nearby (in memory) information will be also accessed in the near future (*spatial* locality)

Figure 1.12 illustrates the phenomena of spatial and temporal locality of a program during its execution by showing the distribution of the addresses emitted by the processor running (this is a symbolic representation: the points within the ovals represent the addresses accessed by the program).

Figure 1.12
Properties of spatial and temporal locality.

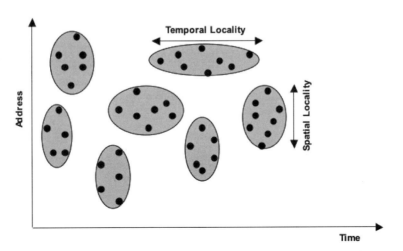

The principle behind caches consists of maintaining, in a level of fast memory, the data which are most frequently accessed at a given moment. The management of the contents of the caches for the fastest levels is implemented in hardware, to maximize performance.

Figure 1.13 illustrates, in a very simplified way, the organization of a simple cache mechanism.

Figure 1.13
Cache mechanism.

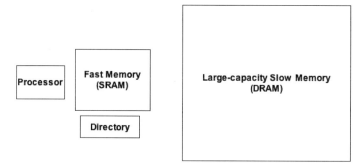

Memory accesses emitted by the processor are "filtered" by the cache directory (which is an associative device); it indicates which storage areas of DRAM are present in the cache. In the event of success (hit) the access takes place directly in the cache. In the case of failure (miss), an access to DRAM is necessary.

One of the significant parameters for the performance of a cache is the probability (the success rate, or hit ratio*)* of finding information sought in the cache (i.e., in the fastest level of the memory). This success rate depends on the behavior of the program, i.e., of the sequence of addresses used by the program during its execution, as well as the design parameters of the cache.

Caches make it possible to hide access time discontinuities in a system; one can thus expect to see a cache each time that there is a significant difference between the access times of two adjacent levels of memory. In servers, we see caches:

■ *Between the processors and the memory*—top-of-the-range microprocessors support two levels of caches: a first level of cache (known as L1, for Level 1) internal to the processor and an external level of cache (known as L2, for Level 2). The general trend is to integrate caches within the microprocessor over the span of successive generations: integration of the first level cache; then of the L2 controller (but not the memory itself); and then the whole of the L2. Along with this integration, one notes an increase in the number of levels with, for example, Level 3 caches sometimes shared between a small group of processors in a tightly-coupled multiprocessor

- *Between memory and disks*—for example, the Disk Cache Buffer of UNIX or Windows' System Cache
- *Between discs and magnetic tapes*—for example, management of a secondary hierarchy of memory between discs and one or more tape libraries
- *Between memory and the network* for accesses to distant data

To show the effectiveness of a cache, consider a situation in which main memory is constructed from DRAM with an access time of 150 ns while an L2 is built from SRAM with an access time of 10 ns. If we assume a hit ratio of 98%—that is, 98% of the time, a memory reference is found to be in the cache—and also assume an L1 cache integrated into the processor, with an access time of 1 ns and a hit ratio of 95%, then the apparent—or effective—access time for the memory system may be computed as:

Effective Access time = 0.95 x 1 + 0.03 x 10 + 0.02 x 150 = 4.25 ns

Thus we have constructed a memory system built mostly from cheap DRAM which offers access time performance close to that of fast, but expensive, SRAM. As the technology improves, the size of caches grows and caches are being integrated within microprocessors. The number of cache levels is also growing; 3 or 4 levels of caches (between the microprocessor itself and the memory) is now common.

A similar equation for the effective access time for a disk system with cache can be constructed the same way. The performance increase is, however, even more spectacular, since the performance ratio between disk and DRAM-based memory is around 40,000 (150 ns for the memory and around 6 ms for the disk).

As mentioned, each level of cache has a mechanism to track what data is held in the cache. For the processor-memory caches, this mechanism is implemented in hardware, while it is implemented in software for the higher levels (such as memory-disk or memory-network).

Caches pose yet another problem, that of data coherence, which we will cover later in this chapter.

1.5.3 Cache Design Parameters

Caches may be characterized by a number of parameters [HAN98]. In addition to the total size of the cache and the size of the cache line or block,[5] which are strong determinants of performance, the most significant parameters are as follows:

Separate caches or unified cache. In the case of separate caches, there is one cache for data (reading and writing) and a separate cache for instructions (reading only). With separate caches, the replacement algorithm (which decides, when new data must be brought into a cache, which data is to be thrown out) can be specific to the cache; for example, the processor writes into (changes the data in) the data cache, but does not change the instruction cache. Thus, when a block is replaced in the instruction cache, there is never any need to copy the block being replaced back to memory. The discussion as to whether a unified cache is better than separate caches has been settled, separate caches provide a higher throughput while a unified cache can provide a better hit ratio.

Figure 1.14
Cache organizations—placement of blocks within a cache.

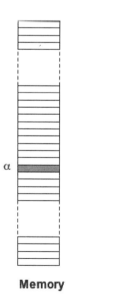

Fully-associative cache
the block at address α can be placed anywhere in the cache

Direct-mapped cache
the block at address α can only be placed in one position, here marked β, in the cache

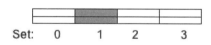

Set: 0   1   2   3

Memory

Set-associative cache (here 4-way)
The block at address α can be placed anywhere in set 1

How blocks are placed in the cache. There are three modes of placement, as illustrated in Figure 1.14:

- *Fully Associative.* In this mode, a block with a given address can occupy any place in the cache

- *Direct-Mapped.* A block with a given address can occupy only one place within the cache (from the point of view of the implementation, there is a fixed relation between the address of a block and the place which it occupies in the cache)

- *Set Associative.* A block with a given address can occupy only certain places in the cache (one indicates this type of associative organization under the name of n-way or n-way set associative, according to the number n of sets or independent storage places offered for a given address by the cache)

For these the last two modes of placement, the position of the block in the cache is given by a function which computes the placement offset from the block address; this function is often called the cache's *hash function*.

Identification of which blocks are in the cache. Associated with the cache is a description of what it holds. This is a sort of catalog, associating the address of a memory block with its address in the cache (if it is present) and providing information on the state of the block. Either virtual or physical addresses may be used for this, depending on whether one first searches the cache for data and then does the virtual-to-real translation or translates and then looks up. Using virtual addresses poses a problem, because virtual addresses are local to each process.[6] Thus, two processes may have different objects at the same virtual address, or (even worse) have the same object at different virtual addresses (this is the *aliasing* problem). In practice, these days one generally finds just physically-addressed caches.

Replacement of blocks in the cache. This case arises when a reference to a block misses—that is, the block is not found in the cache. Under these circumstances, the block must be brought in and placed in the cache—this implies that the current contents of the cache may need to be replaced. In the case of a direct-mapped cache, there is no choice as to where to place the new block, since there is but one placement possible for a block of a given address. For fully-associative and set-associative caches, a choice must be made as to which block to replace. One of the best-known algorithms for making the choice is LRU (*Least-Recently Used*), in which the choice

---

Virtual Addresses and Physical Addresses

From software's point of view, the need to have an abstraction for memory separated from physical reality (a notion we revisit in Chapter 3) has led to the concepts of *virtual addresses* and *physical addresses*. Virtual addresses are those manipulated by software and generated by processors during the execution of program. These addresses are then translated into their corresponding physical addresses, which correspond to the location of data in the memory system. In a running system, only "active" portions of the virtual address space are held in memory, so this translation can lead to a situation in which data to which the processor wants access is not currently in memory, but is held on disk. Since the unit of allocation (and of transfer) between disk and memory is called a page, the situation described is known as a *page fault*. The operating system, told of a page fault, fetches the data from disk and places it in memory, updating the information it uses to map between virtual and physical addresses appropriately. This operation amounts to transparently managing a memory hierarchy (as far as an application program is concerned) between physical memory and the disks. The actual operation of translating virtual to physical addresses is done by specialized hardware, using caches which hold the most frequently used translations.

---

between candidate blocks for replacement is made by choosing the one that was least-recently used.

Write strategy. There are two major write strategies:

- *Write-Through.* The data is written to both the cache block and to the immediately adjacent level of memory

- *Write-Back (also known as Copy Back or more rarely Store Into).* The data is written only into the cache, with the modified block being written to the next level of memory only when expelled from the cache

A cache must remember that a block has been changed by a write to it; such a block is said to be *dirty*. To avoid blocking the processor's progress when writing (whatever the write strategy), it is usual to provide a *write buffer*—fast local storage in which the request to write the cache may be stored quickly, allowing the processor to continue work as soon as the data is captured in the buffer.

Writing to a block missing from the cache. There are two strategies:

- *Write Allocate (also called Fetch on Write)*. The missing block is fetched from memory into the cache and updated there
- *No Write Allocate (or Write Around)*. The data is written to the next level of the memory hierarchy without the block being fetched into the cache

The hit ratio depends on all these parameters, as well as the total size of the cache and the cache line size together with the behavior of the application itself.

We may categorize the reasons for a cache miss:

- *Compulsory*—the very first time a program accesses a block, it will not be in the cache, and so must be loaded (this type of miss is also called *Cold Start Miss* or *First Reference Miss*).
- *Capacity*—since the cache has a finite size, it may not be able to hold all the blocks accessed by the program: thus, some blocks must be evicted and replaced by others during the execution of the program. If an evicted block is referenced later, it will in turn replace another block and be reloaded
- *Conflict*—in the case of Direct-Mapped and Set-Associative caches, a given block has a limited number of places in the cache where it can be held, even if other portions of the cache are empty. When a block of one address needs to be cached and replaces a block of another address, we say that the blocks are in conflict

The subject of cache properties and organization merits a much longer discussion, but this would move us away from the focus of this book.

1.6   The Problem of Memory Throughput

Microprocessors are increasingly demanding in terms of memory through-put, for the following reasons:

- Cache block sizes are increasing

- The frequency of operation, both within the microprocessors and at their interfaces with their environment (for example the processor bus), keeps getting faster

- Some processor performance approaches result in accessing memory either ahead of what would be required by normal execution of the program, or which may not actually be used by the processor (in the case of *speculative execution*)

- Code footprint—the amount of memory occupied by the program itself in memory, without regard to the data it uses—is increasing with emerging instruction set architectures

- The move to 64-bit processing means that in many cases the processor will manipulate 64-bit quantities rather than 32-bit quantities

On the other hand, the changes in memory behavior seem opposed to the needs of the processor:

- The available throughput of memory chips improves only slowly (much more slowly than their capacity)

- As we have seen, improvements in memory technology keep reducing the number of chips needed to construct a memory system of a given size, thereby making it difficult to gain back throughput by increasing the number of chips used

- The number of pins on a memory chip is limited for reasons of cost, which limits the parallelism possible in accessing the data in the chip, and thus the available throughput

This situation, which is hardly new, has led to some discontinuities in the memory marketplace with the introduction both of chips which can deliver several bits in parallel and of new memory technologies.

Some quick explanations will set the scene well enough for our purposes: memory chips can be characterized by a pair of numbers: n, the number of cells in a chip and t, the number of bits per cell; the cell is usual unit of access and transfer. The chip capacity is $n \times t$, and is expressed in megabits (where one megabit is 2^{20} bits—very nearly 10^6 bits—hence the nomenclature). The larger t is, the greater the throughput (at constant access time).

A number of different specifications have been introduced to improve memory throughput: some alphabet soup—for asynchronous DRAM, there have been fast page mode and EDO (for Extended Data Out) while for synchronous DRAM allowing even higher bandwidths we see SDRAM (for Synchronous DRA*M*) and RAMBUS.

A detailed discussion of DRAM technology is outwith the scope of this work, but the interested reader may consult [JAC02].

Looking at it at a system level, Figure 1.15—inspired by [PAT04]—shows schematically several different methods for increasing memory throughput.

The first organization, shown as (a) in the figure, uses a memory whose implementation allows the reading or writing of just one word (32 or 64 bits) on each access. The loading of a block into cache thus requires several sequential accesses to the memory; while this does not reflect real-world practice, it is provided as a basis for comparison.

In the second organization, (b), the memory is able to provide a cache block's worth of data on each access. This organization offers the best potential for performance.

Figure 1.15
Organizations for the improvement of memory throughput.

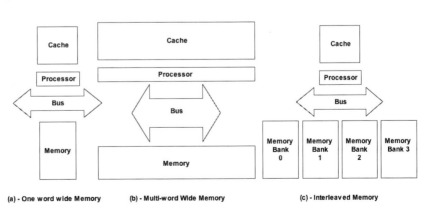

(a) - One word wide Memory   (b) - Multi-word Wide Memory   (c) - Interleaved Memory

On the other hand, the use of many memory chips in parallel implied by this organization presents several disadvantages:

- Modularity of the storage capacity: the storage capacity is a multiple of the product of the capacity of the chips by the width of the memory: with a wide memory, it is difficult to match the possible memory system capacities to the needs of the system
- The increase in the width of the various interfaces and in particular that between processor and memory presents implementation difficulties

The third organization, (c)—known as *memory interleaving*—consists of implementing the memory as a number of limited width *banks*, capable of being accessed in block mode.[7] Data is interlaced across the multiple banks, with (for example) word 0 being in bank 0, word 1 in bank 1, word 2 in bank 0, word 4 in bank 0, etc. With this approach, the widths of the different interfaces can be limited (in this example, to the width of a word). The memory may be organized so that, in the case of a read, the read operations occur in parallel in all the banks. In the same way, for a write, the cache line may be block-transferred and then written into each memory bank. Different optimizations are possible.

This approach is widely used in systems, despite the memory size modularity issues.

To mitigate the differences in performance between processor and memory, an increasingly significant share of the silicon resources within the microprocessors is devoted to the provision of internal caches intended to hide memory latency.

1.6.1   Memory Hierarchy Summary

Table 1.3 summarizes the levels of cache frequently used in information processing systems along with their key characteristics. Read the table in conjunction with Figure 1.11, which shows a general view of system memory hierarchy.

It should be noted that the access times given for disk caches and tape caches are only the access times of the hardware; that is, they do not include the execution time of the software that manages the caches as it determines the presence or absence of cached data, nor the calculation of the addresses of the data involved in the operation.

Table 1.3   *Summary of the characteristics of the various levels of cache*

Cache Type and Properties	Level 1 and Level 2	External	Disk cache	External Storage Hierarchy
Where it's found	Internal to the processor	Between microprocessor and main memory	In memory	Disk
Technology	SRAM integrated into the microprocessor	SRAM	DRAM	Disk
What's cached	External cache or memory contents	DRAM contents	Disk contents	Contents of tape cartridges in a robot
Characteristics				
Capacity	O (10 KB/100 KB)	O (1 MB)	O (100 MB)	O (1 GB)
Granule size	O (10/100 B)	O (100 B)	O (10 KB)	O (100 KB)
Access time	3 ns	15 ns	~180 ns	~6 ms
Bandwidth	O (GB/s)	O (GB/s)	O (1 GB/s)	O (100 MB/s)
Who manages the cache	Hardware (internal to the microprocessor)	Hardware (internal to the microprocessor)	Software; either the operating system, the file system or the DBMS	Software; the memory hierarchy manager

As shown by the table, the first two levels of memory hierarchy are managed entirely by hardware (that is, with no intervention by software). In the case of large multiprocessors, an additional level of cache may be used: a group of processors (for example, four) in which each processor is supplied with its own internal caches may share a large external cache. In this manner, the traffic on the bus or crossbar connecting this group to memory may be greatly reduced. As with internal caches, the management of such an external cache is done purely in hardware. The disk cache in main memory, on the other hand, is entirely controlled by software. In Table 1.3 and elsewhere in the book, the notation O(N) means "of the order of N;" so that O(100 B), for example, means "of the order of 100 bytes—certainly more than 10, and certainly less than 1000." In general, it is the operating system, the file system or the DBMS which looks after the disk cache. The file systems of current operating systems look after all disk cache management (as with the Disk Cache Buffer in UNIX and the System Cache in Windows). However, relational data base managers often take over this responsibility for their own data, using their knowledge of the roles of the various data they are manipulating (for example, it is preferable to keep the indexes in memory rather than the data itself, since the indexes are smaller and are frequently accessed).

Management of the external memory hierarchy involves using disk to cache the data held on tape libraries; this is done by software. This final level of the memory hierarchy is currently much less widespread than the others, but we expect this to change over the next few years.

1.7　Processor—Memory—I/O Interconnect

The connection between the processors, the memory, the I/O controllers and the peripherals is carried out typically by a whole collection of interconnects. Figure 1.16 illustrates these various connections in a generic server architecture.

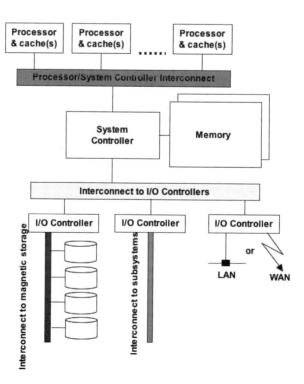

Figure 1.16
Connections within a system

This diagram shows four types of connections:

- The connection between processors and the system controller, which integrates a memory controller and an I/O bridge
- The connection between the system controller and the I/O controllers
- The connection between the I/O controllers and the disks (etc.)
- The connection to specialized subsystems, like those of communication and storage

In the following section, we will look at the connection between processor, memory and bridges; the three other types of connections will be handled in the following chapter, which discusses I/O, and we will spare few words on them here.

1.7.1   Bus and Crossbar Interconnect

The connection between processors, memory and I/O is the first element of this hierarchy. Two types of technologies are usually used for the realization of this interconnect:

- Bus
- Crossbar

The type of connection most usually used is the *bus*. A bus is a means of communication shared between all the elements, each of which connects to the bus. A bus is physically implemented as a number of electrically-conducting wires. Its major advantage lies in its simplicity.

The major disadvantages of a bus are as follows:

- Limitations in terms of frequency of operation, maximum length and in the number of connected elements
- The fact that it constitutes a bottleneck since its potential throughput is shared between the various connected elements

The potential throughput of a bus is a function of the number of bits it can convey in parallel and of its operating frequency. The length of the bus

---

Buses

A few years ago, it was common to organize an information processing system around a bus. Standards were developed: Multibus I (followed by Multibus II) and VME, as well as a certain number of buses specific to a manufacturer. Such buses were called backplane buses, because the systems were constructed from printed-circuit boards interconnected by an electrical bus forming part of the chassis containing the cards. The backplane bus interconnected the various elements of the system, except for the peripherals: processors, memory and I/O controllers.

With the increase in both circuit integration and microprocessor performance, the connection processor/memory/bridge became more specialized, and the industry moved away from the use of backplane buses. Often, each new major generation of microprocessor brings its own bus definition, together with the associated chips (memory controller and I/O bridge).

---

and the number of connected elements are factors which limit the frequency of operation. For example, multiprocessor systems can be organized around a 128-bit wide bus functioning at a frequency of 400 MHz, a maximum length of about fifteen centimeters (or six inches) and connecting to a maximum of five elements (i.e., four processors and a system controller). The theoretical throughput of such a bus would be thus 6.4 GB/sec.

A bus is composed of control lines and data lines. The control lines are used for requests and acknowledgments, as well as to indicate the nature of the information carried on the data lines, which conveys either the data itself or addresses. The operation of the bus is governed by a protocol and a concept of cycle. We will not delve into the inner technical details relevant to the operation of buses, in particular the notions of asynchronous and synchronous buses, bus arbitration, address/data multiplexing, and so forth. The interested reader will be able to turn to [PAT04].

To make this more concrete: a processor's request to read the memory is translated into a request for access to the bus followed by the sending to the memory of the address of the element desired (the control lines indicate that the request is a read request for the memory and that an address is present on the data lines). When the memory answers, the control lines indicate that the operation is a transfer of data from the memory to the processor and that information is present on the data lines.

We can distinguish two types of bus based on how the elements connected to the bus communicate:

- *Synchronous buses,* in which the control lines integrate a clock signal that regulates all bus activities. The simplicity of the protocol requires only a little logic for its implementation; consequently, a synchronous bus can function at a high frequency. On the other hand, the use of a synchronous bus implies that all the elements connected on the bus function at the same speed (with respect to their relation with the bus), and that, because of the phenomena of dispersion, the length of the bus must be shorter, since the frequency of operation of the bus is higher.

- *Asynchronous buses,* in which there is no synchronism constraint between the elements which are connected. The communication between elements implies a synchronization by means of a protocol, known as a handshake, that is implemented by means of specific control lines. Asynchronous buses do not suffer from the same problems of distance as synchronous buses, but they offer a lower throughput.

Different techniques are implemented to increase bus performance, such as:

- *Reducing latency.* To avoid keeping the bus tied up throughout each operation, one uses the concept of a *Split transaction,* which exists, in the case of a read, to emit the request accompanied by an identification of the transaction on the control lines; when the memory responds—with a subsequent, separate, bus operation—it provides along with the data the corresponding transaction identification.

- *Increasing throughput.* Transferring information on a block basis makes it possible to exchange, between the elements connected on the bus, information with a size greater than the number of data lines by minimizing the number of cycles of the bus. It consists of transmitting, in consecutive cycles of the bus, the information after having specified the operation required and the starting address (which uses just one cycle operation/address followed by N cycles of data, instead of the succession of N pairs of cycles of bus-request, command/address and data).

- *Increasing parallelism.* Increasing the number of data lines is limited by packaging constraints and the problems of electrical noise.

These buses are critical elements in system performance, and, as we indicated in the preceding note, are related to the specifications of the various generations of chip sets (microprocessor and system controller) and are thus directly under the control of the originators of these chip sets. This phenomenon of integration makes a *de jure* standard in this field highly unlikely.

The other type of connection used by certain manufacturers is the crossbar. The goal of a crossbar is to remove the contention which is a necessary part of the use of a bus by providing multiple paths between the connected elements. The problems arising from this approach are at the level of the support of a significant number of simultaneous paths and number of pins needed on the chip (the number of pins of the crossbar being directly proportional to the number of connected elements).

We will see in Chapter 4 examples of systems organized around crossbars.

1.7.2 Other Connections

With the advent of the specialized processor-memory buses to replace the standard buses, new standard buses have emerged as I/O buses. These connect the processor-memory subsystem to I/O controllers.

Of the various standards which were proposed and used in this field, the PCI bus—and its extensions—has received the favor of the majority of manufacturers.

As regards connection of magnetic peripherals, another standard—SCSI—currently dominates. Connection of specialized subsystems (specialized subsystems of communication and subsystems of storage) is implemented using high-speed local area network technology, or makes use of the Fiber Channel standard. We will examine these connections in Chapter 2, which is devoted to I/O.

1.8   Parallelism

As we saw in the beginning of this chapter, microprocessor performance increases at a dizzying rate. However, the performance needs, of the top-of-the-range applications for both scientific and technical work and for data management exceed the capacity of standard microprocessors. Wishing to base their systems on the use of standard microprocessors rather than create and maintain their own microprocessors, the majority of systems builders have turned to *parallelism*. Given the limits fixed at any time by technology, parallelism seems to be a good way of increasing performance.

We will illustrate the implementation of parallelism, using an example provided by Informix. In this example, the handling of an SQL request breaks up into four stages. Figure 1.17 illustrates some strategies to accelerate the processing of the request.

This diagram shows, on the left, the traditional (sequential) treatment of a request to join two tables. This operation requires four stages: a seek for the tuples[8] concerned, the join operation itself, a sort of the tuples obtained, and finally writing the resulting table.

A first level of parallelization consists in making the operations proceed in a pipeline: when the search operation has produced the first tuples of interest, the join operation can begin; the first results of the join are then presented to the sort operation; and so on.

Figure 1.17
*Parallelization of
an SQL request
(according to
Informix).*

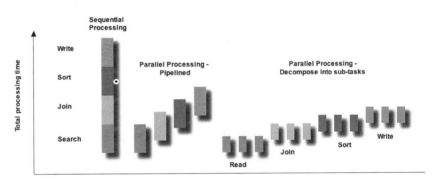

An additional degree of parallelization is obtained with the decomposition of each operation (when it is possible) into several tasks likely to be carried out in parallel.

We now will discuss the definition of parallel systems.

Parallel Systems

Philip Bernstein defined, in 1966, the conditions under which two programs may be executed in parallel. That is to say, given two programs P1 and P2, it is supposed that each program uses variables on entry (E1 and E2) and produces values at exit (S1 and S2). Programs P1 and P2 may be executed in parallel (denoted as P1||P2) if, and only if, the following conditions are observed:

$$\{E1 \cap S2 = \emptyset, \; E2 \cap S1 = \emptyset, \; S1 \cap S2 = \emptyset\}$$

More generally, a collection of programs P1, P2,... Pn is executable in parallel if, and only if, the Bernstein conditions are satisfied. In other words, if Pi || Pj for any couple {i,j} with i # j.

In practice, such conditions are difficult to respect.

Granularity of Parallelism

In the field of parallelism, the concept of "granularity" of parallelism arises. This concept refers to the size of the sections of code likely to be carried out in parallel. One speaks of *fine grain parallelism* when the size of the section represents only some small number of instructions, or of *coarse grain parallelism* when the sequences represent a significant number of instructions.

Sources of Parallelism

The sources of parallelism arise from the type of the problems being handled. There are three forms of parallelism:

- *Data Parallelism.* In this form of parallelism, the same operation is carried out—by different processors—on disjoint sets of data.

- *Control Parallelism.* In this form of parallelism, different operations are carried out simultaneously. This sort of parallelism is available when the program is constructed of independent portions, or when certain control structures (such as loops) are likely to be carried out in parallel.

- *Flow Parallelism.* In this form of parallelism, work on one portion of the data flow is overlapped with work on another portion (i.e., a following operation can be started before the preceding one is finished). This is an assembly line or pipeline model.

Figure 1.18 illustrates the relation between Flynn's classification and the various options as regards architecture. We shall return in the following chapters to these various architectures and their characteristics.

Before discussing the problems of employing parallelism in data base management systems, we should point out that one of the major difficulties—perhaps even *the* major difficulty—in parallel systems is writing the programs. Indeed, writing parallel applications implies synchronization

---

Flynn's Classification of Parallel Architectures

On the level of systems architectures, Michael Flynn proposed a classification of parallel architectures [FLY72]:

- SISD (Single Instruction Single Data), in which just one stream of instructions performs a transformation on a single stream of data (this is the simplest model and corresponds to the computer architecture model described by John von Neumann.)

- SIMD (Single Instruction Multiple Data), in which the same stream of instructions is applied to disjoint sets of data

- MISD (Multiple Instruction Single Data) in which several instruction streams are applied to the same stream of data, (some sources hold that pipelined execution is the closest approximation to this approach, but we feel that this is a somewhat artificial view, since in a pipelined machine there is but one instruction stream)

- MIMD (Multiple Instruction Multiple Data), in which independent instruction streams are applied to independent sets of data (as we will see in the case of parallel DBMSs, the same program (the DBMS) is simultaneously executed, without synchronism on disjoint sets of data one speaks then of SPMD Single Program Multiple Data Stream)

---

operations for access to shared data, and thus *rendezvous* between the various parts of the program. Operating systems provide synchronization primitives as well as effective support mechanisms for intra-application parallelism with the concept of lightweight processes or threads. (See Chapter 4, Symmetrical Multiprocessors (Tightly Coupled).)

Figure 1.18
Relationship between Flynn's classifications and architectural options.

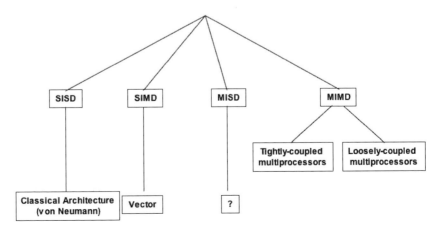

We should note that no tool exists for the automatic parallelization of applications; although such a tool has long been a research topic, few if any concrete results have been obtained. For intensive numerical computations, there are software environments that allow the expression of parallelism within the applications. PVM (Parallel Virtual Machine) has existed for many years, and more recently Open MP (a message-passing interface) has emerged.

However, in business-oriented data processing, these execution environments are hardly used—instead, essentially all the parallelism is provided by an appropriately-parallelized DBMS.

1.8.1   Speedup and Scaleup

We agree with [DEW92]: an ideal parallel system must have two properties linear speedup and linear scaleup.

To illustrate these properties, it is said that a parallel system has

- A linear speedup if n times more resources make it possible to treat a given task in n times less time than the reference system
- A linear scaleup if n times more resources make it possible to deal with an n times *larger* problem in the same time as the reference system

Figure 1.19 illustrates these concepts of speedup and scaleup.

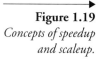

Figure 1.19
*Concepts of speedup
and scaleup.*

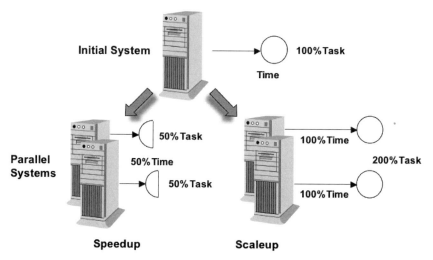

Speedup consists, without changing the definition of the problem to be solved, of decreasing the response time by means of exploiting in parallel the resources of the information processing system; this is done by transforming the execution of a single request into the execution of several independent, but coordinated requests. This is intra-request parallelism. Decision-support systems generally seek speedup through intra-request parallelism; they decompose a complex request into several less complex requests which are likely to be executable in parallel.

An OLTP (On-Line Transaction Processing) system,[9] on the other hand, is more likely to seek scaleup—a system with n times more customers on line will have to handle n times as many requests (and generally not very complex requests) against a database n times as large. Scaleup performance increases for transactional systems are thus done through inter-request parallelism, that is, by seeking to perform the transactions submitted to the system in parallel through optimization of the system resources, such as the processors, the disks, etc.

Further, this is exactly the type of scaleup required by the TPC-C benchmark from the Transaction Processing Council (TPC), wherein the size of the database is proportional to the performance of the system. The TPC, an organization created by manufacturers of information-processing systems and DBMS vendors, has the dual aim of specifying performance benchmarks and of publishing measurement results. The performance of information processing systems will be covered in Chapter 7.

Figure 1.20
Typical Speedup curve (according to [DEW92].

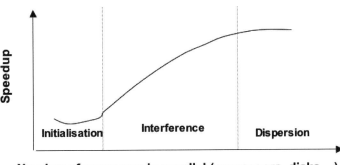

Obviously, the behavior of real systems diverges from this ideal of linear acceleration, as Figure 1.20 shows.

This figure highlights three negative effects:

- *Start-up.* This is the amount of time needed to start up the parallel activities: a process must create the various processes to be executed concurrently, to associate each with appropriate data, and to then collect the results of the simultaneous execution. To manage this, a balance must be struck between the number of parallel processes, the average execution time of each such process, the cost to launch the processes, and the synchronization costs of the processes.

- *Interference.* This is the slowdown caused by conflicts as the various processes access shared data (which varies by application). This slowdown increases with the number of parallel processes.

- *Dispersion.* As the number of parallels processes increases, work carried out by each process decreases, and the variance of the execution time between these parallel processes can become significant compared to the average execution time. The net result is that the time of overall execution is the execution time of the slowest process.

A general law, known as Amdahl's Law [HEN02], expresses the speedup factor resulting from an improvement to just a portion of the system (i.e., an improvement which leaves one portion of the system unchanged and therefore with the same performance):

$$\text{Speedup} = \frac{\text{Execution time of whole task without using the improvement}}{\text{Execution time of whole task when using the improvement}}$$

Amdahl's Law expresses speedup as a function of two factors:

- The fraction of the time that the computation spends in the part capable of improvement

- Speedup of the improved part

To illustrate this law in a simple manner, we will assume that the speedup is proportional to the number of processors run in parallel (in practice, as noted above, this is not true—there is a frictional effect due to interference which increases with the number of processors). The speedup is expressed relative to a system with just one processor.

In general, an application has a portion which must be executed sequentially—for example, the initialization of the parallel tasks and the collection of their results. Suppose a is the fraction of instructions in the application which must be executed sequentially; then the fraction which can be accelerated through parallelism is $1—a$. Suppose P is the number of processors devoted to the execution of the program. Then the maximum speedup available through parallelism is given by Amdahl's Law as:

$$\text{Maximum Speedup} = \frac{1}{\alpha + \frac{(1-\alpha)}{P}} \leq \frac{1}{\alpha}$$

Thus, if the sequential portion of the application is 10%, and we assume we have ten processors in parallel, the maximum speedup is 5.26x, although with an infinite number of processors a 10x speedup would be achievable.

Available speedup falls quickly as the sequential portion of the application grows. As an example, if the sequential portion were to be 20%, then (still with 10 processors) the available speedup is 3.57x falling to 2.17x when the sequential portion grows to 40% and to 1.67x at 60% sequential.

Some intensive numerical calculations are such that the sequential portion may be reduced almost to zero by increasing the size of the problem. Gustavson's Law [CUL98] reflects this situation by recognizing that the parallel portion of such computations is generally made up of data-manipulating loops and so the parallelizable fraction grows along with the amount of data. Consider a program with a sequential portion s and whose execution time a for the portion likely to be parallelizable is a linear function of the size of the problem n. The execution time on a single processor would then be:

$$t = s + a \times n$$

Amdahl's Law gives the execution time on a system of n processors:

$$t = s + \frac{a \times n}{n} = s + a$$

And speedup is therefore:

$$A = \frac{s + a \times n}{s + a}$$

which tends to n as a tends to infinity.

One must also take into account the fact that in practice, the execution time of the sequential portion of an application which has a parallel portion will depend on the number of processors (due to the need to initialize a number of parallel tasks related to the number of processors plus the collection of the data produced by these tasks). Another law has been propounded to represent this situation:

If α_p is the sequential portion of an application being executed on a system of n processors, then the maximum speedup is limited to:

```
Maximum Speedup ≤ P × (1 - αp) + αp
```

An objective of DBMS programmers is to exploit to the maximum the available parallel resources—processors and disks. Thanks to thirty years of OLTP experience, significant results have been achieved in speedup. With current DBMS implementations, however, we are just at the beginning of the learning curve for decision- support systems.

DBMS

Nearly all the data base management systems available on standard systems—a subject to which we will return in Chapter 8—are relational database management systems. Hierarchical databases (like IBM's IMS) and Network databases (Codasyl databases, like Bull's IDS) remain of interest only to proprietary systems, while object-oriented databases have not achieved the penetration predicted by some. We will use the term DBMS henceforth to indicate a relational database management system; the term RDBMS is also used.

It is interesting to note that in the 1980s, Teradata (now a part of NCR) offered a database machine that made a breakthrough in decision support application performance, leveraging a specialized architecture built around the use of standard microprocessors (Intel's 8086) and specialized software (OS and DBMS). These systems were connected to IBM and Bull mainframes. The architecture was able to benefit from improving technology by improving functionality—the ability to integrate application processors running UNIX, for example. A key deployment area for these systems was to complement IBM and Bull mainframes (they have been in Bull's catalog since 1987). NCR's Teradata systems are marketed under the name of 5200, and will be commented on in Chapter 5.

1.8.2 Problems Arising in Multiprocessor Architectures

In this section, we will examine the various problems arising with symmetrical multiprocessor architectures and will present the general principles of the solutions to them. These problems are cache coherence, memory consistency models, and synchronization mechanisms.

Parallel Systems Architecture

As we have seen earlier in this chapter—and handled in greater detail in Chapters 4 and 5—there are two major families of parallel systems:

- *Tightly coupled architectures*, in which all the processors uniformly share the system resources. In particular, memory is shared and data coherence is ensured by the hardware, with just one copy of the OS running the system. Such systems are known as "symmetrical multiprocessor systems," or SMPs.

- *Loosely coupled architectures*, in which the memory is not shared between the processors. In such architectures, the total system is composed of a certain number of interconnected nodes; each node has its own resources and functions under the control of its own copy of the operating system (if a node is itself a small SMP, then the node's memory is shared by the node processors). Clusters and MPP (Massively Parallel Processing) machines are loosely-coupled architectures.

We will limit ourselves to a general presentation of these principles, since a detailed description and comparisons of the various related solutions are beyond the scope of this book. The interested reader will be able to consult the bibliographical references presented at the end of the book.

1.8.3 Cache Coherence

In a symmetrical architecture multiprocessor (SMP, for *Symmetric Multi-Processor)*, all the processors have access to all the resources of the system, such as the memory and the I/Os. Since, for reasons of performance we wish each processor to have its own cache, a given data item may be in the cache of many processors. Thus when a processor updates such a data item in its own cache, we wish to arrange that subsequent accesses by the other processors to their own caches will reflect that updated information. This is the cache coherence problem, illustrated in Figure 1.21.

As shown in diagram (1) in the figure, processors P2 and P3 have each executed a Load Register instruction (Load A) referring to variable A (which has the value 1 at this time) in the block B. These load instructions cause there to be made in the caches of P2 and P3 a copy of the block B. Now, when processor P1 executes a Store Register instruction having as its target variable A (Store 4 -> A, in the second figure) the copies of A in the caches of P2 and P3 no longer hold a correct value for A, and thus should no longer be accessible.[10]

For obvious performance reasons, cache coherence is implemented directly in hardware.

Figure 1.21
Illustration of the problem of cache coherence.

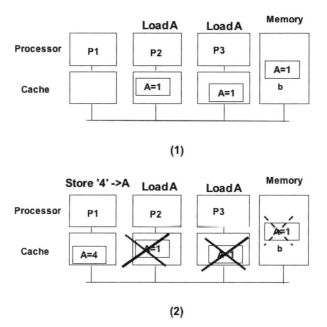

(1)

(2)

Cache coherence protocols have various characteristics:

- Mechanisms to supervise modifications to block
- Update mechanisms for modified blocks
- State diagrams for the blocks

We briefly will examine these various characteristics.

There are two major techniques for managing block modifications:

- *Protocols based on monitoring all traffic (snooping)*. In this approach, each processor observes all transactions on the processor-memory interconnect[11] to see if the transaction refers to a block which it holds in its cache. The state of each block may then be modified appropriately in accordance with the bus transactions. The problem with this protocol is the bus traffic it generates; it therefore offers a barrier to scalability (and so at some number of processors one must instead adopt a directory-based approach, which means that more than one system architecture must be constructed for a product family scaling from very small multiprocessors to fairly large ones)

- *Protocols based on directories (Directory-Based Protocols)*. This approach is based on the idea of a (logically) single "directory" that specifies, for each block in the complete memory system, which caches hold a copy, as well as the state of that copy. Thus, requests to update or invalidate a block may be sent to the cache which has the valid copy, rather than broadcast on the interconnect (whether bus or crossbar). It is easier to support a large number of processors with this approach than it is with snooping.

For interested readers, [HEN02] and [HAN98] provide detailed descriptions of cache mechanisms.

There are two techniques available to maintain cache coherence as blocks are modified:

- *Write Invalidate*. The processor wishing to write the data must first invalidate of all the copies of the data in the caches of the other processors; it may then proceed to update the data in its cache. To do this, the processor wishing to write first puts an invalidate transaction on the bus, specifying the address of the block affected. All the other processors check for the presence of the block in their own caches, and, if it is present, invalidate it. This allows multiple readers for a cache block, but only one writer.

- *Write Update*. Rather than invalidating other copies, in this scheme the updated information is broadcast on the bus, and the other processors update their copies with the new value. This approach has also been called Write Broadcast.

The Write Update approach is similar to that of Write Through (cache management) which we described previously in section 1.6.1 Memory hierarchy summary, since every update to a shared block is propagated to the bus.

In the Write Invalidate approach, only the first write to a given block by a processor will be put on the bus; subsequent updates to that block may remain local to that processor and its cache (since the other copies were invalidated). Thus, invalidation is a more attractive approach than update from the point of view of bus traffic. On the other hand, broadcast has the advantage of reducing latency for the other processors, since they have copies in their cache.

Since the processor-memory bandwidth is a precious resource, microprocessors intended for multiprocessor use employ the Write Back and Write Invalidate techniques.

Most cache protocols belong to a family of protocols called MESI, an acronym which refers to the various states a cache block may be in—Modified, Exclusive, Shared or Invalid. The state diagram for a cache block defines the legal transitions between these states. Our description is inspired by [CUL98].

The four MESI states for a cache line are defined as follows:

- *Modified.* The block is valid, and has been changed by its processor, and is the only cached copy of the data in the system
- *Exclusive.* The block is valid, and is the only cached copy in the system, and has not been modified by its processor
- *Shared.* The block is valid and there is at least one other copy of the block in another processor's cache—all such copies are identical
- *Invalid.* The block is invalid—it does not contain any valid data; any access to this block (in this cache) will lead to a cache miss

Figure 1.22 provides a state transition diagram for a MESI protocol.

As already noted, each block has associated state information held in the cache. Transitions between states are caused by both memory access operations executed by the local processor and by bus transactions from the other processors.

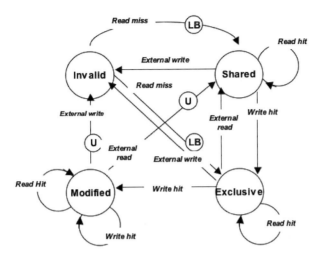

Figure 1.22
*State Transition
Diagram for a
MESI protocol.*

Consider the initials state of a cache. All its blocks are marked Invalid. Any access (read or write) to the cache will result in a cache miss and a loading of the block from memory[12] into the cache.

The block then transitions into the Exclusive state. A read request from another processor for an address within the block will cause it to move to the Shared state (this transition is labeled "External Read" in the diagram). When a processor with a block in the Exclusive state modifies it, the block changes to the Modified state. A block in the Modified state will transition to an Invalid state if another processor emits a request to write to that block (labeled "External Write" in the diagram); this is accompanied by updating the memory. A Modified block becomes Shared (again, with an accompanying update of memory) when an external processor emits a read.

A block in Shared state becomes Invalid if another processor updates the block (External Write). In the cache of the processor doing the modification, the block (which was in the Shared state since there were multiple copies) becomes Exclusive.

1.8.4 Models of Memory Consistency

A memory consistency model for a symmetrical multiprocessor specifies the memory behavior for programmers. Intuitively, a read to the memory should return the last value written to it. In the case of a system with only one processor, the last value of a datum is easily seen from the execution order of the program.

Again, a detailed examination of memory consistency models is outside the scope of this work; interested readers may refer to [ADV96].

To illustrate the issues of memory consistency, we will use a parallel program composed of two processes, illustrated in Figure 1.23 and drawn from [HEN02].

Figure 1.23
Parallel program composed of two processes.

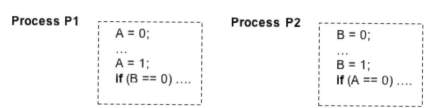

Two processes P1 and P2 function in parallel on different processors. The variables A and B are shared by the two processes. Assume that they were loaded into each processor's cache with the initial value 0, and assume that cache coherence is done through Invalidation. If memory coherence is maintained, then it is not possible for either process to evaluate the tested condition as true (either A = 1 or B = 1)

The continued search for performance has led microprocessor designers to a number of optimizations. One of these is the use of write buffers that allow the processor to execute a write operation and to continue before all the work associated with the write (such as invalidation of a cache block) has been completed. Optimizations like this amount to abandoning the strict order of program execution—that is, the processor does things in an order different from that specified by the program.

A possible side effect, in our example, is that the processes P1 and P2 do not see the invalidations of the blocks containing variables A and B before they evaluate the condition. In such a situation, it is possible for the two processes to both evaluate their conditions to true.

Even in this elementary example, it is evident that the order in which things are done is vital to the semantics of the program.

For symmetric multiprocessor systems, a first approach to a consistency model is the sequential consistency model. This makes it possible to avoid the situation just described, but at the expense of performance.

An SMP is sequentially consistent if [CUL98] the result of any execution is the same as if the operations of all the processors were done atomically[13]—launched one at a time and each allowed to complete—in an unspecified order, and if the operations of each processor appear in such an execution in the same order as specified by the program.

While preserving strict order (the ordering of operations precisely as specified by the program) makes writing and managing the execution of parallel programs straightforward, it hurts performance considerably (the processor must wait for completion of every operation before starting the next one). For this reason, architects became interested in schemes which allowed some relaxation of consistency, to make higher performance possible. The relaxation affects how reading and writing of memory are done. Such models are based on the fact that for programs the exact order of memory operations is—in many cases—no longer fundamental, and also on the use of specific synchronization instructions when appropriate. In practice, this means that accesses to shared data must be protected by the operations of acquiring and releasing locks and that synchronization instructions (such as the sync instruction in PowerPC, which we will see in the next paragraph, or the synchronization barriers seen in other architectures) must be used. Relaxed consistency models thus imply that one must specify such exclusion mechanism when writing the program but that the hardware never has to await completion of an operation except when so instructed by a synchronization operation.

1.8.5 Synchronization Mechanisms

Although shared memory is the most effective means of interprocessor communication, accesses to shared data must be synchronized.

To synchronize their accesses to such data, programs use variables called locks. To access shared data, a process must first acquire the lock associated with that data. Once the lock is acquired, the data may be accessed. After finishing its work with the data, the process must release the lock.

The operations to acquire and release a lock are carried out in modern microprocessors by means of two instructions: load and reserve and store conditional.[14]

How these instructions work may be summarized as follows:

1. The Load and Reserve instruction creates a reservation state for the address of the operand specified by the instruction

2. A Boolean (the reservation bit) associated with this operation is set

3.   Once set, the hardware monitors all accesses to the specified address

4.   If any write is detected to the address, the Boolean is cleared

5.   The Store Conditional is only effective (i.e., will only write to memory) if the Boolean is set (the instruction sets an indicator— a condition code—to specify whether the store occurred or not)

6.   The program then tests the indicator, and if the store failed, it loops back to step one and tries again

With weakly-ordered memory models, the order of memory operations is no longer guaranteed. Weakly-ordered models have higher performance than those with strong ordering.

When it is necessary for memory accesses to be ordered in some specific manner, the programmer uses an instruction that synchronizes the accesses; execution of such an instruction forces the processor to start executing subsequent instructions only when all instructions preceding the synchronization instruction have been completed. Typically, such an instruction is used to ensure that all modifications to shared data have been completed before releasing the lock controlling access to the data. This type of operation is also called a synchronization barrier.

1.8.6 Examples of Implementing Traditional Synchronization Primitives with the Instruction Pair

This description is inspired by [PPC94], which describes the operations within the framework of the PowerPC architecture, but we have taken liberties with mnemonics and have somewhat simplified the code:

- *Test and Set.* The version of Test and Set presented here atomically performs the following sequence of operations
  - load a word form memory
  - test to see if the word has the value zero
  - if it has the value zero, update it to a new value otherwise leave it unchanged:

```
Loop:
    Load_and_reserve r5, r3 // creates a reservation
    Compare_immediate r5, 0 // test if equal to zero
    Branch_if_not_zero continuation // branch not zero
    Store_conditional r4, r3 // store if reservation still
    // held
    Branch_if_not_stored loop // loop if store not done
    // (loss of reservation)
    Continuation:// continue.
```

■ *Compare and Swap.* The following instruction sequence atomically compares the value of a word in memory with a value in a register. If the values are equal, a value held in another register is written to the word in memory. If the values differ, the value of the memory word is provided in the first register and a condition code set. The address of the memory word is held in register r3, the value to be compared is in r4 and the value to be written is in r5. The initial value of the word is returned in r4.

```
Loop:
    Load_and_reserve r6, r3 // creates a reservation
    Compare r4, r6 // test equality of the    // two values
    Branch_if_not_equal Exit // branch not equal
    Store_conditional r5, r3 // store if reservation    //still
held
    Branch_if_not_stored Loop // loop if store not done //
(loss of reservation)
    Exit:
    Movereg r4, r6 // move r6->r4
```

The implementation of this primitive corresponds to the semantics of the IBM S/370 instruction Compare and Swap.

Using these primitives, it is possible to implement lock mechanisms. In the example which follows, the address of the lock is in register r3. This lock controls access to shared data. The lock is clear when its value is zero, and set when its value is one. The following sequence of instructions calls the Test and Set primitive described above.

```
load_immediate r4,1 // indicator lock obtained
Loop:
```

```
Call test_and_set // call the Test&Set
    // primitive
branch_not_zero Loop // test if lock value zero
sync // synchronization
    // the following
    // instructions do not
    // start until all up to
    // here have completed
return // return
```

Unlocking simply consists of setting the lock to zero with a simple store. To ensure that all writes to the shared data have completed before freeing the lock, we must first execute a synchronization instruction:

```
sync // barrier to ensure all
    // data writes have '
    // settled'
load_immediate r1, 0 // put 0 in r1
store r1, r4 // clear lock by storing
    // zero
return // return
```

One finds similar constructs in other microprocessor architectures. It should be noted that the synchronization instruction has a very detrimental effect on performance, and so it is advisable to limit its use to those situations where synchronization is necessary.

1.9   Binary Compatibility Constraints—Java and Architecture Retargeting

While the constraint of binary compatibility is very strong in the world of workstations, it is just as important for servers. Indeed, applications are delivered by their producers in a binary form (that is, as programs compiled for a given environment and in a loadable format); an application can therefore function only on a platform presenting that interface.

A new circle (virtuous or vicious, depending on one's point of view) has been brought to our attention: software vendors, aiming to reduce their costs for support, distribution, qualification, and development costs, tend to concentrate on a small number of targets, generally those with the broadest base. From this results the industry's concentration on the Windows/PC and, to a lesser extent, the Macintosh platforms for workstation software. The market penetration of an architecture depends, in part, on the richness of its applications catalog, which itself depends on the portion of the market represented by the architecture.

There are various levels of compatibility, as illustrated by Figure 1.24.

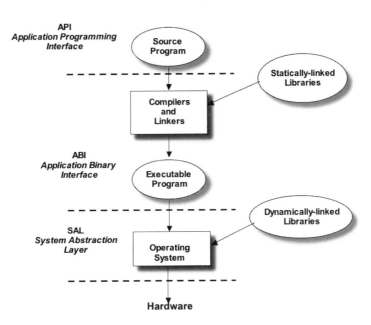

Figure 1.24
Levels of compatibility.

This figure distinguishes three levels of compatibility:

1. *Source level compatibility,* which allows portability of the program to all systems that provide a specific interface standard between applications programs and the operating system (for example, the Posix standards, or the standards published by the Open Group). Such interfaces are referred to as an API (Applications Programming Interface). To port a program between platforms supporting a given API requires recompiling the application. Convenient though this form of portability may be, it provides no protection for the program since the source code is accessible.[15]

Data Representation and Data Exchange

Data representation can pose problems for the portability of programs and the exchange of data between different systems, or even the sharing of data within a system composed of different types of processor. There are two modes for the representation of data in a computer system, differing by how the bytes in a word are ordered. In representing numbers—both integers and floating point—the two modes are little-endian and big-endia. The naming comes from the choice of where the most significant byte of a number may be found in the word.

To illustrate, consider a system having memory organized as 32 bit words, and in that memory assume that there is a data structure containing an integer and a string. The integer has the value 15 (which fits in a single byte) and the string contains the following four characters: UNIX. Their representations in the two endian systems are as follows:

Big Endian

Address of byte 0	0	0	0	15
Address of Byte 4	U	n	i	x

Little Endian

0	0	0	15	Address of byte 0
x	i	n	U	Address of Byte 4

2. *Application compatibility at the binary level,* which represents the interface between the operating system and the applications programs once they have been compiled and linked with the run time libraries. Such interfaces are called an ABI (for Application Binary Interface). Compatibility at the binary level depends on several factors:

- The processor architecture (its instruction set)
- OS-imposed addressing conventions (as an example, the longevity of the 640 KB limit inherited from DOS and the first PC)
- Interfaces between the application and the OS and with the libraries
- Conventions for data representation
  Applications are generally distributed in this form (that is, requiring platform providing the required ABI). This provides two major advantages: protection of the intellectual property represented by the code (reverse engineering the binary to obtain a representation of the

System Abstraction Layer

SAL allows the portability of the operating systems—in binary format—between various platforms based on the same processor architecture. The role of this layer is to hide the specific details of the platform from the operating systems. Among the principal functions of a SAL are:

- The assumption of responsibility of initialization, test and the configuration of the hardware resources of the platform

- Providing the operating system with data structures describing the configuration

- Provision of basic services for resource management, such as choice of which processor will load ("bootstrap") the system; basic hardware error management and error logging

- Hiding differences arising from the use of different processor architectures, or the use of different processors within a single architectural family

For IA-64 systems, Intel has introduced a further layer between the SAL and the hardware; this new PAL (Processor Abstraction Layer) layer is intended to hide the differences between the implementation details of successive generations of IA-64 processors from the SAL. For an operating system intended to be ported across processor architectures, this functionality has its natural home in a SAL.

The concept of a SAL was understood and implemented long before the term itself was introduced. As an example, the manufacturers of both proprietary and UNIX systems developed families of products which had differences in implementation—in particular, for performance reasons—and therefore often had to develop an abstraction layer to facilitate porting the OS between the various models in the range.

In the case of Windows NT, a similar abstraction layer was implemented, called HAL, for Hardware Abstraction Layer

program is far from easy), and easy installation (since the code need not be compiled).

3. *Binary-level compatibility for components of the operating system,* which is ensured by an abstraction layer called SAL (System Abstraction Layer).

Historically, there have been some attempts to get away from the constraints of compatibility; two examples are Architecture-Neutral Distribution Format (ANDF) and, more recently, Java.

Architecture-Neutral Distribution Format

Within the framework of the OSF (Open Software Foundation) created at the end of the 1980s by a group of information processing systems manufacturers, whose initial goal was to develop a UNIX operating system independent of Sun and ATT, there was an attempt to promote a distribution technology independent of processor architecture. However, this technology, called ANDF was not adopted by industry players. It consisted of distributing the applications in a form of intermediate code (compilers produced this intermediate code instead of generating computer code). Installation then required translation of the intermediate code into computer code. One reason for the failure of this approach could be that software vendors using it might have been presented with a support problem, since the approach vastly increases the number of platforms on which the software could be run (to port to a new platform, one needed only a translation program for that platform). The Java approach, which we cover shortly, is different in that it specifies a Java Virtual Machine (JVM) to execute the Java programs., and the JVM is the piece to be validated. However, in the JIT (Just In Time) compilation strategy of Java, one sees a close parallel with ANDF

The most recent attempt to relieve the problems of binary compatibility, and the most promising, is the Java language—and associated products—from Sunsoft (a subsidiary of Sun, specializing in software products). We look at Java section 1.11.

1.10 Compilation and Interpretation

Before looking at Java and architectural retargeting it seems worthwhile to look at the differences between compiling and interpreting. These differences are shown in Figure 1.25.

We have illustrated the case of compilation with a complete chain of events, from program development all the way to execution. In doing this, we have deliberately chosen to assume a rather general software development framework, in which the development environment (for example, Windows 2000 or UNIX) is different from the deployment environment (for example, IBM's MVS). Compiling a program transforms it from a form

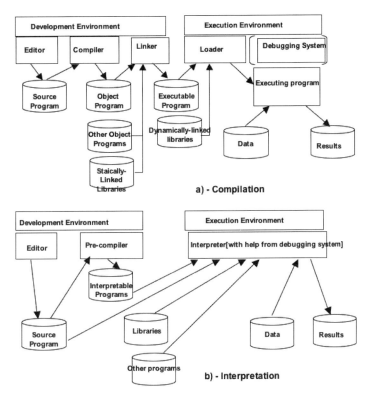

Figure 1.25
*Compilation and
interpretation.*

expressed in a source language (such as COBOL, Fortran, or C++) into a program expressed in the lowest semantic level and which is suitable for execution by a processor. Compiling a program assumes the compiler is able to attach meaning to the statements of the program (see below); the debugging environment is optional.

In the case of interpretation, the program may either be translated into an intermediate format (such as by compilation for a virtual machine) or it may be executed directly. The program—whether in intermediate form or not—is executed by a program called an interpreter, which dynamically assigns meaning to the program statements. As in the case of compilation, the debugging environment is optional.

Reasons for using interpretation rather than compilation include:

■ To ease interactive debugging by making source code changes simple, at the cost of performance. Because of how interpretation works, modifying the source code doesn't result in the long sequence of steps prior to execution needed by compilation. This is typically how one handles BASIC.

- To provide an executable from just one compilation phase, able to be run on multiple platforms provided only that they have an appropriate interpreter. This is the approach taken by Java.

- Because of an inability to attach a meaning to the program source at compile time. While this may at first glance seem a strange circumstance, it occurs when a data type can only be known during program execution (as with APL, for example). In APL (A Programming Language), which was popular in the 1970s, variables are not declared and their type (for example, whether integer scalar or vector float) is determined during execution depending on what is written into them. Thus, one cannot determine during a static examination of the source what "A + B" might mean, since the types of A and B can only be known at runtime. Thus, one does not know whether the operator + is an integer addition or a floating point addition, or even whether it calls for scalar addition or matrix addition. APL is therefore a language which one must interpret.

It should be noted that one may encounter schemes in which compilation and interpretation are intermixed. We will see an example of this in Architecture Retargeting (section 1.12).

1.11   Java

The Java language is an evolution of C++ and presents some interesting characteristics as a programming language. Our intent here is not to cover all aspects of the language—we refer the interested reader to specialist works for that. Java allows programmers to develop their applications, to distribute them in an architecture—independent form, and to get them to run on different architectures provided that these architectures have an implementation of the Java Virtual Machine (JVM).

Support for Java falls among the interpretive techniques. In a client-server architecture, application parts (both client and server) may be downloaded upon demand. Java promoters use the slogan "Write Once, Run Everywhere," meaning that the application is written once and can execute on all systems that support Java execution. Applications of this form for the client side are called applets, and servlets for the server side. An application written in Java is distributed in an intermediate language called byte code.

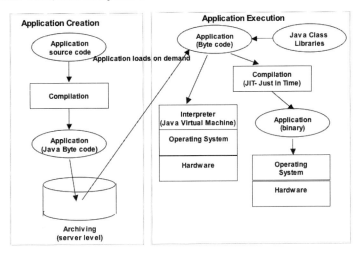

Figure 1.26
Development and execution of Java applications.

This intermediate form is supported by a virtual machine, the JVM, which is emulated on multiple architectures by software. In other words, a JVM executes Java byte code.

Figure 1.26 illustrates the development and execution of Java applications.

Applications developed in Java are transformed by a compiler into intermediate code (byte code). These applications (applets and servlets) are held in the file system and loaded into systems (workstations or servers) upon demand. The application may then be directly executed on the target system by means of the JVM. There are some variations possible from this scheme, depending on whether or not the target systems is entirely dedicated to Java or not (for example, a Java processor and Java system). The diagram assumes a system not dedicated to Java.

It is possible to increase the performance of a Java application by translating it from byte codes into instructions directly executable by the target system. Two approaches are possible to achieve this; one, called JIT, for Just In Time compilation, calls for the program, once loaded, to be translated immediately before execution; the other does incremental compilation during execution (Sun's Hot Spot implements this approach).

1.12 Architecture Retargeting

Because of the very high performance of modern standard microprocessors, it is now possible to host on one architecture the applications and operating systems developed for another. The techniques used for this are termed architecture retargeting.

Generally speaking, one considers this approach when new native implementations of these old architectures can no longer be justified economically.

Among the approaches used for retargeting, we can list:

- *Retargeting compilers to a new architecture.* The languages used to develop the system and its applications are regarded as yet another source language, and then they can be translated by a specially-constructed compiler into the machine language for the chosen standard microprocessor.

- *Emulation.* The instruction set of the old architecture is simulated, by software, on a new architecture. In other words, an interpreter simulates the instruction set of the architecture to be retargeted.

- *Binary Translation.* Existing binaries (that is, programs for the old architectures in a loadable form) are transformed into binaries for the new architecture, either statically (once) or dynamically (during emulation).

From Interpretation to Translation

Static translation takes place, necessarily, independent of any execution of the program. For this to work, it implies that one can determine, by simple static analysis of the program in its binary form, which elements are to be translated and not to be translated—that is, to be able to identify instructions (translate) and data (do not translate). Since such properties cannot in general be identified statically, it is advisable to learn the structure of the program by observing its execution. With the instructions identified, translation becomes possible. This approach, a combination of interpretation and compilation, is called DOCT (Dynamic Object Code Translation).

In addition to these techniques, we should also mention the approach of simulating the system environment. Such a simulation, implementing the facilities of one OS on another, allows an application to be supported on an OS other than the one it was developed for. Such an approach is used in conjunction with other techniques, already reviewed. Thus environment simulation may be used in partnership with emulation, thereby masking differences between the old and new environments by simulating the old primitives on the new system.

Performance is always an issue. Here are some notes:

- Retargeting compilers can give satisfactory results provided that the source language of the original code is of a sufficiently high level that it is effectively architecture-independent, or that the differences between the architectures are not very great.

- Emulation generally results in performance degradation of at least 10x; this can be worsened by differences between the emulated architecture and the support available in the target architecture.

- Binary translation can result in the code footprint growing significantly (the increase being a function of the differences between the architectures). This can reduce performance, simply because cache performance will be reduced.

We now briefly describe some real-world retargeting exercises.

1.12.1 Compiler Retargeting

In October 1991, Tandem announced, as a continuation of a proprietary architecture, two product families (CLX/R and Cyclone/R) based on the MIPS architecture and providing binary compatibility with existing applications.

The migration was carried out as follows:

- Guardian, the operating system, was converted into native MIPS code. Guardian had been written in TAL (Tandem Assembly Language); the TAL translator was retargeted to generate MIPS code.

- The compilers for the new systems operated in two steps. First, they generated code for the proprietary architecture; then this code was translated and optimized for MIPS. Both binaries are kept, allowing the application to run on both types of system

- The existing applications, in binary form, are run by the new systems by means of an interpreter (called millicode)—that is, an emulation of the proprietary architecture on the MIPS machines.

Tandem has been purchased by Compaq, which is turn was acquired by HP, and has moved away from the MIPS architecture for IA-64. Still, the same technology could be used elsewhere.

Bull, for its DPS/4000 line—a mid-range DBMS system characterized by the use of high-level languages in connection with a database—implemented a retargeting to UNIX-based systems built on standard microprocessors. Some of the programmatic interfaces were simulated on UNIX, and others on top of the relational database. Migrating applications programs requires recompilation on the UNIX platform

1.12.2   Emulation

As indicated earlier, this technique consists of emulating one architecture on another. This technique uses an interpreter. Emulation revisits the techniques of microcoding that were widely used for the (complex) processors of the 1960s.

Microprogramming

In the 1960s and 1970s, machines were often implemented using microprogramming. In this sort of machine, the execution unit has its own, very simple, instruction set and is controlled by a program (the microcode or microprogram), which is nothing more than an interpreter for the instruction set specified for the architecture. The structure of the execution unit depends on the performance level required (this affects, for example, the degree of parallelism, the number of bits between the execution unit and the memory, etc.). Microcode is thus specific to each model of machine, but the hardware-software interface is identical for all models in the range. With this type of structure, one could emulate another architecture with specific microcode (for example, emulation of IBM 1401 on the Series 360, or the emulation of direct execution machines on the Burroughs 1700)

For its DPS/6000 line of traditional minis, Bull provided an emulation on PowerPC. The OS and the application programs are executed under the control of AIX (a version of UNIX adapted for PowerPC).

As to binary translation, two cases must be considered, according to whether the translation takes place statically (independent of any execution) or dynamically (during execution).

We should note that architectural retargeting becomes more complicated when live code—letting the program modify its own code—occurs.

1.12.3 Example of Architecture Retargeting Through Emulation: Bull DPS7000

Bull's DPS7000 system is a proprietary system whose implementation started towards the end of the 1960s and which was first introduced to the market in 1973.

This multiprocessor system is used in production environments—transaction processing, decision support and batch. The system architecture, inspired by Multics, provides notions of segments and of rings of protection. A further characteristic is that certain systems functions—such as process scheduling and I/O supervision—are implemented in hardware (using a microcoded approach).

As already noted, a CMOS implementation of the DPS7000 appeared in 1987. While the system was a commercial success, Bull was faced with the endless escalation in development costs of follow-on implementations, a cost which the volumes of the systems sold were not sufficient to amortize—a problem not unique to Bull, since it either has been or will be faced by any vendor of a proprietary system.

With the goal of providing continuity to its customers, Bull chose to provide a software implementation of the DPS7000 on Intel-based platforms (initially IA-32, and subsequently IA-64) running under the control of Windows 2000. This project, code-named Diane, was launched commercially in 2001.

The architecture of Diane and its principal component V7000 (for Virtual 7000) can be summarized as follows (Diane's general architecture is illustrated in Figure 1.27):

V7000 is composed of the following elements:

- *CPU Firmware.* Software that implements the microcoded functionality of the DPS7000 on the Intel processors. A number of these processors are dedicated to GCOS—that is, GCOS allocates the processes to processors. The number of visible processors depends on the number of processors dedicated to GCOS.

Figure 1.27
*Overall
Architecture of
Diane (source:
Bull).*

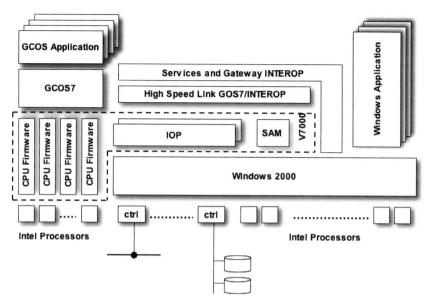

- *IOP.* Windows 2000 processes which implement the I/O functionality of GCOS 7. Actual I/O and peripheral control are left to Windows 2000.

- *SAM* (System Administration Manager). Looks after GCOS' own administrative functions (since the goal is no user disruption, Diane must provide familiar capabilities in system management).

- *DPS7000 Systems.* Have long offered an integrated UNIX port to provide GCOS7 applications with services such as TCP/IP, FTP and Internet access. A module in the Diane version of GCOS 7 provides this functionality. Memory-based communication provides a means for efficient interaction between the UNIX and GCOS environments. INTEROP services and bridge software make these facilities available to GCOS7 applications.

- *Windows 2000 Applications.* Supported natively, these can operate independently of GCOS applications or cooperate with them. The memory-based communication optimizes performance.

Each *CPU Firmware* block is a separate Windows thread, the collection being managed by a further pair of threads: one looking after overall behavior and the other dedicated to time management. Unless an I/O request is issued, the CPU Firmware threads do not call upon any Windows 2000 services.

Again, each IOP is a Windows thread, with a maximum of 8 IOPs. Within each IP, there is a thread per peripheral type.

To simplify recovery, each GCOS disk is a Windows 2000 file, with the GCOS software responsible for management and interpretation of the control structures. With this approach, there are no real limits on the allocation of GCOS volumes—complete virtualization has been achieved.

Administrative functions are based on DCOM (Microsoft's Distributed Common Object Model).

As far as a DPS7000 user is concerned, moving from a real DPS7000 system to a Diane implementation is transparent: there is no need to recompile, reorganize the data, or adopt new operating modes. The approach simultaneously provides a bridge to the new world of standard computing platforms.

The obvious concern with this sort of approach is the robustness of Windows 2000, but in this case that does not apply since Windows is only providing a small part of the functionality. Most of the robustness is driven by the quality of the Bull software implementation and on the stable GCOS itself.

Static Binary Translation

At the introduction of its Alpha architecture, Digital/Compaq presented its evolutionary plan to move from current architectures (VAX for VMS and MIPS for its UNIX products) to Alpha. Unlike Tandem, which moved its proprietary architecture to an architecture not intended to support retargeting, Alpha's design incorporated aspects to support retargeting. As an example, Alpha directly supports most VAX data formats.

Alpha provides the concept of PALcode (Privileged Architecture Library routines), which operate in a special architectural mode (for example, the instructions in that mode have complete control of system state, interrupts are blocked, and so forth) and allow the efficient emulation of a number of complex functions which were part of the VAX architecture

Their retargeting uses the following techniques [SIT92]:

■ Binary translation of applications (both VAX/VMS and MIPS/UNIX)

■ PALcode for the emulation of certain systems functions

Dynamic Translation of Object Code

Digital wanted, as part of its Windows strategy for Alpha, to be able to execute IA-32 binaries on Alpha. It developed a technology it called FX!32

[HOO97], which uses the techniques of both emulation and dynamic translation. Although Alpha and Windows/Alpha are now a part of history, the principles behind the approach remain valid.

Key points:

■ Because it is impossible for a static analysis to distinguish between code and data in an IA-32 binary, FX!32 uses a mixed approach

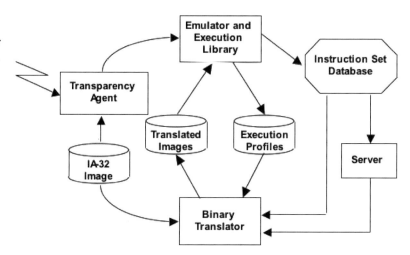

Figure 1.28
General diagram of FX!32 (according to [HOO97].

■ Program execution begins in emulation mode, which makes it possible to identify the portions of the program which are instructions

■ Once the executable instructions are identified, they can be translated into directly-executable Alpha code

Thus, with FX!32, at least two program analyses are required to obtain even a partial translation—an interpretation phase and a translation phase. Figure 1.28 illustrates the operation of FX!32. As shown in this figure, FX!32 comprises several functional parts, as follows:

■ *The transparency agent* which initializes the execution of native IA-32 applications

■ *An emulator,* which makes it possible to execute IA-32 instructions on Alpha, and which records the execution profile (that is, it keeps note of which IA-32 instructions were executed)

- *A translator*, which can generate—given the object code and execution profile—a translation into native Alpha code

- *The database*, which keeps track of execution profiles, translated Alpha binary images and configuration information

- *The server*, which keeps the database updated and launches the translator

- *The manager*, not shown in the diagram, which lets the user control resources used by FX!32

The first time an IA-32 application is executed on Alpha, it is entirely emulated. FX!32 records, in a file associated with the application, the execution profile specifying what portions of code were executed. This information is subsequently used by the translator, which generates Alpha code from the IA-32 instructions (in other words, only IA-32 instructions that were actually executed get translated).

The translated sequences are constructed as DLLs (Dynamically-Linked Libraries). During subsequent executions of the program, if the execution chances upon previously-seen sequences, FX!32 will use the previously-translated code. If, on the other hand, as-yet unexplored branches are encountered, FX!32 updates the execution profile and a later translation is called for.

FX!32: Performance

Published FX!32 performance, measured by the BYTEmark benchmark (from Byte magazine) is as follows:

- On a 500 MHz Alpha system, whose native performance is about twice that of a 200 MHz Pentium Pro, FX!32 provides performance about equivalent to that of the Pentium Pro. In other words, the performance degradation compared with recompiling is about 2x.

- With straightforward emulation code, one would expect a performance degradation of about 10x.

In this way, the execution speed of IA-32 code gradually improves as more code sequences are explored, encountered and translated.

Compared with emulation, this approach provides a significant performance improvement, but with a very noticeable increase in code size (which can have a deleterious effect on the behavior of the caches, and thus on performance).

1.12.4   Example of Dynamic Object Code Translation: Transmeta

In January 2000, a new company—Transmeta—announced a new family of IA-32 compatible processors under the name of Crusoe (after Defoe's Robinson Crusoe), based on a new technology which they called Code Morphing. In the context of this book, we would look upon their approach as an example of a JIT technology applied to IA-32 code.

The key goals of the new family are high performance with low power consumption; embedded applications may be particularly targeted.

The approach is based on a VLIW processor capable of executing four instructions per cycle, and a software layer providing dynamic translation of IA-32 instructions into VLIW instructions.

Unlike traditional hardware IA-32 implementations such as those from Intel, which translate instructions one by one into micro-ups, the Code Morphing approach is able to view a group of IA-32 instructions as a translation possibility, allowing certain worthwhile optimizations.

Translated code is held in a cache in memory; re-execution of already-executed code does not—in general -require retranslation.

Although the initial products are IA-32 compatible, the same processor could emulate other architectures with tuned code morphing software. This seems an interesting approach, although it requires the development of specialized processors. As these words are written, it is too early to make a useful prediction about the success of this approach to IA-32 implementation.

We believe that describing these exercises in some detail is extremely useful, because the extraordinarily fast rate of improvement in microprocessor performance (accompanied by an equally impressive rate of cost reduction) can make such techniques applicable to a wide range of applications still implemented today on architectures with no future development path (for example, architectures conceived specifically for a particular class of application; or a microprocessor architecture whose disappearance in the near future is virtually certain).

1.13 Microprocessor Evolution

In this section we examine microprocessor evolution, which covers two distinct areas:

- Architectural change in instruction repertoire and memory addressing, a subject generally called microprocessor ISA, for Instruction Set Architecture
- Evolution in the implementation of architectures, which is a response to the available technology and to market requirements

We will first look at current performance improvement techniques used in microprocessors, and then look at these two points in turn along with economic aspects. The possibilities will be reconsidered in Chapter 7 once we have laid out various system architecture options, since some aspects of the future path of microprocessors are dependent on the effects of integrating system functionalities into the microprocessors.

1.13.1 Traditional Performance Improvement Techniques

In this section we examine performance improvement techniques used in microprocessors.

In the processor performance equation:

$$\frac{time}{tache} = \frac{instructions}{tache} \times \frac{cycle}{instructions} \times \frac{time}{cycle}$$

the hardware implementation of an architecture—that is, whether it is CISC or RISC—primarily seeks to influence the two terms *cycles per instruction* and *cycle time*. Since both technology and architectural complexity limit the cycle time, microprocessor designers seek to improve performance by concentrating on the other two terms in the equation.

Improving the cycles per instruction term amounts to increasing parallelism at the instruction execution level; this is called ILP (Instruction Level Parallelism). Two effects limit achievable ILP:

- The nature of the applications themselves, reflected in two areas—algorithm choice and the sequential nature of most programming languages
- The processor's ISA

Measurements [JOU89] suggest that the limit of ILP for classical architectures is around five to six; that is, one cannot expect to execute more than five or six instructions in parallel. To circumvent this barrier, two options are available:

1. Create a new ISA which of itself allows a higher ILP than classical architectures; this, while a compatibility break with older architectures, is the goal of the approach taken by Intel and HP in their creation of IA-64.

2. Create more parallelism in the application and the processor implementation to increase the number of tasks being executed at one time. A simple approach is to use technology advancements to implement multiple processors on one chip; this is called CMP (Chip MultiProcessing), or CMT (Chip MultiThreading) and relies on the application being structured as multiple tasks— TLP, (Thread Level parallelism).

In the CMP/TLP approach, there is no need to change the ISA of the processor, and so backwards binary compatibility with prior generations is provided. This approach is attractive to manufacturers of modest means and represents a modest risk. However, it does not allow any specific legacy application to be executed more quickly; it simply provides resources to allow multiple tasks to be executed simultaneously.

To seek to improve ILP through the creation of a new ISA requires a major investment and represents a major risk, in particular from the removal of binary compatibility, a major factor in the acceptability of a product.

Of course, ILP and CMP/TLP are not exclusive; ILP seeks to minimize the amount of time taken to execute the instruction stream, while CMP seeks to maximize the use of hardware resources by executing multiple instruction streams simultaneously. Implementing CMP on a high ILP architecture is entirely feasible.

We have noted one straightforward way of implementing TLP; in fact, there are two major strategies available

1. *CMP,* the integration of multiple processors on one chip. IBM chose this approach with its Power 4 machines

2. *Simultaneous Multithreading,* an approach which enables one processor to have its resources used by multiple threads simultaneously; when one thread is unable to proceed momentarily—perhaps because of a cache miss, for example—other threads continue execution and make efficient use of the hardware. This approach has been chosen by Intel for Pentium 4, where it has been labeled Hyperthreading. There is also another possibility, in which the processor tries to maximize the utilization of its resources internal among a set of threads.

We will look again at these approaches in section 1.13.12 on implementation evolution.

When an architect is forced to improve the performance of an existing architecture, the goal is to obtain the best compromise between performance, cost, and development time; this last sets the introduction date for the product and strongly affects the profitability of the development.

We should note that several key performance enhancement techniques used in modern microprocessors were originally introduced in high-end mainframes in the 1960s. This observation reminds us that there's very little new under the sun[16] and that the large factors in implementation possibilities are technology progress and the effects of high volume production, which make it possible nowadays to deploy in everyday implementations techniques which were once of necessity limited to extremely expensive systems.

The major factors limiting microprocessor performance are:

■ *Data level dependencies.* The execution of a given instruction requires data computed by a prior instruction which has not yet completed execution

■ *Branches.* An unconditional branch breaks the instruction sequence and can result in the next instruction to be executed not being in the cache; and a conditional branch requires that the machine decide which instruction to execute next depending on how the condition was evaluated (this is also an example of a data dependency)

- *Waits caused by interactions with the memory hierarchy.* A cache miss means that the required data must be fetched from a higher level cache or main memory, requiring some time to effect

We will now look at some basic structures employed by microprocessors to improve performance.

1.13.2 Processor Structures: Pipelines and Superscalarity

These fundamental processor structures aim at minimizing the number of cycles per instruction by exploiting parallelism available at the level of instruction sequences.

- A pipeline structure divides the execution of a single instruction into multiple stages and commences execution of the "next" instruction before the execution of "this" instruction has completed

- A superscalar structure is one in which more than one instruction begins execution simultaneously

The following description was inspired by paper appearing in the IEEE Transactions on Computers.

Table 1.4 illustrates instruction sequence parallelism using two simple sequences.

Table 1.4 *Illustration of parallelism in a sequence of instructions.*

Sequence 1	Sequence 2
load r1 <- (r2)	add r3 <- r3 + 1
add r3 <- r3 + 1	add r4 <- r3 + r2
fpadd r5 <- r6 + r7	store r4 -> (r5)
Level of parallelism = 3	Level of parallelism = 1

In the first sequence, the instructions are independent of each other, and so may be executed concurrently (given appropriate hardware). On the other hand, in the second sequence, the execution of each instruction depends on the result of the preceding one: thus, the instructions must be carried out sequentially, each one of them having to await the result of the execution of the preceding one to before its execution may start. The role of a compiler is to optimize the instruction sequences which it generates, in order to maximize parallelism between instructions. Such optimizing compilers were first heavily exploited with RISC architectures and then spread into use with CISC architectures (where there was also need for optimization).

In high-end CISC and RISC microprocessor implementations, the processor tries to improve performance by guessing the outcome of certain instructions (in particular, conditional branches) and proceeding as if its guesses were correct; of course, it must cease such speculation and undo any work it has done if and when it discovers its guesses were wrong. To do this, the processor must detect and track dynamically all the dependencies between instructions, which is a key factor in the complexity of the implementation.

The EPIC (Explicitly Parallel Instruction Computing) concept underlying IA-64 seeks to reduce this complexity by having the instructions explicitly indicate the dependencies to the processor.

We now examine the various implementation choices aimed at improving performance through increased instruction-level parallelism without changing instruction set architecture. The approaches will be compared on the basis of the following components:

- *Issue rate.* The number of instructions issued per clock cycle

- *Operation latency.* The number of cycles necessary to complete a simple operation

- *Instruction-stream parallelism.* The amount of parallelism within the instruction stream necessary to take full advantage of the hardware

To keep the discussion straightforward, we will simplify the problem to one in which there is a perfect memory (that is, which always produces a result within a clock cycle) and in which we consider only single-cycle instructions.

1.13.3   Basic Pipelined Processor

The principle behind the pipeline is straightforward: the work needed to execute a single instruction is broken up into some number of simpler steps, and each step is executed by an independent processor unit, the units being arranged one after the other so that as each unit finishes its piece of the work it hands the task on to the next unit. The effect is that of a bucket brigade. We characterize a pipeline by its length, or number of stages; this is also referred to as the depth of the pipeline. Figure 1.29 illustrates this structure for a processor with a very simple four-stage pipeline.

Figure 1.29
Basic Pipelined
Processor.

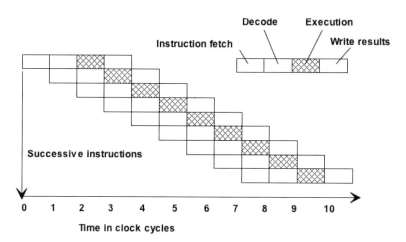

The characteristics of this structure are as follows:

```
issue rate = 1
operation latency = 1
required parallelism = 1
```

In this structure, the processor begins execution of a new instruction every cycle and simple instructions take one cycle to execute; thus a parallelism of one in the instruction stream is all that is needed to take full advantage of the structure. As can be seen in the diagram, starting from a cold start—with no work in the pipeline—the machine takes four clocks to become fully occupied and thus needs eight cycles to execute the first four instructions. Once running, a four-stage pipeline will—in the absence of conflicts—execute instructions at a rate four times that of an unpipelined implementation; a pipelined machine runs faster than an unpipelined processor implementing the same architecture, because each stage of the pipeline has much less work to do and can therefore operate in less time, allowing a higher operating frequency.

Of course, life is not so simple—conflicts can and do occur and result in longer execution times than one instruction per clock. Instruction dependencies and conditional branches can cause the pipeline to wait—referred to as a bubble in the pipeline—for the needed result or for the evaluation of the condition. In general, the longer the pipeline, the greater the impact (in clock cycles) of such a conflict. Compilers attempt to rearrange the instructions needed to perform the computations called for by a program in such a manner that dependencies are minimized (for example, by separating a dependent instruction from its upstream source by several instructions).

Figure 1.30 illustrates two simple cases of conflicts in a pipeline.

Figure 1.30
Illustration of conflicts in a pipeline.

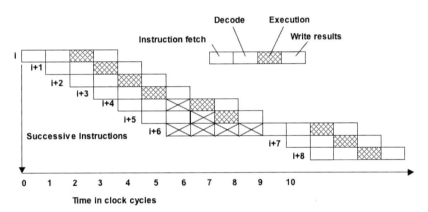

In this example, instruction i+4 uses as operand a result provided by instruction i+3. It is thus necessary to wait until this result is available (at the end of the execution of i+3) before the i+4 instruction can execute. Instruction i+5 is a conditional branch. It is necessary to await the end of the execution of this instruction to know the next instruction to be carried out. There are techniques making it possible to minimize the effect of these conflicts.

A phrase superpipelined was once in vogue. While it implied great skill and cunning in the implementation, it simply referred to an implementation with a large number of pipe stages, and therefore means just the same as pipelined.

1.13.4 Superscalar Processors

A superscalar processor is able to start execution of more than one instruction simultaneously, and is characterized by its degree N, which is the number of instructions it can start at once. Superscalar processors are also generally pipelined—a superscalar implementation of degree N will have N execution units capable of running in parallel and arranged in a pipeline capable of feeding them with instructions and data.

Figure 1.31 illustrates the operation of a degree-2 superscalar machine with a four-deep pipeline.

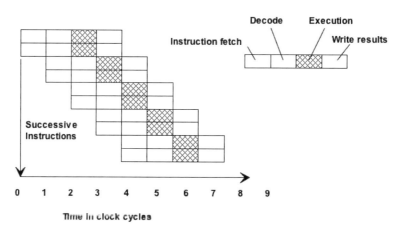

Figure 1.31
Superscalar Processor

The characteristics of this structure are as follows:

```
issue rate = N (2 in the case illustrated above)

operation latency = 1

required parallelism = N (2 in the case illustrated
above)
```

To fully use this structure, N instructions must be executed in parallel; for this to be possible, each pair must be independent. For a degree N superscalar machine, then, there must be parallelism of degree N in the instruction stream. A degree N superscalar machine has N times the throughput of a same clock rate single-issue pipelined machine (again, in the absence of conflicts, etc.). And compared to the simple pipelined processor, the impact of a branch or dependence on performance is much greater and increases with the degree of superscalarity. Currently, implementations of degrees greater than two are common. However, there are diminishing returns as the degree of superscalarity increase. To get an idea of the possible gains it is generally agreed that a two-way superscalar provides a 30% gain, a three-way 10% more and 5% more (although to get these levels of performance requires increasingly aggressive use of other techniques mentioned, such as out-of-order execution and speculation) for ordinary programs, although for tight DSP or scientific loops, significantly higher performance is achievable.

1.13.5 Comparison of the Superscalar and Deeply-Pipelined Structures

Analysis of program execution indicates that in extremely favorable cases a degree of parallelism of five or six can be found in ordinary programs;[17] this sets an asymptotic upper bound to available ILP. To exceed this limit, it is necessary to change the instruction set architecture or to execute, in parallel, several instruction sequences concurrently and to determine dynamically the best option (an example of this is the trace cache, which we will examine in section 1.13.12 Implementation Evolution). In the meantime, we can characterize superscalar and deeply-pipelined structures as follows:

- *Deeply Pipelined.* Adding extra stages to a pipeline does not, of itself, add disproportionate complexity. The most critical implementation issues are the cache and the TLB implementations, but there is another limiting factor, too. A pipelined microprocessor has storage elements (latches) in front of each pipe stage; when the number of pipe stages increases, the ratio between latch electronics and the electronics needed to do useful work in each stage increases, with the result that the increase in clock rate (which is the primary performance driver when increasing pipeline depth) is not as linear as one would hope.

- *Superscalar.* Increasing the degree of superscalarity increases complexity super-linearly, both because of increased control complexity and the need to richly interconnect an increasing number of functional units (the latter is of itself an n2 problem). The increase in complexity, with concomitant area and wiring length increases, could even cancel out through reduced clock rate the extra performance achieved by increased parallelism; certainly, time-to-market is adversely impacted by complexity.

1.13.6 VLIW Processor

With the notable exception of Transmeta, the concept of a Very Long Instruction Words (VLIW) processor has not been exploited in today's general-purpose microprocessors.

In the VLIW approach, each instruction comprises several primitive operations that can be executed concurrently. Early promoters of the approach considered instruction widths of 128 or even 256 bits; if we assume that a useful primitive operation may be represented (as it is in a traditional RISC architecture) in 32 bits, this means that such machines have an inherent concurrency of four to eight operations. This sort of machinery clearly requires the compiler to be able to extract significant ILP parallelism from the source code; since it is often the case that fewer than four or eight such operations can be identified for concurrent execution, VLIW instruction sets always include a no-op primitive operation which does nothing. No-ops are used to pad a VLIW when not enough useful work can be identified to fill the instruction. One effect is that VLIW machines of this nature tend to have code footprints even larger than those of RISC machines, by a substantial factor.

Multiflow, now out of business, built supercomputers based on this approach. In January 2000, Transmeta presented a new microprocessor family called Crusoe, which uses a VLIW ISA with 64- or 128-bit instruction words, each such instruction containing up to four primitive instructions. To hide the complexities and to avoid the problems of backwards compatibility of such a new architecture, they offer their processor packaged with software which provides dynamic translation of IA-32 object code, calling the approach Code Morphing. We discussed this briefly in this chapter.

Figure 1.32 shows a hypothetical VLIW processor which provides three elementary operations per word:

This structure is similar to the superscalar structure, with three differences:

- Instruction decode is simpler in VLIW, because the compiler has explicitly represented in the VLIW instruction itself that the component operations may be executed concurrently; in the superscalar implementation, the hardware has to discover this for itself dynamically

- When the parallelism available in the instruction sequence is lower than the degree of parallelism in the VLIW instruction, code size

Figure 1.32
VLIW processor.

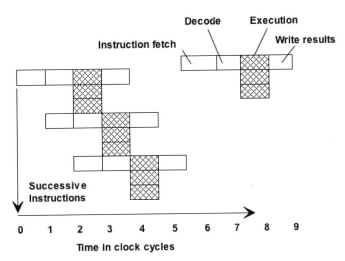

increases because the unusable primitive operation fields in the instruction still occupy space (and are filled with no-op primitive operations) although they do no useful work

■ A superscalar processor maintains binary compatibility across generations as the degree of superscalarity changes. Thus, wide superscalar machines can execute legacy binaries (for example, Pentium 4 can execute binaries generated for the 80386). Thus, for superscalar, the degree of implementation parallelism is a hidden intrinsic property. For a VLIW machine, however, the instruction width specifies the concurrency level; thus, increasing instruction width—in straight-forward VLIW implementations—automatically breaks binary compatibility between the new machine and an older, narrower one, even if they share identical and identically-encoded primitive operation repertoires

As noted earlier, there are no commercially-available VLIW general-purpose microprocessors, with the exception of Transmeta. Intel's IA-64 architecture, called EPIC, is essentially a VLIW architecture with two key differences:

■ The instruction encoding is not constrained by the fixed format of classical VLIW, so the code bloat occasioned by stuffing instructions with no-ops is removed

- Better marketing and sloganeering: EPIC is not tainted by the unsuccessful VLIW tag

We now look at a number of techniques which can be applied to any of these processor structures.

1.13.7 Speculative Execution

As has been seen, a key problem with high performance implementations is the presence of conditional branch instructions. If the machine waits to see which way the branch will go, it will waste processor cycles, and the deeper the pipeline the greater the number of cycles wasted (and the greater the degree of parallelism, the greater the amount of work not done). Avoiding this penalty is thus a key issue in the design of high performance machines. Speculative execution is aimed at exactly this problem. In a machine with speculative execution, a guess is made about the outcome of a conditional branch, and execution proceeds as if the guess were true; to handle the cases when the guess is wrong, the processor has resources that allow it, effectively, to backtrack and try again. This backtracking must be complete; for example, if the machine speculatively executes a divide instruction which generates a divide-by-zero exception, or a load instruction which page-faults, the exceptions must not be acted upon until it is safe to do so, or the machine's backtracking capability must be heroic indeed.

1.13.8 Out-of-Order Execution and Register Renaming

A second key problem in high performance implementations is inter-instruction data dependencies and waits caused by cache misses. Out-of-order execution is a technique that aims to minimize these effects, and register renaming is a companion technique. A machine with out-of-order execution may execute instructions in an order quite different from that obtained by simple sequential execution of the program (although its internal mechanisms will ensure that the results it gets are the same as sequential execution would have provided, of course).

To illustrate this operation, consider the following instruction sequence:

```
load r1 <- x
load r2 <- y
add r3 <- r6 + r7
load r16 <- b
```

```
store r16 -> a
store r3-> z
add r8 <- r1 + r2
```

If we assume that the data for either or both of the first two instructions is not in the data cache, then in an out-of-order machine the following instructions will be executed before the memory hierarchy has delivered the values for the first two instructions. At any time while the machine is executing these, the execution of the first two instructions may be done as soon as the memory hierarchy delivers the desired values. Only when the machine arrives at the final instruction, which is dependent on the first two, does it have to wait (but presumably, in a real program, there are other successor instructions on which it could work).

The maximum number of instructions which can be executed out of order influences performance (and complexity).

But simple out-of-order execution can run into a further limitation—the machine has architected limited number of registers, and while the machine is awaiting the moment to execute an instruction which will write to one of these, an instruction—in principle completely independent at the source code level—may be encountered which, because of the limited number of registers available, requires the re-use of a register already in use. The machine will then need to stall; if it had more registers, then it would have been able to proceed, but adding registers to a machine's instruction set breaks binary compatibility. Register renaming solves this problem by providing more implementation registers than architected registers.

The following example shows the situation:

```
e1:load r3…
add r2, r3…
…
e2:load r3…
sub r3, r4…
…
```

In this example, the code sequence starting at label e2 is logically completely independent of the code sequence starting at label e1, but because of resource limitations it must use register r3 as the destination of a load, just as the code at e1 did. To allow an out-of-order machine to execute the e2 code while awaiting the e1 load to complete, the machine must systemati-

cally map architected registers to internal registers on every register assign-
ment. Thus, it may have mapped r3 at label e1 to internal register 17 (r3:->
ir17), then r2 to ir18, and so forth through the e1 code sequence. By the
time it gets to the load at e2, it may have found ir37 as the next free internal
register, and it then maps r3 to ir37. After a mapping, all references to an
architected register specified in an instruction are replaced by a reference to
an internal register. Thus, with the example values given here, the code
sequence above would be mapped into Table 1.5:

Table 1.5   *Register renaming example.*

Original Instruction	Mapped Instruction
e1: load r3	e1: load ir17
add r2, r3	add ir18, ir17
...	...
e2: load r3	e2: load ir37
sub r3, r4	sub ir37, ir21

It is worth noting that this technique, although widely used in RISC
architectures, can be particularly effective in architectures like IA-32, which
have a very small number of architected registers.

An out-of-order implementation is characterized mainly by the number
of instructions that may co-exist, started but as yet uncompleted; this number is sometimes also called the instruction window.

1.13.9 Branch Prediction

An examination of executing programs shows that conditional branches are
not completely chaotic in their behavior, but rather show correlation patterns. Since conditional branches can be a major performance problem, it is
worth looking at hardware that can track the behavior of conditional
branches and usefully predict their outcome. One frequently used mechanism to achieve this keeps a cache, accessed by the address of conditional
branch instructions, whose entries are the expected next instruction for
each conditional branch cached. As the behavior of the branches changes,
the cached entries are updated. Details of the algorithms used are outside
the scope of this work.

1.13.10   Dynamic Translation of Code

By dynamic translation of code, we mean the technique of representing the actions that a sequence of instructions calls for as a sequence of simpler instructions; the collection of simpler instructions is kept in an appropriate cache, and executed in preference to the original instructions when the original instructions are encountered during execution. The use of simpler instructions make certain optimizations, such as those described above, simpler to implement in hardware. This approach has been used by Intel in its IA-32 processors since the Pentium Pro; AMD has also adopted the technique. Transmeta's Code Morphing—used in their Crusoe processors—is a related approach, although it uses software to effect the translation from complex to simpler instructions. This technique is also applicable to RISC architectures, especially those embodying rather complex instructions despite being labeled as RISC by their manufacturers.

Microprogrammed Architectures and Dynamic Translation

In this note, we discuss a different approach from that outlined in section 1.12, Architecture Retargeting. In the 1960s and 1970s, microprogrammed architectures were commonplace. In such a machine, the central processing unit has its own very simple instruction set, and executes just one program, which is nothing more than an interpreter for the instruction set specified by the machine's architecture. With a machine employing dynamic translation, the microprocessor, rather than interpreting the architectural instructions, transforms them into instruction sequences, caches the results and then executes them. Thus, no interpretation occurs, removing an important source of inefficiency. The effects of increasing silicon density and integration have enabled this more complex approach.

Table 1.6 summarizes some characteristics of a number of currently-available high end microprocessors, showing the rather wide range of performance-improvement approaches adopted.

Table 1.6 Notes: For the AMD Opteron and the Intel Pentium 4, the architectural instructions are decoded and dynamically translated by hardware into a simpler, RISC-like instruction set. These simpler instructions are called ROPs (RISC Operations) by AMD and µops (micro-operations) by Intel. Power 4 converts some of its more complex operations into instruction sequences. The recently announced Power 5 features a dual core implementation along with two-way simultaneous multithreading (SMT),

Table 1.6   *Characteristics of some microprocessors (as of March 2003).*

	AMD Opteron	HP-PA 8700	Intel Itanium 2	Intel Pentium 4 Xeon MP	Power 4	UltraSPAR C III
Architecture	IA-32 plus 64 bit extensions	PA	IA-64 + IA-32 compati-bility mode	IA-32	PowerPC-64 with AS 400 exten-sions	SPARC
SMP/CMP approach	-	-	-	SMT (2 threads)	CMP (2 processors)	-
Clock (MHz)	2000	875	1000	2000	1300	600-1050
Integrated caches (I/D)	L1: 64KB/ 64KB L2: 1MB	0.75MMB/ 1.5MB	L1: 16KB/ 16KB L2: 2566KB L3: 4MB	L1: 12K µops/8KB L2: 256KB L3 2 MB	L1: 16KB/ 32KB L2: 1.5 MB	L1: 32 KB/ 64KB
Superscalar degree	9 ROPs	4	6	6 µops	8 (5 simul-taneous)	4
Pipe stages	12(integer) 17 (float-ing point)	-	10?	20	12	14
Out-of-order execution (number of in-flight instructions)	?	56	yes	126 (µops)	200	no
Speculative execution	?	yes	?	?	yes	?
SPEC 2000 performance (int/ fp)	1202/1170 (estimated)	642/600	810/1427	816/677	790/1098	439/269 @ 900MHz

Table 1.6 *Characteristics of some microprocessors (as of March 2003). (continued)*

	AMD Opteron	HP-PA 8700	Intel Itanium 2	Intel Pentium 4 Xeon MP	Power 4	UltraSPAR C III
Other characteristics	Integrated memory controller; SMP inter-face logic integrated (coherent Hyper-Transport interface)	-		integrated miccro-op cache— holding translated IA-32 instruc-tions	Integrated L3 cache controller; integrated SMP inter-face logic	Integrated L2 cache controller (<= 8MB). Integrated memory controller.

a 1.875 MB integrated L2 cache and a 36 MB external L3 cache. The integrated interconnect allows streamline implementation of a physical 64-way SMP. The size of the L3 cache of the Itanium 2 has been increased up to 6 MB. Descriptions of Itanium 2 and Power 5 can be found in the March-April issue of IEEE Micro. Pentium 4 uses a cache of the translations of recently executed instruction.

It is evident that all the techniques we have described (except for VLIW) have been employed by one-or-other of these processors: superscalar, out of order execution and register renaming, branch prediction and dynamic translation of object code, and, in addition, Pentium 4's translation cache.

1.13.11 Architecture Evolution

There are two key barriers to the introduction of any new architecture for processors aimed at workstation and server applications:

- *Design cost of the new architecture*, which can amount to several hundred million dollars. This amount covers not just the architectural studies and specifications themselves, but also the development cost of chip families (associated microprocessors and, possibly, I/O controllers, if existing controllers are not suitable), plus compilers, operating systems, applications, and so forth. While in general application development is not the responsibility of the microprocessor vendor, to ensure a reasonable chance of success a vendor must engage with software publishers and, often enough, contribute to the cost of the porting and development costs.

- *Binary compatibility.* As we have mentioned several times, a key value of an architecture is the size, breadth, and quality of its associated software catalog. Since software is sold in binary form, it is imperative that architecture changes do not compromise compatibility. This clearly represents a major barrier to the introduction of a new architecture or of changes to an existing architecture.

As we shall see in the section on economic factors, the issue of binary compatibility is usually considered less of an issue for embedded applications. Thus, it seems that the opportunities to define architectures tuned for specific needs are more numerous than in the data processing field.[18] However, such a view must be moderated by consideration of the effects of volume on cost, the effect of which is to lead to a *de facto* standardization of architectures.

A key milestone in architecture evolution is the move to a 64-bit virtual address. Some architectures were designed from the very start with 64 address bits, either in their initial specification or in their first implementations. For example, in chronological order, IBM's iSeries (System/38 when first introduced and AS/400 later on), HP's Precision Architecture (which actually contains three architecture models with 32-, 48- and 64-bit address spaces, although the 32-bit version has never been implemented), DEC Alpha and IA-64.

Other architectures came to life as 32-bit architectures and received 64-bit extensions later in life; key examples are MIPS, IBM's POWER (a stepping stone to PowerPC), and SPARC. The relative simplicity of these RISC architectures and their associated regularity were factors favorable to straightforward extensions to 64 bits.

Intel chose, within the framework of a partnership with HP (which had long experience in the field of RISC architectures and research into highly parallel VLIW instruction set architectures), to introduce a totally new architecture, IA-64.[19] This represents a major gamble for Intel; we will discuss later the basic concepts behind IA-64.

Although this architecture has no direct links with IA-32, the strong constraints of binary compatibility have led Intel to offer an IA-32 compatibility mode on IA-64 implementations. While such machines can execute IA-32 binaries, these binaries cannot benefit from the architectural advances of IA-64, nor can they take advantage of the much larger address

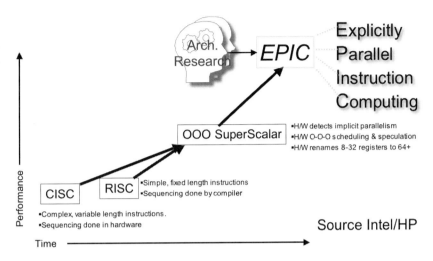

Figure 1.33
*Illustration of the
EPIC concept
(Source Intel/HP)*

space. The first implementation of this architecture, called Itanium, was offered in both system and chip form in the second half of 2001. The next generation, Itanium 2, was introduced in July 2002.

The IA-64 architecture is based on the assumption that compilers can do a more thorough job of identifying fine-grain concurrency than hardware, and that having identified it the available concurrency should be made explicit to the hardware through appropriate instruction encodings. This is reflected in Intel's name for the approach, EPIC (for Explicitly Parallel Instruction Computing). The EPIC concept is illustrated in Figure 1.33, taken directly from Intel/HP presentations.

While this figure has the unmistakable fingerprints of "marketing" all over it, it does highlight some major steps in architecture evolution. Our comments follow:

- *CISC (Complex Instruction Set Computer)* was the dominant architectural concept from the very first days of commercial data processing, with architects constructing increasingly complex instruction repertoires during the 1960s. At that time, the key goals behind architectural change were to simplify the software—seen more at the assembler level than at a high-level language level—and to minimize code footprint (i.e., to minimize the amount of memory required to hold the object code of a program). This latter goal was a reflection of the pressure caused by relatively small main memory sizes, the high cost of memory. Variable length instruction encodings (in which

Looking at the historical record, we can see that processor architectural evolution tends to develop as a repeating two-phase phenomenon—a stability phase being followed by a breakaway phase.

In the stability phase, we see concentration on implementation refinement while the architectures remain essentially unchanged.

- *hardware architectures*, embodying improvements such as the techniques we have discussed

- *compiler improvements*, making it possible to better exploit architectural features

- *instruction set extensions*, but without breaking backwards binary compatibility; examples are the addition of multimedia capabilities, and the extension of addressing capabilities

The stability phase is one in which an equilibrium has been reached.

However, despite the equilibrium, in the background things are going steadily wrong, putting increasing pressure on extant architectures. Examples include the growing gulf between processor and memory speeds; the reduction in memory costs that make program size much less of an issue than before, and the increasing the integration capabilities of the technology. We can qualify such evolutions as being non-homotetic, since they destroy established equilibrium and lead eventually to a break; In other words, pressure is great enough to support a breakaway solution.

Such a breakaway solution is characterized also by a flock of new ideas and thinking, and of questioning of well-established "truths". Two obvious examples are

- The appearance of RISC architectures

- The introduction of IA-64

This view of architectural evolution suggests it proceeds in a manner similar to an earthquake—for a long time, the deep movements are invisible except to those with the appropriate sensitive instrumentation; but eventually the tensions pass a critical threshold and the situation ruptures. A key difference between earthquakes and architecture evolution is that for architectures, the critical threshold keeps increasing, particularly in terms of the size of the necessary investment.

more frequent operations required smaller instruction sizes) were widespread. Although the high-end implementations were pipelined, the compilers often did not generate code that took optimal advantage of the pipeline structures; further, although the architecture provided complex problem-oriented instructions, the compilers of the day were rarely able to take advantage of them.[20] Overall, however, the prevalent implementations, generally microprogrammed and with moderate amounts of pipelining, were an excellent match to the capabilities of the available technology, with these CISC machines offering an attractive blend of cost and performance.

■ *RISC* (*Reduced Instruction Set Computer*). The observation that compilers made very poor use of the complex instructions created for CISC machines made researchers consider a different approach—instead of constructing architectures with complex instructions (where complex means that a single instruction could cause a long sequence of operations to occur), why not look at an architecture in which only the simple primitive operations necessary to construct programs were provided, so that complex operations were represented by a sequence of these basic operations? This allowed the instruction set to have greater orthogonality (or generality). As a result, the job of the compiler was much simplified (because of a major reduction in special cases), and implementation was substantially simplified, with the result that a complete processor could be constructed on a single chip. IBM's 801 design is generally credited as the first RISC. A cost of the new approach was that programs were not encoded as efficiently, and needed more memory to hold their object code than had contemporary CISC machines; however, the inexorable march of Moore's Law was simultaneously driving memory capacities up and prices down, and so the added code footprint was not a significant drawback.[21] RISC machines were always pipelined, allowing higher clock rates for a given technology than classic CISCs; the compiler's job was both made more difficult and more simple, in that while the compiler now had to generate code which allowed efficient use of the pipeline (for example, by generating instructions in a manner which minimized stalls), the target architecture was very regular, removing special-case issues. The very regularity of the architecture also provided the compiler with opportunities to make optimizations in the code which would have been impossible with a CISC architecture.

The search for higher performance for both CISC and RISC architectures led designers to adopt architectures which were capable of detecting

Short History of RISC

It is reasonable to look upon the early CRAY architectures, which strove to obtain high execution rates through the use of simple instructions, as the basis of RISC architectures. The concept was explored in a more general manner inside IBM with the 801 project (John Cocke and George Radin [HOP87], [SHR99]); this project—named after the building in which it was done—was finished in 1979, and its results were published in 1981. Similar studies at Stanford and Berkeley started in the early 1980s, and led respectively to the MIPS and SPARC architectures. The acronym RISC was created by the Berkeley team. The first commercial computers based on these concepts were marketed by start-ups Ridge and Pyramid, who introduced their products in (respectively) 1983 and 1985, followed by HP who introduced HP PA (Precision Architecture) in 1986. Sun's introduction of SPARC-based systems in 1987, transitioning in an exemplary fashion from their 680x0-based product line, was instrumental in the acceptance of RISC concepts.

and exploiting instruction-level parallelism. As we saw in section 1.13.1, traditional performance improvement techniques, superscalar architectures with out-of-order execution both detect and exploit instruction-level concurrency, using speculative execution (involving prediction of the future operations to be executed) and register renaming (in which the implementation provides more registers than specified by the architecture) to provide high performance. EPIC architectures, on the other hand, rely on compile-time detected concurrency explicitly represented in the encodings of the instructions, and offer increased performance more from a combination of concurrent execution coupled with predicated execution.

The objectives of EPIC are as follows:

- *Performance and the potential for continued performance improvement over a long period.* IA-32's architecture has a number of features which make achieving high performance very difficult—for example, the limited number of registers and the stack-based floating point. While IA-32 implementations certainly reach very high performance levels, achieving that performance is extremely difficult, expensive and time-consuming and leads to very complex implementations. IA-64 is intended to remove all such basic performance-blocking features, allowing the architecture to have a long lifespan and for performance to be competitively improved throughout that life, without heroics.

■ *Software compatibility with IA-32 and HP-PA.* Given the amount of software available for IA-32 and the amount of money invested in PA, it is a business necessity for legacy binaries to be executable on an IA-64 computer. IA-32 execution is provided by current IA-64 implementations directly in hardware, while PA compatibility is provided by dynamic translation techniques in software.

■ *Scalability.* The architecture must allow implementations at current technology offering various performance levels; for example, by varying the degree of parallelism in the implementation.

■ *Large address space.* Both very large virtual address space (64 bits) and very large physical address space.

In addition, the IA-64 architects sought to reduce or remove well-understood performance barriers through provision of appropriate architecture and mechanisms. The key issues addressed are:

■ *Branches.* Although high-end microprocessors have effective and elaborate branch prediction mechanisms, a mispredicted branch has a substantial negative effect on performance, particularly for long pipeline machines. Further, when a machine implements branches, it is generally impossible for the compiler to effect optimizations between branch targets; the resulting code chunks (called basic blocks) are rather small, limiting optimization opportunities.

■ *Memory latency.* As we saw earlier in this chapter, there is a large and growing gulf between processor speed and memory speed. Despite the constant increase in cache sizes, cache misses still exist; when a miss is encountered, the processor must eventually stall awaiting the response from memory. Were it possible to ask the memory for data long in advance of it being needed, some portion of the memory latency could be hidden. Unfortunately, in a processor with branches, it is generally impossible to hoist a load instruction out of its native basic block, and a blocks are too small to offer much latency hiding possibility.

■ *Instruction-level parallelism.* Programs are generally written in high-level languages translated to machine code by a compiler; while the compilers "know" the structure of the program (learned as they read and translated it), and thus in principle can identify operations which may be executed in parallel, extant processor architectures offer no way for the compiler to communicate this knowledge of potential parallelism to the hardware. Thus the microprocessor must expend transistors, area, power and complexity to rediscover the inherent concurrency, but with a much more limited view of the program than the compiler had.

A key performance element is simply having enough registers; IA-64 architects 128 64-bit general (integer) registers and 128 floating point registers. The architecture does not specify how many functional units an implementation may have.

Instructions are collected up into groups of three, each group called a bundle. Each bundle contains a compiler-generated descriptor indicating any inter-instruction dependencies in the bundle; the processor therefore has explicit knowledge of possible concurrency, and does not need to spend hardware discovering it.

IA-64 uses predication to reduce the number of branches executed. When one examines the number of instructions actually executed per clock cycle by a superscalar machine, one discovers that the number actually executed is below the amount the hardware is capable of. There is thus spare instruction execution bandwidth available. IA-64 predicated execution takes advantage of this; each instruction contains a predicate field, which specifies one of 64 predicate registers (each one bit in size). An instruction will only be executed if the predicate register it specifies has the value true (that is, 1). So rather than collecting instructions to be executed if a condition is true into one basic block, executing the instructions if the condition is not true into a separate basic block, and using a conditional branch (and likely an unconditional branch too) to arrange for the correct basic block to be executed, IA-64 simply sets specific predicate registers according to the value of the conditional expression, tags the instructions appropriately, and lets the processor see just one bigger basic block rather than two smaller ones.

Figure 1.34 illustrates, according to a presentation of INTEL and HP, this predication mechanism.

As shown in this simple example, an if-then-else is translated, in a traditional architecture, into code which evaluates the condition. A conditional branch is taken if the condition is false (the conditional branch has as destination the code (sequence-2 in the example) which is to be exe-

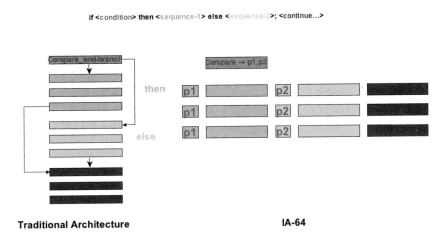

Figure 1.34
IA-64 Predication Mechanism (Source INTEL-HP).

cuted if the condition is false; the conditional branch is followed by the instructions for the code to be executed (sequence-1 in the example) if the condition were *true*. This code is followed by an unconditional branch to the continuation code.

When compiled for IA-64, things are different. The code which evaluates the conditional sets two predicate registers, shown as p1 and p2. p1 is set true if the condition evaluates to true, and p2 is set true if the condition evaluates to false. The instructions for sequence-1 are generated specifying p1 as the controlling predicate register, and the code for sequence-2 is generated with p2 specified; there are no branches needed, conditional or unconditional. Any instruction in sequence-1 is independent of any instruction in sequence-2, and so they may be paired up as in the diagram to be executed in parallel (with only s-1 or s-2 instructions actually having any effect).

To handle memory latency, IA-64 introduces the speculative load operation. This differs from a normal load in that it will never cause an exception, even when a normal load would (badly-formed address, page miss, etc.). Rather than causing an exception, a speculative load notes that an exception should have been generated, and does nothing more.

Because a speculative load has no unpleasant side effects, it can be hoisted (scheduled long before the value it loads is needed). In the code that actually needs the value, a test is first made to see if the speculative load succeeded, or whether it failed. If it failed, a normal load is executed (generally using predication to avoid branches). A speculative load can safely be executed ahead of a conditional branch; if the branch takes a direction in which the speculative load is not needed, the results of the speculative load is simply ignored.

[DUL98] describes these two architectural characteristics of IA-64.

It can be seen that the compilers for the IA-64 carry a heavy responsibility for system performance, and while relevant compiler technology probably benefited from VLIW research, we will most likely see a maturation phase before the compilers offer performance satisfactory to the IA-64 architects.

Good architecture design is guided by the needs of future workloads. While we will see (in the section 1.13.12 Implementation Evolution) that, as ever, the embedded marketplace will represent the vast majority of microprocessors, we are interested here in high-performance processors for servers and workstations.

In a workstation, it is estimated that the user interface consumes a significant share of compute resources, and that this is increasing with the increasing amount of multi-media usage. To match this, architectures have been extended to better support multimedia workloads.[22] Two factors contribute to ensuring that the processors for high-end workstations and processors for servers are the same (well, technically the same; marketing pressures and margin management can create multiple differently-priced processor products from one single processor chassis).

- The emergence of multiprocessor workstations (when previously servers were multiprocessor but workstations were uniprocessor)
- The relatively low volume of servers manufactured (a few million a year, as opposed to a few tens of millions a year for workstations), which means that server-specific development is hard to justify economically

We should note that multimedia extensions can be useful for servers as well, since the extensions may be used to speed multimedia database processing, or even to accelerate entirely different tasks, such as TCP/IP implementations.

To conclude this section, we can say that, overall, any major extension to an existing architecture or any attempt to introduce a new architecture is a very iffy prospect, due both to the weight of existing binaries and the development costs of a new architecture.

On the other hand, we can see that evolutionary improvements purely at the implementation level are a much more attractive prospect, since their only cost is that of the implementation with binary compatibility de facto available.

We can also say that, absent a major change in the model of execution, there is little chance of significant progress in architecture evolution. Even given such a new paradigm, it must still offer substantial performance and price advantages over current approaches. That is, the barrier to entry for new architectures and new computing paradigms is today exceptionally high, except—arguably—for embedded applications.

1.13.12 Implementation Evolution

Previously in this chapter, we reviewed the projections of integrated circuit technology experts. As transistors get smaller, a new problem appears: the internal connections on the chip scale more slowly than transistor speed, and so effectively get slower as the performance improves. The effect is that with a chip of around a billion transistors, it is estimated that a chip crossing will take 20 clock cycles. It is therefore impossible to have a single clock on the chip, and the chip will need to be constructed as a collection of communicating subsystems, each with its own clock. Although a cost-effective (and power-effective) solution to these issues is indispensable for future processor generations, the various approaches are beyond the scope of this work.

We will now provide a quick look at some established implementation approaches together with one new approach. For more details, see [COM97] and [KOZ98]. We should note that some of these approaches are based on the assumption that the transistor budget to hand is on the order of a billion transistors.

High-degree Superscalar

In this approach, one seeks to increase the number of instructions simultaneously executed. This approach is already largely exploited by the top-of-the-range microprocessors (see Chapter 4's table 4.3).

EPIC

This approach, extensively described in preceding paragraphs, relies heavily on compilers discovering and explicitly representing internal concurrency.

1.13.13   Trace cache

This approach notices that if branch prediction works, then one may avoid branches by a taking a different view: simply identify sequences of executed instructions—omitting the branches—and cache the most frequent sequences. Each such sequence is called a trace, and the cache is called a trace cache. Candidate traces are executed speculatively in parallel and the results of the trace which had the same effects as a sequential execution (given the incoming data values) would have had is chosen. Thus, the degree of internal parallelism is increased while branches are removed, at the expense of sometimes substantial cache area.

SMT (Simultaneous MultiThreading)

In this approach, a single processor has sufficient resources (registers, for example) to be able to represent the state of more than one process (or thread). The processor then interleaves instructions from the collection of represented threads so that at any one time, instructions from several threads are executing within the processor.[23] Then, if an instruction in one thread encounters some conflict, further instructions from that thread are no longer scheduled and the processor is dedicated to the other threads; in this manner, even when individual threads stall, it is much less likely for the collection of threads to stall as a whole, and so more work is done per unit time than if the processor were to execute just one thread at a time. This approach does not improve the performance for any one thread, but improves system throughput. It is an example of TLP (Thread Level Parallelism), implementing several "logical" processors with just one physical processor.

IBM's POWER 3 processor (codenamed NorthStar) implemented simultaneous multithreading, and, as already indicated, Pentium 4 implements this concept under the name of hyper threading.

CMP (Chip MultiProcessing)

This is a straightforward approach that simply integrates several processors onto one chip. The processors generally have private first-level caches, and share level 2 and level 3 caches and memory; the implementation generally provides cache coherence, and so the result is a single-chip SMP (Symmetrical MultiProcessor) system (we will discuss SMP in greater detail in Chapter 4). As with TLP, a CMP implementation provides higher performance by taking advantage of thread-level parallelism.

Of course, Chip Multiprocessing and multithreading are not in contradiction. A microprocessor implementation may combine multiprocessing and multithreading (e.g., IBM's POWER 5). IBM's POWER 4 is an example of a CMP integrating two processors. We will see, in Chapter 4, an example of a system built with this microprocessor.

Intelligent Memory

The approach integrates processing elements within a memory chip, and will be described later in the section on Architectural Evolution.

Configurable processors

Rather than a chip being a processor, a configurable processor provides a large number of connected, replicated elements, each with memory for instructions and data, an ALU, local registers, and some configurable logic to decode a (configurable) instruction set. The resources are connected up and configured under the control of software, and can be set up, for example, to be a domain-specific processor (that is, one aimed at a specific task); to be adaptively changed from one domain-specific tuning to another; or to be configured as a massively parallel processor on a chip. With a billion transistors, one could construct a chip with 128 processors and 128 MBytes of memory.

We will take a second look at possible evolutionary paths in section 2.8, after we have looked at architectural options for servers.

1.14 Economic Factors

As mentioned in this chapter, economic issues dominate microprocessor evolution. Figure 1.35 (from [HEN99]) shows forecast volumes for 32 and 64-bit microprocessors in the PC (including server) and embedded markets out to 2003.

For the year 2001, we have the following figures:

- High-performance microprocessors for PCs and servers: $23 billion

- High-performance microprocessors for embedded applications:$10 billion

- DSP's (Digital Signal Processors):$4 billion

Figure 1.35
*32/64 bit PC and
Embedded
Microprocessor
Sales Projections
(Source
[HEN99]).*

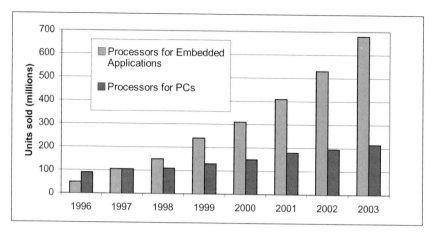

As can be seen, while embedded applications dominate in terms of volume, the PC/server market is where the money is.

8- and 16-bit Microprocessors

Many, many applications use 8- and 16-bit microprocessors, in volumes much higher than 32/64 bit processors. But 16-bit processors (and therefore 8-bit) have no place in the PC market (except as embedded processors in disks and keyboards). Thus, any architectural evolutions in the 8- and 16-bit market have little or no effect on 32- or 64-bit architectures, and so despite their volumes we pay them no attention here.

A significant share of the embedded market shown in the figure is for systems which could be called information appliances—systems that connect to the internet and communicate with sufficient intelligence to organize themselves. Emergence of machines of this class intended for the general public will increase demands for availability (both of the machines and of the servers with which they communicate), maintainability, and scalability. The apparently acceptable behavior of PC users—reboot after a crash—becomes increasingly unacceptable for this class of machines and their users, making it an interesting challenge for systems designers.

A number of different scenarios can emerge, such as:

- Embedded processors are derivations of those intended for the PC market, enhanced by appropriate functional units meeting the needs of specialized applications

- PC processors are derived from processors designed for the embedded market, enhanced as appropriate (for example, larger caches, graphics capabilities, SMP support)

- Two different families emerge at one vendor, and their differences increase over time

- The world crystallizes into an arrangement in which some vendors supply the embedded market, while others supply the PC market

Of course, this list is not exhaustive, and serves merely to indicate the complexity of the real-world situation. The outcomes, however, have a very large effect on the availability and nature of processors for the server world, since server volumes are not such that they can support special development for servers alone within the economics of the microprocessor marketplace.

It would be rash to put to much effort into prognostications here, but it must be said that the enormous volumes of the embedded market are bound to have a large effect on the direction the industry moves. The computer-oriented processor analysts and observers have an unfortunate tendency to concentrate on the brute performance and commercial success of processors in the server arena, and may not pay enough attention to the dynamics of the larger marketplace for silicon.

A key economic aspect is development cost, which (as we have noted) is constantly increasing. Table 1.7, from [HEN99], shows that these costs grew exponentially over time for MIPS processors, a trend not believed to be unique to MIPS.

Table 1.7 *Development cost trends for MIPS processors (source [HEN99]).*

Microprocessor	Year of Introduction	Millions of Transistors	Number of Developers	Project Duration	Project Headcount Cost Estimate ($M)	Verification Cost (Percentage of the project cost)
R2000	1985	0.1	20	15	2.5	15%
R4000	1991	1/4	55	24	11	20%
R10000	1996	6.8	>100	36	30	>35%

The headcount development cost (the cost of the people doing the work) increased over about a decade from a few million dollars to a few tens of millions of dollars. Note that this does not include development costs for associated support chips, or for software; nor does it include associated capital costs and other expenses, such as for workstations, test equipment, prototypes; nor any software investment, such as compiler enhancements needed to take advantage of the new implementations.

We expect that verification, which is itself an increasing fraction of a fast-growing cost, must be even greater for architectures more complex than MIPS.

To remain a credible contender, a vendor must (historically) introduce a new version every 18 to 24 months. For a given microprocessor generation (that is, a given microarchitecture), it is possible to take advantage of one or two semiconductor technology steps without making significant changes to the microarchitecture. Doing this generally results in straightforward improvements (such as higher clock rate and larger caches), and represents a small fraction of the cost of development of an entirely new microarchitecture. A given microarchitecture (for a given general-purpose microprocessor) can therefore expect a competitive life of three or four years. For successful microprocessors targeted at the embedded market—and for processors which migrate from general-purpose into embedded—a much longer lifespan of a decade or so may be expected.

Because design and verification requires increasing amounts of time, and because new design must be produced every three or four years, a vendor must have several designs proceeding concurrently, but at different phases of their life cycles. While we will not perform an ROI (Return on Investment) calculation here, it is evident that playing in the microprocessor market requires significant investment, which can only be amortized over exceedingly large volumes of processors sold.

Table 1.7 also highlights the increasing verification costs for microprocessors. Any fault in a microprocessor has financial impact, since the fault must be identified and corrected, a new mask set constructed and a new batch of processors manufactured and tested in prototypes. To these direct costs must be added the indirect costs of delayed introduction (loss of market share, impact on public image, loss of confidence, loss of time-sensitive customers, and so forth).

For context, it is generally supposed that about half (40 to 50%) of the development cost of an Intel microprocessor is allocated to verification, and about 6% of the transistors on the chip are dedicated to BIST (Built-In Self Test).

The standard approach to verification is to subject the design to specific and to randomly-generated test scenarios, requiring the design to be simulated for many, many cycles and the expected and observed results to be compared. Simulation of a complex design is a slow, computational-expensive process. Clearly, any methodology or technology that promises to sharply reduce the number of bugs remaining in a design and/or the cost of finding them must be of great importance to microprocessor manufacturers. An approach called formal verification seems to offer this opportunity.

1.15 Formal Verification

The adoption of logic synthesis almost universally in integrated circuit design has moved the design bottleneck from design itself to the task of verifying that the design does what it is supposed to do. A large and increasing percentage of the design effort is now dedicated to this functional verification, which is very important, as taping out an essentially correct chip reduces time to market and time to money. However, this verification has traditionally been done by simulation, in which the design is simulated and subjected to a large range of stimuli, with its behavior being compared to what the specification calls for. Unfortunately, simulation performance has not kept pace with the increasing complexity of designs, and so new techniques are becoming more attractive. The most attractive contender for the near future is formal verification.

Formal verification uses mathematical techniques to confirm or refute the hypothesis that a design is equivalent to its specification, thereby avoiding the necessity of generating and simulating billions of tests while promising exhaustive coverage.

1.16 Memory

As indicated on several occasions in this work, a major barriers to increased system performance is current memories characteristics.

Throughout this chapter, we have examined the problems occasioned by memory, along with the current solutions—the use of caches, and organizing memory to provide high bandwidth. These solutions allow us to maintain current systems architecture.

In this section we will look at a proposal—intelligent memory—which suggests a change in systems architecture. The proposal is to integrate with each memory chip some processing capability; as before, systems will comprise several to many chips.

1.16.1   **Intelligent Memory**

Researchers at Berkeley have suggested [PAT97] [KOZ97] that rather than bolting some amount of SRAM, organized as a cache, around a processor, one should add a processor core to a DRAM. They called this approach IRAM, for Intelligent RAM. Since processor and memory coexist on the same chip, extremely high bandwidth connections between them are possible and cheap. When the memory happens to be large enough to contain a complete application and its data, one can then imagine adding serial or narrow interfaces such as HyperTransport, RapidIO or Gigabit Ethernet, and thus avoid expensive, silicon-unfriendly parallel external interfaces. In such a situation, an IRAM chip would have interfaces only for power and network interconnect. A specialized version of the concept, a vector-processing. We summarize the pros and cons of IRAM in Table 1.8.

Table 1.8   *IRAM pros and cons.*

Advantages	Inconveniences
■ High band-width (compared to traditional DRAM) ■ Low latency (compared to traditional DRAM) ■ Energy effectiveness.Compactness	■ Suitability of DRAM manufacturing process for processor (logic) implementation ■ High-temperature operation of the chip (because of high-performance logic), making DRAM refresh cycles very frequent ■ Limiting the memory size of a system to what fits on a single chip ■ No flexibility in the processing power/memory capacity ratio ■ Cost of manufacturing test ■ Industry acceptance

These judgements arose from the IRAM project, and deserve some comment.

- DRAM processes optimize for different capabilities from the high-performance logic processes generally adopted for microprocessors. Therefore, the natural question is: is an IRAM built in a DRAM process (yielding markedly sub-optimal processor performance) or a logic process (yielding markedly sub-optimal DRAM)?

- One may circumvent the memory capacity limitation of pure IRAM by providing interfaces to external memory (perhaps serial, for cost reasons); but then some of the IRAM advantage is lost.

- With the pure IRAM approach, each chip has a well-defined processing and memory capacity. Changing this ratio implies changing the chip. The most natural system architecture for such a device is a loosely-coupled multiprocessor. Note that integrating a message-passing interface (for example, RapidIO) would not change the processing/capacity ratio. An SMP would mean major complicated changes to an IRAM chip, and would strongly affect performance (inter-chip bandwidths are unlikely to match within-chip bandwidths).

- A significant portion of the cost of a DRAM is manufacturing tests. Adding a processor must increase this cost noticeably, but an IRAM cost must be compared with the cost of a processor plus the cost of a memory.

- For an IRAM-like approach to succeed, it must be widely adopted. For this to occur, a major industrial gulf would likely have to be bridged—memory manufacturers (whose economics have long been controlled by commodity-like cost constraints) and microprocessor manufacturers (whose pricing reflects a belief in value-add through superior IP).

We should also note—reflecting the concerns of an earlier section—that an IRAM would likely offer a new instruction set architecture, and would thus run into many more barriers as well; it is possible that a Java-like approach might modify this harsh judgement. An IRAM must also choose to follow DRAM interface standards or not; either course of action will have cost and usability consequences.

And finally, we must note once again that any silicon technology which does not achieve wide adoption is destined to disappear.

1.17 Endnotes

1. In October 2001, Intel announced that it had invested $2 billion in the construction of a new fab at Chandler, Arizona. This fab will construct chips on 8-inch wafers using a 0.13μ technology. Constructing the fab took 18 months and 4,200 workers.

2. For comparison, note that the diameter of a human hair is of the order of 70 μ (70 microns)

3. MicroDesign Resources, publisher of Microprocessor Report, the authoritative publication in the world of microprocessors (http://www.MDRonline.com).

4. Which means that one must plan for an expenditure of a few tens of millions of dollars at the end of the first period and of several hundred million every three or four years.

5. We use the term cache block for the allocation unit of information within the cache. This is also the size of the data transferred between a cache and the immediately-adjacent memory level. A cache block is a collection of consecutive bytes, with a typical size of 64 or 128 bytes; this size has a tendency to grow with successive processor generations. The term cache line is sometimes used instead of cache block.

6. This is the case with the MAS (Multiple Address Space) model that is widely used in low-end or midrange servers. The two models MAS and SAS (Single Address Space) are discussed further in Chapter 3.

7. This technique, which we'll examine more closely when looking at the connections between processor, memory and I/O, makes it possible to increase the bandwidth of the interconnect between processor and memory (a bus in our example). It consists of transmitting in consecutive cycles on the bus data, which specify first the command and the address and then the data—one bus cycle combining command and address, and then a succession of N data cycles—rather than N pairs of cycles each comprising command/ address followed by data.

8. In relational databases, the idea of a database is simply that of a table constructed of identical entries, called tuples, or lines. We reuse this classic terminology.

9.   As already discussed, on-line transaction processing (OLTP) is characterized by the fact that any request for execution is the direct response to a user action.

10. Here, we are assuming a write-back strategy for the caches, which means that the processor holding the valid copy of the data must respond to any access request

11. This continual observation of the bus is what gives rise to the terms snoopy and snooping.

12. To simplify the talk, it is considered that: the strategy adopted for the writing in a block absent is of the type "Write Allocate." i.e., one feeds the block, and that the processor updates the data in its cache—the block was not present in the caches of the other processors.

13. In other words, each operation executes completely or does not execute at all—another instance of the idea of an atomic action central to transactional systems.

14. In somewhat older architectures (mainframes and minicomputers) one used atomic instructions such as Test and Set, Compare and Swap, or Fetch and Add for synchronization operations. These instructions hurt performance, and that prompted architects to move to the new instruction pair.

15. It is possible to offer some degree of protection to source-level intellectual property by subjecting it to a transformation that consistently replaces each symbol (names, keywords, figures, operators) in the source by another other randomly generated symbol having no mnemonic value.

16. One is tempted to remark that there's nothing new except what's been forgotten.

17. We should note that important software codes implementing DSP, heavily mathematical Fortran loops and multimedia are different—much higher degrees of parallelism may be found in these.

18. In this regard, we should also note the approach of extending an existing general-purpose architecture by adding instructions capable of manipulating new data types, rather than creating a whole new architecture for that purpose. This extension approach is one that has been taken by several processor vendors,

particularly in the field of multimedia, examples including IA-32, PowerPC and SPARC.

19. At Microprocessor Forum October 1999, AMD responded to the introduction of IA-64 by offering its own 64-bit extensions to the IA-32 architecture. The first implementation of this architecture, codenamed Hammer, was expected to appear in late 2001, and was introduced in 2003. It is now called Opteron.

20. We are aware of some architectures in which certain such instructions were executed only in self-test programs—that is, programs which exercised all instructions to confirm correct operation of all the instructions implemented by the machine.

21. We should note that this is not necessarily a truth for embedded applications, where RISC architectures can cause most unpleasant cost increases for lower-end systems on a chip which use, say, embedded FLASH memory integrated on the chip. This is what drove ARM to implement their reduced-footprint Thumb instruction set, for example.

22. We should note that the extensions to handle multimedia data have uniformly adopted the SIMD (Single Instruction Multiple Data) architecture [FLY 72], in which a single instruction operates on multiple data items concurrently.

23. Without multithreading, utilization of the execution unit resources of a microprocessor can be as low as 25%.

2

I/O

Neither systems architects nor computer architecture researchers have paid as much attention to I/O as they have to processors. The rationale for this lack of attention is completely unclear to us, since I/O is a key part of a system, being both a driver for system performance and an opportunity for value add—unlike processors, where the economies of scale predominate. As we will see in this chapter, I/O is an area where some interesting work has been done.

In the previous chapter, we provided a generic server model with the purpose of identifying the various interconnects of interest, mentioning the interconnects between processor, memory and I/O.

An I/O system comprises a number of elements, illustrated in Figure 2.1.

As shown in this diagram, the various elements of a classical I/O subsystem are as follows:

- A system controller implementing the connection between processor(s), memory and the I/O bus(es). In practice, this is often a chip integrating two functions—a memory controller and an I/O controller.

- One or more I/O buses. The industry has converged on the PCI (Peripheral Component Interconnect) bus and its extensions.

- I/O controllers connected to an I/O bus. Peripheral devices—for example, disks directly connected to the system, long-distance network connections (WAN, for Wide Area Network) and local network connections (LAN, for Local Area Network) are connected to these controllers.

- Directly-attached magnetic peripherals (a configuration called DAS, for Directly Attached Storage), on specialized buses such as SCSI, which today is the standard for this purpose.

Figure 2.1
The elements of an I/O system.

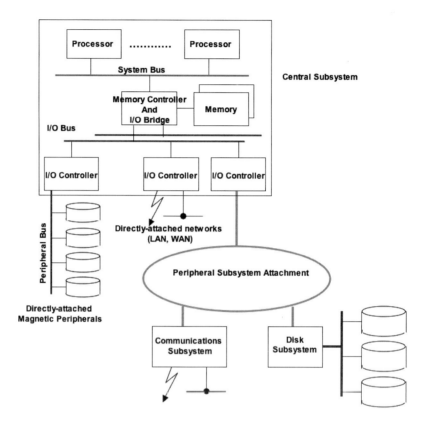

- Specialized networks are used for the connection of peripheral sub-systems, such as disk subsystems (e.g., SAN, for Storage Area Network) or communications subsystems (WAN or LAN). In this domain, the industry is moving to Fibre Channel.

In this chapter we will first be interested in buses used for I/O (principally PCI and its extensions) and in the connections between controllers and magnetic peripherals (SCSI and Fibre Channel—Arbitrated Loop, or FC-AL) and subsequently in Fibre Channel, used to connect to peripheral subsystems.

Later, we will look at the InfiniBand I/O proposal, which has some chance of gaining traction in the years to come. For this success to come about, widespread industry support will be vital; at the time of writing, we are still waiting for confirmation of such commitment from an appropriate spectrum of industry players. For InfiniBand, we will concentrate on the functionality of I/O interfaces and the optimizations appropriate for communications in a loosely-coupled system, with an emphasis on clusters.

Since data is the vital and central element of business information technology, the characteristics of the storage systems used are important factors in the choice of servers. Since data needs to be directly accessible—that is, on-line—permanently, both within a company and outside it (through the Internet), storage systems have become an essential part of a server. Trends in storage subsystems are ever-increasing capacity, performance, and availability, coupled with steadily reducing cost per gigabyte.

Communications support—both local and wide area—also has increasing importance. Reflecting this, specialized subsystems connected to servers have been developed.

Because of the importance of storage, we have dedicated Chapter 6 to discussing the subject in depth. In this chapter, we will limit ourselves to describing the evolution of storage and communications technologies.

2.1   PCI, SCSI, and Fibre Channel

The PCI standard had its origins in the PC world, and has supplanted the two earlier standard microprocessor backplane buses—VME and Multibus. VME is, however, still used in real-time systems and in some process control applications.[1] It started as a 16-bit bus and later grew to 32 bits; for the most part, VME-based systems used Motorola 68000-family microprocessors.

Multibus I was also a 16-bit bus initially, but Multibus systems tended to house Intel processors. While Intel extended the definition of Multibus I to 32 bits as Multibus II, the new version never saw wide adoption and disappeared fairly quickly.

We can summarize PCI's major characteristics as follows:

■ Two data transfer widths—32 bits and 64-bits

■ Two clock rates—33MHz and 66MHz

■ Various available bandwidths (133, 266, and 532 MB/sec), depending on clock rate and data width, and with burst-mode transfers

■ The ability to support both 32 and 64 controllers on the same bus

---

PCI's Origins and Competitors

PCI started as an industry initiative that aimed to overcome the limitations of the then-current PC bus (ISA bus). Initially proposed by Intel, it was developed by a group that included systems manufacturers, component vendors, suppliers of add-in cards and peripherals, and software companies.

Competition for the bus at the time included IBM's MicroChannel Architecture (MCA), introduced on their PS/2 personal computer systems and the EISA bus, promulgated by a PC manufacturers' group.

MCA, unlike the open ISA bus, was a protected piece of IBM intellectual property; the result was that it only ever appeared in IBM products.

EISA suffered from a different problem; since it was backwards-compatible with the venerable ISA bus, it embodied a number of compromises which limited its advantages over the earlier standard.

PCI won against both MCA and EISA through its combination of functionality and its openness.

- The ability to automatically discover the configuration of devices on the bus at system initialization (known as Plug and Play; this avoids tedious parameter setting in control tables)

- The ability to plug in and remove controllers without stopping the system, a capability known as hot plug.

PCI offers—even in its slowest version—substantially higher throughput than the earlier buses (and higher than MCA and EISA, too, which offered 33MB/sec and 40MB/sec respectively).

The significantly greater demands of more recent technologies, such as Gigabit Ethernet or Fibre Channel, have led to a proposal for a first extension to PCI, called PCI-X, with 32- or 64-bit data widths running at 66, 100 or 133MHz. The bandwidth of a 64-bit, 133MHz PCI-X interface is 1064MB/sec. Along with the physical enhancements, the bus protocol has also been improved in order to enhance efficiency.

The capabilities have been further extended into PCI-X 2.0, whose specifications were approved early in 2002. The goals of PCI-X 2.0 may be summarized as:

- Meet performance needs with an interface capable of handling 64-bit data widths running at 266 or 533MHz and with a throughput of 2128 or 4256 MB/sec respectively

- Support the use of earlier-generation cards to protect earlier investments (of course, this simply means that old cards must work with the new bus; a PCI-X 2.0 system with a mix of cards meeting earlier specifications and cards meeting 2.0 specifications will run at the speed of the slowest card)

- Become an industry standard

- Integrate well with the InfiniBand initiative (see below)

These various buses all represent the classical way to connect up peripherals and controllers; in section 2.4—New I/O Structures: InfiniBand—we will examine the limitations of the classical approach and show why a new I/O architectural approach is called for.

2.2   **SCSI and Fibre Channel**

SCSI has long been the *de facto* standard for the connection of magnetic peripherals. It is a parallel interface, and calls for some level of intelligence in the devices, so a SCSI peripheral has, in addition to the logic which provides the connection and the physical device itself, a microprocessor and memory. Data transfers are buffered in the memory—so that, for a read from disk, the data read from the disk are held in this memory. Data integrity is handled, and any errors are corrected. The data is then forwarded on the SCSI bus to the requestor. The existence of the intelligences inside SCSI disks has led researchers at the University of California at Berkeley to develop the notion further and to propose Intelligent Disks, a subject discussed further at the end of this chapter. Noteworthy limitations of SCSI include its fairly limited maximum length for a connection, and bulkiness and weight of the connectors and cables.

Serial interfaces can remove the limitations of both length and bulkiness while preserving the protocol. One such—SSA, for Serial Storage Architecture—has remained proprietary to IBM. FC-AL (Fibre Channel—Arbitrated Loop) has properties similar to SSA, but is an open standard. Further, its definition allows the use of optical fibre as a physical layer, allowing very long distance interconnect (SSA can also make use of optical fibre, with the use of specialist hardware). Because of the advantages of Fibre Channel—longer interconnect distances, perhaps up to several kilometers if optical fibre is used—and the ability to connect many more devices to one interface than with SCSI, industry is moving away from SCSI and towards Fibre Channel. Table 2.1 summarizes the differences between SCSI and Fibre Channel.

Fibre Channel, developed in 1988 by an ANSI Technical Committee, supports connection-level redundancy, and allows the intermixing on the same media of different network and I/O protocols (so that, for example, SCSI and IP can be carried together). Table 2- 1 illustrates the fusion of network-oriented and I/O connections within Fibre Channel.

Table 2.1   *Integration of network and I/O channels in Fibre Channel.*

I/O Channels	Networks	Fibre Channel
Normally implemented in hardware	Normally implemented in software	Implemented in hardware
High speed—O(10 MB/s)	Moderate speed—O(MB/s)	High speed—O(100MB/s)
Low latency—O(μs)	Rich connectivity	Rich connectivity
Short distance	Moderate latency- O(100 μs)	Low latency
Master/slave architecture	Long distance	Long distance (with optical)
Strong data integrity	Peer-to-peer architecture	Both master/slave and peer-to-peer supported
Error detection at very low level (hardware)	Fragile	Strong data integrity
	Error detection at a very high level (in software)	No management station

Fibre Channel has a layered architecture, as illustrated in Figure 2.2, which should not be confused with the layers of the OSI model.

The lowest three layers form the level called FC-PH (Fibre Channel—Physical).

- The FC-0 layer defines the physical interconnect and its characteristics

- The FC-1 layer defines the transmission protocol, including 8B/10B encoding, which equalizes the numbers of ones and zeros in the data stream and both provides stronger noise immunity and simplifies clock recovery at the receiver

- The FC-2 layer defines the transport mechanism—signalling protocol, framing and usage rules. FC-2 supports the three Fibre Channel topologies (see later)

Figure 2.2
*Layered
architecture of
Fibre Channel.*

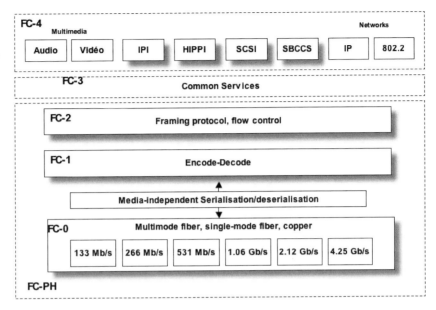

In the FC-4 layer, we find the different protocols supported by FC. The 802.2 protocol is part of the ISO standard, and is in the Data Link Layer. This layer is divided into two sublayers—MAC (Media Access Control) and LLC (for Logical Link Control). The 802.2 protocol corresponds to the LLC sublayer, and manages the communication between equipments on the same physical connection. It provides both connection-based and connectionless services for higher levels, and in particular it permits the support of different protocols on the same physical link.

Fibre Channel supports various types of topologies, illustrated in Figure 2.3.

The diagram shows the three basic Fibre Channel topologies, together with the standard ports. Point-to-point connection is generally used between systems; FC-AL is typically used for peripheral connection; and the fabric connection—which is just a switched interconnect technology— is used to connect storage or communications subsystems to the servers themselves and allows the sharing of the subsystems between servers.

The loop topology is the most widespread today, being able to economically connect up to 126 units per loop; the available bandwidth is shared between the connected devices.

The fabric topology allows the construction of expansible communications networks using switches to connect up to 2^{24} devices, and with the ability to increase bandwidth as desired by replicating connections.

Figure 2.3
Fibre Channel
topologies.

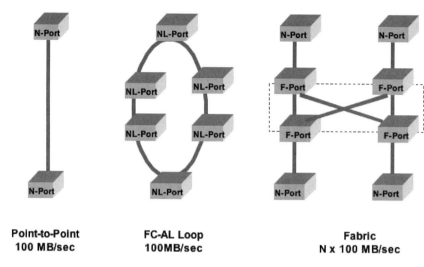

In a company, different activities can go on simultaneously but without necessarily needing to share resources. To simplify the management of resources attached to a fabric FC topology and to increase safety, it is possible to define independent domains, called zones; a zone has the following characteristics:

- It is a collection of interconnected units

- The collection may be divided up into one or more zones

- No unit can communicate with a unit in a different zone

- Each unit can be configured to be in one or more zones[2]

The concept of a zone is supported at the switch level.

A Fibre Channel link has a bandwidth of 100MB/s and supports connection lengths of a few tens of meters (using copper) or kilometers (if optical interconnect is used). Compared to SCSI, Fibre Channel simplifies and improves connectivity. Table 2.2 compares the two interconnects.

Table 2.2   *Comparison of SCSI and Fibre Channel.*

Property	SCSI	Fibre Channel
Number of units per physical connection	15	126

Table 2.2   *Comparison of SCSI and Fibre Channel. (continued)*

Property	SCSI	Fibre Channel
Bandwidth	40, 80, 160 or 320 MB/s	100MB/s
Length of a physical connection	up to 25m (~80 ft.)	Copper: 30m (~100ft) 62.5µm or 50µm fibre[*]: 175-500m (~500-1600 ft.) 9µm fibre: several kilometers (miles)
Nature of the physical interface	68-wire cable	4-wire cable or 2-fibre optical interconnect

[*] to illustrate the fineness of optical fibre, recall that a human hair is about 70µm in diameter

Various classes of service are defined within Fibre Channel, each class meeting some specific needs.

Table 2.3   *Fibre Channel service classes*

	Class 1	Class 2	Class 3	Class 4
Service Char-acteristics	■ dedicated—the whole of the bandwidth is available ■ fixed routing ■ in-order message delivery ■ confirmation of delivery or of failure to deliver ■ end-to-end flow control	■ multiplexed ■ datagram service ■ adaptive routing ■ in-order delivery of packets not guaranteed ■ confirmation of delivery or of failure to deliver ■ end-to-end flow control and per-connection flow control	■ multiplexed ■ datagram service ■ no confirmation of delivery or of failure to deliver ■ flow control available solely at the level of the connection	■ a fraction of the bandwidth is dedicated to transport of real-time data ■ virtual circuits with quality of service guarantee for minimum bandwidth and bounded latency ■ congestion-free ■ in-order packet delivery guaranteed ■ access guaranteed

Table 2.3   *Fibre Channel service classes (continued)*

	Class 1	Class 2	Class 3	Class 4
Communication model	■ connection-oriented ■ circuit-switched	■ connectionless ■ packet-switched	■ connectionless ■ packet-switched	■ connection-oriented ■ circuit-switched

Table 2.3 summarizes their characteristics.

Class 1 service establishes a point-to-point dedicated circuit, with packet delivery being guaranteed by a delivery acknowledgment. Putting aside the time necessary to open and close the connection, Class 1 communications provides the maximum possible bandwidth. Typical applications include video transmission and backup of large amounts of data.

Class 2 is a datagram service. It offers a multiplexed data exchange mode with delivery guarantee, but there is no dedicated link. A regulation policy ensures that latency is low—on the whole, below a microsecond. This service class is used for movement of small blocks of data.

Class 3 is also of datagram type, but without delivery acknowledgment. It provides connection-level flow control. This service class is used for carrying SCSI protocol.

Class 4 creates virtual circuits which have performance guarantees for bandwidth and throughput. This service class is intended for use with real-time data, such as video image transmission.

There is also a Class 5, with characteristics similar to Class 1 but which also supports multicast—the ability to send the same message to a selected collection of destinations. Multicast is differentiated from broadcast, in which one message is sent to all potential destinations.

2.3   ATA

While SCSI has been commonly used in servers, we observed the emergence in servers of disks using the ATA (Advanced Technology Attachment) interface. ATA (also known as PATA, for Parallel ATA) is the *de facto* standard in the PC industry. PATA is being completed with SATA (for Serial ATA). Characteristics of PATA an SATA can be summarized as follows:

■ PATA: flat cable 40 wires, 100 MB/s

- SATA: serial interface 150 MB/s
- SATA II (2004): 300 MB/s

ATA take advantage of the large PC market.

In reaction to SATA, SAS (Serial Attached SCSI) has been proposed. Its characteristics can be summarized as follows:

- 3 GB/s (12 GB/s planned)
- Dual ported drives
- Point-to-point connections
- Extended drive addressability (up to 16,286 devices per port) and connectivity using an expander that allows sharing of drives between several hosts (an expander has 128 links which may connect to several hosts' other SAS expanders or hard disks)
- Capability to connect SATA drives (SATA signals are a subset of SAS signals)

Several protocols have been defined for SAS:

- *Serial SCSI Protocol (SSP)*: transfers SCSI commands
- *SCSI Management Protocol (SMP)*: sends management commands to expanders
- *SATA Tunneled Protocol (STP)*: creates a connection that allows the transmission of SATA commands

According to its promoters, SAS advantages are as follows:

- Simplification (serial interface instead of parallel)
- R&D reduction
- Flexibility: selection of SATA drives for cost, selection of SAS drives for performance

SAS products are expected to be available in first half 2004

Figure 2.4
*Exploiting
properties of SAS
(inspired by
Seagate)*

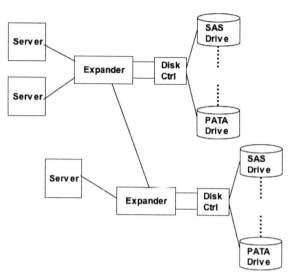

Figure 2.4 is an illustration of the properties of SAS.

As this figure shows, SAS and PATA disk can be supported by the same disk controllers. Expanders allows the interconnection of servers to disks resources.

2.4   A New I/O Architecture: InfiniBand

A few years ago, two I/O architecture and technology initiatives were launched:

- NGIO (Next Generation I/O) promulgated by Intel, Sun, Dell, Hitachi NEC, and Siemens
- Future I/O from Adaptec, Compaq, HP, IBM, and 3Com

The two proposals were very similar in terms of their objectives and basic technology choices, to wit:

- Integration of storage and communication traffic, as well as inter-process communications for processes executing on different nodes
- Improvement of RAS (Reliability, Availability and Serviceability)
- Scalability

In August 1999, these two competing groups buried the hatchet and announced the fusion of their ideas, initially under the name of System I/O, which was rapidly rebranded in October of that year to InfiniBand.

The InfiniBand Trade Association comprised Compaq, Dell, Hewlett-Packard, IBM, Microsoft, and Sun Microsystems. Its objectives were:

- To develop a specification that met the technical needs of users, with an approach based on the concept of a channel and a switch-based communications architecture allowing throughput scalability (from 0.5 to 6 GB/s per link), together with independence from the processor and operating system to ensure interoperability

- To capitalize on existing technology so that technically and economically-viable solutions could be developed and deployed, and to ensure a smooth transition for systems making use of existing standards like PCI and PCI-X

- To adopt a constitution and a steering committee with strong industrial representation in the development process to ensure that the specifications would be reflected in real products

Beyond the Trade Association members, eight further sponsors supported the initiative—Adaptec, Cisco, Fujitsu-Siemens, NEC, Lucent, Nortel, and 3Com.

The InfiniBand specification was published in June 2001.

A cited reason for InfiniBand is the insufficiency of PC-derived I/O technology for large systems, and what is proposed is essentially the integration of standard architectural practices from mainframe systems into low-cost, commodity silicon. Figure 2.5 summarizes the PC model of I/O.

The difficulties with this type of architecture can be summarized as follows:

- The chip integrating the memory controller and the bridge from system bus to I/O bus is complex; this results in difficulties in design and implementation, so development in general tends to be rather slow

- Only five or so controllers could be supported on the I/O bus, so for a richly-connected system, there had to be many I/O buses

Figure 2.5
PC-based I/O architecture.

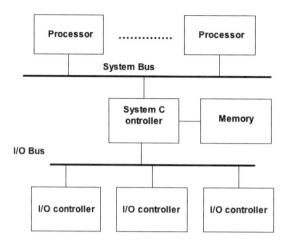

- Lack of failure insulation—the failure of almost any component in the architecture can cause the failure of the whole I/O system

- The I/O bus and the system controller are shared by all the controllers, and so they can be a bottleneck when one attempts to scale up—that is, when controllers are added

- The limited distance permitted between memory controller and bridge is a constraint on system packaging

- A shared I/O bus does not facilitate localization or isolation of faults

- Processor performance is affected by the means used to communicate with the I/ O controllers. In these systems, the controllers are memory-mapped—the registers in the controller which, when written, cause the controller to perform certain actions, and which, when read, report status information are accessed by the processor using ordinary memory load and store instructions. This makes it possible for a controller to corrupt memory, so there is a threat to data integrity and indeed, it is even possible for misbehavior to cause a complete system halt

Given the issues above, it is tempting to rearrange the system as a network of specialized components; processors, storage, communications, I/O controllers). InfiniBand has taken this approach, now called a Systems Area Network—a term not to be confused with the already-existing acronym SAN for Storage Area Network. To avoid confusion, an InfiniBand networks should be referred to as an IBA Systems Area Network (IBA for InfiniBand Architecture).

> Technology changes drove changes to the traditional I/O architecture. Initially, I/O controllers lived on the processor's bus, which connected processor to memory. This structure evolved to the connection of I/O bridges on the processor bus and then to that shown above, with a system controller connected to the system bus. A key driver for this change was the increase in processor and thus processor bus frequency; the higher the frequency, the fewer the number of entities which can be hung on the bus. A further reason was to eliminate I/O traffic from the processor bus.

Figure 2.6 illustrates InfiniBand architecture.

InfiniBand is based on a switch fabric using point-to-point connections. Various types of components may be interconnected, from a collection of low-cost controllers in a chassis to complete processing nodes. To increase connectivity, the switches can be cascaded. A system may be built from subnetworks connected by routers.

InfiniBand provides reliable data transmission with two types of intercomponent communication: message queues and DMA between remote nodes.

The content and semantics of the messages are not specified by InfiniBand, which simply defines the primitives needed for communication. InfiniBand protocols are designed for efficiency; in particular, there is no need for software involvement in the sending and receiving of InfiniBand messages.

InfiniBand components comprise:

- Host Channel Adapters (HCA), which act as the interface for processing nodes (that is, processor/memory combinations) and interface to TCAs (Target Channel Adapters) by means of high speed serial links

- Switches (or fabric, in Fibre Channel terminology), which may be interposed between HCA and TCA to allow the construction of networks

- Target Channel Adapters (TCA), which act as network interfaces for specialized I/O subsystems

- Routers, which allow construction of subnetworks

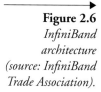

Figure 2.6
*InfiniBand
architecture
(source: InfiniBand
Trade Association).*

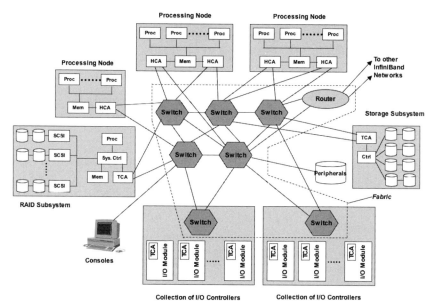

- Management devices (represented in the figure as consoles), which dialogue with agents resident in each network element

The principle of operation is based on command queues being constructed by the computing nodes, with the commands being picked up and executed by the other architectural elements (in particular, by I/O subsystems and collections of controllers). The interface between two active entities (such as processes or threads) is implemented as a queue pair comprising two queues—one for sending operations and one for receiving. In action, an active entity places a work request in the form of a work request entry in the appropriate queue; after the command has been executed, the entity doing the work places an entry in the completion queue. An active entity may have multiple queue pairs in existence simultaneously. Figure 2.7 illustrates this queue structure.

Operations on the send queue fall into three subclasses:

- SEND, an operation for which the WQE specifies the chunk of data in the memory of the sender which is to be sent: where the data must be placed in the receiver is specified by a corresponding WQE in a receiver queue

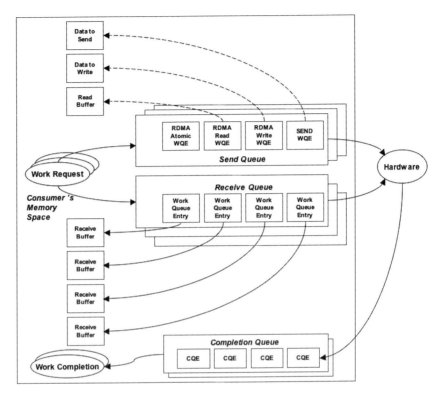

Figure 2.7
*InfiniBand queue
operations (source:
InfiniBand Trade
Association).*

- RDMA (Remote DMA), in which the WQE specifies both sending
  and receiving data size and location: there are three subclasses of
  RDMA:
    - RDMA-WRITE, specifying that the sender's data is to be written
      into the destination memory
    - RDMA-READ, specifying that data from the receiver of the com-
      mand is to be written into the memory belonging to the sender of
      the command
    - ATOMIC, which specifies that a read and conditional store oper-
      ation is to be done upon a 64-bit datum in the receiver's memory,
      providing an inter-node synchronization mechanism
- MEMORY BINDING, which allows mappings to be made between
  the address spaces which take part in the communications

There is only one operation on the receive queue. The RECEIVE operation specifies where the data sent by a SEND should be placed. Whenever
the sender completes a SEND operation, a Completion Queue Entry

(CQE) is created, causing the next entry in the reception queue to be acted upon.

To reinforce system isolation, InInfiniBand allows partitioning.

While InfiniBand doesn't specify the semantics of messages, it does contains the notion of a channel program,[3] a concept whose origin that goes the 1960s and allows off-loading of some of the I/O work from a central processor onto specialized hardware (the channels), which operate independently of the processor proper. How this works is as follows: the processor (under the control of the OS) writes a list of simple commands into memory and tells a particular channel to execute the commands. When all requested work has been done, the channel will inform the processor (or one of the processors, in an SMP) which can then see the results of the operations.

A channel program is a linked list or queue of elementary commands, with each command specifying "command chaining" or "data chaining." Command chaining means that when one command is completed, the next command is to be executed; data chaining means that the same command is to be executed again, but with new data locations—allowing data contiguous in virtual address space but mapped onto discontiguous physical memory to be transferred efficiently (this is one form of a scatter/gather mechanism, which we will revisit in Chapter 6, which covers Storage).

As can be seen, InfiniBand allows efficient memory-to-memory communication between nodes. The efficiency comes in large part because it obviates the need for multiple layers of protocol, such as those called for by TCP-IP, and also because all the data transfer work is done by hardware. To make this work safely, the operating systems on the various nodes must come to a mutual agreement as to which areas of memory are to be used for the communications.

Without going into the details, it seems useful to illustrate the concept of channel programs in the context of InfiniBand. As shown in Figure 2.8, work to be performed by I/O controllers is specified in work queues (see the earlier diagram covering InfiniBand queue operations) stored in the memory of host systems. The items making up the work queues are channel programs.

It should be clear that one of the objectives of InfiniBand is to subsume and replace—over the long term—two current interconnects.

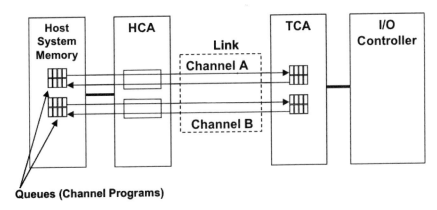

Figure 2.8
*Illustration of the
concept of a
channel program
(inspired by
InfiniBand).*

- InfiniBand should replace Fibre Channel for connection between a processing subsystem and a peripheral subsystem, with FC-AL still being used to connect magnetic devices to the storage subsystem

- InfiniBand should replace PCI, by integrating the controller functionality into the TCA

It is unlikely that such replacement, if it does occur, will happen quickly. PCI and PCI-X have many good years ahead of them, in particular in low-end and mid-range systems. And Fibre Channel will be a stable, long-term infrastructure for storage networks (SANs). A SAN is a specialized high-throughput, low-latency network (covered in greater detail in Chapter 6), used to connect the nodes in a cluster and their peripheral subsystems. Fibre Channel's performance and its widespread adoption will certainly allow it to fend off InfiniBand for quite some time. Interestingly, there is physical-layer compatibility between Fibre Channel and InfiniBand, and the existence of multiprotocol switches could allow the coexistence of the two technologies.

Given all this, we can expect that InfiniBand development will proceed in three successive phases:

- In the absence of acceptable performance solutions based on local area networks (Ethernet, Fibre Channel), InfiniBand allows an improvement in both raw performance and scalability for cluster systems, thanks to its low-overhead RDMA capabilities

- Coexistence of FC and InfiniBand, allowing the use of InfiniBand-equipped hardware in FC systems

- Native InfiniBand

It is projected that the first real InfiniBand products will appear in 2002, with real deployment being in 2003.

Table 2.4—based on Intel material praising NGIO—summarizes the expected benefits of InfiniBand for servers.

Table 2.4   *Expected InfiniBand Server Benefits (inspired by Intel).*

System Aspect	InfiniBand Benefits (expected)
Reliability	Point-to-point links: ■ removes configuration conflicts ■ removes errors arising from incompatible hosts and peripherals ■ removes timing-dependent behavior ■ provides independent error domains ■ separate address spaces for host and controller ■ message send and receive instead of load/store
Availability	■ fault isolation for peripherals ■ hot pluggability of peripherals
Performance	■ low software involvement in operations ■ channel program concept ■ remote DMA between nodes
Serviceability	■ ease of access to peripheral subsystems
Usability	Configuration simplicity: ■ elimination of the possibility of conflicts ■ independence of memory addresses ■ swift automatic discovery as new switches of peripherals are installed
Ease of management	Better management of I/O: ■ error detection ■ error threshold detection and performance monitoring Management of shared resources: ■ storage ■ network Direct management—by SNMP—of peripheral units

As we have noted earlier, a large part of server complexity arises from the I/O subsystems; this complexity, added to the sheer number of peripheral devices in a server system, has great impact on server availability. As noted in the table above, InfiniBand can bring real improvements to key aspects of server operation.

2.5 Virtual Interface Architecture

Virtual Interface Architecture, is the result of a joint initiative between Intel, Compaq, and Microsoft and provides low-latency, high-bandwidth data transfers between nodes and storage subsystems in loosely-coupled systems, such as clusters.

Cluster Architecture Reminder

The concept of a cluster was briefly introduced in the introduction to this part of the book, and is handled in greater detail in Chapter 5.

A cluster may be define as a collection of a limited number (ten or so) of interconnected systems that share resources transparently. Each such system referred to as a node—is a complete system, with its own processor, memory, and I/O, running under the control of its own copy of the operating system.

Clusters are classified as loosely coupled systems, since they almost never share memory between nodes. Contrast this classification with tightly-coupled systems—symmetrical multiprocessors—in which memory is shared with support for coherency.

In a traditional system, communications between subsystems use layered network protocols such as TCP-IP or UDP, which were designed for use in wide-area networks and which are structured to handle all the unpleasantnesses that such networks can encounter. TCP-IP and UDP protocols are not known for their efficiency; a message exchange requires (in many implementations) that the data being sent or received be copied many times between protocol layers, in both sender and receiver. As a result, they are not structured to take advantage of the much better controlled, more stable environment of a cluster, and require the use of all network layers on each message exchange. Because it avoids these copying operations, VIA sharply reduces processing overhead.

The idea behind VIA is to remove these inefficiencies and to make it possible to have data exchange without the involvement of the OS, other than to set up the communication between the two agents. Data transfer is done by DMA, in which a sending agent and a receiving agent specify the memory locations to be sent and where they are to be placed in the receiver's memory. With this information, the transfer proceeds with no further OS involvement.

VIA is to some extent a generalization of this approach, being characterizable as an RDMA (Remote DMA) architecture; this, of course, echoes one of the aspects of InfiniBand. A key goal of VIA is to create an industry standard allowing the interconnection of high volume (and therefore low-cost) systems to allow the construction of powerful clusters. Such clusters could allow the takeover of market segments currently owned by much more expensive mid-range and high-end systems.

A major issue with clusters is the lack of an industry-standard API (applications programming interface) that allows software to take advantage of the multiple nodes. VIA could be such an API. To the extent that platforms suppliers and software publishers support the architecture, the availability of conforming applications could drive its success.

VIA specifies both an API and a hardware interface model, the latter to allow use of standard communications controllers such as ATM, Ethernet, or Fibre Channel, as well as specialized networks such as SAN. Measurements of messages sent in cluster systems showed that 80% of the messages used 256 bytes or less of data, while 80% of the data moved came from transfers equal to or greater than 8KB. The smaller messages are typically remote procedure calls and internal cluster interactions, such as distributed locking (we will discuss the Distributed Lock Manager in Chapter 5). The longer messages are typically transfers of one or more memory pages.

The fact that the majority of messages are short drove a search for a solution with low latency. Further analysis showed that the bottleneck was in the software and that two operations in particular were expensive—one was the context switching between user and OS modes, and the other was copying data between user space and the I/O cards. Reducing latency also allowed a higher usable bandwidth (for a given physical medium).

VIA's approach, illustrated in Figure 2.9, is to strongly limit any use of the operating system in communications.

As shown in the diagram, VIA only calls for invocation of the OS in setting up and tearing down connections, and for error handling. In other words, data transfers do not involve the OS at all.

Key elements of VIA illustrated in Figure 2.9 are:

■ A message-queue model

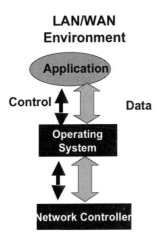

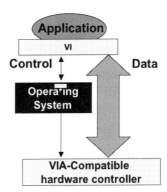

- The operating system is involved only in the
  establishment and tear-down of the
  connection and in error handling

■ Direct, protected access by user level software to the communications
  hardware; the protection is effected by means of the virtual memory
  system

Applications demanding the highest possible performance will interact
directly with VIA's native interfaces. Applications that use standard inter-

---

Applications Wanting to Benefit from a Cluster Architecture

Applications which interface directly to the VIA native interfaces are
called VIA-Aware. Such applications, naturally, are not portable to
(already-existing) non-VIA systems. This illustrates a limitation to the
penetration of new technologies—if the technology quickly gets the
support of software and middleware suppliers, it has a good chance of
success; if not, it is likely headed for an early disappearance.

---

faces can be layered over a VIA implementation, but will obtain lower performance than that obtainable with the native interfaces.

VIA is made up of the following elements:

■ Send and receive packet descriptors that specify scatter-gather operations—specifying where data must be distributed to and collected up
  from—when sending and receiving

- A send message queue and a receive message queue, comprising linked lists of packet descriptors

- A means of notifying the network interface that packets have been placed on a queue

- An asynchronous notification process for the status of the operations requested (completion of a send or receive operation is signaled by writing state information into a packet descriptor)

- Registration of memory areas used for communications: before communications are started, the memory areas for each hardware unit are identified and noted, allowing expensive operations, such as locking the pages, to be used and translating from virtual to real addresses to be done once, outside performance-critical data transfers

As indicated in Figure 2.10, the interface provides two separate sets of primitives. One is a control interface (open, close, memory-map) which allow connections between agents and the declaration of the memory areas

Figure 2.10
*Elements of VIA
(source: Intel).*

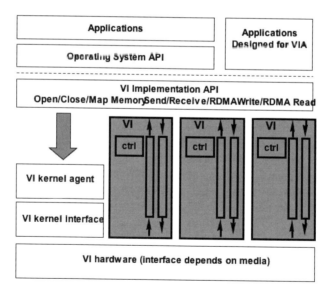

to be used for communication. The other is a data transfer interface and provides primitives for data movement (send, receive) using a DMA device.

It is too soon, at the time of writing, to form a firm prediction as to the success of VIA, but two factors suggest it has a good chance of industry adoption:

- VIA is an effective response to the need for high-bandwidth, low-latency communication as needed by clusters

- VIA's backers are substantial enough to get the attention of ISVs and thereby the industry

As we shall see in Chapter 5, one of the principal properties of a cluster architecture is its natural support for high availability. But as we have already seen, today clusters suffer from the poor performance of inter-node message passing. VIA offers a credible response to this problem; if it does not succeed, it is likely that some similar solution will arise and be accepted.

2.6 Data Storage

In this section we will discuss key characteristics of magnetic disks; we will cover the various architectural options for managing data in files held on disks, storage organizations, backup and restore functions—and a selection of storage product offerings—in Chapter 6.

As a scene-setter, before looking at storage technology we will share information from a project at the University of Berkeley called "How much Information?" [LYM03] examining just how much information is produced in the world. And before embarking on that, we will have a short refresher on the units used to describe data storage capacity. Tables 2.5 defines the units we will need.

Table 2.5   *Units*

Name	Abbreviation	Value
Gigabyte	GB	10^9 bytes
Terabyte	TB	10^{12} bytes
Petabyte	PB	10^{15} bytes
Exabyte	EB	10^{18} bytes

Table 2.6 shows the worldwide production of original information, if stored digitally, in terabytes circa 2002. Upper estimates assume information is digitally scanned, lower estimates assume digital content has been compressed.

Table 2.6 *Worldwide production of original content in 2002 (source: [LYM03]).*

Medium	Content Type	TB/yr Upper estimate	TB/yr Lower estimate
Paper	Books	39	8
	Newspapers	138.4	27.7
	Office Documents	1,397.5	279.5
	Mass market periodicals	52	10
	Journals	6	1.3
	Newsletter	0.9	0.2
	Subtotal	**1,633.8**	**326.7**
Film	Photographs	375,000	37,500
	Cinema	6,078	12
	Made for TV films	2,531	2,530
	TV series	14,155	14,155
	Direct to video	2,490	2,490
	X-rays	20,000	20,000
	Sub-total	**420,254**	**76,687**
Optical	Audio CD	58	6
	CD ROM	1.1	1.1
	DVD	43.8	43.8
	Subtotal	**102.9**	**50.9**
Magnetic	Videotape	1,340,000	1,340,000
	Audiotape	128,800	128,800
	Digital tape	250,000	250,000
	Mini digital videocassettes	1,265,000	1,265,000
	Floppy disc	80	80
	Zip	350	350
	Audio MiniDiscs	17,000	17,000
	Flash	12,000	12,000

Table 2.6 *Worldwide production of original content in 2002 (source: [LYM03]). (continued)*

Medium	Content Type	TB/yr Upper estimate	TB/yr Lower estimate
Magnetic (continued)	Hard disk	1,986,000	403,000
	Sub-total	4,999,230	3,416,230
Total		5,421,220.7	3,493,294.6

The Berkeley study is an ambitious piece of research, and the numbers are not straightforward to obtain from the raw data; the various assumptions and hypotheses used in arriving at the numbers shown are detailed in the report cited. It is best to look upon the resulting numbers as order of magnitude estimates.

One can see that printed matter is a very small fraction of the data produced: just 0.03% of the total. This doesn't mean that paper is dead; rather, it shows that paper is a very efficient form of communication.

It was estimated in 2000 that the volume of information on the public Web at 20 to 50 TB; in 2003 the volume is estimated at 167 TB. Table 2.7 shows the size of the Internet. The Web consists of the surface Web (fixed Web pages) and the deep Web (the database-driven Web sites that create Web pages on demand).

Table 2.7 *Size of the Internet in Terabytes in 2002 (source: [LYM03]).*

Media	2002 TB
Surface Web	167
Deep Web	91,850
E-mail (originals)	440,606
Instant messaging	274
Total	532,897

By 2003, about 31 billion e-mails were sent daily. According to IDC, this number is expected to double by 2006. Average e-mail size is 59 KB, and the annual flow of e-mails represents 667,585 TB.

2.6.1 **Magnetic Disks**

The personal computer, distributed in enormous volumes, has had a marked effect on the evolution of storage peripherals and in particular on disks.

In the 1980s, the disk market was divided into two major portions—on the one hand, large diameter disks for mainframes and minicomputers, and on the other, smaller-diameter disks for PCs. Because of technological advances and the economic arguments from very high demand for the small-format disks, the smaller media soon came to equal and surpass the larger-format disks in capacity, performance, and reliability (current products offer an MTBF of 500,000 hours, or about 57 years).

With the first generations of small-format disks, servers had to use groups of disks to obtain sufficient capacity; this affected reliability strongly, since the failure rate increases linearly with the number of disks used. This observation drove a search to find ways of organizing disks to avoid the reliability problem, and RAID (Redundant Arrays of Inexpensive Disks, now reworded as Redundant Arrays of Independent Disks) technology was introduced as a solution; its use quickly spread. RAID is discussed a little later in this chapter and more extensively in Chapter 6.

To recap briefly, a disk is composed of a number of platters. Each side of a platter has a number of concentric tracks, each of which is made up of a number of fixed-capacity sectors. A disk is equipped with a swivelling arm carrying two read/write heads per platter (one for each side of the platter). Hardware in the disk positions the arm appropriately for the disk surface and track to be accessed, and selects the appropriate head. This structure is diagrammed in Figure 2.11.

The sector access time, from the moment that the command has been received by the disk, is the sum of the following components:

- Seek time—the amount of time it takes to position the arms

- Rotational latency—the amount of time it takes for the desired sector to rotate to be under the heads

- Internal transfer time—how long it takes for the data to be transferred off the disk surface into the disk electronics

- External transfer time—the amount of time it takes to get the data from the disk through the external interface (such as SCSI) to the requester.

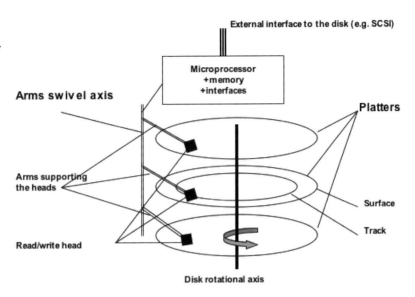

Figure 2.11
*The structure of
a disk*

A typical sector size is rather small, 512 bytes being a current standard. File systems often work on groups of sectors; in such a case, a sector group is a unit of allocation and can also be a unit of transfer (although transfers of less than a group would also be supported).

In UNIX, a group is referred to as a block, with a typical size of 4KB, while in Windows 2000 the same size group exists, but is called a cluster. The following curves from Gartner Group (Figures 2.12, 2.13, and 2.14) shows the shape of the market for "External Controller-Based Disk Storage". According to Gartner's classification, external controller-based disk storage is characterized by the complete physical separation of the disk storage asset from the general-purpose server(s). The RAID controller(s) and disk drives are housed in independent, high-availability external enclosures. This type of storage is typical of midrange to high-end servers.

As the curves show, the recent past is characterized by a collapse in cost per megabyte and an explosion in delivered capacity. As with silicon VLSI, there is a volume-related learning curve for disk manufacturers, and so we can expect the industry to concentrate into a smaller number of disk suppliers: for example, in 2002 IBM sold its disk business to Hitachi.

Note: Price indication for disk drives refers to the cost of the drives themselves. Storage hardware cost must take into account the cost of packaging, power supply, and connections, as well as management software.

Figure 2.12
*Worldwide market
for external
controller-based
disk storage,
$billions (source
data: Gartner
Group).*

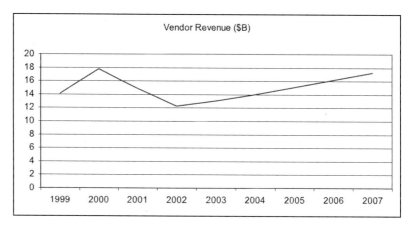

Figure 2.13
*Worldwide capacity
sold for external
controller-based
disk storage (source
data: Gartner
Group).*

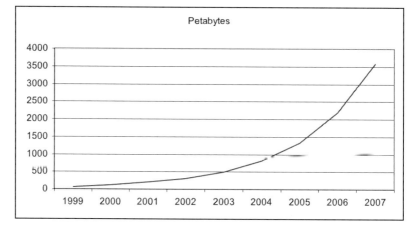

Figure 2.14
*Disk capacity—
price per megabyte
for external
controller-based
disk storage (source
data: Gartner
Group).*

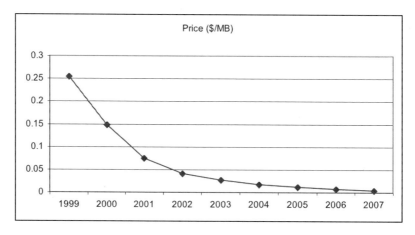

Worldwide market for disk drives was 260 million units in 2003 and about 25 billion dollars by 2001. Cumulative volume is expected to be 2 billion in 2004 and to reach 3.5 billion by 2008. The intensity of the competition resulted in considerable changes in the industry structure: there were 15 disk manufacturers in the 60s, about 136 by the mid-80s and only 9 in 2004 (two of those specializing in disks for Consumer Electronics markets).

Disk capacities have increased by a factor of 100x over the past ten years; at the end of 2001, typical disk capacities were of the order of 70 or 80GB with up to 180GB available—and we speak here of disks available on the market, not the laboratory curiosities which presage the next generation of products. While capacity grew fast, performance—in terms of bandwidth and access time—changed much less and, notably, much more slowly than the growth in processor performance over the same period.

We may summarize the change in disk characteristics over the past decade as follows:

- Capacity increase of 100x

- Bandwidth increase of 10x

- Access time reduced by 3x

- Form factor (physical size) reduced by 5x

Figure 2.15 shows the evolution of disk capacity and access time.

Figure 2.15
Disk capacity and access time trends.

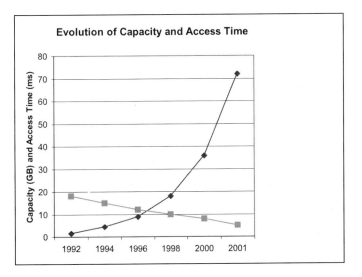

The access time for a disk has several components; for example, for a read operation:

- Arm positioning time (4.9 msec, for instance)

- Rotational time necessary to reach the desired sector (half a turn is 2 msec for a 15,000 rpm disk)

- The amount of time it takes to get the data off the disk, which is related to the density of recording, the speed of revolution and the properties of the internal logic handling the data (typical data rates are around 400 to 700 Mbits/sec, with actual throughput between 30 and 60 MBytes/sec)

- The amount of time necessary to get the data across the interface (for example, on a SCSI bus the data can move at up to 320MB/sec) to the system; this time includes arbitration time as well as the actual transfer time

- The time caused by waiting when there are multiple outstanding requests to the disk or to the I/O channel

Disk rotation rate has increased considerably—today, there are disks turning at 15,000 rpm. With increases in areal density (bits per square inch) combined with the higher rotation rate, data bandwidth has also increased considerably. However, the time needed to move the arm has hardly changed.

There is another side-effect of technological progress, too. Intuitively, an application which makes many disk accesses will, disappointingly, perform worse with modern technology than it did with older disks—in 1996, a 70GB database needed 10 disks, but by 2001 it would fit nicely on just two or even one. But access times have only halved over the period, so the available accesses per second for a fixed-size problem has reduced by a factor of 2.5x.

Figure 2.16 illustrates this phenomenon. It represents the evolution over time of the number of head-positionings per second for a zone of 1 GB. We talk in terms of positionings (this is also termed as access density), because these curves do not take into account the time to move the data.

As shown in the figure, while a 1GB zone could in 1992 receive 37 positionings per second, in 2001 it can receive less than 3. Access to disks

Figure 2.16
Head-positionings per second per Gigabyte.

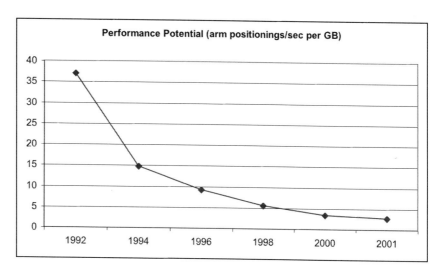

Performance Potential (arm positionings/sec per GB)

becomes, more and more, a very precious resource. A pair of techniques which can help alleviate the problem are:

- Use main memory—or even memory within the disk subsystem—as an information cache

- Partition the data across several disks and access them in parallel so as to reduce data transfer time and the busy time for each of the disks

We introduced the notion of a disk data cache in Chapter 1 section 1.5, Memory Hierarchy. The problem with such an approach is how to do a write operation properly. What happens in a system with a disk cache—like UNIX or Windows—is that a write to a cached portion of a file will not be written to disk until one of the following occurs:

- The disk cache manager finds it needs to reuse the cache block concerned (whereupon it will write modified blocks to the disk)

- A file synchronization primitive is called by the application

- The file is closed

Since DRAM does not maintain data when electrical power is removed, this means that the disk cache contents will immediately be lost in the event of a loss of power.

In transaction-processing applications, the data manager—in practice, the DBMS—will demand that some I/O activities be physically performed—that is, that they write to the disks, rather than to a cache. For this to be possible, operating systems need to provide appropriate primitives to allow forced writes to disk.

To avoid the performance loss arising from direct writes to disk, and to avoid the uncertainties associated with straightforward caching, some disk subsystems provide a "safe cache" for data, by providing redundant controller logic (for example, having two controllers) and a redundant cache with a battery back-up so that power outages can be survived. In such a system, a write operation results in data being written twice, to two independent memory areas in the subsystem. When both have been written, the system requesting the operation is told of its success. The disk subsystem manager eventually decides to purge the cache; it uses one of the copies to do this, so that if a power outage or other failure occurs while writing, there is a second correct copy of the data in memory protected from failure.

We will revisit disk cache techniques in Chapter 6, which covers Storage.

The notion of partitioning of data across many disks was formalized at the end of the 1980s. The research leading to the formalization was triggered by the arrival, in the 80s, of physically small disks with low cost, but also lower reliability than mainframe disks, and culminated in the publication, in 1988, of the University of California at Berkeley's RAID architecture [CHE94].

The idea behind RAID is to form a collection of disk drives that are managed to provide the illusion of a single large disk with high performance and high reliability as an alternative to the use of the more traditional and expensive mass-storage solutions.[4] With the increased availability of inexpensive, small format disks, the use of RAID has spread. RAID spans several ways of organizing a collection of disks; the simplest—RAID 1—was well-known (and used) under the name of disk mirroring before RAID emerged.

A key reason for interest in the technique is its ability to deliver simultaneously high performance and high reliability.

More recently, with the virtual disappearance of large expensive disks, it has been suggested that the I in RAID should be redefined to mean Independent rather than Inexpensive.

We will be looking in detail at these techniques in Chapter 6, where we will also examine:

- On-line data storage on magnetic disks with various systems architectures, including SAN, NAS and iSCSI
- Characteristics of storage devices for backing-up or archiving data
- Various techniques for backing-up or archiving data
- Characteristics of archival media for data and the problems associated with archiving

2.7   **Networks and Communications Subsystems**

Our intent in this section is not to provide a complete, panoramic view of all the technologies associated with communications—many books are available with this information. We will restrict ourselves to the effects that evolutionary change in communications has had and is having on server architecture, although we will provide a brief overview of the emerging generation of switches because of the innovative nature of their architectures.

The communications context for most servers is simply a local area network. Users' workstations are LAN-connected to the server, or—for distant workstations or nomadic devices—through the intermediary of concentrators. In practice, we generally see just a few types of connections to a server:

- LAN connections, typically 10/100Mbit (Ethernet), for attachment of workstations or concentrators for groups of workstations
- High-bandwidth local area network connections (such as 100 Mbit or 1 Gbit Ethernet, FDDI, and Fibre Channel) for connections to other servers within the company, or to concentrators
- Long-distance network connections (such as frame relay) connecting to other systems or to systems in distant sites

The fast growth of the Web has increased connectivity needs, from the point of view of number of users as well as of response time and data throughput. Development of electronic trade will further increase this demand, and such development will rely on systems and communications security.

We will start with a brief examination of network technologies and then look at the problems associated with supporting networks on servers.

2.7.1 Network Technologies

Within a system, multiple communications networks meet—from a chip handling internal connections all the way up to long-distance networks or networks formed from I/O buses and local networks. We will attempt to put the sundry communications technologies into perspective by organizing them by their potential data bandwidths and the distance they are intended to cover. What is usually covered by a discussion of networks is just one part of the whole picture.

Figure 2.17, with no claim to completeness, lists various technologies classified by their distance (point-to-point) and bandwidths.

The very highest bandwidths, over extremely short distances, are the internal communications within a chip.

Figure 2.17
Communications technologies.

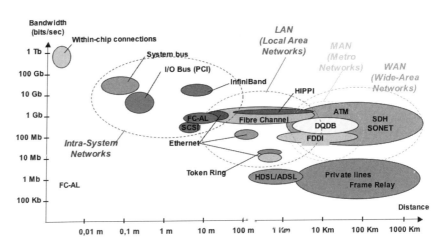

We then encounter a number of technologies which we can group together under the rubric of intrasystems networks, for which the acronym SAN has been used; in that context it meant System Area Network. However, nowadays the use of the acronym has been preempted to refer to network storage, when it means Storage Area Network. To minimize confusion, we shall adopt this latter meaning for the acronym. In the category of intrasystems networks we find:

- Systems buses, connecting processors to memory and I/O, are characterized by bandwidths of several gigabytes per second and distances in the 10-20 cm range—less than a foot

- I/O buses, such as PCI, which connect the processor-memory complex to I/O controllers. InfiniBand might replace PCI for this usage in mid-range and high-end servers. Connecting the processor-memory complex to the I/O subsystems, which would themselves likely still be built around PCI or a derivative

- Connections between I/O controllers and the peripherals themselves, using SCSI or FC-AL

- Connections between the processor-memory complex and a peripheral subsystem, such as disk or tape susbystems or a communications concentrator. Fibre Channel is the current prime example, and it may be joined by InfiniBand. HPPI (High Performance Parallel Interface) offers the same level of performance as Fibre Channel, but its use in practice is limited, essentially, to supercomputers

Beyond the intrasystems networks we find the local area network category:

- Ethernet, offering three classes of bandwidth: traditional Ethernet at 10Mbits/ second, fast Ethernet at 100 Mbits/sec (both these are very widely used) and gigabit Ethernet at 1 Gbit/second, which is finding its place in the market

- Token Ring at 4 to 16 Mbits/sec, which has an advantage over Ethernet in that it offers deterministic behavior. However, it has not had the same marketplace acceptance as Ethernet, probably because it is not an open technology and because of higher prices

- Fibre Channel and FDDI (Fibre Distributed Data Interface) make an appearance in this category as well, often as a concentrator of lower-speed local area networks (such a network is referred to as a *backbone*)

- ATM has pretensions in the field of local area networks as well, with an emulation of a LAN named *Lane* (for *LAN Emulation*)

We then come to metro area networks, which are networks within a single city using technologies such as:

- Fibre Channel

- DQDB (Distributed Queue Dual Bus), which uses a pair of unidirectional bus connections

- FDDI, based on a token-ring technique

- ATM

And finally we see the category of long-distance or wide-area networks with technologies such as SONET (*Synchronous Optical NETwork*), and SDH (*Synchronous Data Hierarchy*) which are standards (ANSI for SONET), and International Telecommunications Union (ITU—once known as CCITT). SONET and SDH both carry ATM packets. For private lines, Frame Relay is also worth mentioning; it extends the capabilities of X25.

In the figure, we also show two technologies used to connect users to telecommunications networks: ADSL (Asymmetric Digital Subscriber Line) and HDSL (High Bit Rate Digital Subscriber Line), are standards in this area. They make it possible to sharply increase bandwidths using existing copper telephone connections, giving up to 52 Mbit/sec for distances up to 300 meters (a bit over 300 yards) and even 1.5 Mbit/sec at distances up to 3 kilometers (around 2 miles).

Alongside the convergence of the different technologies in the areas of distance and bandwidth, we also see a convergence between local and wide-area networks. As an example, ATM technology is as well-suited to LAN usage as it is to WAN. And it incorporates the concept of quality of service, guarantee a user—once a connection is granted—a quality of service (in guaranteed bandwidth, for example) for the duration of that connection.

However, the largest portion of installed networks are IP networks; this domination can only be extended with the advent of the new IPv6 version of the protocol, which considerably extends the address space of an IP network. Given IP's commanding position, any new network technology must support IP if it is to succeed.

2.7.2 Server Support for Communications

Connecting servers to data networks presents a number of problems. The incessant growth in traffic and in demands for reduced response time must be answered in the architecture of communications controllers. Our discussion is based on [MCK99].

Among the problems posed, we note the following in particular:

- *Very large number of interrupts.* Each interrupt means work for the operating system, and handling interrupts takes processing power away from productive work

- *Memory copying.* Data communications—sending or receiving—between user and kernel space implies copying, reflected in both wasted processing power and an increased use of available memory

- *Cache interactions.* Data consistency means that data which is the subject of communications exchange must not be held in the cache

We can illustrate these problems with an earlier figure representing a classical systems architecture (Figure 2.4) as deployed in PCs.

In this very traditional diagram, the communications controller—one of the I/O controllers—is connected to an I/O bus, typically PCI. The processors—under control of the operating system—send commands to the controller by writing them to memory addresses that map the command registers of the controller; included in the parameters of these commands will be the addresses in the memory of the buffers where the data is to be read or written. This mode of communication between processor and peripheral is called memory mapped. Actual data exchange between controller and memory is effected without calling on the processor by means of a separate piece of hardware called a DMA (Direct Memory Access controller). When the DMA completes a transfer, it signals this fact by raising an interrupt, which will be handled by one of the processors.

Direct Memory Access

Typically, a DMA interface comprises a list of descriptors specifying the memory areas involved in the operation. Each memory area is specified by its start address and size. This basic mechanism can be improved, as we shall see later on, by the ability to chain data areas: a given operation can transfer data to (or from) multiple discontiguous memory areas without the processor having to intervene.

Communications software is logically structured in layers according to a model such as that of OSI. Figure 2.18 illustrates this layering and shows the various stages in encapsulating the data.

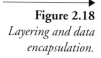

Figure 2.18
*Layering and data
encapsulation.*

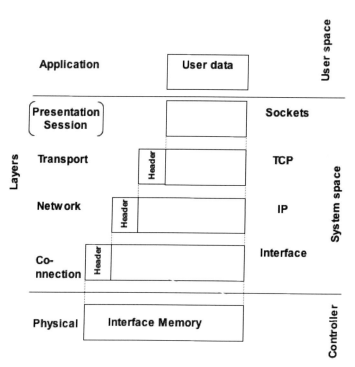

In the case of TCP/IP, the session and presentation layers do not really exist. It is a misuse of language to talk of layers in the case of sockets, since it is simply a programming interface on top of a transport layer.

The diagram shows the movement of data from user space to kernel space, and, for each layer, the encapsulation of the data with each layer's header: TCP header, IP header, and finally a header specific to the communications medium to be used (for example, Ethernet).

Figure 2.19 illustrates the logical processing steps in TCP/IP.

The shading used in the diagram indicates where the processing work comes from:

- White indicates per-message processing: it is the processing load imposed by the system call on the sockets interface, and is independent of the size of the message

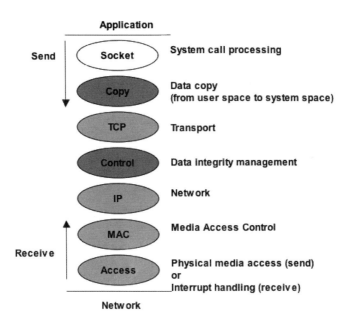

Figure 2.19
Logical processing steps in TCP/IP.

- Light gray indicates per-fragment processing (a long message is broken up into several fragments): this covers TCP, IP, media access and interrupt handling

- Dark grey indicates per-byte processing (actually, per fragment plus per byte in fragment): this covers the data-copying overhead along with computation of the checksum

Few detailed analyses of the performance of network layers have been published, although it seems clear that checksum computation and memory management are expensive.

We will now discuss solutions to the problems posed above.

2.7.3 Reducing the Number of Interrupts

We have seen that we can reduce processor interactions through the use of DMA, but it seems necessary to have at least one interrupt per logical transfer. We can, however, improve on this by enhancing the DMA command set so that it can check the status of an operation and, if that operation is successful, have it initiate a successive transfer without notifying the processor.

With this approach, one specifies two sets of memory descriptors, one for sending and one for receiving. Each collection of descriptors is managed as a circular list, and each descriptor includes status information that shows, for send buffers, whether the buffer has been sent and, for receive buffers, whether they contain data for this system. When a send buffer has been successfully sent, it is free to be used as a buffer for a subsequent transaction. It is the job of the operating system—actually, the TCP/IP layers—to free a receive buffer (by marking it free) after its data has been dealt with. When there are no free buffers, it is best to signal the operating system to handle the received buffers (and thereby free them).

In the presence of caches, certain precautions must be taken to ensure the consistency of data used in I/O operations. The steps necessary are described in Table 2.8 for both cases (simple DMA and optimized DMA).

Table 2.8   *Mechanisms to reduce the number of interrupts.*

Operation	Simple DMA	Improved DMA
Send	■ set up the DMA registers (with buffer address and size) ■ lock the page containing the buffers and purge corresponding addresses in the data cache ■ activate the send command ■ wait until the end of the operation ■ interrupt upon completion of the operation, and free (unlock) the page	■ refill the free buffers with data to be sent ■ lock the buffer page(s) and purge corresponding addresses in the data cache ■ refill a descriptor with the addresses and sizes of the buffers just set up ■ change the descriptor status indicator to "DMA" ■ if the DMA was inactive, wake it up
Receive	■ DMA interrupts processor ■ allocate a page and purge the cache of its addresses ■ set up the DMA registers (with buffer address and size) ■ when the operation completes the DMA will raise an interrupt	■ refill descriptor(s) for receiving ■ purge corresponding addresses in the data cache ■ when a receive operation completes, DMA sets the descriptor indicator to System; the OS can test the status of different descriptors ■ if there are no free buffers, the DMA raises an interrupt

As shown by the table, the number of interrupts is indeed reduced substantially, but at the cost of a considerably more complex DMA engine.

Reducing Copying

As we saw, each layer of TCP/IP adds its own information in the form of a header. In the case of a send, and in the absence of a data assembly mechanism, it is necessary to move data from one layer to the next to add the new header.

Given a DMA engine, we can (for the lower levels of the hierarchy) create a list of descriptors, each referring to a component of the message. In this approach, the first level of optimization is in the software, in avoiding the necessity to copy the data from user to kernel space.

Note that the TCP/IP header has a checksum component (to allow verification that the data has not been corrupted); the computations for this are non-trivial, and can be accelerated by an application-specific chip.

Data Consistency

Having the processor move data means that the data ends up in the processor caches, from which it must be "purged" before the data can be sent.[5] Eliminating processor-controlled data copying through the use of DMA and the movement of the responsibility for header computation into the I/O controllers removes these issues.

Performance Considerations

Since I/O controllers are now equipped with memory and processing capacity, it is tempting to let the controllers handle all or part of the network layers. However, this has not happened; in the case of open systems, the failure is as much the fault of industry environment as of any technical reason. A technical issue was that controllers are relatively long-lived—a controller might be used with two or three generations of processor. The practical effect of this is that one quickly finds an imbalance in performance between processor and controller. It is also the case that the necessary dialog between operating system and controller could become expensive.

Further, since the industry standard is for controllers of little intelligence, any adoption of intelligent controllers would lead to compatibility problems. For high-end servers, this off-loading of network operations is possible—but the intelligences concerned are simply midrange servers. This is, in essence, a resurrection of the old mainframe approach of "front-end" communications subsystems (like the 37xx from IBM, and Bull's Datanet)

This quick overview demonstrates the directions architects have taken to improve communication subsystems performance.

In conclusion, it should be stressed that technological evolution has a strong effect upon server architecture. The technology evolutions themselves are driven by the evolution of the marketplace: a technological advance can drive a rapid market growth, which can attract new investments that fund full development of the technology. The progression of Intel processor performance is a good example of this virtuous circle.

New Generation of Switches

Although switch architecture does not, strictly speaking, have anything to do with server architecture, we will nonetheless provide a succinct overview of the architecture of the new generation of switches. Our motivation for this presentation is that the architectures concerned exhibit some interesting innovations. Such systems support only the software from their suppliers; that is, neither third-party applications nor customer-created applications are supported. Thus, such systems have no binary code compatibility issues. If a value analysis shows an apparent substantial gain from the introduction of a new switch architecture, even if it requires porting or modifying existing software, a vendor can be very tempted by the possibilities.

The unceasing increases in requirements for bandwidths and the growth in network bandwidths (e.g., from 1 Gb/sec to 10 Gb/sec for LANs) results in congestion in switches. To handle this, the industry has developed a new generation of switches said to operate at wire speed; that is, without introducing any delays resulting from the speed of arrival of the messages.

These switches are called Level 4 or Level 7, depending on whether one has the TCP/IP model or the OSI model in mind.[6]

The new switches make it possible to analyze packet content and to arrange to forward them only to the systems for which they are intended. Recall that packet routing is done using routing tables and protocols. There are two types of routing: static (with a fixed association between source and destination) and dynamic (which can change as a result of changes in state).

Two routing protocols are implemented:

- *RIP (Routing Information Protocol).* The various switches periodically communicate among themselves the distances (*Vector Distance*) separating them. The preferred route, then, is the shortest one. The problem with this protocol is that it does not take into account the state of the connections (as an example, it can be better to take a slightly longer route that is lightly-loaded than a short route that is swamped).

- *OPSF (Open Shortest Path First)*. OPSF is decidedly more powerful than RIP and correspondingly more complex. The switches communicate periodically the state of their connections. Thus, each equipment always has a picture of the state of the whole network and can choose the best routing for the messages it handles.

With the new generation of switches, routing is done as a function of:

- The URL being accessed
- The proximity of the sites (i.e., of client and server)
- Network load
- Server load
- The nature of the service requested (since the optimal characteristics vary between, say, accessing an HTML page and providing file transfer)

Figure 2.20 and Figure 2.21 present the internal architecture of two of the new generation switches, one initially developed by Alteon and the other by ArrowPoint; these have been subsumed by, respectively, Nortel and Cisco.

Figure 2.20
Architecture of the Alteon switch.

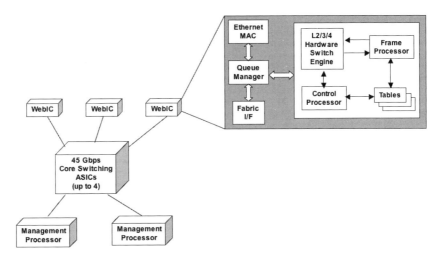

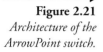

Figure 2.21
Architecture of the
ArrowPoint switch.

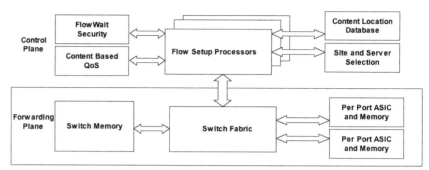

The switch looks at the URL as well as HTTP protocol elements to identify the best server and route. It creates a data flow between client and server and provides appropriate information to the transfer mechanism to enable switching with the minimum of analysis. The level of performance that these switch vendors claim to have reached[7] is related to separation of control and data planes, and relies on implementation of special-purpose hardware.

2.8 Input Output Evolution

We must look at several different aspects in considering the evolutionary path of I/O; we will look at each in turn:

- I/O architecture itself
- The degree of intelligence of magnetic peripherals
- Network connections

2.8.1 I/O

As we noted earlier, I/O has been the poor relation in systems architecture research. With the more or else simultaneous launch of two new I/O architecture initiatives in 1999, the data processing industry finally became aware of the situation, and in August 1999 (as we have seen) the two initiatives merged.

If this initiative meets with substantive success, it will be a major step forward, allowing computer systems to keep pace with the growth of Internet-driven traffic; and standardization around a single proposal should ensure the wide availability of cost-effective silicon implementations.

In addition to interconnect technology, another dimension has emerged—the idea of Storage Area Networks (SANs), allowing optimized management and sharing of storage resources between systems.

While it seems as though the world of SAN has stabilized around the choice of Fibre Channel subsystems and FC-AL interconnect, the arrival of InfiniBand is likely to upset the applecart. But in any case, whatever interface standard ultimately triumphs, standardization at any higher level is less likely, and so interworking between different equipments is unlikely.

2.8.2 Disk Evolution

We expect the rate of improvement in basic technology for disks—storage density and access time—to slow down. Improvements in the architecture of disks and storage subsystems will be able to compensate somewhat for this slowing, particularly for the high-end products, which is where we concentrate our discussion. As a reminder, we note that Chapter 6 is devoted to storage.

Figure 2.22, inspired by [MOO99], summarizes some predictions about disks and storage subsystems.

A few comments are in order, including the observation that the suggested order of events is not to be taken literally.

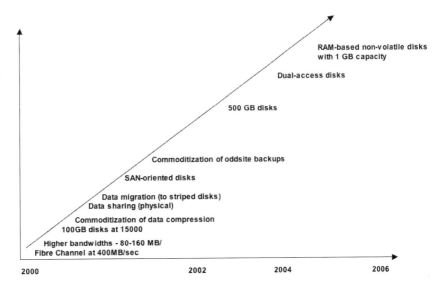

Figure 2.22
Disk and disk subsystem predictions (based on [MOO99] with modifications).

RAM-based non-volatile disks with 1 GB capacity

Dual-access disks

500 GB disks

Commoditization of oddsite backups

SAN-oriented disks

Data migration (to striped disks)
Data sharing (physical)

Commoditization of data compression
100GB disks at 15000

Higher bandwidths - 80-160 MB/
Fibre Channel at 400MB/sec

2000   2002   2004   2006

- The first changes suggested are to do with improvements in the bandwidth of the system interface (with FC projected at 2x2 Gb/s in 2002), or with improvements in bandwidth between the disk units themselves and the disk subsystems (using FC-AL or SCSI at 360 MB/s in 2003), as well as the projected increase in disk capacity (to beyond 100 GB) and rotational speed (moving first to 10,000 rpm and then on to 15,000 rpm). Increasing disk rotational speed improves average access time (which is the time for half a turn of the disk).

- Using high-level interfaces such as SCSI or FC-AL implies the use of a 32-bit microprocessor and a few megabytes of memory in the disk units; the provision of memory allows the disks to provide a cache in a totally transparent manner.

- A spread in the use of data compression is seen. This allows economies in several aspects of disk usage—not only is effective data capacity increased, but also effective bandwidth is increased and latency reduced by the degree of compression attained—at the cost of some processing to effect the compression and decompression. Given the very favorable improvements expected in price-performance for microprocessors, the computational burden imposed by this extra processing should easily be supported, whether in the server proper or in processors embedded in the disk subsystem.

- Physical sharing of storage between servers is currently possible at the subsystem level, and is the basis for SAN.

- As the intelligence in the subsystems grows, it is possible to give them the responsibility for higher-level activities, such as implementing backup and restore: the system initializes as needed, and then the peripheral does the work autonomously.

- Sharing storage at the logical level is significantly more complex a problem than physical sharing, since it means that two different systems (different processor architecture, operating system and data manager) are sharing logical data. Because of the wide diversity of systems and because in many cases the stored data is managed by a DBMS, it is reasonable to suppose that logical sharing is not at all widespread (in heterogeneous systems); it is much simpler to base server cooperation on a client/server-like behavior between applications.

- With disk technology improvements, it is possible for a disk manufacturer to offer multi-disk subsystems, operating as a RAID system and/or as a SAN subsystem; that is, disk manufacturers could become players in the storage world. This would likely hurt the established storage vendors in the same way that Intel moved from being a mere chip manufacturer to a specifier and supplier of systems.

- Data availability requirements and risk avoidance are likely to make remote backup increasingly common, and perhaps commoditized. This could drive a market for companies offering backup storage, with network exchanges taking the place of physical exchanges of magnetic cartridges.

- We can then envision an increase in Fibre Channel bandwidth, and the arrival of 500 GB capacity disks.

- When a system's overall performance is dependent on the performance of its I/ O, the overall performance is (as we have noted previously) liable to drop as improved disk technology becomes available, since as capacity increases the number of physical disks needed is reduced, automatically reducing the amount of parallelism available to the I/O system. Having multiple independent read/write channels on a single disk could claw back some of this concurrency, by more or less doubling parallelism at the disk level.

The last point on the graph is a disk built from DRAM, sometimes called a RAM Disk or a Solid State Disk. For many years, some observers have repeatedly predicted the crossing of the cost prices for DRAM and magnetic storage, and consequently the replacement of disks by DRAM. Beyond the projected cost benefits, the driving force behind this movement is the simple fact that DRAM is orders of magnitude faster than magnetic storage (perhaps 40 microseconds in place of 10 milliseconds). However, cache technology works for disk accesses as well, and a disk subsystem marrying a traditional magnetic storage device to a large DRAM cache can approach the performance of a pure DRAM disk without having to overcome the key issues of cost (since the cost curves have still not crossed and show no immediate signs of doing so) and volatility.

The volatility issue is real; DRAM is volatile—cut the power for more than a rather short interval and all the information is lost. To avoid this, one can provide a battery to keep power on at all times, or look for a better technology. The semiconductor industry is well aware of this and has been developing a number of promising technologies which marry silicon and magnetic effects. Motorola's MRAM [GEP03] seems to be a leader, although more directed at embedded memory than commodity memory chips; IBM's TMJ-RAM (Tunneling Magnetic Junction—Random Access Memory) is also worthy of mention. These technologies promise most interesting benefits: MRAM can be roughly characterized as having the density of DRAM, the access times of a mid-range SRAM, non-volatility and the ability to be rewritten an indefinitely large number of times. Even if costs do not reduce enormously, memory chips built from these technologies could be beneficial for applications requiring very high bandwidths, or for specialized roles such as journaling transactions—that is, recording the journals which track transaction-based changes in a non-volatile memory.

2.8.3 Intelligent Disks

We will now look at yet another proposal from researchers at the University of California at Berkeley, a place with a high output in the field of innovative architectures. Their proposal is to do with making good use of the processing capabilities embedded with each disk drive; they call it Intelligent Disks (or IDISKs) [KEE98].

In the early days of magnetic peripherals, the interface provided facilities closely matched to the operations the disk mechanism could naturally perform. This changed; in the 1960s, with processing power causing a system bottleneck, disk units with autonomous data-handling capabilities began to appear, with a concomitant increase in the level of abstraction supported by their interfaces. An example from IBM in the S/360 family was the *ckd* interface, which, for example, allowed the system to delegate to the disk a key-based search for a record.

The economics of minicomputers and then microprocessors made processing power cheap enough that intelligence began to migrate back into the system proper, and we saw the emergence of standard low-level disk interfaces like SMD and ESDI. The growth of complexity in the peripherals drove the existence of a higher-level interface, SCSI. Implementing SCSI more or less requires a microprocessor and supporting memory, to provide protocol support, cache, local management of the peripheral, management of read/write head positioning, error management, buffer space for SCSI bus transfers and so on. Current technology already makes it possible to integrate, low cost, and low power processing/memory and interface electronics directly with the peripherals themselves, along with system interface support (such as FC-AL). The idea behind intelligent disks is to make greater use of this embedded intelligence, allowing both off-loading of the server and greater computational concurrency. We note here the balance swinging back: new technology allows us to effectively re-implement old ideas.

Various levels of functionality may be envisaged for intelligent disks.; Examples include:

- Off-load database management software, along with necessary supporting OS functions, in a share-nothing architecture implemented across the disks themselves
- Off-load some database management functions onto the disks—for example, searches and joins, with the control of these operations being done by the server-resident DBMS
- Off-load file system activities—for example, optimizing a string of commands by reordering them in the disk to minimize head movement

While there is little quantitative information available for the benefits this approach can bring, the real problem is standardization. Indeed, widespread deployment of intelligent disks would mean that the most widely-used software (from basic file systems with simple access methods, such as those offered by Windows and Linux, all the way up to DBMSs) would be adapted to such machinery. This requires agreements between the players behind this software and the disk manufacturers; an agreement between the disk manufacturers is in the realm of the possible, and is in any case a prerequisite for any larger agreement between software vendors and the disk manufacturers.

These latter possibility seems more remote; we can easily observe that historically, DBMS manufacturers have avoid using the magic features of any system platform, preferring to use extremely low-level interfaces so that they could be certain that execution of vital functionalities is under their control and could therefore be guaranteed across platforms. This view also simplifies porting across platforms and reduces support and development costs for the DBMS.

2.8.4 Networks and Network Connections

As the Internet evolves, we can see specialization increasing in the portions of the systems providing communications support. In the mainframe era of the 1960s, communications were directly supported by the systems. This changed in the 1970s, as needs grew, and led manufacturers to produce semi-autonomous communications subsystems coupled to the main system. These were known as front-end processors, and examples include IBM's 37xx series and Bull's Datanet.

This trend increased with the rise of local area networks, with the emergence of a new generation of network equipment—routers, concentrators and so forth—that off-load a number of chores from the servers.

Nowadays, we do not expect a server to directly support a variety of communications interfaces, but rather to provide a number of high-bandwidth pipes that carry requests for it to operate on the data it owns.

We expect this trend to continue, especially with convergence resulting in the same network carrying voice (and video) along with data, from the point of view of provisioning sufficient physical resources as well as from the IP point of view. Forecasts suggest a continuing significant increase in data traffic, with voice traffic stagnating; thus, the effects of this convergence will likely be felt more in the telephony industry (makers of automatic telephone exchanges and switches) than in the data-processing industry.

Increased use of multimedia will impose further demands on servers, because of the need to observe and guarantee temporal properties. This might suggest deployment of specialized realtime operating systems as well as use of special peripherals, such as disks optimized for this type of use.

The industry has at its disposal a number of technologies, particularly optical, which will allow it to support demand; increasing bandwidth; reducing latency; the address space increase offered by IPv6; the concept of quality of service, and so on.

A key issue, though, is driving new uses that will themselves make use of the possibilities available and allow these technologies to be deployed.

Cisco, the world leader in networking equipment, envisages the emergence of the intelligent network, whose components are:

- Interconnection with proprietary networks like SNA, DSA or others;
- Broadcast or multicast facilities, allowing one message to be sent to many destinations
- Video services (both video conferencing and video-on-demand)
- Cache services
- Administration
- Voice-related services

- QoS (quality of service)-related services
- Security services

Looking at these a little deeper:

- Interworking with proprietary networks is a necessity while these networks exist
- Some applications would benefit from a multicast capability—one message with multiple recipients (examples of such applications include videoconferencing, updating workstation software, Internet "push" technologies, information replication, and more)
- Expect videoconferencing to grow, since it can reduce travel and thus reduce costs and the polluting side-effects of vehicle usage; however, it is a new form of interaction, and there will need to be a learning curve as individuals adapt to it (video on demand, except for specialty niches such as within hotels, should grow at a much lower rate)
- Caching data in the network improves access to information
- It is difficult to overemphasize the requirements for good administration and security in networks
- The concept of QoS appeared a few years ago, and still needs time to develop fully. It is a fundamental parameter for the usability of a system. In use, the quality—in terms of bandwidth, or latency, for example—of a connection is negotiated, and then the network guarantees that level while the connection is open

When a number of disks are assembled within a single enclosure, but without any special organization (such as RAID) being implemented, the collection is known as JBOD (Just a Bunch of Disks).

2.9 Endnotes

1. It is a source of some surprise that VME, which does not provide architected support for data integrity—not even simple parity—should be used in such industrial control applications.

2. This allows a device to be shared between zones.

3. Intel has tried to standardize the notion of channel program with its I2O (Intelligent I/O) initiative, but apparently without success. But even without standardization, the concept is necessary for efficient I/O operation.

4. In general, buffers are not part of user space, but belong to the operating system. So data must be copied from user space to kernel space, which is where the increased processing cost mentioned above in the list of problems posed comes from.

5. Even though all these switches operate in the TCP/IP world, OSI nomenclature is still used. The seven-level OSI model has undeniable structural virtues. One may, however, wonder about the development costs of such a model and its associated specifications, considering just how much of it remains in use.

6. The world awaits measurements—or, even better, standards or benchmarks—that would allow confirmation of these claims and comparison of the effectiveness of such equipment.

7. As we shall see in Chapter 8, when we look at the relationships between server architecture and DBMS architecture, Share-Nothing is one possible architecture. It is a cluster architecture, comprising multiple identical nodes each controlled by their own copy of the software and each having their own locally-controlled storage resources.

3

Evolution of Software Technology

3.1 Virtual Memory and 64-Bit Architecture

The concept of virtual memory, introduced in the 1960s, eases software development by freeing the programmer from some aspects of memory management. Further developed through the 1970s, on minicomputer and mainframe operating systems, including UNIX, it is now standard practice even on desktop operating systems such as Windows.

3.1.1 Virtual Memory

In the absence of virtual memory, the size of any object (data or code) manipulated by program was limited to being no greater than the amount of free memory, set by the amount of physical memory less the amount of memory used by the OS and services such as runtime libraries. To handle objects bigger than available memory, programmers resorted to a technique known as overlays, which was simply the approach of having any one chunk of memory be used successively for a number of different items. The overlay structure was totally under the control of the programmer, and operated at the link-editor level. The link editor inserted into the program system calls which invoked a service to load on demand those portions of the program needed for execution.

Figure 3.1 illustrates the concept of overlays. In this example, the program is composed of several units. A, the main program and includes the data which will always be available to all parts of the program. The parts beginning with B and G execute independently of one another, just as the parts beginning with C and F execute independently, just like parts D and E and parts H, I, and J. These units each contain their own code and data.

Figure 3.1
Overlay concept.

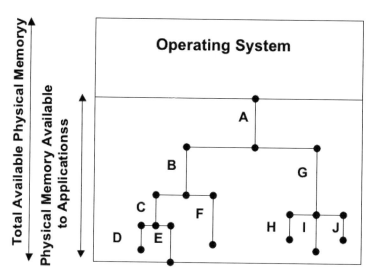

Beyond the complexity of the specification of such structures, having to explicitly load in various portions of the program during execution affected performance. It also meant that whenever the amount of memory changed—for example, when moving to a different computer—then the tuning needed to be reworked. To minimize this performance problem, it is advisable to optimize the structure of the program to avoid too-frequent loading. We should also note that the file system, which handles the loading of portions of files, manages the overlays in their buffers, in which they seek to maintain the most frequently used data to minimize I/O operations. We can see that this collection of activities is nothing more than program-driven memory hierarchy management, either directly by the applications programmer or implicitly by the file system.

Virtual memory gives the operating system the responsibility for managing the memory hierarchy, in a manner invisible to the applications programmer, enabling the use of objects—code or data—larger than the available physical memory without any explicit management activities on the programmer's part. This is done by keeping objects on disk, and bringing necessary parts of them into memory as needed. The most usual approach is that of demand paging in which the address space available to the programmer—the virtual address space—is divided up into units of a fixed size (perhaps four or eight KB), which is both the atom of allocatable memory and the unit of transfer between disk and memory. The actions taken by the operating system to manage the movement of data between main memory and disk is exactly analogous to the activities taken by pro-

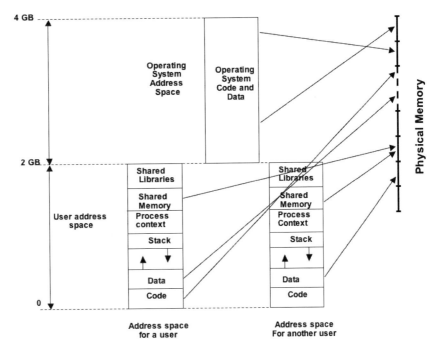

Figure 3.2
Illustration of the concept of virtual memory.

cessor caches, and works for the same reasons—both exploit the existence of spatio-temporal locality in executing programs.

Figure 3.2 illustrates the concept of virtual memory. This diagram represents associated virtual spaces, of one part, with the operating system and, of the other part, with the various active applications on the system. It corresponds, in a somewhat simplified way, to a UNIX system executing on a system offering 4 GB (or 2^{32} Bytes) of virtual memory. The 4 GB of virtual address space is divided into two portions of equal size, allocating 2 GB to the operating system and 2 GB for user programs; as shown in the diagram, all users have their address spaces multiplexed into the same 2 GB virtual address space. We generally refer to an executing program as a process; when a given process is active, the operating system arranges for the process' address space to appear in the global address space. Translation between virtual addresses and physical addresses is done by the processor hardware and uses page-based translation tables. The translation tables contain information managed by the operating system that indicates whether the page is in memory and what its protection attributes are (read-only, read and write, and so on). In addition, the tables contain hardware-managed information, such as whether the page has been read or written; this information is used by the operating system to manage virtual memory.

During process execution, a reference to a page not in memory will cause control to be passed to the virtual memory manager, which looks for a free page in memory into which to place the referenced page. If it cannot find one, it will release an allocated page, writing its contents to disk if it has been modified. On obtaining a page, the operating system loads it from disk and, when this has completed, updates the table entry and returns control to the user process (the operating system allows other user processes to run while this is going on).

A detailed description of the mechanisms of virtual storage for both processors and software is outside the scope of this book; interested readers can consult [PAT04] for a discussion at the hardware level.

Figure 3.2 also shows the structure of a user process's address space, which comprises:

- A portion contain the process's executable code (this portion is called the text segment in the UNIX world)

- A portion for holding the process's data; the size of this portion can vary during execution depending on how the application allocates and frees memory

- A portion holding the stack which holds information on procedure calls and returns;

- a portion in which process state (the values in the processor registers, together with other process-related information) will be saved when the operating system suspends the process in favor of another process

- A portion to refer to data shared between different processes

- A portion for libraries shared between multiple processes

The existence of a portion of memory shared between processes is one source of efficiency for the applications that make use of it, since access requires no more than (perhaps) a synchronization operation followed by normal load and store operations. We will look again at the use of shared data when we analyze symmetrical multiprocessor architectures.

3.1.2   Virtual Address Spaces

In the preceding example, we have implicitly referred to an address space organization known as Multiple Address Spaces (MAS). This approach to address space organization means that the various processes share a portion of the address space provided by the processor (space private to the operating system and shared space), and that each process has its own logically private address space. In fact, all user processes reuse the same virtual address space, and the operating system arranges to have the correct physical address space defined as it runs each process. To avoid ambiguities in such an architectural model, each process is identified by a number (its PID, or Process Identifier); it is preferable that PIDs are unique, but implementation constraints make this impossible, so PIDs must be re-used. When reusing a PID, the system must ensure that all referents using that PID have been removed from the system.

In the MAS model, a virtual address is a doublet:

```
<PID, address within the specified address space>
```

When PIDs are not used in address translation, the operating system must flush the user space translation caches (TLBs, for Translation Lookaside Buffers) on each user process switch.

Using the PID, the operating system can identify the relevant tables specifying the translations for a particular process. Typically, virtual address translation is done through the use of multiple levels of table, often called *page tables*.

The other address space model is the Single Address Space (SAS) model, also known as the *global address space* model. In this model, each process address space is a part of the single, global address space—that is, the address space provided by the processor is shared by all processes. Typically, the translation of virtual addresses to real addresses is done by the use of an inverse (or hash) page table.

In the SAS model, the address of an object is simply its address in the single global address space. From software's point of view, an object is identified by a pointer within this global address space, and items within the object are accessed as offsets from the pointer. Classically, a pointer is held in specific registers that are part of the process context and designated either explicitly or implicitly (for example, by the most significant bits of the virtual address). Unlike in the MAS model, there is no ambiguity about virtual addresses generated by multiple processes, and there is therefore no need to flush the TLBs when changing process.

The MAS model is simple to implement and is widely used in low-end and mid-range servers. SAS simplifies sharing between processes, and is

Figure 3.3
SAS and MAS.

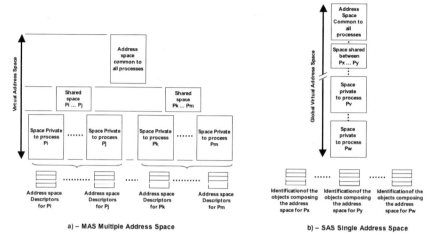

generally found in high-end servers. Figure 3.3 compares the two schemes in a conceptual manner, without being bound to any particular processor or operating system architecture.

As the diagram shows, in MAS the address space of each process re-use the same virtual address spaces, and thus each uses the same range of virtual addresses. One can say that the logical objects manipulated by the various processes are multiplexed into the same address space—with the exception of shared items, the same virtual address in different processes indicates different data items. The potential ambiguities caused by such sharing of addresses is handled by the address space tables. One may see that any shared space, whether shared by all processes (such as the OS) or just by some processes, must have the same virtual address in each process. When handling extremely large virtual address spaces, the page tables also become very large; because MAS must purge the translation caches (when PIDs are not used in virtual address translation) on a user process switch, this results in performance problems for MAS.

In the case of SAS, the different address spaces of the processes are directly represented within a single global address space. Unlike in MAS, where the totality of objects was multiplexed onto an address space of limited size, in SAS all objects exist within the one address space simultaneously; this means that the address space must be very large.[1] To keep virtual addresses to a manageable size (64-bits, for example), the definition of accessible objects is held in special registers, and one portion of the virtual address of the object—for example, the most significant bits of the address—is used to denote which register holds the descriptor for the object.

The choice of address space architecture is a distinguishing factor between both processor and operating systems architectures. Thus, the IA-32 architecture (for Intel Architecture 32 bits, which used to be commonly referred to as the X86 architecture) is built on a MAS model, also adopted by Windows and Linux. On the other hand, HP-PA and PowerPC[2] are able to support the SAS model, and their signature operating systems (HP-UX and AIX respectively) also support SAS.

Implementing an operating system of one address space flavor on a processor architecture which has chosen the other model seems problematic, and gives rise to performance problems.

Since they needed to support both Windows and UNIX (HP-UX and Linux) efficiently, the designers of the IA-64 found themselves needing to support MAS and SAS on the same hardware, and so they defined mechanisms which support both models, as shown in Figure 3.4.

In the IA-64 architecture model, one defines Virtual Regions. A processor must implement between 2^{18} and 2^{24} regions, each identified by a RID (Region IDentifier). Each region may be up to 2^{61} Bytes in size. A process may address no more than eight regions at any one time, and the accessible regions are specified by the contents of the eight region registers. The top three bits (of a 64-bit virtual address) select the appropriate Region Register. Region Register contents form part of the process's context.

With a SAS operating system, the virtual address space is constructed by concatenating the 18 or 24 bits held in a RID selected by the top three bits of a 64-bit virtual address with the remaining 61 bits of that address. In this

Figure 3.4
IA64 virtual memory mechanisms.

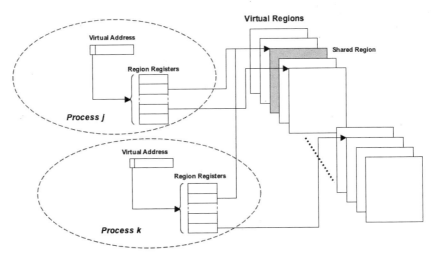

model, the global address space therefore ranges from 2^{79} to 2^{85} Bytes, depending on the number of registers implemented by the processor.

In a MAS-model operating system, the RIDs are looked upon as address space identifiers. To share data between processes, one or more Region Registers must contain the same RID(s).

As touched on earlier, the translation tables contain information on how to translate virtual real information on the permitted accesses to the page (read-only, read and execute, write, etc.) together with information on the state of the page (referenced, modified). As we indicated in Chapter 1, the actual translation is done by associative tables (which are just address transaction caches) done in hardware; these caches are known as Translation Lookaside Buffers, or TLBs. As long as a translation is cached in the TLB, hardware does the address translation transparently. If the translation is not cached, then an exception is raised and software (in general) is given the opportunity to set up the translation table with the necessary information. Again, a detailed description of these mechanisms is beyond the scope of this book.

3.1.3 Virtual Address Translation Mechanisms

There are two main categories of virtual address translation mechanisms:

- Page tables
- Inverted page tables

Figure 3.5 illustrates these two mechanisms.

Figure 3.5
Virtual address translation mechanisms.

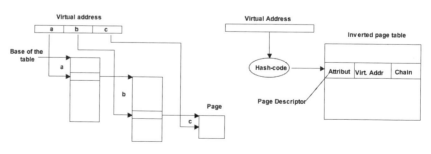

For the classic page table approach, the virtual address is generally partitioned into a number of sections—generally three—used as indices into a hierarchy of tables, which eventually select an entry in a table that specifies the translation. Intel IA-32 architecture processors use this type of structure.

Concepts of Segmentation and Pagination

The terms *segment* and *page* are often used for a two-level page table for virtual to real address translation. Unfortunately, this use of the term segment is historically inaccurate. The term arose in the Multics architecture (and in derivative architectures, such as the Bull DPS 7000 or Intel's 80286). In these architectures, a virtual address was composed of two portions; the first identified an information container (the segment proper) and the second identified information within the container (specifying an offset within the segment). The handling of the two portions was entirely distinct—for example, an overflow in the calculation of the displacement would not cause the segment identifier to increment.

Segments are programmer-visible, at least at the assembler level. In these architectures, it was traditional to specify a length for the segment so that hardware could check the legality of a segment offset.

In architectures where the partitioning of the virtual address does not correspond to an address space of this form, it might be better to refer to the collection of pages selected by an upper portion of the virtual address as a chapter or volume rather than a segment.

However, the misuse of the term is now a *de facto* standard, and so we shall conform to current usage elsewhere in the book.

The size of the collection of page tables is related to the size of the supported virtual address space, and so the amount of memory they require can become very significant. Further, since as described every memory access would require traversing the page table hierarchy (a slow process) microprocessors provide special address-translation caches that appropriately cache page table entry information. As we have said, these caches are generally called Translation Lookaside buffers, or TLBs.

In the case of an inverted page table organization, must search for the address of the page for which we desire a translation in a table that holds descriptions of all the pages in physical memory. For each physical page there is a descriptor in this table that indicates whether the page is currently allocated, and, if so, its corresponding virtual address. To minimize search costs, the whole virtual address is operated on by a function to generate a hash value which is used to index the table. The size of the page table is directly related to the size of physical memory (because there is one descriptor per physical page), resulting in a substantial savings in page table space for systems with large virtual address spaces, compared to systems using the classic page table scheme, together with a lower access cost thanks to the hashing function.[3] This approach is typically adopted by RISC microprocessors.

TLBs are also implemented in processors adopting an inverted page table approach.

In either case, if a translation for a virtual address cannot be found in the TLB, one of two approaches is used to handle the situation:

- The microprocessor automatically proceeds to walk the page table structure, and copies the translation eventually selected into a TLB entry

- An exception is raised, and software (part of the operating system) handles the translation, walking the page table structure to find the appropriate translation, and then selecting a TLB entry and writing the translation into it

The first approach—hardware page table walking—is potentially higher performance but also more rigid (algorithm, structure and format of the page tables are "carved into silicon"). The second approach is much more flexible, and is becoming the more prevalent.

3.1.4 64-Bit Architecture

The increase in size of both the data objects being operated on and physical memory and the need to hide disk and network access times by placing ever more information in the memory-based disk or network cache lead to severe pressure on the addressing ability of 32-bit processors and operating systems, which saturates at 4 GB. Some RISC processors—Alpha and PA from HP, SGI's, MIPS, IBM's Power, and Sun's SPARC) support a much larger address space of 64-bits. Alpha was designed to be 64-bits right from its inception, while the others all began as 32-bit architectures and were extended later in life to 64-bits. In practice, Intel's IA-32 architecture is limited to 32-bit addressing, although AMD has proposed a backwards-compatible extension to 64-bits. (It should be noted that, as defined, the IA-32 architecture allows addressing much more than 32-bits, but structured as

16,384 segments each of up to 4GB, but that no operating systems exist which make use of this feature[4]). Intel's new architecture, IA-64, is another architecture designed from inception to support 64-bit addressing. The first systems based on this architecture appeared on the market in the second half of 2001 with the Itanium processor (which had been code-named Merced). The implementation of Itanium suffered so many delays and problems that many industry observers are of the opinion that the first commercially-attractive IA-64 implementation is Itanium's follow-on, Itanium 2 (code-named McKinley). Systems based on, Itanium 2 appeared in the market in the second half of 2002.

Applications that can make good use of the vast address space offered by 64-bit addressing are primarily databases (particularly for decision support), with scientific applications and CAD programs also able to benefit.

The advantages brought by a 64-bit architecture can be summarized as follow:

- The ability to address, per process and in virtual memory, a collection of objects representing more than 4 GB. This removes the need to manage the memory hierarchy explicitly within the application, and simplifies the ability to take advantage of the continuing increases in main memory size.

- The ability to support directly and efficiently files or filing systems whose size is greater than two to four GB.

- The ability to operate on large files placed directly in virtual memory. With a 64-bit address space, there is sufficient room for a substantial number of very large files to be placed mapped into virtual memory, where software can directly access them with load and store instructions rather than I/O operations and with the processor's built-in address translation hardware doing all needed address translation. And, finally, the movement of data between memory and disk is handled automatically by the demand-paged virtual memory system itself.

- The ability to manage very large physical memories—larger than 4 GB. Memories of such size are principally used as cache for disk-based data; in particular, the performance of database management software depends in large part on their management of the memory hierarchy, which explains why database software generally takes responsibility for the management of disk caches. A DBMS can normally do better than a vanilla memory hierarchy manager, since the DBMS knows a lot about the data it is manipulating (whether a datum is data or index data, for example) and can act appropriately. Simply placing large amounts of (reused) data in memory provides a performance improvement, because it removes the need for the software to perform file-to-memory address mapping and also reduces I/O traffic.

It should however be noted that some 32-bit architectures (hardware and software system) can address physical memories of more than 4 GB and support file systems of more than 4 GB.

Clearly, to make full use of a 64-bit address space one needs—in addition to an appropriate processor—the necessary software: compilers, operating systems, applications. The vendors of 64-bit RISC systems (Compaq, Digital, HP, SGI, IBM, and Sun) offer such a suite. Some initiatives intended to adapt UNIX to IA-64 have fallen by the wayside. By mid 2004, Linux and Windows were the only operating systems planned for Itanium platforms and offered to system manufacturers, although there are 64-bit versions of AIX, HP-UX (available on both PA and Itanium for HP systems), Linux, Solaris, and Windows.

In the second half of 2001, IBM, with its z900 family of mainframe systems, introduced a 64-bit extension to the S/390 architecture, which had its roots in the S/360 system of the early 60s (with a 24-bit architecture).

For servers, 64-bit architecture is a necessity, not a luxury. It acts as a foundation for the systems to support the changing needs of the application space and to take advantage of the opportunities offered by technology.

3.2   Operating Systems

This section looks at operating systems from the perspective of how their market share is evolving, together with the functionality they provide. We need to consider market share because the market for standard systems—by which we mean UNIX and Windows—is conditioned by the availability of applications, which itself is affected by market share; thus there is a feedback effect. Operating systems' functionality is also important, since it affects the ability of an OS to support certain classes of application

Operating System Market Share

The quantitative future estimates from analysts, which we use as the basis for our discussions, must of course—as with any predictions—be taken carefully. Our main goal is to use them to extract and illustrate significant

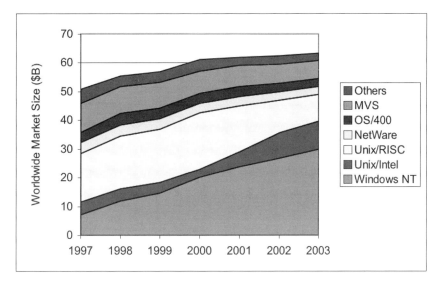

Figure 3.6
*Server sales forecast
by operating system
(source data:
Gartner Group,
November 2003).*

market trends. To start with, consider Figure 3.6, from Gartner Group data from November 2003 and showing server market trends sorted by the operating system provided with the servers.[5]

The strong increase in sales for Linux and Windows is obvious. It is likely that Windows's growth will be mostly in the midrange, as the high end is the hunting ground for proprietary systems and UNIX. Netware is expected to undergo a noticeable reduction in market.

Market Evolution

As is often seen in the data-processing industry, a balancing effect had moved us from the centralized approach—terminals connected to mainframes—to a distributed approach, embodying minicomputers and of PCs. Unfortunately, the distributed approach, while providing more flexibility tended to give rise to inconsistencies in the company's data and was hard to administer effectively. Now the world is swinging back towards a more centralized approach (at least as far as the management of data is concerned). "Upsizing" (or "server consolidation") has the effect of increasing the average size of a server and concentrating a number of independent servers into a single server, whether it be a single large machine or a cluster.

Linux's market share is expected to grow noticeably. This OS seems to have a promising future in the domain of dedicated servers (that is, servers which support a single application).

Among the proprietary versions of UNIX, we see that AIX's share is expected to grow while those of HP-UX and of Solaris are expected to stay stable at best. For HP-UX, the seamless transition offered to customers between HP's PA architecture and IA-64 is a factor in reducing the erosion of HP-UX's market share. Since HP has not announced any intention to give access to HP-UX outside OEM agreements, its market share will be strictly limited to systems developed by HP.

For Solaris, we should note that Sun has an IA-32 port. The battle between the different UNIX vendors will be interesting to watch, not least because it looks as though the players will be fighting over a shrinking field as they lose share to Linux and Windows Server 2003.

This shrink in market share is an effect of the competition that Windows and Linux are offering to UNIX systems in the low-end and midrange. The introduction of systems based on IA-64 (Itanium) is likely to relaunch the sales of UNIX on Intel platforms, in particular in midrange and high-end systems. And we should note that the various UNIX variants have had time and experience enough to reach a level of maturity and reliability that allows them to attack enterprise-critical systems, previously the domain of proprietary mainframe systems.

Economic Considerations in the UNIX World

As in other areas, it is difficult for a systems vendor to bear the cost of development and maintenance for server-class UNIX systems if sales are weak. This leads to consolidations, concentrating the industry around ever-fewer UNIX versions. As the few remaining versions of UNIX differ, their uniqueness gives the UNIX market much of the flavor of the traditional proprietary market for high-end systems. And this, quite likely, will benefit Linux, which is not restricted at all in this manner.

Windows looks set to dominate the market at the lower-cost domain, with its success in the higher end only coming with maturity. The process of maturing is, of course, much aided by the installation of a very large number of Windows systems—provided its vendor can provide the needed support and maintenance, since this exposes the system to a wide range of different situations.

Our thoughts must also encompass the "free software" phenomenon, as evidenced by Linux. Linux has the advantage of being essentially free at the point of acquisition; any problems it might have, compared to UNIX versions sold by the major manufacturers or by major software publishers will be in the level of support available. This risk is being mitigated however, as the same major manufacturers now include Linux in their catalogs and offer support and services for Linux as they do for their own systems. Independent software houses are also offering Linux support and services.

As we have emphasized before, a key element in choice of an operation system is the richness of the applications catalog associated with it. While the talk is encouraging, it remains to be seen just what the actual long term commitment of software vendors to Linux will be. While such vendors are most likely to be interested in the much larger marketplace offered them by Linux platforms, they are not likely to offer their applications in source form to the community.

For certain embedded and specialized systems,[6] Linux has an undeniable attraction. Because such systems rarely are expected to run any extant application, but to execute some well-defined, application-specific applications, the richness of the application catalog is irrelevant. Qualifying such a system is eased by its natural closed character. The applications for such embedded systems may, themselves, be members of the world of free software—for example, the Apache web server, and the SAMBA PC file sharing package.

3.2.1 Operating Systems Functionality

Proprietary systems vendors were, for a long time, considerably ahead of open systems in the level of functionality offered by their operating systems, especially in areas like the number of processors supported in SMP versions, robustness, availability, systems administration, and so forth. But over time, UNIX systems have caught up, and offer SMP, cluster support, and constantly-improving robustness and availability. This maturation of UNIX has thus significantly reduced any functionality advantage proprietary systems may now offer over UNIX (although that very process of maturation has drastically reduced the number of extant UNIX variants). In terms of functionality, we should see the same process happening between UNIX and Windows, as Windows gathers experience.

There are five useful technical areas in which one may compare operating systems. We list them here, and then subsequently discuss them at greater length.

- *Scalability.* As already noted, this is a measure of the ability of a system to match the dimensions of a problem it must handle

- *RAS—Reliability, Availability, and Serviceability.*[7] These characteristics drive the total availability of the servers and thus their capacity to support the uses for which they were acquired.

- *Distributed services and Internet support.* Here, we mean the integration of the basic elements that allow operation in a distributed system (these services are, properly speaking, middleware and do not form part of the operating system). Supporting basic Internet capabilities and supporting PC clients fall into this category.

- *System management.* By this we mean the complete collection of facilities—mainly software—that facilitate the management of the system. One may observe these facilities evolving towards some quasi-autonomous decision-taking capabilities (so that the software can react without further human input), which should lead to lower cost of ownership.

- *Capacity to simultaneously support various isolated workloads.* Since a server is an expensive investment, systems managers are pushed into making each server support many different independent workloads simultaneously. The process of server consolidation, which is the act of reducing the number of (generally distributed) servers deployed in an enterprise to a smaller number of (probably co-located) servers, requires this capability. The management of several workloads according to a given policy (for instance, priority given to certain applications regarding the allocation of resources) is also called workload management. A system's capability to be partitioned into several independent system to support, in complete isolation, different workloads is another approach to server consolidation. Dynamic partitioning capability (i.e., without stopping the complete system) is a key feature.

Scalability

Scalability must provide adaptability in multiple dimensions of the system: computational and data handling capacity (as reflected by the number of processors supported), address space (which means, in practice, a 64-bit address space), physical storage capacity, connection capacity for storage peripherals and subsystems, and finally communications capacity (in terms of both the number of independent ports and the aggregate bandwidth). Scalability in data handling implies the ability to handle growth in the two

Two other dimensions relate to services and total cost of ownership. services is a generic term that refers to a collection of attributes such as: support, business model and practices offered by both hardware and software providers, and the availability of professional services and skills. TCO is a measure that integrates all costs associated with hardware, software and maintenance. A number of factors affect TCO—for example, the characteristics of the software used can affect the costs of usage, along with functionality such as good systems management facilities, RAS capabilities, and performance. Together with availability, TCO is one of the rallying cries of the proprietary systems vendors. We discuss TCO in Chapter 11.

dimensions of multiprocessing: tight coupling (implying SMP adaptability) and loose coupling (implying cluster or massively parallel scalability). These scaling capabilities are referred to as vertical (in the SMP) and horizontal (in the cluster dimension). As we shall see in Chapter 7, which discusses systems performance, SMPs offer significantly greater scalability (within the limits—sometimes restrictive—of system configurability) than do clusters or MPP systems.

Reliability, Availability, and Servicability (RAS)

RAS has as its goal, quite simply, to reduce system unavailability time. Obviously, unavailability can be triggered by hardware failures, and we will restrict ourselves here to discussion of what functions the operating system can provide to limit the impact of such failures. Chapters 9 and 10 cover the architecture of high availability systems.

One of the first characteristics operating systems can implement deals with the managing certain hardware errors:

- The operating system can mitigate the effects of hardware failures, and can—under appropriate circumstances—hide the failures from users; to do this generally implies redundant hardware. It is possible to avoid likely hardware failures—for example, if the single-bit error-correction rate of a region of memory (using ECC protection in the memory) exceeds a given threshold, it is likely that a memory chip is failing in that region; the operating system can avoid any memory failures by marking that region of physical memory invalid so that it is never again accessed. If the I/O subsystem has appropriate redundancy, as much in terms of interconnects as actual storage media, the operating system can again hide the problems.

- Handling a processor failure is more difficult, since such a failure can cause data loss or inappropriate data modifications. Often enough, the failure of one processor will result in the system automatically halting and restarting, with the faulty processor identified and isolated after the reboot self-test phase.

Obviously, the system is completely unavailable during the phases of halting, self-test and reboot, which can take several minutes. This is an area of functionality where the high end systems vendors—including some of their specially-adapted UNIX systems for top-of-the-range machines—have definite advantages over standard systems. Most systems—whether standard or proprietary—adopt cluster-based solutions to improve availability (see Chapters 9 and 10).

Operating systems can also use journaling file systems, which make it possible to accelerate system restart (see Chapters 9 and 10).

Journaling File Systems

In a journaling file system, all actions that change the meta data of the file system (for example, the meta data in a UNIX file system, which is represented by the i-nodes, or the internal data structures of NTFS, the native file system for Windows Server 2003) are managed as transactions, and can therefore be cancelled or re-done without side effects if they do not complete. This approach makes it possible to reduce start-up times for the systems by cancelling or replaying actions which were not completed at the time of the failure incident.

The final dimension of interest is that which describes the ability of the system to be kept in a state of correct operation, and which covers a number of elements, among which we should note:

- *The ability to define recovery points (Checkpoint/Restart).* With this functionality, one may define a procedure that allows one periodically to snapshot all the information necessary to enable a transparent restart of an application, given just this state information. Such information is known as a recovery point. Then, in the event the system fails, one can invoke the extant recovery points and roll the system forward safely and consistently.

- *Resource Management.* To allow better optimization of resource usage, some systems provide resource control at the level of a process or group of processes, driven by knowledge of the process' service objectives.

- *Memory Dump Analysis Tools.* Typically, when an application—or even the operating system—is the victim of a crash, a memory image (a 'kernel dump' or a 'core dump' depending on whether the crash is a kernel crash or an application crash) is automatically generated by the operating system. Some operating systems provide tools to analyze these dumps, so that—given the availability of source code—the root cause of the failure can be pinpointed.

Distributed Services and Internet Support

Let us now turn our attention to distributed services and Internet support. We can identify the following basic elements to do with distributed services:

- *Directory Services.* The increase in the number of users and the number of objects managed in distributed environments means that some form of Directory Services are necessary, and indeed form a central part of such systems.

- *Security.* Distributed systems reinforce the need for security. A detailed discussion of how this can be implemented is beyond the scope of this work, and we will satisfy ourselves with some general security suggestions for distributed systems: Kerberos (an authentication service), firewalls (allowing filtering and monitoring of communications traffic), support for the public key encryption infrastructure, and Virtual Private Networks (VPNs).

- *Distributed File Services.* In practice, this tends to mean implementation of Sun's NFS (Network File System) in the UNIX world, or of CIFS (Common Internet File System) in the Windows world

- *Distributed Time Services.* Some distributed applications need to ensure that their various components running across the distributed system all have the same view of what the time is. To support this, a distributed system service—DTS, for Distributed Time Service— makes it possible for all systems to have essentially the same idea of current time (within some small delta).

- *Inter-program Communication.* Here we mean provision of RPC (Remote Procedure Call), RMI (Remote Method Invocation) or MOMs (Message-Oriented Middleware). RPC allows one to write software in which invocations of distributed services are represented as a simple procedure call; systems software implements some message-passing under the hood to carry arguments and results across the network. Implementing software that uses RPC requires supporting development tools as well as runtime support. RMI is integrated into any distributed object environments, such as CORBA or DCOM/COM+. We will look more closely at the characteristics of these various mechanisms later on in this chapter.

- *Transactional services.* The support of transactions—that is, mechanisms to ensure the conservation of the ACID properties (atomicity, consistency, isolation and durability)—implies the provision of transaction monitors which make it possible to implement, in cooperation with the resource managers (that is, in this case, the DBMS's), a two-phase validation protocol.

While some of these elements are integrated into the operating systems themselves, other, such as the transaction monitors are separate products, such as Tuxedo from BEA.

Distributed services

Examples of these services are NIS (Network Information Service) and NIS+, used in a UNIX context; NDS (Netware Directory Service) used in the Netware context; NTDS (NT Directory Service) integrated into Windows Server 2003; and DNS (Domain.Name Service), which allows the translation of Internet names (such as www.xyz.com) into TCP/IP addresses. We should also mention the support of LDAP (lightweight directory.access.protocol), which is built on a subset of the X500 standard and which makes it possible to interface with various directory services.

A complementary dimension to these services relates to the support of PC clients; here the key services are file sharing and printing services, which must be made available to the PC user in the most transparent manner possible. Windows Server 2003 integrates these functions, while most UNIX systems also offer distributed file services and printing services. An interesting crossover product, AS/U (Advanced Server/UNIX), implements the

---

Distributed Computing Environment (DCE of OSF)

It is useful to point out the action of the Open Software Foundation, (OSF) consortium in the field of distributed systems. OSF was created by hardware vendors with the ambition of providing a UNIX system independent of AT&T (which owned UNIX at the time and had shown a desire to become an player in the data-processing market by taking a participation in Sun in particular). Parallel to this action, OSF had launched, at the beginning of the 90s, a technology research program and an effort at integration for an environment allowing the development and the execution of distributed applications. This environment, called DCE (for distributed computing environment) , had the merit of being almost complete in terms of integrating the various services necessary (directories, security, time, etc.). DCE, probably because of its complexity and also because the OSF partners backed away from their commitments, did not meet commercial success. However, DCE constitutes an architectural model for distributed applications. It should be noticed that pieces of DCE are indeed used in various commercial offerings.

Windows Server 2003 network services on UNIX, allowing a customer to use UNIX systems to provide the needed distributed support for a collection of PCs. SAMBA, an implementation of the Windows file sharing protocols, also merits mention; it allows Linux servers to provide file sharing services to PC clients.

Such PC-supporting systems also need to integrate the capability to manage what software is installed in the client PCs and to allow management of new version updates. This functionality is sometimes integrated into the system management functionalities of the server.

A final element is Java support. This implies the implementation of a JVM (Java virtual machine) that allows the execution of Java programs on the system. The JVM may be supplemented by further functionality, such as Java development tools (JDK, for Java development kit), by a JIT (just in time) compiler to improve performance, and by optimizations in memory management and in support of lightweight processes called threads.[8] Further, the ability of the server to distribute Java applets must be considered.

We now revisit the requirements for Internet support:

- Support for the IP protocols and their extensions: multilink PPP (Point to Point Protocol) that allows multiple physical connections to be ganged together for increased performance; IPv6 addressing (128 bits rather than the classical 32 bits of address in IPv4); and VPN.

- Functional extensions, performance optimizations and tools and services for TCP/IP

- Web servers and browsers integrated into the operating system, which made it easy to create a Web server without the purchase of further software

- Support for e-mail servers: since e-mail is a basic requirement, it is key that the service is provided with the OS in some appropriate manner

- Electronic commerce: After e-mail and Internet access, the likely next wave will be electronic commerce, thus, provision of integrated tools for this should be a key selection criterion[9]

We will say no more about the Internet, important though it is.[10]

Systems Management

As far as systems management is concerned, the operating system must provide facilities for the following:

- *Hardware configuration management.* Automatic recognition of the hardware configuration and its technical state (for example, the version number of the firmware integrated into the controllers), automatic set-up of device drivers reflecting the connected peripherals, and so on

- *Software configuration management.* Recognition of all software modules present and their revision state

- *User Management.* Managing passwords, access rights, etc.

- *Resource management.* Optimization of the usage of the various resources of the system—memory, processors, storage, communications) to best meet user demands.

- *Remote management.*

- *Performance analysis.* Automatic recording of the usage statistics of the various resources.

- *Batch processing optimizations.*

In general, operating systems—especially the standard operating systems—provide fairly weak capabilities in these areas, making it necessary to acquire third-party products.

Simultaneous Support of Various Isolated Workloads

The last area we will examine is the ability of a system to support multiple different isolated workloads simultaneously. As we have noted, servers can be major investments, so those responsible for them will seek to maximize their usefulness, often by requiring that one server support several different independent workloads.

The advent of both distributed client/server computing and a new generation of more affordable servers has led to a proliferation of choices among servers. Because of this, CIOs (Chief Information Officers) are faced with increasing exploitation costs and looking for solutions that reduce the number of servers deployed. The process of reducing the number of servers is called server consolidation, and can take different forms depending on the approach taken; we will discuss these approaches in Chapter 4.

The requirement for supporting multiple applications simultaneously on a single server (creating what we call a multifunction server), as opposed to a set of dedicated servers, calls for certain properties of the platform. The two key properties are scalability and isolation. Isolation has more than one dimension:

- *Resource allocation.* Obeying rules designed to ensure that no one workload hogs resources and starves the others
- *Failure independence.* The failure of any one workload should have no detrimental effect on any other workload

Resource management in a multifunction server is also called workload management. This implies that the OS must be able to allocate resources across an application set in accordance with a set of rules, provided by the system administrator, which reflect business priorities.

Various solutions have been developed to address this problem, ranging from the concept of virtual machines to that of the logical and flexible partitioning of a system; we will look at these more closely in Chapter 4.

3.2.2 **Operating Systems: a Conclusion**

There is a confrontation, in high end servers, between proprietary systems and UNIX; UNIX is being joined by Linux and Windows.

The proprietary systems have the advantage of vast experience. However, such systems are expensive to develop, and to remain viable they must attract a market sufficiently large to amortize the costs of R&D and support. So vendors with relatively small market sizes will be forced, over time, to move their customer base to some other system (preferably while providing backwards compatibility); this is exacerbated by the fact that the high-end market does not seem to be growing.

The inherent functionality of today's high-end UNIX systems (that is, those offered today by high-end server vendors) renders them fully capable of supporting critical business applications. Rather, the concern with UNIX is its diversity; although all UNIX implementations share a common origin, the various vendors added value through divergent versions, so that both functionalities and interfaces can differ across the available systems. This makes application portability difficult. While there have been explicit attempts at reunification, these have not been successful. The diversity has other consequences, too:

- *Market fragmentation.* Software vendors concentrate their efforts on the UNIX versions with large market share, to the detriment of the others. Since richness of application catalog is an important selection criterion, this makes it harder for the lower-volume vendors to survive.

- *Development cost.* Each manufacturer has to amortize development costs of his own version (absent any cooperation between vendors). This requires the sales of a large number of systems.

When IA-64 was announced, there were many announcements in the UNIX camp regarding alliances and focus on a smaller set of UNIX versions. These announcements were driven by the factors outlined above. The attempts at concentration have not been successful.

The use of Linux as a bottom-end and midrange server is growing. With known improvements—number of processors, cluster technologies, etc.)—Linux will be able to address the high-end market as well.

The development of Windows will continue with improvements in various fields:

> **Linux and Enterprise Servers**
>
> The improvement of characteristics such as scalability (number of processors supported in multiprocessor systems, number of nodes supported in clusters), or even the improvement of the availability of the system, are related to the characteristics of the hardware architecture of the system, for example architecture CC-NUMA (see Chapter 4) and will primarily be implemented by systems manufacturers. RAS (reliability, availability and serviceability) and system management are also areas where Linux needs improvement. When the volume of their UNIX sales is no longer sufficient to support the development of their own UNIX versions, manufacturers are likely to turn to supplying Linux instead, since appropriate UNIX versions are available only from other manufacturers little inclined to provide their software outside an OEM agreement—which would require the small vendor to sell the larger company's hardware. Further, the margins available in OEM arrangements are rarely enough to cause excitement to the smaller vendor.

- *64-bit architecture support*. While originally the announced 64-bit targets were PowerPC, Alpha and IA-64, all but IA-64 have dropped by the wayside.

- *Scalability*. The current limitations in SMP processor count and cluster size will slowly improve; such improvements tend to be expensive and require a long time, since they are based on experience.

- *Robustness*. Microsoft demonstrated with Windows Server 2003 that it was serious about the ability to properly support business-critical applications through provision of improved systems robustness (the RAS characteristics discussed earlier). Its further progress is—like scalability—a long, experience-based task.

We foresee that UNIX systems will gain a place in high-end systems because of their robustness and scalability, characteristics based on the fruits of experience and the willingness by the vendor to invest fairly heavily. UNIX's position in the bottom and midrange has been challenged by Windows and Linux; this will continue within the high-end domain as well.

3.3   Client/Server Applications and Middleware

In this section we do not aim to cover every aspect of client/server (there are several excellent works available which do that), but simply to point out the characteristics of various architecture options and to present the principles behind some of the middleware used to support client/server.

3.3.1   Client/Server Architecture Models and Middleware Components

The widespread replacement of dumb terminals (like VT100) and smarter terminals (such as IBM's field-mode 3270 and its successors) by PCs drove a major shift in application architecture towards the client/server model.

The ascent of the Internet and widespread adoption of company intranets also contributed to this change. A key contributor, from the point of ergonomics, was the swift adoption of HTML as a standard, with an evolution towards XML.

We, now quickly summarize various client/server architecture options along with their characteristics. Those interested in the technologies behind client/server systems may consult works such as [ORF99].

Figure 3.6 illustrates the various architectural options as functionalities move between client and server.

The applications are composed of three major parts: data management, the application itself, and presentation. The differences between the models are simply where each portion of the application is executed—on the client or on the server:

- The *traditional* architecture was used by mainframes and minicomputers—all processing (data, application and presentation) was done on the server, while the terminal's duties were limited to display and data entry with little if processing capability—the 3270, for example, could do limited field validation on input. Of course, a workstation running a terminal emulation program falls into this architectural class.

- The *revamping* architecture represents a situation in which the application—and its programmatic interfaces—remain unchanged, while the workstation is used to provide a new and more friendly user interface.

- The *remote access to database* architecture has the application and the presentation layer running on the workstation, while the database—

Figure 3.7 *Client/Server Architecture options (after Gartner Group) .*

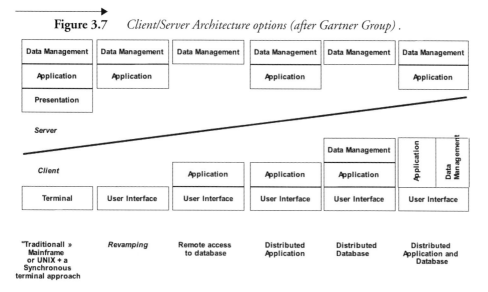

Note: In a Java environment, applications running on the clients are called *applets*, while those running on the server are known as *servlet*

shared between the workstations—runs on the server. The interface between application and database could be either based on access mechanism such as JDBC, ODBC, SQL-CLIS, or, for efficiency, references to procedures stored in the DBMS.

- In the *distributed application* architecture, the application itself is split, part running on the workstation and part on the server; this partitioning has a large effect on system performance and behavior. In general, the two parts of the application will use RPC, RMI, or MOM for communication.

- The *distributed database* architecture has the data distributed between workstation and server. In a transaction-processing environment, this will force the need for two-phase commit protocols, which will reduce performance.

- The *distributed application and database* architecture integrates the approach and characteristics of the two previous architectures. The resulting complexity in design of application and database means that usually this architecture is reserved for use in special circumstances— for example, when data updates need not be synchronized, or when a very rapid response time (at the workstation for actions which do not involve data stored on the server) is the overriding requirement.

The architecture model that seems to have the wind behind it is known as n-tier client/server, with n ≥ 3. In its 3-tier variant, presentation is done on the workstation, with each of application and database executing on separate servers.[11]

The 4-tier version is widespread; it interposes an HTTP support level between user interface and application. This directly supports the need for application access via the Web.

Figure 3.8 is a technical example of a 4-tier client/server architecture.

Figure 3.8
Example of the 4-tier client/server technique

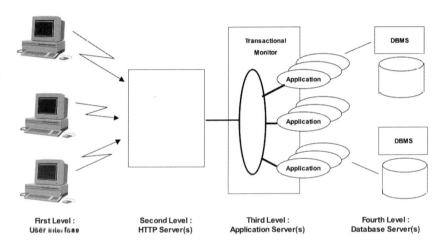

- The first tier consists of the user interface, running on the workstations

- The user requests are handled by the second tier, an HTTP server

- The requests are broken out and transmitted to the application by RPC (Remote Procedure Call), RMI (Remote Method Invocation) or by MOM (Message Oriented Middleware) protocols

- Within the application layer, a transaction monitor handles the user requests; it also optimizes resource usage

- And, finally, all data manipulations are handled by the fourth layer, the DBMS itself

We will discuss the role of the various components in greater detail, but meanwhile we should note that the partitioning shown here is founded on the approach of partitioning by service. Another partitioning, as we will see later, is based around the identification of objects rather than services.

The multi-tier client/server model currently is the best choice for configuration flexibility (the ability to adapt a system to needs) and for evolutionary demands (the ability to adapt a system as needs change). Large software vendors—in particular those selling ERP (Enterprise Resource Planning) solutions have adopted this approach. We will look again at the advantages of the approach later in this work.

For some interesting case studies on 3-tier client/server systems, consult [EDW99].

3.3.2   Components of Client/Server Middleware

We have chosen to discuss a limited number of middleware components, concentrating on just the most important. We are restricting ourselves to them architectural characteristics, and we aim to highlight their impact on server characteristics. For greater detail, the interested reader should consult the reference works on client/server, such as [ORF99].

By middleware we mean the collection of software elements which support the operation of applications—in particular, in a distributed client/server environment—while hiding the specifics of the physical configuration on which the applications are executing.

Figure 3.9 illustrates the various components of middleware.

Although this diagram shows a layer structure, it is not strictly accurate to think of middleware as a layered architecture, because some services interface directly to services not in adjacent layers.

Among the services offered by the operating system itself, we show here process and thread management (used by some middleware), local process communication, and a local file system.

The communications services are built on the operating systems services and are, in the immense majority of cases, TCP/IP services. On these are built network operating systems services—that is, services that make a distributed system feel like a single system to the layers above it. On this level we find RPC (Remote Procedure Call), remote inter-process communications, distributed file services, and so forth. We should comment that, properly done, the distributed file services should allow any user to see all files mounted in the whole of the distributed system (assuming the user has appropriate access rights), and that the file naming should be independent of where the files are; NFS does not, in this sense, qualify as a distributed file system.

Figure 3.9   *Middleware components (source: [MEI99].*

	Internet	Dialogue	Data Access	Transactions	Objects	
Application Services	HTTP S-HTP SSL	HTML, Windows, Applets Java	SAG/CLI, RDA, DRDA, ODBC, JDBC	X/Open (Tuxedo, Encina, CICS 6000,...)	ORB (CORBA, COM+, ...)	● ● ●
Distributed Environment Services	System Administration (SNMP, ..)		Directories (LDAP)	Security (Kerberos) Distributed Time	PVM MPI	● ● ●
Network OS Services	RPC	MOM Message Queues	IPC Remote Inter-Process Communication	Distributed File Systems (NFS, DFS)	● ● ●	
Communication Services			TCP/IP			
Operating System Services	Processes And Threads		IPC Local Inter-Process Communication	Local File Systems	● ● ●	

It is traditional to build, above the various systems that constitute a distributed system, an abstraction which one defines as the network (or distributed) operating system (NOS). The services offered by a NOS are remote procedure call (RPC), a message-based communications service called MOM (Message-Oriented Middleware), a method of remote inter-process communications means, a distributed file system, etc. These services not only provide the illusion of a single system, they also mask any heterogeneities in the lower-level services in the distributed system.

This collection of system and communications services makes it possible to support distributed applications. The services necessary for such applications include:

- A directory service, which makes it possible to abstract away from where resources are situated in the system. That is, the name of an object is independent of where it is resident: if the object moves within the system (perhaps because of a failure of its original host), its name remains unchanged; when a applications refer to it after the move, the directory service locates the object.

- A time service, allowing the various components of a system to have a common time base. This is necessary in some applications—for example, opening markets up at a specified time on widely-distributed sites.

- A security service, allowing authentification and confidentiality (distributed systems are more vulnerable than single systems).

- Communication services between the components of distributed applications, such as PVM (Parallel Virtual Machine) or MPI (Message-Passing Interface). The majority of services offered by DCE are in this level.

We will provide only a short list of applications services:

- Internet-specific services, such as HTTP protocol and its secure version, SHTTP (Secure HTTP), secure sockets, or SSL (Secure Sockets Layer). (We will examine Internet services in greater detail in this section.)

- Man-machine interface support, with elements like HTML, Windows presentation or Java applet technology, which allows the personalization of the dialog

- Distributed database access, using appropriate standards

- Distributed transaction processing (we look at this in greater detail subsequently)

- Services related to distributed objects (also to be covered in greater detail)

Given our focus on server characteristics, we will concentrate on just those elements which seem most relevant:

- Transactional monitors

- Message-oriented middleware (MOM)

- A distributed object model

- Data base access techniques

- A "component-oriented" model for constructing applications

- Technologies used in the construction of Web servers.

3.3.3 Web Servers

With the goal of facilitating Web-based business transactions, the W3C has standardized a number of elements which form a services architecture. Our description is based on [GOT02] and [IBM01].

A Web service is an interface that describes a collection of services accessible over the network by means of XML messages.

The actors, their roles and the operations covered by this architecture are shown in Figure 3.10.

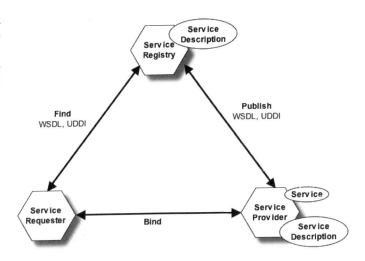

Figure 3.10
*Web services actors,
roles and operations
(source: IBM)*

In the diagram, a service provider has created a service and registered its description with a registration service. This exchange is controlled by a standard called UDDI (Universal Description, Discovery and Integration).

Once the service is registered, the server supporting the registration can respond to users wanting to make reference to the service (*Find*). In response to a request, this server provides to the user both the description of the service in WSDL (Web Service Description Language) and the URL (Uniform Resource Locator), allowing the user to address the service with the appropriate format for its requests (Bind).

A layered architecture, illustrated in Figure 3.11, provides an implementation.

The network layer is the base for this stack. Communication is based on SOAP (Simple Object Access Protocol), which is derived from XML.

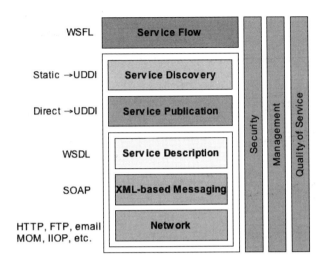

Figure 3.11
*Web services
conceptual stack
(source: IBM)*

The specification of the service which can be invoked by the clients is described in WDSL (Web Services Description Language). This description is in the form of an XML document. These three layers form the basis for Web services and allow interoperability. The higher levels are optional.

Any action that can make an XML document available is called a publication service. The simplest form, called direct publication consists of the service provider communicating the description of the service directly to the requester (for example, by e-mail).

In principle, the discovery of available Web services can be done either during the writing of the applications or dynamically.

It is clear that, with these mechanisms to hand, it is possible to construct new services through compositions of existing services.

The description of different Web services for a domain-specific function can be done using a language such as web services flow language proposed by IBM.

The adoption by the various different portions of the business world of such standards is the key element for the success of e-commerce (particularly for business-to-business commerce).

3.3.4 Transactional Monitors

Let us quickly review the characteristics of transaction-processing applications, as described in the Introduction:

- *Sharing.* The database is shared by the collection of users, for reading and writing

- *Irregular request arrivals.* One cannot predict the individual user requests

- *Repetitive work.* Users call upon a prespecified set of functions, typically a few tens or a few hundreds in number

- *Simple functions.* The majority of these functions are not very complex, typically 10^5 to 10^7 instructions and around 10 I/Os

- *Batch transactions.* Some transactions have as long a duration as traditional batch processing; batch transactions can be differentiated from the vanilla batch work through their preservation of the ACID properties

- *Large number of users.* (human or machine)

- *Intelligent clients.* Workstations, PCs, other systems

- *High availability.* Typically required of a transaction-processing system

- *System recovery.* Data integrity must be automatically assured; recovery is based on the ACID properties

- *Automatic load balancing.* High throughput coupled with guaranteed response times

Transactional monitors were introduced at the end of the 1960s to help solve the problems of supporting transaction processing on mainframes; the problems were processor performance and memory size (in those days, memory was very small and very expensive). At the time, a process-oriented model had been in use but was found to perform inadequately—performance became unacceptable even with a small number of users—and so a new abstraction had to be created, one that was less expensive to manage than a process. Noting that the strong protections assured by the general process model were not needed in this environment, architects constructed the concept of a light process, nowadays called a thread. Then, to manage transactions on a collection of threads, transaction monitors (like CICS on IBM systems, and TDS on Bull systems) were introduced.

Currently available for standard operating systems (UNIX and Windows) there are a number of transaction monitors—such as Microsoft Transaction Server for Windows Server 2003 (MSTS), CICS/6000 from IBM, or UNIKIX from Integris, all offering compatibility with IBM's CISC mainframes and BEA's Tuxedo. In addition, as we shall see, there are transaction monitors tuned for electronic business as well as object-oriented transaction monitors.

The principal functions of a transaction monitor are as follows:

- Thread management, including launching the applications needed to handle user requests (whether users on workstations or requests coming from other systems), controlling their execution and doing load-balancing
- Transaction management (ensuring that the ACID properties are respected) in a context which may be distributed and which can have several database managers involved in transaction execution

In the absence of a transaction monitor, one would allocate a process to each user (or possible user) or create a per-request process as each request arrives. In the former case, the sheer number of processes required could tax even a modern computing system, while the latter has performance problems—the creation and tear-down of a process can require significantly more instructions to execute than a typical transaction requires. A transaction monitor improves efficiency by multiplexing the users, and the applications, onto a number of processes—perhaps a few hundred—that is greatly fewer than the number of users.

Transaction monitors implement a two-phase commit protocol in cooperating with the databases; more details on this appear later.

We will illustrate the operation of a transaction monitor in a distributed system, and then look at its architecture.

X/Open—a group of data-processing vendors now part of the Open Group—has defined a distributed transaction model, as well as the various protocols necessary for the various monitors and database managers to cooperate. In creating the standard, the group participants sought to take account of the needs for interworking and portability, balancing these against the desire to leverage existing work as much as possible. This model is widespread in standard systems, while the proprietary system vendors support these standards in addition to their own private ones (such as IBM's LU 6.2).

Figure 3.12 is inspired by [GRA93], X/Open's DTP (distributed transaction processing) model.

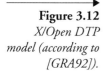

Figure 3.12
*X/Open DTP
model (according to
[GRA92]).*

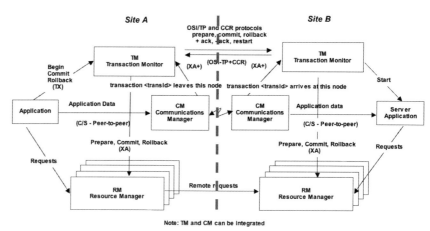

X/Open's Approach

We should emphasize that this approach, which seeks to create a good standard by choosing from existing (or nearly existing) elements, best meets the needs of both users and systems vendors. A standard will, in general, not be adopted until there is at least one implementation (preferably, several compatible implementations) available at a reasonable cost. We all know of very complete standards, with expensive development costs, that went essentially unused.

For simplicity, our example distributed transaction system is shown with just two sites, site A and site B. The key element in the model is the transaction manager (TM). In this model, each data manager (called a resource manager, RM in X/Open terminology) is assumed to have the ability to implement the ACID properties for the resources (i.e., data) it manages.[12]

An application begins a transaction by making a begin call to the local TM. Within the transaction, the application can call upon local resource administrators by means of specific verbs. Since these operations are done within the context of a transaction, the resource administrators make use of two-phase commit.[13] Each such resource administrator must declare itself to the TM, so that the TM knows, when committing (or abandoning) the transaction, just which RMs were involved. The RM-TM interface is known as XA.

When we look at a distributed transaction framework, the application also calls upon services located at other sites, using primative inter-application communications. The exact nature of this interface (shown in the diagram as communication between application and application server) is not central to our discussions, although the key property of the software layer implementing the inter-application communication is that it communicates to the TMs, at the various sites involved in the transaction, that the various actions undertaken on behalf of the application at those sites all form part of the transaction. This allows the collection of TMs to ensure the ACID properties at a global level by coordinating the actions of all the RMs involved in the transaction.

To communicate with the TM, the application has (at the high level at which we present this technology) three verbs:

- *Begin.* The application announces to the transactional monitor that a transaction has just begun and that all the actions on the resources (typically data) must respect the ACID properties.

- *Commit.* The application announces to the transactional monitor that the transaction is complete and should be committed. Two-phase commit must be used in either of the following circumstances:
  - More than one local RM did work on behalf of a transaction (we refer to this as a local two-phase commit)
  - More than one RM, on more than one site, did work on behalf of a transaction. In this case, all RMs involved in the transaction must be involved in the commit.

- *Rollback or Abort.* The application announces to the TM that the transaction must be voided, and thus causes the abandonment of any and all changes effected by all the resource managers involved in the transaction

At the local level, the interface between the transaction monitor and the resource managers is called XA. It too has three verbs:

- *Prepare.* Announce to the various resource managers the beginning of the first phase of two-phase commit: the phase of preparation

- *Commit.* Announce to the various resource managers that it is necessary to commit the modifications which were made within the framework of the transaction

- *Rollback.* Announce to the various resource administrators that the transaction must be cancelled

As shown in Figure 3.12, the communications between two TMs on different sites uses the services of a CM (communications manager). When, within a transaction, an application calls upon the services of another application (the "server" in the figure), the message is relayed by the CM, which informs the local TM that the transaction, identified by the tag <transid>[14] (for transaction identifier), will involve more than one site, and so a two-phase commit should be used.

Symmetrically, the remote CM supporting the application server site will inform its local TM when the request arrives that this site is involved in the execution of transaction <transid>.

Table 3.1   *Interfaces and protocols of transactional models in distributed systems.*

Participating Elements	Protocol or Interface (API)	Organization Involved
Application-TM	TX	X/Open DTP
Application-RM	Specific to RM	RM suppliers
Application-server	client/server type communications	OSI and application suppliers
TM-RM	XA	X/Open DTP
TM-CM	XA+	X/Open DTP
TM-TM	OSI-TP + CCR	OSI

The interface between CM and TM is called XA+.

As indicated in Figure 3.13, the CM can be integrated into the TM.

On a remote site, the TM causes the launching of the application "server" (the primitive start in the figure).

During the commitment or abandonment of a transaction, the coordinating TM (generally, the TM on the site where the transaction began) communicates with the other TMs involved to implement appropriate closure. All TMs communicate with their local RMs to ensure local coordination. The TM-TM communication obeys the OSI-TP standard, similar to IBM's LU 6.2.

Table 3.1 summarizes the various protocols and interfaces, as well as the organizations in charge of their respective definitions.

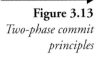

Figure 3.13

Two-phase commit principles

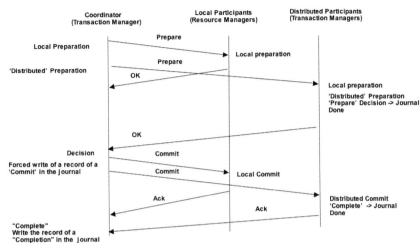

Let us recall that OSI defines protocols and formats (FAP, for format and protocols), needed for interworking. X/Open defines APIs (application programming interfaces), needed for portability.

The client/server communications may take one of three forms:

1.   A transactional RPC (Remote Procedure Call) or RMI (REmote Method Invocation), so-called because the RPC or RMI mechanism (which here is just a CM) must use the XA+ interface to communicate with TM

2.   A peer-to-peer dialog

3.   A message-oriented middleware, or MOM

CCR (Commit, Concurrency Control and Recovery) is an OSI standard. OSI-TP, which is similar to LU6.2, is a standard relating to the interactions allowing two-phase commit.

Figure 3.13 illustrates the general flow of a two-phase commit.

The Commit is made up of two successive phases:

■   preparation

■   commit

Each phase comprises two sub-operations: a local phase and a distributed phase.

We will describe these two phases, under the simplifying assumption that everything works as it should—i.e., no failures occur.

Two-Phase Commit

It should be noted that the validation with two phases makes it possible to ensure the respect of ACID properties in all cases (for example failure of a RM or failure of a site). As we are only illustrating the principle of the validation with two phases, detailed description with the processing of all the cases is beyond the scope of this work. In the same way, the generic organization of a RM, with in particular its journal, will not be described. The interested reader will be able to turn to the reference works previously quoted.

When the coordinating TM is called by the application to commit the transaction (using the commit verb), the TM begins with a local preparation phase while requesting that all the local RMs involved in the transaction prepare to commit. In our scenario, each RM replies to the TM indicating that it is ready to commit ("OK"). If not, the RM indicates its inability to commit, and if that occurs for any RM, the TM can decide to give up on the transaction, which will have the same effects as an abort). In parallel with the local preparation work, TM asks the remote TMs involved in the transaction to prepare to commit. Each of these TMs undertakes a local preparation phase and, when all RMs of a site have responded, the TM records in its journal that it has successfully completed preparation for this phase and then responds to the coordinating TM that it is ready to commit.

When all remote TMs have responded affirmatively, the coordinating TM then records in its journal that it has entered the commit phase.

The coordinating TM then starts the commit operation by first requiring all local RMs to commit; if they do this successfully, each local RM provides an acknowledgment (Ack) back to the coordinating TM. In parallel, it asks the remote TMs involved in the transaction to each undertake local commits; as each TM discovers that its local commit has succeeded, it sends an Ack back to the coordinating TM. When all involved TMs have acknowledged, the coordinating TM notes in its journal the successful completion of the two-phase commit (and thus that the transaction committed).

> **Two-Phase Commit and Performance**
>
> It should be clear that having to resort to a two-phase commit can have a significant (deleterious) effect on performance, and as shown in our example, two-phase commit must be brought into play even in a single system if more than one resource manager is involved.
>
> When sizing a system, it is thus advisable to take into account the performance impact as soon as more than one RM must be involved in a local transaction, and to be even more circumspect with regard to distributed transactions.

To supplement the description of traditional (i.e., not object-oriented) transaction processing with an overview of Tuxedo, a transaction monitor. We discuss the centralized version of Tuxedo.

> **Tuxedo**
>
> Tuxedo was originally developed in AT&T labs on UNIX to meet the needs of telecommunications-related applications. It had two major components: System/T, the transaction monitor itself, and /D, a DBMS. Only System/T was released outside AT&T; it now is owned by BEA. As the name suggests, Tuxedo is a wrapping layered onto a traditional system.

Tuxedo is an example of the architecture of a transaction monitor (centralized case). As shown in Figure 3.14, Tuxedo manages, on one side, relations with clients and, on the other, relations with servers, which are the processes or threads that support the functions (shown as function 1 to function n) available to be called by the clients. The correlation between client requests and available functions is done via the Bulletin Board; Tuxedo uses a directory (BBL) not shown in the diagram to establish the correlations. Service requests are placed in per-function queues, and servers take requests from the queues. Tuxedo therefore integrates a MOM-type queue manager (see later).

The number of processes which may service a queue is parameterizable, and allows load balancing. RM LIB indicates the libraries which maintain the connections with the databases.

Figure 3.15 illustrates the architecture of Tuxedo in the case of a distributed architecture.

Figure 3.14
An example of the architecture of a transaction monitor.

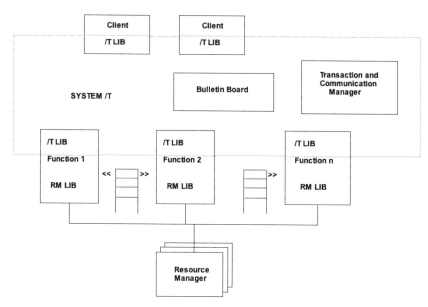

The figure shows the various elements used in the distributed context. The client workstations are managed by the WS Handler process.

The Bulletin Board is based on a directory (BBL) describing, on one hand, the services (applications) available and, on the other hand the message queue associated with each. The queue forms the abstraction of the processes or threads supporting these services. Since a transaction can call upon distributed services, there is also a distributed directory mechanism (DBBL), which makes it possible to forward service requests to the sites providing the requested services.

Figure 3.15
Tuxedo, an example of the architecture of a transaction monitor (distributed case).

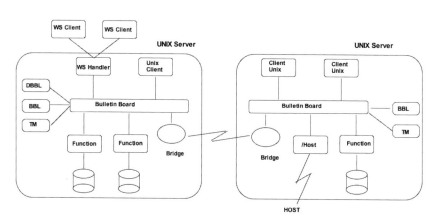

The RMs (in fact, DBMSs) are represented in the figure as disks.

The connection between the sites is carried out by means of a bridge. As we saw with the preceding figure, Tuxedo integrates the functions of TM and RM.

Tuxedo, by means of the function /Host, allows the participation of systems not supporting Tuxedo in distributed transactions, insofar as these systems support the interfaces and protocols of distributed transaction processing. For this to work with a proprietary system, it is necessary in particular that its transaction monitor can be coordinated by an external monitor.

3.3.5 RPC and Message-Oriented Middleware

The rise of the Internet and of electronic commerce, and the widening of the use of servers, has lead to an increased asynchronicity between systems and users. This has made it necessary to introduce architectural means to relax temporal constraints while still guaranteeing data integrity. Electronic commerce has increased the role played by transaction processing in server workloads, and it is important that a message, once delivered to a system, cannot be lost and that it be delivered in a useful form. Thus, one can view the placing of a message in a message queue as itself a form of transaction.

The queues of messages fill this double objective (asynchronism and transactional properties) and are assured of an excellent future with transactional monitors.

The communication between program units can take several forms:

- Peer-to-peer

- Request response, such as the RPC (key aspect of RPC is that the caller awaits the response before continuing (just as with a traditional procedure call; this is a synchronous communication)

- Message-passing, a one-way exchange in which the sender does not await a response before continuing execution; this is an asynchronous communication

- Message queue, or MOM, an asynchronous message-based communication in which messages are held in a queue until processed

- publish and subscribe, a third form of message-based communications in which recipients register with a sender; this allows one sender to service multiple recipients

This section describes RPC, a synchronous communications mechanism. Remote Method Invocation (RMI), is an equivalent synchronous mechanism used in object-oriented environments such as Java. We discuss RMI later, in the section on component-based models.

Figure 3.16 illustrates some of these communications mechanisms.

Figure 3.16
Models of communication between programs.

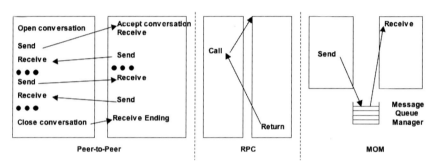

Peer-to-peer communication was introduced when mainframe-based applications needed to cooperate. It is up to the applications concerned to specify the details of their cooperation—for more details, look at the protocols such as IBM's LU 6.2.

The synchronous Remote Procedure Call (RPC) mechanism enables program executing on one machine to call a procedure residing on another machine. Interestingly, the remote procedure could execute on the same machine as the caller, a possibility that is particularly useful during development and testing, since it allows the developer to use one machine rather than several.

With RPC, the caller stops execution until the remote procedure has executed to completion and returned; this is therefore a synchronous mechanism. The use of message-oriented middleware frees us from synchronism—a client deposits his request in a queue and continues execution. We look at first RPC and then MOM, from the point of view of their architectures.

RMI (Remote Method Invocation) is based on mechanisms similar to RPC with, in addition, the notions of object and method. In keeping with the scope of the book, we will only describe RPC and the basics of the distributed model.

3.3.6 **RPC**

The call of remote procedure is based on the concept of call of procedure but authorizes that the called procedure is not on the same site as the procedure.

From the point of view of the programming, the use of the RPC is practically transparent, the only constraint consisting of filing a definition of the heading of the procedures called so that the compilers can carry out certain checks.

An example of the development chain for an application using RPC is illustrated in Figure 3.17.

When creating an RPC-based application, the interface of the server side must be specified to the client side; this is done in a specific language, the Interface Definition Language (IDL). An IDL compiler processes the interface definition and generates the following:

Figure 3.17
Development of an RPC-based application.

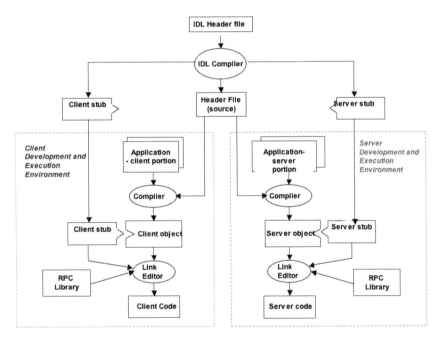

- A header file, describing the server procedure, used in compiling the server portion,

- Two *stubs*, which will be linked into the client and server portions by the link editor. The role of the client stub is to encapsulate the data that will be sent to the server, to effect any data conversions necessary, to call the RPC runtime library, and to await the response from the server. The server stub extracts received arguments, calls the proper server procedure, and then encapsulates the results and calls the RPC runtime library to send the results back to the client.

Figure 3.18 illustrates the operation of an RPC.

Figure 3.18
Operation of an RPC.

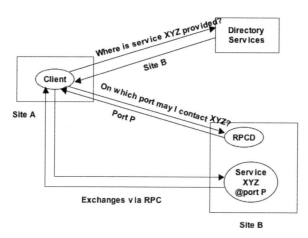

As shown in the diagram, the first step in calling a service—for example, XYZ from an application located at site A is to use Directory Services to discover which site currently supports the service—in our example, site B. Then the second step on site A is to ask that site's RPC Daemon (RPCD) which port to use when communicating with that service—for example, port P. With this knowledge, the client application (via its stub) can communicate with the remote service via RPC. The stubs—along with the runtime libraries—provide all the functionality to call upon directory services and other needed work, including management of errors and subsequent recovery. This vastly simplifies the task of programming RPC-based applications. Note that the diagram does now show the various network layers brought into play in these exchanges.

This scheme allows independence between a service and the location providing that service. When there is redundancy, the backup sites are also made known to Directory Services.

> **Transactional RPC**
>
> In the case of client/server transactional applications founded on RPC, it is advisable to use a transactional RPC (TRPC, for Transactional RPC). In the case of a call of remote procedure using a TRPC, the actions of the procedure called belong to the transaction. In other words, there is an interaction between the TRPC and the transaction monitors of the sites concerned.

3.3.7   MOM: Message-Oriented Middleware

One of the limitations of the RPC is its synchronous nature. MOM allows asynchronism between client and server. It also guarantees data integrity: a message sent will indeed arrive at its recipient. Table 3.2, inspired by [ORF99], compares the characteristics of RPC and MOM.

Table 3.2   *Comparing the characteristics of RPC and MOM.*

Characteristic	MOM	RPC
Metaphor	Mail	Telephones (without answering machine)
Temporal relation between client and server	Asynchronous	Synchronous
Nature of the communications	Queue	Request-answer
Operational state of the server	Not necessary	Mandatory
Load Balancing	Policy of extraction of the messages (priority system)	By means of a transaction monitor
Transaction support	Depends on the product	Depends on the product (required of a transactional RPC)
Message filtering	Possible	No
Performance	Slow if messages are made secure by writing to disk	More effective than MOM, since call parameters are not saved to disk

We will present here, in a very simplified way, MQSeries from IBM, which is one of the most widespread MOMs.

There are several types of files of messages provided by MQSeries:

- Local queues, which reside on the system to which the MOM is connected

- Remote queues, which are managed by the MOM associated with the system where the message queue is managed

- Alias, which decouples the naming of a message queue at program level from the naming at implementation

- Model, which makes it possible to create queues showing certain characteristics

- Rejection, records messages which could not be placed in the destination queue or which the destination server was unable to process (e.g., because of improper message format)

Figure 3.19 illustrates the communication between two remote programs by means of MQSeries.

Figure 3.19
*Communication by
means of
MQSeries.*

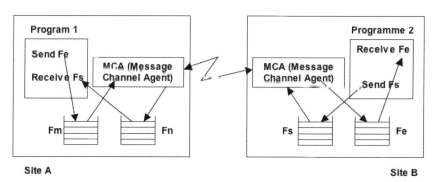

In this example, an application located on site A wishes to communicate with another application. It sends a message to the queue associated with the service requested (let Fe be this queue). It expects to receive the results of its requests on the queue Fs. Since the files Fe and Fs are remote, the MOM makes two local queues, Fm and Fn, correspond to the two remote queues Fe and Fs. The Message Channel Agent (MCA) dispatches the message aimed at the Fn queue towards the destination queue Fe, which the program intended for the processing of the messages (Program 2) reads to withdraw the messages. The results of the processing are deposited in the Fs queue, and the MCA takes care of their routing towards the client and storing them in the Fn queue.

In a way similar to the RPC stubs, the MCA takes responsibility for its operations of data conversion, security, etc.

As with the RPC, the implementation of these operations goes through a number of intermediaries, which mask the underlying complexity and provide basic support for high availability.

There are several possibilities for the activation of the server part of the application. That is to say the server process program is permanently active, and when it scans the queue, or when certain specified conditions on the state of the queue are met, it causes the activation of the execution of the application. These conditions are called *triggers*.

3.3.8 Distributed Object Model

There are two competing models in the object-oriented view of distributed systems—OMG's (Object Management Group, a standardization collective) CORBA model, and Microsoft's DCOM and COM+ products. We will not compare their merits, and choose to present CORBA (despite the diversity of implementations, which have not helped its penetration into the market), with emphasis on its relationship to system architecture. We do not imply at all that CORBA is superior to COM+, nor the contrary. Readers interested in a comparison may refer to [CHU97].

Here we should recall that the concept of an object allows us to concentrate on the properties of an object—that is, what operations (methods) on the object are available to users, with no concern whatsoever as to the internal implementation

Starting from this concept of object, the concept of distributed object was developed. CORBA proposes a distributed object model, illustrated in Figure 3.20.

Let us review the various elements of this model of reference:

- *Application objects.* Specific objects of an application (for example a bill of materials, in a manufacturing application)
- *Common facilities.* A collection of common utilities, such as class (type) catalogs, email, etc.

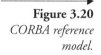

Figure 3.20
CORBA reference model.

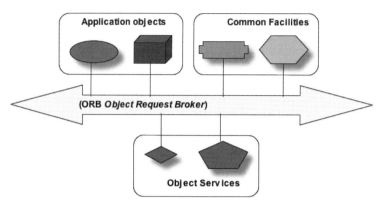

- *Object Services.* A set of optional services which can be used in certain environments. including the creation or the suppression of objects, transaction services, persistence, naming, etc.

- *The object request broker.* A mechanism for the exchange of requests and responses; the ORB makes it possible to send requests to objects, local or distant, regardless of where they are and regardless of their implementation

Figure 3.21 illustrates the exchanges provided by the ORB.

Figure 3.21
Exchanges with the ORB.

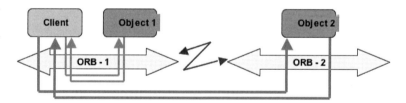

This system example is composed of two ORB implementations, ORB 1 and ORB 2. Using ORB 1, a client can communicate directly with Object 1 via ORB 1, but to talk to Object 2 ORB 1 and ORB 2 must communicate, using the IIOP (Internet Inter-Orb Protocol); i.e., IIOP is bridging the two ORBs.

As with RPC, distributed programs based around CORBA also use an IDL (Interface Definition language).

Figure 3.22 illustrates the way in which clients and objects interact using CORBA (version 2.0).

Figure 3.22
Functional architecture of CORBA.

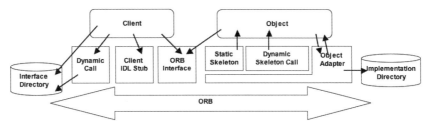

A Client IDL stub is precompiled (using an IDL definition). It represents the object interface to the client—it acts as an agent or proxy for a remote object. Just as with RPC, the stub provides a number of functions including data conversions. Calling the stub is a static call, since the object characteristics are known at program creation time.

There is also a possibility that the application will want to call an object whose characteristics are known only at run time; in this case, the stub call will be a dynamic call. When the application makes the call, the stub will cause the object characteristics to be discovered, using CORBA facilities that allow lookup in an interface directory. The directory is a distributed database which contains the executable definitions of the interfaces.

The ORB interface provides a number of basic services to the client, common to all ORB implementations.

A static skeleton defines the interface through which an object offers its services. They are stubs generated by the compilation of their definition in IDL.

The static skeleton call provides a means, during execution, to ensure the connection between clients and an object. It allows, thanks to the analysis of the request, to determine the object called, to build a request and to address it to the object. In return, it receives the answer which it will delivers to the client.

The object adapter standardizes the interface between the ORB and objects. It provides the execution environment for the objects (activation, deactivation, reference counting, etc.). It records the classes of object that it supports and their instantiations in the implementation directory.

The implementation directory contains the definitions of the supported classes and their instantiations. It also holds state information, which is used in administration, follow-up and audit functions.

In a transactional context, CORBA would be supplemented with a transaction monitor object whose generic name is OTM (for Object Transaction Manager). Its functions are similar to those of a traditional transaction monitor.

3.3.9 Database Access Techniques

The client/server model implies access by applications to remote databases—that is, databases located on another system. Further, there are diverse types of databases to be accessed, the diversity arising from any number of factors, including different decisions being made by different portions of the company, or as a side effect of company mergers; this all implies that it is desirable that access methods for databases are independent of the DBMS's themselves. This is a real problem; although all databases provide SQL as an access method, various vendors have independently extended SQL in different manners compromising portability of applications between DBMS's.

Various approaches have been proposed to meet the need for DBMS-independent access techniques. In this area, as in others, there are examples of scarcely-used or implemented standards, along with proprietary solutions which have the advantage of existing and working but the obvious drawback of instigating captive applications.

The access to a remote database includes the following dimensions: the interface, on the one hand, and FAP (formats and protocols), on the other hand.

As to the interface between applications and a DBMS, two approaches are distinguished:

- Embedded SQL (ESQL), which uses a precompiler to translate SQL commands embedded in the application program; with this approach, calls are fixed at application creation time
- Direct SQL calls (CLI—Call Level Interface), which do not require the application to know at creation time just which DBMS will be used

The work done within the SAG (SQL Access Group) consortium, comprising several DBMS vendors, has resulted in a number of solutions. The first type of solution uses a CLI interface to provide access to a wide variety of DBMS; it is the ODBC (Open DataBase Connectivity) standard proposed by Microsoft.

Figure 3.23 illustrates the ODBC architecture.

ODBC is implemented at the workstation level. For each DBMS to be supported, it is necessary to develop a specific ODBC driver.

The principal difficulty with ODBC is that its specification is controlled by Microsoft and that it keeps changing. There is a similar technique for use in a Java environment, called JDBC, for Java DataBase Connectivity.

A second type of solution implements an open link approach, which converts application SQL commands (whether embedded or CLI) into SQL commands understood by each DBMS. In practice, this requires that the DBMS vendors support a common FAP. There are several competing solutions available of this type, including SAG's RDA (Remote Data

Figure 3.23
ODBC
Architecture

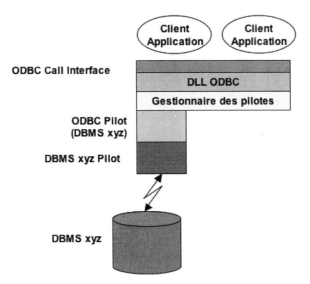

Access), and IBM's DRDA (Distributed Relational Data Access) the latter provides several models for the interaction of the application with database, and also supports two-phase commit.

3.3.10 Enterprise Java Beans—A Component-Oriented Application Model

This section briefly describes Enterprise Java Beans (EJB), a component model for applications offered by Sun. For a detailed description, the reader may refer to more specialized works.

EJB is derived from Java Beans, a software component model and framework for applications; it provides an object-oriented model for the development and deployment of Java applications in a multi-level distributed architecture. The EJB corresponds to the server portion of the application.

The components are generic application parts which can be assembled for the construction of an information system.

The component model of Java Beans is aimed at applet development and does not contain facilities for resource sharing, persistent objects or transaction management.

Figure 3.24 shows the Java technologies used to support EJB in an Internet applications context.

Figure 3.24
EJB Support
Services

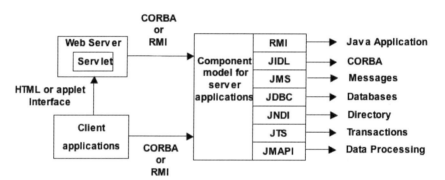

Let us review the various elements of this support:

- RMI (Remote Method Invocation), which we have already introduced, is a means of interacting with a remote object. As with RPC, a Java compiler (RMIC, for RMI compiler) processes the calls and generates the code necessary for communication

- JIDL (Java Interface Definition Language) makes it possible to use the standard CORBA and IIOP interfaces. JIDL empowers communication between applications written in Java and those written in other languages

- JMS (Java Message Service) is an asynchronous communication mechanism, which in fact is just a MOM offering all the guarantees of security to the level of the messages

- JDBC (Java DataBase Connectivity), which provides a uniform access interface to data bases with the help of per-database drivers

- JNDI (Java Naming and Directory Services) is the directory system which makes it possible for applications to locate objects symbolically

- JTS (Java Transaction Service) is a service providing management of distributed transactions for Java. JTS breaks up into three parts:

    - JTS API, a programming interface with which the applications can delimit transactions
    - JTS OTS, which makes it possible to map between the transactional services of CORBA (Object Transaction Service) and the Java language
    - JTS XA, which makes it possible to map the Java language to the resource managers (such as DBMS's) compatible with the XA interface of X/Open's distributed transaction model

- JMAPI (Java Management API) is an interface facilitating the development of business applications

EJB components are executed in the context of a container, which itself is supported by a server

Figure 3.25 illustrates the structure of an EJB container.

Figure 3.25
Structure of an EJB Container

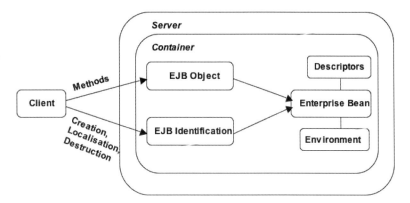

A container encapsulates an EJB and provides a number of services. The operations of creating and destructing an EJB are done using the EJB Identification interface (the Home Interface); naming an EJB is done via the JNDI service. The interface is provided by the Bean's implementor and is an instantiation of the Home Object class, created by the container.

The client-EJB interface is method-based. It is a remote interface, provided by the Bean implementor and comprises the Bean's methods and is unique to a Bean. It is an instantiation of the EJBObject class.

The EJB interface intercepts all calls to the EJB and implements transactions, management of state information, and security in accordance with the definition held in the descriptors associated with the EJB.

The container's management of security and transactions simplifies component programming. If this approach succeeds, it will enable a component marketplace and transform how the industry thinks of and builds applications.

3.3.11 Intranet, Extranet, Internet

The rise of the Internet occasioned a major upheaval in the way systems are used. Prior to the Internet, each system had its own ergonomics and man-machine interface; a user who wanted to use an application or to access data on a particular server had to adopt that system's approach; using services on several different systems was therefore a burden to the user, since each could be different. With the Internet's communications and presentation standards (HTTP and HTML), a much greater degree of transparency was achieved between servers and their users; the industry-wide convergence on TCP/IP as the communications protocol of choice was the first step in this simplification.

The Universal Client

The term *universal client* is even often used to indicate the use of this type of interface, i.e., a client, based on HTML/HTTP, which would be able to access every application, whatever the nature of the server executing them. Many existing applications, in particular on mainframes, can be accessed through the use of a standard browser. When designing a new application, this type of interface is often retained.

To be able to accommodate the new uses and users enabled by the Internet, servers had to support these protocols. In other words, with the rise of the Internet, servers adapted to clients, whereas, in the past, the clients had to adapt to the server.

One can characterize the various Internet variants in the following way:

- *Internet*. Indicates the network upon which applications and information are put available for any public use and with limited security

- *Intranet*. Indicates a network where private applications and information are limited to a "community" (generally a company) and present a high degree of security. Access by people outside the community is not allowed

- *Extranet*. Indicates a network of the type Intranet extended to partners in whom a high degree of confidence is placed Access by people outside the partnership is not allowed. A high degree of security is associated such networks

By May 2004, there were about 786 million Internet users world wide (source: InternetWorldStats.com).

We will not differentiate between Internet, Intranet and Extranet in our description of the technologies used, since the differences are differences between users—employee for an Intranet, employee and partners for an extranet, and everyone in the case of the Internet—not technologies. The user differences give rise to differences in administration and security management, but not at the level of server programming.

The first things that the Internet asks of a server are the properties of scalability and high availability. Scalability, because predicting the number of users in advance is difficult; high availability because in the absence of availability, a customer attempting e-commerce with a site and finding it unavailable will simply go and buy elsewhere—the distance between two electronic shops is just a mouse click.

3.3.12 Basic Technologies Used in Web Servers

As usual, our goal in discussing Web server technologies is to provide an overview, with the aim of allowing the reader to understand the demands placed on server architecture. The reader interested in the technologies *per se* will find many specialized works on the subject.

Figure 3.26, inspired by [ORF99], shows the technical architecture of a Web site in a client/server architecture on three levels with various types of clients.

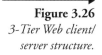

Figure 3.26
*3-Tier Web client/
server structure.*

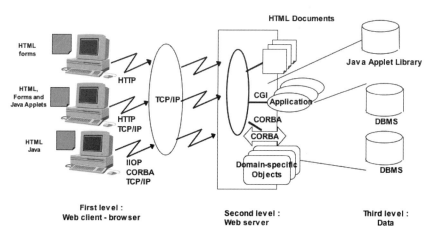

In this illustration, three types of client are shown:

- A basic client who uses HTML with form-filling capability. HTML gives access to various pages, identified by means of the URL (see hereafter). The forms make it possible to activate applications by means of the CGI interface (see hereafter).

- A client using HTML with form-filling capability, along with Java applets. The Java applets are downloaded from the server according to the requests of the workstation. The use of Java makes it possible to personalize the man-machine interface. The portable character of the Java code (examined in Chapter 1) means that the programming of the applet is independent of the type of the workstation used. To execute an applet, it is sufficient that the workstation has a Java execution environment (for example the virtual machine Java- JVM) or a HotJava navigator.

- A client who uses mainly Java applets which interface directly with a universe of CORBA objects.

The dialogue is standard HTML (*HyperText Markup Language*). The user uses a *browser* to access the various pages. The accessible pages are identified by means of a URL (*Uniform Resource Locator*). The Web server responds to the user by sending the required pages.

The dialogue is built on HTTP (HyperText Transport Protocol) which is implemented on top of TCP/IP. HTTP has two fundamental characteristics:

- Character-oriented encodings
- The absence of state (stateless)

The HTTP protocol has a character-based encoding, which simplified its widespread adoption. When data must be transmitted, it is encapsulated.

HTTP is a *stateless* protocol, which means that each request involves the opening of a connection that is closed again after sending the response. HTTP thus generates a substantial processing demand, prejudicial to scalability.

HTTP's statelessness complicates the management of transactions with databases. To mitigate this difficulty, a mechanism makes it possible for the users to fill in forms and deliver requests to applications by the intermediary of an interface called CGI (*Common Gateway Interface*). The parameters provided by the user are sent is identified by a URL. The program, called by the Web server, transmits in return an HTML page.

CGI makes it possible to dynamically generate HTML pages. On the other hand, CGI is not very powerful (interaction with processes supporting the applications, since an application is launched for each request), and there is no management of state. Indeed, because CGI is being "without memory," each action is independent of the previous one, and it is not possible to create a transaction made up of several CGI requests. To circumvent this difficulty, one can use, for example, the technique of *hidden variables*. A hidden variable is a variable placed in an HTML that cannot be seen; to identify the user. Using this identification, the application can manage a context and thus support a concept of transaction.

In a Web context, it is possible to encounter long transactions—that is, transactions which take a long time to be effected—implying a need for asynchronism to which MOM provides a first level of response. But Work Flow[15] techniques seem to offer a better solution to the management of long transactions. Performance considerations lead the designers of such applications to make them operate 'optimistically'; that is to proceed assuming that they will succeed and be committed (but still able to be aborted if need be.)

Some software vendors—for example, Netscape and Microsoft—have proposed interfaces intended to mitigate the difficulties of CGI, particularly the Web-DBMS interface. However, these are proprietary interfaces, whose usage compromises the universal or open character of Internet-related technology.

The final case we are considering is that of the Java applet, which directly interfaces to the domain-specific objects managed by CORBA; that is, in this usage, CORBA replaces HTTP/CGI. The communications between the several ORBs is managed by IIOP, which is always used (in this context) to load applets and HTML pages.

This approach markedly improves both performance and the capability for scalability, compared to a CGI-based approach; it also simply enables transactions.

3.3.13 Script Languages

We must also touch on the important subject of script languages like Perl, Rexx, and TCL. While traditional programming languages are oriented towards the development of programs that manipulate their own data structures, script languages are aimed at integration; they assume the existence of software components and provide a simple means to express their collaboration.

Traditional programming languages integrate—to varying degrees—the notion of *data types*; in scripting languages, this is much less important, with the languages concentrating on ease of expression of inter-component cooperation and on rapid development.

3.3.14 Mobile Code and Data Exchange

With the Internet, disparate systems can be made to cooperate to fulfile the needs of users. Given the diversity of applications, it is not usually possible to equip each Internet-connected computer system with all the applications needed to meet these needs. With Java's portability (byte-code representation) and dynamic loading, it is possible to resolve this problem.

It is usual to associate byte-code program representation uniquely with Java, although in principle compilers for other languages could also generate bytecode and gain the same portability.

The diversity of systems also impacts data exchange, and XML (*eXtended Markup Language*) seems to be stepping forward to fill this gap. XML is a derivative of SGML (*Standard Generalized Markup Language*), a document format description language introduced in 1986. While SGML's usage remained rather limited, another derivative, HTML, has seen much greater success.

XML combines the expressive power of SGML while preserving the attractive characteristics of HTML. XML eases data exchange by accompanying the data with its description; a difficulty arises from the current lack of conventions for data description, making it difficult for different systems to have common interpretations of the data. It is expected that such conventions will be developed, in a manner very similar to what happened with EDI.

3.3.15   Agents

Agent technology can take many forms; we base our description on the approach within the AAA (*Agent Anytime Anywhere*) framework developed by GIE Dyade [DYA00].

The central element of the model is the concept of an agent. The characteristics of agents can be summarized as follows:

- Agents can be executed concurrently (they are active objects)

- Agents have their own state

- Agents do not share memory with the other agents

- Agents communicate and synchronize themselves with the other agents by means of notifications

The notifications (also called events or messages) are typed data structures used for information exchange between agents; notifications are the only means of inter-agent communication.

When an agent receives an event, it carries out a *reaction* appropriate to both the nature of the event and the agent's current state. A reaction is a computation modifying the state of the agent and/or a communication with the other agents.

The event/reaction mechanism is based on a message communications infrastructure (a MOM) that provides both asynchronism and the anonymous nature of the communications (that is, an agent does not know which agents are associated with each event). The concept of *role* makes it possible to dynamically manage the connections between agents and events and to make communication reliable. As part of this management, agents must register (or be registered by a third party) before being able to handle events.

Because of the asynchronous nature of the agent universe, there is no need for all the agents needed for a particular set of actions to be ready at the same time; the MOM will arrange for message routing and delivery as agents become available. This is particularly important for a distributed system, since it eases recovery after failure or unavailability.

In order to ensure recovery, the agents are equipped with the following properties:

- *Atomicity,* which means that the reaction of an agent is carried out in its totality or at all

- *Persistence,* which means that the state of agent is not limited by the execution of the agent; the state of the agent persists after the completion of execution or the failure of the system which supports it

- *Flexibility,* which means that a third party, insofar as it has the corresponding rights, has the ability to change the attributes and the roles of agents without needing to change the programming of the agents

The first two properties are similar to two of the properties which characterize transaction processing—the A and the D of ACID.

With flexibility, it is possible to dynamically change the version of selected agent; to change the structure of an application; or indeed to change the systems that support agent execution.

Communication is central to the agent model since it constitutes the only means of exchange. It has the following properties:

- *Asynchronism,* which means that the messages are delivered only when the agents are ready to be executed;

- *Reliability,* which means that the messages will be delivered even in the event of failure of the network and/or the systems. This is a MOM characteristic which implies that recovery mechanisms are invoked to ensure the delivery of messages to their destinations as soon as the network or the system supporting a destination agent is operational again.

- *Causal ordering,* which means that the events will be delivered to their destinations in chronological order. To illustrate this property, let us consider an agent A1 sending an event E1 to the agents A2 and A3.

The reaction of A2 causes a E2 event which is sent to A3. The respect of this property implies that A3 will receive E1 before E2.

Just how to program agents is outside the scope of this book. The technology has been used in some number of projects, where it proved particularly useful in knitting together existing applications or allowing new applications to interface with existing code.

A rather different approach to agent technology was taken by Apple's Data Detectors [NAR98], which are based upon using grammar to describe the syntax of data. This approach to programming is both simple and effective, and could be used with benefit whenever some processing can be tied straightforwardly to the syntax of input data.[16]

3.4 Security

Security is an important dimension for servers. While a detailed analysis of security would be beyond the scope of this work, we will present the key concepts, review some technologies used in the implementation of solutions, and provide a methodological approach to security implementation. The reader interested in more details may refer to more specialized works.

Before launching into the larger discussion, we will touch upon the smart card, a flexible, economical, secure, and extensible tool (this latter being especially true of cards containing Java technology, which facilitates personalization). Personalization is an important feature for the widespread acceptance of low-cost Internet access devices (so-called Internet appliances or information appliances), since it is appropriate for the appliance to adapt to the user and not the reverse.

3.4.1 Security Concepts

Computer security may be defined [MEI98] as the collection of measurements, methods, and tools charged with protecting the resources (information, functionality, or components) of an information system to guarantee the three attributes of security (the AIC attributes):

- *Availability.* The property of an information system of being accessible and usable upon the request of an authorized entity

- *Integrity.* The property of ensuring that data and components are not altered except by authorized entities within preset management rules

- *Confidentiality.* The property that data is unavailable and undisclosed except to authorized individuals, entities, or processes

Figure 3.27 presents the semantic network covering the various concepts involved in security.

We will explore this network quickly. A system is composed of resources (information, functions, components). Each one of these resources can be characterized by sensitivity—measurement of the importance attached to the protection of the aforementioned resource.

The resources can present vulnerabilities, i.e., risks of calling into question the AIC criteria (or availability, integrity, and confidentiality) for the aforementioned resource.

The vulnerabilities, which are weaknesses or faults of the system, are placed *vis-a-vis* threats.

Figure 3.27 *Concepts of computer security (source. [MEI98].*

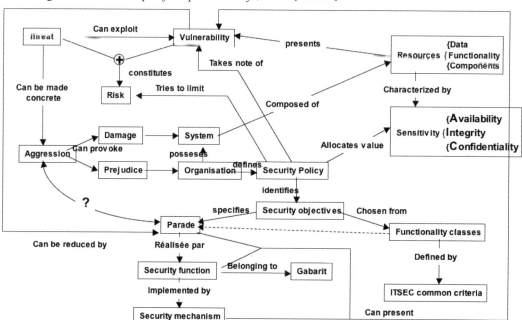

Examples of Threats

Drawn from a concrete analysis made within the framework of a financial institution a list of threats:

- *Passive listening.* Listens to the network, captures data and passwords (means: network espionage)

- *Identity substitution.* Allows a user to inherit the visibility of resources and corresponding access rights of another user (means: falsification of IP address—*IP spoofing*)

- *Replay.* Recording of a sequence of events or commands to replay them at another time

- *Integrity attack.* Modification of the contents of exchanged information

- *Diversion of message to another user* (means: manipulation of network equipment, such as routers, which were not protected)

- *Concealed gate, Trojan horse.* Unauthorized processing under the cover of the execution of an authorized program (means: program substitution)

- *Virus.* Programs which are grafted on files to modify or even destroy files

- *Repudiation.* People or entities deny having taken part in a communication and to have exchanged certain messages (means: the transactions are not accompanied by information allowing control a *posteriori*)

A vulnerability, and the threats that can be associated with it, constitutes a risk. A company's security policy has the goal of limiting the risks threatening security.

When a threat is made concrete, it is an attack (in our discussion, we will ignore whether the attack is intentional or not). Damage (loss of files, outage of a system) is the consequence of an attack at a system level. An attack can cause other losses—for example, trading losses—to the organization owning the system. It is the organization's responsibility to construct a security policy that, aware of the vulnerabilities presented by the resources which it to protect, aims to reduce the risks. From the definition of security policy arise security objectives that specify the *parades* of responses intended to respond to the threats. The parades are implemented by security functions, which themselves make use of other mechanisms (such as encryption).

In Europe, the safety criteria are defined by ITSEC (Information Technology Security Evaluation Criteria) which follow the American TCSEC (Trusted Computer System Evaluation Criteria).

ITSEC allows us to classify a system, from the aspect of security, into one of seven levels (E0 to E6), as a result of positioning the system with respect to the following eight security functions [MEI98]:

- Identification and authorization, allowing the system to establish and verify an identity

- Access control to objects, data, resources and information flows

- Imputability, the recording of the exercise of security-related rights

- Audit capability, allowing detection and analysis of events could represent an threat to the system

- Re-use of objects, which allows control of the re-use of information support

- Fidelity, which guarantees that objects have not been modified except by authorized entities

- Service continuity, which guarantees access to a resource by authorized entities

- Data exchange done in a manner that guarantees their security while being transmitted

We should also note that for some applications, particularly those used in e-commerce, it is best to add to these dimensions the one of non-repudiation, which makes it possible to ensure that neither the receiver nor the transmitter of a message can dispute the veracity of a message nor of its sending and receiving.

Computer security is evaluated by looking at two elements: the target system itself, and the security goals for the system.

The security goals comprise:

- The system security policy

- A specification of the security functions

- A definition of the necessary security mechanisms

- The minimum level of resistance of those mechanisms

- The level of evaluation desired

Evaluation of the security goals includes

- Checking conformity (that the security functions meet requirements). This involves checking that the implementation of the function and the security mechanisms is correct with respect to the security objectives

- Checking the effectiveness of the system security. This involves checking the adequacy of the mechanisms of the target system with respect to the stated security objectives

How well the system meets requirements can be expressed in the form of criteria related to the degree of development of the system as shown in Table 3.3, which enumerates the elements which must be provided to the organization in charge of the evaluation

Table 3.3   *Conformity criteria by development level (Source [MEI98]) .*

	Specification	General Design	Detailed Design	Implementation
E1	Provide security target and objectives	Informal architecture description		Elements of proof of operational tests
E2			Informal detailed design description	Elements of proof of functional tests
E3				Supply of hardware diagrams and source code

Table 3.3   *Conformity criteria by development level (Source [MEI98]) (continued).*

	Specification	General Design	Detailed Design	Implementation
E4	semi-formal functional specification model of security policy	semi-formal architecture description	semi-formal detailed design	
E5				tight alignment with design
E6	formal specification of the security functions	formal architecture description		

In practice, since security has multiple dimensions, a hierarchical classification is not really applicable, and comparisons are difficult. Initial work on security led to the hierarchical classification scheme embodied in the US DoD (Department of Defense) Orange Book.

In the Common Criteria, (the result of a convergence of the American and European criteria), the notion of a profile has been given prominence; this allows one to establish a security hierarchy. Two concepts are distinguished:

- *The security target* is the object of the evaluation, being determined by the desired security objectives for a system and a given environment

- *The security profile* make sit possible to define a hierarchy of security levels, but only within a given application domain; thus, does not provide a general hierarchical classification (however, for any given field one can establish the DoD classification)

3.4.2 Some Security Technologies

We now will review some of the technologies used in the implementation of security.

> **Back Doors**
>
> It seems worthwhile to mention that some technologies suggested in the security field provide a back door, which allows spying on the systems on which it is installed. For this reason, some experts recommend the use of only "open source" software in security applications—that is, software whose source code is available and for which it is easy to make sure that it does not contain a back door. In the same way, one also recommends the greatest prudence in downloading software which could contain undesirable elements such as back doors or viruses.

One of the significant vulnerabilities of the information systems comes from their opening on the networks. The rise of Internet did nothing but increase this risk.

To cure it, two *firewall* techniques are proposed:

- Firewalls with packet filtering at the IP level
- Application firewalls, which are based on the *proxy* technique

The packet-filtering firewalls accept or reject packets based on the packet source or destination IP addresses and the port numbers used, with tables describing acceptable values. For this to be really effective, the firewalls need to have an understanding of user and application; however, it is possible, using rather complicated methods, to firewall at a higher level by inspecting the IP messages. This is the approach taken by the *Stateful Inspection* technology deployed by Checkpoint.

The application firewalls implement a very small number of rather simple applications, *proxies*, which are made secure. For a given proxy, one can specify a security policy that takes account of users rights, the context of the application, and so forth. For a given function, such as email, only the address of the proxy concerned is available outside the security barrier. It is this proxy which handles exchanges with the real users inside the corporate network. Application filters can only act as agents to switch messages to the appropriate proxy. Proxies often have a caching function in addition to security; when, for example, a proxy sees a request for a Web page, it will look within its cache to determine whether or not the page is available locally before sending a request out to the external network.

The fire walls write to journals, making it possible to supervise and audit. In fact, the two firewall techniques are complementary, with the filtering firewall discarding messages as appropriate.

Figure 3.28 illustrates a possible business information system configuration protected by means of the two firewall techniques.

This system has three firewalls: two filtering firewalls (one external, one internal) and an application firewall. When a threat is detected, either on the internal network or externally, the appropriate filtering firewall blocks traffic while the threat remains. The various Internet-related servers are connected to the applications firewall; this sub-network constitutes what has been called a demilitarized zone separate from the corporate network; any incidents occurring there will not propagate to the intranet (although they may affect the ability of the company to make useof the Internet). In addition, one may buy products that can be connected to the network to identify attack scenarios.

We will now take a look at some other technologies implemented in the field of security [WER99]:

- *Encryption* allows one to transmit data encoded in a manner which is impossible to understand without some extra information (the key).

Figure 3.28
Business information system with firewalls.

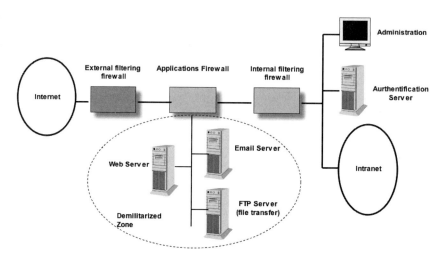

This technique enables information to be kept confidential to an extent depending upon the encryption techniques employed.

- *Certification* provides proof that a user is indeed the originator of a message; it is the electronic equivalent of a signature.

- *Authentification* allows each participant in an exchange to be assured that the others are who they claim to be.

For encryption, there are two major approaches: private key and public key, which we will cover briefly.

In the private key approach, the same key is used by transmitter to encode the message and by the receiver to decode it. Thus, the participants must agree on the value of the key before beginning communication, which in general involves communicating the value by some means other than using the network. The DES (Data Encryption Standard) is widely used; based on keys of 56 or 128 bits in length, it is powerful, but its use is limited because of the problems of securely communicating the key value.

In the public key approach, different keys are used for encoding and decoding. The key used to encode the message is the public key of the intended recipient—that is, that key can be known to everybody and is indeed listed in appropriate directories, while the key used to decode the message is a private key belonging to the recipient. Using this scheme, anyone knowing the pubic key of a correspondent can send a secure message.

It is also possible to run this backwards when the recipient knows who is sending the message (and therefore discover his public key)—then the sender can encode with his private key and the recipient decode with the sender's public key. Most systems support both approaches, that is:

$$D(K_{private}, C(K_{public}, M)) = M$$
$$D(K_{public}, C(K_{private}, M)) = M$$

C indicates the encryption function, and D the deciphering function; is the message.

Figure 3.29 illustrates how public key encryption operates.

The algorithm usually used to implement public-key encryption is called RSA (after the initials of its inventors, R. L. Rivest, A. Shamir and L Adelman). RSA is 100 to 1000 times slower than private key encryption, and this limits its use (today) to the encryption of short messages. Thus it is

Figure 3.29
Public Key Encryption

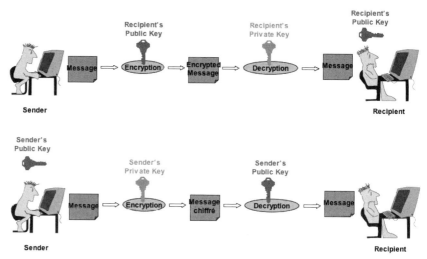

widely used for authentication and signatures. The use of algorithms other than RSA is spreading—Diffie-Helmans, DSA, SHA, for example—because these others do not require payment for use.

Public key encryption (given that the property $D(K_{public}, C(K_{private}, M)) = M$ is true) supports electronic signatures: the message sender computes a signature for the message by hashing it and then encrypts the hash value with its private key. The recipient can then check, by applying the same hashing function to the received and decrypted message, that the received signature is the same as the transmitted one.

One of the major problems posed by the implementation of encryption systems is key management:

- For private key systems, is required a completely-trusted third party to construct the private key and communicate it to the parties.

- For public key systems, the greatest weakness is the potential falsification of a user's public key. It is therefore advisable to be able to check a user's public key.

The public key certificate technique provides a safe key distribution mechanism. The principle behind this is that the message contents (the message being the key to be distributed) are signed by the sender. The message contains:

- The name of the user and his public key

- Additional information, such as the retention period, a unique number identifying the sender, the algorithm used to create the key, and the name of the sender

Public Key Infrastructure (PKI) is an ISO standard (X.509) which allows (*inter alia*) the distribution and management of public key certificates. In PKI, one has recourse to trusted third parties (Certificate Authorities, or CAs) who alone are allowed to issue certificates. To provide scalability, CAs are constructed hierarchically, with the main CA as the root of a tree. Each CA signs certificates for users and for the CAs beneath them in the tree. Thus, two correspondents wishing to communicate must obtain the certificate of the first common CA in the tree. SSL (Secure Sockets Layer) uses X.509 and RSA.

Kerberos,[17] which was developed within the Athena project at MIT, provides a means for authentification in a distributed environment. Kerberos (version 5) is widely deployed, for example as the security infrastructure within Windows. As regards encryption, Kerberos uses the DES (private key) or its extensions and is based on the following entities:

- *Client.* Represents a user or a client application

- *Resource.* An entity (or server) that wishes to make sure that its client is legitimate (i.e., it is indeed that which it claims to be)

- *Key Distribution Center (KDC).* Central trusted entity that knows the totality of the keys (clients and resources)

Clients and resources (servers) use, for their dialogue, shared keys (private) built by the KDC. With each connection, a client and a resource must obtain a key from the KDC.

Figure 3.30 illustrates, with a simplified example of authentification of a client with respect to a resource, the principle of operation of Kerberos [PUJ99].

A client desiring a service requests it from the resource, which sends him a check ticket. The Ticket Granting Ticket (TGT) is provided by the KDC, and contains information such as a session key, the user name, and an indication of a time after which the ticket is no longer valid. This message is

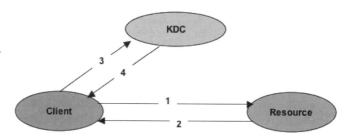

Figure 3.30
*Kerberos example
of principle of
operation.*

encrypted with a key unknown to the client (it is shared by resource and KDC).

To authenticate himself, the client sends the ticket to the KDC, which deciphers it, extracts the session key and deciphers the name of the resource using this key. The KDC checks a checksum to ensure that the same key was used to encrypt and decrypt.

The limited validity time makes it possible to prevent an intruder who has listened to the conversation and recorded it from replaying the conversation.

The client may also ask that the resource authenticates itself; this provides a symmetrical scenario.

To implement security in an application, two interfaces are available:

- SSL (Secure Sockets Layer), a security layer between sockets and TCP/IP, and therefore transparent to an application. SSL supports both encryption and authentication, and is based on the use of public keys.

- S-HTTP (Secure HTTP), located above the communications stacks. Parties use normal HTTP to negotiate the level of security. In addition to RSA-based encryption, S-HTTP allows client and server authentication, as well as supporting the ability to check the servers security certificates and signature.

SSL and S-HTTP are complementary; their joint use makes it possible to reinforce security.

3.4.3 **Methodological Step-by-Step Implementation of Security**

Figure 3.31, inspired by [MEI98], illustrates a methodological step-by-step approach to the implementation of security.

The steps suggested includes three principal phases:

- An analysis phase

- A design phase (which also includes some implementation, not shown for simplicity)

- A deployment and maintenance phase, which allows experience to be used to adapt and change the system (i.e., feedback-driven change)

In the analysis phase, it is first necessary to specify the security target (that is, what elements are to be covered by the project and—equally important—which are not). The sensitive elements are identified and—for each such element—the AIC criteria (Availability, Integrity and Confidentiality) as well as the risks facing the system are identified. That is, the

Figure 3.31
Step-by-step security.

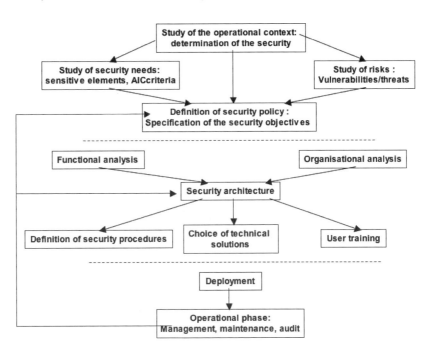

study aims to identify and evaluate the threats to and potential vulnerabilities of the system. From this analysis, it is possible to identify for each risk the likelihood of occurrence and the possible consequences, this making it possible to proportion the security effort to respond to a risk in reasonable proportion to the potential consequences of the risk's occurrence.

A required output from this stage of the analysis is a definition of the security policy for the target system. Involving users (or user representatives) in this phase is extremely important.

After analysis, the design phase can begin. This phase consists of defining a security architecture based on a functional analysis (looking at the sensitivity of the elements to be secured and the security system functions) and an organizational analysis (looking at critical tasks, users, manner of use). The implementation of the selected architecture is also part of this phase: implementation means the operational definition of security procedures, choice of technology components (seeking to avoid inventing what already exists, has been tested, and is already a *de facto* marketplace standard) and user training.

The system is then deployed. It is likely that operational experience will lead to suggested modifications to the security system. The same steps can be followed again, changing details as appropriate in the light of the new desires or evidence.

3.5   Systems Administration

With the rise of e-commerce and inter-company communications, it has become increasingly critical that information systems continue to operate correctly. Quality of service depends—at least to some extent—on quality of systems administration. The challenge and importance of systems administration is increased by the trend to distributed systems, networks, and geographic distribution (not necessarily just within a company, but perhaps caused by a network of partners). The heterogeneity of systems only adds to the complexity of the problem.

Systems administration is and should be considered of strategic importance to companies, for whom it is important not to underestimate the costs and manpower needed to manage the systems so that they perform as required to meet business needs.

Perhaps unfortunately, there are no standards covering systems administration. This results in intense competition between vendors' various products; we will not cover in detail the available offers, but will limit ourselves to covering the functions that any solution should offer, by describing a basic technology on which it is possible to build appropriate systems administration solutions. The material in this section is inspired by [ZAM99].

System administration covers several fields:

- Management of users and their rights with respect to resources and applications
- Management of equipment, work groups, and their rights
- Administration of databases
- Management of the equipment base and associated resources, software in particular, from the point of purchase to their destruction or sale
- Incident management
- Monitoring, optimization, and automation of system usage, in particular for batch processing
- Monitoring, optimization, and automation of the use of networks
- Management workstation (i.e, a single workstation to manage all systems, local and remote), definition of usage scenarios and reconfiguration (in general through the use of scripts)
- Automatic management of backups and restores
- Measurement of quality of service (QoS, publishing reports on QoS, improvement of QoS, etc.)

As shown by this list, systems administration covers several quite different fields of expertise and requires, as soon as the systems involved pass some critical size, the cooperation of several different skills.

One of the factors making system administration complex is the great diversity of the players involved, from systems platform providers, through vendors of applications packages, to the providers of Internet access.

Since quality of service is a major objective of systems administration (the other key objective being cost reduction), it is helpful to define both objectives for quality of service and the associated metrics[18] and the means of collecting them.

Thus, systems administration implies the installation of statistical tools and the generation of associated management reports covering:

- Detection of abnormal operation

- Breakdown prevention—such prevention is based upon the selection of important indicators together with threshold monitoring; an example is when the frequency of errors detected and corrected via main memory's ECC hardware surpasses a predefined threshold. Such a sign is strongly indicative of an incipient failure, perhaps caused by aging, and is a strong signal to replace the erring component before catastrophic failure.

- Contributions to performance optimization

- Capacity Planning—which we will examine in Chapter 7

- Expenditure forecasting

A key support function in an information system is the establishment of a Help Desk, or assistance service, whose role is to provide users with help in solving the problems they may encounter in their work. Installing this service and properly sizing and resourcing it (for example, with the construction of a database of known problems and their associated cures) is the responsibility of systems administration.

From the perspective of systems architecture, the simplest administration solutions are based on the use of the SNMP (*Simple Network Management Protocol*) protocol. SNMP was developed for the management of TCP/IP networks, and allows remote administration of systems. Since SNMP has some limitations, a new version—SNMPv2—was introduced in 1992 and improved on SNMP in some dimensions.

Despite these issues, SNMP is widespread.

SNMP makes it possible to manage arbitrary resources; these can be, for example, network equipment, applications, or servers. Each resource needing management is a *managed object* and has a database—the MIB (Management Information Base) associated with it. A MIB has a tree structure and contains a description of the object with which it is associated, as well as the state of that object. The data structure of the MIB is described by SMI (Structure of Management Information). Each MIB also has an associated agent to manage it.

Figure 3.32 illustrates the principle of operation of SNMP.

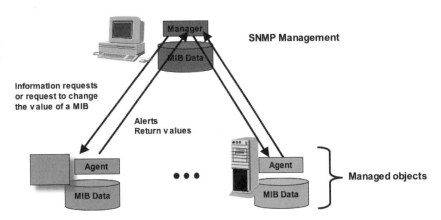

Figure 3.32
Principle of operation of SNMP

As shown by the diagram, the SNMP Manager dialogues with the object agents to obtain or modify specified values of variables in the MIB. Setting values in the MIB, and the associated interpretation made by the agent, causes changes to the managed object.

In the event of an abnormal situation, the agent of a managed object can inform the manager by means of an alarm signal.

Any managed object must have local memory and processing resources.

On the basis of this rather simple protocol systems administration products are built.

3.6 Software Evolution

In this section we look at issues related to software and attempt to draw conclusions.

3.6.1 Economic Model

The size of software continues to grow, matched by a corresponding increase in complexity; as one indicator, Table 3.4 shows the numbers quoted by [MOO99] for the number of lines of code in various operating systems.

Table 3.4   *Number of lines of code in various operating systems (Source: [MOO99]).*

Operating system	Estimate of the Number of Lines of Code (million of lines)
Windows 3.11	3
Windows 95	14
Windows 98	18
Windows NT 4.0	16.5
Windows 2000	35
OS/2	2
Netware 5.0	10
UNIX (average)	12
Linux	5 to 6 (still growing)
OS/400 (v4.r3)	40
MVS (OS 390 and extensions)	9 to 18

These figures must be read with caution, since they can be counting lines for very different creatures. As an example, the lines of code for Windows 2000 undoubtedly include a substantial amount of code for the graphical user interface, functionality absent from MVS. The OS/400 numbers probably include a complete industrial-strength DBMS.

The development and, even more, the support of such complex software constitutes a real gamble for the industry; today's approach is to seek to pay for the costs through very large sales volumes. In this regard, it is interesting to consider two propositions offered by Jim Gray (we have edited the words somewhat). Given that developing an average piece of this sort of software is on the order of 10 million dollars, his two propositions are:

1.   For a vendor of moderate volumes: never develop any software which is expected to sell less than 100,000 copies; given a price/development cost ratio of 10:1, this means the software must be sold for $1,000.

2.   For a high-volume vendor: never develop any software which is expected to sell less than 1,000,000 copies;[19] given a price/

Some comments on these figures:

We must first remark that it is easy to reach the example $10 million development cost with software that is not particularly complex. Assume that a software engineer costs about $150,000 a year (a reasonable number for the US in 2002); then $10 million is a year's work for just 67 engineers. The productivity of the team varies wildly depending on the complexity of the product, individual skills mix, size of the team and so on; so without doing justice to the work on this subject in [PRI98], and simply assuming that annual output is 2,000 lines of code, we can see that the $10 million buys us just about 133,000 lines of code. To set perspective, a version of Word for Windows in 1991 was around 326,000 lines of code.

Most computer companies spend about 10 percent of their revenues on R&D (this ratio varies, being greater for software companies and markedly lower for PC manufacturers, for example). The remaining 90 percent covers cost of administration, cost of sales, cost of support, benefits, taxes, and any profit. Different ratios would not change the overall picture much.

development cost ratio of 10:1, this means the software must be sold for $100.

There is of course something deliberately provocative in Gray's propositions, but that does not alter the fact that high volumes are the most obvious way of amortizing costs. It is true that well-chosen niche strategies can keep much smaller players in the game, but notably lucrative niches tend to attract unwelcome attention from the bigger players.

While this shows industry specialization, it is yet another example of industry concentration. One example is the reduction in the number of commercially-interesting UNIX versions; another is the growing interest in Linux.

3.6.2 Software Development

Software development has long been subject to successive waves of fashion (whimsy might be an even better term). Each new fashion pushed a technique, concept or approach (sometimes with some quantifiable demonstration of usefulness, but always within the context of a small-scale experiment) and was generally presented as a panacea. Each fashion promised to solve the

---

Amortizing Costs and Free Software

In this discussion, recall that free software such as Linux has a different dynamic, being characterized by benevolence in its supply and the fact that development costs are not directly charged to users. However, it would be wrong to suppose that this means that such software costs nothing to develop; rather the costs are hidden, with the software writers using their personal time, or using otherwise (supposedly) idle time at a full-time job. It should be also mentioned that some companies seem to be willing to play the game by offering their own developments to the community. However, such companies are tempted to retain some added value for themselves (along with the associated competitive advantage).

---

whole problem, but in fact addressed just one portion thereof. And very often, a new fashion swept the world even before the weaknesses of the preceding piece of magic had been exposed through usage.

We will not, therefore, propose a new miracle solution, but will simply look at one possible way to reduce development time and cost for software.

The client/server model imposes a structure on software that makes it possible to divide an application up into three parts: the presentation software (the user interface), the logic of the application, and data management (which, to all intents and purposes theses days corresponds to the relational DBMS, or more basic data managers such as indexed sequential data managers). This structure means that the three components can have their own independent evolutionary paths and rates, as long as the interfaces are maintained. Although the market has not yet settled on a choice, middleware technologies such as CORBA, COM+, J2EE, MOM, and so on also drive similar structures into the application.

In practice, the implementation of the presentation and data management portions are constrained by the use of products such as Windows and the DBMS. Thus, the application logic offers the most opportunity for freedom to the designer, although the use of configurable integrated software packages (ERPs, for *Enterprise Resource Planning*) in place of developing a new application is becoming more widespread.

An approach coming into use today involves constructing applications by integrating software components, based upon a hope that the software industry will evolve to the point of supplying standard components which may be composed as needed to address specific application needs. Such components are sometimes called COTS (*Components Off The Shelf*). Since mainstream publishers charge for their products and wish their IP (intellectual property) to be well-protected, such components would be delivered in a binary, rather than source code, form, and could therefore only be configurable through parameter settings.

This approach is one instance of IP reuse; that is, when implementing software for a project, each module is designed with the intent that it can later be used in other applications, thereby simplifying the construction of and reducing the cost and time to market of new applications.

One issue of *IEEE Computer* [IEE98] was devoted to this subject.

A key issue with this approach is to be able to ensure (at reasonable cost) that the system obtained by composing or integrating the modules meets its functionality, performance, and availability goals.

The problems that arise with such an approach include:

- The conformity of the components with their specifications
- Existence of emergent and immergent properties
- Recovery procedures upon failure
- Version synchronization issues among a collection of components
- Dependence on the various providers
- Difficulty in substituting one component for another

We look at these points in turn.

How well the various **components conform to their specifications** is a fundamental issue driving the ability of the overall application to meet its specification. Since one would expect that such components are supplied by third-party vendors, it would seem necessary to have rigorous quality control on the components purchased. This is a recurring cost, since it must be reapplied to new versions, and so must be factored in to the lifecycle cost of the total solution.

Constructing a systems as a composition of components (called subsystems in the immediately-following text) can reveal **emergent properties**. The principle of integration posited in [MEI98] is: "For a decomposition using given subsystems, the overall properties of the system result from the conjunction of the properties of its subsystems, along with the characteristics of the interconnecting network. We call *emergent properties* those properties of the total system which do not arise simply from the properties of the subsystems, and which therefore appear to emerge from the network. The term *immergent properties* is also sometimes used to describe properties of the subsystems which are not found as properties of the system, but are lost or destroyed by the network."

Thus the quality of the overall system's operation can also be very dependent on the quality of the overall system validation, and cannot be guaranteed by simply validating the components one by one.

What can be done for **failure recovery** depends on the characteristics of the components; two situations allow recovery:

- Stateless subsystems
- Transactional subsystems which support a two-phase commit

In the absence of one of these, it is impossible—from outside a component—to make any assumptions about the state of resources managed by the component, and thus to effect a useful recovery.

The problem of **version synchronization** arises because each component has its own life cycle, and coming from multiple vendors with their own delivery rates for new versions, it is most unlikely that the cycles will remain in phase across a collection of components just as happens with bug fixes. The process might be simpler were the components all to come from one source.

There are two possible course of action:

- To live in a permanent state of integration, qualification and version change
- To accept new versions only at controlled intervals—perhaps annually—and thereby accept bugs and functionality issues

Using software components, rather than writing one's own application, means that one is **dependent on an external vendor**; the issue becomes more critical when an application must integrate components from multiple vendors.[20]

Something that would help manage the risks in this situation would be if, for any given component, there were several vendors offering plug-and-play equivalents, allowing the **substitution** of components when necessary (failure of a vendor, unacceptable quality or functionality, and do on). Substitution, however, seems a remote possibility in the absence of standardization, unless it were possible to encapsulate the provided components to create new interfaces (and perhaps fill in or transform functionality differences), and this is likely to introduce problems of its own, such as performance loss and increased integration cost.

Also having an effect will be the economic model adopted by the component vendor—commoditizing the components, market volume effects, reduction of the dependency of a customer on vendors, and so on.

3.6.3 Integration of Enterprise Applications

An enterprise information system is nowadays most likely constructed by the integration of existing applications, whether these be in-house applications or bought-in software packages. A key portion of the integration effort—referred to as EAI (for *Enterprise Application Integration*)—consists of developing interfaces between the applications to allow their cooperation.[21]

The contents of this section were inspired by [OCT99].

The objective of EAI is to allow a company to seamlessly adapt its information system to meet the changing needs of the business, and also to leverage the benefits of new technology, while minimizing the costs of the changes.

One can see analogs of this process in the evolution of cities; this has led information systems architects to use the term **urbanization** to characterize such system evolution. In a city, each separate group of buildings was conceived and constructed at different times, meeting the needs of the day and using then-current technology. The construction of a new group of buildings does not necessarily mean the destruction of an older group, but such new construction can require infrastructure change—improvements in road access; increases in water, gas, and electricity supplies; changes in drainage; and so on. The art of the town planner is to arrange things so that the establishment of such new buildings does not impact the life of existing districts, communication between old and new districts is possible and convenient, and any work needed to improve the infrastructure proceeds without harm to the inhabitants.

Transposing these thoughts from the city to the enterprise information system, we can see a number of rules and principles emerging:

1. Each component of the system is autonomous and can operate asynchronously

2. The various components of the system consume and produce information in a standard format

3. Communication between the various components takes place through a common interconnection network with flow control characteristics

4. And so forth

Figure 3.33, after [OCT99], illustrates the various building blocks which make up an EAI offering.

We will comment on these various technical components.

Figure 3.33
*Technical
components of an
EAI offering
(source:
[OCT99]).*

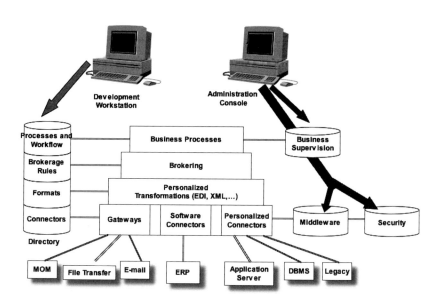

At the highest level of this hierarchy, we find the processes that describe how the company manages its business; these comprise the company's *workflow*. Workflow makes it possible to automate the control of tasks within the company, starting with a description of the rules of operation. These rules apply to the communications between the relevant applications, and supplement information brokers' tasks (ORB, or Object Request Brokers, as seen in this chapter) in processing complex events, managing the states of the various components of the system, management of long transactions, and so forth.

The workflow processes are thus based on brokering, and the brokering is based on rules. It is helpful to separate out the operation rules and routing rules in this manner, since the operation rules are specified in terms understandable by the business folk in the company, while the brokering rules are at a technical level.

We then see the transformation of information. For two applications to communicate and cooperate, they must agree on the data representation. EDI (*Electronic Data Interchange*) was a first approach to a standard in this field—in each branch of industry, companies agreed on a representation of the data they had to exchange. XML should be the next step in data representation, and should also—with its close integration with the Internet—simplify making the standards open.

Connectors constitute the last layer in this architecture, making it possible to interface the various systems and applications which together form the integrated enterprise system. Various types of connectors may be used:

- MOM (Message-Oriented Middleware)
- File transfer (a fair number of existing applications communicate this way; a relatively simple evolution can be to a message-passing paradigm, where the file contents are passed item by item)
- ERP (for Enterprise Resource Planning), which consists of bridges allowing the system to interface to integrated management packages
- Application servers, such as WebLogic or even transaction monitor (Tuxedo, CICS or MSTS, for example)
- Existing applications

We showed two workstations in the diagram; one represents software development and the other system administration. The development workstations mostly make use of the reference material.

While there are several EAI providers, a discussion of their products is outside the scope of this book.

3.7   Endnotes

1.   If, in MAS, an address space of 2^{32} bytes is enough for a mid-range system, a larger address space will be needed for SAS, of about the size of the sum of the address spaces of the active processes. To illustrate the point, consider a system needing to support 1,000 active user processes. In MAS, each of the 1,000 processes uses the same virtual address space; if we say that the per-process private address space can be 2^{31} bytes, then the system can happily get by with a total virtual address space of 2^{32} bytes shared among the processes. In the case of SAS, keeping the assumption that each process needs 2^{31} bytes for its private objects, then we need address space for 1,000 x 2^{32} bytes, which translates into another 10 address bits for a total virtual address of 42 bits—32 for within-process addressing and 10, effectively, for distinguishing between processes.

2.   The extended PowerPC "Book E" architecture (announced in 2000 and aimed at embedded applications) supports both MAS and SAS very straightforwardly.

3.   The technique of hashing is a semi-associative search method usually used in page table search algorithms. One constructs a table containing the things one wishes to look up, and addresses each uniquely by constructing a key from a portion of the contents of each thing (key here has nothing to do with cryptographic keys discussed elsewhere in this chapter). The hash value itself is usually the result of a logical operation performed across the bytes of the thing stored (such as addition module 256 of all the bytes in the item). This numeric value may be used (after a remainder operation to limit the value to the number of entries in the table) as an index into a table each of whose entries is a list of items which share the same hash value. One can then search this list, comparing keys, until the desired item is found. As an example, suppose we have 2048 items; then by computing a hash value for the items in the range 0-255, and assuming a uniform distribution of keys against items and of hash values across items, then one may find a specified item with one hash computation followed by a search of no more than 8 items (just 4 on average), which is a significant performance improvement over linear search of the 2,048 items (which would require a search of 1024 items on average).

4. In fact, in some systems implementations the 4 GB of available address space is split into two 2 GB sections, one dedicated to the system and the other for use by user processes. As shown in Figure 3.3, the user zone is multiplexed among all the different user processes. In other words, each user process occupies the same 2 GB address space and the operating system ensures that the correct address space definition is in play as each such process becomes active.

5. We should note here that these Gartner Group figures cover only sales of base systems, with their operating system, but without any peripherals beyond the system disks, and without any middleware.

6. In the server world, one calls a system managing a single well-defined mission with a fixed set of software (for example, a Web server or a firewall) a specialized or an embedded server.

7. These properties are now one of the warhorses of standard systems in their conquest of the critical functions of enterprise servers.

8. Lightweight processes, or threads, correspond to the possibility of concurrent execution within a single process. The use of threads can reduce system loading, because the cost of switching between threads is much lower than the cost of switching between processes. Threads are a fundamental technology for transactional monitors. We will take a more detailed look at this technology in Chapter 4, within the framework of the study of programming models for SMP architectures.

9. There exists a tendency to look upon electronic commerce as just an issue of making payments secure. In fact, Web technology and security are simply the components of e-commerce.

10. A large number of books and magazines available in the market cover most of these issues, and we prefer to direct the reader to them rather than to give a partial treatment here.

11. We should note that the applications portion and database portion—and, more rarely, the HTTP portion—can all reside on the same server. In such circumstances, we remain in the four-tier model, provided that the interface between application and database does not assume that both are co-resident on the same server.

12.   The description of these techniques, which are based upon journaling, is outside the scope of this work. The interested reader can consult works of reference such as [BER97] and [GRA92].

13.   In fact, in the case of a transactional application that executes on just one site but involves several data managers in the course of a single transaction, there is a need to use a two-phase commit so that all the data mangers properly participate in the transaction's global commit.

14.   In a transaction-processing system, each transaction must have a unique identifier. In the context of a centralized system (just one site) a unique number generator is all that is needed to create these transaction identifiers. In a distributed context, a simple solution consists in forming the unique identifier by concatenating the (unique) identifier of the site with the number provided by a local generator.

15.   Workflow is a mechanism by which the processing of a request (such as a customer's order) can be tracked. So in Workflow, it is necessary to describe the processing steps for the item of interest; several products support Workflow, including Lotus Notes and MQSeries.

16.   This approach of programming is being used extensively in compiler writing since the 60s.

17.   Takes its name from the mythological three-headed dog which guarded the entrance to Hades.

18.   We should remember that in the absence of any metrics it is hard to define quality. But one can always talk about it.

19.   Since PC software—especially Microsoft software—is sold in volumes of several millions, one can see that if these numbers are close to reality, PC software prices could fall precipitously without causing real business difficulties to the vendors.

20.   Here we see the re-emergence of the idea of the *second source* prevalent among vendors and buyers of hardware components. Since the lack of a second source is often judged unacceptable by the customer, vendors work to ensure their existence for the success of their products. We should, however, note that microprocessor vendors have long abandoned the notion of official second sources for their products.

21.   The component approach discussed above also presents the problem of integration.

Part 2: System Architecture Options

Server architecture has been strongly shaped by the realities of technological development. Since the beginning of the 80s, the introduction of the microprocessor and the pace of (particularly) semiconductor technology development has transformed a business once based on the value-add from proprietary systems (solutions developed by one manufacturer just for its own product line) to a market built upon commodity components (components and subsystems used in the PC industry).

As the transformation unfolded, mainframe architectures saw their market share stagnate or even decrease. Minicomputers disappeared completely, replaced by servers based on standard microprocessors. That said, there has in recent years been a notable stabilization of the mainframe market (sufficient for some analysts to pontificate that "the mainframe is back"). Several factors have played into this phenomenon: reduction in mainframe costs because of the adoption of CMOS technology; the use of peripherals from the UNIX and Windows worlds; the acceptance of lower margins by manufacturers to compete with high-end open systems; the basic robustness and maturity of the mainframe systems; the move to server concentration that replaces distributed systems around a company with a smaller number of single-site systems; and the ability of mainframe applications to interwork with other systems through the use of open standards and even to host open applications through the use of UNIX interfaces now available on a number of mainframes.

In addition, we should note that the Year 2000 Problem and (in Europe) the problems of adopting the euro currency have helped mainframe sales in the recent past.

In the world of open servers, a very fast evolution in hardware technology has been evident. Hardware components for commodity products quickly integrated key mainframe (and even supercomputer) technologies: program execution acceleration techniques, multiprocessor support, data integrity mechanisms, caches, redundancy, and so forth. On the other hand, the pace of software capability integration was markedly slower: system robustness in the face of failures, disk-mirroring support, high availability, reconfiguration, support of transaction monitors—these all took much longer to migrate into standard operating systems than did the hardware capabilities.

UNIX moved the industry from the mainframe economic model (in which each provider developed all the basic software for the system, from operating system to DBMS and including compilers and more) to a model where the basic software investment was limited to what was necessary to address the target markets of the manufacturer (since UNIX provided the rest). Indeed, in UNIX, manufacturers were provided with a complete suite of basic software, and the complementary software, such as a DBMS, was available from specialist vendors. However, price pressure meant that this new model quickly hit its limits, and since that point the industry has been concentrated around ever-fewer UNIX versions.

Windows is an extreme example of concentration: just one operating system from one provider, shared by multiple systems vendors.

Open source software suggests yet another model, in which development costs are pooled or shared implicitly; we have discussed this phenomenon in several places already.

UNIX approached the levels of quality and functionality offered by mainframes, but did so at an entirely new price point, supported by amortizing the cost of development over a very large number of systems.

This path has also been followed by Microsoft for Windows, in what is clearly a volume play. The inexorable logic of volume sales, however, leads to a much greater uniformity among supported systems, and thus to somewhat of a levelling of the technical quality of those systems, with a tendency to seek the bottom.

We should note that progress in middleware and application development tools was rather quick in the standard systems.

An example was the pace of introduction of relational databases on UNIX, and now on Windows. Almost every UNIX or Windows system installed has at least one relational DBMS, while the traditional hierarchical databases (such as IBM's IMS) or navigational databases (like Bull's IDS) are nowhere to be seen in UNIX or Windows, despite widespread use on mainframes and minicomputers.

This portion of the book, Part 2, presents and discusses the various options available for SMP systems, clusters, and massively-parallel systems. We will then look at the relationship between these factors and the various architectures and parallel architectures for DBMSs.

We will present the principles behind high availability systems and discuss a number of products.

We will end the section with a view of the future.

4

Symmetrical (Tightly-Coupled) Multiprocessors

Symmetrical multiprocessors made their appearance during the 1960s in the high- end mainframe space, driven by the need for scalability. As we have explained earlier, scalability is the property that makes it possible to adapt a system to the size of the problem to be handled, and while problem size is often equated to the size of the processing problem it should not be forgotten that other dimensions are just as important, storage requirements and communications being key examples.

The processing capability of a symmetrical multiprocessor is adjusted to meet needs simply by installing additional processors until the requirements are met. This allows a customer to increase the capabilities of an installed system by simple addition of processor modules, rather than having to replace the whole machine with a higher-performance version. In a symmetrical multiprocessor, the workload is distributed fairly among all the installed processors.

For simplicity, we will refer to symmetrical multiprocessors by the industry-standard acronym, *SMP*. SMPs are also referred to as *tightly-coupled multiprocessors*.

The SMP approach is an economically-attractive way of implementing a range of systems; the power of the various models in the range is characterized not only by the capabilities of the processors used (for example, internal microarchitecture and maximum frequency) but also by the maximum number of processors that can be installed.

After its introduction in the mainframe world, the approach was adopted by minicomputer manufacturers (in the 1970s) and then in the 1980s for UNIX systems based on standard microprocessors. Windows NT was conceived from the very start to support SMP, and today even desktop PCs are adopting the approach.

The architecture of an SMP system is illustrated in Figure 4.1.

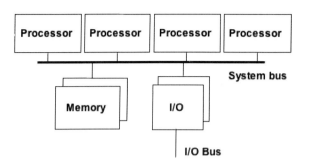

Figure 4.1
*Symmetrical
multiprocessor
(SMP)
architecture.*

> **Terminology**
>
> Describing a system as a "symmetrical multiprocessor" distinguishes it from a different class of systems, also deploying multiple processors, in which specific functions were allocated to specific processors. For example, while in an SMP processing I/O and interrupt handling may each be handled by any processor, in the other class of system, one processor might be dedicated to I/O, another to the file system, and yet a third to handling interrupts.
>
> SMPs are also known as *tightly-coupled* multiprocessors by virtue of the close connection between the processors in the system. This usage is in distinction to loosely-coupled systems, which is used for clustered and massively parallel machines in which the processors in one node have—in the general case—no direct access to memories in other nodes, and have no intimate connections with the processors in those nodes.

By symmetrical, we mean that each processor can access each resource of the system; that is, any processor can play any role in the system. This structure is also known as a *Tightly-Coupled Multiprocessor*.

An SMP functions under the control of one operating system, which manages all system resources.

The attraction of this approach is that a multiprocessor architecture is the most economical way to offer scalability—simply adding one processor card to the system provides a useful increment in processing ability. The programming model for an SMP is straightforward: either the application makes use of concurrency primitives (threads, synchronization mechanisms)—in which case it will naturally take advantage of an SMP to provide either or both of *scale-up* or *speed-up*—or it does not, in which case it will perform in an SMP just as it does on a uniprocessor built from the same processor.

In Chapter 1 we reviewed the fundamental hardware issues raised by an SMP architecture: cache coherence, memory consistency, and synchronizations. We will not revisit those issues here.

We will look first at multiprocessors with a fairly small number of processors—up to ten or so—and then look at systems deploying rather more processors. We will first discuss the hardware limitations of an SMP, and then consider software aspects—programming model, the concept of *threads* and finally the internal characteristics of SMP-oriented operating systems.

4.1   SMPs: Hardware Limitations

Hardware characteristics limit the number of processors that may usefully be used in an SMP, the technology used and the performance of the interconnect being deciding factors. The interconnect must carry all necessary transfers—cache-memory, cache coherence and I/O—and the required bandwidth grows with the number of processors.

Microprocessor internal operating frequencies continue to increase, with current designs offering rates of up to several gigahertz (GHz). Frequencies as high as these can only be sustained over relatively small areas and distances, so the system environment will use substantially lower clock rates—this is visible in the processor specification, which will offer a bus (interconnect) clock rate at some selectable sub-multiple of the internal frequency. As useful as this can be in a single-processor environment—allowing, for example, the replacement of a processor in a PC with a higher clock-rate version while maintaining system clock rates—the approach quickly shows its limitations in an SMP, since while the processor is faster (and can therefore generate more bus traffic), the interconnect remains at the same speed and quickly forms a bottleneck.

On the subject of interconnects, current technology suggests an economic limit for a bus of a around 400 MHz, connecting no more than half a dozen elements, over a distance of no more than 10 or 20 centimeters; little progress is expected in this area.

Luckily, as we will see in this chapter, an alternative interconnect structure is possible—the crossbar. A crossbar provides full interconnect between the elements it connects, unlike a bus (which provides shared interconnection). Thus, in an SMP, while a bus causes the various processors to take turns on the bus when they need to access memory, a crossbar-connected system allows each processor to concurrently access memory.

For reasons of performance and cost, a crossbar for an SMP will generally be implemented as a chip, and so the number of supported processors will be limited by the number of pins that can be supported by the packaging technology for that chip.

We will examine in a later section the techniques necessary to construct systems with a very large number of processors, but we will introduce here an important concept—that of the NUMA (Non-Uniform memory Access) architecture.

4.1.1 NUMA

As we have just outlined, hardware limits the number of processors that can connect to a memory system. So, for configurations with a large number of processors, one is driven to use an architecture in which a group of processors-plus-memories (which we can refer to as a *module*) are interconnected with a coherent interconnect. Such a system allows any processor to access any memory, although there is a difference in the access time to within-module memory and to memory in another module; such architectures are therefore referred to as NUMA (*Non-Uniform Memory Access*) or—for cache-coherent systems—CC-NUMA (for *Cache-Coherent Non-Uniform Memory Access*). The greater the ratio of distant access to local access (this ration is called the *NUMA factor*), the more attention software must pay to memory allocation and usage to ensure acceptable scalability.

4.2   Adapting Software to an SMP

To benefit from the power available from an SMP, appropriate software is necessary, both operating system and application.

4.2.1 Application Software, SMP Programming Model, and Threads

As we have said earlier, software designed for uniprocessor deployment will work perfectly well on a compatible SMP, but the performance available will be unchanged—uniprocessor software cannot harness the power of multiple processors. To leverage the performance of the hardware, the software must be designed appropriately—fundamentally, it must be constructed as multiple units that can execute concurrently.

The SMP programming model is based on the concept of shared memory, which provides a simple and effective way for multiple processes to cooperate. Variables may be shared between processes; when this is done, access to those variables requires some discipline. Operating systems provide mechanisms to declare regions of memory as shared (*cf.* UNIX or Windows shared memory) and to implement the access disciplines necessary. Thus applications may be organized as a collection of multiple elements structured as cooperating processes.

However, while the concept of a process provides useful guarantees of protection and isolation, the overhead of having a processor stop executing one process and begin executing another tends to be rather expensive, to the extent that were a process to be allocated to each user of a system, the system would likely spend the majority of its time in housekeeping and very little in doing the work for which it was purchased.

To avoid the overhead costs while maintaining much of the concept, mainframe systems long ago introduced the idea of a subprocess, which was borrowed and re- used in the UNIX and Windows worlds and renamed as *threads*. The approach simply multiplexes multiple lightweight processes within a single process.

Figure 4.2 illustrates the concept of lightweight processes in the context of UNIX.

In the figure we show both a single-threaded and a multi-threaded process. The available address space of 4 GB (2^{32} bytes) is partitioned into a user space of 2 GB and a kernel space also of 2 GB; the user space is re-used

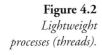

Figure 4.2
Lightweight processes (threads).

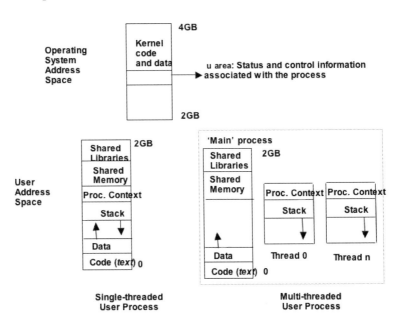

for each process—that is, every time a user process starts execution, the operating system sets up the virtual- to-real address translation tables in the MMU to map the 0 to 2 GB virtual address space onto the portions of real memory that hold that process. In the kernel area, we show a structure (*u area*, for user area) that contains—among other things—the definition of resources allocated to a user process.[1]

The user address space contains:

- Instructions constituting the program to be executed (shown as code in the figure, and called *text* in UNIX terminology)

- Data (this portion can grow and shrink dynamically) also known as the *heap*

- The call stack (contextual information managing procedure calls and returns, and the local data for each procedure)

- Process context (state information for the process sufficient for it to be snapshotted and resumed, containing data such as the contents of the processors' registers)

- Shared data

- Shared libraries

Interprocess cooperation is based on information exchange using shared files or interprocess communications mechanisms, these being themselves either message-based (for example, using *pipes*) or shared-memory mechanisms.

Using shared memory implies that the user processes must declare to the operating system their intent to share memory, whereupon the system arranges a shared region in the virtual address space of the cooperating processes. Access to a shared region requires access disciplines to ensure proper synchronization as multiple processes manipulate the shared data. Interprocess communication by means of shared memory is by far the most efficient mechanism available.

Each lightweight process has its own procedure call stack (as does the owning process) and its own context save area (register contents, instruction pointer, and so on).

The programming interface for threads has been standardized for UNIX (POSIX 1003.4a); lightweight processes may be supported either directly

> **Threads and Middleware**
>
> As we have mentioned previously, some middleware such as transaction monitors (like Tuxedo) and DBMSes implemented their own concept of threads on top of the process primitives offered by the operating system. In the absence of standards for operating-system supported threads, this gave the middleware certain portability advantages. However, it also cuts them off from operating system advances and so calls for new work whenever the hardware characteristics of the platforms changes substantively; an example is adoption of a CC-NUMA architecture, introduced earlier and which we will discuss later.

by the operating system (as in Windows Server 2003), or as a separate subsystem (as in some UNIX variants).

4.2.2 Operating systems

To be able to function usefully, an SMP system must have an appropriate operating system. Such an operating system will—in general—be executed simultaneously by several processors, and so must itself take care in accessing its own shared resources. The standard way of doing this is to protect each resource with a *lock*; any operating system code needing access to such a shared resource must first request permission by requesting the lock. If the request is granted, the needed operations on the resource may be performed and when complete, the lock released. If access to the lock is refused, the code must wait for the lock to be freed. This can be done either of two ways—a *passive wait*, in which the code will wait for (ask the OS to notify it when) the lock is freed; or *active wait* (also known as busy wait) where the code asks for the lock again, in a loop with some bounded number of iterations.

There are two interesting situations to be considered in the design and implementation of the OS, depending on whether the OS was originally designed for multiprocessor deployment or for uniprocessor usage. As examples, while Windows NT and its successors were designed from day one for multiprocessor use, UNIX was originally a uniprocessor system and needed adaptation for multiprocessor use; such adaptation generally occurs in two stages:

- *MP-safe operation.* In this stage, the operating system is modified so that every access to a shared resource is properly protected by a lock, but without attention being paid to performance. Such a system operates correctly, but is of dubious value to a customer.

- *MP-efficient.* In this stage of evolution, careful attention is paid to how many locks should be provided (up to some point, more locks allow greater granularity in access and minimize the likelihood that code running on separate processors will be awaiting the same lock), and to scheduling algorithms. This is not a one-time activity; tuning continues throughout the useful life of the operating system, because the introduction of new microprocessors, new cache hierarchies, the number of supported processors, and the characteristics of evolving software can all affect the tuning needed to get the highest performance from (in particular) the largest configurations supported.

In fact, whether the OS was first designed for MP usage or not, the goal of efficiency will demand constant observation of the system under realistic operating conditions, together with tuning and modifications driven by the observations.

To get a view of the internal architecture of an SMP operating system, the interested reader can consult [RUS00] and [BOS03], which provide descriptions of the innards of Windows 2000 and Windows Server 2003 respectively.

To help illustrate the key issues in getting efficient MP operation from an OS, we will outline the steps necessary to convert a correct uniprocessor OS into an efficient MP OS; this discussion is inspired by [TAL95].

Kernel Characteristics

One of the earliest tasks in the transformation is to transform the kernel from one based on processes to one based on threads; this reduces context-switching inefficiencies in the kernel.

A key performance determinant for a kernel is its preemptability. A preemptive kernel is able to suspend one of its own threads to give preference to a higher priority thread; this improves the response time for interactive applications and can move the OS toward real-time capabilities.

As the scope of the resources controlled by the kernel increases along with the number of users, the size of the code and data representing the OS and its operation can become extremely large. Rather than allocating, once and for all, a massive amount of physical memory reserved to the OS at start-up time (thereby removing that memory from application usage), the kernel itself can be demand-paged. This means that only the pages needed for current operation of the kernel may be present in physical memory at any time; a thread hitting a page fault is—like a normal application program—suspended until the page is available in memory. For this to work, there is clearly some minimal always-resident amount of OS code and data.

Locking

As we have indicated in Chapter 3, the most crucial point in the transformation of an OS from uniprocessor to MP operation is the safeguarding of data structures managed by the system, because the same data can—in an SMP—be accessed simultaneously by code executing on multiple processors. There are two cases of interest:

- Thread-thread conflict, in which the same data is accessed simultaneously by two threads or processes
- Thread-interrupt conflict, in which data is simultaneously accessed by a thread and by an interrupt routine

Data structures are protected by locks.

The notion of *granularity* lets us characterize locking; we distinguish *fine-grain locking* and *coarse-grain locking*. These two styles are distinguished by the amount of time that the resource controlled by the lock is owned by the lock owner.

As to what is managed by a lock, we can distinguish:

- *Locks on code sections*. These are coarse-grained locks, which allow MP safeness to be implemented fairly straightforwardly. Code that manipulates a data structure acquires a lock on entry and releases it at exit. This means that every process or thread executing this section of code competes for the same lock, so that the probability of collision is high. Such a code section is also often referred to as a critical section.
- *Locks on data structures*. Each data structure of interest is given a lock; code wishing to access the structure must be granted the lock before manipulating the data in any way; the code releases the lock when it has finished with the data. This can sharply reduce the amount of collisions and thus improve efficiency.

> **Busy Wait**
>
> In this response to discovery that it has not been granted a lock, the thread simply asks again. This means that the thread, while making no progress, is using up processor resource. Alternatively, the thread can ask the OS to suspend it until the lock is available; the OS will implement this by suspending the thread and adding it to a queue of threads waiting for the lock; this allows the processor to be dedicated to work in another thread.

When a thread is refused access to a lock, there are two strategies available: the thread enters a busy loop, or it suspends, giving up the processor.

Two sorts of lock exist:

- *Simple locks*. When a thread is refused access to a lock, whatever it wants to do to the managed resource, it busy waits until the lock is free. Optimizations are possible and frequently used; for example, if the thread that now owns the lock is not executing, the requesting thread will be suspended until the lock is available.

- *Complex locks*. Semaphores allow a finer granularity than simply controlling any access to a resource. Clearly, if multiple threads which to simply read a shared resource, they may all proceed in parallel; only when one needs to write to the resource is unique access required Complex locks allow this efficiency improvement; like simple locks, a busy wait that proceeds for too long can convert to a suspension.

Usage of these locks can cause an undesirable situation known as *priority inversion* when a high-priority thread attempts to gain access to a lock owned by a low-priority thread (which will likely not get processor time for a while). To avoid the problem of a low-priority thread slowing down a high-priority thread in this manner, any thread owning a lock has its priority increased to at least that of the highest-priority lock requestor.

We will briefly describe two issues raised by lock usage:

- The number of locks and the duration of locking. A system designer must choose between having a small number of locks, each of which will likely be held for some time; or a larger number of locks, each of which will be held for a shorter time (but in general several locks may be needed to do a useful piece of work). A balance must be found between these; that balance will be determined by the characteristics of the sharing of the data to be controlled by the locks.[2] Unfortunately, a solution that is optimal for a small number of processors is unlikely to be optimal for a large number of processors—the larger system will require many locks for maximum concurrency, while the smaller system will pay an efficiency penalty in having to acquire many locks despite not having enough concurrency to benefit from their fine granularity.

- Deadlocks. As soon as there is more than one lock in a system, the possibility of *deadlock* or *deadly embrace* arises. In the simplest case of a deadly embrace, thread 1 wants lock A and already owns lock B, while thread 2 wants lock B and already owns lock A. Neither can continue, so neither ever completes its work and gives up the lock it already owns. Scenarios with more than two threads are also possible, but increasingly harder to discover. There are two ways of dealing with deadlock—avoidance and discovery/recovery. One simple (in theory) avoidance technique is to impose an overall ordering on all locks in the system, and to require any thread which needs multiple locks to request them in that ordering; this approach is rarely used as the only solution. A discovery approach keeps a boolean matrix describing all locks and requires a simple operation thereon (transitive closure) to detect deadlock; once detected, some threads can be forced to fail (transactional semantics allow their work to be safely restarted).

Adapting an OS to an SMP environment also poses other problems:

- Allocating threads to processors. A simple view of the world, taking the promise of "symmetrical multiprocessing" on trust, would allow the OS's scheduler to let threads run on whatever processor became free. However, the existence of large caches changes this view; a large-enough cache can have useful state still present even many milliseconds after a specific thread has been suspended in favor of another one. This leads to schedulers needing to recognize *processor affinity*, which is the rule that the scheduler should, if practical, schedule a thread for execution on the processor that most recently executed it. Were a thread to be scheduled for another processor, there would be a performance hit on both processors—the new one, because its cache would not contain the data/code needed by the thread; and the previous processor, since its cache would (in a sensible cache-coherent implementation) be required to provide data and code to the new processor as it suffered cache misses.

■ If affinity is dynamic—that is, managed by the scheduler in a best-efforts manner—it is possible when necessary in critical applications to create a long-lasting binding between thread and processor. This allows overall system performance to be traded off in favor of better responsiveness.

■ Interrupt management. To keep the load balanced across all processors, it is desirable that the interrupt system should, to the extent possible, direct interrupts to the most lightly-loaded processors in the system. Hardware support for this is necessary.

■ Interprocessor communication. In an SMP kernel, some means for interprocessor communication is needed; such communication should make it possible for one processor to communicate with another specific processor or with all processors.

Many other aspects must be taken into account in getting an OS to work well on an SMP, but we have covered the basics; more discussion is beyond the scope of this work. We hope that our coverage has provided at least a glimpse of the complexities involved.

We will now look at hardware issues, beginning with SMPs with a moderate number of processors.

4.3   SMP Architectures with a Moderate Number of Processors (<= 8)

Given the rate of progress in the industry, one can classify—in 2003—any system with up to eight processors as an SMP of moderate size. Indeed, ready availability of commodity silicon enables systems manufacturers to build systems with up to four processors, with no need to develop the custom silicon components (*chipsets*, or *ASICs*—for Application-Specific Integrated Circuit), needed to knit the processors together into a system. Because of the level of integration needed, together with intimate knowledge of how best to make use of the microprocessors' interface characteristics—it is becoming increasingly the case that for systems of up to

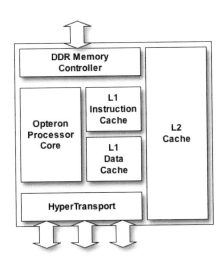

Figure 4.3
Internal structure of the AMD Opteron microprocessor (source: AMD).

eight processors, the microprocessor vendor is the source of choice. This is particularly true of Intel.

In this section we will look at a number of contemporary moderate-sized SMPs.

4.3.1 Four to Eight Processor Servers based on AMD Opteron

Our first example is an AMD Opteron-based server; the internal structure of the Opteron processor is sketched in Figure 4.3.

We will not discuss the internal characteristics of this microprocessor in great detail, even ignoring a particularly interesting aspect of this microprocessor (its implementation of AMD's 64-bit extensions to the IA32 architecture), but, will concentrate on SMP aspects. In this respect, a key area of interest is the integration of multiple HyperTransport ports and their controller into the processor. HyperTransport is an efficient, silicon-friendly, point-to-point interconnect suitable for interconnecting small numbers of processors and I/O subsystems; its integration into the Opteron removes the bottleneck that would be occasioned by the more-traditional provision of a shared bus interface.

Figure 4.4 illustrates the construction of SMPs with four and eight processors.

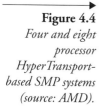

Figure 4.4
Four and eight processor HyperTransport-based SMP systems (source: AMD).

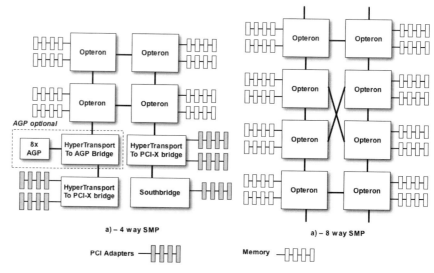

Figure 4.4 (a) shows a configuration with four processors integrating a graphic interface (not typical of a server), connections to memory (attached to each processor), and connections to I/O subsystems.

With three HyperTransport links, it is possible to create, without any additional logic, a system with eight processors (Figure 4.4(b)). Four HyperTransport links are available for connections with I/O subsystems. Each processor has coherent access to the complete memory of the system. The NUMA factor is no more than two, since the worst case involves the need to traverse just two other processors. Although exact figures for a fully-loaded system are not available, there is every reason to suppose that this system is more a "nearly UMA" system than a real NUMA system, and so few if any changes to the software otherwise necessary to adapt to a NUMA system should need to be done.

Although integrated SMP solutions are now available from microprocessor vendors, this was not always the case, and so system vendors were obliged to create their own solutions. Figure 4.5 shows a system architecture developed by IBM for its Intel-based servers.

IBM developed components which allowed the construction of systems with between 4 and 16 processors. Key components included:

■ A memory and I/O controller

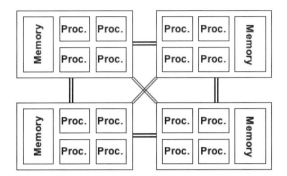

Figure 4.5
*Overview of IBM's
X-Architecture
(source: IBM).*

- A remote I/O controller, allowing a four-processor module to control I/O operations on non-local PCI adapters

- An L4 cache controller integrating three pots (called *scalability ports*) allowing access to the other modules in the system

The scalability ports implemented the system cache coherence protocols.

IBM developed versions of this architecture for both IA-32 and IA-64. This type of approach is running out of time; rather, we expect to see, increasingly, the system dimension integrated into the offerings from the processor vendors.

4.3.2   INTEL IA-32 and IA-64 Based 4-Way Servers

We will present two 4-way processor architectures, one IA-32 based and the other IA-64 based. It should be clear that the business goal of these systems is low cost allied with the ability to be manufactured in high volume—that is, no heroics will be performed in a search for the highest possible performance.

IA-32: Xeon-based Four-Way Servers

Figure 4.6 illustrates the architecture of a Xeon-based four-way SMP server.

The system's backbone is a 64-bit, 400MHz bus providing a raw throughput of 3.2GB/sec.

The processors are MP Xeons, which incorporate technologies that Intel calls Hyperthreading (simultaneous multithreading) and Netburst; we discussed these in Chapter 1. Xeons integrate several levels of cache; in our

Figure 4.6
Architecture of a
4-way Xeon MP-
based Server
(source:
ServerWorks).

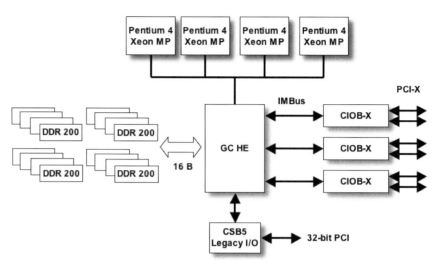

description here we report their sizes as of early 2003—we expect capacities to evolve upwards over time.

Xeon's cache complement includes:

- A cache of decoded instructions called the Level 1 Execution Trace Cache. It holds 12 K micro-ops (a micro-op being Intel's name for the simpler instructions into which IA-32 instructions are decoded)
- A first level data cache, of 8 KB
- A second level shared cache of 512 KB
- A third level of cache of 2 MB

ServerWorks' Grand Champion HE chipset provides the connection between processors and memory. It supports up to 64 GB of SDRAM (Synchronous DRAM) memory, using four channels of DDR200 (200MHz double data rate) with up to four-way interleaving and providing an overall bandwidth of 6.4 GB/s. The memory system (whose structure is vastly simplified in the diagram) has an ECC covering chunks of 128 bits, using 16 bits of detection and 8 bits of correction. The chipset supports memory scrubbing and hot-plugging of memory modules. It also supports Chipkill, a proprietary name for a technology improving the reliability of memory (without going into technical details, let us just say that memory operations are essentially the same as RAID for disk subsystems).

As is traditional with Intel-based systems, legacy I/O subsystems are supported (CSB5). The system also supports six hot-pluggable PCI-X buses, providing an aggregate rate of 4.8 GB/s.

Intel's SPSH4 and SRSH4 server platforms (which differ in their configurability options) are based on this chipset. The business goal of this class of system is high-volume production; indeed, the name of the preceding generation (which was based on Pentium III Xeon processors) was SHV, for *Standard High Volume*.

IA-64: Itanium-2 based INTEL SR870NB4

Figure 4.7 illustrates the general architecture of the SR870NB4, a 4-way Itanium2 based SMP server, whose aims are similar to those of the Xeon-based systems just discussed.

Figure 4.7
Architecture of a 4-way Itanium-2 based SMP Server, the SR870NB4 (source: INTEL).

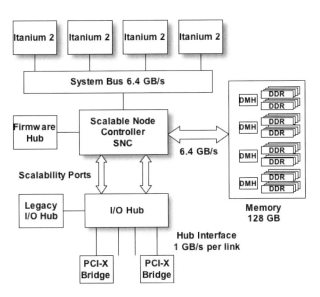

This system's backbone is also a bus, but of 128 bits rather than 64 and running at the same 400MHz, providing double the bandwidth of the Xeon system discussed, at 6.4 GB/s.

The E8870 chipset has a number of components:

■ The SNC (Scalable Node Controller) is the central element of this architecture. It provides the interface between the system bus on one side and on the other memory, I/O and (in large systems) other processor/memory/I/O subsystems

- The SPS (Scalable Port Switch), not shown here, provides coherent connections between modules and I/O Hubs. The SPS provides 6 Scalability Ports, giving a peak bandwidth of some 38.4 GB/s. The coherence mechanisms employ filtering, to improve performance by avoiding sending coherence traffic to subsystems which do not have the storage block in their caches

- The Scalability Port, which is a coherent point-to-point interface

- The I/O Hub, which interfaces to I/O bridges

- I/O bridges, which drive the I/O buses themselves—both PCI and legacy PC I/O

Memory is driven by DDR Memory Hubs (DMH) providing a DDR SDRAM interface at 200 MHz; with four memory interfaces, the maximum capacity is 128 GB (with 4 GB memory chips) and the bandwidth provided is 6.4 GB/s.

We will see a little later in this chapter how these components may be used to construct a 16-way system.

Systems vendors can use this technology, with the support of some custom silicon, to build systems with a rather large number of processors. As soon as a system exceeds four processors, though, the system design moves into the NUMA realm. As we have suggested, the NUMA factor has an effect on the behavior of the system. When the ratio is small, software thinks it is executing on a simple, fully-symmetrical processor, but as the ratio increases care must be taken as to the placement of information and to the scheduling of the work, so as to place data as close as is practical to the processor using it.

Extending the 4-Way Intel Systems

Given a working 4-way system, a simple way (at least, in principle) of extending to much greater numbers of processors is to treat a 4-way system as a module, and build a system by connecting many modules. This approach is the basis of Intel's Profusion architecture, which uses a single component to interconnect two 4-way systems forming an 8-way system.

Profusion was originally developed at Corollary, a company acquired by Intel in 1997, and supported the Pentium III processor family.

Figure 4.8 illustrates the Profusion approach.

> **Evolution in the Industry**
>
> In its early days, Intel produced only memories; it then added microprocessors to its catalog. Over time, these were supplemented by chipsets—further components simplifying the construction of systems—and then by systems components themselves, like the SHV cards[*] and by systems.
>
> Initially, these were offered along a timeline organized as follows: first, the microprocessor; then the chipset; then the cards; then the systems. But over time, Intel has begun synchronizing its offerings so that the whole range is available more or less simultaneously. This makes it ever harder for systems vendors to compete effectively with Intel.

*SHV, which stands for Standard High Volume, was the name Intel used for its 4-way system cards. Such cards were used to build 4-way systems or even larger systems by using specific silicon (see CC-NUMA discussion below).

Figure 4.8
The Profusion Architecture (source: Corollary/ Intel).

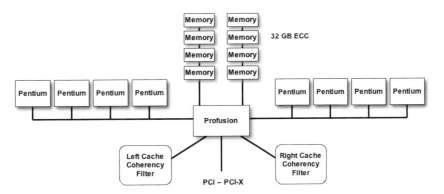

The approach is to glue together two 4-way systems using the Profusion controller chip, which integrates three functions:

- A memory controller, which supports two ECC-protected memory subsystems with a maximum combined capacity of 32 GB

- A directory-based coherence controller, with two directories to minimize coherence traffic on the two system buses

- An interface to two PCI-X buses (at 100 MHz) and PCI (33 MHz), supporting hot-pluggability

The coherence management is interesting, if straightforward. Within each 4-processor subsystem, coherence is maintained by the normal snooping activities integrated into each processor. To avoid the need for each branch of the system to snoop the traffic in the other branch, the Profusion controller tracks in its directories which storage blocks are cached in each branch and can therefore tell if a transaction on one bus needs to be seen on the other bus; when this is necessary, it propagates the transaction. Managing the directories and propagating transactions implies extra cycles and latencies in some activities, and does have an effect on raw system performance, albeit not a strong one.

In architectural terms, other approaches are viable (and have been implemented)—examples are configuring four processors to share an L3 cache; or using cross-bar interconnections rather than buses and bridges. In any decision to construct a custom solution, however, the key issues are economic rather than technical: deciding to design, build, test and deploy a new silicon solution has implications on the product's time to market, and implies an appropriate system sales volume to make economic sense. As the commodity chipsets handle increasingly large numbers of processors, the opportunity for systems vendors to make money through offering better solutions in this space is increasingly limited. And the trend continues; in 1999, commodity chipsets could construct 4-way systems; by 2002, that had increased to eight.

4.3.3 Crossbar-based Architectures

Figure 4.9 shows another way of implementing an SMP, illustrating Sun's Sunfire 3800.

As shown in the figure, the Sunfire 3800 is based on a card which can hold up to four UltraSPARC III processors. The processors, in groups of two, are connected using a crossbar; these processor pairs themselves are connected by a higher-level crossbar. Each four-processor module can contain up to 32 GB of memory, and can be used to construct SMPs with a capacity of up to 24 processors. The crossbar connections are used just for data; addresses are carried by another, dedicated, interconnect.

4.4 Multiprocessors with Many Processors (More than 16)

The preceding section gave an overview of architectures appropriate to systems that deploy a reasonably small number of processors, and in it we indi-

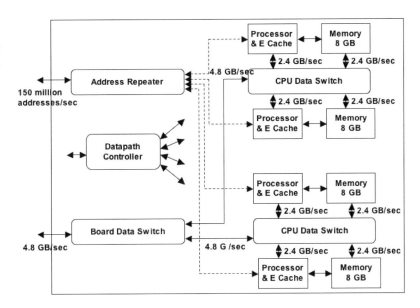

Figure 4.9
Sun Fire 3800 architecture (source: Sun).

cated the physical limitations which constrain the maximum number of processors such systems can support; and we further indicated that the boundary between "small SMP systems" and "large SMP systems" is moving upwards over time as the microprocessor vendors integrate more and more system capability into their silicon.

Because of the physical and electrical constraints, larger SMP systems must use a hierarchy of interconnect mechanisms; in a recursive manner, a large SMP tends to be a collection of smaller systems, each of which is itself an SMP. Such a hierarchy means that memory access times differ—when a processor accesses its own memory, it will see a much shorter access time than when it accesses memory in a distant module. This non-uniformity of memory access times can have a major effect on system behavior and on the software running on it.

The degree of uniformity allows us to distinguish two classes of SMP systems.

- Systems in which access to any memory takes an identical amount of time, or very nearly identical are called (respectively) UMA—for Uniform Memory Access—or nearly UMA[3]

- Systems in which there is a noticeable disparity in access times—a factor greater than two—are referred to as CC-NUMA, for Cache-Coherent Non-Uniform Memory Access

This classification is purely empirical, and its practical significance is that in a distinctly NUMA system, software must—for maximum efficiency—take account of the varying access times. The amount of work needed for this adaptation tends to increase with the NUMA ratio.

We now will present some examples of SMPs with a large number of processors.

4.4.1   Fujitsu PrimePower

Fujitsu's PrimePower family comprises three models—the 800, which can have up to 16 processors; the 1000, which deploys up to 32 processors; and the 2000, with a maximum of 128 processors. The processors used are SPARC64 GP (deployed in 2001 at 450 MHz, and with 8 MB level-2 caches). Maximum memory capacity is 512 GB, and the system can support up to a maximum of 192 PCI adapters. The system architecture is shown in a simplified form in Figure 4.10.

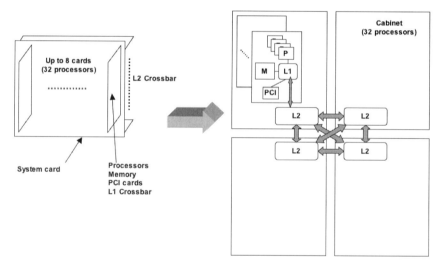

Figure 4.10
Fujitsu PrimePower system architecture (simplified) (source: Fujitsu).

The basic building-block of this system is a four-processor card, connected up using a hierarchy of crossbars. Within the card, the processors are connected with a level-1 crossbar; a cabinet can hold eight cards, which are connected by a level-2 crossbar; and a system can comprise up to four cabinets, connected by a level-3 crossbar.

The declared memory latency is 300 ns when a level-2 crossbar is part of the access path; if we assume a local access time of around 200 ns, it can be seen that the NUMA factor for this system is low. Coherence uses a snooping protocol.

Many system components are hot-pluggable—processors and memories, PCI cards, power supplies, fans, system control cards, and disks. The system may also be partitioned into up to 15 partitions.[4]

4.4.2 HP Superdome

HP's Superdome system is also constructed around a 4-processor building block, called a cell; the architecture of a cell is shown in Figure 4.11.

Figure 4.11
HP Superdome cell (source: HP).

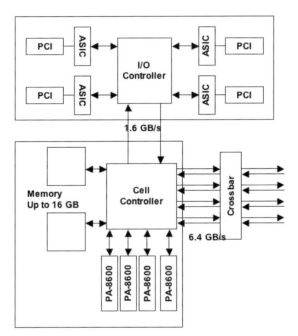

As shown in the diagram, the cell is organized around the Cell Controller, which is a crossbar which interconnects the four processors, the memory, and the local I/O, as well as the next level in the crossbar hierarchy, allowing systems of up to 64 processors to be composed from a number of cells.

Figure 4.12 illustrates the Superdome architecture.

Four cells may be connected via a crossbar to form a 16-processor system; two 16-processor subsystems may be connected to form a single-cabinet 32-processor system. The available crossbar ports limit the system to a maximum of 64 processors in 2 cabinets. Provided enough connections are

Figure 4.12
HP Superdome
architecture
(source: to HP).

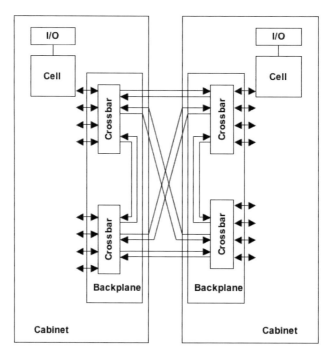

used, the system provides linearly scaled bandwidth: 12.8 GB/s for 16 processors, 25.6 GB/s for 32 and 512.2 GB/s for 64 processors. The system also supports hot-pluggability, and can be partitioned.

Memory latencies for a fully-loaded system[5] are said to be:

- Within-cell: 260 ns
- On the same crossbar: 320 to 350 ns
- Within the same cabinet: 395 ns
- Between cabinets: 415 ns

It seems that available HP's system architects were capable of keeping the NUMA factor well within the comfort zone.

4.4.3 IBM pSeries 690

IBM's pSeries 690 uses the Power4 microprocessor, which integrates two processors per chip and integrates several processors into an MCM, or Multi-Chip Module, whose architecture is shown in Figure 4.13.

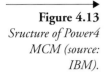

Figure 4.13
Sructure of Power4 MCM (source: IBM).

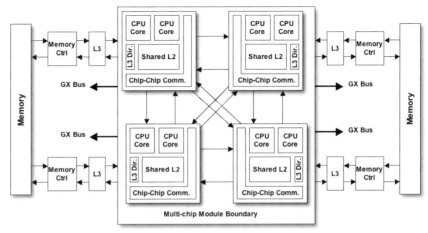

In this 8-processor architecture, each chip contains two processors with a shared L2 cache; a directory; a controller for an L3 cache (whose capacity is 32 MB); inter-processor communication logic (the *fabric bus controller*, which is also the foundation for the construction of larger systems) and a bus controller for the GX bus used to connect to I/O. We do not show the memory controllers in this diagram; each such controller connects between an L3 and up to 16 GB of memory.

There is a second version of this system, 690 HPC (HPC means High Performance Computing, implying large scientific workloads rather than commercial workloads), in which the processor chips have just one processor to remove or reduce memory bandwidth concerns.

Figure 4.14 shows the way in which the system, in its maximum configuration with 32 processors, is built from four of these components.

The interconnect between the MCM offers a bandwidth of 41.6 GB/s. In the largest possible configuration at the time of writing, the memory can be up to 256GB in size, with an aggregate bandwidth of 16GB/s. Although direct connection to peripherals does not form the heart of this class of system—they are more usually connected to storage or communications subsystems than to individual peripherals—the pSeries 690 can support up to 160 PCI cards with dynamic connection and reconnection. The system allows hot-pluggability of its components (processor cards, PCI cards and peripherals), and also supports dynamic partitioning.

Although memory latency figures are not available, it seems reasonable to believe that this system, too, has a very reasonable (low) NUMA factor.

Figure 4.14
*Architecture of
IBM pSeries 690
(source: IBM).*

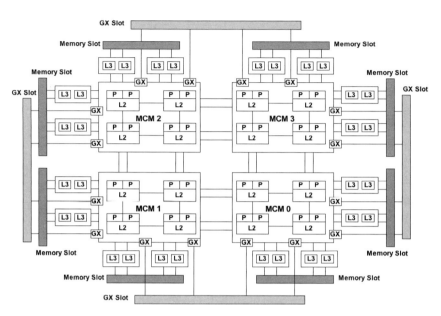

4.4.4   IBM eServer z900

In December 2000, IBM announced a new generation of its S/390 main-frame series, the eServer z900. This new generation makes a significant change to the ISA—while maintaining backwards compatibility with earlier generations, it now supports a 64-bit architecture. We will not comment on this new instruction set architecture—the interested reader can read [IBM00], or a summary paper published in [IBM02]—but will describe the server architecture of this new series. Our description is inspired by [IBM02].

Figure 4.15 illustrates the hardware architecture of the z900.

The diagram does not represent the physical configuration of a machine. An MCM containing 35 chips integrates the major system components: 12 or 20 processors (depending on the model), second level cache, system controllers (not shown in the diagram) that allow connection to memory models, as well as memory bus adapters (MBA) connecting the I/O. The interconnection is a crossbar.

The MCM is 127 x 127 mm, and one MCM dissipates 1300W.

In initial versions of the system, delivered in 2000, the processors had a clock cycle of 1.3 ns, 2.6 ns at the level of the MCM; processors delivered 261 MIPS[6] at an average CPI (clocks per instruction) of 2.95. The 2002 version improved clock to 1.09 ns for the processors and 2.18 ns at the

Figure 4.15
*z900 hardware
architecture
(source: [IBM02]).*

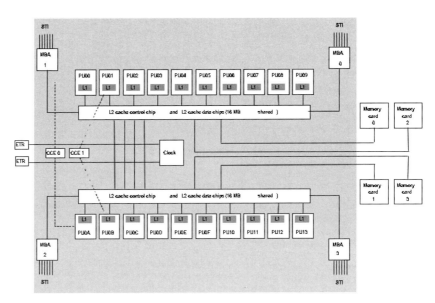

MCM level. The processors have a seven-stage pipeline, significantly fewer than contemporary commodity IA-32 processors.

The machine has a single realtime clock, which has an interface to external time references (ETR) so that nodes may be operated with different time zones when configures as a Sysplex cluster (see Chapter 5). Two groups of 10 processors are used, each with its own L2 cache. IBM uses the word "cluster" to describe a group of 10 processors—to avoid confusion with industry-standard usage (in which the term is sued to describe a loosely-coupled system), we avoid use of the terminology here.

Each logical processor is actually two physical processors, running in lockstep and operating as a self-checking machine (see below). The L1 cache comprises two caches of 256 KB.

Of the number of processors implemented in an MCM, some (16, for the 20-processor MCM) are used to run applications and the remainder used for system functions and may be swapped in the event of an applications processor failing. Since an MCM is always manufactured with the maximum number of processors, a delivered system is configured to use just an appropriate subset matching the configuration purchased by the customer. As needed, additional processors (up to the maximum implemented) may be temporarily allocated to application use, with the customer being billed appropriately. An unallocated processor may be reconfigured to act as a hot spare in the event of the failure of an allocated processor. Allocation and release of processors is done dynamically and at the logical level, without physical reconfiguration of the machine.

The maximum capacity of the memory is 64 GB.

The interface to the I/O controllers is made using STI (*Self-Timed Interface*) cables offering 1 GB/s per interface, with 6 interfaces per MBA. Compared to the previous generation, the z900 offers three times as much bandwidth. I/O controllers are organized in chassis, with 28 controllers per chassis and up to three chassis. I/O programming is done, as is traditional with IBM mainframes, via channel programs. The system may be partitioned (with the concept of LPAR, for logical partition); data may be exchanged between partitions by means of within-system I/O.

To allow direct support of PCI, an adapter is needed to convert between the mainframe world of channel programs and the PCI world of memory-mapped I/O; a PowerPC-based adapter was developed, supporting two PCI cards.

z900's support for Linux occasioned a change in disk I/O, with the introduction of SCSI disk support over Fibre Channel (FCP, for *Fibre Channel Protocol* for SCSI) in addition to the traditional ECKD (*Extended Count Key Data*) which has its origins in S/360.[7]

The standard configuration of the z900 integrates two cryptographic coprocessors (Cryptographic Coprocessor Elements CC0 and CC1), which do not form part of the MCM. Further cryptographic processors are supported as PCI cards.

The z900 designers paid a great deal of attention to high availability, with the result that, by placing the processors in an MCM into self-checking mode (as noted, each logical processor actually comprises two real processors together with extra logic, discussed below), the z900 can survive the failure of a processor. The explanation below is inspired by [MUE99], which describes the RAS (*Reliability, Availability, Serviceability*) aspects of the G5 and G6 processors, which were predecessors of the z900 processor for which the same approach was taken.

Figure 4.16 illustrates the principle of operation.

The model of execution is based on the following concepts:

- As each instruction is executed, the machine state (or execution context) is memorized. As we will see in Chapter 9, this is simply applying the principle of a *recovery point* at the level of instruction

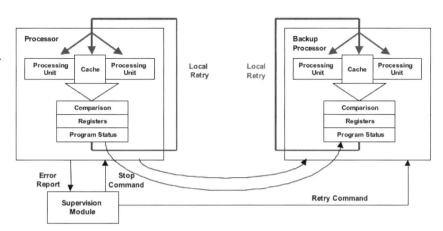

Figure 4.16
*z900 Processor
Principles of
Operation [derived
from IBM]*

execution. A very small number of specialist instructions are not subject to checkpointing

- The instruction is executed by both the processors that make up a logical processor (that is, the processor visible to the process being executed). The two results of execution are compared. When the comparison shows identical results, the machine state is modified and execution proceeds to the next instruction. When the comparison shows a difference, a recovery procedure is initiated

- The recovery process takes place locally—that is, on the same processor duplex as detected the problem—and starts from the memorized state. The operation is basically a sequence of retries, and if the comparison differences persist, a fault is declared and recovery may then be attempted by passing the memorized state to a spare processor in the MCM

The z900 allows hot-swapping certain components, such as I/O controllers and memory blocks. It also employs an N+1 strategy for fans and power supplies.

4.4.5 16-way Intel Server—Itanium 2 plus E8870 Chipset

Figure 4.17 illustrates the architecture of a system with 16 Itanium 2 processors, based on Intel's E8870 chipset.

As with other systems, this shows the hierarchical approach to building systems as collections of 4-processor building blocks, using—here—the

Figure 4.17
*Architecture of a
system with 16
Itanium 2
processors (source:
INTEL).*

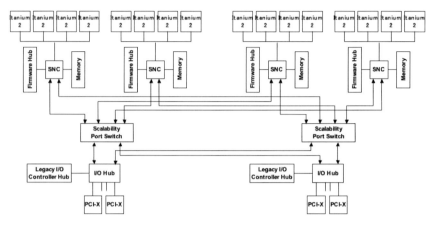

Scalability Port Switch and its Scalability Ports. These provide both connection and coherence, and offer a reasonable NUMA factor—Intel indicates a value of 2.2 for this system. As with the memory, and as would be expected for an SMP, all I/O is symmetrically shared.

4.4.6 Sun 3800, 4800, and 6800

Sun's larger systems are, again, implemented as collections of 4-processor cards; their architecture is shown in Figure 4.18.

Figure 4.18
*Structure Sun's
3800, 4800, and
6800 systems
(source: Sun)*

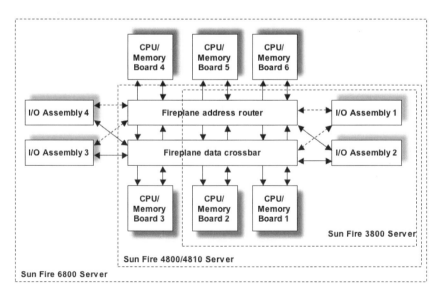

As indicated in the figure, systems of 8, 16 or 24 processors may be constructed using a crossbar to connect up appropriate numbers of four-processor cards, with coherence implemented via snooping. The system supports hot-pluggability of processor/memory cards, power supply modules, fans, disks, PCI cards, etc., and supports dynamic partitioning.

The NUMA factor is also quite good—local memory accesses take 180 ns, while access to memory on another card takes 240 ns according to Sun.

4.4.7 CC-NUMA and COMA Architectures

As seen, the fairly large systems described above have architectures which are close to UMA behavior; however, early implementations of large systems constructed in this manner (as collections of 4-processor subsystems) exhibited very strong NUMA characteristics, with NUMA factors in the four to ten range.

In this section we explore the subject of NUMA a little more deeply, and then look at the COMA (*Cache-Only Memory Architecture*).

Early pioneers in the CC-NUMA field were Data General, Sequent and SGI; we will discuss SGI's system a little later.

COMA is an architecture in which the whole memory is managed as a cache; it has had one public outing, which was not particularly successful.

In our conclusions section, we will also discuss other innovative approaches.

4.4.8 CC-NUMA Architecture

Of the various non-traditional systems architectures, NUMA is worth some attention. As we have indicated, a NUMA architecture is characterized by the distribution of the system memory among a number of processors, in such a manner that a processor sees noticeably different access times for memory connected directly to it and to memory connected to other processors. When a NUMA system provides system-wide cache coherence, it is called a CC-NUMA (Cache-Coherent Non-Uniform Memory Access) system. While it is in principle possible to support cache coherence in software, such systems offer rather poor performance; and thus those interested in SMP systems must focus attention on CC-NUMA rather than NUMA in general.

Early commercial examples of CC-NUMA architectures were the systems offered by Data General and Sequent; these—which we do not

Figure 4.19
CC-NUMA
architecture.

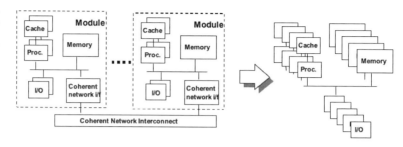

Physical Configuration   **Equivalent Logical Configuration**

describe further—constructed a system by coherently interconnecting 4-processor Intel SHV cards. The SCI (*Scalable Coherent Interface*) is a suitable candidate interface, and is defined by IEEE 1596. The general architecture of a CC-NUMA system is illustrated in Figure 4.19.

On the left of the figure is depicted the actual physical organization of the system, showing a number of SMP modules interconnected by a coherent network. A processor in any module can access both its own memory (that is, the memory within its own module) or memory in any other module; clearly, there is a difference in performance between these two types of access. On the right of the figure is shown the logical configuration, showing that at an abstract level, the system feels like a simple shared-bus architecture, but without the bandwidth limitations associated with that architecture.

From software's point of view, the higher the NUMA factor, the more care must be taken to optimize memory allocation and placement to minimize references to objects in distant memory; these changes will affect both the OS and the DBMSs.

4.4.9 Locality

The system is a simple composition of modules. If code executing on a module accesses only memory in that module, the program is said to have perfect locality, and the system will not suffer any performance degradation compared to what a perfect SMP of the same size with identical but uniform access times to memory would offer. At the other extreme, if code executing on one module has all its data accesses to memory in other modules, the performance compared to the perfect SMP will be seriously degraded. Of course, the hardware seeks to minimize the cost of such distant accesses through the use of caches—the caches in a module will, in this instance, cache data held in other modules.

A key objective for designers of CC-NUMA systems is to make the NUMA factor as low as possible; it is generally considered that a factor above five is liable to make an un-tuned implementation disappointing in performance, while a factor of two or less will have no substantive negative effects of performance, even with software that has not been CC-NUMA tuned.

We now indicate a (non-exhaustive) list of possible CC-NUMA optimizations for use when the NUMA factor is uncomfortably large:

- Affinity scheduling: arranging that a process, once suspended, is rescheduled on the same processor on which it last executed in the expectation that the caches contain useful state from the earlier execution

- When allocating memory, prioritize local allocation (i.e., allocation within the module on which the program is executing) above distant allocation

- When a process has had pages paged out, allocate memory for the pages when paged back in on the same module as the process is executing

To illustrate this sort of architecture, we describe the SGI Origin 3000 systems. A related system, the Altix 3000, was introduced in early 2003; it is built around Itanium-2 processors and provides the ability to construct clusters with shared memory. Other than the processor/memory subsystem, subsystems are interchangeable between Altix and Origin systems. The topology of the interconnect network of the Altix 3000 is different from the Origin 3000; because of its cluster capabilities, we will describe it in Chapter 5.

Figure 4.20 illustrates the architecture of the basic module and the principle of composition of this system.

The basic module is crossbar-based and uses two MIPS architecture processors. These modules are grouped into *CX-bricks* (up to 16 processors per CX-brick); the router integrated into a CX-brick allows the interconnection of 128 processors. With the R-brick (see below) to interconnect groups of 128 processors, the system can grow to an extremely large size—up to 512 processors.

Figure 4.20
*General
architecture of SGI
Origin 3000
system (source:
SGI).*

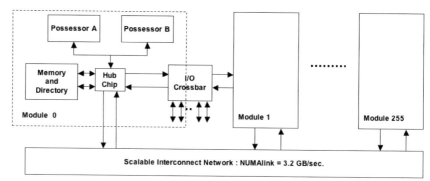

The interconnect network has a Hypercube topology, using bidirectional Craylink links with a bandwidth of 1.6 GB/s in each direction. The network supports coherence, using a scheme developed from the Stanford DASH project.

The system supports hot pluggability of its modules, and can be partitioned; evolution towards the use of Itanium processors rather than MIPS (*cf.* Altix 3000, described in Chapter 5), and the migration to Linux rather than IRIX as an operating system are expected as Linux begins to acquire more of the characteristics of a high end UNIX like IRIX (which is SGI's UNIX).

Physically, the architecture is modular, with the components being referred to as *bricks*.

- CX-Brick: processor/memory module holding 4 to 16 processors, 32 GB of memory and an 8-way router

- IX-Brick: Base System I/O Module; 11 pluggable PCI-X slots distributed over six 64-bit/133MHz PCI-X buses; system disk and a CD-ROM; Gigabit Ethernet

- PX-Brick: PCI expansion module, providing up to 12 hot-pluggable PCI cards distributed over six buses

- X-Brick: an extension module allowing the use of the I/O cards from the Origin 2000 on the 3000, and providing 4 XIO cards

- R-Brick: NUMAFLEX Router Interconnect Module (Metarouter in SGI's terminology) which enables the system configuration to grow up to 512 processors by interconnecting groups of 128 processors

- D-Brick: a disk module supporting up to 12 Fibre Channel disks (with capacities ranging from 36 GB up to 180 GB), managed as either JBOD (*Just a Bunch Of Disks*) or RAID

- G-Brick and V-Brick: graphics modules

- Power Bay: up to six hot-swap power supplies in an N+1 configuration

Interconnect between routers is implemented using cables.

Figure 4.21 illustrates the technology of interconnection of the hypercube type for configurations with 32 and 64 processors.

Figure 4.21
32 and 64 processor SGI Origin 3000 configurations (source: SGI).

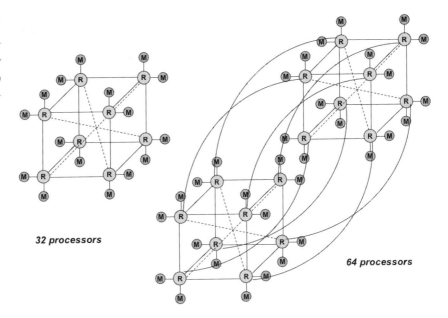

32 processors

64 processors

In this diagram, routers are indicated by the letter R and the dual-processor module by the letter M.

Figure 4.22 shows a configuration with 128 processors.

As to memory latencies, SGI has provided just one figure for the 128-processor Origin 3000, giving the NUMA factor as 2.99. More detailed figures had been provided for the earlier Origin 2000:

- Local memory access: 310 ns

- Distant memory access in a 2-module (4-processor) system: 540ns

Figure 4.22
SGI Origin
3000—128-
processor
configuration
(source: SGI).

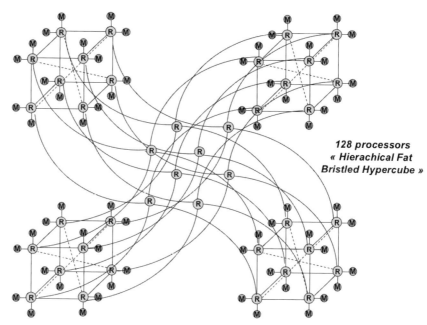

128 processors
« Hierachical Fat
Bristled Hypercube »

- Distant memory access in a 16-module (32-processor) system: 733ns
- Distant memory access in a 64-module (128-processor) system: 945ns

The NUMA factor for 128 processors is close to 3, which implies significant tuning requirements. SGI made hardware changes to mitigate software issues. To take advantage of locality and to help migrate pages to the modules using them, page reference counters were implemented in hardware; the use of the traditional load-linked, store-conditional instruction pair to build atomic operations results in significant contention in a large system—SGI therefore implemented a new synchronization primitive.

4.4.10   COMA (Cache-Only Memory Architecture)

Another architecture intended for use in very large SMP systems is COMA, *Cache-Only Memory Architecture*, in which data doesn't have a fixed place in memory (that is, has no fixed address in the memory of a module), and the memory of each module acts as a cache. Data is moved, by hardware, to where it is being accessed, and data that is shared for reading may therefore be resident in several modules at any one time.

Kendal Square Research, a company which has now disappeared, was the first (and only, by 2003) company to introduce a COMA to the marketplace.

Figure 4.23 illustrates the principle of COMA.

Figure 4.23
*Schematic diagram
of a COMA.*

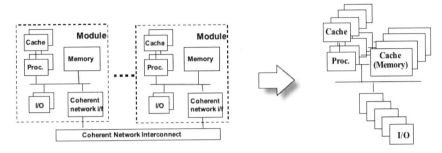

Physical Configuration   **Equivalent Logical Configuration**

This diagram shows, on the left, the physical implementation of a COMA architecture, with SMP modules connected by a coherent network; and on the right, the logical representation of the system. The system depicted is almost identical at the hardware level to the CC-NUMA architecture shown in Figure 4.19 except for the fact that main memory in the logical representation is shown as cache.

In a COMA system, objects are represented only as disk-resident objects, and cached copies of them are extracted and held in memory as the need arises. The various memory units in the modules are looked upon and managed as caches for the disk data; movement of data between memory and disk, and between memories, is managed according to a cache coherence protocol (rather than as a combination of cache coherence for memory-memory management and paging for memory-disk movement, as seen in a CC-NUMA system).

We can summarize the advantages and disadvantages of COMA with respect to CC-NUMA as follows:

Advantages:

■ Because memory is managed as a cache, data is always local to the module using it

■ Many copies of data used read-only may exist simultaneously

Disadvantages:

■ The hardware is more complex

■ Directory sizes increase, as does the time necessary to make allocate data

As originally described, COMA required a specific processor architecture in the area of virtual address translation, that is, in the definition of the MMU. This is the way KSR implemented the concept—rather than to having to create a whole new processor architecture with its substantial investments, research has been oriented towards the use of standard microprocessors. The S-COMA (Simple COMA) project at Stanford University is an example of this sort of approach.

Readers interested in discovering more about shared-memory architectures aimed at supporting a very large number of producers may refer to [LEN95].

4.5   **SMP, CC-NUMA, COMA: a Summary**

In this section we will compare and contrast SMP, CC-NUMA and COMA architectures. Figure 4.24 (after [PAI98]) shows the functional diagrams for these three architectures; we should note that of course CC-NUMA and COMA are simply approaches to implementing an SMP architecture, and that what is meant by Classic SMP in the diagram is a straightforward UMA SMP.

This diagram should make it clear that all the systems implement the objects manipulated by the system in the storage subsystem. The key difference between the architectures is the number of copies of the real objects that may exist in memory simultaneously.

In SMP and CC-NUMA, at most one extract,[8] of a VM object can exist throughout the whole of the physical memory. Indeed, when a processor seeks to access an object (or part of an object) that is not in physical memory, a page fault occurs; the OS allocates a page of physical memory— somewhere in the unified memory for a classic SMP, or (preferably) in the memory belonging to the module which raised the fault for a CC-NUMA machine—and copies the page in from storage to memory. Multiple copies of the object, or portions of it, can be in the various caches of the system (at most one per processor); these copies are properly managed by the cache coherence protocol.

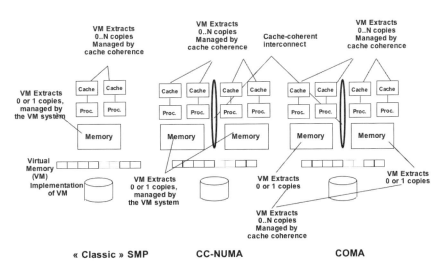

Figure 4.24
*"Classic" SMP,
DC-NUMA and
COMA
architectures.*

« Classic » SMP   CC-NUMA   COMA

In the case of COMA, things are a little different—several copies of the object may be present in memory simultaneously (up to one per processor). As before, when a processor attempts to refer to an object not in memory, the system must allocate memory and copy the object in from storage. It is clear that the performance of the system will be affected by the size of the object transferred, and by the nature of the device (or software) responsible for moving the data from storage to memory. In experimental systems like S-COMA, the size of such portions was the same as a traditional page, that is, several kilobytes, and it was software (the OS) which allocated memory and arranging for necessary I/O.

Coherence between the multiple copies of information placed in the memories of the various modules is ensured by the coherence protocol provided by the interconnect network. Just as in SMP and CC-NUMA architectures, several copies of the same extract of the page (cache granules) can be present in the caches of the various processors. The cache coherence protocol—implemented at the level of interconnect between the processors within a module and at the level of inter-module connection—ensures the coherence of information.

To summarize:

■ The traditional UMA SMP architecture provides the best characteristics as regards memory access time and the simplicity of the required cache coherence protocols

- CC-NUMA's data uniqueness property (0 or 1 copies of an object in memory at any time) simplifies the coherence protocol at the expense of increased access time to data in other modules

- COMA's ability to replicate data copies improves effective access time but results in a greater complexity in the needed cache coherence protocol

4.6   Performance Improvement Provided by SMP

We will cover systems performance and performance standards, in Chapter 7; here we will concentrate on the important property of scalability of SMPs.

A number of factors prevent an N-processor SMP having N times the performance of a uniprocessor. These include:

- Contention for the bandwidth of the processor-memory interconnect increases with the number of processors

- Contention for shared memory increases with the number of processors

- Maintaining cache coherence means that cache line invalidations, and movement of data from cache to cache, must occur

- Reduction of cache hit rate as a result of more context switches

- An increase in the number of instructions that must be executed to implement a given function because of the existence of locks and the contention for them

Just how much these factors affect performance is strongly dependent on the nature of the application; as an example, Table 4.1 shows a more or less linear increase in performance for an SMP system providing up to 24 processors, as measured by its performance on the SPEC_int_rate standard.

These most encouraging results show that a 24-processor SMP can deliver nearly 22 times the performance of a uniprocessor; however, this linearity is due to the characteristics of the benchmark, SPEC_int_rate standard, used for this experiment. The key characteristic of the benchmark is that it consists of multiple independent executions of a single program, and thus almost none of the contention mechanisms mentioned above have any effect—that is, each processor is involved only in accessing its own local

Table 4.1 *Example of improvement of SMP performance (SPEC_int_rate standard).*

Number of Processors	Relative Performance
1	1
4	3.98
8	7.69
16	15.09
24	21.93

resources and the other processors are invisible to it. It is, therefore, straightforward—given a good basic architecture and some tuning effort, to get rather good results with the benchmark; however, one may entertain reservations about the applicability of such numbers to real-world usage.

Unfortunately, there is little publicly available information on the scalability of SMPs on real-world applications. Figure 4.25 shows how the performance of a relational database application on an SMP system improved with from one software release to the next.

Figure 4.25
Evolution of the behavior of a system multiprocessor (transactional application and DBMS), according to the successive versions of software.

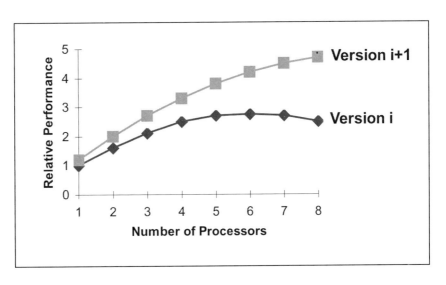

As shown in the figure,[9] with version I of the system and database software performance increases with up to five processors, and then declines. The next release substantially improves both raw performance and its scalability without any hardware changes; the software changes undoubtedly reduced bottlenecks in both OS and DBMS.

4.7   **Advantages and Disadvantages of SMP Architecture**

This section reviews the advantages and the disadvantages of SMP architectures. We will look again at this subject once we have covered cluster and MPP approaches.

Table 4.2 summarizes the advantages and disadvantages of the SMP approach.

Table 4.2   *Advantages and disadvantages of the SMP approach.*

Advantages	Disadvantages
■ Scalability of the system at a moderate cost.	■ Existence of at least one single point of failure—the operating system
■ Simple performance increase by adding a card or a processor module	■ Maintenance or update activities on the hardware and the OS generally require the whole system to be stopped
■ Multiprocessor effectiveness—the system performance increases (within definite limits) as the num ber of processors grows	■ Limitation of the number of processors because of access contention in the hardware (e.g., the bus) and software (operating system and DBMSs)
■ Simplicity of the programming model	■ Upgrade capability limited by rapid system obsolescence versus processor generations
■ Application transparency—single processor applications continue to work (although only multi-threaded applications can benefit from the architecture)	■ Complexity of the hardware
■ Availability: if one processor fails, the system may be restarted with fewer processors	■ Adaptation and expensive tuning of the operating system
■ The ability to partition the system	■ Necessary application adaptation to benefit from the performance available

The principal disadvantage of the SMP approach is the existence of a single point of failure; any failure of the operating system will bring down the complete system. Such a failure may be due to software errors, or to a hardware error that the OS cannot circumvent; as an example of the latter, when a processor fails, the OS has (in general) no means of knowing whether all the changes the failed processor had made to memory have successfully propagated to the rest of the system (in general, of course, they will not have done and will have been localized in the defunct processor's caches). The OS' only recourse is to stop the system, arrange for the failing elements to be removed or locked out of the coherence protocols and from execution, and restart (that is, reboot) the system.

When, as is frequently the case, a single system must support several different applications, one wishes to avoid having the failure of one application kill the others; large systems manage this through the technique of *partitioning*, which we will now discuss.

4.7.1   Systems Partitioning

Partitioning divides a single physical SMP system into a number of independent logical SMPs, each logical SMP running its own OS.[10]

This can be useful in the following situations:

■ When consolidating several servers into a single system (for investment rationalization, for example), while maintaining the apparent independence of the servers

■ Sharing the same systems between independent activities whose balance changes over time

Partitioning is a traditional facility long offered by mainframe systems, and now adopted by high-end standard systems.

Figure 4.26 illustrates partitioning.

Figure 4.26
Example of partitioning.

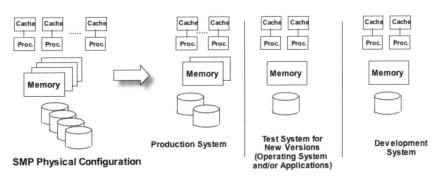

In this example, an SMP system is divided into three independent systems, each dedicated to a specific use: one is the production system, running a transaction system; another is a testbed for new versions of the OS and applications; and the third is dedicated to application development. Each of these systems runs its own copy of the OS. To be useful, the partitioning mechanisms must provide perfect insulation between the systems so that the failure of one has no effect on the others. This approach is of value because of its dynamic reconfigurability—a given investment in an SMP can be reconfigured to meet needs as they change, rather than having to upgrade and downgrade real independent systems.

To give an idea of what the partitioning might look like in practice, imagine that the SMP in the figure has 12 processors. Then under normal circumstances, one might expect six processors to be dedicated to the production system, two for the testbed and four for development. When the testbed system shows that recent changes look solid, it is usual to start stressing the new versions through increased loading. To do this, the development system is stopped and its resources transferred to the testbed—this might be done gradually, slowly stripping the development system of resources and giving them to the testbed, or it might be done "big bang." In a similar way, if real- world load on the production system is expected to increase, resources may be transferred from testbed or development systems to the production system, and given back when the peak has passed.

So partitioning makes it possible to have production, testbed and development running on a system of only 12 processors; an alternative would be a six processor production system, a six processor testbed (so it can match the production system's capacity) and a 4-processor development system. If the alternative was implemented, one might actually need to give the production and testbed systems eight processors to handle peaks, for a total of 20 processors rather than the 12 needed in the partitioning system

In our example we have implicitly assumed that the partitioning is effectively dynamic—that resources can be removed from and added to a system without stopping it. Were this not to be the case, the system would need bringing down and restarting, an activity prejudicial to the effective running of a production system.

We quickly will review some techniques used for systems partitioning.

4.7.2 Techniques of Partitioning

There are three major approaches to partitioning:

- Virtual machines

- Hardware partitioning

- Logical partitioning

The **virtual machine** technique was developed by IBM on the 360/67 with the CP (*Control Program*) system. CP generated multiple virtual machines, allowing multiple different operating systems to run on the computer simultaneously in an appropriate interleaved manner. From this experimental system, IBM developed a commercial product, VM. A time-sharing OS—CMS—had been developed alongside CP, and in conjunction with VM had some success in software development.

This approach is based on a system that makes it possible to define virtual machines and to have them supported on the hardware. The name hypervisor has been given to this class of meta operating systems.

Figure 4.27 illustrates the principle of operation of virtual machines.

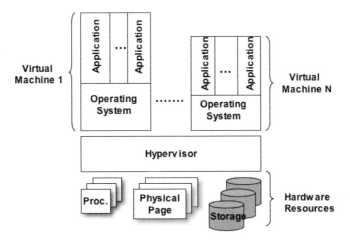

Figure 4.27
Virtual machine principle of operation.

Each virtual machine has its own virtual address space insulated and separate from any other VMs on that computer. Within each virtual machine, an operating system is loaded, which—as is usual—controls application execution. These OSs may all be different. Within a virtual machine, any user mode operations are executed normally, by the computer, at full speed.[11] When supervisor mode instructions are encountered, the machinery traps and the hypervisor emulates the needed operations, mapping the virtual resources of the virtual machine on to real resources.

The normal virtual memory mechanisms ensure insulation between user mode code executed in the various virtual machines. Insulation for privileged instructions is ensured by correct execution of the emulation by the hypervisor.

The virtual machine approach was widely used in mainframes; it exists also for IA-32 systems, an example of which is VMWare's ESX Server (www.vmware.com).

Hardware partitioning consists of defining, for a given physical system configuration, a number of logical systems, each with its own allocation of hardware resources (processor, memory, controllers, and peripherals). As an example, any given physical page is allocated to exactly one logical system. Hardware protection mechanisms make it possible to ensure that resources not allocated to a logical system are inaccessible to that system. A workable technique allocates numbers to the logical systems and to the resources (so that resources available to machine n are tagged with the number n); when a logical machine attempts to access a resource, the logical machine number and the resource tag may be checked.

Logical partitioning does not require dedication of the physical resources to logical systems; rather, the resources are managed by a special operating system that dynamically multiplexes the physical resources correctly between the logical systems. This approach is illustrated in Figure 4.28.

Figure 4.28
Principles of logical partitioning.

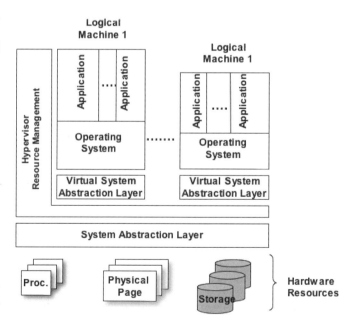

This approach, as illustrated, rests upon the use of a System Abstraction Layer (whose role in abstracting or hiding the details of the physical configuration we saw in Chapter 1). The hypervisor, in cooperation with the SAL and VSAL layers (Virtual System Abstraction Layer), will grant each logical machine the resources it needs. As each logical machine allocates resources, the VSAL maps the logical resources requested to the physical resources (as presented by SAL).

This allocation may be made respecting the various service policies granted the systems. Such an environment, naturally, requires that both the operating systems and the hypervisor support dynamic configuration and reconfiguration.

To conclude our partitioning discussion, we must remark that it is difficult to over-emphasize the necessity for dynamic partitioning, which allows the system to be reconfigured without having to stop and restart it.

Implementing this functionality requires very close cooperation between the hardware resource manager and the operating systems deployed; the complexity of this implementation helps to explain why dynamic partitioning is—even today—still found primarily in high-end systems.

It should also be clear that dynamic configuration vastly simplifies maintenance and upgrading, allowing components to be removed from logical systems, physically replaced, and then reallocated; and the components may be hardware or software, even operating systems. Again, without this capability, the whole system must be halted, reloaded and restarted.

4.7.3 Workload Managers

It is worthwhile to mention here an approach called *Resource Manager*. A Resource Manager is a piece of software that complements the OS, is ensuring that a given application (or applications) can be afforded a guaranteed slice of the actual physical systems resources (e.g., physical memory, processor time.) A Resource Manager reserves sufficient resources to ensure that critical work may be performed as required, while allowing a system to support multiple concurrent applications. When the critical work does not use all preallocated resources, the unused resource slots may be used by other applications.

Finally, it should also be clear that the virtual machine and logical partitioning approaches better lend themselves to dynamic configuration than does the hardware partitioning approach.

4.8   **Endnotes**

1.   Concerning the organization of virtual spaces (see the discussion about SAS and MAS in Chapter 3), we consider here the case of MAS (Multiple Address Spaces).

2.   To give an idea of the maturation process, we can mention that a UNIX system that has just been made MP-safe had around 100 locks, while in its mature, MP-efficient state it has nearly 6,000.

3.   In the PC world, the term UMA also exists, and is also an abbreviation for Uniform Memory Access. But its meaning is quite different, referring to PC architectures in which the memory for the display subsystem is a part of the processor address space, rather than being a part of the address space of a specialist graphics processor with which the main processor would communicate through the means of I/O operations.

4.   Partitioning is a set of hardware and software mechanisms that allow a given SMP to be divided into several (smaller) independent SMPs, each sub-SMP being controlled by its own operating system. The concept of partitioning and its use are discussed later on in a specific section.

5.   We note that only figures for a fully-loaded system are of interest.

6.   For this type of system, IBM has traditionally expressed performance in terms of MIPS—millions of instructions per second. This metric, which we will discuss further in Chapter 7, allows one to make comparisons between a range of machines of the same architecture. IBM's figures are obtained by measuring a collection of workloads across different environments, such as TSO (Time Sharing Option), CICS/DB2, and so on. The benchmarks themselves are described in an IBM report ("Large System Performance Report"), which is regularly updated and gives performance figures for a number of systems. Unfortunately these figures cannot be used to compare IBM systems with other vendors' systems, because the applications are only available on IBM systems. Further, for the zSeries, IBM has not (by the beginning of 2003) published figures for standard benchmarks, such as SPEC or TPC.

7.   EKCD corresponds to I/O with variable block lengths (Count) and identifiable by a Key. At the time this interface was created (in the first half of the 60s, with System/360), off-loading the

work to identify the blocks to the disk controllers noticeably reduced both the load on the main processors and the amount of memory needed (loading blocks into memory and searching for the block matching a key). The sharp and continuing improvement in processor performance and memory capacity has since rather reduced interest in this approach.

8. By the term extract, we mean that elementary information which is allocated in the target memory. The size of such an extract might be a page—several kilobytes—when the target memory is physical memory, or a few hundred bytes in a manner similar to data held in caches.

9. In the figure, we have deliberately removed the actual performance numbers and any information allowing the subject system to be identified, since the shape of the curve and the ability for software changes to improve matters the concepts are important here.

10. Different OSs may be used in such a context. This is frequently the case where a new release of the OS is to be installed: it is first checked before moving production work to it. Different OS may be of interest, e.g., Linux/UNIX in addition to a proprietary OS.

11. We can generally distinguish two modes of operation for a processor: the supervisor (or privileged) mode and user mode. In user mode, only a subset of the machine's instructions can be executed. Instructions that change the fundamental state of the machine—for example, instructions which change a program state descriptor corresponding to the activation of another process; changing of the virtual memory descriptor tables; initialization of I/O operations—may only be executed in supervisor mode. The transition from user to supervisor mode is done by a supervisor call instruction or as a side-effect of accepting an interrupt or an exception. We should note further that not all of the operating system operates in supervisor mode.

5

Clusters and Massively Parallel Machines

In this chapter we will look at both clusters and massively parallel machines, starting with clusters. Both these architectures are often referred to as being *loosely-coupled*, a term based on the observation that the processors in one node do not have any close link with the processors in another node—processors in different nodes do not share memory (in general, although some clusters do support shared memory), and each node runs its own copy of the operating system. Such unshared-memory systems are also sometimes called NORMA, for *No Remote Memory Access*.

5.1 Clusters

The concept of a cluster was introduced towards the end of the 70s, by Tandem[1] with its Guardian systems, and was further exploited by Digital with its VAXclusters, introduced in 1983 [KRO86]. Interested readers may found more on clusters in following reference book [PFI95]. The use of the term cluster in a computing context is a simple extension of a fine English term (Webster's definition: "cluster n. [Old English clyster] a number of persons or things grouped together – vi., vt. to gather or grow in a cluster").

A cluster is fundamentally some reasonable number of systems—around ten is a practical maximum—interconnected so that they can share resources. We will refer to such resources as *cluster resources*. Each system in a cluster is called a *node*. Each node is a real, complete system, with all the resources it needs—processor, memory, I/O devices, and storage subsystem—working under the control of its own copy of the operating system. As we have noted previously, the term loosely-coupled is often used to describe clusters, in contrast to the tightly-coupled nature of SMP systems.

Tandem and Digital were pursuing different goals with the introduction of their respective cluster systems.

■ Tandem wanted to build transaction-processing systems that were failure-tolerant—an application running on a node which failed could be safely and correctly continued on another node. Tandem's applications, being transaction- oriented, naturally provided recovery points (the beginnings of each transaction).

■ Digital, on the other hand, was looking for a performance boost leveraging existing systems, since its next-generation high-end system (based on bipolar technology) had suffered unexpected delays, and Digital needed something to keep customers happy.

The architecture of the VAXclusters (and, to a lesser extent, Tandem's Guardian) served as a basis for both UNIX clusters and Microsoft clusters[2] (Microsoft's offering being MSCS, for *Microsoft Cluster Services*, earlier known by its codename *Wolfpack*). We give a brief overview of some commercial clusters in this section: IBM's HACMP, the Windows cluster, and two examples of clusters supporting shared memory—IBM's Sysplex and SGI's Altix 3000.

Here, we will just give a high-level description of the "clustering" software architecture for HACMP and the Windows cluster; a description of the mechanisms within these systems will be provided in Chapter 10 (hardware and Software Solutions for High Availability).

Cluster differ from distributed systems in three key ways:

■ *Homogeneity*—a cluster is constructed from a number of similar nodes (e.g., processors are the same, each node comes from the same vendor, and so forth) with well-defined configurations and all under the control of the same version of the operating system (albeit a version adapted to cluster use).

■ *Single System Image*—a cluster provides the illusion to the user, and to some extent to the administrator, that it is just one big system, not a collection of systems. As an example, the cluster has but one IP address, so a user establishes a connection with a cluster using just one IP address for the cluster, whichever node actually supports the connection. Efforts to maintain the illusion of a single system in all aspects of the system can lead to substantial implementation complexities and to unwanted inefficiencies. We note that the shared resources within a cluster are referred to as *clusterized resources*.

- *Geographical concentration*—as we have already noted, the various nodes composing a cluster are generally in close physical proximity, so they are not just logically a system, but physically just one system as regards maintenance, access security and so forth.

We can therefore look upon a cluster as a means of implementing a server that is differentiated from a distributed system through the homogeneity of its logical and physical management.

Inter-node synchronization is provided by a Distributed Lock Manager. The VAX Cluster DLM served as inspiration for the various DLMs now available in standard systems.

A cluster operating system may be either a purpose-built OS—as was the case for Tandem's NonStop Kernel—or one derived from an existing general-purpose OS, as was the case for the VAXcluster (based on VMS); for the MVS for IBM's Sysplex, the various cluster-adapted UNIX versions; and for MSCS, the cluster version of Windows.

Even more than the increase in performance, the key advantage offered by a cluster is its high availability. As we shall see, clusters have intrinsic redundancy, making them much less susceptible to failure in the presence of errors and, importantly, in the presence of software errors.

It must be said, however, that the performance increase achieved is not always what one might expect. A number of limiting factors can be relevant:

- Some applications have only a limited amount of parallelism
- Communication between processes running on different nodes is not very efficient
- Development tools and middleware for this class of application are rare and often of limited functionality
- There are no programming standards for parallel applications running on cluster limits portability

However, these limitations have not prevented cluster architectures from figuring prominently in published TPC benchmark results (see Chapter 7). These results, although good, must be interpreted carefully:

- The very design of the TPC-C benchmark means that inter-node communication is rather low, and so scalability can look excellent

- Systems manufacturers and DBMS vendors recognize the attractive power of excellent TPC benchmark results, and expend large amounts of effort tuning for those results

We should note that the question of whether or not such benchmark results translate usefully into the real world is an eternal subject of discussion—but we should remark that publishing the performance results for one's system using recognized benchmarks is a sign of "good system health" (as well as good business practice) for systems vendors.

The performance improvement seen on cluster systems with database systems is at its most pronounced with decision-support applications, since these applications are read-mostly and benefit from the intra-request optimizations easily available on a cluster, while the synchronization required for database updates arising during normal transaction processing penalizes cluster architectures.

Thus, even if they provide an objective means of comparing available systems, the results of the TCP benchmarks cannot be directly mapped into projections of how a business' real-world workload will perform.

The concept of a *single system image* is generally implemented only in a limited way on a cluster system. The reasons behind this are as much to do with implementation difficulties as with the fact that the approach is of limited value for certain cluster characteristics. As an example, although the efficiency of effecting interprocess communication by means of shared memory is well recognized, implementing shared memory within a cluster whose nodes are connected by a local area network provides bandwidth and latency performance hardly different from that obtained by message-passing, while also introducing a single point of failure. Worse still, even if the shared memory itself has not failed, it is not possible to guarantee that such shared memory has not been left in an inconsistent state by the failure of a node, so that in such a system the failure of a node generally implies the failure of the system as a whole and the need for a reboot. Thus, shared memory used in a cluster system destroys one of the cluster's key advantages—high availability.

In many cases, the single system image is limited to certain classes of resources, such as disks; logical volumes (an abstraction of disks); file systems; communications controllers; or a single network address for the cluster. The development of clusterized file systems once posed problems, since this functionality was late to arrive in UNIX systems.

Since cluster nodes are loosely coupled and can be built upon a standard local area network technology, they can not only support several technology generations simultaneously, but also support nodes of different generations within a single system.

To date, apart from databases and Enterprise Resource Planning packages, few applications have arisen that can benefit from a cluster architecture. In databases, Oracle was the first to deliver a clusterized version for the VAXcluster, followed by UNIX versions. Today, most widely-adopted databases are cluster-adapted—DB2, Oracle, and SQL Server among them. We should also note that tools for the support of parallel applications of a scientific nature—PVM and MPI—are well-suited to use on cluster systems.

5.1.1 Example of a UNIX cluster—IBM Cluster 1600

Several years ago, IBM introduced the RS/6000 SP, a massively-parallel system whose nodes were originally built from single-processor server chassis (actually, from uniprocessor workstations) and then later from standard SMP nodes. An SP system comprised multiple racks, each rack holding a varying number of nodes (depending on the nature of the nodes) and containing the interconnect fabric. A system could contain up to a maximum of 128 nodes, although up to 512 could be provided on special order. The systems were intended for scientific applications.

IBM's equivalent offering for the commercial space was HACMP (for *High Availability Cluster MultiProcessing*), which allowed one to connect up a number of standard AIX systems to create high-availability systems and—to a lesser extent—systems with the ability to have modular performance increments (that is, performance improvements through addition of nodes). We will look more closely at this in Chapter 10.

The Cluster 1600 family was born from a convergence of these two systems, although the distinction remains in their naming—"Cluster 1600 for High-Performance Computing" and "Cluster 1600 for Commercial Computing." After introducing a few common concepts, we will describe, the Commercial Computing version. The High-Performance Computing version, with its specific interconnect network, is described in a later section of this chapter, one devoted to massively parallel machines. The architecture of HACMP is covered in Chapter 10.

In the Cluster 1600 for Commercial Computing system, each node operates under the control of AIX, IBM's UNIX offering.

Software components are:

- CSM (*Cluster System Management*) or PSSP (*Parallel System Program Support*) for system management
- GPFS (*General Parallel File System*), a clusterized file system
- Parallel Environment, for the construction of distributed applications

CSM comes from the Linux world, and offers a single console management tool for the cluster as a whole, as well as single-console support for hardware management (HMC, for *Hardware Management Console*).

PSSP is a collection of support and management tools for the system, including:

- Communication Subsystem: support of SP Switch and SP Switch 2 interconnection networks
- Virtual Shared Disk (VSD): creation of logical volumes accessible from any node (that is, construction of a Shared Disk architecture on top of a Shared Nothing architecture)
- Recoverable Virtual Shared Disk (RVSD): allowing continuity of accessibility in the event that a node fails

GPFS creates a single file system for a collection of nodes and makes it possible to exploit the processing power of different nodes. GPFS provides journalizing (that is, transactional handling of changes to the file system's metadata) to reduce both the amount of time needed to restart the system after a failure, as well as replication of the metadata to improve system availability.

A key component of Parallel Environment is LoadLeveler, which allows system resource optimization through both dynamic scheduling of jobs and load balancing.

Figure 5.1 illustrates a simple cluster configuration based on AIX, with the application making use of a parallel database (Oracle); the system makes

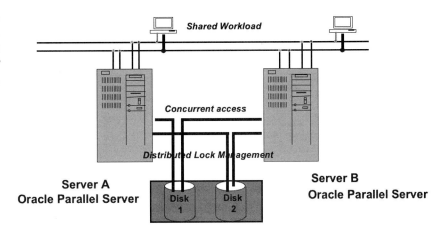

Figure 5.1
Example of an HACMP configuration.

use of HACMP to add cluster capabilities. As with other UNIX systems, the configuration is not limited to just the two nodes as shown here.

In this system, the clusterized resources are the disks, the WAN and LAN networking and the DLM (*Distributed Lock Manager*), whose implementation is distributed across the nodes of the system. System interconnect is Ethernet or FibreChannel- based, and can be replicated to increase availability. System workload is distributed between the servers.

The general architecture of the HACMP software is shown in Figure 5.2.

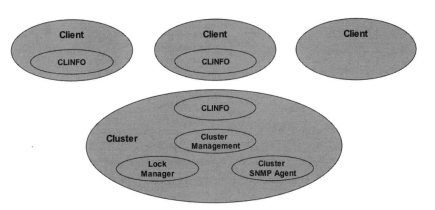

Figure 5.2
General Architecture of IBM's HACMP/ 6000.

The various components of the HACMP/6000 architecture are as follows:

- *Cluster Manager.* Active on every node in the cluster, it has the responsibility of keeping up-to-date information on the cluster and on the state of the interconnect network. It also handles reporting the operating state of the cluster with respect to other systems.

- *CLINFO.* Cluster Information Services are optional on both client and cluster nodes, it provides an API to allow clients to query the state of the cluster, that information is also communicated to the SNMP agents.

- *Cluster SNMP Agent.* SNMP (*Simple Network Management protocol*) is a distributed systems administration standard in the UNIX world. The Cluster Manager provides information to the Cluster SNMP agent, which makes that information available through SNMP.

- *Lock Manager.* The cluster Lock Manager provides a distributed synchronization service to the various services and applications executing on the cluster; it is a implementation of the concept of a DLM (Distributed Lock Manager) introduced in the VAX Cluster.

A detailed account of this architecture and how it works is provided in Chapter 10.

In version 4.4, HACMP offers various levels of functionality:

- *Classic,* a base level of service at which HACMP detects and reacts to software failures sufficient to cause a failure of the system

- *Enhanced Scalability* (HACMP/ES), which provides improved availability by being built on top of RSCT (*Reliable Scalable Cluster Technology*). RSCT allows administrators to manage a significant number of AIX servers—up to 32—without the need for expensive communications equipment

- The *Concurrent Resource Manager* (CRM) allows concurrent access to shared disks

- The C-SPOC (*Cluster Single Point of Control*) and *Dynamic Reconfiguration* software, which allow actions such as the attachment of new resources or the creation of new users to be carried out without having to stop and restart the system.

In addition, other software complements HACMP proper:

- *LoadLeveler* provides load-balancing across multiple users

- *Parallel System Support Program* provides a single point for administration

- *GPFS* (*General Parallel File System*) provides a clusterized file system

PSSP offers also particularly useful services in the construction of high-performance clusters, such as VSD (*Virtual Shared Disks*), which provides visibility of logical volumes that can be supported by disks distributed on various nodes of the cluster, along with an associated recovery service.

5.1.2 Microsoft Cluster Service (MSCS)

Microsoft developed a cluster version of its Windows operating system under the codename *Wolfpack*. Originally called MSCS (*Microsoft Cluster Server*) it was renamed Microsoft Cluster Service in 2002.

The development stages for Cluster Server were:

1. End of 1996: publication of the APIs for cluster programming and availability of the associated SDK (Software Development Kit), allowing software producers to develop applications making use of the first version of Cluster Server

2. First half of 1997: the first version of Cluster Server, limited to just 2 nodes

3. August 1998: the beta 2 version, with extended functionality

4. The Windows 2000 Datacenter Server supports up to four nodes, each node comprising four or eight processors (for a maximum configuration of either 16 or 32 processors), while Windows NET Data Center supports up to 8 nodes

The Microsoft Server 2003 cluster supports up to 8 processors in the Enterprise Edition and up to 32 processors in the Datacenter Edition. The key objective of the earlier versions was to support high-availability configurations, while the later ones also began to address increased performance—that is they began an evolution towards participative redundancy[3] as illustrated in Figure 5.3 (inspired by a Microsoft white paper).

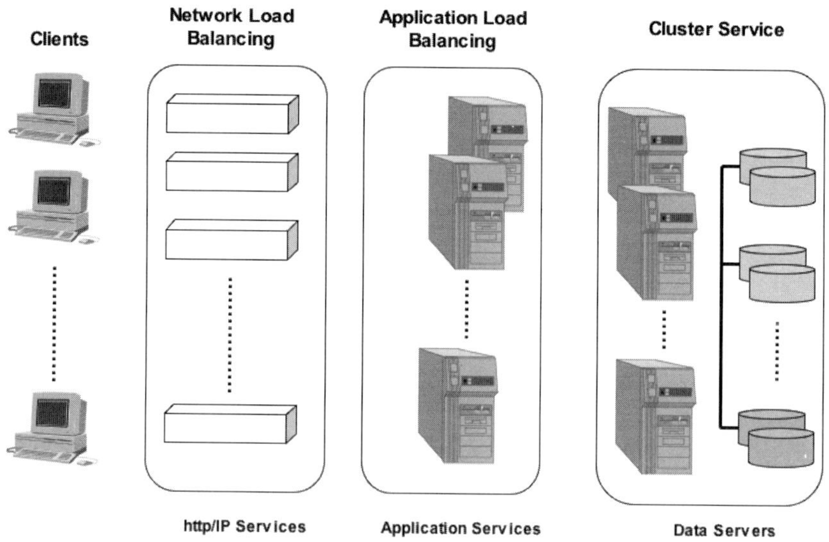

Figure 5.3
*Example of use of
Windows Cluster
(source: Microsoft).*

Figure 5.3
*Example of use of
Windows Cluster
(source: Microsoft).*

This example shows a 4-level architecture, in the context of Windows 2000. Three technologies are used to support this configuration: Network Load Balancing, Component Load Balancing, and the Microsoft Cluster Service itself.

The NLB (*Network Load Balancing*) level handles processing HTTP protocols, the standard Web communication protocols. The cluster architecture provides both high performance and high availability. NLB uses just one virtual IP address to which client requests are addressed. Although a basic premise is load-sharing between the nodes, it is possible to specify that certain classes of traffic—such as ftp requests—are to be forwarded to specific systems.

In the event of a failure, the remaining servers take over handling requests. A server may be dynamically reinstalled in the cluster. Up to 32 nodes can be used for the NLB level.

The CLB (*Component Load Balancing*) tier is provided by the Microsoft Application Center 2000 product. It uses COM+ (a distributed object environment supplemented by transactional services) as well as the Cluster Service (see later). Up to eight nodes may be used for the CLB level.

The components of CLB are:

■ *CLB Software*, which provides load-balancing

- *Router*, which provides routing between the Web portion and application servers

- *Application servers*, which support COM+ components

Load balancing is based on measurements of response times across the various application servers.

The Data Services portion is based on Cluster Services, and can support up to 8 nodes.

Cluster Service has the goal of providing high availability; in the event of failure of one of the nodes, resources managed by the node may be instantiated on another node (this is covered in greater detail a little later).

Microsoft chose the *Shared Nothing* architecture for its clusters, as opposed to the *Shared Disks* model. This choice is not limiting; software such as a DBMS, which assumes a shared disk architecture, can simulate such a model layered on top of a *Shared Nothing* system, for example through the use of the notion of *remote I/O*. These architectural options are covered in Chapter 8.

The Windows cluster is based on the following concepts:

- *Cluster Services*. A collection of software implemented on each node, managing cluster-specific activities

- *Resource*. A canonical resource managed by the system. Cluster Services looks upon all the resources as opaque objects, since it is not interested in the operations supported by any particular resource. As examples of resources, we may list physical resources (disks, communications controller cards); TCP-IP addresses; applications; and databases

- *On-line resources*. A resource is on-line in a node when it is providing services on that node

- *Group*. A collection of resources managed as a single entity. In theory, a group contains all the elements necessary for an application. Groups ease an administrator's workload—an administrative act on a group applies to all the resources in the group

Cluster Services are presented at client workstations in the form of virtual servers. Connection takes place using an IP address; this address is interpreted by the Cluster service as a resource that is part of the same

Figure 5.4
*Components of
Cluster Service
(source: Microsoft).*

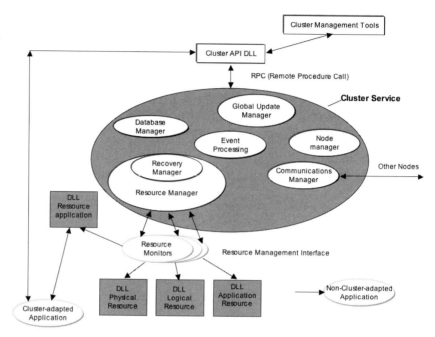

group as the application in use. If a node fails, the Cluster service moves the whole group to a new node; the client detects the failure of the session and requests a re-connection; with the IP address available on the new node, connection is re-established in the usual manner.

Microsoft Cluster Server architecture is depicted in Figure 5.4.

Cluster Service components are as follows (derived from [MIC03]):

- *Node Manager.* Manages the membership of the node in the cluster and monitors correct operation of the other nodes in the cluster by means of heartbeat messages. In the event another member of the node does not respond in time to a heartbeat message, each active member of the cluster checks the complete cluster state to reconfigure it appropriately.

- *Database Manager.* Maintains the database representing the cluster configuration. Entities represented in this database are the cluster itself, cluster node membership, resource types, resource groups, and descriptions of specific resources, such as disks and IP addresses. Each Database Manager running on each node in the cluster cooperates to maintain consistent configuration information across the cluster.

- *Checkpoint Manager.* Ensures that Cluster Service can recover from a resource failure by checking registry keys when a resource is brought online and writing checkpoint data to the quorum resource (see below) when the resource goes offline.

- *Log Manager.* Ensures, in cooperation with the Checkpoint Manager, that the recovery log on the quorum resource (see below) contains the most recent configuration data and change checkpoints.

- *Failover Manager.* Responsible for stopping and starting resources, managing resource dependencies, and for initiating failover of resource groups according to the state information provided by Resource Monitors and the cluster node.

- *Global Update Manager.* Replicates changes to the cluster database across cluster nodes in an atomic (i.e., all or none) and serial (total order is maintained) fashion. Backup/Restore Manager. Backups or restores of the quorum log file and all checkpoint files.

- *Event Log Replication Manager.* Replicates log entries to all cluster nodes.

- *Resource Monitors.* Implemented as processes, they communicate with Cluster Service by means of RPCs (Remote Procedure Calls). They check that resources are operating correctly, using callbacks for this purpose. They also provide transformations for calls on resources.

- *Event Service.* Sends events to and from applications and the cluster service components running on nodes in the cluster.

- *Time Service.* Implemented as a resource, it provides a homogeneous time across the cluster.

To be strictly accurate, the last three components are not part of the Cluster Service.

In order to insure proper cluster operations, each cluster has a special resource known as the *quorum resource.* Such a resource (often a disk) provides a means for arbitration leading to membership and cluster state decisions (tie breaker) and provides physical storage to store configuration information (of course, information consistency, insured by Cluster Services, is key).

Chapter 10 provides more details on this architecture and its operation.

5.1.3 **Shared-memory Clusters**

Cluster architectures that share memory or other resources have been the subject of both research projects and commercial products. While the research projects are interesting, we will concentrate on just the commercial products, and in particular IBM's Sysplex and the more recent SGI Altix 3000.

5.1.4 **IBM Sysplex**

IBM's Sysplex is a cluster architecture built on the S/390 mainframe and the z/ Series, and has had reasonable market success: IBM reports that there were more than 1,600 customers by the end of 1999, and more than 600 of them used data sharing in their systems. A logical view of the architecture is given in Figure 5.5.

Figure 5.5
IBM sysplex logical architecture.

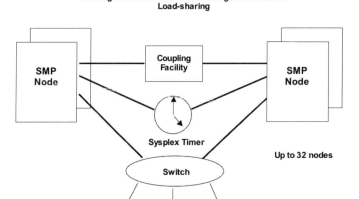

As shown by the figure, a Sysplex configuration comprises a number of nodes (up to 32), interconnected as follows:

■ *Coupling facility.* Its basic elements are a data cache shared by the nodes (with global cache coherence) and control structures that make it possible to implement shared data queues, along with a distributed locking mechanism.

- *Sysplex Timer.* A centralized time server that distributes the same time base to the cluster nodes.

- *Switch.* The connection to the disk subsystems, allowing storage resources to be shared by the cluster nodes. Two connection technologies may be used: Escon, an IBM proprietary technology whose capabilities are similar to those of Fibre Channel (Escon was introduced before Fibre Channel had demonstrated its reliability) or Fibre Channel itself.

The figure gives just one logical view—in reality, a number of physical configurations are possible for the coupling facility, increased even further with the series z900, which now supports the following possibilities:

- *z900 system Model 100.* A specialized system proving just the Coupling facility, with up to 9 nodes

- *ICF* (Internal Coupling Facility). This is the Coupling Facility supported within a z900 avoiding the need for a specific system; it may be used as a backup to an external Coupling Facility (i.e., a z900 Model 100)

- A *logical partition* within a z900 system

With regard to the connections between systems, various technologies exist:

- *IC Channel* (Internal Coupling) within the same node with a bandwidth of 1.25 GB/s

- *ICB-3* (Integrated Cluster Bus), between nodes, on a copper connection: 1 GB/s and 7 meters (7 yards or so) maximum length

- *ISC-3* (InterSystem Communication), between nodes, on monomode fibre: 2.125 GB/s and 10 kilometers (a little over 6 miles)

ICB-3 and ISC-3 benefit from the STI interface (*Self-Timed Interface*) of the z900.

The timer facility can be used either to synchronize all the nodes in a system, or to synchronize each node to a different time zone. This is the purpose of the ETR (*External Time Reference*) components mentioned in Chapter 4 in the discussion on the z900.

There are two types of Sysplex cluster:

- A *local cluster* (Parallel Sysplex) in which all the nodes are geographically close

- A *Geographically Dispersed Cluster*—GDPS (Geographically-Dispersed Parallel Sysplex)

GDPS can be used to satisfy the objectives of Disaster Recovery; it can therefore be used in conjunction with the data duplication techniques PPRC (*Peer-to-Peer Remote Copy*) and XRC (*eXtended Remote Copy*), which are covered in Chapter 6. According to IBM, the following objectives can be met with these techniques:

- GDPS/PPRC: less than one hour recovery time, no loss of data, and a maximum distance of 40 kilometers (about 25 miles) between sites

- GDPS/XRC: approximately 30 minutes' recovery time, a window of opportunity for data loss not exceeding one minute; and no distance limitation between sites

Sysplex relies on two z/OS technologies for resource management:

- PR/SM (*Processor Resource/System Manager*): supports the creation of (up to 15) logical partitions (LPAR) within a single machine. PR/SM allocates processor, memory and I/O resources (I/O resources may be shared) to the specified partitions. The allocation is dynamic. Processors may be allocated to a partition, or shared between partitions.

- WLM (*Work Load Manager*): a workload manager driven by specified objectives within a partition managed by z/OS.

IRD (*Intelligent Resource Director*) synergises the existence of PR/SM and WLM by managing resources between the various partitions of a Sysplex cluster.

To provide transparency to the users, the VIPA (*Virtual IP Addressing*) functionality makes it possible to provide address independence and allows load balancing between the nodes of a Sysplex cluster.

Several further modules simplify the operation and management of a Sysplex system; three examples are the *Sysplex Failure Manager* (which allows parametrization of the failure detection intervals and associated recovery actions), *Automatic Restart* (which speeds up restart after a failure) and *Single System Image* (which facilitates the management of the Sysplex system).

A number of IBM data management products, such as VSAM, IMS (a hierarchical DBMS), and DB2 (a relational DBMS), have been ported to Sysplex and support data sharing between cluster nodes via the coupling facility.

> DBMS are a key element in servers, and their availability on an architecture is vital. Many innovative architectures failed when DBMS support was not forthcoming, and have since disappeared completely. Such decisions by DBMS vendors are market-driven; market share and costs of support and of porting to such innovative architectures are the deciding factors. In the case of Sysplex, we note with interest that only IBM DBMS products were ported.

A number of other products have been ported to Sysplex:

- *Batch Processing.* Batch processing performance can be critical for some applications—for example, it may be necessary to complete batch processing by some specified time or date—and Sysplex' parallel processing can provide sufficient power to guarantee this.

- *DB2, IMS/DB and VSAM RLS (Record Level Sharing).* Sysplex makes it possible to manage the coherence of data caches used by these DBMSs; it also minimizes—by caching data in the coupling facility—disk accesses.

- *Transaction Monitors.* CICS and IMS/TM (the transaction monitor for IMS). Sysplex allows transparent (to the users) load distribution between different instances of the transaction managers.

- *Work Load Manager.* (see above)

- *WebSphere*, based on technologies (such as CICS) which have been ported to Sysplex, exploits Sysplex capabilities. WebSphere is an environment to support client/server applications in an Internet context; similar products include BEA's WebLogic and Microsoft's .NET.

Shared Memory and High Availability

As we have indicated earlier, the very presence of shared memory compromises system availability. This is because in the event of the failure of one of the nodes, it is impossible in the general case to determine how to undo the changes made by the failing node to the shared memory to recreate a coherent/self-consistent state for the memory. The author hypothesizes that Sysplex could deal with this problem by allowing only the system components (i.e., the OS and the data managers) to have access to the shared memory, and by ensuring that all update accesses to that memory are based on the concept of transactions. This makes it possible to cancel the effects of any transactions which were in process—i.e., not yet committed—at the time of failure.

5.1.5   SGI Altix 3000

In January 2003, SGI introduced the Altix 3000, which builds on the Origin 3000; indeed, the only change is in the processor. The Altix C-brick is a 4-way Itanium 2 SMP.

In its first version, this system supports up to 64 processors and 512 GB of memory. A future version should extend these limits to 512 processors and 4 TB of memory.

Figure 5.6 illustrates the internal architecture of the C-brick.

The C-brick contains four Itanium 2 processors, 32 GB of memory and two proprietary chips called SHUB. Each SHUB provides the interface between two processors, their memory, their I/O and the other SHUB. Communication between processors in one module and processors or memory in another module is done via the SHUB, using NUMALink, a CC-NUMA interconnect based on the Origin 3000 NUMAflex interconnect; these connections use cables.

While Origin 3000 was based on a hypercube interconnect, Altix 3000 makes use of a "fat tree" topology.

We can look at an Altix 3000 as either:

- A CC-NUMA SMP

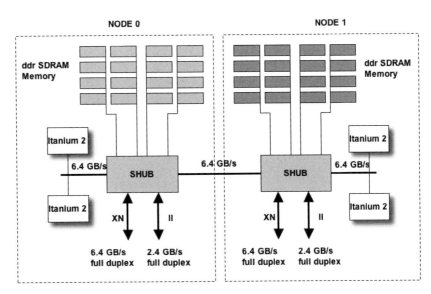

Figure 5.6
Architecture of the Altix 3000 Itanium-2 based C-brick (source: SGI).

- An SMP-based cluster, making use of CC-NUMA for any node larger than 4 processors, with shared memory

Figure 5.7 (from SGI), illustrates three interconnect topologies providing 8, 16, and 64 processor systems.

As shown by Figure 5.7, an 8-processor system can be built by interconnecting SHUBs with NUMALink4 connections.

The 16 processor configuration uses an 8-port crossbar router and NUMALink3 connections.

The 64-processor system is a fat tree, with replicated interconnect for performance and availability, making use of four 8-port crossbar routers interconnected by XpressLinks.

According to SGI, an access to memory going through one router sees a 45 nsec overhead.

To optimize NUMA performance, SGI made a number of extensions to Linux, providing commands that make it possible to control both processor and memory affinity (processor affinity manages the likelihood or requirement that a processor executes next on the processor it most recently executed on). The standard MPI (*Message Passing Interface*) and SHMEM (*Shared Memory*) interfaces were implemented to make the hardware capabilities (the BTE—*Block Transfer Engine*—provides fast data movement and synchronization operations) straightforwardly available to applications.

Figure 5.7

Some examples of configurations Altix 3000 (Source SGI)

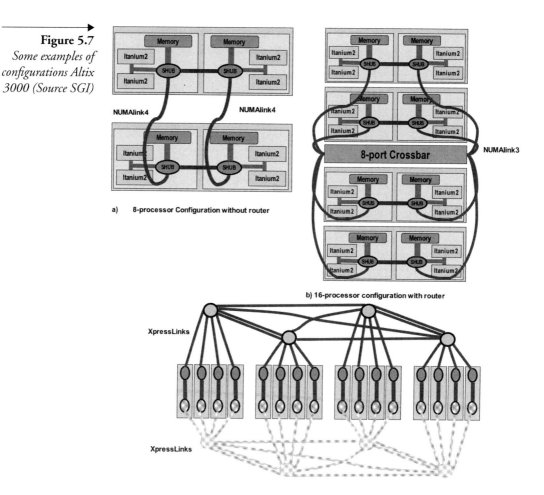

a)   **8-processor Configuration without router**

b) **16-processor configuration with router**

c) **64-processor Configuration**

5.2   Advantages and Disadvantages of Cluster Architecture

In this section we briefly review the advantages and disadvantages of the cluster architecture; we will revisit the subject at the end of the chapter, including SMP's in the equation, after we have described MPPs.

Table 5.1 summarizes cluster advantages and disadvantages.

Since each node has its own resources, the failure of any one node does not result in the failure of the other nodes. However, extreme care must be taken in the design and implementation of clusterization software, to avoid

Table 5.1 *Advantages and disadvantages of the cluster approach.*

Advantages	Disadvantages
■ High intrinsic availability (independence of the nodes) ■ Simple hardware implementation ■ Application-level compatibility with uniprocessors and multiprocessors ■ Increase in performance for DBMS (OLTP if there are few interactions between nodes, Decision Support always) ■ Easy integration of new technologies (processors and OS versions) ■ Transparent sharing of "clusterized" resources ■ Ease of maintenance	■ Multiprocessor effectiveness limited (compared to SMP) ■ Implies the need for changes to the OS (making Single System Image more difficult) ■ Applications must be modified to take advantage of cluster performance increase (i.e., to give the application the ability to exploit several nodes concurrently) ■ In practice for commercial applications, the most common software tuned for clusters has been DBMSs (e.g. Oracle, DB2, SQL Server) ■ The standards for writing parallel programs are still in their early stages ■ The upper limit to the size of a cluster is only of the order of ten interconnected systems ■ Difficulties administering the cluster

problems such as a *cascade* of crashes—a situation in which the failure of one nodes directly leads other nodes to fail. Clusters are mainly used to build high-availability solutions.

A node in a cluster is basically the same as a single isolated system: it must provide the same layers of software, a connection (perhaps replicated) to a fast local area network such as Ethernet or FC, and disk subsystem connections of a form suitable to allow the disks to be connected simultaneously to several systems, so that in the event of a node failure, another node can take over the disk subsystem. Thus, implementing a cluster does not require any hardware out of the ordinary, which means that cluster hardware prices should be pleasantly low.

Any application that already works on a uniprocessor or multiprocessor will function correctly on a single node of a cluster; however, to take advantage of the promise of high availability offered by a cluster, modifications must be made to scripts (that is, procedures written in the OS's command language, such as UNIX shell commands) and to resource declarations.

Applications adapted to leverage cluster capabilities—that is, making use of the message-passing paradigm—will see a performance increase when run on a cluster (compared to a uniprocessor). Few management-oriented applications have been ported to clusters—just DBMS and some ERP packages come to mind. Minimizing node interactions allows higher performance.

Because the nodes are independent, inserting new technologies is relatively straightforward. In particular, it is simple to mix CPU technology generations in a cluster; this is in stark contrast to an SMP, in which—in practice—all the processors must be identical, and so adopting a new microprocessor generation usually requires complete system infrastructure replacement (even down to swapping motherboards). In a cluster, an incremental migration from one operating system version to another can be done, provided that the system can live with nodes being managed by different versions of the OS.

Node independence also simplifies maintenance—to be able to work on a node, one must simply tell the cluster configuration that the node is no longer part of the system; then necessary maintenance or upgrade activities may take place on the node. Once completed, the cluster can be told to reintegrate the node.

A key disadvantage of a cluster is that its multiprocessor efficiency or effectiveness is less scalable and effective than an SMP, because of a cluster's reliance on message-passing rather than the SMP's shared memory. We should note that with the adoption of VI (*Virtual Interface*, covered in Chapter 2), the multiprocessor effectiveness of clusters should improve.

Software must be adapted to work well on a cluster; this affects both OS and some applications (such as a DBMS). Since the key purpose of a cluster is high availability, it should be clear that these changes need very careful validation.[4] This represents a significant R&D cost for rather limited units of the software, so cluster software can be quite expensive.

Applications must be modified, perhaps quite extensively, to be able to exploit the cluster's resources—for example, to be able to execute concurrently on a multiplicity of nodes. In practice, we see that just DBMSs—such as Oracle, DB2, and SQL Server—have been thus adapted.

Development of applications for clusters has been slowed because there are no mature, established programming standards for such software. The diversity of UNIX clusters was certainly not an incentive for software companies to move their applications to cluster architectures.

The properties of the standard interconnect networks used to connect nodes in a cluster limit the upper size of such systems to a fairly small number, around ten or so. This is changed for MPPs, as we will see later.

The final problem with a cluster is that despite strenuous efforts by the systems vendors, administering a cluster is still more difficult than administering a single system.

5.3   Massively Parallel Machines (MPP)

A massively parallel machine (or *MPP*, for *Massively Parallel Processing*) can be defined as a (potentially large) collection of systems (from several tens to several hundreds) called nodes, connected by a specialized interconnect network. As in a cluster, each node is a complete system unto itself, with the usual collection of resources—processor, memory, I/O controllers, and its own copy of the operating system.

As far as hardware is concerned, MPPs differ from clusters as follows:

- The maximum number of nodes supported by the system. A cluster can comprise up to about ten nodes, while an MPP can contain hundreds or even thousands of nodes.

- The system packaging (that is, its physical organization, such as equipment racks) for MPPs is designed to support a very large number of nodes and to make addition of further nodes straightforward. This is much less of a concern for clusters, since their size is much more limited.[5]

- A specialized high-performance interconnect, rather than the fast LAN used in a cluster.

MPPs have evolved since their appearance in the early 90s; while initially an MPP node was a uniprocessor, it is more usual nowadays for the node to be an SMP.

MPPs are aimed at highly-parallel applications, which exploit parallelism and—in general—are specifically developed for deployment on MPPs.

Although one of the first commercial MPPs to hit the market was Teradata's RDBC (*Relational DataBase Computer*) in 1984, the prime target for MPPs today is intensive numerical computation rather than decision support.

MPPs competed with—and vanquished—traditional vector supercomputers. Based largely on standard technology—standard microprocessors and memories, and using widely-available operating systems—MPPs offered a much more attractive price/performance ratio than did the vector supercomputers. The principal barrier to their adoption was (and is) the need to develop (or adapt) software specifically for the parallelism in an MPP platform. This move to parallel systems implemented around standard components had a significant effect on the supercomputer industry. SGI absorbed Cray Research, while other manufacturers (like Cray Computer) simply disappeared and start-ups (like Chen) failed. The survivors of this era are Cray, Fujitsu and NEC. We will note in passing the approach of adding a vector coprocessor to a standard microprocessor; such systems, however, rarely offer the same data bandwidths as those provided by the classic vector machines, and so do not offer the same performance potential.

We will look at a vector machine, the NEC SX-6, in a later section.

Failure was not limited to the vector vendors—companies created to develop MPP systems also disappeared or changed direction, while many projects undertaken by existing manufacturers also failed. Examples of failure include Kendal Square Research, Thinking Machines, N-Cube, and Intel's Paragon systems.

Currently, MPP usage in business applications is limited to decision support, an area that is increasing slowly. DBMS have been adapted to employ parallel processing on extremely large volumes of data.

An MPP's architecture is characterized by its interconnection network.

For a massively parallelized application to best exploit the system, it is vital that the interconnect network is not a bottleneck. A parallel application will generally exhibit a combination of two activity phases—communication phases, in which data is exchanged with other nodes, and computation phases. A slow interconnect can easily limit the performance of such an application.

We may characterize an interconnect network as follows:

- Network topology

- Maximum number of supported nodes

- Interconnect latency and bandwidth

- The simplicity and generality of the hardware/software interface

- Whether the network is blocking or non-blocking

- Cost

- Failure resistance. The interconnect network is generally redundant. In normal use, the two networks are used in a load-sharing manner, and in the event of a failure in one, the other carries all the traffic

- Conformity with, or the possibility of establishing, a standard

Figure 5.8 shows some example interconnect topologies.

Figure 5.8
Examples of interconnect topologies.

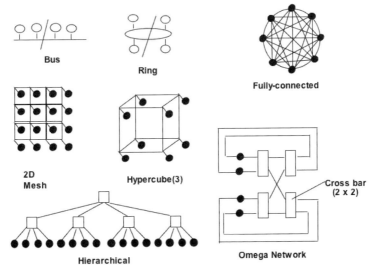

The performance of a network can be characterized with just two parameters: its latency (the time necessary for a message to get from the address space of one process to the address space of another) and bandwidth (the number of bytes per unit time which can be communicated). Both these figures must include all contributory costs from both hardware and software.

The bandwidth of a network may itself be characterized in two ways:

- *Total bandwidth.* This is the bandwidth of a single link, multiplied by the number of links in the system. Unfortunately, this does not characterize the system itself particularly well, since it assumes that all links are always used, and that there are no conflicts in link usage.

- The *average bandwidth* actually usable by a node. The *bisection bandwidth* is used to characterize the average bandwidth. The bisection bandwidth is described as follows:

  - For a symmetrical network, cut the network into two equal subsystems; the bisection bandwidth is the bandwidth available between the two halves
  - For an asymmetrical network, the bisection bandwidth is the minimal bandwidth observed on all feasible cuts of the network

An "ideal" interconnect network would have the following characteristics:

- A constant latency (independent of the number of nodes). That means that the time necessary to route a message between any two nodes is independent of the number of nodes of the system.

- A bisection bandwidth growing linearly with the number of processors. That means that each addition of a node to the system contributes a constant share to the average band-width.

Figure 5.9 shows how the latency and bandwidth of an interconnect network varies with the number of nodes for a typical cluster and for an ideal MPP.

Figure 5.9

Comparison of the interconnect characteristics of a cluster and an MPP.

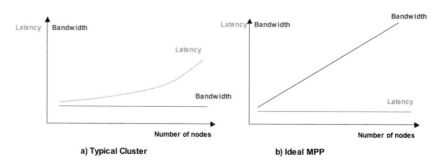

For the cluster, based on a local area interconnect, latency increases with the number of nodes, because there is increased contention for the fixed amount of available bandwidth. In the case of the MPP, the interconnect implementation seeks to approach the ideal of constant latency and bandwidth increasing with the number of nodes.

We expose the difference between this ideal and reality in the following few figures and examples.

There is a relationship between the topology of an interconnect network and its bandwidth. Table 5.2, from [PAT04], compares, for a 64-node system, the bandwidth and cost of several topologies.

Table 5.2 *A comparison between several interconnect networks used in a 64- node system (source: [PAT04]).*

Criterion		Bus	Ring	2D Mesh	Hypercube (6)	Fully connected
Bandwidth	Total bandwidth	1	64	112	192	2,016
	Bisection bandwidth	1	2	8	32	1,024
Cost	Port by switch	N/A	3	5	7	64
	Total number of links	1	128	176	256	2,080

The unit of bandwidth chosen is the bandwidth of a single link. Figures are shown for total bandwidth, for bisection bandwidth, for the number of ports needed for each connecting element, and the total number of links. A fully-connected system is one in which each node has a direct link to every other node in the system.

The table highlights the distinction between bisection bandwidth and total bandwidth. It also shows that as far as the interconnect is concerned, the number of ports and the number of links determine cost.

We should note that the crossbar switches used in SMP architectures construct fully connected systems.

In practice, the choice of a topology is made by trading off needed performance against cost.

5.3.1   MPP Interconnect Network Characteristics

Figure 5.3 shows the characteristics of SGI's Spider hypercube interconnect network.

Table 5.3   *Characteristics of SGI's Spider interconnect network (source: [GAL97]).*

Number of Nodes	Average Latency (NS)	Bisection Bandwidth (GB/s)
8	118	6.4
16	156	12.8
64	274	51.2
256	344	205.0
512	371	410.0

While this network shows ideal behavior in bisection bandwidth, which increases linearly with the number of nodes, latency is far from ideal, also increasing with node count. (The figures shown are pure hardware latency and do not show any software overheads).

Figures published [GIL97], and [MAY98] on the latency of interconnect networks suggest that the latency for the routing of short messages is around 25 µs (in a system based on 332MHz PowerPC 604e processors) using an appropriate interface and communication protocols such as MPI (*Message-Passing Interface*). Hardware latency is around 1.2 µs for systems of up to 80 nodes, and 2.0 µs for systems having between 81 and 512 nodes.

Traditional communications protocols, such as UDP or TCP, used on FDDI interconnect at 100 Mbits/s, display latencies around 80-160 µs on a system built with an 300 MHz Alpha processors.

These last two results show that latency is software-driven. Thus, optimization of interfaces and communications protocols is a key element in wringing the best possible performance from the system. This is the reason that VI is of interest, since it removes software overhead in message routing.

5.3.2   IBM Cluster 1600 for High Computing Performance

This system, which follows the RS/6000 SP (SP means *Scalable POWER-parallel*) is a massively parallel system whose nodes are built from standard SMP systems with minor modifications. A system is built from a number of racks, each rack containing a number of nodes (the number depends on the node deployed) and holding the interconnect network.

Cluster 1600 can have from 16 to 128 nodes, depending on node type; node types can be mixed as long as the limit is not exceeded. As with the SP range, larger configurations are available to special order.

The system can make use of several different interconnect types:

- 10 or 100 Mbit Ethernet or Gigabit Ethernet
- SP Switch2, a second-generation interconnect network having a peak bandwidth of 500 MB/s in each direction; the interconnect may be replicated for both performance (through load-sharing) and availability (in the event of the failure of one network)
- SP Switch, an earlier generation with 150 MB/sec bandwidth in each direction, for customers already owning SP systems

Over simplifying slightly, there are three types of node:

- *Thin node*: 2 or 4 Power3-II processors running at 375 or 400 MHz
- *Wide node*: 2 or 4 Power3-II processors running at 375 or 400 MHz
- *High node*: up to 16 Power3-II processors running at 375 MHz

The SP also accepts POWER4-based nodes. Thus, it is possible to place 16 pSeries 655 servers in a standard 24-inch rack. The pSeries 655 is based on the biprocessor POWER4 chip, and is available in two configurations: a 4-way SMP using 1.3GHz processors, or an 8-way SMP with 1.1 GHz processors, each with up to 32 GB of memory.

Depending on the physical size of the nodes, a rack can contain from 4 to 16 nodes.

Each node functions under the control of its own copy of AIX (IBM's UNIX).

The first generation of the SP interconnect used an Omega topology built from 4 x 4 crossbars. Each node has a bidirectional interface to the interconnect. The physical bandwidth of the link is 150 MB/sec in each direction; this is a peak bandwidth, and less is available in practice.

A second generation of interconnect, called Switch2, was introduced in 2000; PCI and PCI-X adapters were introduced in 2001 and December 2002 respectively. Several types of interface are available with Switch2, including MPI (Message-Passing Interface), TCP/IP, and LAPI (Low-Level Application Programming Interface), a proprietary IBM protocol

An IBM report [IBM03] provides performance figures for Switch2; we excerpt some of these figures here.

Table 5.4 summarizes the Switch2 hardware performance (peak performance).

Table 5.4 *Switch2 hardware performance (source: IBM).*

Number of nodes	Latency (μsec)	Bandwidth (MB/s)	
		One-way	Bidirectional
Up to 16	1.0		
From 17 to 80	1.5	500	1000
From 81 to 512	2.5		

The report studied two different modes of use:

- Use of the MPI library between two Fortran applications (therefore functioning in user address space)
- Use of sockets with TCP/IP

For MPI, both latency and bandwidth were measured. Latency corresponds to the time needed to send a zero-length message (mpi_send) from one node to another. Bandwidth was measured using long messages (several megabytes in size); because bandwidth increases asymptotically with message size, measuring with long messages gives a better estimate of the upper limit to bandwidth.

With pSeries 655 nodes, PCI-X adapters and just one MPI task per node, measured latency is 18 μs and bandwidth is 239 MB/s unidirectional and 245 MB/s in each direction when operated bidirectionally. When

Switch2 is replicated, and with several MPI tasks running per node, bandwidth reaches 400 MB/s.

Using TCP or UDP is more expensive, because these protocols provide extra services (such as guaranteed delivery of messages). The following table gives some performance figures on the same configuration as was used for the MPI figures.

Table 5.5 *TCP/IP bandwidths with Switch2 (source: IBM).*

Number of TCP/IP sessions	Bandwidth (MB/s) Single Interconnect		Bandwidth (MB/s) Dual Interconnect	
	Unidirectional	Bidirectional	Unidirectional	Bidirectional
1 or more	238	259	-	-
1	-	-	449	495
2 or more	-	-	435	491

These figures illustrate the differences between the raw performance and achievable performance in the context of real applications.

The various software components described earlier for the Cluster 1600 are also available for the SP.

The SP is used in a number of applications:

- Intensive numerical computations

- Decision support, using large databases, and a parallelized DBMS

- LAN consolidation (server consolidation)

The use of MPPs in this last application deserves comment. First, some history: the introduction of the PC into businesses resulted in a loss of control in the company information system. Rather than re-establishing company-wide IT coherence, small islands of coherence were created on a per-department basis, like manufacturing and research and development. The systems deployed, often called departmental servers, are of medium capabilities, and tended to be deployed on the approach of "one application, one server." The proliferation of these servers poses administration problems, and perhaps even information coherence problems.

Regrouping such departmental systems within a single physical system can be seen to simplify aspects of administration—physical security, uninterruptible power supplies, backup and restore, and so on). MPPs are sometimes used for this purpose, a choice which is incomprehensible to us since *de facto* the consolidated systems have little communications requirements between nodes, and a cluster architecture would seem a much better fit: the MPP provides unneeded interconnect bandwidth; all that is needed is the ability to contain a fairly large number of nodes. A rack-mount cluster seems a much better fit, all the more so since it offers high-availability facilities often unavailable on an MPP.

5.3.3 **NCR WorldMark 5250**

This system is an evolution of the system introduced by Teradata in 1984; that machine's target was computerized decision-support systems, and it was used connected to the mainframes of the day (IBM, Bull). A production database from the mainframe was loaded onto the Teradata, which provided decision support, using several hundred processors to manage databases ranging in size up to several terabytes.

Originally, the machine was built around Intel 8086 microprocessors and a proprietary DBMS. An intelligent interconnect network, YNET, was used. Figure 5.10 illustrates the general operation of these early systems.

Figure 5.10
Operation of the first Teradata systems.

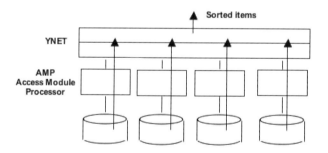

A request is broken up into sub-requests, which are given to the AMPs (*Access Module Processors*). An AMP is a disk controller with a processor, a memory, an operating system, and software that supports data access and filtering (that is, selection of data items which meet certain criteria). An AMP presents items that it has selected to the YNET interface, which chooses the order in which it will communicate items based on the value of a key in the item. This sorting capability is what leads us to describe the network as "intelligent."

The original systems made use of a number of generations of Intel hardware. The WorldMark 5250 system uses a standard NCR server as a node; this system is an SMP with 4 Xeon processors. The system supports up to 128 nodes, giving a maximum size of 512 processors.

On the software side, industry-standard components are used, particularly UNIX; however, on the RDBMS front, the Teradata DBMS is still being used.

Figure 5.11 illustrates the general hardware architecture of the World-Mark 5250 system (Source: [SWE02]).

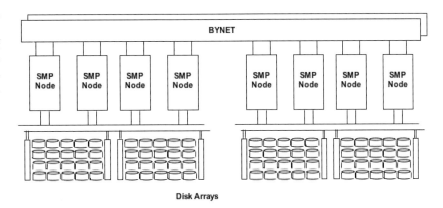

Figure 5.11
General architecture of the NCR WorldMark 5250 (source: [SWE02]).

As shown, each node has two BYNET connections. A BYNET connection runs at 120 MB/s, and only one BYNET connection is used at a time. The other one is for redundancy. 64-way switches are used. Each node is attached to two switches. Up to 128 nodes can be connected over two 64-way switches. To go beyond 64 nodes, two 8-way expansion switches are used to interconnect the 64-way switches (see Figure 5.11). In a 64-node configuration, bisection is = 7.86 GB/s (120 MB/s × 64).

For the maximum configuration (128 nodes or 512 processors), four 8-way expansion switches are used. The bisection bandwidth is only 1.92 GB/s (16 × 120 MB/s).

BYNET is simpler than YNET; it omits the sorting capabilities. A structure using *Virtual Processes* (called VPROCs) is used instead as shown in Figure 5.12.

Requests are still broken up into sub requests, which are dealt with by processes running on the system nodes. The results of the sub requests is passed to BYNET for sending on to the consuming processes.

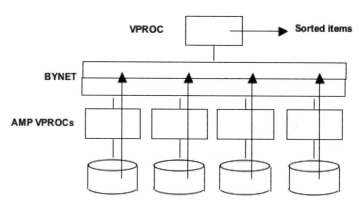

Figure 5.12
*Concept of virtual
process VPROC.*

It seems likely that this change in interconnect philosophy is another example of Moore's Law in action. At the time of the first Teradata machines, the available processors (Intel 8086) were slow, and the memories of low capacity. It therefore made sense to distribute processing between processors and the network. With the march of technology, processors became very fast and memories became very large making a simple, highly-scalable interconnect network more attractive and relying on fast processors and large memories in the nodes to do the sorting.

> A general comment: it should be noted that software vendors rarely, if ever, directly supported any hardware architecture innovations. Even in the field of DBMS, where several system manufacturers offered some relevant innovations, take-up was almost zero. Of course, if a DBMS manufacturer had adapted its product to the specific hardware capabilities offered by just one system manufacturer, it would quickly have been confronted by the costs for support and for future development for the platform. The effect is substantially increased cost with rather low unit volume, an unattractive proposition to the DBMS vendor. Thus, judging that the hardware innovations did not compensate for increased costs and their adoption would not improve market share, such innovations were consistently ignored by the DBMS vendors.

5.4   **Advantages and Disadvantages of MPP Architecture**

This section reviews the advantages and the disadvantages of the MPP architecture. As noted earlier, we will revisit this subject at the end of the chapter, bringing clusters and SMPs into the equation.

Table 5.6 summarizes the advantages and disadvantages of the MPP.

Table 5.6 *A summary of the advantages and disadvantages of MPP.*

Advantages	Disadvantages
■ Favorable cost/performance ratio compared with traditional vector supercomputers for scientific applications ■ Performance scalability limited only by the degree of parallelization of the application (that is, the MPP does not have the size limits (in terms of number of processors) that clusters and SMPs have) ■ Potential of high performance in decision-support applications (given an adapted DBMS) ■ High availability (potentially)	■ Area of effectiveness is limited ■ Non-standard specialized interconnect networks ■ An emergent technology, not a mature one ■ Implies modifications of the system (e.g. SSI) ■ Emerging programming standards for parallel applications ■ Limited number of applications available ■ Difficulty of writing parallel applications ■ Difficulties in administering the system

MPPs key advantage over traditional supercomputers was cost, because MPPs are designed and manufactured using standard (commodity) components available at very low cost—together with some custom components built as ASICs—while the supercomputers tended to use niche technologies such as GaAs (Gallium Arsenide). For domains with a small number of applications, capitalizing on the knowledge available in a company to develop or tune software—for example, in specialist areas such as software modeling the aerodynamics of an aircraft, or modeling automobile crashes, or the combustion process in an automobile engine—was a very reasonable course of action, thereby creating valuable software for the new architectures. We should note that the subsequent adoption of CMOS technology by the vector supercomputer vendors (as in the NEC SX6) has somewhat reduced the price differential.

An MPP application's performance limits are those imposed by its degree of parallelization. In Chapter 1, we introduced both Amdahl's Law and Gustavson's law, which describe limits to the speedups available through parallelization.

For DBMS-oriented applications, the potential performance is available only in decision support; transaction processing suffers from too many inter-node synchronizations caused by the necessity of lock operations.

High availability is not a dimension normally exploited by MPPs— although the hardware tends to have the necessary redundancies (such as replicated network connections), the OSs provided do not exploit the dimension of continuity of service.

Because all inter-node interactions involve the use of the interconnect network, any software layers in the message sending and receiving can have a serious impact on performance. However, the impact of such software involvement is less than for clusters, since the MPP networks have better scalability (and other characteristics) and the communications protocols used are optimized. As we have said before, the use of VI is of interest in this area.

The interconnect network of an MPP is generally proprietary; thus, one tends to be locked into that vendor unless one is prepared to write off all investment in already-owned MPPs.

During the 90s, MPPs were a hot item, giving rise to many start-ups and offerings from established companies; however, most of these have now disappeared from the field. Thus, before choosing an MPP, one must give due consideration not only to the continued existence of the vendor, but also to the vendor's commitment to the product line. As we shall see later, the rise of products built around networks of small servers and workstations may provide an attractive alternative to MPPs.

As is the case for clusters, MPPs are handicapped by the fact that standards for writing parallel programs are still in their infancy; the wide variety of approaches and the small available market make it difficult for a software vendor to port an appropriate application to an MPP.

This is further exacerbated by the difficulty of adapting existing programs to make use of a high degree of concurrency.

And—again, just as with a cluster—administering an MPP is more complex than the administration of a single server.

5.4.1 Networks of workstations, Computing Grids, Global and Peer-to-Peer Computation

In the second half of the 80s, the observation was made that workstations were rarely used to 100% capacity, even during working hours, and that for the remainder of the day they usually remained powered up but idle.

> **Differences between Clusters and MPPs**
>
> The similarities between clusters and MPPs should by now be apparent. From the outside, the adaptations necessary for an OS are the same whether the target is an MPP or a cluster: same software services, same clusterization layers, and so forth.
>
> The major differences arise simply from the differing goals:
>
> - Clusters are aimed at high availability
> - MPPs are aimed at high performance
>
> Thus, in principle, there could be just one generic version of an operating system, with two derivative versions aiming at the two goals.
>
> Some vendors chose, nonetheless, to create the cluster and MPP versions of their OSs as two independent tasks.

This gave rise to the idea of making use of these "idle cycles" through some form of LAN based distributed processing, and software (such as Condor) making it possible to distribute, synchronize and control tasks on such systems was developed. Such distributed systems have now been operational for many years, and are generally referred to as NOW (for *Networks of Workstations*).

The continual increase in workstation performance, coupled with the emergence of high-bandwidth, low-latency networks such as Gigabit Ethernet, MyriNet or SCI[6] (*Scalable Coherent Interface*), made such solutions increasingly attractive within the context of a single company or campus.

This general approach has been the subject of much development effort, resulting in the ability to harness workstations (which, these days, are generally PCs) on a national or even continental scale to solve extremely large problems (such as sequencing the human genome). We will review the principles behind NOW and then briefly examine the related approaches of Grid Computation, Global Computing (GC) and Peer-to-Peer Computing (P2P).

5.4.2 Networks of workstations

Our discussion of networks of workstations is based on the treatment in [CAP98].

As we noted earlier, commercial massively parallel machines are generally based on standard microprocessors, the very same devices used in workstations; such MPPs have prices in the quarter million dollar plus range, an amount of money that would buy considerably more processors—maybe 5 times—in the form of workstations.

Table 5.7 presents the bandwidth and latency figures for the interconnect used in NOWs.

Table 5.7   *Bandwidth and latency of NOW interconnect networks.*

Type of Network	Flow	Latency
Ethernet (10Mbit)	1 MB/s	1 ms
Myrinet	125 MB/s	10 µs
SCI	500 MB/s	1 µs
Spider (SGI) with 16 nodes	12.8 GB/s	156 ns

This table highlights the three classes of networks:

- Ethernet, whose latency is much the same in its 100 Mbit and 1 Gbit versions

- Myrinet and SCI, which are used for networks of workstations with bandwidths from 125 to 500 MB/s and latencies from 1 to 10 µs

- MPP interconnect (here, SGI's Spider), with much better bandwidth and latency than SCI or MyriNet and which are also more scalable

Connection with these fast networks is done by means of a simple PCI card. The connections themselves can require the use of specific cables and switches, the unit remaining, in any event, of a moderate cost compared with an MPP interconnect network.

Using these interconnect technologies it is also possible to construct networks of workstations with essentially the same topologies as MPPs; the University of California at Berkeley's NOW Project [CUL97] is an example.

The disappointing Ethernet latency is due to the use of the traditional TCP/IP protocol stack. For the specialized interconnects, new protocols have been developed, such as active messages or fast messages. Performance is gained at the expense of the properties that one would want in a general-purpose local area network (such as sharing, flow control, error handling, and so forth).

Such systems require tools as much at the system level (i.e., above the OS) as at application programming level.

The first of the system level tools covers management of the collection of workstations making up the configuration, and one sees similar adaptations to those done of cluster-oriented operating systems (VMS, UNIX, Windows, IBM's MVS). As is probably clear, administering a NOW is simplest when all stations are running the same operating system. Monitoring workstation loading is a typical example of a tool used at this level. A tool such as Condor allows unused workstations to be used for batch processing.

As with clusters and MPPs, for applications to exploit the power of a NOW system, they must be adapted or specially written to make use of parallelism.

For such environments, the programming model perhaps best fitted to the problem is message-passing. In principle, calls to distributed systems services could be used—RPC (*Remote Procedure Call*), CORBA, or COM+. However, these paradigms are not common in the community that most uses NOW systems, and so message-passing is used. Some experiments have been conducted on distributed shared memory in this context, but the problems we noted for this approach when used in clusters apply here, too.

Two message-passing libraries are in use: PVM (*Parallel Virtual Machine*) and MPI (*Message-Passing Interface*) [SNI96].

PVM is the *de facto* standard, and there are many tools available to ease design and implementation of applications.

5.4.3 GRID Computing

The term grid computing covers both large scientific calculations and clusters. A grid is likely to contain up to 100 nodes or more. The nodes in a grid are well-identified and stable—that is, it is rare for a node to be added to or removed from a grid. The operation of a grid relies on there being no special reason to have security between grid nodes—so that the nodes belong to a single company or consortium. Node cooperation requires adherence to the same collection of protocols and services. The majority of current grids uses the services supplied by the Globus Toolkit. To develop and promulgate standards, the Global Grid Forum, or GGF, has been created (www.gridforum.org); it works in a manner similar to the IETF (Internet Engineering Task Force). We will not go in further details about grid computing. The interested reader may refer to specialized work such as [FOS03].

> With the projected increase in transistor budget over the next few years, there are now research projects—such as the CART project [CAR03]—that propose to implement grid computing on a single chip.

According to their usage, several types of grids can be distinguished :

- Compute grids
- Data grids
- Instrumentation grids
- Application grids

Compute grids are aimed at numerical intensive applications. Data grids are managing large data sets and are servicing requests for data. Instrumentation grids are related to large and distributed scientific experiments. Application grids provide to users with a set of applications.

5.4.4   Global Computing (GC) and Peer-to-Peer (P2P)

These are in some sense the opposite of grid computing, being very large-scale distributed systems containing perhaps tens of thousands of workstations (mainly Linux and Windows systems). Such systems have little configurational stability (that is, the members can change fairly frequently) and robustness is limited. Applications suited to these configurations include sequencing the genome, investigation into cancer drugs, the cracking of RSA, the search for extra terrestrial intelligence (SETI@home).

Figure 5.13, from [CAP02], illustrates Global Computing and Peer-to-Peer.

In the Global Computing model, client workstations have the task of

- Launching requests to the servers, with the requests containing the code and data needed to satisfy the request
- Collecting and organizing the results returned from the servers

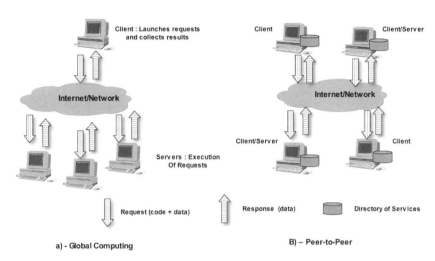

Figure 5.13
Global Computing and Peer-to-Peer models.

The distribution of code and data is done over the Internet or a private network. The servers execute the code provided and return results to the client.

Some applications use this model and there are also commercial products such as Entropia, Parabon and United Devices.

In the Peer-to-Peer model all workstations have an equal role—they can be clients *and* servers. Each server offers to the community the services that it can provide. A workstation connecting to the community will both hold a directory of the services offered by other participants and offer a description of the services it can provide. The participants communicate directly with the workstations whose services they wish to use. The operation of such a system is strongly dependent on the protocols used; the establishment of such protocols is the goal of a number of different projects.

5.5   Networks Used to Build Supercomputers

This section will focus on network technologies used within a datacenter for high-speed data transfers between systems or cluster interconnects. Network technologies used today for personal computers and broadband circuits are covered in other materials.

The top 500 supercomputers are compiled on the Web site www.top500.org every six months. This Web site publishes the results of a LINPACK performance test used to simulate real-world computational intensive tasks and provides good examples of leading edge hardware solutions and specifically advanced networking techniques. The supercomputer list represents most hardware manufacturers and contains clustered and non-clustered systems. In November 2003, 39 percent of the top 500 supercomputers used Myrinet cluster interconnect, a specialized high-bandwidth low-latency network. Many of the supercomputers are built using hundreds or thousands of systems connected with high-speed interfaces. The network enables many small systems to perform complex tasks not possible with a single system. In June 2004, 58 percent of the top 500 supercomputers contained some type of clustered configuration. These clusters range from the low-cost commodity Intel hardware to the more expensive SMP systems clustered together.

Table 5.8 shows a four-year trend and the classification for the top 500 supercomputers. Academic- and research-type installations have increased, while the classified-, government-, and vendor-type installations have decreased. The cost of these solutions has decreased significantly. Academic supercomputers are more affordable today. The network is a significant part of this success; it allows commodity low-cost computers to be connected together forming a single large supercomputer.

Table 5.8   *The supercomputer classification trends over one year.*

Installation Type	June 2003 Percent Share	June 2004 Percent Share
Academic	16.4	19
Classified	6.2	3.8
Government	1.2	0.6
Industry	52	48.4
Research	21	23.2
Vendor	3.2	5

A wide range of choices for networking is available today, from low-cost, commodity-based solutions to high-speed, more proprietary options. Ethernet is probably the most universal networking option, available in nearly every type of personal computer and server. Standard 100 Mb/sec Ethernet can be used in clusters with a few nodes. The high latency of standard Ethernet makes it almost impractical for large cluster installations. Gigabit Ethernet improves the overall throughput but has the same high latency of 100Mb Ethernet. Example of low-cost clusters might include databases or high-availability solutions.

Many of today's modern SMP computers utilize internal system buses that transfer data between processors and memory at speeds reaching 256GB/sec and I/O bus speeds near 32GB/sec. That is more than 13,980 times faster than a standard 10Mb Ethernet network. A system bus is capable of moving one terabyte of data every six seconds.

Note: One terabyte of data is equal to 20,000 four-drawer filing cabinets filled with typewritten pages.

Gigabit Ethernet is considered a commodity interface and is available for nearly every type of computer. The term *commodity* means that the technology is available in large volumes and, because of the volume, the price will reduce dramatically. Today gigabit interface cards are less expensive than the first 100 mb Ethernet cards, five years ago. High-speed interfaces such as InfiniBand, Quadrics, and Myrinet can costs thousands of dollars, require special driver software, and use specialized switches supplied by the vendor.

Network interfaces that operate beyond the normal gigabit Ethernet speeds are typically used to transfer large amounts of data between systems at very low latency. The most common use of a high-speed network or cluster interconnect is in a clustered database or grid computing. A clustered database like Oracle passes messages and data between servers. A database cluster with only a few nodes can use some of the low-cost options, but a cluster built with tens or hundreds of nodes will slow down with these standard interconnects.

How much time does it take to move this data through popular networks, factoring that the disk transfer speeds will not slow the network down? See Table 5.9 for relative network and standard device transfer speeds.

Table 5.9   *Amount of time required to move 1 TB of data.*

	MB/sec	Minutes	Hours	Days
56k Modem	0.05	327,235.6	5,453.9	227.2
T1 (DS1)	0.18	94,937.4	1,582.3	65.9
USB	1.20	14,563.6	242.7	10.1
10Mb Ethernet	1.25	13,981.0	233.0	9.7

Table 5.9 *Amount of time required to move 1 TB of data. (continued)*

	MB/sec	Minutes	Hours	Days
T3 (DS3)	5.36	3,257.9	54.3	2.3
100Mb Ethernet	12.50	1,398.1	23.3	1.0
Firewire 400	47.68	366.5	6.1	0.3
USB2	60.00	291.3	4.9	0.2
ATM 622Mbps	74.15	235.7	3.9	0.2
Firewire 800	95.36	183.3	3.1	0.1
Giganet (VIA)	100.00	174.8	2.9	0.1
Gigabit Ethernet	119.00	146.9	2.4	0.1
2 Gbit Fibre Channel	200.00	87.4	1.5	0.1
Myrinet (Myricom) GM/MX	250.00	69.9	1.2	0.0
SCI (Dolphin)	284.00	61.5	1.0	0.0
InfiniBand	300.00	58.3	1.0	0.0
QsNet (Quadrics)	335.00	52.2	0.9	0.0
4 Gbit Fibre Channel	400.00	43.7	0.7	0.0
GSN	800.00	21.8	0.4	0.0
10GigE	1,000.00	17.5	0.3	0.0

The network choice is a balance of cost, functionality, and performance. For some solutions, multiple network choices are available, with no single best answer. Some questions to ask during the network planning process are:

- What is the expected throughput requirement?
- Is the network internal or private, or will it be routed to other systems?
- What are the distance restrictions?
- Is high-availability important?
- What is the budget for this project?
- Is future expansion important?

5.6   SMPs, Clusters, and MPPs—a Summary

This section offers an initial attempt at comparing the various server options, including possible evolutionary paths. Chapter 7 compares the performance capabilities of SMPs, clusters, and MPPs.

One can compare architectures using any number of criteria. For our purposes, we feel that the best comparisons are those that are visible to the system users, and by users we mean those responsible for the data processing systems in a company—the administrators and so on. Table 5.10 summarizes the system characteristics we feel are important here.

Table 5.10   *Summary of the characteristics of SMP, Cluster and MPP systems.*

Characteristics	SMP	Cluster	MPP
Acceleration (speed-up) or Increase (scale-up)	Scale-Up	Scale-Up	Scale-Up
Load-balancing	Implicit	Requires software intervention	Requires software intervention
High availability	Typically not	Principal objective	Possible (is generally not an objective)
Large configurations (100 processors and beyond)	Limited availability in commodity technology; proprietary hardware is needed for large configurations	Limited by the characteristics of the interconnect network (often of commodity technology)	Principal objective (custom interconnected network)
Single System Image	Complete (by definition)	Limited	Limited
Resource Sharing	All (including the memory and the operating system)	Limited (typically discs and network connections)	Limited (typically just network connections)
Programming	Single process or multiple processes and threads allowing exploitation of parallelism	Custom programming necessary insofar as the objective is to exploit parallelism	Custom programming necessary in order to exploit parallelism (a more crucial issue for MPPs than for clusters)
Flexibility in integrating different generation technologies	Very limited	Yes	Limited
Ease of mainte nance	Limited (often implies first stopping the system)	Easy (no need to stop the system)	Easy (no need to stop the system)

By considering just the dimensions of scalability (under which rubric we include both scale-up and speed-up) and availability, we can position the various architectural options as shown in Figure 5.14 (borrowed from Compaq).

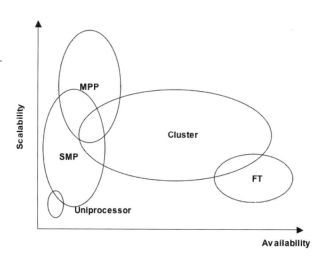

The figure shows that MPP systems have the highest potential *scalability.*

Clusters offer greater *availability* than any systems except for the Fault-Tolerant systems (we prefer the term High Availability; such systems are covered in Chapters 9 and 10). As we shall see in those chapters, a system described as Fault Tolerant normally is one that bases its availability on hardware mechanisms. Such systems suffer from two major drawbacks—limited scalability and inability to survive software failures.

We should note that it is risky to draw too many conclusions from a diagram such as this: to set a useful perspective, the following sections discuss the positioning of the architectures in these two dimensions, and touch on other characteristics mentioned in Table 5.10.

5.6.1   Scalability

An SMP's principal performance objective is scale-up and, to a lesser extent, speed-up (because this is limited by the number of processors). The system's ability to meet its objectives is dependent on its ability to execute several different tasks independently; that is, its ability to implement *inter-task* parallelism.

To obtain speed-up rather than scale-up, an individual application must be structured as a number of cooperating processes or threads that may be distributed to multiple processors and executed concurrently, thereby decreasing total execution time. This is *intra-task* parallelism.

Applications that are implemented as just one process, with just one thread, will not run faster on an SMP; nonetheless, the system capacity is greater than that of a uniprocessor because it can execute many such tasks simultaneously.

These same characteristics are as true of clusters and MPPs as for SMPs—scale-up is a natural property of the system, while software needs adaptation to enjoy speed-up (although the adaptation tends to be different for clusters and MPPs than for SMPs—message passing, rather than shared memory).

Total system performance is strongly affected by inter-node interactions. To illustrate this, consider a DBMS being used for transaction processing: in such a system, any update of the same block of storage by two nodes requires a dialog between these nodes (via the network and/or the disks), which results in a loss of performance. In other words, the scalability of a cluster or MPP for transaction processing is very dependent on the distribution of accesses to the databases—that is, on the probability of accesses by different nodes to the same data.

A number of DBMS, have been ported to both clusters and MPPs, allowing substantial performance improvements in the following cases:

- Speed-up for decision support
- Scale-up for transaction processing, provided that data access conflicts are rare

In Chapter 8, we will look at the changes necessary to a DBMS necessary for it to exploit the data-handling capacity of clusters and MPP systems.

The principal goal of an MPP is speed-up, and applications (particularly for computation-intensive problems) are being and have been developed to take advantage of this class of platform.

As we have said before, an SMP's principal advantage over clusters and MPPs lies in its ability to incrementally increase its data-manipulation capacity at low cost—simply by the addition of a processor or card (up to the limits imposed by the system). Since the nodes of a cluster or MPP are often SMPs, these systems have a two-dimensional growth path—add a processor to an SMP node, and when all nodes have reached their maximum configuration, add nodes. This dual dimensionality has implications for application design—for SMP behavior, the application should be a collection of cooperating threads (so they may efficiently share address space) while for cluster/MPP behavior, they should be constructed as groups of multiple processes (so each can have its own address space on a node); within a group, the processes may be implemented as threads and rely on message-passing rather than shared cache-coherent memory for communications.

5.6.2 Load Balancing

It is clear that for load-balancing—that is, the ability to optimally distribute the workload across the available processors—the SMP is best, since load-balancing is in essence part of the computational model of an SMP. All processes share the same memory, all information necessary to their scheduling and execution is available equally and at low cost to all processors so that a process awaiting a resource may be scheduled as soon as that resource comes available.

But load-balancing in a cluster or MPP is more difficult, and relies on the software making an up-front decision as to where to execute which portion of the workload. If the placement turns out to be unsatisfactory, it is difficult to have the tasks migrate from one node to another. Such migration requires the processes representing the task on one node to free all resources used on that node, and the reacquisition of those resources on the second. This is a fairly complex operation, and one that is expensive in execution time. The dilemma is then in choosing between an unsatisfactory load-balance and an expensive migration, with little knowledge of the future behavior of the migrated task.

5.6.3 High Availability

SMPs have weaknesses in the area of high availability, since the single copy of the operating system and its data structures represent a single point of failure (*SPOF*) for the system—that is, were the OS as a whole to fail, or some key data structures become corrupted, then the whole system fails. Since the SMP model is basically the symmetric sharing of all hardware resources (such as the bus or cross-bar connecting the processors, the I/O controllers or the memory system) any failure of such resource will—in the absence of redundancy, as is usually the case in low- and mid-range servers—lead to the halting of the system. The search for high availability therefore starts with the identification and elimination of any SPOFs (see Chapter 9). While replicating key hardware resources for improved availability makes sense, replicating the OS does not.

Some hardware failures (for example, the failure of a processor) can lead directly to system failure, as can failure of system software. However, in certain cases, such as processor failure, the system can be reinitialized with the failing component "configured out," or removed from the system. However, doing this usually requires the system to be brought to a halt and rebooted, which will entail a gap in availability of at least a few minutes.

Some high-end UNIX servers implement a traditional mainframe functionality to sidestep this problem—they provide partitioning, which allows the system as a whole to be logically decomposed into independent subsystems called *domains*. The failure of a domain then will not affect the proper execution of the other domains.

Clusters, on the other hand, have high availability as their prime goal. While it is not a prime goal for MPPs, the failure rate of a system increases linearly with the number of components, and therefore a large MPP that pays no attention to high availability is likely to suffer an unacceptable failure rate. We may therefore expect considerable convergence between cluster and MPP operating systems.

The similarity of clusters and MPPs means that the same base technology can be used for both, with the systems differing fundamentally only in their optimizations (availability for clusters, performance for MPPs).

5.6.4 Configurations with a Large Number of Processors

As we have noted previously, in the absence of a custom hardware architecture (which is difficult to implement and expensive), an SMP is not scalable to extremely large numbers of processors. However, the CC-NUMA architecture presented in Chapter 4 presents interesting opportunities, although its success will rely on the extent to which the hardware and OS are able to hide the asymmetries in access time.

In general, not only the OS but also key applications, such as the DBMS, must be adapted to work effectively on a system with a large number of processors; without this, any advantage from the increase in the number of processors is likely to be marginal at best.

Clusters and MPPs can both support a large number of processors; however, the available performance depends strongly on the nature of the applications as well as the skill and expertise that the software developers brought to bear on optimizing the applications. As we have already mentioned in this chapter, spectacular TPC-C and TPC-H benchmark results were announced for clusters; but the very nature of these applications means that—given sufficient effort in optimizations—inter-node interactions can be minimized to the benefit of performance. This may not be true for real-world applications, and so it is always appropriate before making a system choice to observe the performance of a cluster or MPP on one's own workloads.

The principal objective of the MPP is speed-up, and the realization of this goal relies on carefully written applications aimed at the platform. The main usage of MPP has been in scientific computing and decision support. The difficulties of programming these systems has limited their penetration: many pioneering companies, such as N-Cube, Thinking Machines, and Kendall Square Research encountered serious difficulties, which resulted in either their disappearance or a significant shift in their business model.

5.6.5   Single System Image

Because an SMP operates under the control of a single copy of the operating system and has a shared coherent memory, it provides by definition a single system image (SSI for short).

The extent of a single system image tends to be somewhat limited for clusters. The limitations arise from implementation difficulties (such as a clusterized file system) along with the inapplicability of certain aspects of a single systems image. Consider attempting to provide an SSI view of a shared common memory visible to user processes. The interconnect network is usually a LAN technology, such as 10 or 100 Mbit Ethernet or 100 Mbit FDDI; implementing such a view on a cluster would be complex and would bring substantial inefficiencies—writing to memory would then need to be done via the network, and synchronizations through the use of a distributed lock manager rather than by direct memory access.

Further, a single image for processes (such that all the processes running on the nodes form a single group) accompanied by cluster-level memory sharing could be catastrophic for the availability of the system, since, if a process were to fail on one node, we would have no way to guarantee that processes on the other nodes were not affected; thus, the failure of one node would necessitate the failure of the cluster.

For these reasons, a single system image is normally limited to a subset of resources, such as the disks, an abstraction of disks as logical volumes, a single network address for the cluster, or the file system (a functionality that took some time to become available on UNIX clusters).

5.6.6 **Programming Model**

We should first re-emphasize that there is no single universally-adopted programming model for clusters and MPPs. The issue is less of a concern for clusters than for MPPs, both because of the generally lower number of processors and because the prime goal of a cluster is availability rather than application speed-up.

MPPs and clusters have in common the fact that in many cases their application programs are supported by a DBMS that exploits system resources; in addition, the applications are often structured as multiple tiers running on multiple servers. Since the servers in this model may be system nodes, this class of application drops naturally and efficiently onto clusters and MPPs—with the support of the last two levels on the servers, and with the ability to make use of the potential for high availability.

A number of different middleware products support distributed programming for both clusters and MPP—examples include RPC, MOM, and CORBA.

For scientific computing, software has been developed to simplify the writing of distributed applications, with the objective of minimizing the complexity of programming and implementing such systems. PVM (*Parallel Virtual Machine*) is the *de facto* standard, with MPI (*Message-Passing Interface*) the emerging standard.

5.6.7 **Integrating New Technologies**

The combination of technology improvements and industry dynamics drive low-end and mid-range SMP products. From the technology aspect, chips with two processors on them appeared in 2002, with the expectation that this number would grow to four. Industrial pressures encourage chip manufacturers to move into the card business, both uni- and multiprocessor—and all this before multiprocessor chips appear (consider Intel). For the manufacturer, the lure is a higher margin than that available from pure chip products, but this is at the expense of the systems vendors. Clearly, any contribution by dataprocessing systems companies in the low to midrange is made very problematic. Companies that provide microprocessors and system logic chips have a clear advantage; they can drive the moment of introduction of processors, system logic and even card-level products integrating these. Thus it is clear that the opportunity for value-add for systems manufacturers is extremely limited in this domain and will reduce further over time.

We will look again at these issues in Chapter 12.

The close coupling between processors and the rest of the system seen in an SMP leads to a rather short commercial life for a given SMP compared to more loosely-coupled systems like clusters. By lifespan, we mean the ability to upgrade these systems by simply upgrading a card or a processor across several processor generations.

Clusters—because of their loosely-coupled nature, using standard LAN interconnect—can support several generations of processor across their various nodes within the one system; this is relevant to high-end clusters, where the cost of system infrastructure is quite substantial.

The SMP's tight coupling can often impose more stringent constraints on mixing technologies than does a cluster. An MPP that integrates—for performance reasons—its interconnect onto the processor subsystem will be less tolerant of technology mixing than a cluster, or an MPP that uses PCI cards for its interconnect. Thus, for the integrated interconnect, a new card must be developed before new technology can be integrated; in a cluster, the use of standard interconnect makes this a moot point.

In the big architectural picture, we have seen that clusters and MPPs are very closely related, with the differences being mainly the upper limit for the number of nodes in a system (around ten for clusters and hundreds or thousands for MPPs); packaging issues; and the use of specialist interconnect technologies in MPPs.

Some clusters make use of custom packaging, such as rack mounting with integrated interconnect. Given such a rack system, it is clearly possible to connect up multiple racks; thus, the distinction between clusters and low-end MPPs is rather blurred.

As we have seen in this chapter, a number of fast interconnect technologies are currently being offered. These have given rise to a number of high performance projects which interconnect workstations or high-end PCs using plug-in fast network interface cards; these projects are aimed at scientific computing and are based in research laboratories. The thinking behind this approach was the notion of using the unused cycles on high-performance workstations to avoid having to spend substantial sums on any form of supercomputer. We expect some technologies from this domain to become industry standards, which will present the pure-play MPP vendors with some difficulties. Most likely, the outcome will be a convergence between clusters and MPPs.

Such convergences should also improve the OS situation by focusing attention and resources on a smaller number of platform types. As we have noted, it seems likely that a single generic operating system can be tuned judiciously through relatively minor optimizations to provide, separately, both cluster and MPP variants.

5.6.8 Ease of maintenance

For an SMP with no mainframe-like logical partitioning, any maintenance activity implies or requires the stopping of the system. Given partitioning, it is practical to halt operations on just the affected partitions. Software update for an SMP almost always involves stopping the system. Some high-end SMP systems support various forms of hot-plugging of some components; if the OS understands this, then downtime may be reduced.

Both clusters and MPPs provide a natural redundancy and independence of the nodes. This makes hardware maintenance simpler, because a node can be halted without halting other nodes. Software update, in particular any update of the OS, is more problematic, since the updates must be made incrementally, node by node, to avoid bringing down the whole system.

5.7 Flexible SMP-Cluster Architecture

With three-level client/server architectures, the information systems architects must choose—for both application and data management levels—the processing capacity and the amount of needed redundancy. The difficulties in this decision come from the changing requirements of the system over its operational life, requiring configuration changes to be made with minimal impact on system availability. We have seen earlier when looking at SMPs that support for logical partitions can provide a response to this need for flexibility.

In the domain of configuration flexibility, some systems designers offer partitionable SMPs with very fine granularity. Unisys' ES7000 system, introduced in 1999, is an example. Its code name was CMP (for *Cellular MultiProcessor*); the SGI Altix 3000—already described in this chapter—is another example.

Figure 5.15 illustrates the architecture of Unisys' ES7000.

Figure 5.15
Unisys' flexible
ES7000
architecture
(source: Unisys).

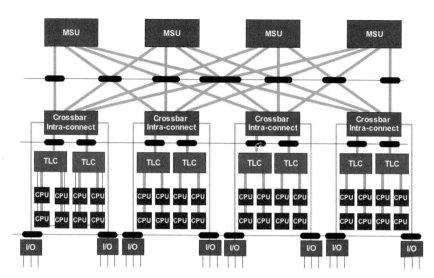

This architecture, introduced with Pentium III Xeon processors, will evolve to IA-64. The system can include up to 32 processors.

The basic building block is a 4-processor module. Each pair of processors is connected by a bus and shares a third-level cache; recall that the processor integrates both first- and second-level caches.

The memory interface is provided by non-blocking crossbars. Each of the four crossbars manages two level-3 caches, forming a group of 8 processors. Further, each crossbar connects to the four storage units and the two I/O bridges. Each I/O bridge connects to 3 PCI buses, each capable of supporting 4 controllers, giving a total capacity of 24 PCI buses and 96 PCI controllers.

Each memory subsystem can support up to 16 GB, for a total memory capacity of 64 GB. The cache coherence relies on a directory-based scheme.

To ensure high availability, the most critical hardware components are replicated, and a number of systems components are hot pluggable.

System partitioning is supported at the hardware level, with fault detection in the event of any access attempting to touch components outside specified limits.

The diagram provides some idea of the available bandwidths in this system.

The system provides great flexibility in configuration. A given collection of hardware may be configured as any of:

- A 32-way SMP

- An 8-node cluster, with 4 processors per cluster

- Any combination of SMP systems with a granularity of 4 processors, each able to be a component of a cluster

The choice between these various configurations is made by the systems administrator, starting from a definition of the general configuration and the desired protections/isolations between the domains, and requiring the installation of the appropriate versions of the OS on the various nodes of the system.

Because of its flexibility this type of system is likely to achieve reasonable success, always provided that manufacturers manage to control costs so that the systems can be sold at reasonable prices.

5.7.1   Note on Server Consolidation

As previously mentioned, with the advent of affordable servers based upon standard technologies, there were a proliferation of departmental servers. Facing with a strong pressure on costs, information managers are looking for solutions to reduce the Total Cost of Ownership (TCO). Several approaches are proposed, such as:

- Physical concentration, where several servers are regrouped in the same location, possibly in a cluster configuration (offering high availability if needed)

- Concentration, where all applications distributed on several servers are supported on a single system (i.e., in a way similar to the "traditional" mainframe). Several technologies can support this type of consolidation:

  - Virtual machine approach, where a single system supports several virtual machines, each with its own operating system and a dedicated set of applications
  - Workload management, where a single operating system supports several applications simultaneously. Resource sharing between applications is managed according to a set of stated rules

- Datacentric, where data is supported by a single (high-availability) system, offering to application servers the data service (application servers do not support data)

- Application integration, where various applications and associated data are concentrated on a smaller set of servers to facilitate cooperation between applications

The choice of a solution depends heavily on the characteristics of the existing configuration and the set of constraints. Obviously, reducing the number of servers contributes to reduce the TCO. Both cost and business continuity issues may prevent attempts to go further than physical concentration.

Vector Architecture Example: the NEC SX-6

As we have noted earlier, massively parallel systems based on standard microprocessors have driven out the classical vector supercomputers in most application domains. However, the supercomputers still dominate in some areas, aided by their recent adoption of the same technologies as these processors—that is, CMOS, rather than relying on exotic materials technologies (such as GaAs) or circuit technologies (such as ECL). This has sharply reduced the costs of ownership and operation, at least at the hardware level.

The cost of ownership and operation of such systems necessarily includes the cost of acquisition of the applications of interest (collision codes, combustion models, etc.), so the vendor of an innovative (and thus different) supercomputer architecture must bear the costs of negotiating with the vendors of such software even before the system can be brought to market. If the new system has a massive price/performance advantage over existing products, payment can be avoided, or at least reduced substantially; otherwise, the supercomputer vendor must cover the NRE and opportunity costs for the software vendor. Similar reasoning applies to a company that uses supercomputers with internally-developed application software. This (fairly obvious) issue is probably the reason for the commercial failure of a number of companies whose major characteristic (beyond the traditional substantial delay between planned market introduction and actual introduction) was a major break with existing programming models. The converse is also true; for a substantial amount of time, CRAY-compatible (or CRAY-like) systems had a notable success in the marketplace.

Before looking at the NEC SX-6, a quick recap on vector architectures is in order: a vector machine exploits a form of data parallelism. A key to its utility is the transformation of a simple (appropriately-formed) loop into a form which can leverage the machine's capabilities.

As an example, consider the following source code:

```
DO i=1, 256
Z(i)=X(i)+Y(i)
ENDDO
```

On a non-vector machine, this is represented as a loop, with the machine doing the following steps:

```
initialize I =1
test: see if the loop has finished; if so, branch to the end
of the loop
calculate X(i) + Y(i)
place the result in Z(i)
increment i
jump to label test
end of loop:
```

The SX-6 has 8 computational units, and so this computation would have its housekeeping and calculation steps parallelized across the multiple units, allowing the necessary computation time to be reduced by a factor of 8. Loop control would be effected by the SX-6s scalar processor. To achieve improvement in performance by a factor of eight, the vector units must be fed an uninterrupted stream of operations and values; the SX-6 has a carefully-designed memory architecture to support such behavior, with a bandwidth of 256 GB/s per node, coupled with a high degree of memory interleave, to keep the *vector registers* fed.

A vector architecture has *vector registers*, intended to hold vectors (in the following example, a vector register is indicated by a name such as r-v*N*) along with instructions that operate on vector values held in these registers. To illustrate, here is how the computation from the preceding example could be arranged for the SX-6:

```
Load the 256 values of X[] into r-v1
Load the 256 values of Y[] into r-v2
Perform the vector addition of r-v1 and r-v2 into r-v3
Store the 256 values in r-v3 into Z[]
```

This sequence clearly requires fewer instructions and removes all tests and conditional branches, actions which are performance problems in high-performance machines.

SX-6 is a vector-optimized system. Looking at its architecture at the highest level, the system combines a tightly-coupled SMP system with n processors, each equipped with a vector unit sharing the same memory and a cluster architecture with distributed shared memory, providing a very high bandwidth between processors and memory (a crossbar, providing a maximum bandwidth of 32 TB/s).

Table 5.11 summarizes the characteristics of the SX-6 range.

Table 5.11 *SX-6 family characteristics.*

	Single node	Multiple nodes (cluster)
Peak performance	64 Gflops	8,192 Tflops
Number of processors	8 (each of 8 Gflops)	1024
Number of nodes	1	128
Maximum memory size	64 GoB	8 TB

As is usual for vector machines, performance is expressed as the maximum number of floating point operations per second that the machine can provide; the number quoted is the peak power, which is the machine's capacity provided that all its units are busy continuously. This is an optimal circumstance, and so represents a "cannot exceed" performance value rather than that expected to be available in normal use. Nonetheless, for appropriate classes of problem and for programs written with the vector model in mind, vector machines can deliver close to peak performance on real applications. In general, a machine optimized for short vectors will provide close to peak performance over a wider range of applications than a machine optimized for long vectors (since long vectors are encountered less frequently than short vectors).

Figure 5.16 shows the general architecture of an SX-6 node.

An SX-6 node contains up to 8 processors and 4 I/O processors (IOPs). The memory and I/O bandwidths were the subject of very careful attention during the design of the SX-6, since the performance of such a system depends to a very large extent on the ability of the memory system to keep the function units fed with data. The capabilities of the I/O system is also

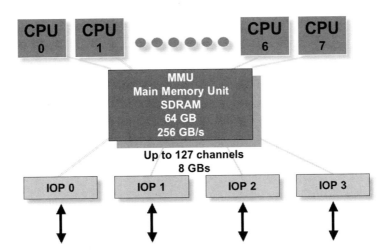

Figure 5.16
Architecture of an SX-6 node (source: NEC).

important (recall that big vector calculations may well contain data sets too large to fit in even a memory of the size supportable by the SX-6).

Figure 5.17 illustrates the internal architecture of an SX-6 processor.

The main memory unit (MMU) is connected to each processor through a Load/Store unit that handles transfers between memory and the vector registers. Memory bandwidth is provided by both a crossbar and a high degree of interleaving. Memory itself uses SDRAM chips and is arranged as a number of independent blocks in such a manner that successive addresses fall into successive blocks (wrapping round modulo the block count). Thus,

Figure 5.17
Internal architecture of an SX-6 processor (source: NEC).

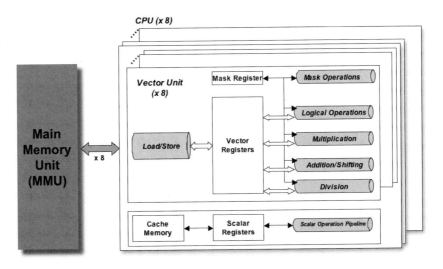

successive addresses can be accessed and fetched concurrently. This reduces latency and is optimized for short vectors.

A processor itself comprises two elements—a vector unit and a scalar unit; these can work in parallel. The vector unit consists of vector registers and a set of eight pipelines for logical operations, multiplications, adds, shifts, and divisions (load/store) on the vector registers. The vector registers may be looked upon as an explicitly-managed cache (managed by software). Each pipeline executes a vector operation, and all pipelines may operate in parallel. Making effective use of the machine's vector capabilities is best done through use of appropriate languages and compilers; FORTRAN 90, HPF, and C++ all provide automatic vectorization capabilities.

The scalar unit is a 4-issue superscalar design.

The performance potential of the machine lies in effective use of the vector unit; thus, it is the ratio of vectorizable to normal computation that sets limits on the performance advantage of such a machine over a non-vector design.

NEC's SUPER-UX (an SX-6 UNIX version) was optimized to guarantee a bandwidth of 75 MB/s per HIPPI channel for large blocks (a frequent occurrence in scientific workloads).

Bull [NIV00] is deploying these systems in non-scientific applications domains, in particular for use as a high-performance decision-support system (DSS). The general approach (which is the subject of a patent application) is as follows: at the cost of a particular encoding, the fields of a table may be represented as elements of a vector. Thus, computations on table fields may be implemented as vector computations. Measurements on a prototype system, using requests that span the complete database, show very promising response times, as well as a price/performance ratio several tens of times better than those obtained with "classical" technologies (i.e., a standard RDBMS running on an SMP based on high-performance microprocessors).

5.8   Endnotes

1.   Tandem was a computer systems manufacturer specializing in high-availability systems. It was initially bought by Digital and now belongs to HP.

2.   Dave Cutler, the architect of Windows NT, came from Digital.

3. We distinguish participative redundancy—in which nodes cooperate to share the workload after a failure—from standby redundancy, in which spare node(s) are held ready for use in the event of a failure but are not used for processing until such failure occurs.

4. This cost increase is more obvious in the UNIX systems offered by proprietary systems vendors, because although all such systems have more or less the same functionality and capability, developments and thus development costs are unique to each manufacturer. Linux clusters may change the equation.

5. In the case of clusters, one also encounters the need to simply add a further node. Thus, some cluster implementations are in the form of racks, and a node is a rack-mounted unit. In such implementations, the interconnect network may be pre installed in the rack, so that the insertion of a new unit into the rack connects it into the cluster.

6. In this context, SCI is used as a very fast communications network; its capability of providing a coherent distributed memory is generally not used.

6

Data Storage

In Chapter 2 we looked at how I/O technology evolved, with particular emphasis on two issues: the effect of technology on magnetic disk data access and problems in the software layers of network access. In this chapter, we focus on the issues of data storage, looking at both data storage architecture options and the issues surrounding data backup and restoration. We will also look at some storage subsystems.

Unlike the realm of processor architecture, the field of data storage is characterized by innovative architectural solutions. Note: The field of communications also displays substantial innovation.

As we noted earlier, one explanation for this richness of innovation is that a storage subsystem generally only needs to run software provided by its vendor—there is no requirement to run other software, and so there are no within-subsystem compatibility issues. Thus, if a change in technology drives the subsystem vendors to change architecture, it is a private issue invisible to the end customer; if there is a good reason to change architecture, then a subsystem storage vendor is likely to make the jump to the new approach.

As we have noted before, end-user compatibility, while a boon to the end user through economies of scale, is a major barrier to the introduction of new architecture.

6.1 Data Storage

Since data is the central, vital element in business data processing, the characteristics of storage systems are significant issues in the choice of servers. The need to make information available—generally, continuously available—as much within a company as outside it (via the Internet) has made storage subsystems an essential component of servers. The general trend is for larger and larger subsystems with ever-increasing performance and avail-ability and ever-decreasing cost per gigabyte.

In our discussion of storage, we will begin with an overview of the prob-lems whose solutions justified the rich variety of approaches and technolo-gies in data storage. We start by looking at the architecture and functionality of centralized and distributed file systems, examining NFS and CIFS. We will look at optimization possibilities, both at the level of the file system itself (optimizing for writes) and in looking at the possibilities offered by new I/O architectures such as DAFS and at the performance improvements available with parallelized file systems.

Because storage systems rely on magnetic disks, reliability is an issue; we will look at how disks are organized in RAID (*Redundant Array of Inexpensive Disks*) systems.

We will look at techniques to virtualize storage which can simplify resource management.

We will analyze and compare architectural options for RAID and stor-age virtualization, and will look at a number of storage subsystem approaches:

- NAS (*Network-Attached Storage*), a storage system using a network interface
- SAN (*Storage Area Network*), a network tuned for the connection of storage, carrying data-access commands that reflect low-level disk commands, such as SCSI commands
- iSCSI, allowing access to remote disks over the Internet
- Simultaneous support of both SAN and NAS architectures

We then compare the properties of these various architectures.

6.2   Storage Issues

Table 6.1, from Horison Information Strategies (www.horison.com) gives very useful numbers regarding storage.

This table has been compiled by Horison Information Strategies from various sources. It confirms several facts, such as the growth in storage requirements, the importance of data storage issues for servers and the need

Table 6.1 *Storage facts, figures, estimates, and rules of thumb (source: Horison)*

Average annual storage demand rate (primary occurrence of data, all platforms)	50-60%
Amount of disk data stored on UNIX, Windows 2000 and Linux systems (estimate)	85%
Average disk allocation levels for z/OS (eSeries mainframes using DFSMS suite)	60-80%
Average disk allocation levels for iSeries (AS/400 servers)	60-80%
Average disk allocation levels for UNIX/Linux	30-50%
Average disk allocation levels for Windows 2000/NT	20-40%
Ratio of block data to file data	1.5/1
Average annual disk drive capacity increase	60%
Average annual disk drive performance improvement (seek, latency, and data rate)	<10%
Increase in disk drive capacity per actuator since the first disk drive in 1956	39260x
Increase in native tape cartridge capacity since the first tape cartridge in 1984	1250x
Average multi-user server utilization (% busy)	25-40%
Average tape cartridge utilization levels for virtual tape systems	60-85%
Estimated range of disk data managed per administrator (distributed systems: Windows 2000, UNIX, Linux)	500 GB – 1 TB
Estimated range of disk data managed per administrator (z/OS, mainframe)	> 30 TB
Estimated range of automated tape data managed per administrator (all platforms)	40 TB + External Backup (varies widely based on library size)
Average CAGR of e-mail message size	90%
Average growth rate of e-mail spam	~350%
Estimated percentage of SANs that are homogeneous (the same OS)	75% (UNIX and Windows 2000 systems only)

Table 6.1   *Storage facts, figures, estimates, and rules of thumb (source: Horison) (continued)*

Average size of e-mail message and attachments in 2002	50 kb
Average size of e-mail in 2007 (estimate)	650 kb
Number of e-mails sent daily in 2001	12 000 000
Number of e-mails sent daily in 2005 (estimate)	>35 000 000
Percentage of all e-mail traffic that is spam (also known as bandwidth burning)	62% (and growing)
Annual growth in all Internet traffic	80%
Percentage of digital data stored on single user systems	56%
Percentage of digital data stored on removable media (tape and optical)	>80%

for software suites to manage storage, specially in the environment of standard systems.

Gartner Group published a report in June 1999, that suggests that more than half of server expenditure goes to data storage, and this proportion is growing. This is illustrated by Figure 6.1, which shows how the allocation of money between I/O, data storage and computational capability has changed over time.

This analysis highlights three application categories with differing storage requirements:

- *Data Intensive applications*, which concentrate on making directly accessible more or less all of the enterprise data, without paying much attention to what media the data is archived to (magnetic tape, microfiche, etc.). Decision-support systems, in which the amount of data to be managed grows with the age of the company, are an example.

- *I/O Intensive applications*. Transaction-processing applications (OLTP) are critically reliant on disk update performance; the number of available disks[1] is a key factor. These applications tend to have a workload proportional to the size of the company.

→

Figure 6.1
Allocation of expenditure for servers (source data: Gartner Group).

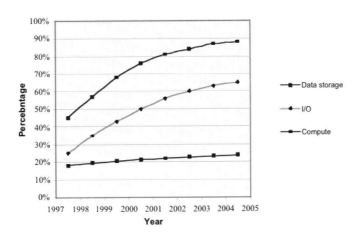

Allocation of expenditure for servers

■ *Compute Intensive applications.* These are applications that do not have such extreme requirements on either storage performance or storage size.

Given that key factors in the performance of an enterprise server are its data storage and I/O subsystems, it is not surprising that more than half of server expenditures go to I/O and storage, and it looks like this proportion will continue growing over time. This leads us to comment that information systems decision-makers should put a very high priority on how they select storage systems and should consider the possibility of using multiple vendors for their servers. [2]

Data storage for servers must meet a number of objectives, among which are:

■ The availability and reliability of the data

■ Performance (response time, bandwidth)

■ Scalability

■ Ease of operation and administration

■ TCO (*Total Cost of Ownership*)

■ Backup and restore

Data archived and managed by servers must not only be accessible, but must also be protected against access by unauthorized users and unwanted modification.

We may use several parameters to express data storage performance: latency (how long it takes to respond to a data request), the maximum number of concurrent requests, and the maximum data bandwidth that can be guaranteed.

Storage scalability is characterized by its ability to grow in capacity as well as in performance, since a balance must be maintained between the capabilities of the processor (both processors proper and their memory) and of the I/O system when making changes to the system configuration.

Ease of operation and administration has an obvious effect on both total cost of ownership and the quality of service. TCO reduction has become one of the flagship claims of systems suppliers (servers, storage, etc.). We will reconsider this aspect in Chapter 11.

The combination of the enormous growth in the volume of data to be managed and the requirement for availability has made data backup and restore a critical issue. This is exacerbated by the move to electronic commerce, which is reducing and perhaps removing the window of time available for regular daily or weekly backup operations. The amount of time necessary to restore service after a technological (hardware, software) or human error (operation, software) drives the available quality of service. We will examine data backup and restoration later on in this chapter.

Figure 6.2, inspired by [BUL99], illustrates the problems of data storage in a traditional client/server environment.

As shown in the diagram, the architect of an information system is faced with a number of issues:

- *Reducing the load on the local area network*. The effect of caches in the client workstations is the reduction of the load on the network. Data backup and restore operations load the network, and this leads one to consider solutions which avoid the use of the network.

- *Optimizing response time*. Response time is a function of a number of factors, including client performance, the performance of the communications protocols in use, the intrinsic performance of the data storage subsystems along with the caching subsystems in the clients, as well as the storage subsystems.

Figure 6.2
Storage issues.

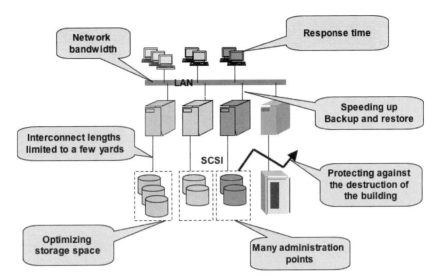

- *Reducing backup and restore times.* Given the increase in the amount of data stored on a server, backup times can become unacceptably long. Several approaches can be used to improve the situation: avoiding having the data stream through other servers and/or the network; backing up only modified data; backing up open databases (i.e., not requiring the databases to be closed during backup).

- *Limited distance between processor and the peripheral subsystem.* As an example, SCSI—still a widely used standard—limits the distance between the device and its controller to just a few yards. For servers with very high capacity and with multiple servers sharing a given storage resource (for example to provide high availability), this distance can be a major constraint.

- *Protecting against catastrophes.* Putting the processors and storage in the same location leaves the system vulnerable to catastrophes such as fire and flood. To protect against the effects of such catastrophes, it is important to be able to put the storage somewhere other than co-located with processing and to put backup and restore mechanisms in place (this will be discussed in Chapter 10).

- *Optimizing the use of storage space.* As we have just shown, the cost of storage dominates the cost of an information system.[3] As a result, there is pressure to centralize storage and share it among the several servers in an information system. An example of this is the practice of meeting the storage needs of a given system by making use of unused storage in other systems.

■ *Simplifying administration.* When each server has its own storage resources, an administrator must handle each system separately. Centralizing resources simplifies both their administration and their optimization.[4]

To address these issues, information systems manufacturers and storage subsystems suppliers and have proposed systems that allow the sharing of storage capacity between different systems within the context of a local area network, a specialized network, or even the Internet.

6.3   Functional Levels: File Systems

In this section we will review the different software components involved in accessing data held on a storage system.

We start by providing an overview of the major characteristics of a file system, and will look later at the various levels of software within a system involved in file access.

To recap briefly (see Chapter 2), a disk is composed of a number of platters. Each side of a platter has a number of concentric tracks, each of which is made up of a number of fixed-capacity sectors. A disk is equipped with a swivelling arm carrying two read/write heads per platter (one for each side of the platter). Hardware in the disk positions the arm appropriately for the disk surface and track to be accessed, and selects the appropriate head.

The sector access time, from the moment that the command has been received by the disk, is the sum of the following components:

■ *Seek time*: the amount of time it takes to position the arms

■ *Rotational latency*: the amount of time it takes for the desired sector to rotate under the heads

■ *Internal transfer time*: how long it takes for the data to be transferred off the disk surface into the disk electronics

■ *External transfer time*: the amount of time it takes to get the data from the disk through the external interface (such as SCSI) to the requester

A typical sector size is rather small, 512 bytes being a current standard. File systems often work on groups of sectors; in such a case, a sector group is a unit of allocation and can also be a unit of transfer (although transfers of less than a group would also be supported.

In UNIX, a group is referred to as a *block*, with a typical size of 4 KB, while in Windows 2000 the same size group exists but is called a *cluster.*

This short disk recap should serve us well in comprehending the concepts presented later in this chapter.

Figure 6.3 illustrates the functionality of a file system.

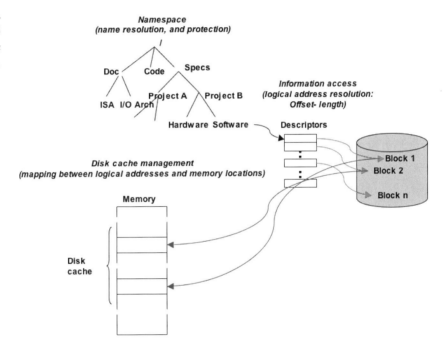

Figure 6.3

File system functionality.

This diagram shows the three major functions performed within a file system: resolving the file names, resolving logical addresses (offset and length) for data access, and managing the disk cache. The data access method illustrated is basic, since it does not assume any specific data organization within the file. However, more complex access methods may be constructed on top of such basic access, such as index-sequential access (as used in C-ISAM and VSAM).

For simplicity, we did not make any explicit representation of the operating system in the diagram. In practice, the file system is generally part of the operating system, although the DBMS generally is not.

A file system, then, has three major functions:

- *Name resolution and access right management.* As has been the case since the Multics[5] system, the file namespace in a system is tree-structured. Thus, to specify an item, one essentially lists the sequence of directories needing to be traversed from the root directory or a subdirectory to the leaf node or directory representing the item itself. An example in the diagram could be /Specs/Project B/Software.

  When an application wishes to access a file, it does so by using its symbolic name; then the file system maps this into the elements that describe the implementation of the file on the disk.

- *Managing the representation of files on the disk.* In systems such as UNIX or Windows, a file is a continuous succession of bytes (numbered from 0 to N-1). The representation of the file on the disk is as a collection of blocks (of, for example, 512 or 1024 bytes). The description of the file's implementation is done by means of a table—the inode structure in UNIX is an example of this. A reference to an element of a file (an offset from the beginning of the file, and the length of the element) is translated into blocks using this form of table.

- *Management of the disk cache in memory.* As we saw in Chapter 1, a cache can improve performance by holding in memory those blocks most likely to be accessed. The mapping between the logical addresses of the file elements and the memory addresses of the cached copies is maintained by the file system. In the case of memory-mapped files, hardware (the MMU) manages the address translation and demand-paging manages the cache contents. In the case of no translation (that is, the page is absent), the mapping table, which describes the layout of the file on disk, is consulted to provide the needed information.

Through an unfortunate choice of language, the term "file system" refers both to the collection of files in a system and to the software that manages those files. A disk unit (physical, or logical if a level of abstraction is placed on top of the physical layer) contains one or more file systems—that is, one or more collections of files. Figure 6.4 shows the general structure of a UNIX file system.

The *Boot Block* occupies the first part of the file system and can contain the system bootstrap code that initializes the OS. Typically, when started a system first executes code held in read-only memory (PROM or EEPROM), and this code causes the Boot Block of a specified file system to

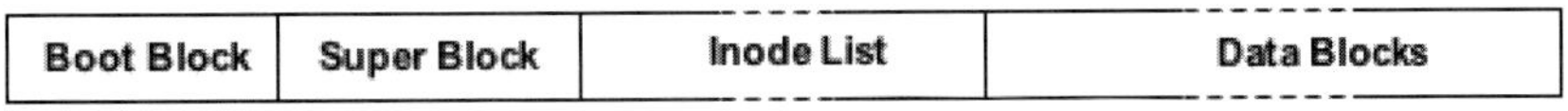

Figure 6.4
General structure of a UNIX File system.

Boot Block	Super Block	Inode List	Data Blocks

be loaded. The Boot Block code is not the operating system proper, but simply code that will load the first part of the OS into memory and then transfer control to it.

The Super Block contains information describing the file system and its representation on the volume. A volume is the storage space allocated to a single file system. In some works, the term file system is used instead of volume, adding to confusion.):

- The size of the file system

- The number of unused (free) blocks in the file system

- A list of the free blocks

- The index of the first free block

- The size of the list of file descriptors (inodes)

- The number of free inodes

- The list of free inodes

- The index of the first free inode

- Locks for the lists of free blocks and inodes

- A flag indicating that the Superblock has been modified

The free block list is often represented by a *bit map*, where each bit represents a block and its value indicates whether the block is free or allocated. With such a structure, looking for a collection of N free blocks is transformed into looking for a vector of N contiguous free bits.

Inodes are file descriptors, and specify the blocks composing the file. The structure of an inode is shown in Figure 6.5.

As shown in the diagram, the inode structure can economically represent the structure of a file. A list of 13 descriptors is associated with a file, the first ten of these directly specifying a block, and the last three providing pointers to secondary lists with one, two, or three levels of indirection. We

Figure 6.5
Structure of an
inode.

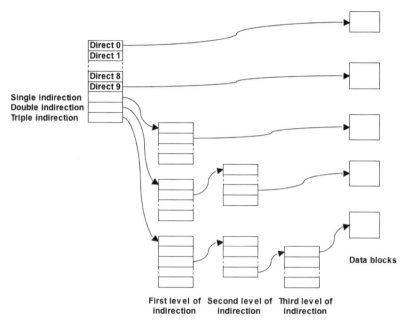

will not spend any more time on the inode structure; those interested in greater detail can consult more specialized works such as [SIL01]. We should note that although this structure is space efficient, it has the disadvantage of fragmentation—that is, scattering the blocks of a disk across the disk. This impacts performance, since to read logically contiguous blocks the heads may need to be moved to many different tracks. To avoid these issues, file systems targeted at efficiently managing very large files have been developed.

The information contained in the SuperBlock and in the inodes forms the file system's *metadata*. Correctness of metadata is vital for file system availability, so although the metadata is cached in memory, file systems also duplicate this information and use transactional logic for any operation that changes metadata. The transactional logic uses journaling mechanisms that allow any change that has not properly completed to be undone, and then replayed to be properly effected. Such file systems are said to be *journaled file systems*; many UNIX systems implement this approach, as do Windows (with NTFS) and Mac OS X (in 10.3 and subsequent versions).

The elements that support the mapping of a file name to its inode, along with protection information, are also vital to a file system. Two different means of representing the mapping information are commonly encountered:

- Information contained in standard files

- Information contained in specific files

The diagram in Figure 6.6 represents, at the system level, the various elements used within a system to effect file access; the system example has directly attached disks using the SCSI interface.

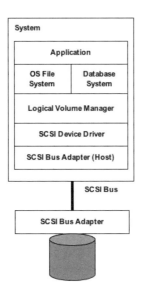

Figure 6.6
Functional Levels in data access.

File system requests come directly from applications (via calls to the file system) or are created as a side effect of requests addressed by applications to the DBMS.

A file system can be layered on top of a *Logical Volume Manager.* The role of an LVM is to provide the file system with an abstraction of the concept of a storage volume. Many operating systems, such as UNIX in its early days, built upon the notion of a physical disk as the basic storage unit. The consequence of this was that a file system could not be spread over multiple disks. The introduction of the logical volume allows multiple disks to be organized as a single volume, allowing in turn a single file to span multiple physical disks.

The LVM provides a layer of abstraction: block addresses (corresponding to a logical address—an offset within the file) are addresses within a logical volume. These logical addresses are translated into physical addresses by the logical volume manager and provided to the I/O system.

An LVM may also organize multiple disks into a RAID system (we will look further at the notion of a software RAID—a server-supported RAID—later on in this chapter).

It is frequently the case that as much for reasons of performance as for integrity, a DBMS is often built upon a notion of a logical volume rather than on top of a file system. Prior the introduction of the LVM, DBMSs were typically using an interface providing direct access to peripherals. The raw I/O functions of UNIX are an example of this class of interface. This allows the DBMS to have complete control of all I/O operations needed.

In thinking of integrity, we must remember that in normal operation, a write by an application to a file does not result in data immediately being written to the disk; rather, the data is written into memory in the disk cache, with the actual write to the disk only being done when the block is purged. But some operations, such as writing to a journal, must be completely finished before processing can continue. Some LVMs allow and support this mode of operation, along with providing RAID capabilities, multi-volume partitions, incremental backup, recovery points, and data restoration.

For performance reasons, a DBMS will usually implement its own caching, since it has knowledge of the types of cached information; for example, it may choose to keep in cache index tables rather than data.

Disk I/O requests are managed by appropriate drivers, and are passed to the disks themselves through the intermediary of the SCSI adapter. Some I/O-oriented optimizations may be done in the driver (for example, minimizing head/arm movement by reordering the incoming requests). Some operating systems have an I/O supervisor, whose job is to manage I/O requests and to ensure their proper operation.

6.4   Optimized File Systems: Log Structured File System

Performance issues encountered in file systems have led, since 1989, to proposals for file systems optimized for writing. First described in [OUS89], the concept of *log-structured file systems* has been described by others, including [ROS92]. Implementations of this approach have been described [JOH96], [WHI96], and [CZE00]. The performance of such systems has been studied and reported in [MAT97].

Network Appliance's WAFL (*Write Anywhere File Layout*) (HIT00) is an example of a file system inspired by these proposals.

To recap: the capacity of memory chips increases by a factor of 2 roughly every 18 months, so for a memory system built from a constant number of chips, servers double their memory system capacity every 18 months. Operating systems make use of this increasing memory capacity by using it as a cache for disks. Putting data in an in-memory cache avoids the need to go to the disk itself when data is reused; the caches exploit the spatio-temporal locality properties of data and program access. While using caches for reading data poses no system issues, writing is another matter entirely. Some writes really must be to the disks themselves rather than to a memory cache. The DRAM memory, after all, is volatile; its contents will disappear if the power goes away, and thus there could be no record of the data written in the event of a system failure, if the data were written to cache rather than disk. An effect of the trend in increasing cache sizes is that the ratio of disk writes to disk reads is also increasing over time.

In an OLTP environment, accesses tend to be random—that is, there is no discernible pattern in the sequence of disk addresses and files accessed, and the amount of data written is often less than the size of a disk block. At the hardware level, this access pattern has a bad effect on performance, since it means that there are many head movements involved in satisfying the requests.

The log-structured file system approach directly addresses this issue. The core notions in the approach are:

- No in-place modification of data
- Replacement of several random operations by one sequential I/O operation, collecting up all the blocks that need writing

This is reminiscent of the journaling approach used in OLTP systems [GRA92]. An implication of the adoption of this approach is that file descriptors (inodes) for the files whose blocks are not updated in place must be modified to reflect the new organization of the data on the disk.

We will provide a generic description of the technique, as the description does not correspond to any specific implementation. The key operations of a log-structured file system are shown in Figure 6.7.

As shown in the diagram, the update of modified blocks does not occur in-place. The inode marked *file inode* acts as an index for the 'real' file inodes. Rather than modifying blocks, new blocks (both data and meta-

Figure 6.7
Log-structured file system operation.

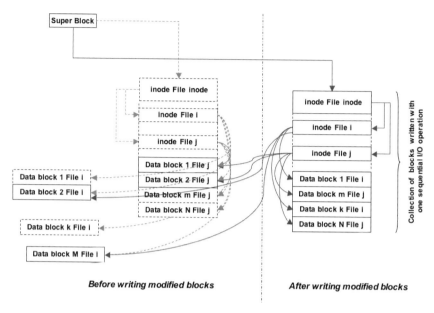

data) are written as a contiguous sequence, and the pointer in the Super-Block is updated to point at the new file inode.

The diagram shows the state of some files after a new update has been made and assumes that prior updates have already occurred. For simplicity, we show just one prior update (itself having been preceded by earlier updates). We assume in the diagram that the earlier updates had affected only file j. The new update provides new values for:

- Blocks l and k in file i
- Blocks m and N in file j

Logically, effecting the update requires two I/O operations: updating the SuperBlock and then writing the collection of blocks representing the updated data and the inodes describing them. To ensure the integrity of the file system, the file system manager must ensure the atomicity of this pair of operations.

To avoid head movements entailed by SuperBlock updates and the writing of a journal, it is possible to use a strategy of not always updating the SuperBlock. The system maintains in memory the valid *File inode*. Rebuilding a file system (following an incident) then involves the following of the journal formed by the sequence of blocks pointed at by the SuperBlock held on disk.

To simplify disk space management, the notion of a *segment* is introduced; a segment is a sequence of contiguous blocks, typically of a size of 512 KB or 1 MB. The space for writing journals is allocated within a segment.

Blocks that are no longer valid (because new blocks contain the updated values of data once held by the invalid blocks) may be reclaimed by a background operation, which examines the disk structures, identifies invalid blocks, collects them up and compacts the data.

The log structured file concept makes backup simple; we will revisit this issue later in the chapter when we discuss backup and restore operations.

To make a *snapshot* of a file system, it is only necessary to make a copy of the inodes describing the file contents. The operation is shown in Figure 6.8.

Figure 6.8
Making a snapshot of a file.

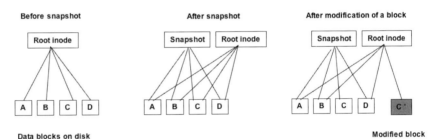

The time needed to make a copy is just the time needed to copy the inodes. We should note that this operation could be implemented in a file system not based on journaling (although it would be necessary to architect the structure so that file inodes did not have fixed positions).

A log-structured file system simplifies the implementation of a number of different backup operations:

- Complete backup
- Incremental backup—backing up only data blocks modified since the last incremental backup (or since the last complete backup for the first incremental backup; restoration involves applying the incremental backups in order up the desired point
- Differential backup data backing up blocks modified since the last complete backup—restoration involves applying first the latest com-

plete backup which preceded the point for that restoration is wanted, followed by applying the appropriate differential backup

The basic principle of the log-structured file system is that of the incremental backup. When the interval between incremental backups is longer (perhaps daily) than that implemented for the journal (for example, several hours), it is necessary to fuse several journals to obtain the backup.

The implementation of an incremental backup also depends on the fusing of journals.

Table 6.2 compares the advantages and disadvantages of Log-structured file systems and classical file systems.

Table 6.2   *Comparison of "classic" and log-structured file systems.*

	Log-Structured File System	"Classic" File System
Advantages	Improved write performance due to minimizing head movement Simplification of backup operations (snapshot, incremental, differential,.)	Widespread adoption Well-proven technology
Disadvantages	Requires custom, complex implementation Parameterizing the free-space reclamation operation	Write performance Backup is more complex

Log-structured file systems have been implemented particularly in specialized file servers, particularly NAS servers. The advantages of the approach should allow it to migrate into general-purpose servers.

6.5   Parallel File Systems

In cluster environments and MPPs, some file systems have been optimized to take advantage of the processor and memory resources represented by the nodes forming the cluster or MPP.

IBM's General Parallel File System (GPFS) is an example of a parallel file system; it can be used on AIX clusters (HACMP), MPPs (IBM SP) or Linux clusters. Our description of GPFS is based on [HEG01].

GPFS's major characteristics are:

- A clusterized file management system allowing transparent cluster file access (that is, program running on any node transparently accesses files, even if they are stored on another node)
- Scalability: GPFS has the ability to make use of processor, memory (used as a disk cache), and I/O resources of the nodes
- Failure-tolerant: GPFS provides journaling for metadata changes and data replication

In the SP implementation, GPFS is built on a software layer called *Virtual Shared Disk* (VSD). VSD allows disk blocks to be routed over a network, either an IP network or the interconnect network of an MPP. To this extent, VSD can be looked upon as a form of SAN (Storage Area Network), which we will discuss later.

GPFS is installed on the system nodes; it is possible to configure some nodes as specialist storage nodes. Data is shared by the applications running on the nodes provided with GPFS instances. Data is cached on the client nodes.

GPFS distributes data over the available disk, providing an effect similar to *data-striping*, which we will discuss later in the section on RAID systems.

Figure 6.9 illustrates the general architecture of GPFS in an SP environment.

Apart from AIX, the major software components of this architecture are the components of PSSP (*Parallel System Support Programs*), which are specific to the SP environment. The major elements are:

- VSD: *Virtual Shared Disk*, which provides the ability to access logical volumes as if they were local to the accessing node.
- GS: *Group Services*, which provides notification on the event of failure of a node or process, along with recovery of programs executing on the failing nodes on surviving ones. These services also initialize information necessary to VSD's operation.
- RVSD: *Recoverable Virtual Shared Disk*, which makes it possible to prevent access by a node to certain disks during recovery phases of the node.

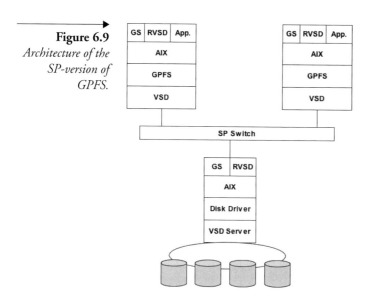

Figure 6.9
*Architecture of the
SP-version of
GPFS.*

AIX also includes a component called VFS (*Virtual File System*), which allows applications' file access requests to be directed to the appropriate file system (e.g., JFS (AIX's journaled file system) or GPFS) transparently, depending on the type of the file.

6.6   Remote File Access: NFS, CIFS and DAFS

There are a number of options for accessing distributed file systems: NFS (*Network File System*) and CIFS (*Common Internet File System*) are the most widespread. In addition, DAFS (*Direct Access File System*) allow systems to take advantage of the possibilities offered by VI or InfiniBand within the context of a local network.

We will look at NFS and CIFS before addressing DAFS.

6.6.1   NFS Network File System

Figure 6.10 shows the layers involved in NFS access to local and remote files.

The diagram is somewhat simplified to enhance comprehensibility. While the diagram assumes directly-attached disks, the SCSI bus used to connect them is not shown.

The left of the diagram shows a normal access to local files (i.e., with no NFS involvement).

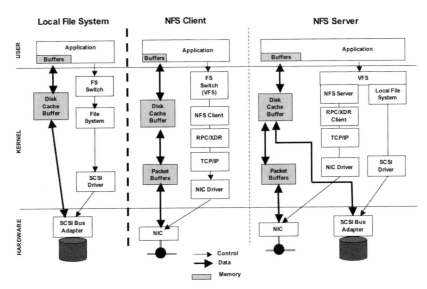

Figure 6.10
Software and hardware layers in NFS.

A system that accesses remote files by means of NFS is called an NFS Client. In such a client, the File System Switch (underneath the file system API) determines whether a file access is local (making use of the local file system with SCSI I/O operations) or remote (via NFS, making use on the client of local area network I/O operations). As shown in the figure, data is moved between user and system space.

In the case of remote access, NFS is used. If the request cannot be satisfied from the client's cache, a message is sent to the system that contains the desired file. The server calls are implemented as RPCs (*Remote Procedure Calls*). XDR (*eXternal Data Representation*) is a layer that provides freedom of data representation, which can differ between systems, by transforming all data into a standard representation. The TCP/IP layers manage data transport.

At the remote system, the NFS server, the request is received by the TCP/IP layers. It is passed on to the NFS service by means of an RPC. The XDR layer is also used in the server, at the cost of data conversion, to avoid data representation problems. For generality, we also show on the NFS server local access to files by a local application. All these operations involve substantial data movement, and often also require dynamic memory allocation.

6.6.2 Common Internet File System

We would be remiss in our descriptions of remote access file systems were we to omit mention of CIFS, which is used in Windows systems for remote file access.

CIFS is an improved version of Microsoft's SMB (*Server Message Block*); proposed by Microsoft, CIFS was offered to the IETF (*Internet Engineering Task Force*) for adoption as a standard.

CIFS, installed on a PC, allows that PC access to data held on UNIX systems.

There is an important difference between NFS and CIFS. NFS is *stateless*, while CIFS is *stateful*.

This means that an NFS server does not need to maintain any state information on its clients, but a CIFS server must. Thus, in the event of a failure in either the network or the server, recovery is much more complex for a CIFS server than for an NFS server. NLM (*Network Lock Manager*) was provided to implement lock operations in NFS, but its use is not widespread. Version 4 of NFS supports locking.

Examples of products implementing CIFS include:

- Samba (free software);

- ASU (*Advanced Server* UNIX) from AT&T

- TAS (*TotalNET Advanced Server*) from Syntax

UNIX file systems need extensions to support Windows file semantics; for example, the "creation date" information needed by Windows and CIFS must be kept in a UNIX file system in a complementary file.

Figure 6.11 shows the layers implemented in CIFS for both client and server.

This diagram follows our practice of omitting some components for simplicity. We do not show the TLI (*Transport Layer Interface*) nor the NDIS (*Network Driver Interface Layer*), for example, nor do we show local accesses on the server. NTFS (*NT File System*) is the Windows 2000 native file system.

The I/O manager determines whether an access is local or remote; the request is either directed to the local file system or handled by the CIFS

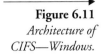

Figure 6.11
Architecture of CIFS—Windows.

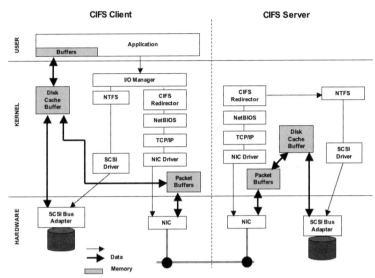

Redirector. This checks to see whether the data is available in the local cache and, if not, passes the request on to the network layers for forwarding to the server holding the file involved.

6.6.3 DAFS: Direct Access File System

DAFS (*Direct Access File System*) emerged from an initiative by a number of companies. It is a new access protocol for distributed file access in a local environment; Network Appliance was a key driver in the effort. The goal of DAFS is to take advantage of new interfaces such as VI (the *Virtual Interface Architecture*) and Infiniband. Our description of DAFS is inspired by [CAR00] and [KLE00].

The key functional goal of DAFS is to minimize the overhead of file access; the software layers involved in DAFS accesses are illustrated in Figure 6.12.

There is a DAFS-specific API, which is layered on top of VIPL (*Virtual Interface Provider Library*).

As we saw in Chapter 2, VI offers the ability to do DMA (*direct memory access*) in loosely-coupled systems like clusters. The memory accesses involved are called RDMA (for *Remote DMA* and, of course, the capability to use the built-in RDMA feature offered by InfiniBand or VIA). DAFS is a protocol based on NFSv4, which uses the properties of VI, to provide applications with efficient access to shared file servers.

Figure 6.12
*Software layers
involved in DAFS
file access.*

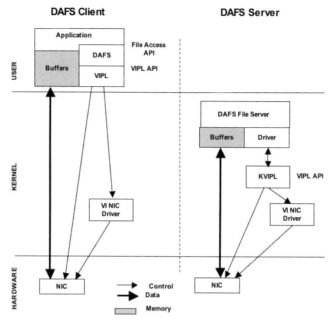

DAFS supports the following transport styles:

- VI over IP
- VI over Fibre Channel
- InfiniBand

DAFS provides direct application access to memory-to-memory transport. Thus, data transfers operate completely within user memory space and without the intervention of the operating system.

We can summarize DAFS characteristics as follows:

- File access protocol with data sharing
- Direct application access:
  - Direct transfer of data to/from application buffers
  - Without OS intervention
  - With file access semantics preserved

- Optimized for both low latency and high bandwidth (taking advantage of VI and InfiniBand)

- High-performance lock capability

- Support for failure and recovery by both clients and servers

- Isolation capabilities (the ability to restrict access by a system to specified peripherals)

Initial testing shows substantial performance improvements over vanilla NFS.

The first DAFS products appeared in the first half of 2002 from Network Appliance; the number of suppliers is expected to grow.

Figure 6.13 illustrates various possible implementations for DAFS.

Figure 6.13
DAFS implementation options.

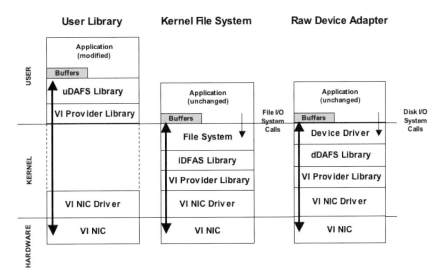

The various implementations are distinguished in two dimensions: whether the implementation is user or kernel space, and the level of the application/DAFS API—whether the API is a special one, requiring application modification, or a standard one for file access and making use of raw I/O. When DAFS is implemented in user space, applications must be modified to make use of DAFS functionality, particularly the file-sharing capabilities; doing this provides the highest possible performance.

When the file system is implemented in kernel space, there is no need to make any changes to the application. As a result, applications are unable to make use of the complete set of DAFS capabilities, and there is little performance advantage compared to the use of a standard file system operating on local files.

As pointed out before, DBMSs usually require direct peripheral access, so that they can precisely control their interactions with the system resources (a write to the journal must be completed, rather than just written to the disk cache, before processing can continue).

6.7　JBOD, SBOD, and RAID Disk Organization

As we described in Chapter 2, the arrival of cheap, small disks with lower reliability led researchers at the University of California at Berkeley to propose in 1988 an architecture for using variously-organized collections of disks. This architecture would provide higher performance and improved reliability at costs much lower than traditional for mainframe storage systems. This RAID approach [CHE94] was initially called *Redundant Array of Inexpensive Disks*, later modified to *Redundant Array of Independent Disks*.[6] Over time, physically small disks have become the norm, and the use of RAID organizations has grown significantly.[7]

While RAID is widely used and known, there are other ways of managing collections of disks; we will look at these now.

6.7.1　JBOD and SBOD Disk Organization

If a storage subsystem comprises a number of disks contained within a single physical unit—for example, 16 disks in a rack—without the disks being organized in any particular way, the collection is referred to as either a JBOD (Just a Bunch of Disks) or SBOD (Switched Bunch of Disks), depending on their interconnection. Clearly, a RAID organization can be imposed on a JBOD or SBOD.

The first JBODs used dual SCSI connections (for redundancy), although nowadays FC-AL is more usual.

Our description of JBODs is based on the account in [HAM02]. There are two topologies usually employed to construct a JBOD, and these are illustrated in Figure 6.14.

The *daisy chain topology* is traditional, and with FC-AL the maximum number of units connectable is 125.

With a *hub-based topology*, the disks forming the JBOD are star-connected to two hubs; again, with FC-AL the maximum size is 125 units. To handle more units, hubs can be cascaded.

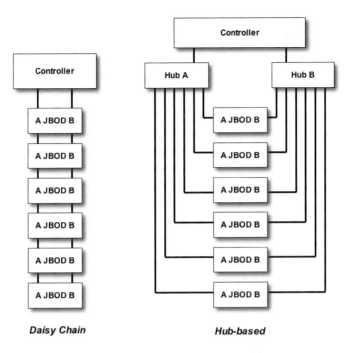

Figure 6.14
JBOD topologies.

These topologies have the following problems:

- *Reliability*: the daisy chain topology is not very reliable—a fault in any unit can compromise the whole JBOD, and diagnostic capabilities are generally rather limited

- *Scalability*: a JBOD contains some number of disks (e.g., 32), all connected to a controller; the disks share the bandwidth of the interconnect segment used to connect them

SBOD seeks to avoid these problems. Figure 6.15, from [HAM02], compares JBOD and SBOD architectures.

Figure 6.15
Comparison of JBOD and SBOD architectures (source: [HAM02]).

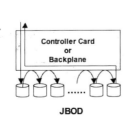

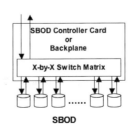

In the figure, the JBOD disks are connected as a daisy chain, while in the SBOD an X-by-X switch matrix is used to provide redundant interconnection of the disks. This allows each disks to be independently connected to the controller, improving both reliability and performance.

6.7.2   RAID Organization

We will provide an overview of the basic principles of RAID, followed by a description of the various types of RAID and their applicability.

Figure 6.16 shows a number of RAID organizations, some of which are in widespread use. The areas shown shaded indicate the data used for redundancy.

Figure 6.16
RAID Architecture

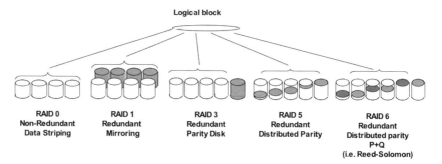

RAID architectures are based on the following two principles:

- *Distributing the data across several disks* capable of being accessed in parallel; this action is called *data striping*. This improves the effective information bandwidth, since the disks involved can supply data concurrently, while latency is hardly affected at all. The necessary synchronization waiting for the end of an operation can provide some performance degradation.

- Using redundancy (except for RAID 0), so that the failure of a disk does not affect the availability of the data.

RAID 0 does not offer redundancy, and simply exploits data striping to provide higher bandwidth data transfers.

RAID 1 uses the disk-mirroring technique: each disk has a mirror disk; writes to a disk proceed in parallel to its mirror, and reads can be made to either a disk or its mirror.[8] The figure shows two groups of disks, but for even greater availability, greater degrees of mirroring can be deployed. As the diagram makes clear, RAID 1 combines data striping with mirroring, but in an unfortunate terminology choice, it has become usual to use the term RAID 1 exclusively for mirrored systems; systems that use both mirroring and data striping are often referred to as RAID 0+1.

RAID levels 3 and 5 are based on an *exclusive OR* (XOR) parity generation scheme, illustrated in Figure 6.17.

Figure 6.17
XOR-based
redundancy
scheme.

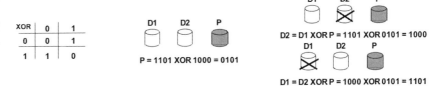

In the figure, the redundancy information is shown as a shaded disk; this information is simply the XOR of the data it is protecting. The disk containing the redundancy information can be called the *parity disk*. By constructing the XOR of the protected data, it is possible to reconstruct data in the event of failure on any one disk at a time, using the data on the remaining disks and the parity information, so that if a sector or even a complete disk fails, data can be recovered. If the parity disk fails, it may be replaced and the parity information reconstituted.

Some disks have integrated controllers that are able to do the XOR operation, thereby improving performance.

The choice of which RAID level to use depends on what task is being attempted:

- RAID 0: use when performance is needed and redundancy (data availability) is not an issue.

- RAID 1: provides higher performance reads because of parallel access, while writes only terminate when all of the individual disk writes have completed. Effective but expensive redundancy, as twice as many disks are required as are needed to hold the data.

- RAID 3: offers cost-effective redundancy (one parity disk for *N* data disks), and high performance for large data transfers. On the other hand, updates require recalculation of parity and access to the parity disk, which rapidly becomes a bottleneck.

- RAID 5: offers cost-effective redundancy (as with RAID 3, a total of $N+1$ disks are needed for N disks of data) and high-performance data transfers. The distribution of data and parity among the disks removes the parity disk bottleneck of RAID 3, minimizing the cost of updates.

- RAID 6: same basic characteristics as RAID 5, but with the ability to survive the concurrent failure of two disks rather than just one. The probability of a disk failure increases linearly with the number of disks, so RAID 6 is well-suited to larger disk collections. RAID 6 uses the P+Q redundancy technique based on Reed-Solomon codes, and doubles the amount of redundancy information compared with RAID 5.

6.8   Storage Virtualization

A simplistic application of the RAID concept would lead to providing the user with one very large very reliable disk (built from many physical disks). Since a disk unit is a natural unit of allocation for an operating system, such an approach would lead to an extremely large allocation unit. In 2003, typical server disk size was at least 72 GB, and disk sizes have been growing ever since and will continue to do so. This view of storage hardly simplifies management of disk space, and leads naturally to the desire to offer virtual disks—disks with desirable properties provided by an appropriate RAID level chosen for each subcollection, the choice matching the frequent-case usage of each such subcollection. Because virtual disks can be smaller than physical disks, a given physical disk can be involved in several different RAID schemes concurrently. This approach is called *storage virtualization*.

Virtualization brings these advantages:

- It provides to the system's operating system(s) with a view of storage as a collection of virtual disks whose sizes and RAID functionality can be chosen to match their usage. As an example, one 20 GB RAID 1 virtual disk for the system and several RAID 5 virtual disks for the database

- It seamlessly supports several RAID systems built from different disk sizes or technologies, or technology generations, or that come from different vendors, as virtual disks.

■ It takes best advantage of the installed physical resources. Consider the case where we already have a collection of five disks that may be accessed concurrently, and we wish to add another five disks that are similarly concurrently accessible. Using the concept of virtual storage, to provide maximum performance, we could choose to provide a virtual disk distributed across the ten physical disks.

We first encountered the notion of overutilizing storage earlier in this chapter when we discussed the Logical Volume Manager. As we shall see, there are several ways to support storage virtualization.

Storage virtualization will allow us to specify more precisely several notions related to RAID implementations. Figure 6.18 shows a RAID implementation underneath a virtual disk, using RAID 3 to keep the discussion simple (the concepts map into other RAID levels).

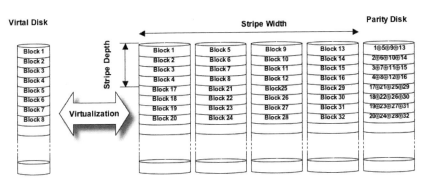

Figure 6.18
RAID implementation with virtual disks.

A block is a collection of some number of sectors. The number of disks put in parallel to hold the data (i.e., ignoring the parity disk) is called the *Stripe Width*; naturally, this sets the maximum concurrency for data access. The number of consecutively-allocated blocks on a disk represents the *Stripe Depth*; *Stripe Size* is the product of Stripe Width and Stripe Depth. To compute the address of a block to be accessed, the virtualization algorithm simply divides the virtual block address by Stripe Size to identify the disk, and uses the remainder from this operation to identify the block on that disk.

It should be noted that although the diagram shows Stripe Width and Stripe Depth both as four, in practice width and depth may be independently chosen.

There are several options in implementing storage virtualization. We shall examine these possibilities in the section in which we discuss the architectural options for supporting RAID functionality.

6.9 Scatter Reads and Gather Writes

A usual optimization in a file system is to take a collection of elementary I/O operations, to regroup them as a single command as far as the peripheral subsystem is concerned, and to do the operations in an order that minimizes head movement and rotational delays (that is, make use of a channel program to effect multiple I/O operations while looking like a single operation to the application. We discussed channel programs in Chapter 2). A disk write operation can involve data from several noncontiguous memory zones, a situation that can also occur as a normal side-effect of the operation of virtual memory, wherein logically contiguous addresses may be physically completely disjoint.

A similar effect occurs in reads, when a single logical block must be "scattered" across several noncontiguous physical pages.

If these *Scatter Reads* and *Write Gathers* were implemented by the processor, performance would suffer, so generally these operations are done by specialized circuitry that implements a *DMA* (Direct Memory Access) controller. When an I/O operation is initiated, it is necessary just to provide a number of descriptors to the DMA controller, specifying which memory zones are needed for each portion of the I/O operation, and the DMA machine will manage the various operations needed, whether gathering or scattering. Figure 6.19 shows scatter/gather operations on a mapped file (that is, a file whose data the application has requested to the operating system to map into its virtual address space, so that data accesses, rather than file I/O, can be done on the file). In the diagram, we have made the simplifying assumption that the virtual memory page size and the disk block size are the same.

6.9.1 Data Update

When one or more storage blocks are updated in a RAID system with redundancy, the parity information must also be updated, which suggests that the related but unmodified blocks must be read so that the parity may be computed.

However, if just a small number of blocks are being updated, or just data within one block, then parity calculation need not involve reading blocks on other disks. Suppose we have three data disks and one parity disk and that we wish to update a block b_2 on data disk 2. Its associated blocks are data blocks b_1 and b_2 on the data disks and b_p on the parity disk.

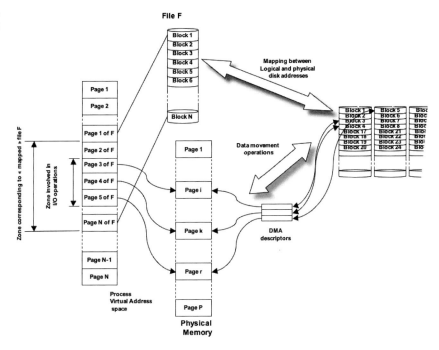

Figure 6.19
Scatter/gather.

We need to calculate

$$\text{new } b_p = b_1 \oplus \text{new } b_2 \oplus b_3$$

We know that XORing a number with itself gives a result of zero.
We observe that:

```
old b₂ + old bₚ = old b₂ + old b₂ + (b₁ + b₃)
```

which is just $b_2 + b_3$.
Thus,

```
new bₚ = new b₂ + b₁ + b₃
```

so

```
new bₚ = new b₂ + old b₂ + old bₚ
```

Thus, provided one has the old value of the block(s) to be modified to hand, there is no need to read the associated data blocks, although the old parity block must be accessed. With disks whose electronics can implement the XOR, the logical steps in updating b_2 are as follows:

Read the value of old b_2—the block to be modified

Calculate new b_2 + old b_2

Send this value to the parity disk, with the request to XOR it with current b_p value:

```
new bp = old bp + (new b2 + old b2)
```

For RAID organizations making use of parity (RAID 3, 5, and 6), it is vital that a write operation is completely done, or that if an interruption occurs during the writing, that any modifications can be undone. This is complicated by the fact that such a system needs at least two write operations: one for the data update, and one for the parity update.

To guarantee the integrity of the data in such a system, it is necessary that:

- Writes are atomic
- Data passes from one consistent state to a new consistent state
- Any intermediate states of the data must be invisible to other operations; they must be isolated
- The effects of the write be durable

These, of course, are simply the ACID properties necessary for OLTP.[9]

To provide these properties, at the beginning of every write—whether a write creating data or updating it—an entry in a journal is created indicating the commencement of the write. Each data modification gives rise to a journal entry for each changed block, containing sufficient information that any operation that did not complete properly can be completely cancelled, or be replayed.

There are two approaches to creating such a journal, one making use of specialized hardware:

- System-supported journal on disk

- Nonvolatile memory

System-provided journaling capabilities do not require special hardware, beyond the use of dual-channel connections to the disks for redundancy.

The use of nonvolatile memory does require some form of specialized hardware, usually battery-backed DRAM, again with dual access means for a high-availability system. The journal is written into the DRAM.

6.10   Comparing the Various RAID Levels

Table 6.3, a modification of information from VERITAS [VER00], compares the various RAID levels under the following assumptions:

- A RAID system uses *N* disks

- Mirroring is of order M (with M =2 being the usual case)

- Comparisons are against storage on a single disk, unless otherwise indicated

Table 6.3   *Comparison of the most popular RAID organizations.*

RAID Type	Name	Storage cost	Relative data availability	Large sequential read speed	Large sequential write speed	Random read bandwidth	Random write bandwidth
0	Data striping	> 1	Lower than that of a conventional organization	Higher— Depends on the number of parallel disks	Higher— Depends on the number of parallel disks	Higher	Higher
1	Mirroring (of order M; M=2 usually)	x M (see note [10])	> RAID 3 & RAID 5 < RAID 6	Up to M times a single disk	Lower than a single disc	Up to M times a single disk	Lower than a single disc

Table 6.3   *Comparison of the most popular RAID organizations. (continued)*

0+1	Striped mirror (of order M; M=2 usually)	$M \times N$	> RAID 3 & RAID 5 < RAID 6	Up to M times a RAID 0 equivalent	Can be higher than that of the single disc as a function of N	Up to M times a RAID 0 equivalent	Lower than equivalent RAID 0
3	Parity disk	$N + 1$	>> conventional disk	Higher Depends on the number of parallel disks and the need to compute parity (< RAID 0)	Higher Depends on the number of parallel disks and the need to compute parity (< RAID 0)	Higher	Lower than equivalent RAID 0— requires calculating and writing parity
5	"Spiral" parity	$N + 1$	>> conventional disk ~ RAID 3	< RAID 0 because of the parity check	< RAID 0	Higher > RAID 3	>> RAID 3
6	Double "spiral" parity	$N + 2$	Higher than all the other types	Slightly > RAID 5	< RAID 5 (2 parity blocks)	Slightly > RAID 5	< RAID 5 (2 parity blocks)

In the table, performance is characterized in two ways: one for bandwidth for large transfers and the other for random transfers. Large reads and writes are typical of decision-support applications, as well as numerically-intensive computations for which computational time is the key factor. Random reads and writes are typical of OLTP, for which bandwidth is the key factor.

Some comments on the table:

- For RAID 0 (Data Striping), the cost of storage is higher than for a single disk (assuming that a single disk has sufficient capacity) since using several disks (regardless of their ability to provide more storage capacity than a single disk) increases costs for items such as racks, cables, controllers, power. Data availability is lower than for a single disk, because MTBF for the RAID is the MTBF of a single disk divided by the number of disks used—that is, a RAID 0 of N disks has an MTBF N times smaller than the MTBF of a single disk. Reading and writing large blocks on a RAID 0 using N disks takes less time than for a single disk (at best N times less, limited by the fact that the disks are not in general rotationally synchronized). This reduces the occupation time of the disks and allows higher bandwidths. The same is true for random reads and writes.

- For RAID 1 (Mirroring), the storage cost is proportional to the number of copies of the data kept (the factor M in the table). Most often, mirroring is simple replication (M = 2).[11] As to availability, it is clear that RAID 1 has higher availability than RAID 3 or RAID 5, since it has complete data replication rather than a parity disk per N physical disks. Reading, whether of large transfers or random transfers, has higher performance because the data can be read concurrently from multiple disks. Concurrency is less effective for writes, whether for large transfers or random transfers, because of the need to not signal completion until the last write on the last disk is complete.

- RAID 0 + 1 (Striped Mirror) has more or less the same properties as RAID 1, with just one further comment on write operations: the time for write operations for large transfers can be lower than for a single disk, if the time saved as a result of distributing the data across N parallel disks is greater than the extra cost of synchronizing completion across M groups of disks.

- RAID 3 (Parity Disk) availability is ensured through the use of parity information. Large block reads offer similar performance to RAID 0, with any differences attributable to the need to compute parity for the information read, along with any required correction. Large block writes are slower, because such transfers involve both the calculation of parity and writing the parity values to the parity disk, whose busy time can be greater than those of the collection of data disks, since there is just one parity disk. Random reads require a parity disk access, calculation of data parity, parity comparison, and any necessary correction. A write operation implies calculation of parity and its writing to the parity disk. Performance compared with a single disk depends on the performance advantage obtained by distributing the data across multiple disks.

- RAID 5 (Spiral Parity) offers essentially the same availability as RAID 3. Again, large transfer performance is impacted by the need to calculate parity and apply correction as required. Random reads and writes are generally better than for RAID 3 because of the distribution of parity information over multiple disks, reducing contention on parity updates.

- RAID 6 (Double Spiral Parity) provides higher availability than RAID 5, since it can survive two concurrent independent failures. RAID 6 has slightly higher read performance than RAID 5, since double parity reduces contention and thus wait time for parity writes (only slightly higher performance, since the number of disks grows only from $N + 1$ to $N + 2$). Write operations, on the other hand, are slower, suffering from the increased burden of double parity computation and writing.

A complete comparison would also include the cost of writing journals for all the cases above. When the journal is written into non-volatile memory, the performance impact will be minimal.

Vendors have created further RAID organizations from these basic categories. Examples include RAID 53, RAID S and RAID 7.

6.11 Performance

The performance of more or less any system can be expressed by in two dimensions:

- *Response time*, that is, how long it takes to complete an operation
- *Bandwidth*, that is, how many operations may be done per unit of time

Depending on what an application needs to do, one or the other of these measures will be of prime interest (keeping in mind that they are not completely independent); for an OLTP application, response time is key, while for decision support, bandwidth will generally be key since the latter requires analysis of a great deal of data.

To illustrate the connection between the two dimensions, consider an OLTP system using RAID 0. Because the amount of data updated per operation is small—generally less than a disk block size—distributing the data across multiple disks does not improve response time. However, distributing the data in such a manner does help reduce wait time and thus response time (compared with a system with no distribution) since disks are busy less often. As a result, bandwidth also increases, since more operations per unit time are completed.

Figure 6.20, derived from [VER00], provides this performance relative to a single disk information. For simplicity, we distinguish just two types of RAID: RAID 0 (without any redundancy), shown as a group of 4 disks, and RAID with parity (RAID 3 or 5), depicted as a group of 5 disks.

Figure 6.20
RAID performance positioning.

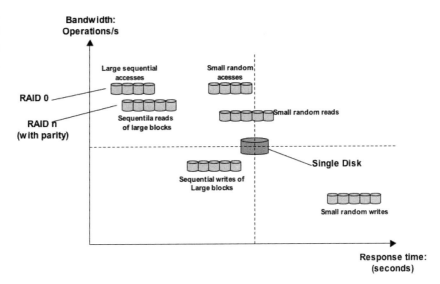

The diagram is qualitative. Choosing the best organization for an application requires performance measurements of candidates made under relevant well-established conditions, or perhaps more conveniently performance measurements made with knowledge of key application parameters.

SPC (for *Systems Performance Council*), an initiative that saw the light of day in June 2001, should help simplify some of these comparisons. Formed by a group of storage vendors, the SPC promotes a new family of standards allowing performance comparisons between storage solutions. The first standard, SPC-1, characterizes the performance of storage subsystems in an application environment combining OLTP, databases and e-mail; such a mix emphasizes random I/O operations. SPC-1 measures the systems in this environment in the two dimensions we have been discussing:

- Bandwidth, as the maximum number of I/O operations per second (SPC-1 IOPS) under the constraint of maintaining a reasonable response time

- Response time under a small load (Least Response Time, or SPC-1 LRT)

6.12 MAID

The concept of MAID (*Massive Array of Inactive Disks*) has been recently introduced. It refers to a collection of low-cost SATA (or even PATA) disks drives that are not active until they are accessed. Once a disk is going to be accessed, it is activated. This results in a lower acquisition cost and a lower operation cost, owing to the reduced electrical consumption. Of course, response time is heavily increased as compared with active disks, since the typical starting time of a disk is about 10 seconds. MAID can be used wherever access time is not a key factor; for instance, a MAID can serve as a cache to a tape library or as an alternative to tapes.

Intelligent Discs

We must also discuss a proposal from University of California at Berkeley researchers. The proposal addresses making use of the intelligence embedded within today's disks. They call the proposal *Intelligent Disks* [KEE98].

The rationale is straightforward: as the industry migrates towards higher-level interfaces such as SCSI or FC-AL, disk drives needed to embed greater processing power, nowadays typically making use of a 32-bit microprocessor and several megabytes of memory. The suggestion is simply to move some file system or database functionality onto this microprocessor.

Clearly, there is a question of balance; during IBM's introduction of the S/360, processors were relatively slow, and thus there was substantial pressure to off-load tasks from them. This lead to the use of intelligent disk controllers allowing disk searches to be done according to specified criteria (the interface was called CKD or ECKD). As time passed, minicomputers and early microprocessor systems became rather higher performance and cheap, driving the adoption of simple, low-cost disk interfaces such as SMD and later ESDI. These interfaces had limitations, and once more an intelligent interface, this time SCSI, was introduced to overcome them, necessitating the presence of microprocessors and memory in the disk drives themselves. Choosing commodity low-cost processors provided much more computer power than was needed by the task, but kept costs down.

The success of this approach, however, does not rest on hardware technology but rather requires that the industry adopt the standards, that operating systems support it, and—perhaps most significantly—that the major database vendors also adopt it. We have discussed this subject in Chapter 2.

6.13   Architectural Options for RAID Implementations

In this section, we first examine various system-level architectural options for implementing RAID systems, and then do the same for storage virtualization.

We can see three major architectural options for RAID:

- RAID functionality implemented by software within the server

- RAID functionality implemented by a specialist controller, connected via the standard I/O interconnect such as PCI

- RAID functionality implemented within the storage subsystem itself, connected to the server with a peripheral interface such as SCSI or FC-AL

These three options are shown in Figure 6.21, using a RAID 3 configuration for illustration, and their various merits are summarized in Table 6.4.

Figure 6.21
System architecture options.

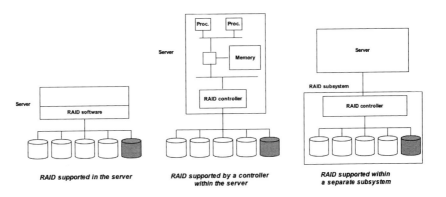

As shown in the table, the choice of a server-implemented RAID functionality is an entry-level solution. A usefully higher performance level, still at reasonable cost, is obtained through the use of a server-resident hardware RAID controller. The use of a specialized RAID storage subsystem brings

Table 6.4   *Comparing System Architecture Options for RAID.*

	RAID supported by the server	RAID supported by controller in server	RAID supported within a specialized subsystem
■ Advantages	■ Low cost ■ High connectivity (i.e., the server's innate connectivity) ■ Scalability (increasing server performance increases RAID performance) ■ High availability (no extra hardware elements involved)	■ Moderate cost ■ Good execution times and good bandwidth (specialized hardware)	■ Connectivity usually high (constrained by the subsystem) along with the possibility of connecting multiple subsystems ■ High bandwidth (specialized hardware) ■ Good write performance, if a write cache is available ■ High availability (doubling internal controllers and multiple access paths) ■ Independence between host interconnect (e.g., FC-AL) and disk (e.g., SCSI).
■ Disadvantages	■ Server performance is impacted by the extra load of implementing RAID functionality ■ Data availability demands mean that the disks must have dual access interfaces to allow recovery after failure of the server	■ Number of disks supported constrained by the connectivity capabilities of the controller ■ Data availability demands mean that the disks must have dual access interfaces to allow recovery after failure of the server or the controller	■ Specialist hardware (redundant secure cache) ■ Higher cost ■ Better response time than a pure server-based solution, thanks to the server/subsystem interconnect

even higher bandwidth, lower latency, and better availability, but at a substantially increased cost. Some of these subsystems provide a secure write cache, using battery-backed memory, which substantially improves response time. The battery-backed memory is replicated; a write operation writes into both memories, and the write operation is signaled as complete as soon as these have both completed.

Figure 6.22 from Gartner Group shows the evolution of the market for RAID support options.

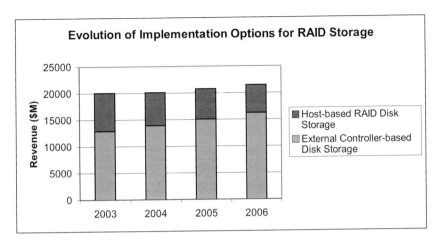

Figure 6.22
Evolution of the market for RAID support options (source data: Gartner Group 2004).

The market share for RAID support within external controllers is growing—from 64% in 2003 to nearly 76% in 2006.

6.14 Architectural Options for Storage Virtualization

System architectural options for storage virtualization are illustrated in Figure 6.23, based on an assumption of a SAN (Storage Area Network) environment; we discuss these later. SAN designates specialized high speed networks directly connected to storage elements; SANs are designed to support the exchange of large amounts of data at high speed in a distributed system and are independent of host systems. In practice, a SAN solution is not deployed without storage virtualization.

These four options have differing properties, which we summarize in Table 6.5, inspired by VERITAS [VER01].

When storage virtualization is implemented within the client systems, it relies on functionality generally implemented at the level of a logical volume manager; such technology is well understood and well proven. It is also possible to integrate virtualization within the file system or DBMS, allowing these to benefit. Since these solutions make the storage globally visible, clusterization techniques must be employed so that a single view of the storage is maintained despite the presence of multiple virtualization managers. The difficulties in administration arise from the need to coordinate the multiple virtualization managers.

Implementing virtualization within the storage subsystem hides storage heterogeneity, but there are as many administration points as there are storage subsystems. Virtualization solutions are proprietary to each vendor,

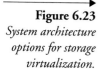

Figure 6.23
System architecture options for storage virtualization.

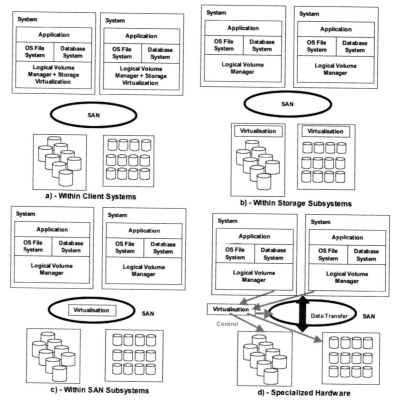

and the cost of each subsystem is impacted by the need to support virtualization. The complexities arising from heterogeneity make qualification difficult.

Integrating virtualization within a SAN allows seamless support of different clients, since the virtualization is hidden behind the SAN interfaces, but again use of different subsystems means that clusterization techniques must be used: availability requirements means that the subsystems (unless they provide internal redundancy) must have a common view of the totality of system storage. SAN equipment cost is impacted by the need to provide virtualization (i.e., processing resources, memory resources, and virtualization software). When the equipment is sourced from multiple vendors, interoperability issues can arise.

The final option is related to the SAN-based approach but uses a special subsystem to implement virtualization. This sort of architecture is called "out of band," as opposed to the other options, which are "in band." The subsystem provides a central control point and offers the potential of higher

Table 6.5 *Comparison of system architecture options for storage virtualization.*

	Client systems	Subsystems of storage	SAN Subsystem	Specialist hardware
Advantages	■ Virtualization based on proven principles	■ Allows the support of heterogeneous storage (technology and vendor independence)	■ Ability to connect diverse clients	■ Centralized control
	■ Narrow integration with File Sys tems and DBMS			■ High performance due to separation of control and data transfer
				■ Supports heterogeneous clients
Disadvantages	■ Global visibility of storage means that clusterization techniques must be used	■ Multiple points of administration	■ Global visibility of storage means that clusterization techniques must be used	■ Requires special drivers in the clients
	■ Administrative complexity	■ Solution proprietary to each vendor	■ Need to use clusterization techniques for availability	■ Difficulty of qualifying the solution in a heterogeneous environment
		■ Global visibility of storage means that clusterization techniques must be used ■ Qualification of the solution	■ Limits choice to hardware that can support virtualiza tion	■ High availability requires redundant equipment
		■ Cost of the various subsystems	■ Interoperability concerns between different vendors	■ Complexity of connection

performance, since it separates control and data paths. The immediate effect is that specialist drivers are needed in all client systems. The potential diversity of connected systems (both clients and storage) can lead to problems in qualification. The subsystem needs internal redundancy to avoid being a system single point of failure (SPOF). Separating control and data interconnects, if implemented at the physical level, will drive up complexity and cost.

The choice of a solution will be based on a combination of these properties and the constraints of the environment (clients, SAN equipment, and storage subsystems).

6.15   Storage Architectures

We can distinguish several storage architectures by the ways in which the storage is connected to the system and the visibility given to the software which manages storage resources. This perspective is independent of any notion of RAID.

We show these different options in Figure 6.24, adapted from IBM's Red Book.

Figure 6.24
DAS, NAS, SAN, and iSCSI (source: IBM's Red Book).

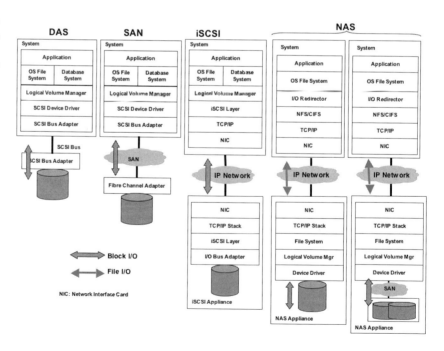

We can characterize these architectures as follows:

- DAS, for Directly Attached Storage, indicates storage resources directly connected to a server and reserved for its exclusive use. It has a Block I/O access interface, and the file system is implemented on the server itself. Physical interface is usually SCSI or FC-AL.

- NAS, for Network-Attached Storage, refers to storage resources which are distributed and network-accessed using high-level protocols such as NFS[12] or CIFS. It uses File I/O to access data. The abstraction presented to client systems is that of a file system; clients emit read and write requests to the remote files, with only a mount operation being necessary beforehand to connect to the file system.

- SAN, for Storage Area Network, indicates specialized high-speed local networks used to connect storage systems, and in practice will always be used with storage virtualization. SANs use Block I/O for data transfers. As specified by the SNIA model (discussed later), while the use of Fibre Channel is not mandated for SANs, it is the most prevalent. We show this by noting SAN FC (for Fibre Channel SAN) in the diagram.

- iSCSI allows a server to access remote storage over the Internet. It uses Block I/O for data access. iSCSI implements the SCSI protocols within an IP wrapper; one may view this as a SAN using Internet protocols.

> Although we describe certain architectures as not having shared storage resources (DAS, for example) in practice the need for availability results in multiple connections between a server and its storage resources, or indeed between multiple servers and storage resources. In normal operation, just one connection (one server) will access the resources over one interconnect; interconnect the other would be used when the primary server or interconnect suffers a failure.

We summarize the properties of these options in Table 6.6.

Connection type does not merit much discussion. Remote connections are native with NAS and iSCSI; they are possible with SAN but generally limited to a few miles distance.

As to the maximum **distance** between clients and storage, both DAS and SAN are limited by the characteristics of their interconnect, with dis-

Table 6.6   *Comparison of DAS, NAS, SAN, and iSCSI*

	DAS	NAS	SAN	iSCSI
Type of Connection	SCSI FC-AL	Fast Ethernet Fibre Channel	Fibre Channel	Internet
Remote Connection	Typically no	Yes	Possible	Yes
Type of I/O	Block	File	Block	Block
Performance	High	Limited by the network	Higher	Limited by the network
Data Sharing	Implies NFS or CIFS	Native	Difficult (in 2002)/ Future	Difficult (in 2002)
Cost Reduction	No	Yes	Ψes	Yes
Investment Separation	No	Yes	Yes	Yes
Scalability	No	Yes	Yes	Depends on network support
Data Availability	Limited	Yes if redundant	Yes if redundant	Yes if redundant
Centralization of Management and Support	Typically no	Yes	Yes	Yes
Management	Traditional	SNMP	Difficult (in 2002)	Difficult (in 2002)
LAN-Free Backup	No	Depends on NAS server	Yes	Depends on iSCSI server
Server-Free Backup	No	Depends on NAS server	Yes	Depends on iSCSI server
Security	By the server	By the servers and the network	By the servers and storage network	By the servers and network
Installation	Specific to the server	Simple	Difficult (in 2002)	Difficult (in 2002)

tances being variously from a few yards to a few miles. Neither NAS nor iSCSI have such limitations.

By **data sharing** we mean sharing at the level of file content. With DAS, systems wanting to share data need to support distributed file systems like NFS or CIFS, and to implement a common model allowing file-sharing and lock operations.

Such sharing is of course native with NAS. For SAN and iSCSI, it is necessary to implement structures supporting a metadata server (such as NFS or CIFS) to implement the transformation between file-oriented access and block-oriented access. We will see an architecture of the type later in this chapter.

NAS, SAN, and iSCSI allow **storage investment to be shared** (so that any added disk can be used by all clients) while also allowing **separation of investmen**t in processing capability (processors and memory of the client systems) from storage. With these approaches, it is also possible to have centralized administration and support for all the storage resources; naturally, this is not feasible with DAS.

With DAS, **scalability** is limited to the capabilities of the system to which the storage is attached. Systems with great scalability are often extremely expensive, and those in charge of IT have no guarantee, when making the choice of solution, that they will ever need a system configuration close to the maximum possible from such a scalable system. On the other hand, with a NAS approach, one can federate several NFS or CIFS servers and distribute files between them. With SAN, it is straightforward to add subsystems that will give client systems visibility of greater disk space (both in capacity and in number of drives). For iSCSI, scalability depends on the capabilities of the Internet network deployed.

The subject of **data availability** calls for several comments. For a DAS system, disks attached to one server must be accessible from others so that recovery from server failure is possible. With the other approaches, data availability depends on the redundancy properties of the servers supporting them. One may therefore simply limit the redundancy to the servers themselves (NAS, SAN, or iSCSI). We should also note that availability, to be useful, implies integrity. In the update situation, the best way of ensuring data integrity is to use transactional applications; this point was discussed in detail in Chapters 9 and 10, which discussed high-availability systems.

With a SAN approach, **storage management** is naturally centralized. With NAS or iSCSI, administration is done by means of SNMP (or perhaps software built on top of SNMP). For DAS, administration must be done on a server-by-server basis. Because SAN products are relatively young, their administration is not yet mature and can be more difficult than for the other approaches. This is particularly evident in heterogeneous environments (that is, with equipment from multiple vendors). On the other hand, iSCSI leverages TCP/IP.

SAN solutions allow backup and store to be both **server-free** and **LAN-free**; that is, neither the servers nor the LAN proper need be burdened by backup and restore operations. NAS and iSCSI can offer the same properties to the extent that they are layered on top of a SAN solution. We will discuss the notions of server-free and LAN-free later, but here we should note that the servers referred to in the term server-free are the client servers, not the specialized storage server. For DAS, the server to which the disks are attached must clearly be involved in backup and restore operations, as must the LAN to which the server is attached (assuming magnetic tape drives are LAN-connected); this has an effect on overall system performance.

In the area of **security**, the DAS system, with locally-connected devices, is naturally more secure than the other, distributed, solutions, which face all the security issues of a distributed system compared to a centralized one.

While **installation** of storage resources in a DAS system is dependent on the characteristics of the server used, NAS installation is very simple because of the high-level access protocols used. The lower-level protocols block I/O rather than file access) necessary for SAN and iSCSI, along with the relative youth of the technology, makes installation of these approaches somewhat less straightforward than a NAS server.

Figure 6.25, from Gartner Group (2003) shows how the market share of the various solutions is expected to change over time for external storage (i.e., for storage integrated within subsystems, which is typical in medium-to large-size servers).

The total worldwide market was estimated at $14 billion in 2001, rising to $17.3 billion in 2007. The forecast clearly shows an expected drop in the

Figure 6.25
*Worldwide market
for external storage
(source data:
Gartner Group
2003).*

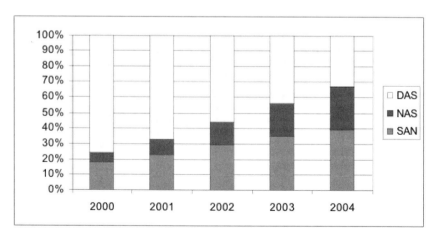

DAS (falling from 83% in 1999 to just 23% 2007) to the benefit of NAS (up from 4% to 17%) and SAN (up from 13% to 60%).

Integrated DAS solutions are most prevalent in entry-level servers, although they are also used for the system disk (containing copies of software and providing paging capacity) in bigger systems. The rise of SAN and NAS is driven in large part by the desire to rationalize costs.

6.16 The Integration of Fibre Channel and the Internet

With iSCSI we saw the integration of the IP protocol and disk access. Figure 6.26 shows a possible integration of Fibre Channel and the Internet.

Figure 6.26 (a) shows access to a storage subsystem with a Fibre Channel interface over the Internet. The iSCSI controller encapsulates the SCSI commands within IP packets. The IP/Fibre Channel bridge sends the SCSI requests to the storage subsystem.

Figure 6.26 (b) shows the interconnection of multiple SANs via IP. The FCIP (*Fibre Channel over TCP/IP*) protocol enables a system to access resources on remote SANs. The FCIP gateways both encapsulate Fibre Channel commands in IP packets, and extract them from received IP packets. The FCIP specification is still being validated.

Figure 6.26
Integration of Fibre Channel and the Internet.

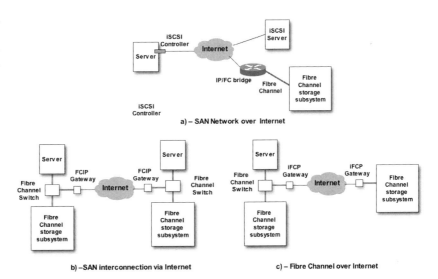

Figure 6.26 (c) shows the extension of a SAN by use of the Internet. Another protocol, iFCP (*Internet Fibre Channel Protocol*) exists for this usage, and is in the process of validation. Its advantage over FCIP is that it removes the need for a Fibre Channel switch on the remote storage site.

6.17   Integration of SAN and NAS within a Single Architecture

SAN and NAS architectures have often been seen as opposites, since they offer distinct functionalities. However, one can look upon the two as complementary; for example, a NAS server could access storage resources over a SAN, and nothing makes it impossible for the SAN to be common to the clients of the NAS server.

Vendors have proposed approaches allowing the integration of the two concepts within a single systems architecture. From the point of view of implementation, there are two architectural options:

- Direct, in which each client system has a copy of necessary metadata and is therefore able to map file accesses into I/O requests on the SAN

- Indirect, in which file access requests are sent to a specific server—the metadata server—which does the mapping from file accesses to SAN block I/O

SAN and Server Consolidation

Concentrating and sharing storage resources between the systems that comprise a complete information system is an example of the *Server Consolidation* phenomenon. In this, the servers, once scattered across a company, are relocated into just one geographical site, saving on space, air conditioning, power, security, and other elements of the cost of ownership. Server consolidation relies on SAN and storage virtualization to work.

Figure 6.27 illustrates the indirect approach.

As shown in the diagram, NFS and/or CIFS requests are directed to the metadata server; the requests are accompanied by the addresses of the memory zones on the clients which are involved in the accesses. The metadata server translates the file-level access requests into block I/O commands and

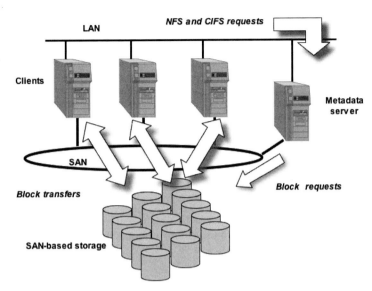

Figure 6.27
Integration of the concepts of SAN and NAS.

issues them to the SAN-based storage, which implements the desired transfers. Tivoli's SANergy is an example of this type of architecture.

A direct implementation saves the cost of sending the request to a metadata server, but at the price of needing synchronization between the systems to maintain metadata coherence.

6.18 Storage Architecture Options: Summary

In Figure 6.28, we summarize storage architecture options

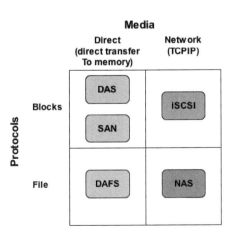

Figure 6.28
Summary of storage architecture options.

We have sorted the options according to two criteria:

- Information access protocols
- Information transport mechanism:

NAS and DAFS are both file access protocols, but they differ in the in transport mechanisms: NAS uses a TCP/IP network, and DAFS makes use of direct memory access in a loosely-coupled system.

For the block-level access protocols (in which the entity initiating the transfer specifies the block or blocks concerned) iSCSI differs from DAS or SAN because it uses the Internet as a transfer mechanism, rather than DMA (whether local or remote).

It should be clear that the highest performance is available from the DAS, SAN, and (especially) DAFS side of the diagram.

6.19   SNIA Architecture Model

The SNIA, Storage Network Industry Association, was formed from a group of storage industry players who had the goal of providing a common framework within which to describe various storage architectures. The SNIA has created and published an architecture model: "Shared Storage Model—A Framework for Describing Storage Architectures" [SNI01].

Figure 6.29 illustrates this model.

The SNIA model is very general, and avoids implementation assumptions. The various necessary functions are described in a generic manner in this model, with the goal of establishing a terminology markedly less ambiguous than that in general use in marketing materials from the various vendors. As an example, the term "virtualization" is not used in the model.

Because the model has not seen widespread adoption as of this writing, we have not used it as the basis for our storage architecture discussions.

One interesting point arising from the model is that it highlights the area of storage management, an area in which there is room for improvement across the industry. In this area, there are some interesting initiatives—we will look at one from EMC in the next section.

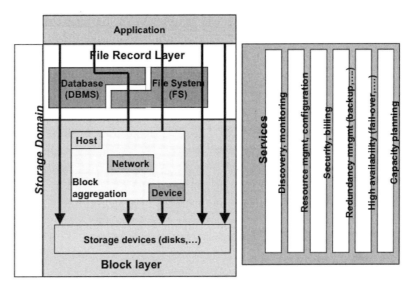

Figure 6.29
SNIA shared storage architecture model.

6.20 Storage Management

At the beginning of this chapter we saw that expenditure on storage represented more than 50 percent of total system expenditure for OLTP and information server systems; thus, managing these resources is an important issue this is, unfortunately, more complex than would be wished, because of the added complexities offered by heterogeneous systems (that is, systems with storage subsystems from different vendors, a variety of administration software packages).

META Group published a report in December 2001 which stated that in a large datacenter (by which they mean one with more than 1,000 MIPS of processing capability) it took one administrator to manage 6 TB of storage, provided that the installation was a mainframe. For UNIX or Windows systems, efficiency is lower, although this will change over time as improvements are made to these systems. By 2005 or 2006, we can generally expect a ratio of around 20 TB per administrator. As we have already pointed out, this ratio is very application dependent.

At the end of 2001, EMC launched WideSky, a middleware product that offered the various storage industry players a single interface allowing their products all to be managed by EMC's ECC/OE (EMC Control-Center/Open Edition). WideSky's architecture is shown in Figure 6.30.

The components of this architecture are:

Figure 6.30
*General
architecture of
WideSky (source:
EMC).*

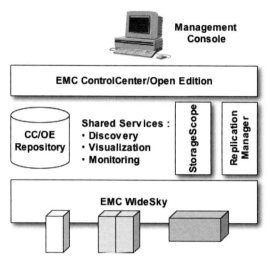

- The middleware WideSky, which provides a homogeneous vision of the various storage equipment

- ControlCenter/Open Repository Edition, a database containing information on the collection of elements

- A number of services shared by the offer's components—configuration discovery, visualization, operational monitoring

- StorageScope, tool for reporting of the use of storage resources

- Replication Manager

- ControlCenter/Open Edition, a centralized management tool for storage resources

At the time these lines are written, it is difficult to determine the success of this product; nonetheless, such an offer is a useful step towards unified management of storage subsystems.

6.21 Data Compression

Moving data costs bandwidth; storing data costs storage space. To reduce the storage and bandwidth needed, compression techniques may be used.

In addition, encryption techniques may be used to improve data confidentiality.

Using these techniques will generally have a performance impact; some systems, therefore, use specialized hardware to do encryption. Our treatment of encryption in Chapter 3 will not be expanded on here.

6.21.1 Data Compression

Data compression techniques have long been used in an attempt to counter the fact that the amount of data to be stored seems to be growing continuously. Using compression can provide the following advantages:

- An increase in the amount of available storage capacity, because each stored item is smaller than before

- Reduced time needed for I/O operations, since there is less data to be transferred

- The opportunity to move stored data up the storage hierarchy (e.g., to keep an item on disk rather than on magnetic cartridge in a robot)

This section draws from a number of sources, including [JAY] and [LEL], as well as [SAY00], a reference book.

There are two major classes of compression:

- *Lossless compression*: data is compressed without losing any information

- *Lossy compression*: data is compressed, but information is lost

Lossy compression techniques are used particularly for images and audio and video stream compression, and make use of both our senses' capabilities and the information pattern in the data. Standards exist; key ones including JPEG (*Joint Picture Experts Group*) for images and MPEG (*Motion Pictures Expert Group*) for video and film. While servers must store lossy-compressed images and video, the underlying technologies—including the need to keep multiple channels synchronized—are a specialist topic we will leave to other works; we will concentrate here on lossless compression.

Hardware devices make it possible to accelerate the functions of compression and decompression.

Obviously, the choice of compression technique depends on the nature of the data to be compressed. The criteria used in the choice of technique are:

- The *effective compression ratio* (the size of data before compression/size of data after compression)

- The *complexity of the compression* function (affecting the time and resources needed for compression)

- The *complexity of the decompression* function (affecting time and resources necessary for decompression)

The achievable compression ratio depends on both the compression algorithm and the details of the data to be compressed. While the ratio will vary across data types, in practice a value of approximately 2 is achievable for non-text files (higher for text). When choosing a technique, tests with representative data will be very helpful.

Some comparative data has been published; look at the Web site [ART01] for some results.

6.21.2 Compression Techniques

In this section we will examine a number of compression techniques, but before diving into the discussion some background may be helpful. A key point is that compression of a file may be applied at several levels: the raw data bits; characters (whether 8 bit ASCII or 16 bit UNICODE); or words (character sequences, usually 2, 4, or 8 characters). Our somewhat simplified discussion will restrict itself to characters and sequences of characters. Such techniques can be applied at other levels—bits and sequences of bits, for example, or words and sequences of words.

6.21.3 Dictionary-based Compression

This technique applies to texts in which the same words frequently occur. To apply the method, first build an ordered dictionary (or list) of the frequent words. Then, in the text, replace each word with its index in the dictionary. To distinguish such indices from ordinary characters, it is usual to prefix an index with a character which is certain not to be in the document. Decoding the document requires the dictionary, so the dictionary is added to the front of the document, with its extent delimited by specific markers.

6.21.4 Fixed Bit Length Packing

This technique applies to files whose characters use only a limited subset of all possible values. An example is a file of decimal values; each character can take only 10 values (with a few more needed perhaps for delimiters), thus 4 bits is sufficient to encode each character. Again, the map must be saved with the document.

6.21.5 Run Length Encoding (RLE)

This technique, which has many variants, is well-suited to documents with repetitive sequences of characters. It works by replacing a *run* (a sequence) of identical characters by a character indicating the number of repeats, followed by the character itself. Thus the sequence

```
AAAABBBBBBCDDD...
```

can be replaced by the following sequence:

```
4A5B1C3D......
```

A global use of this technique—that is, preceding *every* character by an occurrence count) can lead to a file size explosion (since the file may contain areas of no repetition). Thus, the technique is generally applied only to long-enough sequences, which means that the encoding must distinguish between character counts and characters. While several alternatives have been developed to do this, we will not describe them here.

6.21.6 Huffman Encoding

Huffman encoding is based on the frequency of occurrence of characters in a file; more frequently used characters are encoded with a smaller number of bits than less-frequently-used characters.

In general (that is, not specifically related to Huffman) there are two classes of encodings:

- *Static*, in which the relationship between a character (or a character sequence) and its encoding is fixed for the whole of the file and is known before the file is transmitted

- *Dynamic*, in which the encodings can vary within a single document

6.21.7 Static Huffman Encoding

The Huffman algorithm builds a complete binary tree of non-negative values, each of which represents the frequency of occurrence of a character in the file to be compressed, and are sorted in decreasing order. Two methods can be used to build this tree for a specific file:

- *Two passes*: the compression algorithm performs two passes over the file, counting occurrences in the first pass, and then in the second pass, with the tree built, encoding the text. The encoding specification must be added to the file to allow decompression.

- *Use of a preset tree* selected on a per-file-type basis. To do this, one examines many files of each file type of interest, and constructs a tree for each file type that works well across the files examined. The compressed file then must contain an indication of which tree was used for encoding. This method requires just one pass over a file.

6.21.8 Adaptive Huffman Encoding

The general principle behind adaptive Huffman encoding is to dynamically vary the encoding as a function of the symbols encountered during compression, while still maintaining optimal compression. Two techniques are well-known, each named after its inventors: FGK (after Faller and Gallagher, with improvements by Knuth) and V (Vitter).

A key property of these methods is that they require just a single pass through the file. The compressor and decompressor have each to build and keep updated a coding tree during their operation.

6.21.9 LZ77 Encoding

This encoding was created by Lempel and Ziv in 1977. It is based on a sliding window and a read-ahead buffer. It is in very wide use, being the basis of the zip, gzip and pkzip compression formats, among others.

The basic principle is to identify, in the portion of the file already processed, sequences of characters that occur in the portion currently being processed. The sliding window contains the slice of the already-processed text under consideration, and the look-ahead buffer contains the text being processed. A typical size for the sliding window is 4,000 characters.

To illustrate the operation of the algorithm, consider the example drawn from [JAY], which uses a window of 10 characters and a look-ahead buffer of size 5.

Assume that we are observing the algorithm in its steady-state phase just before the end of file is reached- a fair amount of the file has already been processed and the sliding window is full, containing the ten most-recently read characters from the file, with the preceding characters already having been processed and output. We will represent this encoded output as *{encoded earlier portion}*

The situation, then, for the input file is as follows

```
AAAAAAAAAA      BABAAAAA
==========      =====
Sliding Window  Read-ahead buffer
```

Now we look in the window for a character sequence of at least length 2 which appears in the buffer starting at the leftmost position in the buffer. However, there is no such sequence and so we simply write B into the output buffer and advance the sliding window by one character, losing the leftmost A and moving the B into the rightmost position.

Our output buffer now contains:

*{encoded earlier portion}*B

And the input looks like this:

```
AAAAAAAAAB      ABAAAAA
==========      =====
Sliding Window  Read-ahead buffer
```

Again, we look for a sequence of characters in the window that matches a sequence in the look-ahead buffer, and we see that the sequence AB is the longest such sequence. In the window, the sequence has length 2 and starts

Data Compression

2 characters from the end of the window, and we therefore write this as
<2,2> (meaning length 2, distance 2) into the output buffer. We then
advance the sliding window and the read-ahead buffer by the length of the
sequence, 2, giving us:

Output buffer:

```
{encoded earlier portion}B<2,2 >
```

Input:

```
AAAAAAABAB          AAAAA

==========          =====

Sliding Window      read-ahead buffer
```

We now see that the read-ahead's AAAAA sequence already exists in the
sliding window; it starts 8 characters from the end of the window and has
length 5, so again we update the output appropriately with <5,8>. Since we
have read all the input, we're done.

Output buffer:

```
{encoded earlier portion}B<2, 2><5, 8 >
```

Decoding is simple. One reads the compressed file character by character, simply copying to the destination file until one encounters a <length,
distance> pair. When that occurs, one simply copies the appropriate characters from the text already read in the file being decompressed into the destination file.

For our example, it will work as follows. We have already decoded
{encoded earlier portion} into the destination file and are now looking at the
B in the compressed text:

```
{encoded earlier portion}B<2, 2><5, 8 >
```

While we will have as decompressed text the sequence:

```
AAAAAAAA
```

We copy B to the destination, which becomes

AAAAAAAAAB

and encounter <2,2> in the compressed file.

Looking back two places in the decompressed file, and copying two characters, we see AB, giving us

AAAAAAAAABAB

We now encounter <5,8>, which tells us to look back 8 characters and copy a sequence of length 5, giving the decompressed file the correct contents:

AAAAAAAAABABAAAAA

As with other schemes, the encoding of the compressed file must allow us to distinguish characters from <length, distance> pairs.

In this description we have simply described the basics; real-world implementations improve upon this is a number of ways, for example by employing Huffman encoding.

6.21.10   Lempel-Ziv-Welch Encoding (LZW)

This encoding was developed by Lempel, Ziv and Welch. It works well with repeated data.

It makes use of a dictionary containing strings. At initialization, the dictionary is set up with the first n entries containing the characters that can be encountered in the text. The encoding works as follows[13]: it maintains a pair of input variables, a string, and a character. Initially, the string is empty. Then the input file is read character by character. As each character is read, we look up the string formed by concatenating string and character; if the resulting string is present, we concatenate character to string, otherwise we output the dictionary index for string, concatenate string and character, and allocate a new dictionary entry for this new string.

This description assumes a dictionary of unbounded size; in practice, the dictionary is of fixed size and so one can annotate dictionary entries with frequency usage, and cast out least popular entries when capacity is reached.

6.21.11   Arithmetic Coding

A new technique, arithmetic coding, has emerged and can give better results than Huffman. The encoding, which is covered by patents held by AT&T, IBM, and Mitsubishi, requires a license for commercial use.

6.21.12   Closing Comments

The techniques discussed can be combined. For example, an RLE encoding can employ Huffman encoding to further compress the <length, symbol> information. The implementation of the various zip tools supplement the Lempel-Ziv basics with Huffman encoding, resulting in fixed-length encodings. Naturally, these techniques work best when the text to be compressed contains long sequences.

6.21.13   Considerations in Implementing Compression

Compression algorithms can be implemented by software running on traditional processors or by specialized hardware. As usual, these options have the following considerations:

- Performance is higher with the specialized processor, there are costs involved in the development of the compression cards to which must be added the development costs of the processors themselves

- Doing compression on a host or subsystem processor in software will have a performance impact on that processor's ability to do its other work; to recover, it may be necessary to increase the number of processors. Development cost is unaffected, unless the compression software needs to make use of an SMP platform rather than being a simple uniprocessor implementation. Using standard microprocessors to implement this task means that overall performance improves as the processors improve.

An example of the use of specialized processors is provided by the cryptographic processors of the IBM z900.

From an architectural point of view, we can distinguish two classes as regards implementing compression:

- within host systems

- within storage subsystems

Table 6.7, derived from [BMC01], compares the advantages and disadvantages of these two options.

Table 6.7   *Comparison of host-based compression and storage subsystem-based compression (derived from [BMC 01]).*

	Host-based Compression	**Storage Subsystem-based Compression**
Advantages	■ selective compression (e.g., one does not compress system data, file catalog etc.) ■ ability to choose the compression technique to fit the characteristics of the data ■ reduction in I/O traffic between host and disk subsystem ■ does not require any special capabilities in the storage subsystem	■ best use of the storage capacity provided by the storage elements ■ improvement in host system performance (due to off-loading the compression task)
Disadvantages	■ performance impact, unless either specialized coprocessors are used or the number of processors is increased, either of which increases host system cost	■ inability to be selective in what gets compressed and how it is compressed ■ no reduction in host-subsystem I/O traffic ■ disk occupation not known until data is compressed by the subsystem

Some elements of he comparison merit further comment.

- The system knows the purpose and nature of some of the data it is handling, and it can therefore know what data should not be compressed (e.g., system data) and also what compression techniques should work best (e.g., using lossy compression with audio-visual data).

- Doing compression in the host will reduce I/O traffic on the connection between host and the storage subsystems; this might make it possible to use lower-cost storage (reduced requirements for data handling and memory size, since it does not have to implement compression).

- Implementing compression in the storage subsystem allows optimal use of the capacity provided by the storage elements.

Choosing a compression solution will require experiments with representative data; this will allow the benefits in terms of storage capacity to be estimated. Only with this information can an ROI analysis be done between architectural options.

The general selection criteria (discussed in Chapter 11) apply as well.

6.22 Commercial Storage Subsystems

As we have noted previously, because storage subsystems are embedded systems whose internal details are hidden through the use of standard interfaces, they are a hotbed of innovation. In this section, we describe a number of recent systems.

6.22.1 Auspex Series 3000

Figure 6.31 shows a simplified view of the Auspex Series 3000; these are NAS servers, supporting both CIFS and NFS.

Figure 6.31
Auspex Series 3000 hardware architecture (source: Auspex).

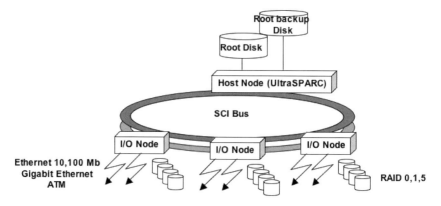

The architecture is organized around a double SCI (*Scalable Coherent Interface*) ring with a 400 MB/sec bandwidth. An UltraSPARC IIi at 300 MHz, along with 576 MB of memory, controls the system. The system supports various Ethernet bandwidths and ATM as client connections. The architecture of an I/O node is shown in Figure 6.32.

Figure 6.32
Architecture of Auspex Series 3000 I/O node (source: Auspex).

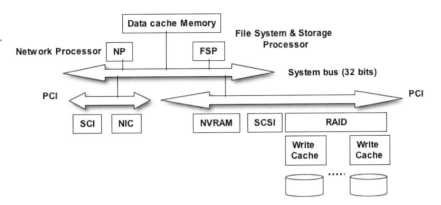

The I/O node provides both network and storage functionality, and uses two processors and shared memory to do so. The network processor and the file and storage processor are both Intel Pentium IIIs running at 833 MHz with 3 GB of shared memory (more can be supported).

RAID 0, 1, and 5 are implemented in hardware; RAID 0 and 1 can also be implemented in software.

A journalized file system (FastFLO) ensures quick reboots (avoiding the need to run *fsck*).

Writes are accelerated by a non-volatile write cache of 384 MB.

The system supports data replication between systems, along with data snapshots (discussed later in the section on backup and restore).

6.22.2 BlueArc

BlueArc has developed a rather original NAS data server, implementing in hardware the layers normally provided in software through the use of FPGAs (*Field Programmable Gate Arrays*). The architecture of the BlueArc SiliconServer Si7500 is illustrated in Figure 6.33.

The goal of the system designers was to remove the bottlenecks encountered with a traditional server, including

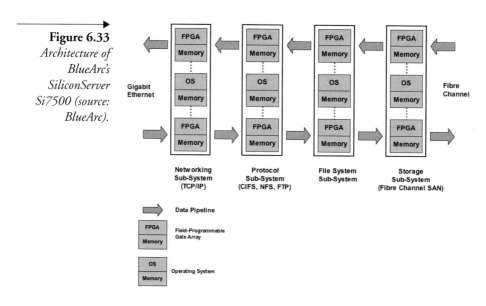

Figure 6.33
*Architecture of
BlueArc's
SiliconServer
Si7500 (source:
BlueArc).*

- Processor-memory interface
- I/O-memory interface
- I/O bus (such as PCI)

The system organizes its functionality as a pipeline of components, each component with its own copy of the operating system and its own memory; data is moved between the components by hardware.

Each subsystem uses FPGAs to operate on and move data, a solution that offers higher performance than a traditional solution using software layers.

Traditionally, solutions of this nature encounter two sorts of problem: the circuit density of FPGAs is lower than for mainstream microprocessors (and thus limits the complexity of functionality that can be implemented), and the fact that what would be a simple software change in a traditional implementation now becomes a hardware change. However, although densities are lower than in microprocessors, they are growing at the same rate, and rather complex implementations are feasible. Updating the hardware, given the dynamically-reprogrammable nature of the technology, may not be a significant issue—one can imagine remote hardware updates, for example, which involve no software whatsoever.

The protocol subsystem supports NFS, CIFS, and ftp, and uses a file system proprietary to BlueArc. The file system is a journaling file system;

for performance reasons, metadata is held in memory, but any actions causing updates to the metadata are treated as transactions and journaled. As we explained in Chapter 3, a journaling file system reduces restart time after an failure. Walking through the journal after restart allows actions which were in the course of being executed at the time of the incident to be cancelled or replayed.

The storage subsystems support Fibre Channel interfaces and also tape libraries. They support LAN-free backup and restore using NDMP.

According to BlueArc, the server is capable of providing a total bandwidth of 2 GB/sec.

6.22.3   EMC Symmetrix/Celerra

EMC has introduced Celerra, a CIFS/NFS file server, complementing its Symmetrix RAID family. Figure 6.34 shows Celerra in the context of a previous generation of Symmetrix systems; the new generation is covered in the next section.

Figure 6.34
EMC Symmetrix/
Celerra
architecture
(source: EMC).

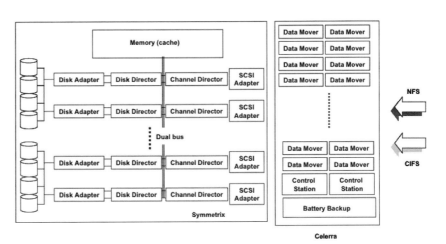

The Symmetrix disk subsystem is organized around a double bus and a cache memory. Although it is not clear in the diagram, the architecture is redundant. The configuration comprises a number of disk directors and channel directors, arranged in pairs so that if one fails, the other can take over.

The very large cache memory—several gigabytes—is replicated and backed up, allowing high speed write operations; that is, the host is told of the completion of a write operation to disk as soon as two copies of the data have been written to the cache. The cache is battery-backed to ensure correct operation in the event of power failure. The cache management algorithms have been the subject of particular care.

In the Celerra, the Data Movers are autonomous file servers (CIFS or NFS). The Control Stations run under a UNIX OS, and do system management: updates, configurations, and control of the Data Movers operation (but they do not intervene in the Data Movers' normal operations).

The Celerra file system journals the metadata, allowing quicker restart after a failure.

The Celerra architecture integrates redundancy. A Data Mover may be specified to replace one or more damaged Data Movers (an *N*+1 approach). The Control Station is replicated.

6.22.4   EMC Symmetrix DMX Series

EMC, known for its Symmetrix and Clariion storage subsystems, introduced a new generation of the Symmetrix family at the beginning of 2003. The new Symmetrix DMX (*Direct Matrix Architecture*) Series differs from the previous generation through the use of a direct-connection matrix between its component subsystems, rather a pair of buses.

Figure 6.35 illustrates the architecture of the DMX family.

Figure 6.35
Symmetrix DMX
architecture
(source: EMC)

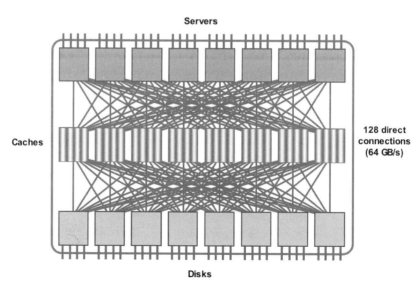

Just as in the earlier generations, the DMX makes widespread use of caching. It uses a matrix interconnect to reduce contention for data traffic between the various elements (cache and the *Channel Directors*—controllers allowing connections to host systems or disks); there are 128 independent paths between cache and the Channel Directors.

The maximum size for the cache is 128 GB; it can be organized as a number of independent caches (up to 32). The Cache Director provides 32 independent access ports, each with a bandwidth of 500 MB/sec (for a total bandwidth of 16 GB/s). The cache makes it possible for the Symmetrix DMX to implement fast writes—as soon as two copies of data to be written to disk have been stored to the cache, the write may be considered complete. The cache is battery-backed. The cache management algorithms have been the subject of much attention.

The host connections can be either ESCON (for IBM systems) or Fibre Channel; the connections to the disks are Fibre Channel. Although the diagram does not show it, the architecture is redundant to improve availability.

6.22.5 IBM ESS

The IBM ESS (*Enterprise Storage Server*) is a data storage subsystem supporting both IBM proprietary environments (zSeries S/390 and AS/400) and standard systems (UNIX, Windows). Figure 6.36 shows its architecture.

The ESS is composed of two processing subsystems (*Cluster Processor Complex*) which operate independently. Each is a 4-way SMP built from 64 bit RISC processors, 16 GB of cache, and one non-volatile memory (NVS)

Figure 6.36
IBM Enterprise Storage Server (ESS) architecture (source: IBM).

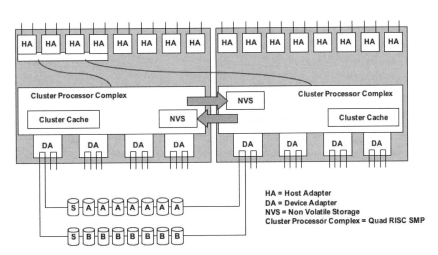

and supports four peripheral controllers (*DA*). The cache is managed by specialized algorithms. On a write, data is stored in the cache (*Cluster Cache*) of one cluster processor complex, as well as in the non-volatile memory of the other Complex. The NVS is battery-backed, with the batteries having a 7-day backup capability. In the event of one Complex failing, data is available in the other, ensuring continuity of operation.

Peripheral connections are organized as shown in the figure, allowing access by controllers in different complexes. The peripheral connection is SSA (Serial Storage Architecture) at 160 MB/sec. Each controller has 4 SSA interfaces. Disks can either be treated as a JBOD, or organized as a RAID 5.

The host-connection controllers (HA) are SCSI, ESCON, or Fiber Channel. For availability, these controllers are each connected to both complexes.

The ESS offers standard systems a number of services, including:

- Sharing data between DBMSs running on different host systems (any needed synchronization must be done by the DBMSs)

- Data copying between remote sites (~60 miles) and called PPRC (*Peer to Peer Remote Copy*) and is used for disaster recovery

- FlashCopy, a data snapshot

FlashCopy was once available only for IBM systems; now it is available for standard systems.

6.23   **Data Backup and Restore**

Because data is so important for the running of a company, proper backup is a necessity. Backing up data allows a company to be protected from the consequences of incidents such as:

- System failures

- Data destruction, for example by a fire

- Incorrect software operation (OS, DBMS, or application)

- Human error

In this chapter we have seen that RAID allows a system to be protected from disk failures.

NAS, SAN, and iSCSI (and indeed cluster architectures) allow other systems to access data belonging to a failed system

In the case of a disaster, such as fire, recovery depends on having a copy of the data at a remote site unaffected by the disaster. This copy could have been created by a remote data replication function, such as a remote mirror.

These various techniques are all in widespread use, but do not protect against software malfunction or human error. This is because data can be corrupted by the malfunction of an application, or of one stage in a multi-stage operation, and data replication, whether local or remote, will simply store the incorrect data.

To protect against these sorts of problems, one must have data copies made at extremely well specified moments in time—for example, immediately before starting an application or the next step in a multi-stage operation. This allows one, after correcting the problems, to re-run (correct) processing on a correct copy of the data.

In the same way, to protect against human error, one needs data copies made at well-specified moments such that, after restoring the data, the operation can be re-run correctly.

Note: Backup and Restore operations are just a part of a more general problem, which is the Business Continuity Plan (see Chapter 10 in the Disaster Recovery section). There are two important objectives which have a strong influence on the choice of a backup solution, namely:

- Recovery Point Objective (RPO) the point at which the system state must be restored

- Recovery Time Objective (RTO) the time allowed for restoring system operation (full or degraded service since all the applications are not critical from business continuity point of view)

As we shall see, such backup and restore operations are complementary to techniques providing data redundancy (such as RAID and remote copying).

We shall also see that backup and restore offer fundamental problems. A backup requires, obviously, an amount of time proportional to the amount of data to be backed up; given the continual growth in data size and the need for 24 × 24 and 7 × 7 system availability, it is necessary to minimize the impact of backup operations. We are thus driven to techniques that reduce the amount of data to be backed up and that allow the backup operation to proceed in parallel with normal operations.

A backup solution is composed of a number of elements:

- The choice of backup technology (support type, robot type)
- The choice of backup policy

We gave a description of the hardware technologies available for backup (cartridges and robots) in Chapter 2. Here, we will concentrate on how the technologies can be used to provide backup and restore.

There is also a serious issue in managing backup of data local to the workstations. Approaches relying on actions by the users quickly show their limitations, and so there has been a search to automate workstation backup. Products such as Legato and Ontrack have been developed for this purpose.

6.23.1   Incremental Backup

Incremental backup is illustrated in Figure 6.37.

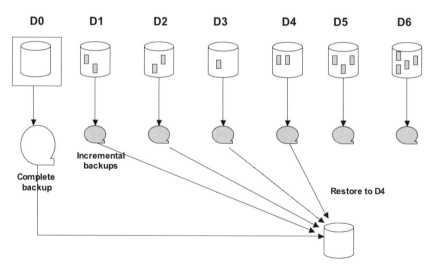

Figure 6.37
Incremental backup

The diagram makes an assumption that the backup policy in force is a complete backup of all files considered necessary once a week, along with a daily backup of updated data. Thus, on Day D0 (for example, Sunday) a complete backup is done of all necessary files. And then at the end of each day, files that have been modified since the previous backup are themselves backed up.

Restoring data to the state it had at the end of a specific day, in the example, D4) involves

- Restoring data from the most recent complete backup
- Successively restoring data from each incremental backup, up to the desired day

While the amount of data transferred during an incremental backup can be rather small, a restore involves many more data transfers, since it requires a complete restore and multiple incremental restores.

6.23.2 Differential backup

Differential backup is illustrated in Figure 6.38.

In the figure, we again suppose weekly complete backups with daily differential backups. Differential backup differs from incremental backup in

Figure 6.38
Differential backup

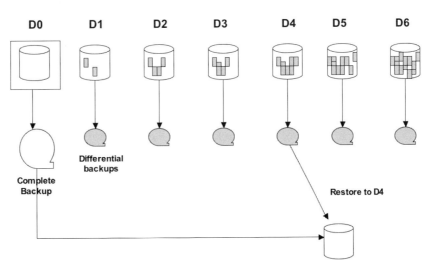

that each daily backup (in the example) is a backup of all changes since the last *complete* backup. Each differential backup therefore tends to be of larger volume than the previous one.

Restoring is quicker than for incremental backup, requiring just two restores:

- Restoration of the last complete backup
- Restoration of the appropriate differential backup

6.23.3 Incremental and Differential Backup

A mix of incremental and differential backup provides advantages over either. The mixture is illustrated in Figure 6.39.

Figure 6.39
Incremental and differential backup.

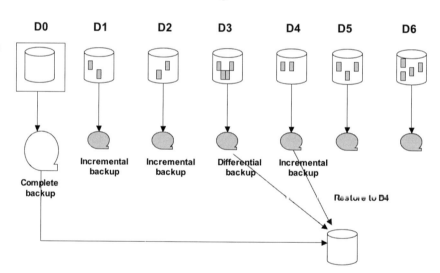

Again, the illustration assumes weekly complete backups and daily partial backups.

The basis of an incremental and differential backup policy is to regularly do incremental backups, interspersed with occasional differential backups. The differential backup is, again, a backup of changes since the last complete backup.

Restoring consists of restoring the most recent complete backup, the most recent differential backup, and then, successively, the appropriate differential backups.

6.23.4 **Progressive backup**

Progressive backup is based on ordinary incremental backup, but differs in restore when only the relevant incremental backups are used in the restore. Figure 6.40 illustrates the backup operation of a progressive backup.

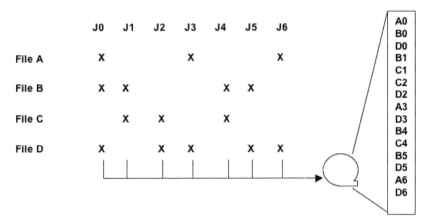

Figure 6.40
Progressive backup:
backup operation.

Progressive backup differs from incremental in that each successive copy of a file is indexed by its backup time; a database keeps track of the file versions. Figure 6.41 shows the restore operation.

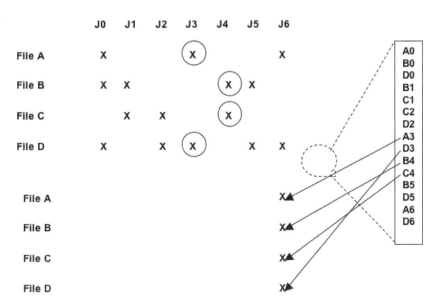

Figure 6.41
Progressive Backup:
restore operation.

In the restore operation, the database is consulted to identify exactly those backups needed to restore to the specified point, thus (in general) reducing the amount of data transferred and thus the time necessary.

The techniques described here apply to files; if the system is able to track modified disk blocks, backup/restore could be done at the block level reducing the amount of data being moved and thereby speeding up both backup and restore.

6.23.5 Fast Complete Backup

Creating a complete backup is an expensive operation that can perturb normal system operation, for example by reducing performance. To alleviate this nuisance, it is possible to implement a complete backup by starting a backup whose destination is not the "active" disk space, as in a normal restore, but a new archive. This approach can be used for different types of backup; we examine some of them now.

6.23.6 Complete backup in a RAID 1 environment

In a RAID 1 (disk mirroring) environment, a complete backup can be done with minimal disturbance to normal operation. Figure 6.42 illustrates this operation.

To ensure that there is no data loss in the event of a failure during backup, the disk mirror should be configured with three copies. To make a complete backup, one "detaches" one copy, so that it no longer receives updates; the detachment must be done at a carefully-chosen time (when no

Figure 6.42
*Complete backup
in a RAID 1
environment.*

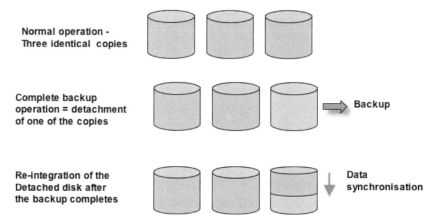

Normal operation -
Three identical copies

Complete backup
operation = detachment
of one of the copies   Backup

Re-integration of the
Detached disk after
the backup completes   Data
                                                              synchronisation

updates are in progress—perhaps immediately before launching an application, or between processing steps).

The detached image may then be backed up normally to magnetic tape or cartridge without perturbing the system (unless resources are shared between normal operation and backup). At the end of the backup operation, the detached disk is reintegrated into the disk system and synchronizes its contents with the "live" copies on the other disks. This operation is standard in a RAID system, being the operation done when a failed disk is replaced by a new one.

The drawback of this approach is the extra cost—a mirroring system of this nature requires 3 times the number of disks rather than 2 times for normal mirroring.

6.23.7 Data Snapshot

We have already looked at log-structured file systems, which are journal-based. As we have noted earlier, this sort of file system lends itself perfectly to the implementation of data snapshots (although one can also implement such an approach on a traditional file system).

Figure 6.43 re-presents the figure we used earlier (Figure 6.9) to illustrate the process.

Figure 6.43
Snapshot mechanism.

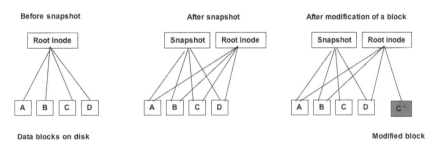

Snapshotting the data involves simply making a copy of the current inodes of the file, which completely captures the state of the file at that moment.

To make a complete backup of a file, then, one simply snapshots it at an appropriate moment, and then walks the captured inodes to determine which blocks are to be copied to tape. The snapshot operation itself is very fast, although clearly there will be some contention between application and backup in accessing the unmodified blocks.

The snapshot technique imposes only a moderate extra cost in disk space, since the space needed for backup is limited to just those blocks which have been modified (as opposed to a complete duplication of the file).

6.23.8   **Backup and Restore in a DBMS Context**

The techniques we have discussed backup and restore files; to use them on a database would require that the database be closed before backup. To avoid the resulting system unavailability, it is possible to use an "open database" backup technique, which is illustrated in Figure 6.44.

Figure 6.44
"Open Database"
backup with
Oracle.

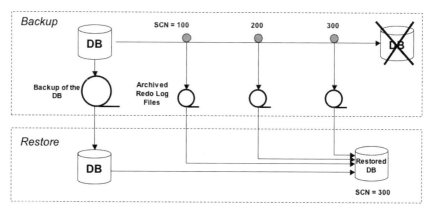

SCN = System Change Number

The principle is based upon periodic complete copies being made of the database and the periodic memorization of updates caused by transactions.

Starting from a complete copy[14] of the database, the DBMS periodically backs up the changes made by transactions. These changes are stored in the transaction journal; this journal contains *after images* (images of the items (tuples) after update). This journal is called the "*redo log*." Each transaction is identified by a unique number—its SCN (for *System Change Number*).

To rebuild the database following a loss due to a system incident, application malfunction, or human error, one chooses the SCN from which the rebuild should be done. The process then applies the journaled transactions successively to the last complete copy of the database, in a manner analogous to incremental file backup/restore.

6.23.9 **Real-time Data Copy**

Properly speaking, this is not a backup/restore technique, but rather one that allows recovery after a disaster. The approach is that of maintaining a remote copy of data; the copies are synchronous and operate at the volume level (that is, this is a RAID-like approach). The inter-site connection is typically a high-bandwidth fiber link.

The approach has been implemented in a number of proprietary systems, such as

- IBM's PPRC (Peer-to-Peer Remote Copy) and XRC
- Hitachi's Remote Copy—HRC and HXRC
- EMC's SRDF—Symmetrix Remote Data Facility

We will illustrate the different functional modes of these techniques. Figure 6.45 shows the synchronous remote copy operation.

Figure 6.45
PPRC/HRC/SRDF Synchronous Copy.

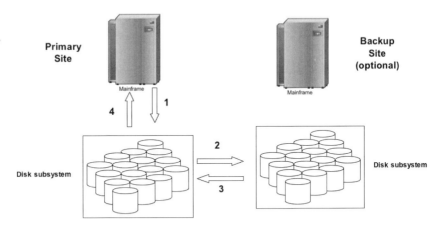

The numbered arrows depict the logical progression of the remote copy operation. The performance impact should be obvious; the host system sees the completion of a write only at action 4. Performance can be improved by the use of the differential update technique illustrated in Figure 6.46.

In this approach, each data update on the primary system incorporates a timestamp. As far as the primary system is concerned, a write is completed as soon as it is written into local stable memory (normally the battery-backed-up cache in the disk system). The data, with their timestamps, are

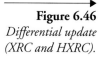

Figure 6.46
*Differential update
(XRC and HXRC).*

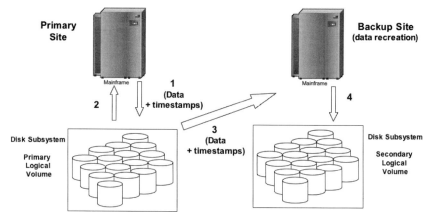

then forwarded to the backup site in whatever order; at the backup system, they are sorted into timestamp order and applied there.

This substantially improves primary system performance, since there is no need to wait for a round trip to the distant site before declaring a write complete.

A further variant is to implement the data copying within the disk subsystem, which avoids the need for a similar computer system at the remote site. This is illustrated in Figure 6.47.

Figure 6.47
*Differential update
within the HARC
disk subsystem.*

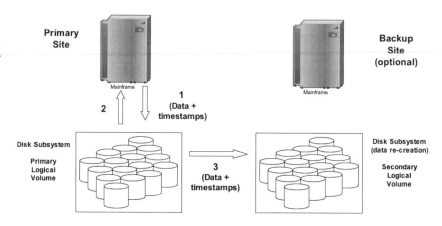

While this approach removes the need for a remote computer system, it does require that local and remote storage susbystems be completely compatible, which means in practice that they come from the same vendor.

6.24 Resource Optimization in Backup and Restore

As was made clear in the introduction to this chapter, when we discuss storage problems, backup and restore operations are potential consumers of processing resources (using servers for the control of the operations and especially for data movement) and communications resources (use of the local network for data movement between disks and tapes).

The SAN (*Storage Area Network*) concept offers the possibility of avoiding these constraints with the notions of Server-Free Backup and Lan-Free Backup (and, despite terminology, doing so for both backup and restore). This is illustrated in Figure 6.48, which shows both a classic environment with DAS storage and a SAN-based one.

Figure 6.48
Server-free and lan-free backup/ restore.

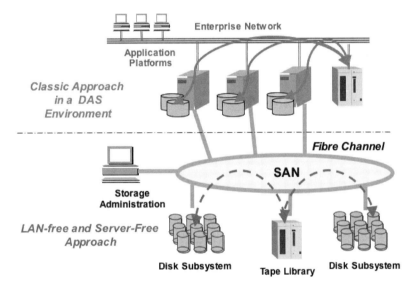

In the "Classic" approach, backup and restore necessarily involves the servers in data access to storage and in network accesses for data movement.

With a SAN environment, one can choose to not disturb the classic setup but to use the SAN to off-load servers and network. In this approach, shown at the bottom of the figure, backup and restore operations are managed by a storage administration system (for simplicity, shown attached to the SAN; in practice, this may be no more than an Ethernet-connected PC).

Backup and restore requires coordination between servers and tape libraries, To make this more straightforward, a standard called NDMP

(*Networked Data Management Protocol*) has been created. The NDMP architecture assumes a server (not necessarily dedicated) and NDMP agents distributed among the various platforms. The operation of NDMP is shown in Figure 6.49.

Figure 6.49
NDMP operation.

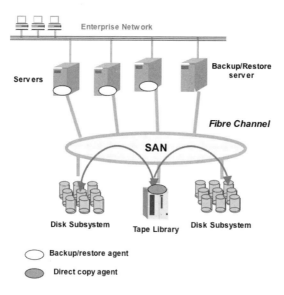

A backup/restore agent plays its part in the NDMP protocol by creating (for backup operations) a coherent state for the data to be backed up (a snapshot). It preserves this snapshot despite the updates that servers can effect upon its data, and constructs and then implements the necessary direct copy commands.

A direct copy agent is implemented within the tape library robot (or within a SAN-connected server) and provides data transfers across the SAN between disks and the robot. This agent, which is in effect the backup server, makes use of SCSI's *Extended Copy* command.

The backup/restore server controls the backup operations and has a picture of the global state of those operations, with the various agents advising it of peripheral status, and status of their current operations.

Data Life Cycle

The data life cycle used to be based upon frequency of access. After a certain period of time, frequency of access to data decreased, and data was a candidate for migration towards lower cost media, or even deletion. There are now other factors to consider, such that government regulations for retention of data or the value of data.

Classical life cycle was composed of three stages:

- Online: retrieval time in ms, life time about 7 days, typically kept on disks
- Nearline: retrieval time in seconds, life time of about 60 days, typically kept on low-cost disks such as MAID or tape library
- Archival and/or deletion (CDs, etc.)

As retrieval activity decrease, the volume of stored data increase.

6.25 Technologies Supporting Backed-up Data

Traditionally, magnetic tape was used to hold backup data, but the increase in data volume made the manual handling of the tapes slow, tiresome, and error-prone. Magnetic tape has now, for the most part, been superseded by the use of robots and magnetic cartridges.

There are two major backup media technologies:

- Magnetic media, used to hold backup data for reasonably short periods—perhaps a few days to a few weeks
- Optical or magneto-optical media, used to hold backup data for extended periods—a few years.

Magnetic media have limitations in the amount of time they can reliably hold data, but are simple to re-use. Typically, therefore, they are used for regular backup operations in which use the backup data will be kept for short periods from a few days to a few weeks. Further, the cartridges are well suited to shipping data to other sites—for example, sending a copy of daily backups (incremental or differential), and a copy of a complete backup to a remote site.

Several technologies are competing for the cartridges and their associated readers; their properties, deployed in a robot, are summarized in Table 6.8.

Table 6.8 *Comparison of various magnetic cartridge technologies (Source [QUA03]).*

	SAIT-1	SDLT320	Ultrium LTO (Generation 2)
Capacity (native)	500 GB	160 GB	200 GB
Capacity (compressed)	1.3 TB	320 GB	400 GB
Transfer Rate (native)	30 MB/s	16 MB/s	30-35 MB/s
Transfer Rate (compressed)	72 MB/s	32 MB/s	60-70 MB/s
MTBF at 100% duty cycle	>300,000 hours	250,000 hours	250,000 hours
Media Formulation	AME	MP	MP
Media Form Factor	Single reel, half-inch cartridge	Single reel, half-inch cartridge	Single reel, half-inch cartridge
Media Length	600 m	600 m	600 m
File Access Time	70 s	70 s	52 s
Media Load Time	23 s	40 s	15 s
Memory in Cassette	Yes	No	Yes
WORM Capable	Yes	No	No
Published Roadmap # of Generations	4	4	4
Roadmap Maximum Capacity (Native)	10 TB	1.2 TB	1.6 TB
Roadmap Maximum Performance (Native)	240 MB/s	100 MB/s	160 MB/s
Multiple Manufacturing Sources for Drives and Media	Yes	No	No

In addition to these parameters, it is helpful to consider positioning in terms of price and performance. Such a comparison should cover:

- Cost per GB of storage ($/GB)
- Cost per unit of bandwidth ($/MB/s)

The cost per GB must include the cost of the robot, the read/write units, and a number of cartridges sufficient to minimally stock the robot (or, better, more, so that some cartridges may be stored elsewhere for disaster recovery). The number of read/write units to be considered will be a function of the amount of data to be backed up and the usage of the backup unit—whether a shared or a dedicated robot, frequency of backup and restore, and so on.

It should be clear, then, that the choice of a backup solution can only properly be made in the context of specific needs. Different vendors' offerings should be compared on a TCO basis. Among the elements that should be considered are:

- Amortizing the acquisition price of the hardware (robots and any computer system(s) necessary for running the robot)
- Hardware maintenance costs
- Cartridge price and cartridge replacement costs (taking into account their likely/average lifespans)
- The cost of backup management software for the servers, along with the price of any agents needing to be installed on various client systems
- Software maintenance cost
- The cost of personnel necessary to implement the solution
- The cost of keeping the system operational
- The cost of using the system—for example, the cost of repetitive verification tasks, such as checking that the overnight backup worked properly—and the cost of export/import of cartridges between the home site and a backup site, or a cartridge storage site.

Doing this evaluation will teach many lessons, probably resulting in questioning received wisdom on real cost allocation. However, the few studies that we carried out in this field did not cover a large enough range of usages for the results to be statistically significant, and thus do not deserve to be published.

6.25.1   **Tape RAID (RAIT)**

Noting the advantages of RAID organizations for disk, one can choose to do an equivalent thing with tape, thereby constructing RAIT systems (for *Redundant Array of Independent Tapes*).

In such a system, a number of tape units are grouped in such a manner as to appear as one unit. This organization (which we will not detail further here) provides the same advantages as for disk, offering higher transfer rates when data can be distributed across the multiple tape units, along with greater reliability against tape unit failure, thanks to redundancy.

6.25.2   **Tape Virtualization**

Just as tape can be RAIDed, it can be virtualized. In this section, we present a backup peripheral virtualization introduced by Neartek in 2002: the VSengine (*Virtual Storage Engine*), whose functionality we can summarize as follows:

- Independent of any particular backup peripheral
- Supports simultaneous, sharable backups for heterogeneous hosts
- Centralized management of resources and of their sharing
- Fast data backup and restore, thanks to a RAID cache
- The ability to provide multiple volumes on a single cartridge (Dynamic Volume Stacking)
- Automatic volume duplication
- Compatible with the most widely-used backup software, such as Netbackup, ArcserveIT, TSM, Networker, etc.

Peripheral independence is achieved through virtualization of storage resources (cartridges, robots). VSengine lets systems "see" the peripherals that suit them, and maps these virtual peripherals onto the available physical peripherals.

Different host systems (mainframes, iSeries, UNIX, Windows, and Netware) can share common backup resources safely.

VSengine manages the necessary support operations for backups—regeneration operations, copy operations, and so forth—in accordance with strategies set by the administrator.

Performance is improved over a pure tape-based system by using a RAID-organized set of disks as a cache: the backup operation proper transfers data to the RAID system, and once complete the data is copied to cartridges. The amount of time that data is kept on disk is parameterizable, so for backups intended to protect data at crucial processing steps, the time to regenerate the data after failure can be substantially reduced because the data is still disk-resident.

In some environments, cartridges are sparsely used, with a cartridge having a capacity of tens of GB being used to backup a disk volume of just a few gigabytes. Using the RAID cache as a staging storage unit, and with the help of proprietary software, VSengine allows several volumes to be stored on a single cartridge for backup and restore.

Given the RAID cache, it is simple and fast to create multiple copies of a backup (on the same or different units).

Table 6.50 illustrates the general architecture of VSengine.

Figure 6.50
VSengine
Architecture
(source: Neartek).

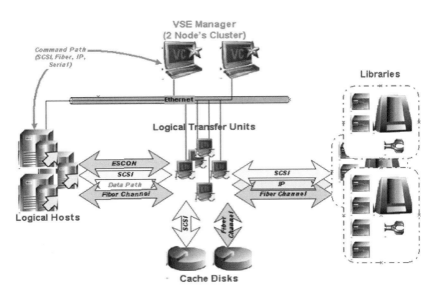

The architecture is based on two types of unit, the VSE Manager and the Logical Transfer Unit (LTU). Scalability is provided by the ability to use multiple LTUs. High availability is based on Microsoft cluster technology, using two VSE Managers in a cluster arrangement.

VSengine uses standard PC hardware running under Windows, along with standard RAID units.

6.26 Data Archiving

The lifespan of backed-up data is usually rather limited, since its purpose is to restore data after some upset, such a a major server failure, a fire, or the untimely deployment of a new software version. The timespan involved with such usages is generally limited to a few weeks, so backup lifetimes are usually a few weeks or perhaps a month or two.

There are however reasons to keep data longer than that, for reasons including government regulations (such as medical records, government records, etc.) or for strategic reasons (for example, to do data mining to improve the performance or functioning of a business). For such usages, one speaks of "archiving" rather than "backup," and in general somewhat different technologies are deployed than those we have discussed.

To set context, it may be helpful to provide some figures.

The Berkeley study "How Much Information," [LYM03], from which we provided some results in Chapter 2, suggests that 92% of new information is stored on magnetic media, primarily hard disks. Further, it is generally considered that most of the data stored is unchanging; EMC estimates that the market for archiving such data amounts to around $3 billion in 2003, and more than $10 billion in 2005.

The Enterprise Storage Group [ESG02] introduced the term *Reference Information* to designate such unchanging data; more exactly, they use the term to mean *"digital asset retained for active reference and value."* The following figures come from the same study.

Growth of Reference Information among new information:

- 37% in 2001
- 51% in 2004
- 54% in 2005

Average growth rate of the volume of information between 2001 and 2005:

- 61% for traditional data

- 92% for reference information

The same study shows that users' most important needs for stored data is the ability to access it straightforwardly, along with systems TCO.

The need to keep data for very long periods of time—perhaps for legal reasons—on the one hand, and the need to simply make use of reference data has given birth to two types of approach for archiving:

- The classical approach to archiving, prioritizing attaining a very long life above swift or simple access

- A commodity-based approach (i.e., PC-based) prioritizing simplicity of access over cost

We now examine these two approaches.

6.26.1 Traditional Archiving

In traditional archiving, one looks for very low-cost, very long-life technologies; while access to the data is important, it is prioritized below cost and lifespan. In general, this leads to the use of robots and specialized software. Because of the rather extended access times for this sort of storage, it is generally referred to as "near-line" storage (not quite on-line nor off-line). In implementing an archiving solution, technology (type of support, choice of archiving software) is not a key determinant, since the issues that will need resolving occur at the level of the functioning of the organization and the necessary changes to it.

Table 6.9 provides an overview of the major characteristics of several archive technologies.

There is a debate over lifespan. Tape vendors (Super DLT, LTO Ultrium) claim lifetimes of around 30 years, but data is lacking to confirm these claims. Any longevity claim must also take into account the operational practices as well as the hardware and software in use. As an example, a 100-year media lifetime would be meaningless if all machinery able to use it had disappeared within 20 years of its introduction. Over such long periods, the issue of who should have access to the information can become a dominating problem, since the media may outlast its users.

Table 6.9   *Summary of the characteristics of several archiving technologies.*

Technology	Capacity (GB)	Longevity (years)	Use
12" WORM	30	50 to 100	Very long-term archiving
5.25" Mag-neto-optic	9	30	Fast access to archived material
CD and DVD 120 mm	3	30	Low cost archiving
Tape	200+	10	High capacity, short lifespan

Thus, successful archiving is likely to include an element of re-engineering, with periodic migrations to new technology and careful attention to access rights.

6.26.2 Storage of Reference Information

A number of systems for Reference Information storage have been introduced; we concentrate here on EMC's Centera system, which is a *Content-Addressable Storage* system.

In Table 6.10, we give EMC's comparison of SAN, NAS and CAS solutions.

Table 6.10   *Comparison of the characteristics of SAN, NAS and CAS (source: EMC).*

	SAN	NAS	CAS
Typical application	OLTP Decision support	CAD/CAM Collaborative work	Management of contents
Nature of information	Modifiable		Fixed
Technological Difficulty	Performance	Modifiable file sharing	Scalability Longevity
Access method	By address		By contents
Type of data stored	Volume	File	Object with meta-data

We have already provided quite detailed descriptions of the SAN and NAS approaches and will not repeat them here. The typical usage for which CAS is targeted is access to reference information, and particularly access by content.

Reference information is produced and accumulated in a CAS; thus a CAS must be able to manage an ever-increasing amount of information and to preserve that information over very long periods of time, since changing the system would likely result in an unacceptable time to reconstitute the data on the new system. Access to the information is by content, not by address; an example would be looking up an individual using a digitized fingerprint. The system enables this by storing objects accompanied by metadata, which is in XML format.

The functional architecture of Centera is illustrated in Figure 6.51.

Centera stores objects as BLOBs (*Binary Large Objects*). Applications deliver data objects to the Centera API (*Application Programming Interface*); from object binary representation, Centera computes CA (*Content Address*), a 128 identifier. The BLOB is stored (along with a mirror copy). The CA and metadata about the object (such as file name, creation date, etc.) are stored in an XML file called CDF (*C-Clip Descriptor File*), which in turn has its content address calculated. The C-Clip is the union of the CDF and its content object. The C-Clip CA is returned to the application after two copies of it have been stored. Applications use C-Clip CA to access stored documents.

Figure 6.51
Overview of Centera functionality (source: EMC).

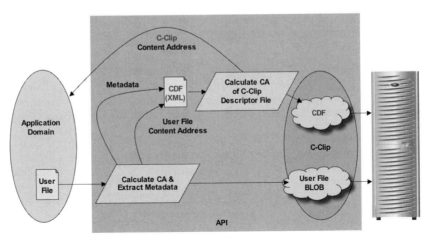

CDF = C-Clip Descriptor File

The CA is a unique identifier for the object; the system detects duplicate objects (since their identifiers match) and stores just one copy. The identifier also serves as a digital signature, making it possible to confirm that the object has not been modified. EMC had not, at the time of writing, published any information on how the unique identifiers are computed.

The system architecture of Centera can be described as a RAIN (*Redundant Array of Independent Nodes*), and to keep costs down it uses commodity PC technology. It is illustrated in Figure 6.52.

Figure 6.52
Centera Architecture (source: EMC).

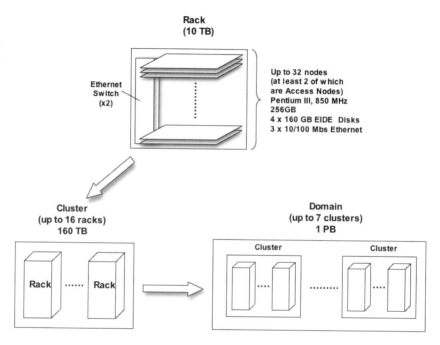

The basic component is a node based on an Intel microprocessor, Ethernet interfaces, and EIDE disks, showing an emphasis on cost rather than performance. A rack holds up to 32 such nodes, at least two of which are Access Nodes, managing interfaces with the outside world (that is, they handle host requests). The Access Node disks are managed as caches, and do not hold data permanently. RAID techniques are used to ensure storage persistence.

6.27 Endnotes

1.   Arranging that the needed disk accesses are spread over a large number of disks increases performance. However, in practically

all applications, it turns out that one cannot make use of all available storage space because performance constraints require that the number of disks deployed is far in excess of the needed storage capacity.

2. There is a risk that the success that server vendors have had in creating a culture of dependence amongst their customers may be repeated by the storage subsystem vendors. While this dependence may not be as blatant as its predecessor, it will be just as real. The existence of current an emerging standards such as Fibre Channel and Infiniband militate against the success of such a strategy.

3. This practice is an example of the Server Consolidation phenomenon, in which servers scattered all over a company are relocated into a single location. This reduces overhead costs (the amount of space needed is reduced, physical security is easier to provide, and environmental issues such as air conditioning and uninterruptible electrical supplies are simpler to address). Such concentration builds upon approaches based on a SAN.

4. Jim Gray [GRA03] reports that at Google in 2002, a staff of 25 people was administrating a 2 petabyte (215 bytes) database and 10,000 servers spread across several sites. This ratio is very application-dependent, other figures are given in the "Storage Facts Figures, Estimates and Rules of Thumb" table.

5. Multics [ORG72], developed towards the end of the 60s and the beginning of the 70s by MIT, on General Electric's GE 645 hardware. GE later became Honeywell, after the purchase of GE's computer business. The 645 was derived from a standard machine (the GE 600) and had an addressing system based on both segmentation and paging, with ring-based protection. Despite its technological advances and benefits, Multics never saw commercial success but was the inspiration for many system architects, with the result that several of its concepts can now be seen in many systems—UNIX being the obvious example.

6. This change came about because after a while, all disks were physically small and inexpensive, and the legacy physically large disks disappeared from the market.

7. We should note that a simple RAID organization, RAID 1, had been known and in widespread use under the name of Disk Mirroring before the popularization of RAID in general.

8. Compared with a disk system which does not use mirroring, a mirrored system suffers a minor performance degradation because, again, of the need to wait until writes to all mirrors have completed. Read performance can be improved because the data may be read from the disk and its mirror concurrently, and because a

choice of which disks to use for a given transfer may be made to minimize head movement.

9. When choosing a RAID vendor, it is impossible to exaggerate the importance of obtaining from the competing suppliers precise information on the capabilities of their product in this area. Your data's integrity relies on these capabilities. For example, in the absence of proper ACID support the RAID subsystem could detect an inconsistency between data and parity, and inappropriately "correct" the situation by incorrectly overwriting the data.

10. If redistributing the data across a number of disks is unnecessary, use of the simple mirror results in a doubling of the number of disks required for data storage. It is also possible to have more than 2 mirrors (the number M is used in the table to specify the number of mirrors).

11. High-order replication can be of interest for backup operations. For a system which must offer both very high availability and minimal disturbance during backups, one could imagine using an order 3 mirror. In such a usage, when a backup operation starts, one of the 3 images is "detached" (that is, updates to this image are no longer allowed), and the backup uses this image for source data, accessing it in parallel with the system's normal accesses to the other images. After backup has completed, the detached image is re-integrated into the RAID system, which involves updating it with the new modified data now on the other images. Image synchronization speed is generally a parameter for the re-integration operation.

12. Arranging the needed disk accesses by spreading over a large number of disks increases performance. However, in practically all applications, it turns out that one cannot make use of all available storage space, because performance constraints require that the number of disks deployed be far in excess of the needed storage capacity.

13. The server vendors' success in creating a culture of dependence among their customers risks being repeated by the storage subsystem vendors. While this dependence may not be as blatant as its predecessor, it will be just as real. The existence of current an emerging standards, such as Fibre Channel and Infiniband, militate against the success of such a strategy.

14. This practice is an example of the Server Consolidation phenomenon, in which servers scattered all over a company are relocated to a single location. This reduces overhead costs (the amount of space needed is reduced, physical security is easier to provide, and environmental issues such as air conditioning and uninterruptible electrical supplies are simpler to address). Such concentration builds upon approaches based on a SAN.

7

Systems Performance and Estimation Techniques

A system's performance can be expressed in two related dimensions:

- Response time
- Throughput

From the user's perspective, the response time is the time between issuing a request and the reception of the corresponding response. Many factors, from the network to the hardware components involved, affect response time.

Again, from the user's perspective, system throughput is the number of requests that the system usefully services per unit time.

The two dimensions are not independent: when request rate is increased, response time will also lengthen. This happens because the requests have to contend for the same system resources. This is illustrated in Figure 7.1.

The data for this graph was obtained by increasing the number of requests per second until the system saturated.

"The system illustrated here is just an example of a Web server on which the rate of incoming requests has been varied up to the saturation point. As we shall see in this chapter, every system has a bottleneck—the component whose throughput limits the systems capabilities. As can be seen from the curve, which is typical in shape, approaching the system saturation point quickly drives response time to unacceptable levels.

System users are very sensitive to response time, not only in its absolute value but also in its variability. Large variations in response time for similar requests are a source of deep annoyance for users. In a transactional system, the goal is to provide essentially uniform response times.

Figure 7.1
Response time as a function of throughput.

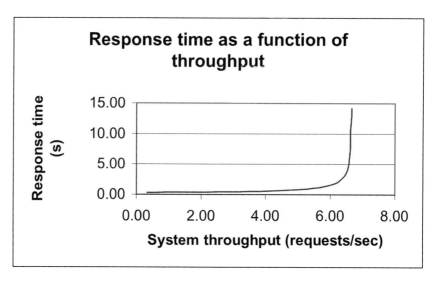

To ensure such uniformity, it is clear that the operating point of the system must be far away from saturation. This requires some planning of system resources and capabilities; we will examine some tools and an approach that enables us to estimate system performance, specially for a non-existent system.

Although response time and latency are simple to understand and measure, their values depend on a very large number of interacting systems parameters. It is not possible to estimate them by simply listing processor performance, memory throughput, or disk latency and so forth. Such numbers, though useful in describing the capabilities of each component of the system, are not sufficient to show how a particular application will perform when running on that system. Because customers need to compare systems, industry players (e.g., computer system manufacturers, providers of middleware and operating systems, transactional monitors, database managers, and Web servers) have jointly defined sets of benchmarks, each of which covers a particular class of application of interest. Each benchmark is intended to be usefully representative of its application area. Later, we will discuss to how well this works in practice, and the limits to the interpretations one should make from benchmark performance.

By benchmark, we mean a specification giving precise instructions of what measurements should be made and under what conditions. In addition to these testing specifications, the source for the program to be used in the measurements may also be provided.

Performance Figures

Although system performance is expressed in figures, we will not be providing any absolute performance figures for any systems, for the simple reason that any published figures rapidly become outdated. Rather, we will indicate Web sites where results are regularly published. We encourage those interested in systems performance to visit these sites.

It is useful to distinguish two major performance indicators: processor performance and system performance. Processor performance is a predictor of how well applicationsthat use only the processor(s) will perform, while system performance incorporates all major components of the system, including software: DBMS, operating system, I/O subsystems, and more.

We show the elements behind processor and system performance in Figure 7.2.

Figure 7.2
Characterizing performance at the levels of processor and system.

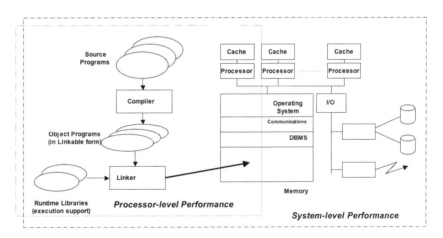

As shown in the figure, only a very small part of the system is involved in processor performance. Specifically, processor performance depends on:

- The compiler and the code optimizations of which it is capable (better compilers provide optimizations at both the structural level and at the machine level, in the latter case understanding the characteristics of the processor microarchitecture (e.g., pipeline details, degree of superscalarity, etc.)

- The quality of the runtime execution support libraries
- The processor itself
- The design of the memory hierarchy (caches and memory)

It should be noted that for some classes of benchmark—for example, the SPEC benchmarks aimed at processor performance—only the cache portion of the memory hierarchy is relevant, since essentially the whole of the benchmark(code and data) will fit in the cache hierarchy of a modern microprocessor. There is no multiprocessor aspect to these benchmarks, since they are targeted as just one processor; similarly, the operating system is also not a factor.

On the other hand, system-level performance depends on more or less every system component.[1] An example of a system-level benchmark is TPC. TPC exercises both software components—the operating system, the DBMS, and the communications subsystem (i.e., the TCP/IP protocol stack) as well as the processor and memory hierarchy. TPC also exercises the hardware components—the processor(s), multiprocessor behavior, the memory hierarchy, and the I/O subsystems.

In this chapter, we will look in greater detail first at processor-level performance, and then system-level performance. We will then look at a data-storage specific benchmark.

After we have finished looking at benchmarks,[2] we will look at performance aspects of a number of system architectures—SMP, clusters, and MPPs—for both OLTP.

Performance is often a neglected factor in the design of systems. We present a modeling-based methodology that allows system performance to be properly integrated into system design. And we offer an operational analysis approach that will, starting from simple-to-observe data, allow the prediction of system behavior and its limits.

We then present some empirical rules for the sizing of systems, and finish the chapter with a short discussion of capacity planning.

7.2   **Processor-level Performance**

Processor-level performance for a given processor-intensive application depends primarily on the processor itself, its caches, and the quality of the compiler. At this level, the characteristics of main memory, the operating system and the I/O subsystems are irrelevant, since they are little exercised.

A short historical digression: for a long time, mainframe and minicomputer performance was expressed in MIPS (millions of instructions per second), a measure that is about as useful (given the diversity of instruction set architectures) as comparing cars by noting how fast their wheels (which vary in diameter form 10 to 18 inches) turned over undefined routes with undefined road conditions. Eventually, MIPS fell into disuse, and the general practice became based on comparing execution times of real programs.

> To be of any value whatsoever, MIPS-based comparisons must be for machines of the same instruction set architecture; even then, the numbers are useful only if the instructions being measured usefully reflect the characteristics of a real program of interest. The acronym MIPS has sometimes been interpreted as *Meaningless Information about Processor Speed*, and more cruelly as *Meaningless Information Provided by Salesmen*.

We can distinguish four classes of such programs:

- *Synthetic programs.* These programs are created specifically to reflect the behavior of real programs. Real programs are observed, and the most frequent constructs identified. In the synthetic program, the constructs are used, each with a frequency reflecting its frequency of usage in the real programs. The constructs are source-language constructs, and thus independent of processor architecture. Dhrystone and Whetstone are examples of synthetic benchmarks.

- *Kernels.* As with synthetic programs, kernels are derived from observations of the execution of real programs. However, rather than identifying all constructs used in the programs of interest, the goal here is to identify the portions of the programs of interest which are most frequently executed. The benchmark then consists of these program portions. This approach is most often used for scientific (numerically-intensive) programs, in which the heart of the program is often limited to a small number of important loops. Linpack is an example of a kernel benchmark.

- *Toy programs.* These are extremely small programs, so small that they can be translated by hand into the instruction set of any machine (whether existing or not), and then be used in simulation. An example toy program is the Towers of Hanoi puzzle.

■ *Real programs*. A benchmark based on real programs is generally a collection of existing programs provided in source form (C or Fortran, often as not). The programs are compiled and executed on the machine one wishes to evaluate. The SPEC benchmarks are an example of this class.

The first three types have fallen into disuse in favor of the SPEC benchmarks. SPEC (System Performance Evaluation Cooperative) was formed by systems manufacturers and microprocessor vendors with the aim of defining useful processor performance measurements. SPEC members are committed to making measurements and publishing them in accordance with a charter.

The definition of the benchmarks, evaluation rules and published results (these being frequently updated) are all available on SPEC's Web site http://www.spec.org

Reflecting a real-world application split, SPEC measures processor performance in two domains, integer and floating point. Depending on the applications one is interested in, either or both of these will be of interest. As an example, the integer results influence operating system and DBMS performance.

SPEC benchmarks have evolved over time:

■ *SPEC89*. The first version was a collection of integer and floating point programs enabling one to express the performance of a processor in terms of the performance of a VAX 11/780, which had performance one by definition for both integer and floating point.

■ *SPEC92*. It was discovered that the program selection and the definition of measurement conditions for SPEC89 made it possible to distort the results. SPEC aimed to circumvent these problems with SPEC92, a new set of six integer and fourteen floating point programs. The unit of performance remained a VAX 11/780.

■ *SPEC95*. To keep ahead of systems vendors, who had learned how to teach their compilers to optimize for SPEC92, SPEC again defined new programs and new evaluation rules. The unit of performance was changed to a SPARCStation 10/ 40 (40MHz SuperSPARC, no L2 cache, 64 MB of memory).

■ *SPECCPU2000.* To get the suite to better represent real workloads, the SPEC95 collection was modified and supplemented. The new unit of performance is the Sun Ultra5_10 (300 Mhz UltraSPARC, 256MB of memory), which was assigned the performance of 100 for both integer and floating point.

SPEC has been guided by two important principles in this evolution: a desire to have representative benchmarks on the one hand, and a desire to be able to express the results properly on the other.

Reflecting Real-World Practices

As an example of the latter, consider SPEC89. One of its floating point programs was matrix300, a program susceptible to major optimizations. Although the floating-point SPEC number was a geometric mean of the floating point results, the effect of the optimization of matrix300 soon came to dominate the floating point results. Some systems vendors took advantage of the behavior of matrix300, using a preprocessor on the source to effect this optimization, which thereby distorted their SPEC floating point results. As a result, SPEC92 omitted matrix300. In the same spirit, SPEC95 changed the rules for use of compiler optimization options, since inappropriate practices had become widespread with SPEC92. We should note that use of a preprocessor or an exhaustive search through compiler options is not representative of real-world use.

As these words are being written, SPEC is working on the next-generation benchmarks, to be called CPU2004.

Whenever a new SPEC standard is established, the rules say that results obtained with prior versions are null and void. The performance scalings of the various versions of the standard (base 1 for SPEC95 and 100 for SPECCPU2000) make confusion between the more recent versions unlikely.

SPECCPU2000 is a collection of reference programs, which are real applications. The two portions are:

■ *CINT2000*, a collection of 12 programs—11 in C and 1 in C++—representing the integer workload

■ *CFP2000*, a collection of 14 programs—6 in Fortran77 and 4 in C—representing the floating point workload

- The SPECCPU2000 evaluation procedure may be summarized as follows:

- Measure the execution time of each program on your system (calculate the mean of three executions)

- Calculate the SPEC ratio for each program (with two different sets of rules for compiler options— ,more detail will be provided later):

```
SPEC_ratio = (execution time on Sun Ultra 5_10/
execution time on system) x100
```

Calculate the following values:

- *SPECint2000*: the geometric mean of the SPEC_ratios for the integer programs, with any compiler options for any program
- *SPECint_base2000*: the geometric mean of the SPEC_ratios for the integer programs, with identical compiler options for all programs
- *SPECfp2000*: the geometric mean of the SPEC_ratios for the floating point programs, with any compiler options for any program
- *SPECfp_base2000*: the geometric mean of the SPEC_ratios for the floating point programs, with identical compiler options for all programs

There is no simple mapping between SPEC95 scores and SPECCPU2000 scores, since the programs are different. However, as some indication, we can say that a Sun Ultra 10 Model 333 (333MHz UltraSPARC III) has SPEC95 of 14.1 (integer) and 18.3 (floating point), while its SPECCPU2000 numbers are 133 for integer and 126 for floating point. Since processor performance doubles roughly every 18 months, in accordance with Moore's Law (or, in practice, somewhat less frequently), we provide no comparative processor performance table here—it would rapidly be out of date. As we noted earlier, up to date SPEC results are available on the SPEC Web site, http:// www.spec.org.

[HEN00] describes both how the benchmarks evolved and the technical aspects of SPECCPU2000.

7.3   **Embedded Systems**

While our focus is on server systems, the commoditization of technologies can provide substantial overlap between servers, PCs and embedded systems. It is therefore interesting to take a quick look at benchmarking for the embedded world.

Specific benchmarks have been developed to compare processors (and compilers) for embedded applications. For far too long, the Dhrystone benchmark (which fits entirely in the caches of almost all processors) has been used. To have a more accurate way to compare processors, the Embedded Microprocessor Benchmark Consortium (EEMBC for short) wasn launched in 1997; their first certified results were published in 2000.

The EEMBC benchmarks can be qualified as "algorithm-based benchmarks". They sit somewhere between "kernel benchmarks" such Whetstone or Linpack and "real application benchmarks" such as SPEC CPU2000. The most significant part (in terms of performance, that is the part of the application on which most of the time is spent) is extracted from real-world applications; the choice of which applications is made as a result of a consensus process. Unlike other benchmarks, EEMBC presents a specific feature: results can only be published after the benchmarks have been run by the EEMBC Certification Laboratories (ECL).

Several benchmarks have been defined targeting various applications: automotive/industrial, consumer, networking, office automation, telecommunications, Java, MP3, MPEG, VoIP (Voice over IP), eight- and sixteen-bit microcontroller, etc.

Information on benchmarks and results are available on the EEMBC Web site, www.eembc.com.

7.4   System-level performance

Attention to standardizing systems level performance measures preceded efforts at the processor level. Until the first half of the 1980s, manufacturers tended to publish system performance numbers using private benchmarks, which made comparisons impossible. A first attempt at standardizing system performance was made in the second half of the 80s, with the so-called Debit/Credit benchmark, or TP1, which was modeled on a simple banking transaction. The lack of rigor in the definition of the benchmark, together with the mischief that could be done to the published results in the absence of ethical behavior, led the various players to create an association, the TPC (Transaction Processing Council), whose objective was (and remains) the definition and promotion of benchmarks for business applications, along with the publication of results.

In addition to their processor-level benchmarks, SPEC has also specified some system level workloads; the SPEC system benchmarks are non-transaction, and complement those of the TPC.

7.4.1   **SPEC system benchmarks**

Just as with the processor-level benchmarks, companies measure their systems using SPEC-provided specifications and programs in source form. They communicate their results to SPEC, who publishes them on its Web site. SPEC does not do any measurement itself.

The following benchmarks comprise the SPEC system level suite[3]:

- **SPEC "rate" benchmark**. This benchmark aims to characterize the throughput of a system and to give an evaluation of the effectiveness of the multiprogramming and multiprocessor implementations of systems for workloads that are processor bound. The benchmark simply consists of running the SPECint and SPECfp workloads concurrently on multiple processors, and so exercises a very limited portion of the system—in particular, I/O is never exercised. The metrics are SPECint_rate2000 and SPECfp_rate2000, respectively. It is therefore not useful for characterizing server systems.

- **SPEC SFS97 (system-level file server)**. This measures how well a system performs as an NFS server in a local-area network, software-development environment. It is based on the LADDIS tests.

- **SPECjbb2000**. This measures how well the system executes the server portion of Java applications—that is, how well it executes servlets.

- **SPECweb99**. This measures the performance of the system as a Web server, and is based on observations of the profile of requests to Web servers. The configuration of the server depends on its throughput; this allows one to characterize scalability.

- **SPECjvm98**. This measures the performance of Java applets, generally on client workstations. It provides a measure of the implementation efficiency of the JVM (Java Virtual machine) on the platform.

- **SPECjAppServer2002**. This measures the performance of Java Enterprise Application Servers using a subset of J2EE APIs in a complete end-to-end Web application in a client/server environment.

- **SPEC_HPC2002**. The HPC stands for High Performance Computing, which means numerically-intensive, scientific computational workloads. This benchmark can be used to characterize the performance of high-end systems and is based on three real-world applications: seismic models, chemical modeling, and weather forecasting. It was developed to allow the evaluation of parallel and distributed architectures. Unlike Linpack-type benchmarks, SPEChp96 measures sustained performance, not peak performance.[4]

- **SPEC OMP2001**. SPEC OMP comprises two benchmarks aimed at characterizing the performance and the scalability of SMP systems. The two benchmarks are composed of parallel processing applications and are related to different system sizes: OMPM2001 for SMP systems up to 32 processors, and OMPL2001 for systems up to 512 processors. Programs use the OpenMP standard for shared memory multiprocessor systems.

- **SPECmail2001**. This benchmark characterizes the performance of a system as an e-mail server.

While the SPEC rate benchmark deservers no further mention in our context, the others merit some commentary since they compare system performance in realistic uses.

SPEC is developing new standards. As these lines are being written, SPECappPlatform is under development. SPECappPlatform is designed to measure the scalability and performance of enterprise platforms (such as J2EE and.NET) running Web services. SPECappPlatform will include features that are typical in customers' enterprise applications, such as transactions, persistent services, Web services, and messaging. Improved versions of existing standards are also under development. Our advice to the reader is to refer regularly to the SPEC Web site to look for both new published results and the emergence of new standards or new versions of existing standards.

7.4.2 SFS system level file server

The SFS workload is derived from observations of more than 1,000 servers used in different application environments, and showed that 60 percent of the usage profiles were similar. This benchmark was created in 1993, and updated in 1997. Figure 7.3 shows an SFS test configuration.

The test consists of attaching an NFS file server to a local area network environment and generating requests to it in accordance with the observed

Figure 7.3
Example of a file server configuration for SFS benchmark.

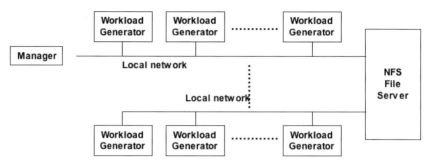

traffic. Workload generators running on LAN-connected clients generate the requests., and the load is increased until server response time reaches 40 milliseconds (reduced from the 50ms of the previous version).

SFS provides the following results:

- Average number of operations per second
- Average response time per operation

SFS exercises the system's I/O (network and discs).

7.4.3   SPECjbb2000

SPECjbb2000 (Java Benchmark Business) provides a basis for comparing servers' abilities to execute the "server" portion of Java applications.

The model, inspired by the TPC-C benchmark (see later) is that of a three-tier client/server application, with only the application portion being measured. The client and database portions are simulated in a simple manner: the "clients" are request generators (each representing a warehouse), and the "database" is modeled by tree-structured data (B-trees) held in memory with about 25 MB per warehouse (without any explicit disk I/O).

This benchmark exercises Java support (whether JVM or JIT), garbage collection, and thread support, and therefore exercises several aspects of the OS. It makes it possible to characterize processor performance, memory hierarchy, and scalability for SMP systems.

The benchmark result is the average throughput of the server expressed as the number of executions of the application per unit of time, the server being subjected to request rates loading it well beyond saturation.

The evaluation procedure can be summarized as follows:

- Vary the number of warehouses (that is, traffic generators) from 1 to $2N$, where N is the number corresponding to the maximum throughput the system is capable of. Each measurement (for any given number of warehouses) lasts for two minutes.

- The SPECjbb2000 value is the average of the throughput for the measurements corresponding to N to $2N$ warehouses.

7.4.4 SPECjAppServer2002

This benchmark corresponds to the SPECjAppServer2001 benchmark but uses the EJB 2.0 specification instead of EJB 1.1.

The purpose of this benchmark is to characterize the performance and the scalability of EJB servers and containers. The benchmark emulates a manufacturing, supply chain management (SCM) and order/inventory system. Four domains are considered: Supplier, Service Provider, Customer, and Corporate. For the size of the business under consideration, it is assumed that each domain has separate databases and applications (likely implemented on different systems). 24×7 operations are assumed. The benchmark assumes relational databases are accessible via JDBC.

A mix of operations is defined on these domains.

- The Customer domain is based on OLTP. Order entry is an application running in this domain with the conventional operations: adding new orders, changing an existing order, and retrieving status of a particular order or of all orders for a particular customer. Approximately 57 percent of the system's work is related to orders from distributors (i.e., they contain a large number of items). and 43 percent is related to individual customers' orders.

- The Manufacturing domain models the activity of production lines in a manufacturing plant. There are two types of production lines: Planned lines and LargeOrder lines. The Planned lines run on schedule and produce a pre-defined number of widgets. On the other hand, the LargeOrder lines run only when a large order is received from a customer, such as a distributor.

- SPECjAppServer2002 expresses performance in terms of two metrics:

- TOPS (Total Operations Per Second), which is the number of order transactions plus the number of manufacturing work orders divided by the measurement period in seconds

- Price/TOPS, which is the price of the System Under Test (including hardware, software, and support) divided by the TOPS

A Web layer will be introduced in the next version of the benchmark (dubbed SPECjAppServer2003).

7.4.5 SPECweb99

Although SPEC had specified a Web server benchmark, SPECweb96, in 1996, it felt the need to update the benchmark in 1999 to reflect changes in Web usage—in particular, the rise in the use of dynamic pages and persistent connections.

SPECweb99 measures the maximum number of simultaneous connections that a server can support.

These connections generate traffic in accordance with the observed profile, and the number of connections used in the benchmark must be adjusted so that the average throughput of the system must be between 400 Kbits/sec (50 KB/s) and 320 Kbits/sec (40 KB/sec).

The benchmark takes account of both the traffic profile and the profile of file sizes observed in real-world use. The file sizes observed led to the following file classes:

- Class 0: 35 percent of the requests concern files smaller than 1 KB

- Class 1: 50 percent of the requests concern files between 1 KB and 10 KB

- Class 2: 14 percent of the requests concern files between 10 KB and 100 KB

- Class 3: 1 percent of requests concern files between 100 KB and 1 MB

Because a higher-performance server can serve more files, the number of different files is required to be proportional to the server performance. The files are grouped in directories, each containing nine files per class for a total of 36 files per directory. The size of the files in each class varies in increments of 0.1 KB, 1 KB, 10KB and 100KB respectively per class.

The number of directories is related to the server performance as follows:

```
number of directories = (25 + (400000/122000) * number of
simultaneous connections)/0.5))
```

During execution of the benchmark, the file accessed per class is selected using a Zipf distribution, making it possible to reflect the fact that some files in a directory are accessed more often than others. We show the access frequency for the nine files of a given class in a directory in Table 7.1.

Table 7.1 *Directory file access frequencies in SPECweb99*

File Number	Access Percentage
0	3.9%
1	5.9%
2	8.8%
3	17.7%
4	35.3%
5	11.8%
6	7.1%
7	5.0%
8	4.4%

As can be seen, file 4 is most frequently accessed, and file 0 the least.

Table 7.2 shows the requests made by the benchmark and their frequency distribution.

It is worth noting that the definition of SPECweb99 is profoundly different from that of its predecessor, reflecting the desire of the SPECweb participants to reflect current, real Web usage as accurately as possible, and thereby be a useful systems comparison tool.

Table 7.2 *Request distribution in SPECweb99*

Type of request	Percentage
Static GET	70%
Standard dynamic GET	12.45%
Standard dynamic GET (cgi)	0.15%
Specific dynamic GET	12.6%
Dynamic POST	4.8%

SPEC has added to its Web benchmarking capabilities by adding SPECweb_SSL to the mix in addition to SPECweb99. The goal is to characterize secure Web server performance using HTTP 1.0/1.1 over the SSL protocol. It is based on the same test harness and uses the same workload and filesets as WEB99. It is a complement but not a replacement for SPECweb99.

7.4.6 SPECjvm98

The objective of this test is the characterization of the performance of a system for the execution of Java applications. The benchmark is mostly relevant to client workstations (where the applets are executed) but also has some significance for servers (wen executing servlets).

The benchmark is composed of eight different tests, of which five are real applications or derivatives of real applications.

SPECjvm98 consists in measuring the time needed to load the program, to verify the classes used by the loaded program, to complete the program's JIT compilation, and then to execute the program.

Each component program is executed several times, allowing best-case and worst- case performance numbers to be collected. The final result is a geometric mean, and system performance is expressed as a number with the reference system, a workstation containing a PowerPC 604 running at 133 MHz, which is given the score of 1.

Since the implementation of virtual memory has an effect on Java execution, the results are subdivided into three sets depending on workstation memory size: 0 to 48 MB (although 32 MB is considered to be a minimum size), 48 MB to 256 MB, and more than 256 MB.

7.4.7 SPEC_HPC2002

As we indicated above, SPEChp2002 comprises three program suites, all taken from the real world: a quantum chemistry application (SPECchem), a weather research and forecasting model (SPECenv), and an industrial application that performs time and depth migrations used to locate gas and oil deposits (SPECseis).

SPEC_HPC2002 benchmarks can be executed in serial or parallel mode. Parallel mode is based on Open MP or MPI standards (SMP or clusters/MPPs systems).

SPEC_HPC2002 provides both a speed measure (how fast given tasks are accomplished) and a throughput measure (how many tasks can performed during a given 24-hour period). SPEC_HPC2002 allow the publishing of results for four different problem sizes (S, M, L, and X).

It is reasonable to ask how well SPEChp2002 can act as a basis for comparing the various architecture options. In practice, the users of such applications generally have a rather limited number of applications, and the speed of execution and the throughput of these programs is indeed a key parameter for them (in order to meet Time to Market objectives). System performance is a defining factor in the development time for products, and the systems are often used to run just one application at a time, or perhaps some small number of applications simultaneously.

Unlike with SPEC95, it is legitimate to apply optimizations to SPEC_HPC2002, since it is considered that this is normal practice for the users of such applications. However, it is not allowed to replace source with hand-coded assembler.

7.4.8 SPEC OMP2001

In June 2001, SPEC finalized SPEC OMP2001, a new benchmark intended to characterize the performance of systems running scientific programs (intensive numerical programs) in a parallel processing environment based on shared memory and using the Open MP programming standards (visit http://www.openmp.org for information on this standard). The benchmark does not make use of disk I/O or network throughput. The applications are taken from SPECCPU2000 and modified to use OpenMP directives to provide concurrency, as there are 11 programs in the suite.

SPEC OMP2001 is a first step, intended for systems in the range of 4 to 32 processors. A subsequent version, SPEC OMPL2001, is in preparation;

it employs larger datasets and is intended for systems up to 512 processors. The reference machine for SPEC OMP2001 is a four-processor SGI 210, clocked at 350 MHz. The speed of a system is expressed relative to the reference system, with two types of results: peak, when aggressive compiler optimization options are being used, and base, when conservative optimization options are being used (an approach similar to SPEC CPU2000). The corresponding measures are: SPECompMpeak2001, SPECompMbase2001, SPECompLpeak2001 and SPECompLbase2001 respectively.

7.4.9   SPECmail2001

This benchmark measures systems performance when acting as a mail server using the standard SMTP (Simple Mail Transfer Protocol) and POP3 (Post Office Protocol version 3) protocols. It models e-mail users supported by an ISP (Internet Service Provider), in which 90 percent of the users are connected by 56 Kbit/sec modems and the remainder by local area networks. The traffic profile used is derived from measurements made on real systems.

The metric is the number of messages per minute (MPM) with the constraint that 95 percent of messages must be sent in less than 5 seconds, along with some QoS (Quality of Service) constraints relating to modem usage, message delivery time and the mail server error rate.

The profile of use is derived from the observation of the traffic on mail servers.

7.5   The TPC

As noted earlier, the first attempts at standardizing a systems-level benchmark took place in the second half of the 1980s, with the introduction of the debit/credit benchmark, or TP1.

To mitigate deficiencies in the definition of this benchmark and to establish a rigorous basis for systems comparison, a group of computer systems vendors and DBMS vendors formed the Transaction Processing Council (TPC). The TPC aimed to both define a benchmark for transaction-processing systems and to specify rigorous publication rules for the results. Each TPC member is committed to obeying the rules, which require results to be accompanied by publication of a detailed report. Reports are subject to audit.

TPC then published a new benchmark to characterize decision support applications, and then, later, one for Web-based transactional applications. The history of TPC benchmarks can be summarized by the following list (benchmarks shown in **bold** were current at the beginning of 2002):

- TPC-A (1989): a simple transaction which does one update to a bank account
- TPC-B (1990): the "database portion" of TPC-A
- **TPC-C** (1992): a benchmark involving multiple, complex transactions
- **TPC-D** (1995): decision support
- **TPC-H** (1999): decision support
- **TPC-R** (1999): decision support
- **TPC-W** (2000): Web-based transaction processing (e.g., electronic commerce, B2B, etc.)

The TPC benchmarks allow systems to be compared in two ways:

- Performance (for example, number of transactions per unit of time)
- Price/performance (for example, total cost of ownership over a three-year period per transaction per minute)

The benchmark is not specified by source code, and so it is the responsibility of each TPC member who wishes to characterize a system to implement the benchmarks for those systems.

The TPC does not measure systems itself.

As far as the benchmarks are concerned, system cost comprises the cost of acquiring the system from the vendor (hardware and software) along with the costs of maintenance for three years. The transactions called for must be implemented properly, respecting the ACID[5] properties of atomicity, coherence, insulation and durability.

Information on the activities and the standards issued by the TPC, as well as the published results of measurements, is available on their Web site at *http:// www.tpc.org.*

7.5.1   TPC-C Transactional Benchmark

The first standard defined by the TPC was TPC-A, in 1989. It exercised the whole system, including the processors, database and telecommunications.

TPC-A defined two metrics: transactional performance (measured as the number of transactions per second under the constraint of a specified response time) and cost, measured as $tps-a (representing the cost of acquiring and owning the system for five years per transaction per second).

TPC-A and TPC-B History

TPC-A formalized the original TP1, or Debit/Credit benchmark. Because TP1 was not precisely defined, computer systems vendors spent a lot of energy on optimizing the performance of the benchmark on their systems, doing things which were increasingly unrepresentative of real-world transaction processing. It was in reaction to these unhelpful activities that the various players decided to produce a much more precise test specification, resulting in TPC-A.

Because running a TPC-A measurement was an expensive exercise, the TPC created TPC-B in 1990. TPC-B was a cut-down version of just the database portion of TPC-A (that is, with no communications workload).

Because measurements of TPC-A were expensive, and because TPC-A transactions were too simple to be realistic, the TPC introduced TPC-C to replace both TPC-A and TPC-B in 1992.

TPC-C is, arguably, a reasonable representation of a transactional application. It has five different transaction types applied to nine tables (TPC-A and -B had but one transaction type). It exercises the whole system: processor, database and telecommunications.

As for TPC-A, two metrics are specified, one for performance and one for price performance. Performance is measured in tpmC (transactions per minute) and cost/ performance as $/tpmC (with the cost being, as said, acquisition cost plus the cost of three years' maintenance).

The size of both the database and the communications subsystem to be used for the measurements depends on system performance. Response times must meet constraints: for each transaction type, 90 percent of the responses must meet the constraint.

The dimensioning of the database and the subsystem of communication depends on the performance of the system.

Revision 5 of TPC-C, in February 2001, made some significant modifications to the benchmark:

- Data need not be maintained on-line for 180 days, as had been the case, but for only 90 days

- The system amortization period was reduced from five years to three

- The maintenance agreement cost (which must be figured in) is now for 24 hours a day, 7 days a week rather than 8 hours a day, 5 days a week

- The cost of the networking equipment (hubs and switches) is not included in the cost of the system

Given these fairly large changes, it would be unwise to compare systems using results from two different versions of TPC-C.

Significance of TPC-C

A key aspect of TPC-C is its use of system scalability. The performance of an OLTP system is expressed as the number of transactions per second, subject to some response time constraint; the larger the system throughput, the greater the number of clients it can serve. Plus, the size of the database grows linearly with the number of customers. TPC-C, then, requires a configuration whose size reflects a combination of system throughput, database size and number of clients: for each tpmC (measured in transactions per minute), the system must support one client and an additional eight MB of database.

We should note the linearity of the scaling factors here: the size of the system in terms of disks and communications subsystem depends linearly on the performance of the system.

7.5.2   The limitations of TPC-C

TPC-C is not completely representative of real-world applications. Two Oracle white papers [ORA02a] and [ORA02b] highlight its limitations. Table 7.3 shows the differences in complexity between TPC-C and example commercial packages.

As the table shows, TPC-C is nowhere near as complex as commercial business packages. The goal of TPC-C was to capture and represent certain key characteristics of transactional applications while remaining relatively

Table 7.3   *Comparison between TPC-C and commercial packages (source: [ORA02b])*

	Number of Tables	Number of Primary Key Indexes	Number of Alternate Key Indexes	Number of Unique SQL Statements
TPC-C	9	9		20
PeopleSoft	7000+	6400+	900	100,000+
Oracle eBusiness Suite (ERP only)	8000+	1600+	5100	290,000+
SAP	2000	16000+	2800+	273,000+

simple to implement—TPC-C is not defined by an implementation (source code), but by a specification, which means that anyone wanting to run the benchmark must first consult the definition and then implement a conforming benchmark. Because of the real-world costs of measuring a system on TPC-C—hardware and software to be acquired and fired up, people skills to be set to work—one can easily see that too complex a specification for TPC-C would have been a serious barrier to its adoption. It's worth noting that a number of benchmarks have been proposed by vendors; it's also worth noting that while the commercial packages in the table above have enormous numbers of components, although in actual execution a rather small subset of the SQL orders are invoked against a subset of the tables.

Another characteristic of TPC-C turns out to be helpful for "share nothing" clusters—by partitioning the database on the Warehouse_ID key, and thereby assigning specific warehouses to specific nodes, one obtains most excellent spatial locality, as shown in Table 7.4.

Table 7.4   *Locality Characteristics of TPC-C (source: [ORA02a]).*

Transaction Type	% of Mix	% of "Local" SQL
New Order	45	99.5
Payment	43	95
Order Status	4	100
Delivery	4	100
Stock Level	4	100

As the table shows, about 98 percent of the transactions are local—that is, they only touch data managed by the node on which the transaction is executed. This explains the excellent scalability of cluster systems on TPC-C. There is little chance that this situation would be seen with "real" applications.

7.5.3 TPC-H and TPC-R: decision support benchmarks

The increasing importance of decision-support applications led the TPC to define TPC-D, issuing the standard in April 1995. This was followed in 1999 by two new benchmarks, TPC-H and TPC-R. As with TPC-C, the benchmarks are provided as specifications, and parties wanting to execute them must provide their own implementations.

Rather than modeling an application in some branch of industry, TPC-H represents a workload for a company operating worldwide. The situation modeled is as follows:

- Database available 24/7: seven days a week, 24 hours a day[6]

- Database content tracks (with some small time delay) the state of the production database (that is, the database being used by the OLTP system), using an update procedure that batches the changes requests and updates are concurrent, and so must respect the ACID properties

- The trade-off between performance and operational needs—for example, when it is desired that the decision support system track the production system with a smaller time lag—may be specified once and for all by the database administrator, through the specification of the level of locking to be used and the concurrency between requests and updates.

The application environment modeled by TPC-H is shown in Figure 7.4.

The size of the decision-support database is parameterizable, but unlike TPC-C, it is not linked to system performance. The approach is rather to quote performance with various database sizes—the database contains eight tables, and six of these have sizes set by a scale factor. Typical database sizes are 100 GB, 300 GB, 1 TB and 3 TB, although by December 2003, results for 10 TB sizes have been reported. Sizes of 30 and 100 TB are expected to be reported in the next few years.

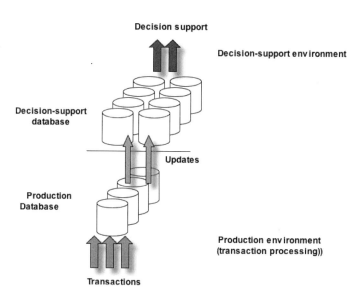

Figure 7.4
*TPC-H
application
environment.*

The database operations of the benchmark involve 22 request types and 2 update types. Two metrics are specified, linked to database sizes:

- Performance: QphH@<database_size> (Composite Queries per Hour)—a measure of the system's throughput in terms of decision support; it describes several aspects of the system's performance: database size, decision support performance with sequential requests (that is, just a single stream of requests) and performance with multiple concurrent request streams

- price/performance: $/QphH@<database_size>—ownership cost for a five-year period, divided by the performance of the system for a specified database size

TPC-R differs from TPC-H only in that it is considered that the requests executed against the database are known in advance, and thus optimizations are possible. The -R metrics are QphR@<database_size> and $/QphR@<database_size>.

Almost all published results are for TPC-H; by January 2003, only two systems builders had published TPC-R results. Thus, there is not yet sufficient information to be able to form an idea of what the effect of optimizations on TPC-R results might be.

There has been criticism of TPC-H, centered on the number of simultaneous users required by the definition (Revision 2.0.0, July 2002); the requirements are given in Table 7.5.

Table 7.5 *Minimum Required Execution Streams (source TPC)*

Scale factor	Number of request streams
1	2
10	3
30	4
100	5
300	6
1000	7
3000	8
10000	9

Some observers believe the number of simultaneous streams is much too low. Only seven streams—seven virtual users—are needed to exercise a 1 TB database.

7.5.4 TPC-W: commercial web applications

TPC-W aims to compare performance and price/performance for systems implementing Web-based electronic commerce. It models three types of client requests:

- Information search, followed by purchase—*B2C*, for Business to Consumer
- Information search
- Web-based transactions—*B2B*, for Business to Business.

The application has eight tables and five interaction types:

- Browse—information search
- Shopping cart—item selection

- Purchase

- Recording of customer information

- Searching for information on an item

The transactions must respect the ACID properties, and each interaction has an associated time constraint. The size of the database (which reflects the size of the virtual store and corresponds to the number of items in the store) is parameterizable, but, unlike TPC-C and like TPC-H and -R, it is not linked to the system performance. The size of the benchmark is specified by the Scale Factor, which sets the number of items for sale: it can be 1,000, 10,000, 100,000, 1 million, or 10 million.

The benchmark requires that data concerning purchases must be maintained on line (i.e., on disk) for 180 days.

The following metrics are specified:

- *Performance*, expressed in WIPS@<scale_factor>—WIPS (Web Interactions Per Second) measures the number of requests per second, ignoring network time (time is measured from entry of the request into the server to the time the response exits the server)

- *Price/performance*, expressed as $/WIPS@<scale_factor>—the price is the cost of acquisition and of three years' ownership of the system

- *Transactional performance*, expressed as WIPSo@<scale_factor>—the number of transactions per second

- *Browsing performance*, expressed as WIPSb@<scale_factor>—the number of browse requests per second

As for SPEC, the definition of TPC benchmarks evolves over time, and new definitions are proposed as old one are retired. This process represents the continuing search both for benchmarks that are representative of the real world (in the sense that their results are useful predictors of system behavior across real-world examples of the domain being benchmarked) and for the creation of a reliable base for comparisons.

TPC-E: an Interesting Attempt

We should mention TPC-E, even if only to regret its failure. This was an attempt by the TPC to create a business systems benchmark; however, the proposal was not approved, probably because of the complexity of the proposal and the expected measurement costs.

Although the benchmark was not approved, its characteristics (which reflect those of a business system) deserve some comment:

TPC-E was to be able to express a system's capabilities in:

- Supporting a very large number of users, with strict response time constraints

- Providing batch services concurrently with the transactional workload and its time constraints; the batch requests also had time constraints

- Supporting a large, complex database with frequent high-throughput requests

- Recovering after a system failure

TPC-E marked an interesting evolution from TPC-C, since it called for overlapping the transactional behavior with a batch workload, and measured recovery capabilities. It is to be hoped that this benchmark, or an improved equivalent, will eventually be approved.

7.6   Storage Subsystems Performance

In 2001, a new initiative aimed at creating performance standards for storage was born: the Storage Performance Council.

Their first standard, SPC-1 (SPC benchmark 1), relates to SAN environments (and is therefore block-oriented, rather than the file-oriented standard one would expect for a NAS environment). SPC-1 models the I/O part of application environments, such as transactional, database and e-mail. It uses *random* profiles (rather than *sequential* profiles, in which one sequentially explores the elements of a file or a database).

Figure 7.5 represents the environment modeled by SPC-1.

In this system environment, SPC-1 covers the performance of the storage subsystems. It comprises a set of eight streams, each referred to as an *execution instance*; the collection of all eight streams is a *Business Scaling Unit*, or BSU. To simulate increases in load, one increases the number of BSUs.

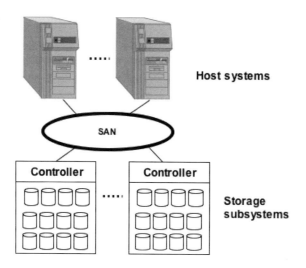

Figure 7.5
*SPC-1
environment.*

Of the eight streams, five are random reads and writes, two are sequential reads and the remaining stream is sequential writes. The request profile, in terms of operations per second, is shown in Table 7.6.

Table 7.6   *SPC-1 I/O streams*

	Reads/s	Writes/s	Total (operations/s)
Random	14.5	16.2	30.7
Sequential	5.3	14.0	19.3
Total (operations/s)	19.8	30.2	50

A stream generates a total of 50 I/O requests per second.

SPC-1 results reflect the performance of a storage solution in two performance dimensions—response time and throughput. It characterizes two situations:

- SPC-1 LRT: the response time under low load
- SPC-1 IOPS: the maximum throughput provided by a storage subsystem

The system measurement procedure consists of first determining the maximum number of I/O operations per second that the system can sustain, by increasing the number of BSUs until performance saturation is achieved. The I/O rate at saturation is SPC-1 IOPS. The load is then reduced by successive stages to 10 percent of this load, and the response time measured; this measurement provides the SPC-1 LRT.

This process is complemented by two further tests: the first test checks that the storage subsystem provides information persistence—that is, that the data is non-volatile. The second checks for repeatable and reproducible performance results.

SPC is currently defining SPC-2, a new standard to be used to characterize the following applications:

- Web server

- Sequential workloads

- Backup and restore operations

- Data streaming, such as for video

- NAS server

SPC also intends to develop other standards. Information on their activities and on SPC standards can be found on their Web site, www.storageperformance.org

7.6.1 Benchmarks: final words

There are other systems benchmarks, some of which are product-specific (such as SAP benchmarks) or platform-specific (such as those for PC-based servers). The description of such benchmarks is beyond the scope of this book, however.

Perhaps the most remarkable aspect of system benchmarks and the organizations that support them—such as SPEC and the TPC—is their model of operation. These organizations are based on a continuing search for better representation of real-world applications, coupled with evaluation/test procedures that ensure the credibility of the results.

We can observe a pattern in the life-cycle of a standard benchmark; initially, it is reasonably representative of the workloads in the domain it is assessing, but the representation decreases over time, due to the effects of improving technology and changing applications. This situation is countered by the introduction of a new definition, which offers greater representation of the workloads while simultaneously limiting the possibility of behaviors that could distort the results.

Measuring a high-end system can be a very expensive activity. For TPC-C and TPC-H, the cost of high-end configurations runs well into the millions of dollars. Thus, only systems companies whose finances are in good order are able to mount such an activity, involving as it does the use of a great deal of expensive machinery and people.

Turning this point around, the fact that a systems vendor publishes the results of industry-standard systems benchmarks indicates both that the company is likely to be financially sound and that it has confidence in the competitiveness of its solutions.

7.7 Comparing the Performance of Architectural Approaches

In this section, we use the TPC-C results available in January 2003 on the TPC Web site to compare architectural approaches in terms of performance. While the absolute values for systems performance are liable to change for the usual reasons (e.g., improved microprocessors, improved system logic, DBMS improvements), we expect that the majority of the conclusions and comments in our analysis will remain valid.

Our comparison looks only at performance, since the price/performance dimensions are prone to non-architectural, non-technical factors, such as changes in pricing policies by hardware and middleware vendors undergoing competitive pressures.

We performed a similar analysis with TPC-H results, but were not able to form any useful conclusions.

7.7.1 Analyzing TPC-C results

Several comparisons were done:

- A comparison of the performance levels achieved by each of the major architectural approaches (SMP, cluster, and MPP)

- A comparison of the effectiveness of each architectural approach, expressed in terms of efficiency of use of a processor

■ A comparison of the effectiveness of processor architectures (to do this, we compare the measured performance, in tpmC, to the theoretical performance, estimated by the number of processors in the system multiplied by their performance, as measured by SPECint 2000)

■ A final comparison shows the change in tpmC performance between February 1999 and January 2003

Figure 7.6 shows the absolute performance of SMPs and clusters of various sizes, as measured in tpmC.

Figure 7.6
SMP-Cluster TPC-C performance comparison (source data: TPC).

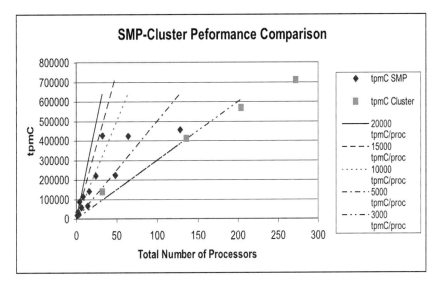

This graph highlights just how well SMPs perform for moderate numbers of processors: SMPs outperform clusters very noticeably (a 16-processor SMP matches the performance of a 36-processor cluster). Clusters catch up in configurations of 128 processors, after which no SMP results have been published; at 128 processors, the SMP has only a 10 percent performance advantage over a 136-processor cluster. Clusters have had results published for configurations of up to 272 processors. As we noted before, with properly-partitioned data, TPC-C should scale more or less linearly with the size of a cluster; this can be seen in the graph, although only at a rate of around 3000 tpmC per processor. An SMP, on the other hand, offers a reducing tpmC per processor, falling from around 25000 tpmC for a four-processor system to 3561 tpmC for the 128-processor configuration.

Figure 7.7
*SMP and cluster
scalability (source
data: TPC).*

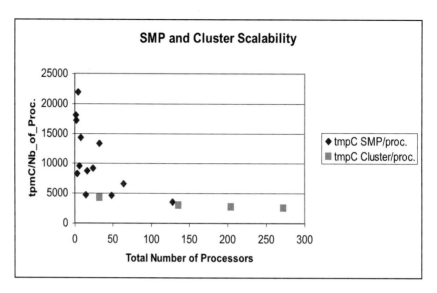

This linearity is shown more clearly in Figure 7.7, which shows the data as tpmC per processor.

This figure shows that the per-processor performance of an SMP, although initially very high, drops quickly as the number of processors increases, while clusters have a much shallower scalability line. These observations are important more for the trends they show than for the absolute values; system performance depends on intrinsic processor performance, and these will change over time. Indeed, the figure shows systems built around a number of architectures. Alpha, Intel IA-32, PA, SPARC, and PowerPC are all represented. The constant tpmC per processor for clusters indicates that these configurations took advantage of the TPC-C data partitioning optimization mentioned previously.[7] The relatively low per-processor performance offered by small-configuration clusters reflects the cost of internode communication, while the high performance per processor for SMPs reflects the low cost of communicating via shared coherent memory.

The trends must be looked at with some caution, because of differences in hardware, operating systems,l and DBMS.

Two factors contribute to the trends we see. The first is the traditional multiprocessor scalability phenomenon; that is, the performance increase provided by an additional processor falls as the number of processors grows.

- Within an SMP, this occurs because of contention for hardware resources—the system bus, the I/Os—and shared data.

- Within a cluster, the addition of a processor to a cluster is subject to the same physics as in an SMP. The addition of a node implies the need for more communication and synchronization with existing nodes, reducing their efficiency.

The second factor is that in TPC-C, the size of the database grows at a linear rate with system performance, but unfortunately we do not have access to published data which allows us to estimate the effect of this requirement. For that, it would be necessary to actually perform measurements to see the effect of size on performance; but since a system configuration on which to properly measure TPC-C is extremely expensive, and systems vendors are most interested in publishing the largest possible number for tpmC (or the lowest cost/performance figure), the reason for the lack of data is evident.

Intuitively, there should be some relationship between the system performance (as measured by TPC-C) and the intrinsic processor performance (as measured, for example, by SPECint2000, probably the most representative benchmark of processor performance for processors used in transaction processing). To investigate this, we standardize, using the number of processors and the SPECint2000 value; we look only at SMP systems, because of a paucity of published results for clusters and MPPs.

In Figure 7.8, we try to show the effectiveness of the various processor architectures for a transaction-processing workload. To do this, we show the relationship between SMP performance on TPC-C and an estimate of the raw power of the system computed from the processor's integer performance.[8]

The interpretation of this data is clouded by the fact that the DBMSs used differ between the architectures. Nonetheless, one can clearly see the reducing scalability as the system size grows, and there appear to be some patterns visible.

PowerPC is noticeably more efficient than the other architectures—look at the points with 8 and 24 processors. Different versions of the same DBMS were used for these three systems. We can explain the advantage over the other architectures as a combination of three factors: large caches, tuning of the OS to the hardware and tuning of the DBMS to the hardware.

Figure 7.8
*Architectural
efficiency for TPC-
C (source data:
TPC and SPEC).*

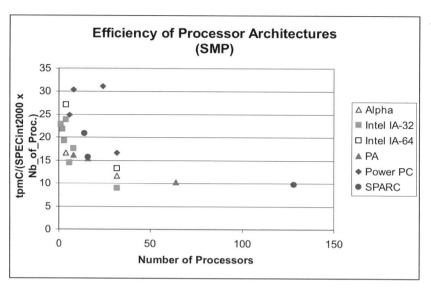

Figure 7.9 shows the changes in architectural efficiency in TPC-C over a four-year period, for SMPs and clusters.

As usual, a word of caution is advisable; the definition of TPC-C changed during the period shown. We should also note that the SMP and cluster figures with 128 processors for 2003 are more or less indistinguishable.

Nonetheless, we can probably draw the following useful conclusions:

Figure 7.9
*Evolution of
architectural SMP
and cluster
efficiency with
TPC-C (source:
TPC).*

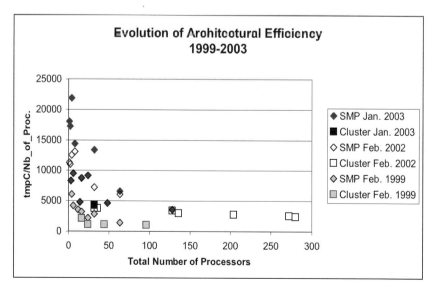

- Per-processor performance for SMPs increased by a factor of about 4.6 between 1999 and 2003

- While there were few cluster results between 2002 and 2003, performance more than tripled between 1999 and 2002

- The largest SMP reported doubled in size (from 64 to 128)

- Cluster size substantially increases (from 96 in 1999 to 280 in 2002)

The performance increase can be explained by four factors:

- Processor performance (which is doubling roughly every 22 months, as previously mentioned)

- Hardware improvements

- DBMS improvements

- OS and transaction monitor improvements

In the absence of more detailed information, it is difficult to estimate the relative importance of these factors.

The increase in processor count is an ongoing phenomenon. As far as published results go (which may not reflect marketplace reality), the increase is much more marked—both in number of results published and the performance levels achieved—for clusters than for SMPs. From this, one can conclude that the evolution of cluster technology will drive the future evolution of TPC-C. With the arrival of InfiniBand and VIA technologies, we should see confirmation of this hypothesis. Nevertheless, SMPs will continue their dominance in output (that is, tpmC per processor) in their domain of excellence, which is in the smaller to midrange in terms of processor count. The upper limit to this domain will also increase slowly.

7.8 Performance as a First-Class Citizen

Far too often, in the design of a system (whether it be the system as a whole, subsystems, software, etc.), considerations of performance are left until the last minute, and then, as often as not, are only taken into account when problems have already surfaced.

This approach generally results in panic measures that yield mediocre or even disastrous results for the system architecture. The search for improved performance frequently leads to a destructuring of the system—for example, the virtualization layers, which were introduced to provide an appropriate amount of hardware and software independence,are simply ripped out. Typically, the resulting solutions are at best partial fixes, and often lead to an increase in costs, a delay in availability, and a negative impact on system maintainability.

Not understanding system performance makes it difficult to predict system behavior, both in the face of changes to hardware (such as the effect of a processor or network change on system response time) or software, or in the workload it is required to perform. It also makes it more difficult to analyze and cure performance issues encountered during the life of the system.

In this section, we offer a methodology that makes performance estimation tractable, using modeling techniques.

Modeling a system makes it possible to study the behavior of the system using models, rather than the real system. When technology or mission changes are proposed, their effects can be gauged using the model. Doing this requires exercising the model using appropriate data, which may come from measurements or from estimates.

Measuring and modeling are two different but complementary activities. They are a necessary aspect of a system architect's job, and bring a quantitative aspect to what is all too often a qualitative activity. Modeling can be done throughout the life cycle of a project, from the initial concept stage to operational use. A system will see many changes in its operational phase—its mission will change and evolve, and the implementation technologies will alter. It is most convenient to be able to evaluate the effect of these changes before being forced to bring them about in the real system.

We can summarize the contributions modelling can make throughout the lifecycle of a system as follows:

- Design phase
- Choice between various architectural approaches
- Sizing the various components of the system
- Sensitivity analysis, looking at the sensitivity of the system as various parameters change
- Implementation phase
- Analysis of changes in architecture or the sizing of various components

- Analysis of the implications of not reaching certain performance objectives (for the system components) on the overall system performance
- Operational phase
- Analysis of the impact on changes in the system mission, or of component replacement
- Assistance in analysis of any performance issues encountered

One can distinguish three major methodological approaches in the field of performance

1.   Intuition

2.   Measurements

3.   Modeling

Intuition is based on experience, It is inexpensive, but is limited both in the degree of complexity that can be handled and the reliance that can be put on its results.

Measurements, on the other hand, are accurate, but difficult and potentially expensive to make. Interpreting measurements can be difficult, since it is often forgotten that a proper interpretation relies on a good understanding of how the system works. The major drawback, however, is that to make measurements, one must have the system itself (or a late prototype) available.

Modeling can be seen as a compromise between intuition and measurement. It is more reliable than intuition, because it is based on real system dynamics, so side-effects can be detected. It is more flexible than measurement, since significant changes require only changes to the model or its parameters. It has the major advantage over measurement of not requiring the system to exist.

We can summarize the advantages of modelling as follows:

- Reliable results
- Rigorous formalism
- A global view of the system, its architecture, and its behavior
- Improved communication between teams

We expand on these points.

Because of the tools used, and particularly for mathematically-based formal modelling approaches, the results are reliable, although some care must be taken with simulation-based methods.[9] In the formal approach, the behavior of the system is expressed concisely, at an appropriately high level of abstraction.

Constructing a model requires a global view of the system, of its elements and how they interact. A model can thus naturally act as a basis for dialogue between the various teams developing the system, and is likely to improve interteam communication. The individual or team responsible for modeling can have a very large effect on such communication.

The obstacles to successful use of modeling can be summarized as:

- A little-known area
- Knowledge of tools is not widespread
- Necessity of understanding how the system works
- Difficulty in getting needed data
- Temptation to go measure instead

The practical consequence of the fact that modelling is little known (and little taught) is the absence of the reflex "performance (or availability) is a critical part of this project, so we *have* to model." A further consequence is that there is a shortage of practitioners and that modelling tools are little known and not very widespread.[10]

The fact that it is necessary to understand the operation of the system as a whole (unsurprising as that may be) can also constitute a barrier to the approach. This problem should disappear with time, since system design methods increasingly use UML notation, which provides the means to describe the dynamic behavior of systems.

Making use of models requires setting the values of parameters with values that may be difficult to obtain—measuring things requires the existence of a system, and estimating them based on experience and extrapolation may not be robust. Avoiding the problem by measuring something real is always tempting, but requires the existence of a system sufficiently close to the one under consideration. And taking this approach implicitly places one in a reactive mode: one reacts to problems, rather than having antici-pated them.

Operating systems keep statistics on a number of their activities, and from these numbers one can learn quite a lot about what a system is doing as it runs.

Sizing a system is complicated; some empirical rules exist which can be helpful as a first step, although this work needs to be complemented by experiments with models and real systems; we will discuss this later.

Our discussion of modeling concentrates on the performance aspects of a system; however, it is a general methodology which can also be applied to estimate availability (for example, comparing repair strategies and their effect on availability), and for the costs and times of development. [JAI91] is a good reference for performance issues, including measurements. A more recent and very readable work is [MEN02], which is recommended for readers interested in the practical aspects of modeling. For client/server sys-tems, we recommend [LOO97], which integrates performance consider-ations starting from the concept phase of a system.

Our modeling overview is structured as follows: first, we introduce the concept of a model. Models allow us to study and validate the impact of modifications. Our modeling technique is based on queueing theory, using queueing networks (networks of interconnected queues). We show two modeling case studies: one starting with a blank sheet of paper, and one handling an existing system. Many real modeling scenarios will be some-where between these two limits. We discuss selection criteria for a modeling strategy.

We then look at operational analysis, a technique that allows us to draw useful conclusions from sets of measurements. We then cover some tools available on standard operating systems, which can be used to collect the figures needed for operational analysis.

We conclude the chapter by presenting some empirical rules that have been proposed for sizing systems, followed by a methodology for capacity planning.

Figure 7.10 illustrates the concept of a model.

Figure 7.10
The concept of a model.

As suggested by the figure, the process of modeling consists of constructing a model which reflects the key characteristics of the system. This approach allows one to study the impact of changes by modifying the model rather than the system, and therefore to experiment and understand before implementing changes in the real world.

A number of techniques are available for constructing models, including queuing networks, stochastic Petri nets, discrete event simulation, and operational analysis.

Petri nets and queueing networks have software support, allowing the system architect to study system behavior from initial systems concept through implementation and into deployment. Our discussion of networks of queues will be made concrete through the use of the MODLINE software (and its queueing network analysis tool QNAP2).[11] As will be seen, operational analysis is simple enough that it can be done with a pocket calculator.

Figure 7.11 illustrates the concept of a queueing network.

The figure shows a simplistic interactive system, with multiple client PCs connected, via a LAN, to a server consisting of a network controller, a CPU, a disk controller and a disk. The figure also shows a representation of the system as a queueing network.

The queueing network is built on the concepts of *customers, stations,* and *transitions.* The customers ask for services, and they move from station to station. In this example, the customer is the request issued by a client PC. A station consists of a *queue* and a *server,* the server being the entity that

Figure 7.11
The concept of a queueing network.

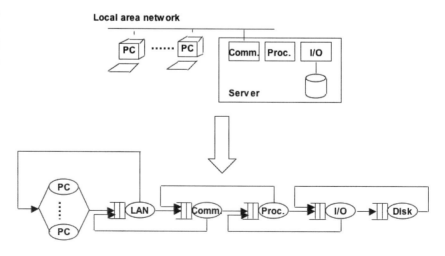

implements the service requested by a customer—so a server might represent a processor, a controller, a disk, and so on. When a server is busy, a customer is placed on the queue; the model may specify any one of several queue management disciplines. Once the customer has received the service requested from a station, it moves to a subsequent station, an operation known as a *transition*.

Along with the notion of a customer, there is a complementary idea—the concept of a *class* of customer. Classes allow customers to have different behaviors; for example, message sizes can differ, or the transitions can differ. An obvious use of classes is to distinguish requests (say, of class IN) from responses (of class OUT). A message of class IN would be consumed by a processor, which would create a message of class OUT in response. For simplicity, we avoided the use of classes in Figure 7.11.

The queueing network specification includes not only the topology of the network (the connections between the stations) and the service requests for each station, but also the definition of transitions. Queueing network resolvers make it possible to determine, for each station, the average number of clients queued up at the station, as well as the average response time (the average amount of time a customer takes to be serviced at a station) along with the load utilization of each station. Figure 7.12 annotates the previous figure with notes on the parameters that must be specified to solve the model.

A station takes an amount of time to service each request; this time is specified as a statistical distribution, and the queueing model requires that the distribution be completely specified—for example, for an exponential

Figure 7.12
Queueing network parameters.

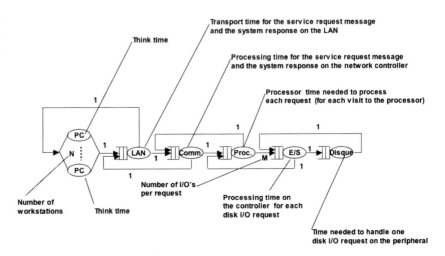

distribution the average must be specified. The workstations' behavior is specified by stating the interval between the reception of a response and the initiation of a new request. This time is called the *think time*, from the terminology of time-sharing systems. The N PCs constitute what is known as an *infinite server* (or *delay-type server*); there is always a server available to service a user request, regardless of the number of requests (this is the natural consequence of there being one user per PC, issuing one request at a time). For each station, one must specify how long it takes to service a request, and also each customer's transitions. An example of transition specification is when the network controller receives a request from a PC and sends a response back to that PC: the transition values are therefore 1 and 1 (i.e., one transition for the processor for an incoming request, and one transition for the LAN for an outgoing request). For the central process, there are M I/O requests per transaction.

There are several queueing network solvers. MODLINE (QNAP2) uses a unique formalism to support more than one solution mechanism: exact methods (analytical methods, Markov chains); approximate mathematical methods; or discrete event simulation. The use of each method requires that the queueing network under study have certain properties—discrete event simulation is the least restrictive in this regard, but requires a highly-detailed description of the system, resulting in rather bulky models. We recommend that, when possible, analytical methods be used.

We will describe the process of modeling an information system; as noted before, we will consider two cases:

- Blank sheet of paper development
- Development starting from a set of existing components

We'll examine these two situations successively, realizing that in the real world we'll often find ourselves closer to the second than the first.

7.8.1 Blank sheet of paper systems design and modeling

This situation is ideal and rarely encountered—the opportunity to design a system from the ground up with no inherited constraints; i.e., working from a "blank sheet of paper." The goal in modelling in such a situation is to be able to completely understand and validate the behavior of the system, prior to its implementation, to the extent that the effects of any change can be understood and quantified. Such changes including changes in the applications, as well as qualitative changes, such as choosing an MPP rather than a cluster or SMP organization, or quantitative questions, such as the effects of a faster processor or different disks.

To model this situation, one must:

- Define the system's mission and select an architecture for it (for example, a three-tier client/server system architecture; where the databases live; whether or not a two-phase commit is to be used), along with related quantitative information (such as the average number of instructions executed per transaction, number of I/Os per transaction, and so on). The system mission must be regarded as unchangeable,[12] while it is possible to change architecture (for example, use of a two-tier architecture instead). Any changes in the mission must result in renegotiating the contract between the system owner and the system implementors.

- Develop a model of the system.
- Study the behavior and properties of this model.
- Validate the application structure and system architecture using the model.
- Validate the model as soon as possible against the actual system, starting when the first system components become available. Keep adjusting the model as needed until implementation is complete.[13]

Figure 7.13 and Figure 7.14 illustrate the two major phases of this activity.

In this phase of system design, the key interests are to confirm the choice of system and application architecture and their sizing. The quantitative data used in the model are often estimates based on experience, although they can also be actual data from existing systems or already-validated models.

The model is iterated, making changes to architecture and sizing until satisfactory results are obtained. Performing a sensitivity analysis (see later) is recommended to obtain a higher level of confidence in the results and to provide some guidance for performance measurements during system development.

Figure 7.13
Ideal case: design phase.

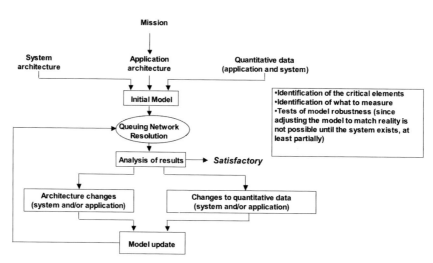

The figure calls for identification of the performance-critical elements of the system. This can be done in the model by varying parameters within ranges (for example, process switch time, or the amount of time the execution of the sequential portion of the application takes) and looking at the effects on system performance. A simple form of sensitivity analysis can be done to identify the critical elements; this analysis can be used to create a measurement plan for the real system, to check that it is working as desired. If it is not, corrective actions can be planned. In constructing the model, some simplifying assumptions will have been made; these assumptions can also be validated by making changes in the assumptions and again doing a simple sensitivity analysis.

The goal of this stage is to construct a model that reflects system behavior as accurately as possible; having done this, the model must be validated against actual observed system behavior as soon as portions of the system become available and can be measured in conditions similar to expected usage. This work is the subject of the second phase of modelling, as shown in Figure 7.14.

During system implementation, measurements should be made as soon as relevant portions of system and application are available. This makes it possible to refine the quantitative data used in the concept stage, and allow both architectural and sizing changes to be proposed. Changes can arise from external sources, such as the unexpected unavailability of a processor or a new, improved version of the software. Such changes can be wrapped into the model while it is being tuned to match reality. At the end of this

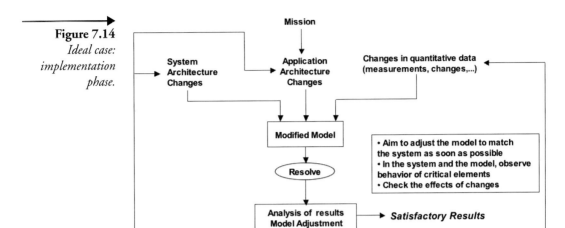

Figure 7.14
*Ideal case:
implementation
phase.*

phase, one is left with a complete system, and a reliable model of it (that is one that reflects real system to an appropriate degree of accuracy).

The model can then be used to assess the impact of changes—architecture, sizing and even mission—before they are made to the real system.

Ideally, the modeling activity does not stop when the system moves into operational use; rather, as the system evolves through maintenance, technology change,s or mission shift, it should be tracked by the model. If this isn't done, the model loses its utility as a predictive tool.

7.8.2 Modeling starting from an existing system

A far more frequent case is one in which an existing system needs to be extended or otherwise developed. We will illustrate this situation with an example in which a team has inherited a legacy system, designed elsewhere, and must extend its capabilities. To get it right, they choose to model the system to provide a basis for change. This is a challenging situation; before embarking on investigating the possibilities, the team must identify and capture concisely the system mission; its architecture; the architecture of the application; and the key metrics describing its behavior.

To build the model, the team will need to measure the system running the application. To choose the right things to measure, they need to understand how the application is structured, what it does, and what the system architecture is. This can be an interactive process; each measurement made can provide more insight into what's going on, so that understanding of the application and system architecture grows over time.

The task can be described in the following way:

- Having obtained a first-level understanding of the system, a first model is built. To be able to build this model, one requires a clear understanding of the dynamics of the system,[14] along with good estimates of some of the numerical values which parameterize that behavior.

- Then the model is adjusted to match the observed behavior of the system. This involves successive refinements of the structure of the model, and modifications to the values of the parameters.

- Once there is a good match, it is possible to study the effect of changes by introducing them into the model rather than the system.

- As the system evolves, the model must be kept up to date (for example, to match changes made through maintenance activities, or through the effect of replacing obsolete components).

Figure 7.15 illustrates these activities.

As shown in the figure, it is necessary to run the system with a workload as close as practical to the one called for by the system mission. One would observe system behavior with the twin goals of collecting data on system structure—how it is organized, the flow of data and control from one com-

Figure 7.15
*Modeling an
existing system.*

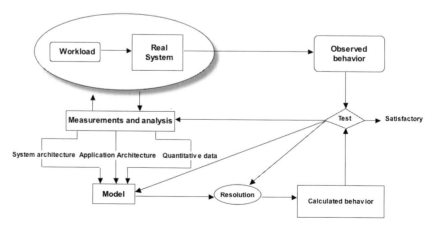

ponent to another, and so forth—and quantifying the numerical parameters of the system.

Understanding the system architecture and its dynamics can be accomplished by a variety of means, including:

- Interviews
- Code analysis
- Execution and I/O traces

Interviews are very helpful, but can only be done if the original system designers or implementors are available, which is often not the case. And even if the implementors are available, they are often unable to describe the system dynamics—even if each has a clear and deep understanding of the portion of the system that he or she implemented, it is rare for implementors to have a clear vision of the whole system. Thus, one must proceed by creating some initial hypotheses about how the system works, and checking these hypotheses carefully during the interviews. This is, clearly, an iterative process and one in which patience is necessary.

In the absence of the designers and implementors, one may have recourse to reading the source code of the application. By studying this, the application's operation should become comprehensible, and its demands on the system should become clearer. This type of review can lead to sufficient understanding of the system as a whole, so that a model can be constructed and iteratively refined. But reading (and understanding) the source for a large system is a challenging task.

As a last resort, traces—logs of the instruction and data addresses used by the program—can be examined. By varying the workload, one can begin to correlate changes in trace behavior with system activity. However, working backwards from traces to system behavior, with no source code and no access to designers or implementors, is extremely difficult and laborious.

These three approaches—interviews, reading the source code and examining traces—are growing more difficult as means of gathering sufficient information to allow the construction of a model.

As soon as the first version of the model has been built, it should be exercised with a workload and configuration equivalent to the system being observed, and its results compared with actual measurements. The divergences between modeled and observed results will lead to a further iteration of information-gathering: interviews, source analysis or trace creation and examination, and new measurements made on the system itself. These measurements will be made to confirm or refute hypotheses constructed to explain the model's behavior, or to obtain better estimates of the numerical quantities parameterizing the model—for example, the processor resources used for a disk or network I/O request.[15]

In constructing a model, a number of simplifying assumptions must be made. As the refinement of the model proceeds, these assumptions must regularly be reexamined in the light of observed system behavior, and themselves refined to allow the construction of a model that appropriately matches the observed system behavior. Similarly, the technical approach used in solving the model may need to change over time.

We must emphasize the fact that that selecting an appropriate abstraction level (or level of detail) is key in building a model for an existing system. The abstraction level must be set in accordance with the objectives of the performance study. One piece of advice to help set an appropriate abstraction level is to have some homogeneity in the model: the various components selected to describe the system must be of a similar level of accuracy and must have execution times of a similar order of magnitude.

7.9   Modeling Strategy

We now look at modeling strategy [KER99]. As we have said earlier, there are two major approaches to constructing performance models described as queueing networks: analytical models (whether exact or approximate) and discrete event simulation.

The analytical methods allow a simple expression or representation of the model, with the queueing networks' properties generally required to meet fairly strong constraints—for example, that they have no synchronization phenomena. Discrete event simulation, on the other hand, tends to result in somewhat more complex models, since the model must capture all the important behavior of the system. In general, a discrete event simulation model will have a significantly greater execution time than an analytical model.

Different models (and modeling technologies) offer varying degrees of accuracy and varying construction and execution costs. An appropriate compromise between these factors must be struck. The space available for choosing the compromise is illustrated in Figure 7.16.

A good model must have the following properties:

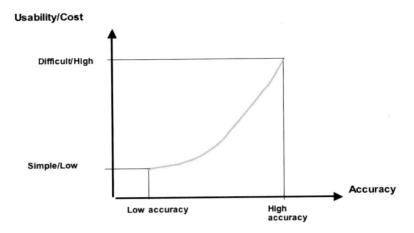

Figure 7.16
Search space for an
appropriate model.

- Utility
- Homogeneity
- Simplicity
- Comprchensibility

It should not be necessary to say much about *utility*; a model should be constructed to meet a specific need (who would construct a model to satisfy an unspecified set of requirements?[16]).

Homogeneity means that, in general, the various portions of the system should be represented to about the same degree of accuracy, and that the timescales involved in describing the system and its components should not cover many orders of magnitude. Thus, it would generally be inappropriate to describe in the same model the inner microarchitecture of a microprocessor and an approximate model of a TPC-C transaction.

Simplicity is important, since it makes the model robust and modifiable. A key purpose of the model is to see the effect of changes, so ease of modification (and confidence that the changes made reflect what we wanted to change) is important, and made more difficult by complexity.

Since a model is a representation of reality, it provides a means of communicating the system behavior between a number of people and teams. The model must therefore be *comprehensible* to a fairly wide range of specialists, who should themselves be capable of communicating with the modeling team leader to ensure understanding of system changes, or, in simple cases, to create a new model or edit an existing one. It is not helpful for only the modeling team to be able to modify the model.

There is therefore a necessary choice between the use of analytic models that have short execution times and fairly simple construction, but constrain the phenomena that can be modeled, and an approach requiring rather detailed descriptions with long execution times, but with no constraints on what can be modeled.[17]

In reality, information systems exhibit some phenomena that is straightforwardly captured by the analytical approach, and some others that can only be handled by simulation.[18] An appropriate response is to construct a hierarchy of models, in which analytic methods are used at the highest level of abstraction and simulation at the lowest, most detailed levels. As an example, Ethernet cannot be modeled using the analytical approach. The approach is to use discrete event simulation for Ethernet using typical distributions for message size (for the application being considered) and varying the load up to saturation. We then get a curve showing the behavior of Ethernet depending on the load (for the message population under consideration). The whole Ethernet subsystem can be then integrated into an analytical model as a single station whose service time depends on the utilization.

We can describe the steps of a defining a modeling strategy as follows:

- Examining each system component and deciding whether it should be modeled analytically or with simulation

- Defining an appropriate hierarchy of models, from simulation (if necessary) to analytic at the highest levels

- Defining the models and the parameters they require for characterization

- Obtaining numerical values for the parameters through either measurement or estimation (any estimates should be checked later)

- Evaluating and adjusting the models, progressing from lowest level up to the most complete

- Evaluating and adjusting of the whole model

At the end of the process, the resulting model[19] represents the system well enough, and changes to mission, configuration, sizing, hardware components etc can be studied on the model with confidence that the behavior it shows is a good prediction of what will happen on the system.

There are tools supporting these techniques. Operational analysis provides a first approach and only requires the use of simple calculations.

7.10 Operational Analysis

Operational analysis provides a first approach to modeling, being an easy-to-implement technique based on simple relationships between measurements taken from a system. Our description makes use of [JAI91] and [MEN02].

The concepts of operational analysis were identified by J.P. Buzen in 1976 [BUZ76] and refined by P. J. Denning and J.P. Buzen in 1978 [DEN78]. The motivation for the work was to bring structure to the study of time-sharing operating system performance.

The term operational simply means that the values used in the analysis are directly measurable:

- With a single experiment
- With a finite time duration

Operational analysis establishes relationships between the values measured (see below). It can be applied to any physical system, as illustrated in Figure 7.17, and has the benefit that its use allows checking of the self-consistency of the measurements made on a system.

For such a system observed for a finite time T, the values measured for any resource as well as for the whole system are: the number of arrivals (Ai),

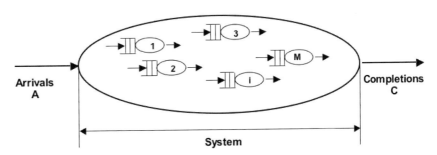

Figure 7.17
Operational analysis concepts.

the number of completions (Ci), and the time the resource was busy (Bi) during the observation period.

Let us precisely define the purpose of the system analysis and thus its limits. As shown in the figure, a system comprises some number of elements represented here as stations; these are called resources in the terminology of operational analysis, and each comprises a server and a request queue.

Operational analysis assumes that the following assumptions are true:

- Arrival/completion equilibrium—the total number of arrivals is matched by the number of completions (this assumption is known as the job flow balance or Flow Equilibrium Assumption)

- Stepwise change—the state of the system changes only as result of an event at a time, arrival or completion

- Resource homogeneity—the completion rate of a resource depends only on the arrival rate (provided the resource is not saturated); at saturation, the completion rate depends on the service time of the saturated resource

- Homogeneous routing—the routing of requests inside the system is independent of the state of the system

Figure 7.18 illustrates the various types of models.

Figure 7.18
Types of models.

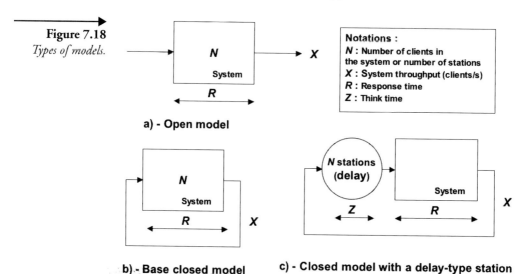

a) - **Open model**

b) - **Base closed model**   c) - **Closed model with a delay-type station**

Figure 7.18(a) shows an open model that receives requests, which it processes, and then produces outputs that are sent to recipients. There is no connection between the inputs and the outputs of the system. This captures the behavior typical of a Web server in the absence of any notion of session.

Figure 7.18(b) shows a basic closed model, in which the processing of an input request always produces a new input request.

Figure 7.18(c) shows a more realistic closed model. In this model, workstations (or, indeed, other independent systems) create requests for a server. Having generated a request, an individual workstation awaits a response. Once it has received the response, it waits for some time (the think time, denoted as Z in the figure) and then generates another request.

The values collected in an operational analysis (termed as operational quantities) for a resource (resource i) during a time (T) of observation are as follows:

- Arrival rate λ_i = number of arrivals/time = A_i / T
- Average throughput Xi = *number of completions/time* = C_i / T
- Utilization U_i = *total utilization busy time/time* = B_i / T
- Average service time S_i = *total service time/number of clients served* = B_i / C_i
- Total service demand D_i = $S_i V_i$ (client requests multiplied by the visit ratio to the resource, as explained below)

A_i, B_i, C_i, and V_i are thus the values which must be measured for each resource. V_i is defined as the ratio of the number of completions by resource i (C_i) and the total number of completions by the system, denoted C_o (thus $V_i = C_i / C_o$). C_o relates to the whole system; it is the global number of completions during the observation period T. X_o, which is defined as C_o/T, is the average throughput of the system. In other words, V_i is the number of visits to the resource i within the framework of the execution of a request.

These operational quantities are measured during a finite observation period. Values relate to a single experiment—one series of measurements of the system. The relations defined between them are called the **Operational Laws**. These relations hold only if all the measurements came from the same experiment.

The **Utilization Law** defines the *utilization* (sometimes called busy factor), which is defined as the fraction of time the resource is busy.[20]

$$U_i \quad = B_i / T = C_i / T \quad \cdot B_i / C_i$$

or

$$U_i = X_i \; S_i$$

The **Forced Flow Law** defines the average throughput of a resource in terms of the average throughput of the system.

$$X_i = C_i / T = C_i / C_o \quad \cdot C_o / T$$

or

$$X_i = X \; V_i$$

C_o is the number of completions over the period of observation, and C_i / C_o is the visit ratio V_i.

Little's Law defines the average number of clients (Q_i) of a resource with response time R_i and throughput X_i. For a closed system, it is expressed in the form:

$$Q_i - X_i \; R_i$$

For an open system, it is of the form:

$$N = XR$$

N is the number of clients in the system, X is the system throughput and R is the system response time (i.e., how long it takes for the request to traverse the system).

From these operational laws one can derive a formula which allows one to calculate the response time of a system. An interactive system is composed of two parts:

- A processing system (also known as the central subsystem)

- A collection of terminals submitting requests to the processing system and expecting responses from it

The terminals can be real workstations, or autonomous subsystems (such as ATM machines). The key feature of a terminal is that it is not shared between clients—that is, each client has a terminal and so no client ever has to wait to use it—so a terminal, in the modeling space, is an infinite server, and there is never any wait to use it. The central subsystem, on the other hand, is shared between all the clients. Figure 7.19 illustrates such a system.

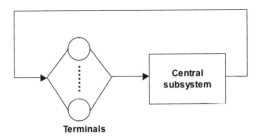

Figure 7.19
Interactive system model.

Terminals

A client/server environment perfectly matches our definition of an interactive system. Since, at this level, the arrival/completion equilibrium (or job flow balance) assumption holds, we can apply **Little's Law**:

$$Q = XR$$

Q is the total number of clients in the central subsystem, X is the system throughput, and R is the system response time.

Applying Little's Law to each resource, we obtain:

$$X\ R = X_1\ R_1 \quad + X_2 \quad R_2 \quad +... + X_M \quad R_M$$

If we divide both sides by the system throughput, X, we get the visit ratios. By then applying the conservation law ($V_i = X_i/X$) we obtain the **General Response-Time Law**:

$$R = \sum_{I=1}^{M} R_i V_i$$

In an interactive system, the users repeatedly generate a request and await its response. Having received a response, the user waits a certain amount of time (called think time, because of its origin in the behavior of real users connected to time-sharing systems). Since the response time of the system and its throughput will vary with the number of users, we seek a law connecting throughput, response time and number of users.

If the central subsystem has a response time of R, then the time for a request/response cycle is $R + Z$. Each user generates $T/(R + Z)$ requests in a time period T.

So system throughput, given N users, is:

system throughput = total number of requests/total time, or

$$X = \frac{N\left(\dfrac{T}{R + Z}\right)}{T}$$

And we can construct the **Interactive Response Time Law** as

$$R = \left(\frac{N}{X}\right) - Z$$

This law applies only to closed systems with delay-type stations.

Starting from these laws, one can effect a bottleneck analysis, in which the first step is to identify the most heavily-loaded resource[21] in the system. Since the resource utilizations are proportional to the service requests, the heaviest-utilized resource is the one with the highest service demand *Dmax*. This resource, which we indicate with the resource index b (b as busiest), is characterized by:

$$D_b = D_{max} = Max_i\{D_i\}$$

System response time and throughput, for a closed system with delay-type stations, are given by the following relations:

$$X(N) \leq Min\left\{\frac{1}{D_{max}}, \frac{N}{D + Z}\right\}$$

$$R(N) \geq Max\{D, ND_{max} - Z\}$$

Given the scope of this book, we will limit ourselves to simply pointing out the measurements on which the demonstration of these two formulae are based.

- Regardless of the resource considered, its utilization will always be less than one

- The response time of a system with N users cannot be shorter than the response time for one user; this defines the lower limit of system response time

- The Interactive Response Time Law allows us to convert a system response time to a system throughput and vice versa

For an open system, we can see that the throughput is limited by the most heavily loaded resource:

$$X(N) \leq \frac{1}{D_{max}}$$

For a closed system with delay-type stations, the two formulae (for throughput and response time) each define two asymptotes—one of these is a horizontal line, the other is a sloping line. The asymptotes for response time and for throughput both intersect at the same x-axis point (that is, both intersect at the same number of clients) and the intersection point corresponds to a system with some number of users N^* at which the system's performance is about to become saturated (the knee of the performance curve).

We shall illustrate the use of operational analysis by using it on the simplified system shown in Figure 7.20.

Figure 7.20
Interactive system example.

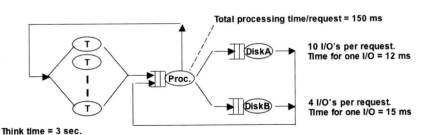

Total processing time/request = 150 ms

10 I/O's per request.
Time for one I/O = 12 ms

4 I/O's per request.
Time for one I/O = 15 ms

Think time = 3 sec.

This (vastly-simplified) interactive system comprises a number of workstations issuing requests to a computer system composed of a central processor and two disk subsystems (Disk A and Disk B). The think time at each workstation is 3 seconds. (Recall that all values are average values).

Processing a request requires 150 milliseconds of processor time, 10 I/Os to disk A and 4 I/Os to Disk B. Disk A has a service time of 12 milliseconds and Disk B's service time is 15 milliseconds

Knowing that for 10-client workstations the utilization of the processor is 0.4311[22], we wish to discover:

- The utilization of DiskA and Disk B

- The average response time for 10 users

- The bottlenecks and the asymptotes for response-time and throughput, along with the maximum number of workstations that can be supported before the system saturates

- How the asymptotes change if the processor is replaced by one that is twice as fast, along with the new maximum number of workstations which can be supported before saturation

7.10.1 Resolution of the problem

The visit ratios for one user request for the various resources of the server are:

$$V_{DiskA} = 10$$
$$V_{DiskB} = 4$$
$$V_{proc} = V_A + V_B + 1 = 15$$

The number of visits to the processor is the sum of the number of visits to Disk A and to Disk B, plus one, which corresponds to the transition to the workstation.

Service Requests $(D_i = S_i \cdot V_i)$ are:

$$D_{proc} = 150 \text{ ms}$$

$$D_{DiskA} = 12 \cdot 10 = 120 \text{ ms}$$

$$D_{DiskB} = 15 \cdot 4 = 60 \text{ ms}$$

Resource utilizations are deduced from the utilization law:

$$U_i = X_i \cdot S_i = X \cdot D_i.$$

That is to say:

$$U_{proc} = 0.4311 = X \cdot D_{proc} = X \cdot 0.150$$

from which we obtain:

$$X = 0.4311/0.150 = 2.874 \text{ requests/second}$$

$$U_{DiskA} = X \cdot D_{DiskA} = 2.874 \cdot 0.120 = 0.3449$$

$$U_{DiskB} = X \cdot D_{DiskB} = 2.874 \cdot 0.060 = 0.1724$$

The **average response time** for 10 users is determined by the following formula:

$$R = N/X - Z$$

That is to say:

$$R = 10/2.874 - 3 = 0.48 \text{ second}$$

With regard to the analysis of the behavior of the system, wee determine that **the processor constitutes the bottleneck** since

$$D_{max} = D_{proc} = 0.150 \text{ second}$$

Response time asymptotes are obtained using the formula:

$$R \geq \text{Max} \{D, N \cdot D_{max} - Z\},$$

where D_{max} corresponds to the processor. The lower limit of the response time is:

$$R_{min} = D_{proc} \, D_{DiskA} + D_{DiskB} = 0.15 + 0.12 + 0.06 = 0.33 \text{ second}$$

The asymptotic behavior is defined by the line:

$$N \cdot 0.15 - 3$$

Throughput asymptotes are obtained using the formula:

$$X \leq \text{Min}\{1/D_{max}, N / (D + Z)\}.$$

The upper limit for throughput is:

$$X_{sup} = 1/0.15 = 6.67 \text{ requests/second}$$

The behavior is defined by the line :

$$N / (0.33 + 3)$$

The maximum number of workstations that the server can support before the beginning of saturation is:

$$N^* = (D+Z)/D_{max} = (0.33 + 3)/0.15 = 22 \text{ workstations}$$

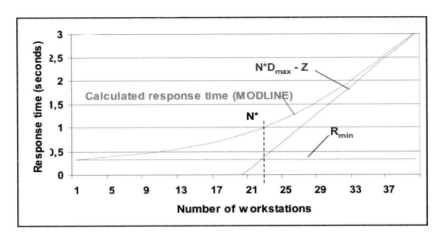

Figure 7.21
Interactive system behavior.

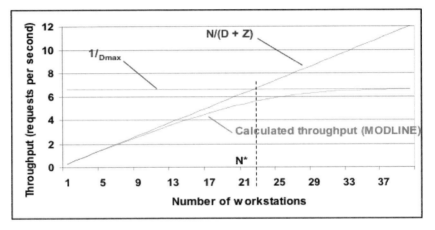

Figure 7.21 shows the response time and throughput asymptotes calculated by means of operational analysis, along with the behavior curve calculated by the MODLINE (QNAP2) tool.

When the processor is replaced by one which is twice as fast, the most heavily loaded resource is Disk A (0.120 seconds).

The asymptotes become:

a) the response time is

$$R_{min} = D_{proc} + D_{DiskA} + D_{DiskB} = 0.075 + 0.12 + 0.06 = 0.255 \text{ second}$$

The asymptotic behavior is defined by the line:

$$N \cdot 0.12 - 3$$

b) for throughput

$$X <= Min\{1/D_{max}, N/(D+Z)\}$$

The upper limit of the throughput is:

$$X_{sup} = 1/0.12 = 8.33 \text{ requests/second}$$

The behavior is defined by the straight line:

$$N/(0.255 + 3)$$

The saturation knee is with:

$$N^* = (D+Z)/D_{max} = (0.255 + 3)/0.12 = 27 \text{ workstations}$$

Figure 7.22 shows the throughput and response time asymptotes, along with the calculated behavior from MODLINE(QNAP2).

Working through this very simplified example allowed us to show the use of operational analysis, demonstrating how the use of some simple measurements and simple calculations can obtain some very useful system properties. Note that the system model could be much more complex; for example, including the network used to connect the workstations to the server, or a communications controller, without affecting the reasoning.

7.10.2 **Taking measurements**

As we have just seen, operational analysis establishes relationships between values measured during a single experiment; from these measurements, one may draw useful conclusions about the system's behavior, and make simple projections of the effects of changes.

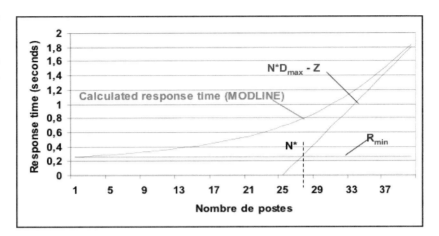

Figure 7.22
Interactive system behavior after doubling processor performance.

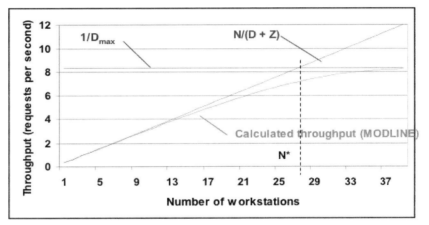

We have seen that it is necessary to quantify the parameters of performance models. There is a large variety of performance analysis tools; however, we will not discuss these, contenting ourselves with mentioning that standard systems (UNIX and Windows) provide integrated instrumentation capable of providing a number of measurements useful for performance analysis, allowing one to analyze the systems behavior, construct a model, or take measurements suitable for use in operational analysis. The Windows 2000 measurement tool is *Performance Monitor*, while the UNIX tool is *sar* (System Activity Report). We will provide a short overview of the Windows tool, based on articles published in Windows 2000 Magazine [NT00].

Performance Monitor provides the ability to measure and record a number of aspects of system performance:

- For logical and physical disks:

    - Number of transfers per disk per second
    - Average length of a disk transfer
    - Average length of a request queue
    - Utilization

- For processors:

    - Utilization (with the details of the percentages spent in user mode and system mode)

- For memory:

    - The number of pages swapped per second
    - The average number of bytes of memory available
    - The utilization of the paging file

- For the system:

    - The average length of the processor queue

- For the network:

    - The utilization

Given that one takes the precaution of subjecting the system one wishes to study to a repeatable workload (one provided by a workload generator would seem to be a sensible choice) for a long enough time (compared to the processing time necessary to handle the transactions one wishes to study) that the assumptions of operational analysis hold (equality of the number of arrivals and completions), then reliable figures will be obtained.

These figures can be fed to a model to answer questions about system balancing or used for operational analysis. Using the operational laws, it is possible to derive figures from the measurements and to evaluate the effect of configuration changes (increasing the number of disks, using faster processors.) on the saturation knee.

For the system to be balanced, it is generally considered that a load factor of around 60 percent (an empirical rule) and that the presence of more than two clients in the request queue of a physical disk suggests that the disk is a bottleneck. These are examples of *empirical rules* governing system sizing; we look at these rules in the next section.

7.11   **Empirical Rules of Systems Sizing**

In the second half of the 1960s, Gene Amdahl formulated a list of empirical rules for sizing systems. Jim Gray and Prashant Senoy recently revised these rules [GRA00]; our discussion is based on their work.

Because the technologies used in computing systems is developing very quickly, it has deep consequences for systems architecture and thus on how to dimension a balanced system. As an example, Moore's Law predicts that the density of integrated circuits doubles roughly every 18 months. This has the following consequences:

- Every ten years, the storage capacity of a DRAM memory increases 100 fold

- A system will need an extra bit of physical address space every 18 months

Illustrating the second point, systems had 16 to 20 bits of physical address space in 1970, and around 40 bits by the turn of the new century. If this trend continues, we will need 64 bits of physical address by 2036 or so.

Disks have also undergone a significant technological revolution, which perhaps strangely (as we have discussed in earlier chapters) represents performance disadvantages despite providing increased density and capacity. Here are some examples: disks increased in capacity by a factor of ten during the decade 1990-2000. In 2002, SCSI disks existed with capacities greater than 70 GB, while speeds increased by a factor of 3 over 15 years, and throughput by a factor of 30 over the same period. Disks with rotational speeds of 15,000 rpm were available in 2003, with internal throughputs of up to 80 MB/sec. Average access time dropped by a factor of only 3 over the same 15 years, from 18 milliseconds to 6 ms. The physical size of the disks reduced by a factor of 5 over this period, with the cost reaching about $0.05 by 2002.

Even with the improvement in access time, the capacity of disks has grown so much that it takes about 45 minutes to completely explore a disk (in 2002). Such an activity is required when restarting a system after a crash (UNIX *fsck*, or file system check), to identify errors in the on-disk data that describe which blocks belong to each file and which are on the list of free blocks. Blocks that do not belong to a file and are not on the free list are "orphan" blocks, and must be identified before disk usage resumes. The 45 minutes represents an unacceptable amount of time for a system restart, which is why operating systems have started providing journaling file systems (one in which any change to the metadata—the data which describes the structure of the data on the disks—is treated as a transaction, which can be completely and safely cancelled in the event of a crash halfway through a modification, or replayed to safely re-effect the changes).

Unfortunately, the improvement in disk density was not matched by improvements in accesses per second, nor by throughput. From the numbers just cited:

- The ratio of disk capacity to the number of accesses per second increases by a factor of 10 every 10 years
- The ratio of disk capacity to the disk throughput increases by a factor of 10 every 10 years

The result of this is that disk access becomes an increasingly critical resource in a system. System architects use the following techniques to counteract this problem:

- Intensive use of caching techniques
- The use of log-structured file systems, which replace multiple updates to portions of a file with the writing of large, contiguous, sequential blocks of data at the end of a file (with updates to the allocation tables reflecting the updates)
- The use of disk mirroring (RAID 1) rather than RAID 5—an update on a RAID 5 storage subsystem requires the reading of data distributed across several disks to allow parity calculation and then the writing of both the data and the parity information

While data storage has always been arranged hierarchically in data processing systems, it is only recently that managing the hierarchy has become automated. Historically, there has been a price per megabyte ratio of 1:10:1000 between memory, disk and tape ($1 of tape holds $10 of disk data and $1000 of memory data).

Automation was introduced in the form of robots to avoid the need for humans to handle tapes. The cost of the robots affects the effective cost of tape; further, the cost of RAM has dropped by a factor of 10 in 10 years. As a result, the price per megabyte ratios are now considered to be roughly

- 1 for tape
- 3 for disk
- 300 for RAM

As can be seen, the preferred storage place for information is moving from tape to disk, and to some extent from disk to memory, although the use of memory presents the problem of memory loss when electrical power is lost, as well as the problem of providing access to the memory by another system, in case o the system containing the memory fails.

Thus, these changes mean that now it is not unusual to see the use of a disk mirror (RAID 1) as backup, with the mirror being remote to avoid failure in the event of a catastrophe.

The cost of administering storage tends to exceed the cost of the storage hardware, a phenomenon already seen with PCs, in which the cost of hardware plus software is less than half of the total cost of ownership of the machine.

In 1980, it was reasonable to have one person allocated per gigabyte of data (which cost around $1 million to buy). In 2000, the ratio is about one person per 30 TB of data (which also costs abut $1 million).

Because of the changes in the capabilities of system components and changes in their relative costs, Amdahl's rules for the sizing of a system need revision. The revised version is as follows

- *Parallelism*: if a task has a sequential portion taking S to execute and a parallelizable portion which takes P to execute, then the best possible speedup is $(S + P)/S$.

- *System balance*: a system needs about 8 MIPS of delivered processor performance for each MB/sec of I/O throughput. However, a TPC-C workload will cause a processor to average around 2.1 clocks per instruction executed, while TPC-H will let it run at about 1.2 clocks per instruction. The difference between the workloads must be taken into account in assessing the delivered MIPS.

- *Memory/Processor*: a system should have about 4 MB of memory for every MIP delivered by the processor (this used to be 1 MB; the trend to increasing MB/ MIPS is expected to continue).

- *I/O*: a system will execute about 50,000 instructions per I/O operation for a random I/O profile, and about 200,000 instructions per I/O operation for a sequential I/O profile.

The first of these rules is unchanged form the original formulation; since you cannot remove the sequential portion of a task by parallelizing it, that provides an upper limit to the speed up available through parallelizing.

The second rule relates processor power and I/O throughput, and again is not changed. However, with increased complexity in the available processors, the 8 MIPS must refer to the *delivered* MIPS in the application, not the MIPS available in principle. There is almost a factor of two in the clocks per instruction observed on an Intel IA-32–based server between a transactional and a decision support workload—thus, the transactional system needs nearly twice the raw processor power for a given I/O throughput than does a decision support system with the same I/O throughput.

The third rule couples processing power and memory size; this has changed by a factor of 4 from the original formulation. Several factors explain this increase:

- Software functionality has increased, and thus so has its size

- Intensive use of memory-based caches speed up disk performance

- RAM costs have sharp reduced

While processor performance and memory capacity are increasing much faster than disk access time and throughput (and processor and memory costs are falling faster), the trend of increasing MB/MIPS is expected to continue.

The fourth rule couples processing capability and I/O throughput. The original formulation quoted a flat 50,000 instructions per I/O, but with the intensive use of disk caches in memory, the number of instructions per I/O has grown to about 200,000 per I/O.

For networks, the rules of thumb are:

Measuring Processor Performance

These laws all use instructions per second as a measure of processor performance. As we have seen in the section on benchmarks, this is not a very powerful characterization. At best, one can use MIPS to compare the performance of machines of identical architecture and varying resources and organization on identical benchmarks. However, this limitation does not affect the general usefulness of the laws, since the ratios are simply indicators of rough orders of magnitude. However, as we have noted, it is worthwhile to consider the MIPS requirements to be *delivered MIPS* in the application, rather than *available MIPS*.

- Gilder's Law (1995)

- Installed throughput triples every year

- Interconnect throughput quadruples every three years

- I/O

- A network message costs 10,000 instructions plus 10 instructions per byte

- A disk I/O costs 5.000 instructions plus 0.1 instructions per byte

- The cost of a SAN message is 3000 clocks plus 1 clock per byte

George Gilder predicted in 1995 that the installed throughput of networks would triple every three years for the next 25 years, a prediction which has held true up to now. However, the rise of the Internet and the effect of deregulation on the world of communications caused the trend to accelerate, and around the turn of the century it was considered that the tripling occurs annually.[23] Technological improvements mean that component throughputs improve at more or less the same rate as semiconductor densities—quadrupling every three years.

For I/O, the numbers refer to a server using its own resources. The cost of an I/O operation over the network to a disk on a remote server is not included in the number.

Although there has been progress in network hardware—including moving some processing to the network card, using DMA, usingf specialist circuitry for checksum calculation, and so forth—the cost of a network message is still higher than the cost of a disk I/O. This suggests the use of disks as network caches.

The cost of a SAN message shows an additional optimization over the cost of direct disk I/O (in terms of server path length, but not necessarily in terms of latency). The numbers show why there is interest in using a SAN to connect cluster nodes.

The final rules cover the management of RAM-based disk caches. In doing a comparative analysis of the costs of storage and related access times, Jim Gray arrived at the following rules:

- *Five-Minute Rule* for random I/O: for a disk whose pages are accessed randomly, cache the pages that are re-used within a 5-minute window

- *One-Minute Rule* for sequential I/O: for a disk whose pages are accessed sequentially, cache the pages that are re-used within a 1-minute window

These rules express the lifetimes of cached data, and suggest increases in cache sizes.

7.12 **Capacity Planning**

This section touches on the issue of predicting how loaded a server will be. It discusses techniques developed during the early days of data processing. The techniques' objective is to satisfy the needs of future use by predicting the extensions needed by the system, based on measurements of the existing system. This approach allows future expansion to be planned.

In doing the work, various system parameters must be taken into account: processing capability, memory size, capacity of the storage subsystems and of the disks themselves, and communications subsystem capabilities.

There are two major approaches, depending on whether or not a system model (as discussed earlier) is available:

- An approach based on the existence of a model of system behavior, a characterization of the application, and a forecast of expected changes to the application (the desired parameters are injected into a model, and the needed system parameters are obtained through an iterative process, as discussed later)

- An approach based purely on system measurements and their expected changes

When a model is available, the task is very similar to the modeling task as it is already described—one must understand system operation and have a reasonable prediction of future needs.

Figure 7.23 illustrates the principle of capacity planning.

Figure 7.23
Capacity planning.

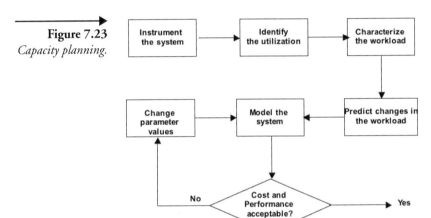

Instrumentation allows one to characterize the real-world utilization of the system and translate this into a loading for the various system elements.

To the extent that one can precisely describe the change in load in terms of its effect on the various resources, it is possible to predict the change in loading and (if a model is available) to predict the performance of the system under the new workload. If it turns out that system performance is unacceptable, the model can be used to investigate changes to system configuration with the aim of achieving acceptable performance. This is an iterative process, which should allow identification of a good compromise.

In the absence of a model, one must depend upon measurement tools to gather system information and tools to help manipulate the measurements. Such tools can suggest system changes based on observed system behavior changes; thus, they embody an implicit and empirical model of system behavior.

There are many load prediction tools; the quality of the results they produce is strongly dependent upon the level of understanding of system operation that their designers have captured from their years of experience.

7.13   Endnotes

1. Clearly, processor performance contributes to system performance. And some systems benchmarks do not exercise all the system components - for example, the communications subsystem.

2. In accordance with the nature of the book, we will not present any benchmarks aimed at scientific (numerically-intensive) applications.

3. SPEC defined the SDM91 (Software Development Multitasking) benchmark, with the goal of characterizing the efficacy of multitasking, multiprocessor systems for program-development applications with a large number of users. The benchmark is based on the simultaneous execution of program-development scripts, which contain the classic commands used in developing software (e.g., make, cp, diff, grep, man, mkdir, spell, etc). Two test environments were specified: one using a file as input and the other using captured keystrokes. The software development style represented by this benchmark is somewhat out of date, making the benchmark unrepresentative; as a result, it has fallen into disuse and few results have been published (with no results published after September 1995). At the end of 1996, SPEC announced that it was working on a new benchmark, SPECsmt97 (smt for Systems Multi-tasking), but this effort appears to have ceased.

4. Peak performance (sometimes called advertised performance) is the speed reached on a program specially written to exhibit the best possible (or maximum) performance. Sustained performance is supposed to represent the performance which can be expected on real-world applications. Some cynics describe peak performance as the performance level that the system is guaranteed not to exceed.

5. This properly reflects how a company operating worldwide must work - in such a situation the notions of day (in which the production OLTP system is active) and night (when the decision support database is updated) are meaningless.

6. Recall that we have previously shown that a simple intuitive optimization of TPC-C can result in around 98 percent of the transactions accessing only "local" data - i.e., they do not result in any interaction with other nodes.

7. We estimate the raw performance of the system as the product of the number of processors in the system and the SPECint2000 performance of each processor. Such an estimate is completely theoretical, and takes no account whatsoever of the interprocessor interactions that occur in a real system. Although this sort of approach is used in the domain of scientific processing, the number obtained must be looked upon as a peak value, or perhaps as a marketing performance.

8. This is an observation based on experience. While we touch on the matter later in the chapter, the key issues in our warning really come down to a strong recommendation to look before you leap—getting an understanding of the key system components and how they interact can often be captured in a manner appropriate for handling by formal methods. The extra detail needed for simulation should, generally, be added after the big picture is understood, and only when necessary. Such extra detail can be difficult to understand (when represented in the model) and difficult to validate.

9. There are specialist areas outside server modeling - especially in embedded systems - where quite the opposite is true - for example, DSP experts typically describe the mathematics of their problem in MatLab, and compile them automatically to C for use in deployed systems. The same practices apply to folk designing systems to control automotive engine control systems.

10. The use of these tools makes the discussion more concrete; however, the discussion is not constrained in any way by these tools; the reader will find that the methodology can be implemented straightforwardly using other tools.

11. It should go without saying that to change the system mission to what a proposed system can do is not a recommended approach.

12. It may be necessary to keep modeling even longer, into the maintenance phase of the system, if quantitative or qualitative changes are a possibility then.

13. By the dynamics of a system, we mean the logical flow of data and control within the system to perform the required actions. As an

example, consider the logical processing of a File System request: search the cache for the required block; if absent, look at the file's inode to identify the required disk blocks; form an I/O request (i.e., construct the command chain for the needed I/O); and send the I/O request to the I/O supervisor. The I/O supervisor issues the I/O request on a command per command basis, handles I/O interrupts, etc.

14.   It is worth mentioning at this juncture the applicability of the statistical discipline known as Design of Experiments, along with the analytical processes such as ANOVA (analysis of variance) and cluster and correlation analysis, in making sense of the results of any experiment.

15.   While there are instances of requirements driving the construction of documents that never lead to anything useful, or that could not possibly lead to anything useful, it is best in a technical field to limit one's activities and work on things which are useful.

16.   While the benchmark specification calls for this availability, it does not provide any verification procedures to ensure the test system has this property, nor does it offer any metrics for availability. Only examination of systems configurations can allow one to form an opinion on the actual availability capabilities of these systems.

17.   In practice, simulation capability (in terms of the ability to get results from the models) is constrained by two factors—the size of the task of programming the model and the runtime necessary to have the model produce plausible results (or, in the domain language, to "converge").

18.   It is very difficult or impossible to construct robust, credible mathematical models of complex subsystems using a theoretical approach. Rather, one builds discrete event models that capture their characteristics, and then essentially curve-fit a mathematical model of appropriate accuracy to the data obtained.

19.   The complete model, which might embody a hierarchy of submodels.

20.   By definition, the utilization is less than or equal to one (utilization is often expressed as a percentage). It is only in the case of human beings, and engineers or managers in particular, that one hears stories of utlizations above 100 percent. As a rule of thumb, for information systems, the utilization should not get above 60 percent or so for good system behavior.

21.   Delay-type stations are not to be considered in bottleneck analysis, since such a station, by definition, cannot be a bottleneck.

22.   The value of 0.4311 is chosen arbitrarily for this exercise; in the real world the utlization is a measurement that should be easily obtained using the performance tools available on most systems.

23.   This prognostication has not been renovated since the great telecom crash; probably, by 2003, the curve has returned to match Gilder's predictions.

8

DBMS and Server Architectures

The objective of this chapter is to analyze and compare architectural options for servers and look at the architecture of database management systems. A DBMS has a privileged relationship with data storage (magnetic disks), broken down into two areas: data management and the caching of data. The nature of the interconnect between system and disk—whether it be a single system, an SMP, or a multinode system such as a cluster or MPP—provides a further dimension of characterization alongside the architectural choices. DBMS vendors have made architectural choices; we will examine these choices, along with their characteristics and also look at the architectures of selected parallel databases.

We will conclude the chapter with a look at applications characteristics and the choice of architecture with respect to scalability.

8.1   Architecture Models

We can distinguish three major classes of architecture in the area of system-disk interconnect. Figure 8.1 illustrates these options.

The diagram shows the three main architectural choices as regards disk connection. There is a fourth possibility, of sharing memory between nodes. This is the approach used by the IBM Sysplex design, a mainframe cluster system covered in Chapter 5.

In the *Share Everything* approach, all the processors in the system run under the control of exactly one copy of the operating system, and an I/O operation can be initiated by any processor to any disk. This approach is typical of SMP systems (symmetrical multiprocessors).

The *Share Nothing* architecture has each node running under the control of its own copy of the operating system, with exclusive access to the disks

Figure 8.1
Architecture options in system-disk interconnect.

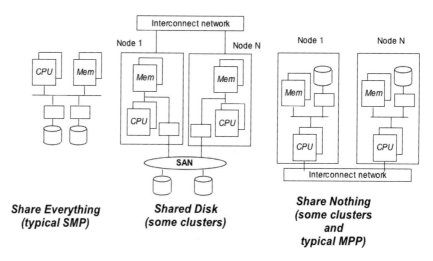

attached to the node. This model is typical of MPPs, and is adopted by some cluster systems.

The *Shared Disks* architecture again has each node controlled by its own copy of the operating system, but in this model the disks are shared so that any processor can initiate I/O to any disk. This model is adopted by some cluster systems.

In the diagram for *Shared Disks*, we used a Storage Area Network (SAN) as the means by which the disks are attached to the system. A SAN—discussed in greater depth in Chapter 6—could have been used in the *Share Nothing* case as well. We should note that in the case of a *Share Nothing* system, some means must be provided to "recover" disks normally attached to a node that has failed.

It is also worth mentioning that in the *Shared Disks* architecture, it is not unusual for each node to have some private disks as well as access to the shared disks. Such a private disk (or disks) is known as a *system disk*, and will generally contain the operating system plus disk space to support demand paging, and often the most frequently-used applications as well.

These three models reflect different perspectives on load balancing and data sharing. The analogy of customers queued up in lines waiting to be served lets us see the differences between the models. This analogy is represented diagrammatically in Figure 8.2, from [PAP98].

This analogy maps the system behaviors into models of customers (processes or threads) waiting for agents at service counters (processors) to pro-

Figure 8.2

Illustration of the differences between the models.

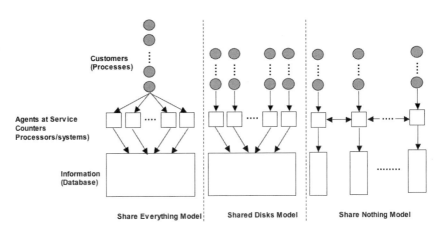

Customers (Processes)

Agents at Service Counters Processors/systems)

Information (Database)

Share Everything Model   Shared Disks Model   Share Nothing Model

vide them with a service. To fulfill the service requests, the agents have to access information files (databases).

In the *Share Everything* model, all customers wait in a single, common queue. As soon as an agent at a counter finishes some work, the first customer in the queue presents himself at the counter and the agent busies himself with satisfying the customer's request. We see that this approach provides natural load-balancing, with customers (processes) being automatically distributed to agents (processors) according to their availability. Every agent can access all the files (the database is equally accessible to every processor). Synchronization between the agents for updating the files takes place by direct interagent dialogue (the processors share memory). The system's capacity is limited by the number of agents one can arrange to have working in parallel and the bandwidth they need to have access to the files (the system is limited by the number of processors supported by the SMP and by disk I/O bandwidth).

The model *Shared Disks* doesn't work quite as straightforwardly. There must be another agent, not shown, who has the job of directing customers to the appropriate queue, so that the work remains reasonably balanced between counters. In computing systems, this role is fulfilled either by software that measures the load on each node and directs requests appropriately, or by load-balancing equipment. Again, every agent has access to all the files (each node can see the whole database). Synchronization for file updates requires conversations between the various counters; in the information processing system this conversation is carried over the interconnect network, and is less efficient than an equivalent dialog through shared memory.

The *Shared Nothing* model also has a non-automatic allocation of customers to agents. Because each agent has access to only a subset of the files, a customer must wait in the appropriate line (e.g., the line corresponding to the first letter of his or her surname). Load-balancing is strongly affected by the distribution of files to agents and the distribution of customer requests with respect to this data. Access by an agent to files owned by another agent is possible, but requires data exchanges between the agents.

Such a request can take two forms:

- *Data Shipping*. The agent handling the request for the customer asks the other agents to send him the needed data. The first agent executes the requested operation and manages any needed data updates by sending the new data back to the owning agents.

- *Function Shipping*. The agent handling the request for the customer forwards that request to the appropriate agent, who will, upon completion, return appropriate data, if needed, back to the originating agent.

As we shall see, DBMS which have chosen the *Shared Disks s* approach choose the *Data Shipping* methods, while those who selected *Share Nothing* tend to choose *Function Shipping*.

Regardless of which of these choices are made, message exchange on the interconnect network is required and is a source of inefficiency.

Table 8.1 compares the characteristics of the various models.

As shown in the table, the *Share Everything* model (which corresponds to SMP system architecture) has excellent properties except for limited scalability and the difficulty of ensuring availability. As we have discussed, in the event of hardware or software failure in an SMP, one must generally halt the system and reboot.

The *Shared Disks* model provides attractive high-availability properties and, to a lesser extent, also has good scalability. In practice, system performance is strongly dependent upon the data update rate from the applications, since if several nodes seek to update the same data, synchronization operations and data exchange between nodes must occur; these occur over the interconnect network, whose performance is very similar to that of a standard local-area network.

Table 8.1   *Compared characteristics of the various models*

	Share Everything	Shared Disks s	Share Nothing
Advantages	■ Simplicity for both interrequest and intrarequest parallelism ■ Good use of resources ■ Natural load-balancing ■ Efficient interprocess communication through coherent shared memory ■ Solution rapidly becoming commoditized at the low end	■ Good availability ■ Good scalability (100 or more processors) ■ Low cost because of reuse of standard components ■ Good load balancing (heavily shared data can be replicated)	■ Good availability ■ Extremely good scalability (several hundred processors) ■ Low cost because of reuse of standard components
Disadvantages	■ Difficult to ensure system availability ■ Limited scalability (upper limit of a few tens of processors)	■ Interaction between nodes needed to synchronize data updates ■ Saturation of the interconnect network because of node-disk traffic ■ Cost of maintaining coherence across multiple copies of the data (if replication is used), especially if there are frequent updates	■ Difficulties in load-balancing ■ Difficult to administer and optimize because of data partitioning ■ System performance strongly dependent on interconnect characteristics ■ Cost of parallelizing requests, even for simple requests ■ Cost of maintaining coherence across multiple copies of the data (if replication is used), especially if there are frequent updates

The interconnect between nodes and disks is shared by all the nodes and can constitute a bottleneck.

Some internode cooperation mechanism must be provided to allow load-balancing. This can be as simple as watching the amount of load on each node. To avoid having frequently accessed data bottleneck the system, it is possible to replicate the data (i.e., make multiple copies of it and distribute these across multiple nodes). This of course gives rise to some difficulties when the data must be updated; the use of a two-phase commit solves the problem, but at a cost in performance.

The *Share Nothing* model offers, as does *Shared Disks*, attractive availability and scalability properties. However, in these systems the interconnect network between nodes and disks rarely poses a performance problem, since its capacity is normally matched to node performance rather than overall system performance.

Again, the performance of such a system is strongly dependent on both the data distribution across the nodes and the distribution of requests for the data. Since a client must in general be allocated to a specific node, this means that either there is *a priori* knowledge of the binding between client request and node, or that a further agent must be involved to select the appropriate node.

Administering the data in a *Share Nothing* system is a significant task, and the optimizing the overall behavior of the system depends strongly upon it being done well.

Frequently-accessed data can be replicated, but as before, coherent update of all copies will require the use of an expensive two-phase commit protocol.

In summary, we can characterize the *Shared Disks* and the *Shared Nothing* architectures as follows:

- *Shared Disks* relies on the assumption that the node-to-disk interconnect is fast enough to avoid the need to distribute data

- *Share Nothing* relies on the assumption that the data is distributed so as to optimize I/O bandwidth and data handling capacity

Table 8.2 shows the architectural choices supported by the principal DBMS.

Table 8.2   *Architectural choices supported by the principal DBMS*

Architecture Model	Share Everything (SMP)	Shared Disks (some clusters)	Share Nothing (some clusters and MPP)
DBMS	IBM DB2 Informix* Microsoft SQL Server Oracle Teradata (NCR) Sybase	IBM DB2 for OS/390 and z/OS Oracle Real Application Cluster	IBM DB2 for Linux, UNIX and Windows Informix Microsoft SQL Server

*   Informix was bought by IBM in 2001. XPS is the parallel version of Informix (Extended Parallel Server), a product positioned by IBM for Decision Support systems, particularly on MPP systems.

As shown in the table, all the DBMSs have been tuned to work on an SMP. However, only DB2 (on mainframes) and Oracle have also decided to support *Shared Disks*. All the others have decided to support *Share Nothing*. Later in this chapter, we will look at the operations of Oracle and DB2 (for standard systems).

> **Distributed Databases**
>
> Some DBMS versions said to be tuned for parallel architectures are simply distributed databases, in which multiple instances of the DBMS execute on multiple nodes and cooperate to provide the effect of a single database. This is the case for Microsoft's SQL server, for which the descriptive term federated databases is used.

We should make the following three comments on these architecture models:

- In *Share Nothing*, if the disk connections are specific to each node, other connections must also be provided so that, in the event of a node failure, another node can take over the management of the failing node's disks. These alternate connections are not used in the course of normal operation.

- The *Shared Disks* and *Share Nothing* are simply schematic representations; in practice, choice of system architecture is driven by choice of

DBMS. If one's hardware is a *Shared Disks* system, it is straightforward to make this a suitable host for a DBMS, which assumes *Shared Nothing* by using software to partition the disks. In the same way, a *Shared Nothing* platform can simulate a *Shared Disks* system by using the Remote I/O abstraction. In this case, the OS of a node redirects I/O requests for disks not directly connected to the appropriate node. Compared to a physical *Shared Disks* implementation, a Remote I/O-based solution results in a significant loss of performance, as much for its impact on latency (two OS interventions and forwardings) as for its impact on bandwidth (greater use of the interconnect).

■ Given the introduction of SAN storage networks, the distinction between *Share Nothing* and *Shared Disks* becomes strictly functional, since every node connected to the SAN potentially has access to all the storage resources on the network. Thus, any distinction is made at the level of the OS.

> **Significant remark:** *Shared Disks* and *Share Nothing* architectures depend on both the architecture of the node-disk interconnect and the operating system. Some operating systems simply do not support the concept of *Shared Disks*. As noted above, if the OS imposes an undesired model, it is possible to layer the desired architecture on top by partitioning (to convert *Shared Disks* to *Share Nothing*) or by using Remote I/O (to convert *Share Nothing* to *Shared Disks*), although the latter brings substantial inefficiencies.

As we indicated in our opening words in this chapter, some systems also offer memory shared between cluster nodes. IBM's Sysplex is one such system. Sysplex's architecture is supported by a number of IBM data management products: IMS (basic hierarchical data management system); VSAM (index-sequential), and DB2.

Table 8.3 summarizes the advantages and disadvantages of this approach.

This approach has had but one, very limited, success beyond IBM's Sysplex. The reasons for this are mostly market-size driven (the DBMS vendors, in particular, do not wish to target a small market), together with the concerns raised by the single point of failure provided by the shared memory. As we have noted earlier, in such a system the failure of a node can result in failure of the complete system, while for clusters, proper robustness and high availability is a natural strength.[1]

Table 8.3 *Advantages and disadvantages of the shared memory approach*

Advantages	Disadvantages
■ Good performance because of communication by shared memory ■ Scalability (depending on the implementation of shared memory)	■ Shared memory constitutes a single point of failure ■ No standards in this domain ■ Very limited availability of software to make use of this architecture ■ Limited willingness on the part of software vendors to embrace this architecture

8.2 Problems of Parallel DBMS

Parallel versus Distributed DBMS

Let us first make a distinction between a parallel DBMS and a distributed DBMS. A parallel DBMS seeks to make maximum use of the resources of a system through the use of parallelism, while a distributed DBMS aims to make a collection of databases (whether homogeneous or not) supported by different systems look like a single coherent database.

Two system components have a key effect on system performance in a DBMS environment: processors and I/O (both disks and controllers). Two further components, memory (in terms of capacity and access time) and communications, also have an influence (note that here, by communications, we mean the interconnect network as is found in MPPs and clusters, not the communications subsystem dealing with remote systems and client workstations). In this section, we concentrate on processors and I/O.

The goal of parallelization is to improve performance, whether in throughput or in reduced response times, by increasing the number of components in a system and operating them concurrently. However, as we saw in Chapter 1, searching for a high degree of concurrency brings its own problems: the overhead involved in managing the parallelism, execution-time dispersion,[2] and difficulties in balancing the workload.

In a system with a high enough load that it is saturated, we can observe two types of behavior:

■ *Processing saturation*: the situation is then said to be CPU bound

■ *I/O saturation*: the situation is said to be I/O bound

If all the data were held in memory, the natural situation would be to be CPU bound. But in practice, fetching the data needed to complete a request can require frequent disk access (for example, to the indices) and one is more likely to be in an I/O-bound situation. Although, as we have seen, processors roughly double in performance every 20 to 22 months (or every 18 months if you believe the industry's puff)—a much faster growth rate than for disks—system architects still seek to make systems CPU bound. While disk capacity growth has indeed been remarkable (a factor of 100 over the past decade), bandwidth has only improved by a factor of 30, and access times by no more than a factor of 2. As noted earlier, the increase in capacity has a negative effect on system performance, because for a given system storage capacity requirement, fewer disks are needed, reducing available parallelism and directing a larger number of requests to each disk.

To process a complex request, there are two possible parallelization approaches [MOH94]:

- *Parallel processing*: the request is broken up into atomic requests, which are executed in parallel

- *Data parallelism*: the data is partitioned into subsets, which are processed concurrently

Both these forms may be implemented on any of the architecture models presented in the preceding section   *Share Everything*, *Shared Disks* and *Share Nothing*.

For parallel processing, a request can be decomposed into an *execution plan*, which generates a partially-ordered collection of operators (such as indexing, data access, sorting and join). The number of operators in an execution plan depends on the complexity of the request; the theoretical degree of concurrency available is the number of operators. In practice, available parallelism is less than this, because of dependencies between the operators. Further, the operators are executed inside threads, and the cost of initializing these, and of communicating and synchronizing between them, also must be taken into account.

In practice, parallel processing is used in tandem with data parallelism.

Data parallelism, which in general offers a much higher potential parallelism than parallel processing, is obtained by subdividing a table (or relation) into a number of partitions—perhaps ten or so. The request is then executed against each partition concurrently. Clearly, each such request can make use of parallel processing providing further concurrency opportunities. A detailed description of the techniques behind parallelizing requests is beyond the scope of this work.

We now describe the internal architecture of two commercially important DBMSs, each corresponding to a different system architecture choice.

8.3   Architecture of Parallel DBMS

In this section we first introduce the principles behind a parallel DBMS and then look at the architecture of two such DBMSs—IBM's Universal Database Extended Enterprise Edition for Linux, UNIX and Windows (*aka* DB2 Parallel Edition) and Oracle Real Application Cluster (*aka* Oracle Parallel Server).

As we have said before, we can distinguish two forms of parallelism in a server

- Inter-request parallelism
- Intra-request parallelism

In inter-request parallelism, the DBMS simultaneously executes several requests submitted by different clients. In intra-request parallelism, a request from a single client is transformed into a number of subrequests, which can likely be carried out simultaneously. Obviously, these two forms of concurrency are not exclusive; it is general practice to manage requests from multiple clients, each request being broken down into subrequests.

The diagrams in this section make the assumption that the system has enough processors to be able to execute all the work given to them at any given moment.

Figure 8.3 illustrates inter-request parallelism.

A typical case in which inter-request parallelism arises is in transaction processing in which the DBMS and, possibly, the transaction monitor (e.g., Tuxedo) are asked to manage simultaneous client transactions.

Intra-request parallelism breaks up one request so it can be executed concurrently in several processes. As we saw in the preceding section, data

Figure 8.3
*Inter-request
parallelism.*

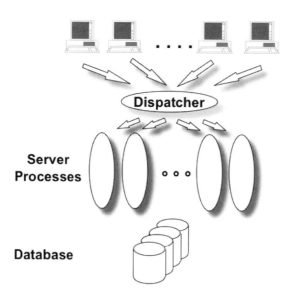

parallelism has agreater potential concurrency than parallel processing. Data parallelism implies the *partitioning* of the data.

Figure 8.4 illustrates, according to [RUD98], the concurrent execution of a request making use of data partitioning.

For simplicity, we show here the request broken into just three steps; the execution times shown are chosen just to indicate the (rather theoretical) performance improvement available from this approach. In the strictly

Figure 8.4
*Intrarequest
parallelism,
illustrating
partitioning a
database.*

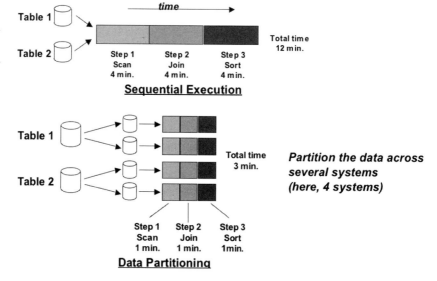

sequential system, each step lasts four minutes for an overall time of twelve minutes. By partitioning each of the two tables into two subtables, we obtain four data subsets on which the operations may be executed concurrently. Assuming perfect parallelization (with zero cost of concurrency management and synchronization), each step now operates on a quarter of the data and lasts a quarter of the time, allowing the execution of the request to be also reduced fourfold to just three minutes.

Partitioning the data can be combined with pipelining execution of the request, as is shown in Figure 8.5.

Figure 8.5
Combining data partitioning and pipelined execution.

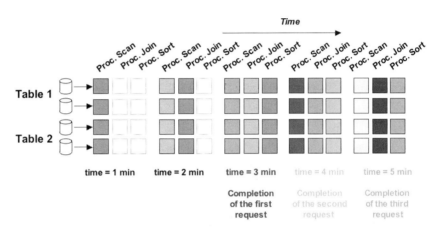

On the assumption that we have twelve processors available in the system, and that the request can be broken down into the three steps outlined above, we can combine data partitioning and parallel processing in the following way. We have four copies of each of the Scan, Join and Sort processes running for a total of twelve processes on the twelve processors. As soon as each process has finished processing a step from one request, it is able to start processing the next request. On the assumption of no conflict between requests, and in an absence of contention between the requests, we can now do multiple requests in a pipelined manner, providing an overall theoretical speed-up of a factor of 12.

It should be made clear that the factor of 12x is a theoretical upper limit for this example.

8.3.1 Data partitioning

Data partitioning is one of the most important issues within a parallel database, and is particularly significant in the case of *Share Nothing* architectures. In a *Shared Disks* architecture, partitioning data also has an effect on system performance if it is possible, through judicious directing of requests to nodes, to create an affinity between node and data to improve the effects of data caching. This arranges for given data to be repeatedly accessed by a given node and the data cache on that node has, therefore, an increased probability of finding the data in memory rather than on disk.

Partitioning seeks to achieve the following goals:

- *Reduction of system load at the level of disk access.* Several resources operating in parallel are put at the disposal of the system to reduce the likelihood that applications access the same resources
- *Load balancing.* Processing is distributed across the nodes matching the partitioning of the data
- *Capacity increase.* The system's work capacity is increased through the ability to have nodes work in parallel

Data can be partitioned in either of two ways:

- Vertical partitioning
- Horizontal partitioning

Figure 8.6 illustrates these two partitioning methods.

Figure 8.6
Horizontal and vertical data partitioning.

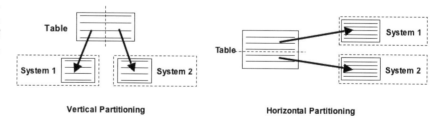

Vertical Partitioning   Horizontal Partitioning

Partitioning is based on an attribute—a field or a column of a tuple—called the *partitioning key*. The partitioning key is not necessarily the same as the database key.

With vertical partitioning, the attributes of a relation are distributed between a number of systems (two systems in the diagram). Using this style of partitioning can have an effect on how applications are programmed. There are two cases to consider—whether the partitioned data is or is not managed by a distributed DBMS. The latter case can arise if the partitions are managed by different DBMSs, or if the DBMS in use does not support distributed databases. As long as the DBMS supports distributed databases, the partitioning is invisible to the application. But if it does not, the application must be written to explicitly take account of the partitioning. In both cases, any updates to the partitioned data will have a performance impact because of the need to have a two-phase commit.

In horizontal partitioning, tuples are distributed across nodes according to the value of the partitioning key.

Vertical partitioning can only be done with the applications' needs in mind. Horizontal partitioning does not have the same constraints at an application design level.[3]

Figure 8.7 illustrates some methods of data partitioning.

Figure 8.7
Examples of methods of data partitioning.

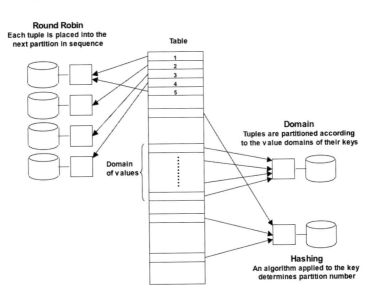

It should be clear that the choice of a partitioning algorithm is of great importance to the behavior of the system. A characteristic required of any algorithm is that it use results in balanced partitions; unbalanced partitions result in performance degradation.

We will examine some properties of the algorithms presented in Figure 8.7.

- Partitioning the data based on value domains of the key allows optimizations because it is possible to steer requests to an appropriate node through examination of the key. However, this approach is open to misbalancing the partitions and thus the system load. To illustrate this partitioning method, assume the keys are all names and that partitioning is done on the basis of the first letter of the names: thus, names beginning with A to E could be assigned to the first partition, F to J to the second, and so on.

- Round Robin balances partitions automatically. On the other hand, load-balancing is not guaranteed since that depends on the distribution of accesses to the data in the partitions.

- The hashing-based approach raises the problem of what hash function to use. An example which generally provides useful results is as follows: look upon the key as being a variable length integer binary number; and compute the hash function as the result of long division by a prime number. A hash function should both be quick to compute and result in well-balance partitions. A hash- based partition will not work optimally for a search based on a value domain for the key—for example, for keys with first letter in the range A to E).

There are other partitioning algorithms, too. As an example, the list approach consists of regrouping the tuples whose keys are members of a list of values; e.g., with the country name as key, collecting up within a single partition (as example, "Europe") all the tuples whose country is a member state of the EEC.

It is also possible to use a combination of methods—for example, first by field and then hashing within fields.

We should note that in addition to partitioning, we can seek to gain extra performance by replicating the data—that is, placing the same data on more than one disk. Read access times will improve since the accesses may be distributed to occur concurrently on multiple disks. Again, however, updates require the use of expensive two-phase commit protocols.

Readers wishing to know more about partitioning may refer to [UNW93].

For a *Shared Nothing* architecture, there are (as we have noted previously) two ways for a node to access data managed by other nodes. Figure 8.8 illustrates these functional models.

Figure 8.8
Functional models in a share nothing architecture.

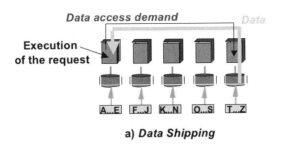

a) *Data Shipping*

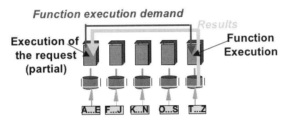

b) *Function Shipping*

In the *Data Shipping* model, a node needing to perform an operation on data managed by a distant node sends a request to that node asking for the data. The distant node performs the accesses and forwards the data to the servicing node over the interconnect network. Other than the remote data access, all processing needed to complete the request is performed on the servicing node.

In the *Function Shipping* model, a node needing to perform an operation on data managed by a distant node sends a request to that node to perform the required operation (or function) on that data. That node accesses the data and performs the requested operation, and then sends the results data back to the servicing node over the interconnect network. Thus, the execution of a single request can be result in work being executed on a number of nodes.

As one might expect, the relative advantages and disadvantages of these two approaches depends on the amount of data needing "exporting" and the amount of processing "exported".

8.4   IBM DB2 UDB Enterprise

This section describes the architecture of IBM's DB2 Universal Database Enterprise – Extended Edition (DB2 UDB EEE) for parallel architectures, specifically the version with the Data Partitioning Option intended for loosely-coupled machines operating under Linux, UNIX, and Windows. Equivalent versions intended for IBM systems exist, both for the z Series mainframes and the integrated iSeries servers (AS400s).

For legibility—and where there is no risk of ambiguity—we will shorten this name (DB2 UDB EEE with DPF) to the simpler DB2.

We noted earlier that DB2 has chosen a *Share Nothing* architecture, and uses (as does Informix) *Function Shipping*.

For partitioning, DB2 uses a hash function along with a parameterizable means of distributing data among partitions. Of course, this description as well as the illustrations are based upon DB2 documents (white papers, manuals) from IBM. Figure 8.9 illustrates DB2's partitioning approach.

Figure 8.9
Data partitioning in DB2.

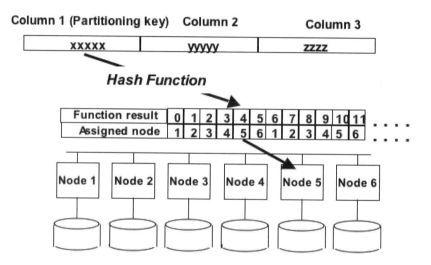

Partitioning is based on the value of one of the attributes of the relation. This attribute, called the partitioning key, is not necessarily the relation's key. The hash function returns values in the range {0..4095}. For each of these values, a table provides the corresponding node for placement of the tuples. Thus, the partitioning key has the hash function applied to it, the result is used to index the table, and the entry thus accessed specifies the node to which the tuple belongs.

Figure 8.10 illustrates the implementation of the concept of *Function Shipping* in DB2.

During its compilation phase, DB2 associates several execution plans with a single request and selects the one having the minimum execution time. The cost function for plan selection takes into account both the

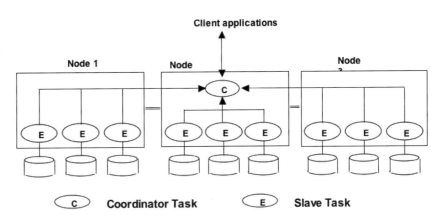

Figure 8.10
Function shipping in DB2.

inherent parallelism in the execution plan and the cost of inter-node communication. Thus, DB2 takes account of data partitioning.

The execution of a request is carried out under the control of a task known as a Coordinator. This task distributes the processing work to slave tasks, and collects the results.

Some examples of request optimization:

- Parallel search on a relation

  SELECT Customer_name FROM Accounts WHERE Balance > 2000

  DB2 creates a Coordination task and slave tasks. There is an instance of the slave search task on each node where there is a table partition.

- Aggregation

  SELECT CustomerAgency, COUNT (*) FROM Accounts WHERE Balance > 2000 GROUP BY CustomerAgency

  Compiling this request generates slave tasks. These select the relevant tuples in the database partitions, gather them sorted by the value of their CustomerAgency field, compute a local total for each such group and pass on the result of the selection along with the local total to the coordinator task. This computes the overall aggregation from the data provided by the slaves.

Figure 8.11 illustrates various join strategies exploited by DB2.

A local join makes use of two table partitions co-residing on the same node.

Figure 8.11
DB2 join strategies.

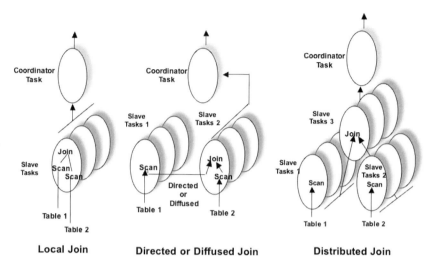

In a directed or diffused join, the table partitions are on separate nodes. Tuples selected on one node must therefore be directed to the other node so that it can perform the join. A *directed join* is the situation in which the other node is known in advance. When the other node is not known in advance, the tuples are diffused to other nodes. This last case, called *distributed join*, is a tree-organized distributed join in which slave *scan* tasks send their results to slave *join* tasks.

DB2 offers a number of facilities along with its multiprocessor implementation:

- Administration tools
- A single system image (as far as the database is concerned)
- A database loading utility which can operate in parallel
- Parallel backup and restore (in parallel with production use)
- Ability to restructure the database concurrently with production use
- High-availability functionality

The usable high-availability features depend on the platform capabilities.

While IBM has published results (in 2000) for the performance of DB2 on a 32-node Windows 2000 system (each node comprising four processors), for TPC-C (transaction-processing) and TPC-H (decision support) using a terabyte of data, most systems have in practice significantly fewer nodes.

8.5 Oracle Real Application Cluster

In this section we present the concepts behind and architecture of Oracle 9i Real Application Cluster, or RAC for short. We shall use the term RAC for readability. Previous versions were known as *Oracle Parallel Server*.

RAC chose the *Shared Disks* philosophy.

A short discussion on Oracle terminology is necessary before delving into the architecture of RAC. Of course, this description as well as the illustrations are based upon RAC documents (white papers, manuals) from Oracle. An *Oracle instance* is the association between the processes implementing Oracle and a global data zone, called SGA (System Global Area). In a non-RAC version of Oracle, there are as many Oracle instances as there are open databases. In RAC, several instances can share the same database. Figure 8.12 illustrates these points.

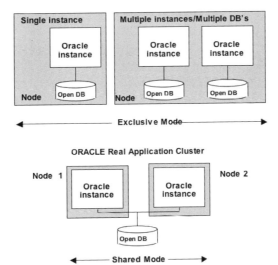

Figure 8.12
Illustration of Oracle terminology.

Note that, for simplicity, the diagram shows just two nodes; RAC supports many more nodes than this, as in configurations used for the TPC-C transaction processing benchmark.

RAC allows several instances to share a single database.

Figure 8.13 shows the general structure of an Oracle instance.

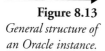

Figure 8.13
*General structure of
an Oracle instance.*

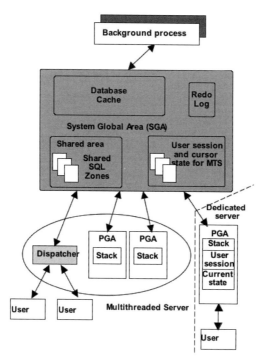

This diagram shows both the structures associated with a user connected to Oracle by means of a dedicated server and the structures associated with users managed by a multithreaded server. In the dedicated server, the PGA (Program Global Area) is a data structure is associated with the user. The PGA contains user information: the stack (holding the nested procedure call linkage and parameter-passing information), along with session-related information and the cursor.[4]

In the case of a multithreaded server, a PGA is also present for each user but contains only a subset of the dedicated server PGA, with session and cursor state being held in the shared SGA. The database cache contains the most-recently accessed data blocks as well as updated data blocks that have yet to be written to disk. The Redo Log contains information that allows transactions that updated the database to be replayed. The shared memory area contains information such as that associated with users who have all asked for execution of the same SQL statement.

Figure 8.14 shows the structures associated with a multithreaded server.

The multithreaded server allows the sharing of a small number of processes between multiple users. It uses an Oracle-specific implementation of the thread concept. Threads, as we have noted previously, are a more effi-

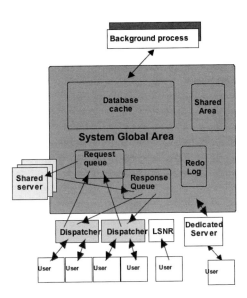

Figure 8.14
Structure of a multithreaded Oracle instance.

cient implementation of concurrency than processes because of lower overheads (resulting from the lower number of processes to be managed) and lower-cost thread switching (compared to process switching).

The necessary multiplexing between the users and the shared servers is implemented by the dispatcher process. Two message queues, one for requests and the other for responses, provide the interface between the dispatcher process and the servers. The LSNR (Listener) process awaits requests from users, and connects them upon request to either a dedicated server or to a dispatcher process.

Figure 8.15 shows Oracle's background processes.

The processes shown implement Oracle's major functionality; their roles are as follows:

- arch (*archive*). Archiving process that records the Redo Log. The database state may be reconstructed using this journal to replay transactions on a backup copy of the database. This recovery is associated with an instance.

- ckpt (*checkpoint*). A checkpoint process that signals dbwr that a checkpoint (or recovery point) is to be done and updates the database files as well as the control files.

- dbwr (*database writer*). A process that asynchronously writes cache blocks which have been modified to disk. In the context of OPS, the

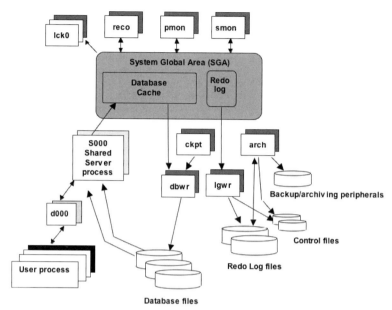

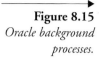

Figure 8.15
*Oracle background
processes.*

dbwr of one instance writes to disk the data blocks required by other instances.

- lgwr (*log writer*). A process that allocates space in the log files and also writes journals.

- pmon (*process monitor*). A process that ensures the recovery of a user's process in the event of failure.

- reco (*distributed transaction recovery*). A process that ensures recovery of transactions in the event of network or system failures.

- smon (*system monitor*). A process that ensures the recovery of an instance.

- lock0 (*lock process*). A process that manages locking; up to 10 lock processes may be used.

- d000 (*dispatcher*). A collection of processes that provide the multiplexing of user requests among the server processes.

- s000 (*server*). A collection of processes that support the execution of user requests.

The following pair of techniques are used to improve transaction processing performance:

- *Fast Commit/Deferred Write.* During a transaction commit, Oracle only updates the log. The database proper is updated only when modified blocks are written back to disk.

- *Group Commit.* Log updates for several transactions are gathered up so that recording several commits requires just one log update. In other words, commit is delayed until enough have been encountered, or until a specified time quantum has expired; the log file is then updated with just one I/O operation.

Figure 8.16 shows the architecture of RAC.

Figure 8.16
Architecture of RAC (Oracle 9i).

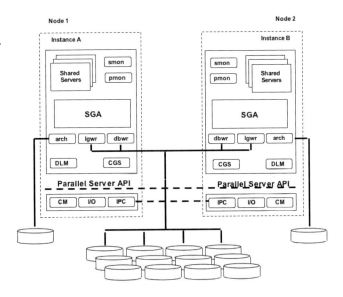

In this diagram, two Oracle instances, A and B, are executing on two nodes (node 1 and node 2) and are sharing the same database. As each instance has its own SGA, which is basically a cache, a cache coherence protocol must be implemented between the two Oracle instances. Management of the parallel environment is provided by the two principal components of RAC: PCM (*Parallel Cache Management*) and CGS (*Cluster Group Services*).

PCM uses DLM (*Distributed Lock Management*) to coordinate access to resources required by the instances; DLM is also used to coordinate access to shared resources such as the data dictionaries (metadata), journals, and so on. CGS interworks with the Cluster Manager to supervise cluster state.

RAC interfaces with the platform by means of a specific API, the *Parallel Server API*. Providing the basic services under this API (CM, for *Cluster Manager*, I/O, and IPC) is the responsibility of the platform provider.[5] CM watches the state of the nodes forming the cluster and tells the software using the cluster the identity of the component nodes.

The diagram does not depict the Oracle background processes, although it does show a typical configuration in that each system has its own archiving disk storage.

From a conceptual point of view, one can say that RAC implements a cache coherence protocol. The basic idea behind the protocol is that only one instance at a time can modify a storage block. Thus, a block being modified by one instance and needed by another instance will be communicated to the second instance. In RAC, the name *ping* is used to denote this communication. In early versions, a ping implied that the block was to first be stored on disk before being read by the second instance. The performance impact of this process can easily be imagined. From Oracle 8i onwards, however, some optimizations (described later) were implemented.

The locking processes (**lock0**) manage distributed locks, which make it possible to ensure coherence of storage blocks between the various instances. A lock protects one or more storage blocks. Intuitively, the more blocks protected by one lock, the more likely it is that a request for a block will require a ping. Since this operation means that all the modified blocks covered by the lock will be communicated to the requesting instance—not just the wanted block—it is said to result in a *false ping*. Thus, a balance must be struck between the cost of managing many locks and the cost of having too many false pings.

The optimization of RAC was based upon the idea of reducing the cost of managing cache coherency (the term *cache synchronization* is also used). This is the key objective of the *Cache Fusion* concept introduced with Oracle 8i, which is illustrated in Figure 8.17.

Four cases are handled to reduce overall ping cost:

■ *Read/Read*. Instance A wishes to read, on behalf of a user, a storage block recently read by Instance B that is in B's SGA;

■ *Read/Write*. Instance A wishes to read, on behalf of a user, a storage block recently written by Instance B that is in B's SGA;

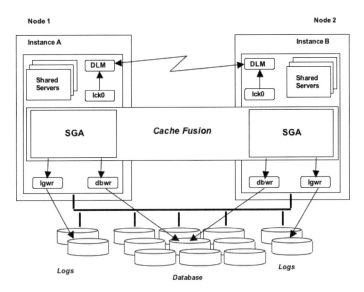

Figure 8.17
Cache fusion concept.

- *Write/Read.* Instance A wishes to write, on behalf of a user, a storage block recently read by Instance B that is in B's SGA;

- *Write/Write.* Instance A wishes to write, on behalf of a user, a storage block recently written by Instance B that is in B's SGA.

The Read/Read case does not require any coordination between the instances; instance A may simply read the storage blocks into its own SGA from B's SGA (i.e., using the interconnect network) or using a disk read operation. Of course, had the block been modified (and not yet written back to disk), coordination would be necessary.

Note that this scheme is based on the assumption that an inter-SGA exchange over the interconnect network is cheaper than accessing disk. Any such advantage is more substantial when the interconnect is optimized, such as in the case of an MPP, or a cluster using high-performance interconnect such as VIA (discussed in Chapter 2).

In the Read/Write and Write/Write cases, a coordination between the instances is necessary to ensure consistency (read/write) or integrity (write/write). In either of these situations, the current possessor of an up to date version of the data sends it to the requester over the interconnect network. This saves the two disk I/Os implied by a ping. RAC implements appropriate data redundancies to ensure recoverability in the event of a failure.

In the case of Write/Read, the instance that last read the data block (and has a copy in its SGA) sends it over the interconnect network to the instance that wants to modify the data. This avoids a read access to the disk.

It should be noted that RAC uses two types of locks:

- Locks specific to transactions, or *transactional locks*
- Locks used to manage the parallel cache, or *parallel locks*

Both versions of Oracle, parallel and non-parallel, treat transaction-specific locks the same. In other words, there are two types of locks, and they are handled separately. Parallel locks are managed by Oracle instances, and not by transactions. A transaction being executed on a node can update a tuple in a block, even if another tuple of the block is being updated by a transaction being executed on another node.[6] Thus, information relating to transactional locking is bound to the storage block and accompanies that block as it migrates between instances.

There are other types of locks beyond transactional locks; since such locks do not have anything to do with the control of parallelism, we have lumped them all together under the rubric of *nonparallel locks*. These concepts are illustrated in Figure 8.18.

This figure shows two lock spaces: parallel and non-parallel. Transactional locks belong to the nonparallel space, as do other locks used by Oracle (other than the management of the parallel cache), such as locks relating to the data dictionaries.

Figure 8.18
Concepts of nonparallel and parallel locks.

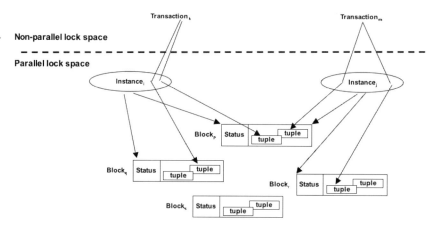

As shown in the figure, transaction K locked two tuples: one in block p and another in block q, while transaction M also locked two tuples, one also in block p and the other in block r. When a block, such as block p, migrates from one instance to another, the transactional locks travel with it.

The efficiency of inter-node synchronization is a key element of performance. Such synchronization depends on three major factors:

- The number of messages required for each synchronization
- The frequency of synchronization
- The latency of each communication

The number of messages required is reduced through the use of services (Global Enqueue Services and Global Resource Directory), which allow the management of a resource to be quickly localized.

Two elements work together to reduce the frequency of communication:

- Dynamic migration of resources, based on data access profiles—that is, the node which accesses the data most frequently. By migrating the data to its most frequent user, the majority of accesses may be made local.
- The use of two levels of locking (that is, transactional locks and parallel locks).

There are several ways to optimize RAC, among which are:

- *Identify data locality.* Partition transactions and the data they most frequently accessed so that inter-instance migration is minimized (that is, ping minimization).
- *Minimize false pings.* The ideal situation for this is that one parallel lock protects exactly one block. As noted earlier, however, a balance must be struck between the cost of managing many locks and the cost of false pings.

Completing our discussion of RAC, we will briefly describe how it ensures continuity of service (continuity of service as a general topic is covered in Chapter 10).

We should note that Oracle introduced the concept of partitioning in version 8. The provision of partitioning does not require application modifications. The goals of partitioning are to optimize performance as a function of the application characteristics by exploiting locality. Partitioning is handled by the DBA (*Data Base Administrator*)—a burden requiring that the DBA has a good understanding of the applications concerned and their usage profiles.

As far as an application is concerned, the failure of a node is transparent: the application migrates to another node, and connections with the database are automatically re-established. This continuity requires that the applications be transaction-based. The failure of an instance (perhaps through failure of the node running it) abandons all transactions in the course of execution.

In RAC, the recovery logic can be described at a high level as the following sequence:

1. Several RAC instances are active on a number of nodes.

2. A node fails; its failure is detected, and connections between the clients of that node and its instance are migrated to instances on surviving nodes.

3. The Cluster Manager (CM) and the Cluster Group Services (CGS) reconfigure themselves to eliminate the failing node. During this process, new service requests from clients are suspended, as are requests in the process of being handled (until recovery is completed).

4. The lock database is reconstituted, and the database and the locks associated with resources are redistributed to the surviving nodes.

5. Cache recovery and exploitation of the logs are done.

6. Access to the database is once more permitted while recovery continues with *Fast-Start Rollback*.

The resulting configuration has a lower performance than the original system; if that had N nodes, the degradation is about approximately $1/N$ and varies with application profile.

Recovery takes a few minutes.

As for other parallel DBMSs, successive RAC versions support ever-larger configurations. To provide perspective on systems configurations, the following may be helpful.

In January 2003, the best published systems performance results for Oracle (i.e., the Top Ten in terms of performance) were:

For TPC-C:

- an 8-node HP Proliant DL-580-PDC cluster with 4 processors per node

for TPC-H:

- 100 GB with a 4-node HP AlphaServer ES45 Model 68/1000 cluster with 4 processors per node
- 300 GB with a 4-node HP AlphaServer ES45 Model 68/1000 cluster with 4 processors per node
- 3000 GB with a 2-node Sun Starfire Enterprise 10000 with 64 processors per node (a result from April 2001)

Even if in practice the number of nodes deployed is rather lower, looking at the top ten results for Microsoft SQL Server (Top Ten in January 2003) shows that configurations with a large number of processors were measured for TPC-C—three cluster configurations of the HP Proliant DL760-900 with an 8-processor node and having successively 16 nodes (for 128 processors), 24 nodes (for 192 processors) or 32 nodes (for 256 processors).

There are no SQL Server cluster results published for TPC-H.

As written in Chapter 7, the basic characteristics of TPC-C make it scale well on clusters. However, the number of nodes deployed in production clusters for mainstream dataprocessing is much lower than the numbers used in TPC-C benchmark exercises.

8.6   Summary: DBMS Architecture Comparisons

In this section we summarize the characteristics of the various DBMS architecture options.

Parallel DBMSs have the dual goals of performance improvement and availability. As we discussed in Chapter 1, performance can be increased by either speed-up or scale-up; and an ideal parallel system has the following two properties:

- *Linear speed-up.* A system has linear speed-up if providing N times more hardware resources allows a given problem to be completed in N times less time.

- *Linear scale-up.* A system has linear scale-up if providing N times more hardware resources allows a given problem of N times the size to be completed in the same time.

In general, we want scale-up for transaction systems and speed-up for decision support. We will cover both characteristics under the name of scalability.

We have already looked at the relationship between architecture and scalability. But the characteristics of the applications themselves also affect scalability, as shown in Figure 8.19.

To characterize an application, we use the two dimensions of the degree to which the database may be partitioned, and the rate of updates to the database.

Figure 8.19
How application characteristics affect scalability.

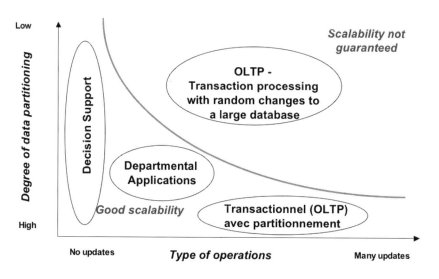

For reasons of efficiency and security, it is usual that the database used in a decision-support application is distinct from one used as a production system in the running of a business. A decision-support database is read-mostly.[7] It does need occasional updates; these may be done using data in the production database or from external sources, and the updates can be performed while the decision-support system is not in use (for example, at night). If the database needs to be continuously updated, that can often be done in a grouped manner so that logs are copied and the updates applied as a single operation, rather than as a sequence of operations.

For such decision support systems, higher degrees of partitioning lead directly to greater scalability.

By their definition, departmental applications partition both data and processing. The barrier to good scalability is the need for access to data common to several departmental systems. This is worsened by the need for updates to common data to use a two-phase commit.

The same thinking on partitioned data applies to transaction processing. The better the locality of the transactions, with respect to data partitioning and the nodes managing the data (*Share Nothing*) or having almost exclusive affinity (if *Shared Disks*), the better the scalability.

Transactional applications with no locality working with very large databases are unlikely to have good scalability.

Table 8.4 summarizes the relations between application characteristics and architecture approaches.

Table 8.4 *Comparing Application Characteristics and Architecture Approaches.*

		Decision Support	Departmental Transaction Processing	Partitioned Transaction Processing	Transaction Processing
Share Everything	Advantages	■ Intra-request parallelism provides speed-up ■ Requests may easily be optimized	■ Inter-request parallelism provides scale-up	■ Not applicable	■ Efficiency (scale-up)

Table 8.4   *Comparing Application Characteristics and Architecture Approaches. (continued)*

		Decision Support	Departmental Transaction Processing	Partitioned Transaction Processing	Transaction Processing
	Disadvantages	■ Limited maximum number of processors	■ Limited maximum number of processors ■ Not failure-resistant	■ Not applicable	■ Limited maximum number of processors ■ Not failure-resistant
Shared Disks	Advantages	■ Intra-request parallelism provides speed-up ■ Data partitioning not needed	■ Intra-request parallelism provides speed-up ■ Data partitioning not needed	■ Efficiency of transaction processing	■ Intra-request parallelism provides scale-up ■ Data partitioning not needed
	Disadvantages	■ Disk interconnect a potential bottleneck ■ Data partitioning needed for performance increase ■ Difficult to optimize requests	■ Disk interconnect a potential bottleneck	■ Partitioning makes applications difficult to design	■ Disk interconnect a potential bottleneck ■ Data partitioning needed for performance increase ■ Difficult to optimize requests
Share Nothing	Advantages	■ Intra-request parallelism provides speed-up	■ Inter-request parallelism provides scale-up	■ Efficiency of transaction processing	■ Inter-request parallelism provides scale-up
	Disadvantages	■ Data partitioning needed for performance increase ■ Difficult to optimize requests	■ Difficult to optimize requests	■ Partitioning makes applications difficult to design	■ Partitioning makes applications difficult to design ■ Controlling data distribution makes database administration difficult ■ Difficult to optimize requests

8.6.1 Share Everything architecture (SMP)

Within the limits of its configurability, this architecture provides an attractive mix of good scale-up and speed-up;[8] its major weakness is its inability to survive failures without a restart.

8.6.2 Shared Disks architecture

This architecture does not require data partitioning, making system administration very straightforward. It offers good speed-up. Its major weakness is its disk interconnect, which can be a bottleneck (in both hardware and software). This issue can be avoided by data partitioning and/or data replication, although replication causes difficulty for updates.

8.6.3 Share Nothing architecture

This approach offers attractive scalability properties in both speed-up and scale-up. Its major weakness is the need to partition the data, and the resultant difficulties in administration. Also, the system performance is very dependent on data distribution and so for some applications the data must be redistributed.

8.7 Endnotes

1. Having said this, we must comment again that it is possible to make such shared memory systems failure resistant by modifying the software so that every update to the shared memory is done in a transactional manner (i.e., maintaining ACID properties). Unfortunately, this makes the implementation even more specialized and further reduces its attraction to software vendors. In the case where the system vendor is also a database vendor, providing the transactional updates to shared memory can be done, making the system much more failure resistant.

2. A simple term for a complex issue: in searching for the highest practical amount of parallelism, the work is broken up into ever-finer "atoms". However, it is very difficult to make these atoms all the same size - and performance is usually set by the time for the longest atom.

3. We should note here that when a transaction requires updates to data in more than one partition, a parallel DBMS needs to imple-

ment a two-phase commit protocol between its different instances (that is, the DBMS instances managing the various affected partitions) in order to maintain the ACID properties of the database as a whole. This version of a two-phase commit is a little less damaging to performance than the general case between heterogeneous DBMS's.

4. A cursor is a concept in SQL (Structured Query Language) identifying a set of ordered tuples; this concept has been created for interfacing with languages that do not support operations on sets of objects. A cursor can be viewed as a type of pointer that allows a program to get sequential access to a set of tuples returned by a SELECT order. Thus, cursors are a part of user state.

5. A practical consequence of requiring the platform provider to implement the services under the API is a de facto standardization in platform architecture, since operating systems vendors seek to minimize their development costs. This is yet another example of a phenomenon tending to favor industry concentration.

6. It may be noted that the transactional locks apply to the tuples (a locking approach known as row locking). This level of locking optimizes performance, since the finer the locking level, the greater the degree of available intertransaction concurrency.

7. As we have mentioned earlier, some decision-support systems require updates. These are applications which are used for "what if" analysis, which must update the contents of the database to reflect the decisions taken in playing through the scenarios. The characteristics of such applications make them more like transaction processing.

8. Since SMPs (Share Everything) are becoming commoditized, system prices are dropping. The other side of the coin is that such commoditization results in a reduction in innovation, so that the systems offered by the various vendors tend to be almost identical. This is a trend which could in the end result in monopoly situations.

The Terminology of High-Availability Systems

Increasingly, activities—business and government, among others—rely on data-processing resources to fulfill their missions. The availability of these resources (that is, their ability to deliver the specified services) and the degree of confidence users can place in the availability of these services, therefore, become requirements for and essential properties of these systems.

The following few definitions help to crystallize the important concept of *system reliability*:

- Reliability allows a user to have a justified confidence in the services delivered by the system

- Reliability is the time-bound property and characteristics of an entity which give it the ability to satisfy needs both explicit and implicit for a given period of time under specified conditions (X50-125, standard of management of quality and quality assurance, standard ISO 8402)

- Reliability is the collection of a product's capabilities, enabling it to provide the specified performance, at the time desired, during a specified time period, without damage to itself or its environment.

Any function of a system or of a subsystem for which the property of reliability is a necessity is known as a *critical function.*

A system's reliability is characterized by a number of properties:

- *Reliability.* A measure of the continuity of the services rendered. This is a common property of critical systems, such as the data processing or embedded systems used for air traffic control, monetary exchange systems, military command-and-control systems, and so forth.

- *Availability.* A measure of the system's ability to deliver its capabilities when needed. The availability of a system is not only a function of the system characteristics *per se*, but also depends on its maintenance. The availability of a system is measured by the ratio of the time it is available for its purposes to the sum of this time and the time during which it is unable to perform the required services.

- *Maintainability.* The ability of a system to be kept in operating condition, and also the ability to be repaired and modified, possibly concurrently with normal operation.

- *Safety.* Or environmental security. Corresponds to the lack of any phenomena having undesirable consequences on the system's environment. This is a property to which users are increasingly becoming sensitive.

- *Immunity.* Corresponds to the ability of a system to resist external attacks, which may be accidental or deliberate. For an information-processing system, immunity is measured in three categories: system *availability*, data *integrity* and data *confidentiality*. These categories describe the continued system availability, the absence of inappropriate changes to the data, and the absence of unauthorized access to the data. In this chapter, we will only look at the availability category.

In a later section we will revisit some of these definitions and describe metrics for them.

Before going into greater detail on the definition of these systems, it is worth looking at the business impact of system unavailability. In Table 9.1, we show figures from Meta Group 2000 on the estimated revenue loss for one hour of system unavailability for various classes of business.

We should note that, in reality, the financial impact of unavailability depends on a company's size. The cost of avoiding unavailability (which we examine further in Chapter 10) must be consistent with the costs of suffering unavailability; this explains why some companies spend substantial sums on high-availability systems, and other do not.

[GRA91] proposes a terminology for classifying systems according to their availability.[1] The computations assume that the system needs to be available 24×7 (all day, every day). The scheme is presented in Table 9.2.

As an example of the computation, consider a class 5 system. This has five minutes of unavailability every year. A year is $60 \times 24 \times 365$ minutes, or 525,600 minutes, and so the system is available for 525,595 minutes a

Table 9.1 *Average Hourly Impact on Various Businesses (source: Meta Group 2000 [MET00]).*

Industry Sector	Revenue/Hour
Energy	$2.8 million
Telecommunications	$2.0 million
Manufacturing	$1.6 million
Financial Institutions	$1.4 million
Information Technology	$1.3 million
Insurance	$1.2 million
Retail	$1.1 million
Pharmaceuticals	$1.0 million
Banking	$996,000

year for an availability of 525,595/525,600, or 99.999% availability. The availability class of a system is the number of nines in its percentage availability score.

Perhaps unsurprisingly, information processing systems vendors exercise a few degrees of freedom in classifying their own systems. In practice, during negotiations for the purchase of a system, the availability classification must be precisely defined. As an example, the table above ignores planned downtime that would allow hardware and software updates and necessary

Table 9.2 *A Classification for Systems based on Availability (source: [GRA91]).*

Type of system	Unavailability (minutes per annum)	Availability (%)	Availability Class
Unmanaged	50,000	90	1
Managed	5,000	99	2
Well-Managed	500	99.9	3
Fault-tolerant	50	99.99	4
High Availability	5	99.999	5
Very High Availability	0.5	99.9999	6
Ultra High Availability	0.05	99.99999	7

maintenance activities. In general, such planned downtime is not included in an availability calculation (although contractual terms may specify that they are to be so considered).

A number of manufacturers are now offering class 4 and class 5 systems (fifty or five minutes of unavailability per annum).

9.1 Basic Terminology and Concepts

To keep within the scope of this book, we will limit ourselves to the presentation of general concepts related to high-availability systems and to the approaches currently in use to provide high availability. Readers interested in a more complete discussion can refer to [LAP90].

A *Computer System* or *System* is a coherent and autonomous collection of hardware elements, basic software, and application software, perhaps placed in a network environment. Its required behavior is specified in a reference document. This document is of cardinal importance in establishing the availability of the system, since any variation of behavior from that specified in the document makes the system effectively unavailable for its specified purposes.

A System's *environment* consists of those parameters which are external to the system and of their variations over time. External parameters may be physical measures, such as temperature or relative humidity; or abstract measures, such as the behavior of users or other systems. In other words, environment is defined by exclusion: environment is everything which is not part of the system. We should note that this definition of the boundaries between system and environment embraces a certain arbitrariness. In practice, it will be convenient to specify very precisely the system boundaries—and thus where responsibilities lie.

- *Expected service* is the collection of results and the conditions under which they are delivered, as specified in the reference document, that the system is to provide to a user in a specified environment

- *Provided service* is the collection of results and the conditions under which they are delivered that the system actually provides to a user in a given environment

In operation, a system is seen by its users as being in one of three states:

- *Proper service*, in which the results provided and the manner of their delivery is in accordance with the expected service

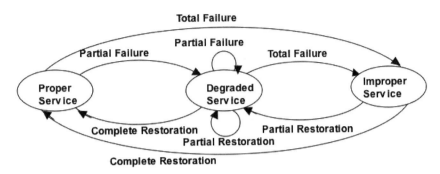

Figure 9.1
*Service concepts
(source: Bull).*

- *Degraded service*, in which the results provided are in accordance with the expected service, but the manner of their delivery is not

- *Improper service*, in which the results provided are not in accordance with the expected service

Figure 9.1 illustrates these concepts.

This figure introduces the concept of failure: *Failure* is a discordance observed between the provided service and the expected service. Failure may be detected either by the system user (whether a human or another system) or by the system itself. The figure shows several levels of failure:

- *Complete failure* occurs when the system is unable to deliver the results expected, for example because of an operating system crash.

- *Partial failure* occurs when the manner of delivery of the results is not as expected, for example loss of performance or support of fewer users.

Failures are caused by *errors*. An error, in an information processing system, is the discordance between a value or a condition (calculated or observed) and the corresponding expected value or condition. An error can involve a failure.

A *defect* or *latent error* is an inappropriate or missing component of the information processing system. The activation of a defect produces an error.

Generally, one distinguishes classes of defects—for example, physical defects, design defects and so forth. A reliability study should specify the defect classes of interest, and how to distinguish the classes.

A *fault* is a failure of the system, or of the human beings in charge of the production of the information processing system, or of the system surrounding the information processing system under consideration. A fault can introduce a defect into the information processing system.

Figure 9.2 illustrates these concepts.

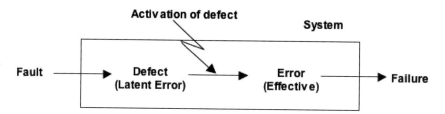

Figure 9.2
Illustration of the concepts of defects, error, fault and failure.

As shown in the figure, the consequence of a fault, whether of human origin (e.g., a design or programming error) or not, is the introduction of a defect into the system. A defect is also known as a latent error, since as long as the defect is not activated (examples of activation include the execution of erroneous code; or use of a variable which was wrongly initialized; or use of a misspecified constant), nothing occurs at the system level. As soon as the defect is activated, an error exists—that is, the latent error is transformed into an effective error. An effective error can lead to a system failure. It is important that the amount of time between the occurrence of the effective error and its detection be as short as possible.

In the next section, we will examine system failure modes.

In analyzing the causes of system failures, one is driven to a classification of defects. In practice, it is clear that some errors are easily and systematically repeatable, regardless of the manner in which the module containing the error is exercised, while other errors are simply not reproducible in a systematic way. This latter class contains defects that can be activated only under particular situations (with a specific conjunction of phenomena); these defects are frequently observable in software. They are also seen in hardware, where they are known as *transient defects*.

Abstracting, one may consider that one is in the presence of either perfectly deterministic defects, or of completely random defects. These classes have been dubbed respectively *Bohrbugs* and *Heisenbugs*, after the models of the atom proposed respectively by Niels Bohr and Werner Karl Heisenberg.

We can illustrate the terminology thus:

- *Bohrbug*: retrying will result in the same error (and possibly a failure)

- *Heisenbug*: retrying may or may not result in the same error

The retry must be done with the same environmental parameters. A Bohrbug is systematically reproducible, and that a Heisenbug is not.

To deal with a Bohrbug, one should remove the defect and thus correct the fault which resulted in the defect. In practice, for software this implies waiting for a new version, obtaining a special update from the vendor (*patch*), or—in extreme cases—selecting another vendor.

The case of a Heisenbug is more complex. Retrying the execution of the function can proceed correctly, if, as is often the case, the activation environment is not exactly the same as the environment which caused the error. If it is possible to capture the parameters to the activation of a function, replaying very often leads to a correct result when the function contains a Heisenbug. In practice, the difficulty is that it is not known, *a priori*, whether one is in the presence of a Bohrbug or a Heisenbug, and therefore one cannot tell whether a replay should be attempted. However, since capturing function parameters is quite straightforward in hardware (or, for a device driver, at the level of the interface between hardware and software), the replay strategy is often brought into play. In software, it is a bit more complicated, since the implication is that one must be able to easily and effectively return to an earlier state. However, transactional applications, with their intrinsic ACID properties (atomicity, consistency, isolation, and durability) make it straightforward to restore the context to allow a replay. We will look further at this point when we look at solutions.

9.2 Failure Modes

The failure mode classifications provided here (from [CRI91]) apply both to complete systems and to system components, and so the term "system" applies equally to systems and subsystems.

Recall that a failure is behavior that does not conform to the specification; thus, the specification of correct behavior is of prime importance. In its absence, it is impossible to differentiate normal from abnormal behavior. Any such specification should cover the system's results:

- The results are a function of the initial state of the system and of initial data values

- The results should be provided within a specified timeframe

- The system should then be in a specified state

- The values of data provided by the system should be specified

We can distinguish several failure classes:

- *Omission Failure*. This failure class is characterized by an absence of response from the system following a request

- *Timing Failure*. This failure class is characterized by the fact that the system does not provide a result within the specified timeframe. There are two sub-classes: *early timing failure* and *late timing failure*, depending on whether the system responds earlier or later than specified.

- *Response Failure*. This class of failure is characterized by the fact that the system provides an incorrect value (*value failure*) or the fact that the system is now in an incorrect state (*state transition failure*).

- *Crash Failure*. If, after its first failure to provide a response, the system provides no further responses until it has been re-booted, the failure is deemed a crash failure.

When designing a complete system, one must determine the most probable failure mode for the component under review and adopt an appropriate recovery strategy.

9.3   System Availability Characteristics

A number of metrics are used to quantify systems availability; we will consider here just those metrics[3] appropriate to our discussion of solutions.

Before going deeper into the metrics, we should recall their inherent random nature. Software failure, unlike most hardware failure, is not due to the random failure of components but to the propagation of errors arising from either the faults of surrounding systems or from design faults. However, we look upon them as random, since their occurrence generally has a random quality. Hardware, too, can suffer from design faults: the example of the floating-point error in the Pentium processor comes to mind. This had a noticeable (negative) effect on personal computer sales, since it was discovered shortly before the end-of-year seasonal buying spree.

We must further note that the term *mean time* used in the various definitions indicates the mathematical expectation of the value of the random variable in question, not simply the arithmetic mean of the first few occurrences. That arithmetic mean can be reasonably looked upon as an estimate of the mean time, provided that the sample over which it is calculated is representative. The sample may be considered representative provided that:

- It encompasses a large enough number of events (that is, that the measurements were made over a long-enough period of time that one may place appropriate confidence in the results)
- The occurrence of failures is a homogenous Markov[4] process (that is, a memory-less process)

Metrics related to the concept of failure

- *MTTF* (Mean Time to Failure). Expected value of the operational life to the first failure. This time is estimated by the cumulative sum of intervals of failure-free operation divided by the number of failures observed over the time interval under consideration.

- *MTBF* (Mean Time between Failures) Expected value of the time duration between two failures. This time is estimated by the cumulative sum of intervals of failure- free operation, plus the cumulative sum of the time necessary to restore the system to proper operation after failures, divided by the number of failures observed over the time interval under consideration.

Differentiating MTTF and MTBF

MTTF and MTBF should not be confused. A key differentiator is that the time needed to restart or restore the system to operational state is involved in the estimate of MTBF. A first approximation (approximate, since the situation is more complex for systems with redundancy) is that

$$MTBF = MTTF + MTTRes$$

where MTTRes (see below) is the mean time to restore correct operation.

Metrics related to the concept of maintainability

- *MTTRes* (Mean Time to Restore, or Mean Time to Recover). Expected value of the time until the system is restored to proper operation. This time is estimated by the cumulative sum of the times needed for restoration divided by the number of times restoration occurred in the time interval under consideration.

- *MTTRep* (Mean Time to Repair). Expected value of the time until the system is repaired. This time is estimated by the cumulative sum of the times needed for repair divided by the number of times repair occurred in the time interval under consideration.

Note that MTTRep characterizes the amount of time needed to repair a component, while MTTRes characterizes the amount of time for the system to be properly operational. While systems designers look for components with low MTTRep values (since it helps with the economics of system maintenance and repair), it is system MTTRes that characterizes behavior at the system level. If a system has good self-diagnostic capabilities and a good stock of spare parts, then given some minimum training for the support staff it is possible to remove the MTTRep component from MTTRes, since defective components may simply be swapped out (and sent away for repair) for the spares.

Metrics related to system availability

- *Availability.* The probability, expressed as a percentage, that service is available at any moment.

Knowing MTTF and MTTRes, the *technical availability* (At) is expressed as follows:

$$At = MTTF/MTBF$$

or:

$$At = MTTF/(MTTF + MTTRes)$$

Technical availability is a measure of the availability of the system alone; another metric, Au (*user availability*), measures the availability of the system to the user, thereby incorporating the effects of the environment.

An ideal system has, by definition, an availability of one. If such a system can suffer failures, the only way to keep an availability of one is for the time to restore (MTTRes) to be zero. In practice, this can be done by ensuring that the system can continue operating in the presence of some number of failures, and that these can be repaired without deteriorating the service provided by the system. This point shows the importance of maintenance, a subject to which we will return later in this chapter.

Repair Tolerance

In an analogy to failure tolerance, one may also speak of *repair tolerance*—that is, the ability to repair a running system. Some systems implement this in hardware to allow, for example, replacement of processor cards, memory boards, or I/O controllers (an example of this is PCI's hot-plug capability). Doing this requires the hardware to be designed appropriately. However, it is far from easy to implement this concept for software, particularly for operating systems.

Metrics related to the concept of service

- *MUT* (Mean Up Time). Expectation of the length of time during which the system provides the expected service during the time interval under consideration. This time is estimated by dividing the total amount of time during which service is provided as expected by the total number of interruptions to service (deliberate or accidental, functional or non-functional) during the time interval under consideration.

- *MDT* (Mean Down Time). Expectation of the length of time during which the system does not provide the expected service during the time interval under consideration. This time is estimated by dividing the total time during which service was not provided by the number of interruptions to the service (deliberate or accidental, functional or non-functional), whether caused by the system or its environment during the interval of time considered.

9.3.1   Summary diagram

Figure 9.3 illustrates the various intervals to be taken into account in all these measurements.

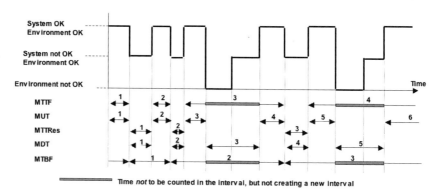

Figure 9.3
Intervals to be taken into account in measurements (source: Bull).

Each annotated line identifies the intervals to be considered for the estimation of the corresponding metric. Some of these lines contain intervals that should not be taken into account in the estimation of the metric: for example, in the estimation of MTTF, the period in which both system and environment are non-operational should not be counted since the system is not providing services during this interval—MTTF is defined as the ratio of sum of times of service to the number of service interruptions over the time considered. It can be seen that the intervals ignored in the estimation of MTTF are counted as part of the estimation of MDT.

9.3.2   Analysis of failure causes

Following [GRA96], we can give some broad-brush ideas of what causes system failures.

- *Hardware modules*: 100,000-hour MTTF and 10-hour MTTRes. Hardware is also subject to transient faults in which a retry will succeed, avoiding any need to repair.

- *Software*: A general number seems to be about one defect per thousand lines of well-tested code. This can reduce to 0.1 defects per thousand lines of code for mission-critical software, such as space applications. In such systems, the project cost is dominated by software validation. In practice, rates greater than one per thousand lines of code are seen; a significant portion of these manifest themselves as Heisenbugs, and rebooting will likely result in correct operation.

Little data has been published on the availability of information-processing systems. This is not for want of data—most systems include automatic incident-recording facilities allowing their behavior to be characterized under real operating conditions, so this data is available to the manufacturers. In general, however, they choose not to publish the data.

However, Tandem broke ranks and twice published interesting data in [GRA85] and [GRA90] from customer systems. Although these results are old, they are still useful sources from which to draw lessons for current and future systems. The results are shown in Figure 9.4

Figure 9.4
Evolution of the causes of system failures (source: Tandem).

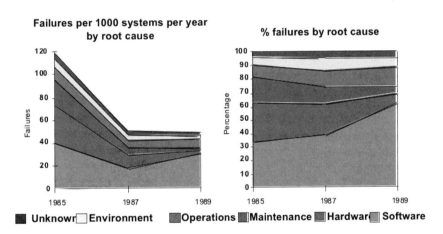

The two graphs highlight:

- A significant reduction in system failure rate per year from 1985 to 1989, followed by a plateau

- Substantial change in the causes of failure over the same period

[GRA90] suggests that failures are underestimated. The change in failure root cause can be characterized as follows:

- The spectacular fall in hardware-caused failures (from 29% to 7%) is fundamentally due to the use of increasingly-integrated components;

the effect of this is substantial even against a backdrop of increasing numbers of systems installed, each generally with increasing memory and storage capacity

- The corresponding reduction in the complexity of the hardware similarly drives a matching drop in failures caused by maintenance, from 19% to just 5%

- A marked increase in failures due to software, from 34% to 62%

This shifting pattern in failure causes calls for some comment. For hardware, an increase in level of integration translates into a reduction in the number of components used to construct a system of given capacity (for example, a reduction in the number of processors, number of memory cards, magnetic peripherals, or communications controller cards), as well as similarly reducing associated interconnect hardware. The failure rate reduces more or less linearly with the component count. Integration also generally increases the expected life of the affected components. Further, improvements in design and development of hardware, including the ability for the most recent systems to use formal verification (discussed in Chapter 1), has notably improved the quality of implementations despite increasing complexity, and also contributes to a reduced hardware failure rate.

A separate dimension of reliability improvement is due to the increasing use of facilities such as error correcting and detecting codes, data integrity mechanisms, and so forth, which once were deployed only in proprietary mainframe systems but now are provided in standard commodity components.

Hardware maintenance profits from this technology evolution: fewer components per system (and consequently less interconnect hardware), software-assisted maintenance operations, and improved localization of failing components all contribute to reduced maintenance demands. Modern systems increasingly tend to implement automatic "health" monitoring capabilities, which can provide suggested reconfiguration and maintenance actions to the support staff. This concept is implemented in high-availability systems, and will spread to standard systems over time.

The increase in percentage of system failures due to software is caused by two independent trends; one is the sharp reduction in hardware failures, and the other is the increasing complexity of the software.

Software Component Qualification?

Unfortunately, software cannot take advantage of any equivalent to increasing hardware integration. One might hope that, given progress in the field of software component validation and of software interworking, it will one day be possible to build systems with high availability starting with standard off-the-shelf software components (this is an approach sometimes called *COTS*, Components off the Shelf). However, software component qualification remains a thorny problem.

The search to construct systems that combine increasing ease of use with increasingly reliable operation results in software of increasing size and complexity. These increases in size and complexity drive up the number of potential defects in software and thus contribute to an increasing failure rate.

Any increase in system availability depends, in its foundations, on some low-level software actions.

In 2000, both Standish Group and Gartner Group published analyses of failure causes in data-processing centers. The Standish Group's results are shown in Figure 9.5 , while Gartner's are given in Figure 9.6 .

The first two (pie) graphs show the causes of failures noted on two different systems: Compaq's UNIX clusters (Digital TruClusters) and IBM Sysplex clusters. The results are, overall, rather similar. Planned stops, it can be seen, are included in the failure causes despite being excluded from many of the official failure metrics. Again, this highlights the importance of having a clear definition of what must be recorded for each measure.

The third (bar) graph summarizes results for a number of systems: UNIX clusters, IBM Sysplex clustes,r and Tandem/Compaq Himalaya high-availability clusters. The excellent availability of the Sysplex and Himalaya clusters is evident (this availability covers hardware and basic software). A surprise is the application unavailability for the reported IBM systems; perhaps these figures reflect the use of legacy applications whose control is somewhat beyond the reach of the data-processing staff.

The Gartner results reflect application-level availability, so direct comparison with Standish results is difficult; indeed, these results paint a different picture from the Standish numbers.

The intent behind showing these figures is to provide a quick look at the general availability of real systems.

Figure 9.5
*Standish Group
results (source:
Standish Group).*

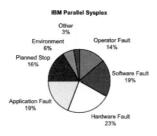

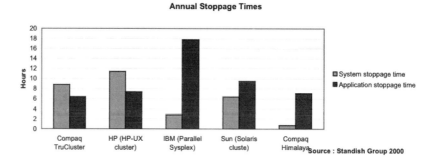

9.4   The Principles of High-Availability Systems Design

This section briefly presents the basics behind high-availability systems design, along with architectural options for such systems. These options are illustrated with real-world examples in the next chapter.

9.4.1   The concept of system state

From an external point of view (that is, as seen by a system's users) a high availability system must conceal any failures. To accomplish this the system

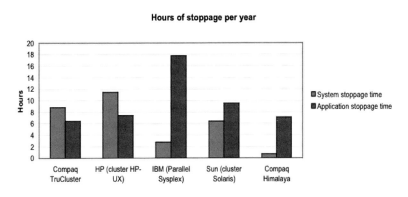

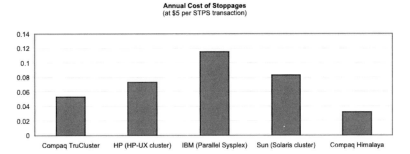

must, after a failure, continue operation from some specified correct state.
Two approaches are possible:

- The system *permanently* maintains several versions of the current state
  of the system, and in the event of a failure continues execution from
  one of them (this approach is used in Stratus' systems)

- The system maintains states from which processing can be
  restarted—the technique of recovery points (as used by Tandem's systems, and by cluster-based solutions)

A solution in which any processing in progress at the time of failure
would be abandoned, with reinitialization of the system, does not meet the
criterion of transparency.

Clearly, any solution involving keeping multiple contexts implies some
form of redundancy, at least at the hardware level. Reconstructing a context
to allow resumption of operations imposes constraints either on software

(through explicit specification of recovery points) or on hardware (implicit definition of recovery points).[5]

9.4.2   Principles of design

The design of high-availability systems follows a number of principles, which we now present; these principles are derived from [GRA91].

Modularity

Modularity is a well-entrenched principle of good design, and is not limited to use in the construction of high-availability systems.

A system consists of a collection of modules; the systems' decomposition into its component modules is a result of the design of the system. A module is a service unit, providing fault containment and setting repair boundaries.

Fail Fast

A module that respects the Fail Fast principle is one that either functions correctly or immediately stops execution upon the detection of an error. A number of technologies related to this exist—notably *fail safe*, *fail silent* and *fail stop*.

A system or subsystem is termed *fail safe* if the consequences of its failure are, from the user's viewpoint, of the same order of magnitude to the benefit that the user can obtain from its correct operation. Such a system is said to suffer *benign failures*. The concept is a little fuzzy and subjective, since the loss of an operation can have very different consequences in different applications: compare the differences in perceived costs between (i) a system performing a large number of experiments for statistical purposes, and (ii) financial transactions.

A system or subsystem is said to *fail silent* if the only result (that a user can observe) of a failure is that the system crashes.

A system or subsystem is said to *fail stop* if the only result (that a user can observe) of a failure is that the system stops.

The *fail fast* concept implies that a system (to the extent that it has any redundancy) continuously watches all its components to distinguish between correctly-operating modules and failed ones. In practice, this is generally implemented by requiring the components to exchange messages on an appropriately-frequent basis to indicate correct operation. This type of monitoring is often called *heartbeat*.

Independence of failure modes

The various modules constituting a system and their interconnections must be designed so that the failure of any module does not affect the other modules.

Redundancy and repair

Redundancy is a basic technique in the construction of high-availability systems. Replacement modules (at the physical level) must be installable during normal system operation, along with whatever is necessary to deploy them (at the logical level). In other words, installation must be possible in advance of need. Thus, when a module fails, the system can immediately make use of the pre-installed emergency module. Symmetrically, modules must be removable from the system—again, both physically and logically. This allows failing modules to be removed, repaired at leisure and subsequently reinstalled without any break in service. Other than some effect on performance, the removal and installation of modules has no observable effect on the operation of the system.

Redundancy and repair are key elements in systems availability. In addition to the ability to remove a failing module and repair it without interruption to system operation, the greater contribution to availability is the ability to remove and repair a module as part of planned maintenance, rather than a response to a failing module. As an example, providing a collection of spare parts at a site, along with a scheme which collects modules needing repair for delivery to a centralized maintenance center, provides somewhat greater availability compared to a scenario in which maintenance staff were required to go to a site to swap out failing components.[6]

An important feature integrated in many systems is the Phone Home capability, in which the system automatically calls a maintenance center when some system component reports an error. The maintenance center is then able to enter a dialogue with system's maintenance software to determine the cause of the error and to launch proper actions (e.g., sending spare parts, etc.).

Eliminating single points of failure

A *Single Point of Failure* (or SPOF) is a module whose failure automatically results in the failure of the complete system. Identifying and eliminating SPOFs contributes to availability. Some examples of SPOFs include:

- The electrical power supply for a system without an uninterruptible power system

- The bus in an SMP

- The operating system in a uniprocessor or SMP system; failure of the OS causes the system to stop, requiring a reboot to regain normal operations

Within a given system, many SPOFs may be eliminated through appropriate use of redundancy. However, some SPOFs resists such an approach—the operating system is a prime example. To handle these, complete system-level redundancy can be required; thus, the system comprises the primary system and a backup system.

9.4.3 Implementation of the principles of design

This section reviews the way the principles stated above are implemented at the software and hardware levels. Table 9.3 summarizes this information.

Table 9.3 *Implementing the design principles*

Concept	Hardware	Software
Modularity	Traditional	Traditional
Fail fast	Self-checking Comparison	Self-checking N-version programming
Independent failure modes	Inter-module coupling methods	Inter-module coupling methods
Redundancy and repair	N+1 module replacement approach Hot-swapping of modules	Redundancy for some software modules Replacement executing software
Elimination of single points of failure	Redundancy	Redundancy

Since the concept of a module simplifies design, development, maintenance and reuse, modularity is generally used in both hardware and software. It is, however, exploited more systematically in hardware, where the rather abstract concept of a module maps easily into a physical reality. The principle of modular design consists of conceiving of a system (or an application, or a subsystem) as a collection of cooperating units, each unit fulfilling a well-defined subfunction of the whole.

Two techniques may be used to implement the fail fast property. While the same terms are used to designate these techniques in both hardware and software, the actual techniques involved differ substantially.

For hardware, the two techniques can be characterized as follows

- *Self-checking*. A module implements not only its required functionality, but also sufficient extra work to be able to assure itself that its state is valid. Error correcting codes that detect and correct errors, and cyclic codes used in communications, are examples of this technique

- *Multiple implementations*. A function is implemented in several modules (for example, in multiple processors), and the results from all are compared to ensure that they are identical (or that a majority are identical).

Self-checking techniques are deployed very widely. As an example, almost all servers have ECC-protected memory (using 72 bits to represent 64 bits of data) allowing any single-bit error to be corrected and any double-bit error to be detected.

Multiple implementations are frequently used at the hardware level in systems used in mission-critical applications; systems from Tandem and Stratus are examples, as are IBM's mainframes.

Systems using majority voting are used generally only in systems whose availability is extremely critical—autopilot systems, for example. We should note that at the beginning of the 90's Tandem introduced the Integrity S2 system, which depended on majority voting. The system is no longer available, although the principle is used in Stratus' ftServer series (which will be further discussed in Chapter 10).

For software, the two techniques may be summarized as follows:

- Self-checking represents a particular design style for software modules in which the input parameters are checked for validity upon entry, and the results are checked for plausibility (e.g., range checking). The module code may also be decorated with *assertions* which require certain properties to be true; this allows appropriate assumptions about the module's correct functioning to be checked during execution. This sort of approach is termed *Defensive Programming*.[7]

- Multiple implementations in software involve implementing the same functionality in several different ways and comparing their results. If the results differ, execution may be suspended; if there is an odd number of implementations, one may choose majority voting over requiring unanimity. This approach has been called both "*n*-version programming" and "design diversity."[8]

All of these approaches have the major disadvantage (for both hardware and software) of both increased development cost (the extra assertions and checks for defensive programming; and the extra implementations in design diversity) and reduced performance. Thus, these approaches are used only where absolutely necessary.[9]

In practice, the diversity approach is not used for hardware; rather, multiple copies of the same design are allowed to execute on the same inputs, and their outputs compared. While this allows breakdowns to be identified and circumvented, it cannot handle design errors.

The independence of failure modes implies that there is little or no coupling between modules. Thus, any inter-module interaction—whether by messages or shared memory—must have its integrity protected. This has obvious implications for development costs and performance. At the hardware level, shared-memory-based communications must be protected by mechanisms similar to those provided by a classical MMU implementing virtual memory. For software, in practice protecting shared memory communications generally amounts to converting the communications into a message-based approach. This clearly loses the efficiency of shared-memory communication.

The principles of redundancy and repair are frequently implemented at the hardware level. To increase systems availability, one is increasingly driven to use systems in which components can be removed, exchanged, or added without stopping the normal operation of the system. As we have noted, the term "repair tolerant" is sometimes used to describe such systems. Such components are called *FRU* (Field Replaceable Units) or *CRU* (Customer Replaceable Units). Use of such an approach eliminates (or at least limits) the need for onsite maintenance staff.

In a number of high-end servers, almost all the components may be exchanged while the system is powered up: memory boards, processors, I/O controllers, disks, fans, power supply modules, and so forth. Such systems are based on the *N+1 principle*: if *N* components of a given type (for example, fans) are necessary to the proper operation of the system, the configuration provides *N+1*. In the event of the failure of a component, the extra component is immediately configured in (and the failing component arranged to be removed for repair and replaced) without any halt to systems operation. As soon as the replacement is installed, the system again has an *N+1* configuration and can again survive a failure of that class of component.

For software the situation is more problematic. Redundancy implies the availability of software modules capable of taking over upon the failure of a software module; this requires capture of all relevant system state so the failed operation can be retried with the new module. We will see that clusters can provide, under certain circumstances, this sort of capability. A significant related point: clearly, the replacement of a software module should not require system restart.

The elimination of single points of failure *(SPOFs)* is implemented in hardware by redundancy of both components and their interconnects. Here, we should recall that a SPOF is a component within a system whose failure necessarily implies the resulting failure of the system.

The complete elimination of SPOFs is generally extremely expensive. Thus, systems vendors tend to construct systems with a small number of SPOFs that each have very high reliability (i.e., components whose probability of failure is essentially negligible, compared to the expected failure rate of other components).

In software, elimination of SPOFs is also handled by redundancy. We will see that with cluster-based solutions, the SPOFs represented by the OS and the DBMS can be circumvented in some cases.

In the next chapter, we examine some commercial high-availability solutions.

9.5   Endnotes

1.   We should note that, even today, the value provided for system availability is subject to wide variations. But it is much better to base the availability value on a well-defined usage basis than on terminology used in advertising brochures.

2.   We should note that this definition of the boundaries between system and environment embraces a certain arbitrariness. In prac-

tice, it will be convenient to specify very precisely the system boundaries—and thus where responsibilities lie.

3. These metrics are accessible and measurable. Like any useful metric, these need to have the following properties: to be representative (of the phenomenon under review), interpretable, consistent, accurate and useful.

4. Markov processes are considered in Chapter 10, in the section on modeling systems availability.

5. It is worth recalling at this point that distributed systems pose particular difficulties in any recovery-point or system state capture approach, because of the difficulty of capturing a consistent, coherent global state for the collection of systems forming the distributed system.

6. Consider the term MTTRes (Mean Time to Restore) in the formula defining the availability of a system: At = MTTF/(MTTF + MTTRes). MTTRes does not include the value of MTTRep (Mean Time to Repair), since repair takes place off-line. Thus, MTTRes can have an extremely low value, incorporating only enough time to allow integration of the replacement module into the system.

7. These design styles imply both a higher development cost and slower execution. Often, a form of defensive programming is used during development, with the checks and assetions "#defined out" for the operational version of the system.

8. The cost of development and maintenance for such systems is a multiple of that for a simple classical system. A simple example: the minimalist majority voting solution requires three separate implementations, with a resulting software cost of about three times the simple solution.

9. The cost to be considered in such systems is not just the initial cost, but the costs of maintenance and evolution. And it should be noted that to gain full benefit from this approach, it must be applied to every component of the system, including: system platform (hardware and OS, communications layers), DBMS and applications programs.

10

Hardware and Software Solutions for High Availability

In this chapter, we will present some examples of high-availability systems solutions offered by both manufacturers of information processing systems and operating systems suppliers.

We can divide these solutions into two main categories:

- Hardware-based
- Software-based

We should note that theoretically these two types of solutions are non-exclusive and that it is possible to combine the two approaches within a single system. In practice, however, systems tend to end up in one or the other of the categories, for reasons of development cost. We proceed then to a comparison of these solutions. Here we must note that implementing a software-based solution requires that the hardware platform have a number of properties, in particular in error detection, but also in the areas of redundancy and repair tolerance. That is, one cannot use a software-only approach to make just any hardware platform capable of continuous service.

Hardware-based solutions aim at tolerating hardware failures, and rely on redundancy to do so. Their effect is to make hardware failures invisible to the applications (although there may be some perceptible slow-down immediately following the detection of a hardware failure, the system rapidly resumes normal performance levels). A pure hardware-based approach cannot hide software failures.

Software-based solutions aim at tolerating both hardware and software failures. For software, whether system or application, faults tend to be transient—that is, *Heisenbugs*. To provide *Bohrbug* tolerance would require a solution that, in effect, ran multiple different software solutions concurrently, using (for example) majority voting to select actions at appropriate junctures. Such solutions do exist, but are deployed only when absolutely no failures may be tolerated and when cost (of both system and the design) is not a concern.

This chapter provides an overview of the strengths and weaknesses of both hardware- and software-based solutions, discusses disaster recovery, examines ways to evaluate systems availability, and then finishes with some discussion of future possibilities.

10.1 Hardware-based Solutions

In this section we review hardware-based solutions for high availability. The number of such solutions is diminishing over time; a fair number of manufacturers—both well-established companies and start-ups—once offered products that met with only limited commercial success and have since disappeared. Later, we will examine the reasons for this reduction in vendors.

In this section we will look at systems from Stratus and from Sun, and will look at the approach implemented by IBM in the processors of its zSeries servers.

10.1.1 Stratus

Status's first systems were based on the *Pair and Spare* approach—that is, providing two instances of critical resources and providing the ability to swap one out. While Stratus's newer systems adopt an approach similar to that chosen by Sun, it seems appropriate to discuss the Pair and Spare approach first.

Pair and Spare

This approach is based on the two following principles:

- *Pairing of units.* The Pair concept consists of executing a function concurrently on two processors within the same unit and continuously comparing the results

- *Replicating units.* The basis of Spare (for example, the processing unit)

Figure 10.1 illustrates the principle of Stratus' processor architecture.

In this architecture, a logical processor unit is made up of two physically independent processor cards. The two processor cards execute the same process in a synchronized manner; at each clock beat, the two cards see the

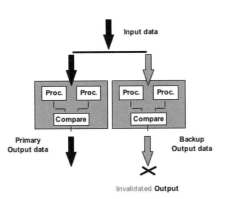

Figure 10.1
Pair and spare concept.

Input data

Primary Output data

Backup Output data

Invalidated **Output**

same data and the same instruction. One of the cards is the *primary* card, and its data outputs—any writes to memory or I/O—are validated. The other card is the *backup* card, and its data outputs are not validated. Each card contains two processors, which work in lockstep with comparison hardware. The comparison hardware continually compares the data outputs of the two processors on the card; if there is any difference, the whole processor card is declared faulty and removed from the configuration, and outputs from both of the card's processors are ignored. Meanwhile, the backup card—whose processors are also running in lockstep with each other, and (up to the moment of fault detection) with the primary card—has its data outputs accepted in place of the primary card's. That is, upon detection of the fault in the primary card, the primary is disabled and the backup card seamlessly becomes the primary.

When the primary card fails, it is removed from service and the backup is marked as the primary. If the backup card's comparison hardware detects an difference, the backup card is simply marked as defective. When a failure is detected, tests—the execution of which is managed by a *service processor*—are executed to determine the nature of the failure: permanent or transient. A card which is currently not in use (for example, one just plugged in to replace a failed card) can be dynamically integrated into the system and used as a backup—that is, configured-in and synchronized with a primary card.

This is an example of an approach which permanently maintains two system states.

The system elements are all hot-pluggable.

Figure 10.2 illustrates the architecture of the Stratus Continuum 4000, which is based on this principle.

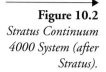

Figure 10.2
Stratus Continuum 4000 System (after Stratus).

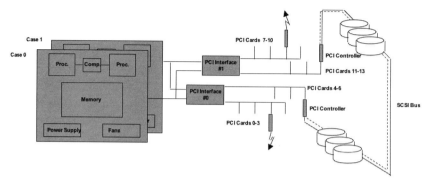

This system uses HP PA (*Precision Architecture*) 7100 or 8100 RISC (*Reduced Instruction Set Computer*) microprocessors. The processing unit is supplied in the form of a rack and includes two microprocessors, the comparison hardware, up to 2 GB of memory, the power supply and fans.

Each rack has access to two standard PCI (*Peripheral Component Interconnect*) I/O buses. The system's disks are double-connected to SCSI controllers on both PCI buses, so that the disks are accessible in the event of the failure of either of the PCI buses or controllers.

The communications controllers are also redundant, with two PCI buses, two controllers and two communications ports.

The system runs under either VOS (*Virtual Operating System*), an OS proprietary to Stratus intended for transactional applications, or under HP-UX, HP's version of UNIX.

10.1.2 Stratus ftServer Series

Stratus' new family, code-named Melody, is based on Intel IA-32 processors and runs under Windows 2000; a major goal for Stratus for these systems is to be able to offer systems at a lower price.

Two types of configuration are supported:

- DMR (Dual Modular Redundancy);
- TMR (Triple Modular Redundancy).

The system is built from processor/memory modules which operate in lockstep. In the event of a failure of one module, continuity of operation is assured by the surviving module (in the DMR configuration) or the surviving two modules (in the TMR configuration). Each module is an SMP able to support up to four processors. The same set of processes is executed by both modules; upon each I/O request, the state of the modules is compared. In the event of divergence, then:

- In the DMR configuration, the determination of which is the faulty module is based upon an analysis of the module history - that is, which faults each module has already encountered. The faulty module is isolated and processing continues with the remaining module

- In the TMR configuration, there is a majority vote and the losing module is isolated. Operation continues in DMR mode with the two remaining modules.

It should be clear that the I/Os and the interconnects between modules and I/O are replicated. Hardware units may be exchanged without stopping the system.

This is an example of a system which maintains several system states permanently.

- Stratus made improvements to portions of the system software—e.g., device drivers, availability manager, the ability to preserve the state of a portion of the system memory while the system is being reloaded— and also in the area of maintainability.

Stratus offers a low-end system, the ftServer 5200, with two processors (logical, because to form a dual processor system, one needs two two-processor modules for DMR, or three two-processor modules for DMR).

Stratus expects that eventually future versions of this system will use the IA-64 architecture.

10.1.3 Sun Microsystems System NETRAft 1800

Early in 1999, Sun announced a system capable of providing continuity of service making use of hardware redundancy. This system, SPARC-based, adopts an approach offered by IMP, an English company acquired by Sun. The system is primarily aimed at the telecommunications market.

The system is a member of the Sun server family, sharing some hardware subsystems and the Solaris operating system.

The systems design is modular, and is made up from redundant processing and I/O subsystems. The modules can be removed and replaced without stopping the system.

Figure 10.3 illustrates the architecture of the system.

Figure 10.3
NETRAft 1800
system architecture
(after Sun).

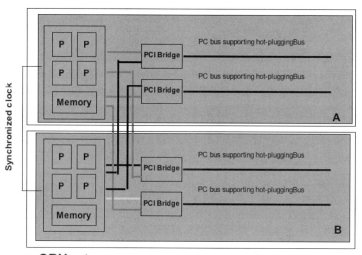

The system is composed of two principal cards (motherboards), each comprising a processor/memory unit called a *CPUSet*, along with two PCI buses supporting hot-plugging (i.e., the ability to remove or plug-in a PCI card without halting the system). Each CPUSet can contain up to four UltraSPARC processors and 256 MB to 4 GB of memory.

The CPUSets may also be swapped in and out without halting the system, as can the power supply. This architecture is of the *Spare* type. The CPUSets are synchronized by a common clock, but do not have comparison hardware at the processor level: the processors in the CPUSets execute software in such a manner that corresponding processors in each CPUSet execute the same code, and comparison between the CPUSets is made only when an I/O request is made. When a difference is seen, the system enters a diagnostic mode to determine which of the CPUSets is faulty. Once done, the faulty CPUSet is isolated, and processing continues with the remaining

CPUSet. It should be clear that challenge in this approach is determining the faulty CPUSet.

The system is said to take about 200 ms to recover from a processor error. Bringing up a new CPUSet is a background task, done in parallel with normal operation, so the system's availability is not affected by the need to copy the memory of the operational CPUSet into the new module.

The I/O subsystem is based on PCI, and the controllers can be exchanged while the system is under power and running. Hardware performs a validity check of memory writes. The controllers use virtual memory addressing, and the hardware checks that the addresses are indeed legal addresses for that controller. The virtual address is translated and the memory access is communicated to both CPUSets. If the address was illegal, the memory access is refused, the PCI controller marked faulty and an interrupt raised on both CPUSets. The disks are mirrored.

This system is an example of the approach which keeps two system states permanently.

The hardware runs under the control of the Solaris operating system. In Solaris, specific adaptation to the hardware is done outside the OS proper; Solaris is structured as a collection of PIM (*Processor-Independent Modules*) and PDM (*Processor-Dependent Modules*). The PDM Modules are not purely processor-dependent, but also dependent on the system architecture.

Figure 10.4 illustrates the software architecture of the NETRAft system.

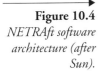

Figure 10.4
NETRAft software architecture (after Sun).

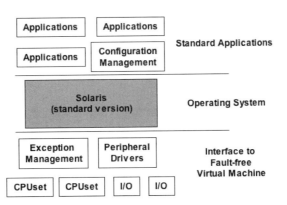

As shown in the diagram, hardware configuration management and all aspects of provision of continuous service are handled outside Solaris. The system has the advantage of using a standard version of Solaris for SPARC, and of being able to make standard applications hardware fault-tolerant.

10.1.4 IBM zSeries

In the microprocessors developed for the S/390 architecture IBM integrated a large number of error detection and correction mechanisms, such as replicating the processing units within each processor and adding comparison hardware. Our description of the continuity of service mechanisms implemented in the previous generation of processors (G5) is based on [SLE99]. According to IBM, these extra mechanisms account for 20 to 30 percent of all the logic in the implementation.

A similar approach is used for the zSeries, which incorporates various characteristics which contribute to high availability, including:

- the concept of a backup processor able to be used to replace a faulty processor

- the ability to swap out faulty components while operating: hardware, microcode

- an *N*+1 strategy for power supplies and fans.

Figure 10.5 illustrates the recovery mechanism at the instruction level in the event of processor failure.

Each instruction is executed in parallel by the two processors, forming a single logical processor. The state of the processor before execution of the instruction is preserved. The results produced by the two processors are compared. When the resulting state is identical, the execution of the

Figure 10.5
zSeries processor recovery mechanism (after IBM).

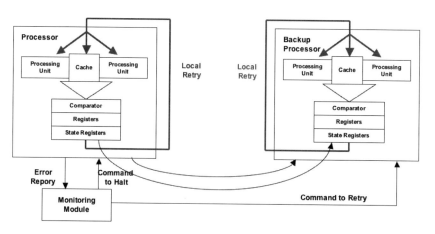

instruction is validated, the state of the processor is updated and execution proceeds to the next instruction. In the event of divergence, re-execution is attempted a number of times. If the divergence persists, the monitor module is informed, a backup processor brought on-line, the initial state (i.e., the processor state immediately before the execution of the failing instruction was attempted) is provided to the backup processor and execution continues on the backup processor.

This is an example of the approach which permanently maintains a state from which execution can restart, applied at the lowest practical level of the hardware.

We shall see that software-based solutions adopt a similar approach, albeit with the information necessary for recovery being at a much higher functional level.

10.2 Software-based solutions

The basis for software-based continuity of service solutions is the memorizing of system states from which execution may correctly continue in the event of a failure. As we have noted previously, the snapshotting of system states is a natural side effect of transaction-based processing, being the system state upon normal completion of a transaction. Our discussion centers on such transactional systems.

A transaction-processing system is usually built on top of both a transaction manager (for example CICS in IBM mainframes, Tuxedo for UNIX systems and MTS (Microsoft Transaction Services) on Windows systems) and a data manager (such as DB2, Oracle, SQLServer or Sybase). In the event of a failure, the transaction manager uses its journals to cancel the effects of any transactions which had not been committed at the time of failure. More information on programming transaction-processing systems is available in works such as [BER97] and [GRA92].

We will look at three systems types: firstly, a system aimed specifically at transaction processing; then cluster solutions (which are simply adaptations of standard UNIX or Windows systems) and finally a software solution capable of allowing standard systems and their applications to offer continuity of service.

10.2.1 Tandem's Himalaya S7000 NonStop System

Figure 10.6 represents the architecture of Tandem's Himalaya S7000 Non-Stop system.[1]

Figure 10.6
*Tandem Himalaya
S7000 NonStop
system architecture
(after Tandem).*

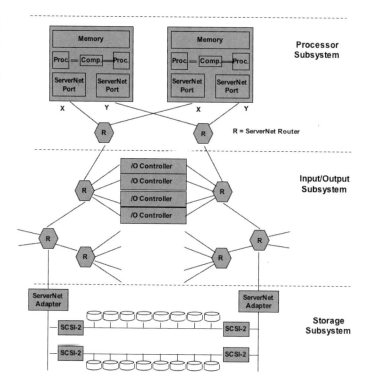

This system is organized around ServerNet, the system interconnect network (which used to be called SAN, for *System Area Network*[2]). ServerNet has the necessary integrity and redundancy mechanisms. The processors have a Pair functionality—that is, each card contains two processors, executing the same software in lockstep, along with comparison logic to compare the results. However, there is no *Spare* functionality; rather, recovery is based on specific resumption points in the software.

Because the system is based on the use of standard microprocessors, Tandem had to implement the comparison logic itself. (Some Intel microprocessors integrate this capability, but—as far as we know—this has never been used in a server).

The system architecture is of the *Share Nothing* type, being composed of a number of independent nodes, each node having its own memory, its own copy of the operating system and its own peripherals. Nodes communicate over ServerNet.

The operating system, NonStop Kernel, is proprietary to Tandem, but comes equipped with a UNIX interface layer. It is a cluster solution, providing a single system image for distributed resources such as files,

The system provides a proprietary basic data manager called NonStop SQL/MX, which provides the users with a single image of the database despite it being distributed across the systems nodes. The SQL/MX instances ensure the synchronization of their operations, giving users a system with the ability to grow in processing power and I/O connectivity with the addition of more nodes. NonStop SQL/MX also takes advantage of the natural parallelism of the cluster by breaking complex requests into simpler sub-requests, and distributing the execution of these across the nodes responsible for the needed data.

For continuity of service we concentrate on the transaction processing dimension. The Tuxedo transaction monitor (see Chapter 3) was ported to NonStop Kernel, and is used as the transaction framework providing two-phase commit in the distributed environment of the system.

The processor card has two MIPS family processors, which operate in lockstep and are connected to comparison hardware. The use of IA-64 processors is planned for 2004. The processors execute the same process and as soon as the comparison logic detects a divergence between the two, it notifies the OS which declares the card as failing and immediately withdraws it from the system. Having recorded this in a journal, the system runs a number of tests on the card to determine the nature of the failure and to decide on its possible replacement.

Various system elements (cards, peripherals, power supply modules, fans, etc.) may be changed without stopping the system.

Continuity of service is based upon the concepts of a primary process and a backup process, illustrated in Figure 10.7.

As shown in the diagram, for each process running on a server (the primary processes) there is a corresponding backup process running on another server. Information allowing the resumption of a primary process (for example, primary process A on system 1, and primary process B on system 2) is recorded on stable storage (generally mirrored disks, or disks arranged as a RAID system) via messages sent over the interconnect network.

When a failure causes the primary process to stop, the backup process is activated (through recovery functionality implemented in NSK) and starts

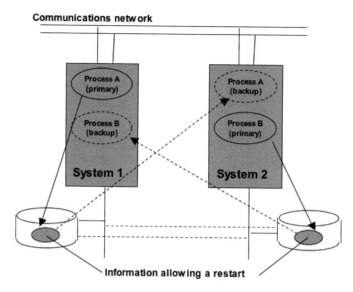

Figure 10.7
*Tandem NonStop
Kernel (NSK):
concepts of primary
and backup
processes (after
Tandem).*

execution from the saved state, thereby becoming the primary process. A
new backup process may then be initialized on another system in the configuration (that is, on another node). Note that for simplicity the example
shows only two nodes; NSK is not limited to such a configuration.

For transactional applications, the transaction points—for example, *start
work* and *commit work*—are the natural points at which recovery information can be saved. At every point when such points can be defined for software components of the system and/or the associated middleware, the
primary/backup process mechanism can be used. The operating system or
the transactional subsystem provides the necessary programming interfaces.

Inside NSK itself, this mechanism has been used for critical processes—
for example, writing to disk.

The systems nodes watch each other using a heartbeat mechanism (refer
to the sections on AIX HACMP and Windows MSCS)

With this approach, it is possible not only for transaction-structured
applications to survive hardware (and some software) failures, but also for
the capability to be extended to other applications (as long as they make use
of appropriate programming interfaces) and to critical system functionality.
This may, of course, only work for Heisenbugs.

In our example, a hardware or software failure in one of the servers halts
execution of the applications running on that server. The applications may
be automatically re-activated on the backup server, with the applications

being responsible for correctly handling any files in use. Of course, for transactional applications, this step is taken care of transparently by the combination of database manager and the transaction manager (e.g., Tuxedo).

10.2.2   UNIX and Windows Cluster Solutions

Inspired by the architectural approaches of Tandem's Guardian (the Himalaya system just discussed is a successor to the Guardian) and Digital's VAX-Cluster, UNIX systems vendors began, around the end of the 1980s, to develop similar systems. Microsoft followed suit with its Cluster Server (MSCS, for *Microsoft Cluster Server*), which had been codenamed *Wolfpack*.

In this section we look first at a UNIX cluster, and then a Windows cluster. For the UNIX example, we choose IBM's HACMP (which is also supplied by Bull under the name *Power Cluster*). UNIX clusters offered by other vendors have very similar functionalities and architecture.

10.2.3   UNIX Cluster Example: IBM's HACMP

Figure 10.8 is a simple example of IBM's HACMP (*High Availability Cluster Multi Processing*), part of their *Cluster 1600 for Commercial Computing* offering. HACMP manages cluster systems based on AIX (with uniprocessor and multiprocessor nodes). Although the diagram shows just two nodes, HACMP—like the majority of other offerings—is not limited to such a configuration. We will not reconsider here the subject of clusters *per se*; this was covered in Chapter 5.

Note: To make it easier to read this section, we repeat here an overview discussion of HACMP, rather than forcing the reader to divert to the appropriate parts of Chapter 5.

In this example, the clusterized resources (by which we mean the resources available to software running on any node without regard to their actual connections, and which are managed globally at the cluster level) are disk drives, communications networks (both LAN and WAN), and the Distributed Lock Manager (DLM). The cluster interconnect makes use of LAN technology (e.g., Ethernet), which may be replicated to improve system availability. The workload is distributed between two servers. A clusterized file system (GPFS, for *General Parallel File System*) is available. Software components (VSD, for *Virtual Shared Disk*) allow disk sharing and continuity of disk access (RVSD, for *Recoverable Virtual Shared Disks*)

Figure 10.8
*HACMP
configuration
example (after
IBM).*

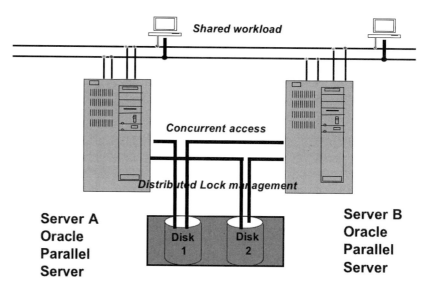

in the event of the failure of the local node to which the physical disks were attached.

HACMP can manage both pSeries servers and logical partitions of these servers. An HACMP cluster can include from 2 to 32 nodes.

Products complementary to HACMP include the clusterized file system (GPFS); Workload Manager, which provides load balancing; and two disaster recovery products, GeoRM and HAGEO.

GeoRM (*Geographic Remote Mirror*) provides data replication between remote sites. A GeoRM target site can support up to seven source sites. There are three mirror types:

- *Synchronous.* Identical data is maintained between local and remote sites. This implies a synchronization on every source write.

- *Synchronous with mirror write consistency.* This uses a two-phase commit protocol to maintain consistency, and can offer a higher performance level than the simple synchronous mirror while also affording a high level of data integrity.

- *Asynchronous.* The source writes data without waiting for the mirror to be updated. This provides the highest possible source performance but poses risks to data integrity.

HAGEO (*High Availability Geographic Cluster*) is based on GeoRM and adds the dimension of automatic recovery in the event of failure. HAGEO manages two sites with a maximum of eight nodes, and provides three recovery modes similar to HACMP (whose modes will be described later).

HAGEO provides:

■ Remote hot backup, in which the remote site guarantees the ability to resume primary site applications

■ Remote mutual takeover, in which pairs of sites play symmetrical roles, with each acting as backup to the other

■ Concurrent access, in which the site applications operate on the same database

The general architecture of the software supporting cluster operation is illustrated in Figure 10.9.

Figure 10.9
IBM HACMP
architecture (after
IBM).

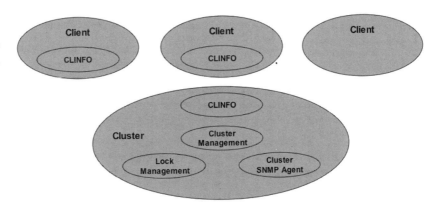

The various components of the HACMP/6000 architecture are as follows:

■ The *Cluster Manager*. Active on every node in the cluster, it has the responsibility of keeping up-to-date information on the cluster as well as the state of the interconnect network. It also handles reporting the operating state of the cluster with respect to other systems.

■ *CLINFO*. The Cluster Information Services are optional on both client and cluster nodes; CLINFO provides an API to allow clients to query the state of the cluster, which information is also communicated to the SNMP agents.

- *Cluster SNMP Agent.* SNMP (Simple Network Management protocol) is a distributed systems administration standard in the UNIX world. The Cluster Manager provides information to the Cluster SNMP agent, which makes it available through SNMP.

- *Lock Manager.* The cluster Lock Manager provides a distributed synchronization service to the various services and applications executing on the cluster; it is a implementation of the concept of a DLM (Distributed Lock Manager) introduced in the VAXCluster.

Figure 10.10 illustrates the architecture of the cluster manager.

Figure 10.10
Cluster manager architecture (after IBM).

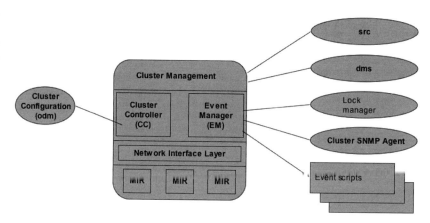

The cluster manager includes the following functional elements:

- The cluster manager proper, which works with an *src* (*System Resource Controller*) and provides a collection of services facilitating the creation and control of subsystems.

- The *Cluster Controller*, which is the main component of the cluster manager. It receives cluster information via network interface layer (NIL) and network interface modules (NIM).

- The *Event Manager*, which runs scripts associated with events. It also takes responsibility for notifying events to the cluster SNMP agent and the lock manager.

- The *Network Interface Layer* (NIL), whose principal role is to control the network interface modules. NIL determines the heartbeat frequency (KA, for *Keep Alive*), depending on configuration details. NIL also manages multicasting (the sending of a message to multiple recipients).
- *Network Interface Modules* (NIMs), whose role is the sending and receiving of messages, such as those indicating network failures.

In HACMP terminology, a *subsystem* is a unit (a single program or a collection of programs; a single process or a collection of processes) that accomplishes a given function. The cluster manager also works with a system service to allow fatal situations to exit. This service is *dms* (for *Dead Man's Switch*), which is based on the following technique: a counter is initialized, and must be updated regularly. A failure to update is looked upon as a demonstration of system failure, which causes the system to stop.

The *Cluster Controller* is responsible for keeping track of the membership of the cluster as well as the state of the interconnect network. It maintains the cluster configuration by means of *odm* (for *Object Database Manager*). odm contains configuration information along with per-resource information for each resource managed by the system. Decisions regarding which systems must interchange regular messages to demonstrate that they are still functioning correctly (KA—for *Keep Alive*—messages, in HACMP terminology; and *heartbeat* messages in other systems) are based on information managed by odm.

Within a cluster we can distinguish two message types:

- Exchanges between Network Interface Modules (*NIM*). These are KA (or heartbeat) messages, allowing each module to see that the other modules are working correctly. How many of these messages are sent per second is parameterizable, as is the number of messages which may be unanswered before the system concerned is declared as failing.
- Messages required by the normal cluster activity.

The various functional modes of an HACMP cluster (as regards continuity of service) are illustrated in Figure 10.11.

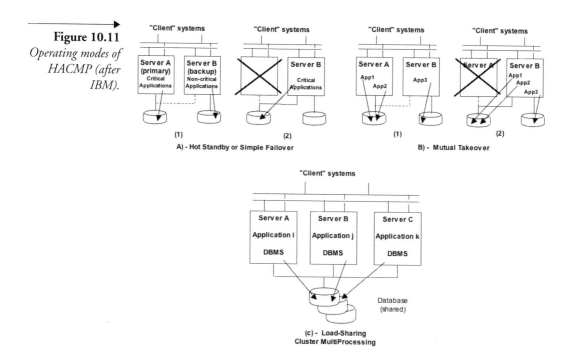

Figure 10.11
Operating modes of HACMP (after IBM).

We look at the three scenarios in turn.

10.2.4 Hot standby, or simple failover

The application runs, in normal operation, on one of the systems (the *primary*). Another system, the *backup* system, is either inactive or executes independent non-critical tasks. A configuration in which one of the systems is dedicated to being a backup (whether or not it runs non-critical tasks) is know as an *active/passive* configuration. If and when the system on which the critical application is executing has a failure, the backup system takes over, perhaps also suspending execution of its non-critical tasks. When the primary returns to operational capability, it takes over the execution of the critical applications, and the backup returns to its passive role.

An alternative version of this approach exists; in this scheme, called *Rotating Standby*, the roles of primary and backup are not fixed. In such a scheme, when the failed primary is returned to operational capability, it resumes as backup.

10.2.5   **Mutual takeover or partitioned workload**

In this mode, the whole system participates in executing the application. The application must be partitioned in such a way that separate systems (Server A and Server B in the figure) share no information whatsoever (in particular, so they share no files). In the event of failure of a system, its workload—applications and resources—is picked up by the other system. This two-way example may be extended to a system of several nodes.

> **Recovery**
>
> Neither the simple failover mode nor the mutual takeover mode offers any guarantees upon recovery of the state of files which were being updated. AIX's journaling files system (JFS) guarantees, thanks to the transactional nature of its internal data management, that the metadata (i.e., the data describing files, such as inodes) is correct; but that guarantee does not extend to the data. For the data to be guaranteed correct, the applications themselves must be designed following a transactional model.

10.2.6   **Cluster multiprocessing**

In this mode, the applications running on the cluster share a single database. This type of configuration, in which all the systems contribute to the primary system mission, is known as *active/active*.

In the event of a failure of one of the systems, another system will pick up the workload and resources of the failing system. Each system in the cluster has an active instance of the database manager. Each DBMS instance accesses, concurrently, the database on behalf of the applications running on its system. The DBMS instances synchronize themselves using a Distributed Lock Manager (DLM). This mode obviously assumes the availability of an appropriate DBMS. An example of such a DBMS is Oracle Parallel Server (discussed in Chapter 8).

In addition to its high-availability capabilities, this sort of configuration provides modular growth; each system added to the cluster provides an increment of resources and performance. The mode provides a participatory redundancy.

When the applications are transactional in nature (that is, they respect the ACID properties), a failure of the system is equivalent to the abandonment of the transactions that were in course of execution at the time of failure. Data integrity is guaranteed because of the transactional properties. Since any users of the system will be automatically reconnected, upon system failure, to another system within the cluster, any failure is invisible to users except for the abandonment of a transaction, or if response time increases noticeably. We should note here that transactions can be abandoned in normal operation—that is, in the absence of a system failure; an example would be abandonment upon the detection of a deadlock.

In this mode, with implicit recovery points (provided by the transactional semantics) and participative redundancy, HACMP is similar to the Tandem NonStop Himalaya S7000 system discussed in the previous section.

The implementation of these systems obviously requires that the disks of a given system can be taken over by another system, and that network connections are also shared between systems.

As regards the implementation of these solutions, it is generally necessary to write or to modify procedures written in the system control language (*shell scripts*, in the UNIX terminology). Such procedures are used to control operations at system command level, such as halting, launching applications and more.

10.2.7 Microsoft Cluster Server (MSCS)

Microsoft has developed a cluster version of its Windows Server operating system; code-named *Wolfpack*; the OS is called Microsoft Cluster Server (MSCS). The following description is based upon [MIC03].

Note: To make it easier to read this section, we repeat here an overview discussion of MSCS, rather than forcing the reader to divert to the appropriate parts of Chapter 5.

Microsoft's architecture choice for MSCS is *Share Nothing*, as opposed to the *Shared Disks* model. It is, however, entirely possible for software—such as the DBMS—to simulate the existence of shared disks on a *Share Nothing* architecture, using, for example, the concept of *Remote I/O*.

The concepts on which MSCS is based are as follows:

■ *Cluster Services*. A collection of software implemented on each node of the cluster; it manages the cluster-specific activities of the system.

- *Resource*. Any entity managed by Cluster Services. Cluster Services looks upon all resources as opaque objects (that is, it has no interest in the operations one may perform on the objects). Resource examples include physical resources (disks, communications controllers, etc.), TCP/IP addresses, applications, and the DBMSs.

- *On-line Resource*. A resource is said to be on-line on a node when it provides its services on that node.

- *Group*. A group is a collection of resources managed as a single entity. Usually, a group contains all the resources an application needs. The existence of groups simplifies an administrator's workload, since an operation on a group applies that operation to all its member resources.

Cluster Server services are presented as virtual servers to a client. Connection makes use of an IP address, which is interpreted by Cluster Services as a resource in the same group as the application. If a node fails, Cluster Services moves the affected group(s) in their entirety to another node. The client detects the failure of its session and requests a reconnection; since the old IP address is now available on the new node, the connection is remade and service continues.

Figure 10.12 illustrates the architecture of MSCS.

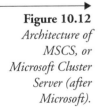

Figure 10.12
Architecture of MSCS, or Microsoft Cluster Server (after Microsoft).

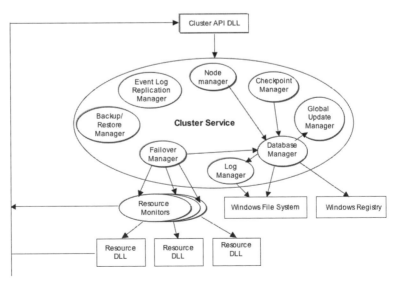

The specific components of Cluster Services are as follows:

- The *Node Manager,* which manages the node's membership of the cluster and watches for correct operation of the cluster's other nodes. This monitoring uses the *heartbeat* technique. If a cluster node fails, each of the remaining active nodes checks the state of the cluster to make reconfiguration possible.

- The *Database Manager,* which maintains a per-node database representing the cluster's state. Entities represented in this database are the cluster itself, its nodes, resource types, groups, and the resources themselves. The various Node Managers cooperate, using a protocol, to maintain a coherent view of the databases across the nodes.

- The *Resource Manager/Failover Manager,* which manages resources and groups and initiates appropriate actions when needed—such as starting, restarting, and recovery.

- The *Event Processor,* which provides connections between the components of Cluster Services, and deals with common operations such as controlling the initialization of Cluster Services.

- The Communications Manager, which looks after communications with other nodes.

- The *Global Update Manager,* which handles updates for Cluster Services components.

- *Resource Monitors,* which are implemented as processes and communicate with Cluster Services by RPC (*Remote Procedure Call*). They check that resources are operating correctly through *callbacks* to the resources. They also perform appropriate transformations between generic resource calls and the specific calls needed for each resource type.

- *Time Service,* which maintains a homogeneous view of time across the cluster. It is implemented as a resource.

These last two components are not, properly speaking, part of Cluster Services.

Resources are implemented as *DLLs* (Dynamically Linked Libraries), loaded into the address space of the resource administrators. A resource may depend on another resource, and a resource is put on-line only when the resources it needs are already on-line. Each resource has associated with it a local restart policy that defines the actions to be taken if the resource cannot continue execution on the current node.

Cluster Server provides as standard DLLs for resources such as physical volumes, logical volumes (composed of one or more physical disks), files and shared printers, network names and addresses, applications or generic services, and an Internet server service.

The interfaces to the resource DLLs are public and are supported by development tools (SDKs). This allows application providers to present their applications (or components of them) as resources and thereby allow the applications—or their components—to be recoverable and thus failure-tolerant.

10.2.8 Functional overview of Cluster Services

As noted above, Cluster Services uses *heartbeats* to supervise the operation of the cluster.

If a resource fails, the resource administrator can decide to restart it or to take it and the resources upon which it depends off-line. Putting a resource off-line indicates to the recovery manager that the resource must be restarted on another node. This can also be done by the cluster administrator.

When a node fails completely, the resource groups it supported must be removed from the node and be re-installed on one or several other nodes. Deciding which nodes to move the resources to is done by inter-node negotiation, based on a number of parameters including node capacity, current load, or a preferences list. After deciding where to place the resources, the node configuration databases are updated.

When a node returns to activity, again resources may be moved around in the system. The decision to do so is based on a preferences list associated with a group. The actual migration of the group is subject to a time delay, in an attempt to avoid the situation in which a system fails at every attempt to start the moved group, causing the group to oscillate between nodes.

The creation of a cluster starts with the execution of initialization software on a single node, which becomes the first member of the cluster. Then initialization proceeds on all the other nodes, with the difference that each such initialization specifies the name of the cluster it wishes to join.

During system restart on a cluster node, Cluster Services are automatically executed. Any shared peripherals attached to the node must be off-line, since they can be accessed by other nodes. The restarting node executes a *discovery procedure* to identify the other members of its cluster. Each such member authenticates the new node and, if all succeed in so doing, the restarting node has successfully joined the cluster and all node configuration databases have been updated.

If the discovery process cannot detect a cluster, the restarting node attempts to form a new cluster. To do this, it must get access to a *quorum* resource. This special type of resource, often a disk, is used to avoid the situation in which the members of a cluster all attempt to form a new cluster in the event of communication failure.

A node can leave a cluster; to do this, it sends a *Cluster Exit* message to all members of the cluster and then proceeds to stop all of its resources.

Switching time—the time needed to move resources from one node to another—is generally about a minute. Obviously, using MSCS does not protect against failure of any single points of failure which might exist in the system, such as lack of backup power supplies, unmirrored disks, and so on.

From the user's point of view, whether a recovery is visible depends on the characteristics of the applications concerned and on how clients connect to the applications. For a *stateless* connection—for example, using a standard browser—any failure and recovery is invisible if it occurs in between two requests. If it occurs during the handling of a request, then any notification and other activity are the responsibility of the *client* portion of the application. Thus, whether the failure is visible or not depends on how the application (both client and server portions) was programmed.

In the case of a *stateful* connection, the user must reconnect, although it is possible to write the applications in such a manner as to have a transparent reconnection.

Transactional Logic

To ensure data integrity and to provide a coherent state to the data following a failure/recovery, the application must be built on *transactional logic* [GRA92]. If this is done, actions being performed by the application at the time of a failure are transactions, and those that fail may be rolled back safely during the rebooting of the data manager (generally a DBMS). The transactions must be retried, but it is possible to make this automatic with appropriate programming of the client portion of the application.

The concept of continuity of service, as seen by the users of a cluster, is thus strongly dependent on the way in which the applications were designed and implemented. When applications are designed with cluster architecture in mind, they are said to be *cluster-aware* applications.

10.2.9 SafeKit

SafeKit is a generic technology making it possible to build solutions offering continuity of service on standard systems, including client/server systems operating under Linux, UNIX (AIX, HP-UX and Solaris), or Windows operating systems. The technology is the result of a collaboration between IRISA[3] and Bull, and allows a service established on a number of servers to continue to function in the presence of hardware or software failures. A number of solutions have been built on this technology, including a firewall, Web server and others.

The technology is provided as a number of software components, whose operation is controlled by a control automaton. The components include a virtualization of IP address, a distributed redundant file system, systems monitoring mechanisms, reconfiguration mechanisms, and load-sharing mechanisms.

SafeKit is not a turnkey general solution but a set of building blocks to be used to satisfy the needs of an application. It works for systems (UNIX and Windows) that are connected by a local area network, and requires no modifications to the standard hardware or software of such systems. For an application to benefit from the use of SafeKit, its behavior must be analyzed and, in some cases, the application must be modified. Such modification is not always necessary (it was not required in the Web server described later). It is also possible to develop an application with the attributes and capabilities of SafeKit in mind.

Figure 10.13 shows the architecture of SafeKit.

The control automaton, implemented as a finite-state machine, configures the SafeKit software components according to the state of the servers. The automaton's state transitions occur upon the reception of events: a change of state in another system, or a local event such as a software failure. A state transition can result in the execution of a script to reconfigure the system modules. The automaton also monitors correct operation of the other systems through a heartbeat technique.

Mechanisms taken from network management allow several systems to simultaneously share the same IP address, thereby allowing clients to see just one network address. This virtual address has two operating modes: *primary/backup* and *load-sharing*. In the primary/backup mode, the network

Figure 10.13
*SafeKit
architecture
(source: Bull).*

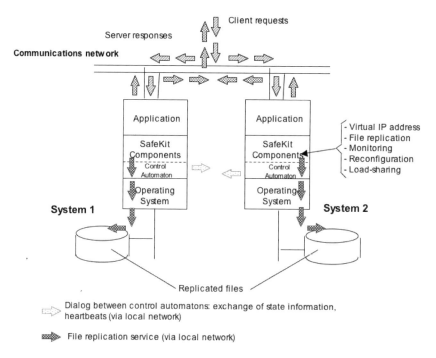

traffic from the clients is seen by both servers but handled by just one, the primary. The backup server monitors the primary and replaces it in the event of failure. In the load-sharing mode, all servers see all the traffic, although in general each handles just a portion of it.

The management of redundant file systems on a network is similar to managing a mirrored disk system; the differences arise from the fact that the replication is done on a different system. It has the following advantages over straightforward disk mirroring: better insulation from system failure, faster recovery time (since there is no need to switch the file system between systems), and the ability to better survive natural disasters, since the systems can be installed in different buildings (limited by the reach of the local area network). Replication can be partial, allowing only critical application data to be replicated rather than complete file systems, although this requires a detailed analysis of the application.

In addition to the usual mutual monitoring mechanisms for hardware, basic software, and network, the system monitoring mechanisms can be parameterized to a fairly fine grain to support mutual monitoring (for example, at the application software level).

The reconfiguration mechanisms allow reconfiguration within a system or between several systems on the network. When a failure is detected on a primary server (or on any server when in load-sharing mode) the applications are restarted on the backup server. The state of the replicated files used on the new system corresponds to the last data written by the failed server. TCP/IP connections with client applications are stopped and then must be restored, which can be done automatically through appropriate programming. For client applications using connectionless protocols (such as NFS clients, or SNMP agents) the failure of the primary server is invisible.

If the server failure was caused by software, the server is automatically restarted. After it has started (or, in the case of a hardware failure, been repaired and restarted), its shared file system is automatically resynchronized with a copy running on an active server. When this is accomplished, the restarted server becomes a backup server (or, in the case of load-sharing, takes its place as a server in the server pool) and the system as a whole returns to being a high-availability system.

The ability to share the load between several networked systems allows not only high availability, but also tuning of the overall system for high performance.

SafeKit technology has been used to make existing applications fault-tolerant. Examples, from work done at Bull, include a firewall (SafeNet-Wall), a Web server (HighWeb) using a commercial Web server, and administration software from the OpenMaster suite.

10.3 Disaster Recovery

This section deals with *disaster recovery*—that is, recovering after a catastrophic failure.

Servers supporting company information systems are prone to a number of risks wherever they are situated. Examples include natural disasters, such as earthquakes, hurricanes, or floods and situations such as fires, attacks, or riots. The effect of any such catastrophe on a server is essentially that its site is neither operational nor accessible. Disaster recovery consists of the techniques, products, and procedures put in place to minimize the consequences of a catastrophe.

Clearly, these techniques must involve geographical redundancy—redundancy between well-separated sites. Since disaster-recovery solutions tend to be expensive, it is important that the risk of catastrophe be estimated fairly well, along with the costs of recovery and the impact of such a catastrophe on the business. A key element of the solution is replication of one site's data at other sites, along with a backup system of roughly the same capability as the one affected by the catastrophe.

The choice of a solution is driven by consideration of the following factors:

- The amount of variation that can be allowed between the state of the data on the system suffering the catastrophe and the state of the data on the backup system
- The time needed to get the backup system to resume processing
- The cost of the recovery system

Figure 10.14 shows the general architecture of a recovery solution.

Figure 10.14
General architecture of a recovery solution.

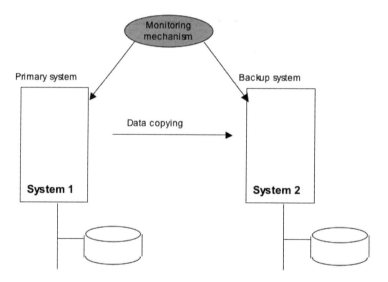

In the diagram, the system providing service in normal times is shown as the primary system, with the other being the backup. Where these systems are sited must be carefully considered to minimize the probability of both being affected by catastrophes at the same time.

The primary system is there to supply the resources needed by the application, while the backup system is there only for use in recovery. To avoid wasting resources on the backup system, several approaches can be considered, including:

- The backup system has more or less the same capabilities as the primary system, and is used in normal times for day-to-day tasks

- The backup and primary systems are both operational systems, each being, symmetrically, the backup for the other

- The company contracts with a service provider with a pool of systems available, one of which can be made available when needed

The first two options lead to operations similar to high-availability clusters, such as IBM's HACMP and Tandem's NonStop Himalayas. The choice of solution is affected by the acceptable amount of time for recovery—choosing the third option results generally in a longer recovery time.

Another significant point in the choice of a solution has to do with the data replication strategy between the sites. In an analysis of replication strategies and recovery practices, Gartner Group distinguishes the following levels of data replication, in ascending functionality order:

- *Level 0.* No recovery

- *Level 1.* Backups, but without checking the backups

- *Level 2.* Backups of the complete contents of storage, at arbitrary times, with a check of the backup contents

- *Level 3.* Systematic backups (for example every evening) of the complete contents of storage, with a check of the backup contents

- *Level 4.* Systematic backups of only the data managed by the critical applications, backing up only the modified data, with a check of backup contents

- *Level 5.* Systematic updates of data modified by the application on the backup system as the application executes, with a check of the backup contents

A point not discussed in this list is where the backups are sited.

Here is an example of a Level 1 solution: some solutions make use of companies that specialize in the keeping and movement of backup data (from ferrying magnetic cartridges by courier to electronic data transfer). Periodic backups are entrusted to such a service provider. In the event of a catastrophe, the company is requested to deliver all relevant files to a backup site. In this scenario, there has been no systematic check that the backups are sound. This approach, although it can provide a measure of independence to the backup site, must necessarily result in a rather long recovery time.

The highest place in the replication hierarchy occurs when the data is updated on the primary server and simultaneously sent to the backup. Transmitting data on the occasion of every transaction results in high communications costs, and is likely to exert a performance penalty on the primary system because of a need for a two-phase commit between the sites [GRA93]. In recompense, recovery time is markedly reduced.

The backup operation is managed by a monitoring system, which must assure itself of the correct operation of both primary and backup systems, as well as arranging for data replication. The monitoring system further manages swapping the roles of primary and backup upon failure and eventual recovery. A catastrophic event at a primary site must not have any impact on the monitoring mechanism (beyond having the event noticed).

Unfortunately, there is no standardized disaster recovery solution; a choice must be made, driven by the needs and costs pertaining to the business's needs.

Business Continuity

We should point out that disaster recovery as described here, along with systems offering continuity of service, comprise just the technology portion of a more general problem, which is *Business Continuity*—the ability to continue operations after a catastrophe.

Disaster recovery is the ability to restore the operation's critical systems to their pre-catastrophe state; operations continuity is the ability to continue to supply critical services in the presence of unplanned interruptions in systems service.

It is therefore vital that companies develop *Business Continuity Plans*, which would include identification of the functions critical to the operation of the business, a quantification of the risks associated with the loss of these functions, a definition of processes and procedures to avoid or limit such risks, the choice of technologies and products to be implemented and the effective implementation of the plan at all levels of the company.

As previously stated (see Chapter 6), two important objectives must be clearly defined:

- *Recovery Point Objective* (RPO), the point at which the system state must be restored

- *Recovery Time Objective* (RTO), the time allowed for restoring system operation (full or degraded service, since all the applications are not critical from business continuity point of view)

10.4 Estimating the Availability of Systems

This section examines the methods most frequently used for the qualitative and quantitative estimate of systems availability. These methods are useful not only for systems providers (data-processing systems manufacturers or systems integrators) but also for IT executives who need to specify the architecture of an information processing system that must provide a high degree of availability. Part of the description which follows is inspired by [MEI98].

10.4.1 Predicting faults: Failure Modes and Effects Analysis (FMEA) and Failure Tree Analysis (FTA)

Predicting faults involves estimating the creation and presence of faults, as well as examining their consequences and how critical they are. With this analysis in hand, one can study ways of avoiding the faults or tolerating them.

Two qualitative approaches can be used: FMEA (Failure Modes and Effects Analysis) and FTA (Failure Tree Analysis). While these methodologies were initially conceived to handle faults and failures in physical components, they have been extended to also deal with software design faults. They can also be applied to errors related to human behavior.

NASA has published a proposal covering similar ground; the *NASA Software Safety Guidebook* [NAS02] is intended for systems whose characteristics are dominated by software behavior. This publication uses the term *Software Failure Modes and Effects Analysis*.

10.4.2 Failure Modes and Effects Analysis (FMEA)

In this process, one determines for each function or component of a system the possible failure modes and the consequences of such failures [DUN02], [GOB98]. If one can further quantify—even if only in a rudimentary way—the probability of a failure occurring, or the seriousness of its effects, one can then make an estimation of the criticality of the failure.

Such an analysis may be used at all levels of system design. It makes it possible to identify necessities and weaknesses as regards ensuring continuity of functionality and to identify appropriate actions to reduce the risks. Examples of such actions include employing defensive programming to provide fault tolerance, extensively verifying the software; and choosing a maintenance strategy.

The process consists of building a table, whose structure is shown in Table 10.1.

Table 10.1 *Structure of a failure modes and effects table*

FUNCTION (Component)	Failure Mode	Cause	Effect (Consequences)	Means of detection	Probability (P)	Gravity (G)	Criticality (P G)	Actions

Each line of such a table contains, for each function or component, the following information:

- *Identification of the possible failure modes.* These were discussed in the section "Failure Modes", at the beginning of Chapter 9 (examples: failure by omission, and temporal failure)

- *Possible causes of the failure.* This identifies the reasons that could cause the appearance of this failure

- *The effect of the failure* (which can be limited to the component or to relate to a subsystem or the system as a whole) *and its consequences to the system.* For example: partial degradation of service (increased response time), loss of a subsystem, critical loss of function, etc.

- *Possible means of detection.* It is important to emphasize the value of the earliest possible detection of failures, since a late detection often has the consequence that erroneous system state has propagated, which will make recovery significantly more difficult

- *Probability of occurrence of the failure.* This probability, even if it cannot be quantified, can be qualified in the following way: low, very low, average, frequent, high

- *The seriousness, or gravity, of the failure.* The failure can be qualified in the following way (in the absence of a more precise evaluation): minimal, minor, awkward, serious, very serious

- *Criticality.* Criticality is expressed as the product of the probability of occurrence and the gravity of the failure

- *Risk-reduction actions* that can be considered

The contents of such a table can be summarized in the form of a diagram having as y-coordinate the seriousness of the failure and as x-coordinate the probability of occurrence. Further information can be conveyed by adding a third dimension to capture difficulty of detection.

The purpose of such a figure is to reveal the most critical failures; an example is given in Figure 10.15.

Figure 10.15
Criticality matrix
(source: [MEI98]).

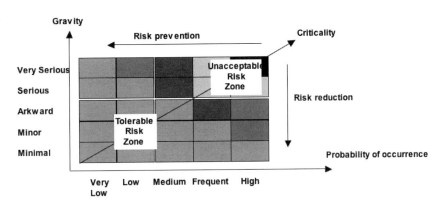

10.4.3   Failure Tree Analysis (FTA)

In order to handle combinations of failures, a *failure tree analysis* can be used [BED01], [NRC81]. This description mechanism allows us to identify combinations of events that could lead to an unwanted event, such as a failure. The principle consists of working one's way up through the possible causes and combinations of causes of an unwanted event, capturing the combinations as AND and OR combinations. Given the failure rates of the system components, it is possible to compute a useful statement of systems reliability; this is called *Risk Analysis* (RA).

10.4.4   Quantitative estimate of availability

Risk Analysis (RA) allows a quantitative estimate. RA is based on FTA, where the failure probabilities for the various components (hardware, software and even operators) must be determined [DUN02], [BED01].

Quantitative estimates of system availability can be derived from the above approaches, but there are tools with a more formal basis, built on Markov chains and stochastic Petri nets.

Markov chains, discussed in greater detail below, consist of capturing the various possible system states and associating a probability with each state transition (which are themselves related to the reliability characteristics of the system components). The resulting model provides the probabilities of the system being in various stationary states. This approach can also handle the representation of repair strategies and be used to estimate availability improvements brought about by different repair strategies.

This type of modeling can be applied to the whole system—hardware as well as software—although the difficulty of obtaining useful estimates of software failure rates can be a barrier.

10.4.5 Markov Chains

Markov chains provide a formalism that enables the quantitative evaluation of system availability.[4] The following description follows was inspired by [SIE92].

The two basic concepts are a *state* and a *state transition*. The state of a system is characterized by the states of its components, which are either *operational* or *faulty*. Over the course of time, the system state changes as its components pass from an operational state to a faulty state, and then return to an operational state after a successful repair. The changes from one state to another are called *state transitions*.

Figure 10.16 illustrates a model of a very simple system, made up of only one component.

Figure 10.16
*Markov model
with two states.*

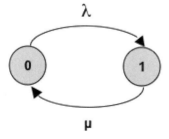

In this model, the system can be in two states: an operational state (state 0) and a non-operational state (state 1). The failure rate is λ and the rate of repair is μ. A set of linear equations can be obtained from a Markov model, allowing one to calculate the probability that the system is in a particular state; more information is available in [SIE92].

Figure 10.17 illustrates a model for a dual system with repair.

Figure 10.17
Markov model of a two-component system.

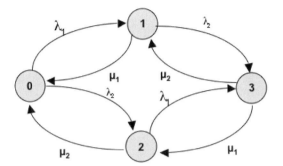

The system has four states: two systems in operating condition (state 0), one of the two systems failing (state 1), the other system failing (state 2), and finally both systems failing (state 3).

More generally, in a system having N components (each one of them either being in an operating condition or failing) the Markov model has 2^N states, which corresponds to a system of 2^N equations that must be solved to compute probabilities for the system being in each of the various states. There are techniques making it possible to decrease complexity, and it is possible, when searching for the solutions to the model, to restrict oneself to the subset of states that are of interest.

10.4.6 Models of growth of the reliability of software

We can construct from such quantitative estimates a model of the growth in reliability of software. Such a model allows one to estimate average time to failure, as well as the number of remaining errors in software.[5] Models have been proposed (Musa, Littlewood, Goël-Okumoto, etc.); these models differ in how they apply statistical laws.

Figure 10.18 shows a model of growth of software reliability.

In practice, these models are used to estimate how much more effort needs to be put into testing to provide the desired reliability. Making use of the models implies that extensive statistical data are maintained on developed applications.

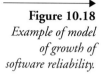

Figure 10.18
Example of model of growth of software reliability.

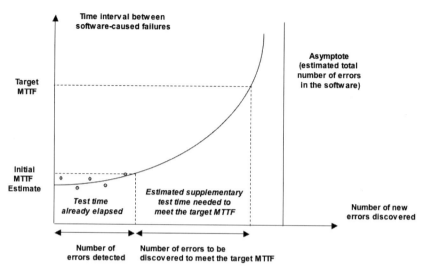

10.5 High-Availability Systems: Conclusions

As we have seen in this chapter, there are various approaches to obtaining high availability. The solutions described each have their own characteristics and areas of application. In this section, we provide some selection criteria to aid in choosing a solution.

The first issue in-systems availability is formulating the requirements for availability. These requirements can drive a first level of choice; for example, were the system to be required to never stop, then one would need to replicate the system and to provide the ability to reinstate a system after repair or software update. This drives the requirement that the system as a whole would need to work properly, even when different versions of system software were running in different parts of the system.

Of course, a business must balance the costs of avoiding system failures against the business impact of suffering such failures.

Table 10.2 provides a partial comparison of the properties of the various solutions put forward in this chapter.

Software-based solutions make it possible to tolerate some software failures, a capability not provided by hardware-based solutions. The software failures which may be tolerated are transient errors (*Heisenbugs*)—none of the solutions can tolerate *Bohrbugs*.

Table 10.2 *Partial comparison of the properties of different high-availability solutions.*

	Hardware Solutions	Recovery Points (software)	Cluster (software)	SafeKit Execution environment (software)
Tolerates Hardware failures	Yes	Yes	Yes	Yes
Tolerates failures of system software	No	Yes (Heisenbugs)	Yes (Heisen bugs) if no sharing of data	Yes (Heisen bugs) if no sharing of data
Tolerates failures of application software	No	Yes (Heisenbugs)	Yes (Heisen bugs) if no sharing of data	Yes (Heisen bugs) if no sharing of data
Applications need special programming	No	Yes (transac tional pro gramming)	Yes, if data is shared and update	Yes, if data is shared and updated
Performance degradation after failure	No	Yes	Yes	Yes
Tolerates repair	Yes (necessarily)	Yes (implicitly)	Yes (implicitly)	Yes (implicitly)

Cluster solutions, and solutions that provide an execution environment (such as SafeKit), can only provide continuity of service when data is shared and updated concurrently by multiple applications running on different nodes if the updates use transactional logic (and, in this case, a distributed transactional logic).

Applications that use transactional logic provide, implicitly, recovery points. We find it hard to overemphasize a recommendation to use transactional logic for *every* data update when there is a need for continuity of service.

Other areas of comparison include performance, recovery time, and cost.

For performance, the price/performance ratio is generally of more interest than raw performance. All the solutions employ hardware redundancy (and in some cases software redundancy), which results in a higher price for a system.

Recovery time—the amount of time necessary between a failure and a return to normal service—can be key in some applications. For example, in a stock exchange, a substantial recovery time can result in significant financial losses.

Table 10.3 provides a comparison for some of the solutions in the areas of cost, performance and recovery time. The reference system, listed as the *Basic System* in the table, is a standard system with no high-availability characteristics whatsoever.

Table 10.3   *Comparisons of performance, cost and recovery time.*

	Performance	Recovery Time[*]	Cost
Basic system	1	Not applicable	1
Hardware Solution	< 1	O(second)	> 2 or 3
Standby System	~1	O(minute)	~2
Participative redundancy (two systems sharing the workload)	< 2	O(minute)	~>2

[*]   O(x) means "of the order of x"

The cost comparison in the table is only for the basic hardware platform—processor, memory, and I/O controllers. It does not include the cost of peripherals or software. The cost estimates are based simply on the cost of the components, assembly, and test. The *prices* of the systems can differ significantly more than these hardware costs suggest; for example, the R&D needed to create hardware-based solutions is significant, and so amortizing this cost over the relatively small number of systems sold for high-availability use may drive the prices up considerably.

We now quickly discuss the systems compared in the table:

The basic system

The base system has no redundancy and is used as the baseline reference for the comparisons. Its recovery time estimate is marked as *Not Applica-*

ble, since any recovery will be a long process including diagnosis of the failure, repair, rebooting the system and then recovery/repair of application and data.

Hardware-based solutions

These are *DMR* or *TMR* solutions, such as those offered by Stratus or Sun. The approaches use two (DMR) or three (TMR) processor/memory subsystems to execute each process.

The table shows these systems as having lower performance than the base system. This arises from two independent root causes, the first architectural and the second the extended development time:

- *Architectural.* The processors must synchronize at a very fine grain, and this results in a lower frequency of operation than non-redundant systems built from the same technology.

- *Extended development time.* Because developing a hardware-based solution is a complex design task, it is usual that by the time the system is ready for the marketplace, the processors used in the system have already been supplanted in the base systems by a newer generation of processors offering higher performance.

Recovery time for these systems is some small number of seconds, which is how long it takes to do the diagnosis of the failure and the necessary reconfiguration.

System cost for these systems must be at least two or three times (for DMR and TMR respectively) the cost of a base system. In practice, the price will be higher than that, because of the need to amortize the substantial R&D costs over a small production run.

Standby systems

The performance of such a system is slightly lower than that of the base system, since the primary system must spend some processing and I/O capacity updating the backup's state. The table makes the assumption that the backup system is used *only* as backup; in practice, this is not usually the case, since often enough the workload can be partitioned and distributed among available servers, and the whole configured so that each server both does useful work and acts as a backup to another. If this is done, then each server can either be sized so that it can carry the workload of both itself and its backup or, given that failures are rare and that some degree of performance reduction may be allowable for a time (long enough to repair the backup system), sized to manage somewhat less load than the combined workloads.

When a standby system is configured so that all its servers are doing useful work, then its performance will be somewhere between one and two times the base system (the table assumes a two-server standby system), rather than the ~1x shown in the table.

Recovery time is some number of minutes, longer than for the hardware-based solutions. The extra time comes from the need to check the consistency of the file system on the backup system, and to launch the applications on the backup.

In this situation, we should note the advantage of journaled file systems over traditional UNIX file systems. In a traditional UNIX file system, when an incident occurs the file system must do a complete check of all the blocks on the disks to rebuild metadata correctly; this can take tens of minutes (a time which increases as disk capacity increases), and must be completed before the system can restart.

A journaled file system avoids this problem. In such a system, each change to the file system's metadata is handled as a transaction, and a log (or *journal*) of the changes is kept. Then, while rebooting, the file system can merely cancel all transactions that started but did not complete; this restricts the work needed to examining a rather small number of disk blocks and reduces the time necessary from many minutes to a few seconds.

As noted, the transactional protection of a journaling file system applies only to the file system's metadata—the information it uses to manage the files—and not to the data in the files themselves. To protect these, the applications must also use a transactional model, and have storage manipulations implemented by a subsystem using transactional logic (such as a relational DBMS).

The cost of a standby system, given that essentially everything is replicated so that standby and primary systems are of similar capability and each is as capable as the reference base system, is a little more than twice that of the base system.

Participative redundancy/load-sharing

In these systems, all the servers do useful work, sharing the data. Although the overall system performance increases (with two servers rather than one), the overhead of sharing the data means that overall performance does not scale linearly with the number of processors, and is therefore less than two times the performance of the base system.

Given that the applications are transactional, recovery from incidents is almost transparent, with a recovery time of several minutes in which time the system diagnoses itself, reconfigures itself, and recovers the shared database.

As with the standby solution, the cost is a little more than twice the cost of the base system.

10.6 High-Availability Systems: Future Trends

Increasingly, industrial and commercial activities rely on computer systems, with the result that the desire for continuous availability of those systems also continues to increase. A few examples:

- Web-based 24/7 information access

- Customer-company and company-company interactions increasingly being done online and in real time

- Increased dependency of the company's operations on anytime access to company data, from geographically-distributed sites

The shape of future high-availability systems will be driven by the capabilities of technology and by considerations of cost.

A side effect of the improvements in hardware technology is, as we have already seen, an increase in the basic reliability of components. This arises from several factors:

- An increase in the level of integration of VLSI[6] devices. With the improvement of technology, circuits become physically smaller and so more functionality can be packed into one chip. A simple way to leverage this is to combine what used to be several chips into the one, resulting in a lower system-level component count and fewer interconnects. These reductions directly increase reliability

- Integrating redundancy and/or error detection and recovery into the components. An example is the addition of error correcting codes and redundancy into the cache memories of microprocessors.

- Manufacturing and quality-control improvements.

- Improvements in the tools for verifying the design of VLSI components, allowing the industry to begin approaching "zero defects" in design and allowing the first implementations of designs to work flawlessly.

- Increasingly sophisticated techniques (integrated into the hardware) for monitoring components and initiating their replacement before they fail. An example of this is the monitoring of the bit error rate of a DRAM memory subsystem. As the error detection rate increases beyond some threshold, the subsystem may be marked for replacement; the OS can arrange to remove all data from that subsystem during normal operation, and the memory subsystem can be replaced without a failure having occurred. This technique provides some subsystems with an essentially infinite lifespan.

As shown in [GRA90], the percentage of failures attributable to hardware has fallen significantly; this trend is expected to continue.

This technology trend tends to make hardware-based high-availability solutions less attractive over time, although there will be a place for such systems in applications (such as financial markets) where almost any outage results in very high costs, or when human lives are at stake. But most systems—especially those connected with Web activities and electronic trading—want high-availability systems with costs as low as possible.

The technological trend for software is quite different from that for hardware. Systems contain more and more software, and the size and complexity of the software is increasing. Increasing size and complexity are factors that drive up the number of residual faults in software. As we have indicated earlier in this work, the cost of driving quality to below one residual fault per thousand lines of code is a dominating factor in the cost of software.

Although there have been improvements in methodology and in associated tools, it has not been possible to completely hide these cost increases. While much effort has gone into the creation of tools that can automatically create code, much less attention has been devoted to tools that automatically generate tests. Thus, software verification (often considered, wrongly, as an activity of little value) is still primarily a mental task unsupported by tools and automation, and one whose cost is not decreasing

Improving this situation requires solutions to be looked for in a number of areas:

- *Design of failure-resistant software*, with defensive programming; error detection, correction and recovery when domain knowledge allows it; the use of transactional logic where justified; appropriate software architecture; and so forth

- *Designing software for testability*; this means that testability, both at the unit level and integration level, must be part of the specifications

- *Re-use of standard software components*, as a number of researchers are looking at the use of COTS (Components Off The Shelf) to build systems; given the existence of appropriate re-usable libraries, the efforts of software development in design and test can be better used to construct systems that use the components.

This list is not intended to be exhaustive, but to indicate major directions in which work is already being done. We could also add to the list the development of formal validation methods for software, which are already being used in some places.

An effect on the industry is that the likely evolutionary path for high-availability systems is a reduction in the number of hardware architectures used, and thus a continuing reduction in the number of suppliers of such systems.

Several factors drive this concentration of suppliers:

- A stagnation in the size of the hardware-based high-availability market, accompanied by a growth in cluster-based solutions that are now able to offer comparable levels of availability

- High system cost, driven by the need to replicate hardware and to amortize high R&D costs over a small number of systems

- Improvements in hardware reliability (discussed above)

- Appearance of high-availability features in mainstream servers, as some standard high-end servers allow the removal and replacement of subsystems (processor cards, memory boards, I/O controllers, power supply modules, fans, etc.) without the need to stop the system—this trend is spreading

- Difficulty of tracking technology; it takes time to engineer a hardware-based high-availability system, and by the time the work has been done the world of standard microprocessors has moved on to a new generation

10.7 Endnotes

1. Tandem was accquired by Compaq, itself later acquired by HP.

2. This nomenclature can create confusion with Storage Area Network, presented in Chapter 2, which is a network intended for connection between servers and their storage subsystems. Since ServerNet did not become the success hoped for by its promoters, in this book we use the term SAN to mean Storage Area Network, meaning the interconnect network for peripheral subsystems.

3. IRISA is part of INRIA (Institut National de Recherche en Informatique et en Automatique, or National Institute for Research into Information Technology and Automation) and is located in Rennes, France.

4. Given that one has estimates of the various parameters (repair and failure rates described below), Markov chains can be used in the systems design phase (that is, before the system exists).

5. These models apply only to already-developed software, since they are based on measurements taken during testing.

6. VLSI (Very Large Scale Integration) indicates the technology used for highly-integrated chips (processors, memories, etc.).

Selection Criteria and Total Cost of Ownership

In this chapter we first take a brief look at appropriate selection criteria for servers, and then moves on to discuss a key economic element of server choice: a system's total cost of ownership.

11.1 Selection Criteria

Over the course of the book, we have compared various architectural options: symmetrical multiprocessors (tightly-coupled machines) in Chapter 4, clusters and massively parallel machines (loosely-coupled machines) in Chapter 5, servers and DBMS in Chapter 8, storage in Chapter 6 and performance in Chapter 7.

We shall not revisit the conclusions and commentaries of those chapters here, but rather will concentrate on user needs and thus the choice of appropriate selection criteria.

Selection criteria are driven by requirements, such as those expressed by the staff in charge of a company's information systems. These needs include:

- Availability of applications and development tools
- Data integrity
- Availability
- Performance
- Scalability
- Price
- Client/server support

- Maturity of architecture

- Perenniality of the investments

Table 11.1 shows how the various architectural options match up to these needs.

Table 11.1   *How Architectural Approaches Match User Needs.*

Need	Symmetric multiprocessor (SMP)	Cluster	Massively Parallel Machine (MPP)
Availability of applications and development tools	***	*	*
Data integrity	*** (Depends on the DBMS and transactional monitors)	*** (Depends on the DBMS and transactional monitors)	*** (Depends on the DBMS and transactional monitors)
Availability	** (reduced due to single points of failure)	*** (key goal of the architecture)	* (generally not a goal of an MPP)
Performance	*** (Within the limits of system configurability)	** (Depends on application characteristics)	** (Depends on application characteristics
Scalability	*** (Within the limits of system configurability)	* (Depends on application characteristic)	* (Depends on application characteristic)
Price	*** (small and medium configurations)	**	* (due to cost of system interconnect and innovative architecture)
Client/server support	**	*** (multiserver architecture)	** (multiserver architecture)

Table 11.1 *How Architectural Approaches Match User Needs. (continued)*

Need	Symmetric multiprocessor (SMP)	Cluster	Massively Parallel Machine (MPP)
Maturity of architecture	*** (More than thirty years of experience)	** (More than fifteen years of experience)	* (Emergent technology)
Perenniality of investment	** (Limited to one, perhaps two generations)	*** (possibility of mixing multiple generations in one system)	* (Emergent technology)

We now will comment on these various points.

When we speak of the **availability of applications and development tools**, we mean the availability of applications and tools designed for the architecture's unique capabilities. Provided that an SMP's, cluster's or MPP's operating system is compatible with the base operating system for a same-instruction set architecture uniprocessor, then applications in the standard catalog (and in-house applications developed by a business) may also run on all these systems. However, this approach will not take advantage of the applications' unique capabilities, especially scalability.

Because of widespread acceptance of its programming model, many applications have been adapted for SMP systems.

As we saw in Chapter 5, the various cluster solutions available are differentiated perhaps more by the differences in the details of their programming models than anything else. This wide variety limits the number of applications adapted to any one cluster API, with suppliers tending to concentrate on systems that represent a large-enough market. This phenomenon is also visible, perhaps even more strongly, with MPPs. DBMS vendors have strongly embraced the cluster model, and also support those MPPs with large enough market size.

The emergence of Windows clusters might attract significant investment from software vendors, because of the combination of potentially large volumes coupled with the use of one API.

None of the various architectures offers any special advantage or disadvantage as regards **data integrity**, because this is in the hands of both data managers (DBMS, generally), which have control over the integrity of their databases, and transactional monitors, which own the task of ensuring coherence across the multiple databases affected by a transaction (that is, they are responsible for the total coherence of the data).

The fact that there is just one copy of the operating system and its data structures in an SMP makes the OS an obvious single point of failure (SPOF); an OS failure stops the whole system, necessitating a reboot and giving SMPs a low mark for **availability**. Removing hardware SPOFs in an SMP is also difficult. With the exception of a small number of high-avail-ability systems vendors who deploy hardware-based mechanisms, most sys-tems vendors concentrate on fault detection and error recovery, along with "repair tolerance" (for example, the ability to swap system components without stopping the system). High availability is a natural property of clus-ters, and is widely exploited. MPPs constructed from interconnected nodes, each running their own copy of the OS, also have the same property, but it is not as widely exploited, since the key goal of most MPPs is performance rather than availability.

On the **performance** front, SMPs offer the best potential (within the limits of the maximum system configuration) because of the simplicity of their programming model (shared memory with multiple processes and threads) and the efficiency of their communication and synchronization mechanisms (the use of simple instructions on shared data). Because clus-ters and MPPs generally use message-based communications, synchroniza-tion uses the interconnect network and therefore the software overhead of using that network. The performance of clusters and MPPs depends strongly on the nature of the application and the distribution of data and data accesses in the system. As a result, the potential performance of a clus-ter or MPP is lower than a similarly-provisioned SMP. This inefficiency is, however, counterbalanced by the much bigger (in processor count) systems possible with clusters and MPPs than with SMPs.

For **scalability**, SMP also wins (again, within the limits of the maximum configuration), since it is easy to add processors, memory and I/O control-lers. As we showed in the analysis of TPC-C results across the architectures, SMPs offer the highest efficiency (in terms of performance per processor). Again, MPPs and clusters can make use of many more processors, and even-tually the larger numbers outweigh the lower efficiencies for these architec-tures, provided that the application characteristics make it cluster-friendly.

Our analysis of **price**[1] in the table is based on the fundamental costs of the various approaches, rather than a study of this week's pricelists. The com-moditization of SMP architectures makes small- and mid-sized SMPs very attractive in terms of price: the processors and chipsets used in these systems are used in workstations and high-end PCs, and the development cost of any custom components is amortized over a very large number of systems. On the other hand, very large SMP systems (for example, CC-NUMA systems) engender large development costs for both hardware and software. These costs are amortized over significantly fewer systems (although this will change as these technologies also become commoditized).

Since clusters are generally constructed of collections of standard systems (usually small- to medium sized SMPs), they too benefit from the effect of commoditization on costs. Rack-mounting clusters offers potential improvements in terms of square footage of facilities needed for the systems, extensibility, and maintenance simplicity.

Because of their innovative nature, MPPs have to amortize their development costs—specifically interconnect network and hardware packaging—over a rather smaller number of systems.

Client/server support is driven by the availability of appropriate middleware. Because of their widespread acceptance (and the simplicity and efficiency of their programming model), SMPs score well in this area. On the other hand, applications requiring several applications servers (such as some Enterprise Resource Planning packages) result in the servers sharing resources, which can pose problems of scalability and failure resistance in SMPs. Clusters and MPPs offer a better solution for such applications, but MPPs suffer from a potential lack of appropriate middleware.

One of our selection criteria is **architectural maturity**. A major factor in determining the amount of confidence one may have in an architecture is how well sorted it is, which can be measured to some extent by the amount of investment already made in that architecture. Any confidence in an architecture will be driven to a low level by the appearance of new architecture that replaces it. SMPs have the longest architectural life of the options we have discussed, first appearing in the 1960s. Clusters followed in the mid-80s. Although the first Teradata systems (MPPs) also date from the mid-80s, MPPs are regarded as a less mature approach. Neither clusters nor MPPs have replaced SMPs; indeed, SMPs are used to construct both clusters and MPPs, these being (at the hardware level) nothing much more than collections of connected SMP systems. Grid Computing and Global Computing can be viable alternatives, in some applications, to MPPs, and can be viewed (in those domains) as a possible replacement architecture for MPPs.

Investment perenniality is a key issue when making a choice of solution. Several factors contribute to this:

- *Architectural maturity.* The more mature the architecture, the higher the probability that it will continue to be useful and supported. Nonetheless, it is wise to keep an eye open for the appearance of replacement architectures and technologies, and to be on guard for low investment in their products by vendors who are content just to maintain their position in the market.

- *Financial strength of the vendors and their ability to finance continued development.* This is a factor for all the vendors of a server system—hardware platform, OS, middleware, DBMS, development tools, and applications. The failure of just one link in the chain can put the whole system at risk.[2]

- The *availability of application developers* and, more generally, the availability of personnel trained in the relevant technologies.

It is not only advisable to take as many precautions as possible when making a choice, but also to keep vigilant for the upcoming appearance of technological discontinuities.

This technology watch should cover technology *per se*, but should also watch the development of the industry. As one example of the latter, it is interesting to analyze how new technologies get established in the industry and so, in the following section, we look at the traditional technology life cycle.

We then look at a different life cycle—that of the *perception* of the potential of a new technology. This is a real issue in portions of the industry that are particularly media-driven (such as the computer industry, where hype, unfortunately, is a major factor).

We present both these life cycles, because for a technology watch to be useful, it must both get to grips with the technology and its possibilities, but also understand the effects of fads and fashions on the outcome of innovation.

11.2   The Traditional Technology Life Cycle

In this section we show and discuss (albeit in a sketchy manner) the traditional life cycle associated with the introduction of a new technology. Our purpose in doing this is to establish in the reader's mind the usefulness of a technology watch.

At a macroscopic level, the potential of any specific technology has a life cycle that follows a curve very similar to the industry itself. The curve is illustrated in Figure 11.1.

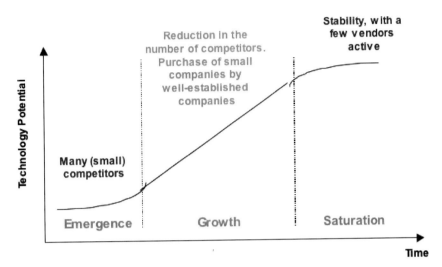

Figure 11.1
Evolution of the potential of a new technology.

When a technology is first available, in its *emergent* phase, there is a profusion of solutions based on it and many competitors, often start-ups. Once the technology has attained a degree of maturity and the market has taken off, then as often as not fewer companies are left, fated to become market leaders, be bought by other companies, or disappear completely. By the third phase, just a handful of companies will remain in existence.

> **Start-ups**
>
> Start-up companies are often born within large companies, when a team's proposals were unsuccessful in obtaining management support and funding; or within universities, when researchers decide to cash in on their work. The birth of such companies is underwritten by venture capital firms. In some markets, VCs are best convinced of the business value of a concept or business plan by the commitment of the founders—for example, by their taking out a second or third mortgage on their house.

If a technology can deliver on the promises made by its promoters, it will transition from emergence into the *growth* phase. The technology then becomes a strong marketplace differentiator, which brings it to the attention of well-established companies along with the (possibly new) markets that it addresses. Such a company can address the market either by deploying its own products (which would suggest that it had planned for this situation) or it can enter into a relationship with one of the pioneers as a distributor, a licensee or partner. During the growth phase, a number of the small companies will disappear, either because they never managed to attract a large-enough market share to survive, or because they were acquired.

Throughout the growth phase, the number of companies playing in the field decreases. By the time it reaches the *saturation* phase, the technology is no longer a marketplace differentiator, and competition now becomes based upon the ability to manufacture and distribute at low cost, with just a handful of companies active in the field.

Choosing a technology when it is in the growth phase can provide an IT director with a competitive advantage (as an example, perhaps the system could provide a better response time, which would give it a better image among its users, better reactivity, reduced application development time, and so forth). Nonetheless, any technology choice implies a technology dependence, in general for several years; and the risk associated with such a choice is whether the technology will remain available and competitive throughout that extended period.

11.3   Perception of the Potential of a Technology

Figure 11.2 illustrates the evolution of the perception of the potential of a technology.

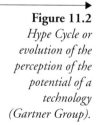

Figure 11.2
Hype Cycle or evolution of the perception of the potential of a technology (Gartner Group).

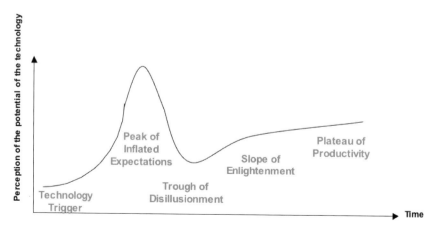

This type of lifecycle has recently been introduced by the Gartner Group and termed as the Hype Cycle.

Starting from the first appearance of the technology, which might be the production of a new device or the outcome of some experiments, investment is applied. However little the technology claims to solve a highly-visible problem, its claims are vastly amplified to the extent that expectations rise, possibly to levels that can not be supported by the technology or the actual outcome of the experiments.

A number of phenomena are involved in driving hope to an unrealistic peak. Among these are: articles in the specialist press, PR (whether press releases or well-placed articles) from the companies investing in the technology, experiments attempted by large companies or organizations, and so on. As to the last item, major companies often experiment with new technologies in an exploratory manner, to evaluate them; it is fairly straightforward for interested parties (marketing folk and the press in particular) to represent this involvement as an endorsement of the technology and a strategic choice for the future by the majors.

Of course, one day the bubble bursts, perhaps because the experiments don't pan out as hoped. In the mirror image of the climb to the unrealistic peak, all hope disappears in a crash of disillusionment. At the very deepest part of the trough of disillusion, it can happen that the technology, having had the benefit of all the money thrown at it in the overoptimistic phase, attains a measure of maturity and begins to be able to demonstrate useful results. This gives birth to a technological life cycle very similar to the one discussed in the previous section. Such a cycle corresponds to a technology which is actually adopted to some extent. There are many technologies which disappear with little or no trace.

11.4 Total Cost of Possession

This section is partly based on the Gartner Group's TCO methodology, whose first work on the subject appeared in 1987 [BER98].

Adopting the TCO methodology enables companies to analyze the different components of cost, measure them, perform appropriate simulations, and make decisions that will lead to reduce costs.

Comparing one company's costs with data on equivalent costs in similar companies ("benchmarking") should not be the only measure, unless the equivalent data is from the whole of the industry.[3] However, within-domain comparisons do provide some points of reference and provide a background for interpreting the numbers measured and what they mean.

The methodology can be supported in-house by tools as simple as spreadsheets and databases, or through services from outside companies.

Any such analysis must cover all the associated costs, not just the server costs—everything from the server and its peripheral subsystems to the workstations and the network must be counted.

The costs identified fall into two main categories:

- *Direct costs, or budgeted costs*. This class covers investment and amortization, the headcount necessary to run the system (administration, development and support), subcontractors, purchases, the training of people who will use the system, maintenance, and communications. These costs are reported annually.

- *Indirect costs, or costs that were not budgeted (sometimes called hidden costs)*. These costs provide an indicator of how well the investment and of the efficiency of the management of the information system meet the needs of the users. As an example, one component of indirect costs is the proportion of the time spent by users training themselves on the system, or helping their colleagues to use it.

We will provide a short discussion of these two classes of costs.

Direct costs include:

- *Hardware and software*. Covers the investment and amortization of the purchase or cost of renting workstations, peripheral subsystems, and communications

- *Administration*. The total cost of administration for the various pieces of equipment and any needed external services (such as for specialist expertise)

- *Development*. Covers the totality of costs associated with application development (design, implementation, test, documentation, etc.)

- *Support*. This is the cost of the help desk, training, etc.; measures of the effectiveness of a help desk include the ratio of users to the number of people in the help desk; call rate; average problem fix time; and so on

- *Communications.* The total cost of communications associated with the information system: renting telephone lines, calls from nomadic workstations, Web usage and so forth

Evaluating the **indirect costs** is not simple, but is necessary. With the goal of reducing direct costs, it is very tempting to forego a number of services. This, however, can result in an information system which is inefficient overall, because of the time wasted by each user, who then needs to practice *self-support*—that is, to research solutions to their problems themselves, or to provide help to colleagues. Either of these can lead to an effective reduction of the availability of the information system. The resulting increase in indirect costs can match or swamp any reductions in direct costs.

There are two main categories of indirect costs: those to do with the users, and those to do with the unavailability of the system.

Among the **user-related indirect costs** we can mention:

- *Self-support and mutual aid.* The total time spent by users in finding the causes of their problems, either by themselves or with the help of colleagues, and finding ways to circumvent or avoid the problems, rather than calling support staff
- *Self-training.* Total time spent by users searching within documentation (nowadays, happily, generally available on-line) rather than taking advantage of structured training offered by the organization
- *Script-writing.* Total time spent by users writing scripts and parametrizing products when such activities are not part of their official responsibilities (that is, not the work that they are being paid to do)

To obtain a measure of these costs, it is best to resort to surveys and questionnaires of the users themselves. The costs can be expressed on an annual basis, for example average time spent by a user in discovering the cause of a problem and how to cure it.

The **indirect cost of unavailability** is measured by the loss of productivity due to the unavailability of any of the components of the system: workstations, servers, networks, helpdesk, or applications. It is usual to distinguish between planned and unplanned. We have already touched on these notions in Chapter 10, discussing high-availability systems. These costs are also expressed on an annual basis.

Planned unavailability corresponds to the periods when the system is stopped for preventive maintenance, software updates and so on. The planning of these stops means they will have zero impact on users (for example, planned stops at night when no users are connected) or minimal impact (as in a company with 24×7 use). Sources of data to help analyze the costs associated with unavailability are:

- Analyzing system journals
- Administrator reports
- Help desk reports
- Surveys of users

The costs can be expressed in a number of complementary ways: total cost per user, support cost per user, cost per megabyte of data managed, etc. Once the data is collected, the choice of how the costs should be shown is driven by the type of analysis wanted.

If there is a desire to benchmark the company (against others, or against best of breed), it is best to have some measure of the relative complexity of each system component, and to make use of companies that offer such comparisons as a service and have already gathered data from appropriate comparison companies.

One needs a complexity measure for the following elements:

- The organization of the information system (from a simple centralized system working just during normal working hours, to a distributed worldwide system working 24×7)
- Services provided by the system and the associated procedures
- The characteristics of the organization within which the system users work
- The characteristics of both infrastructure and application software
- The characteristics of the various pieces of hardware (for example, the degree of heterogeneity of the server platforms)

Complexity is expressed on a simple grading scale. Combining these different factors provides a complexity signature for the system, allowing an appropriate comparison set to be selected.

Whether one implements the comparison or not, it is advisable to identify the elements that can help resolve the most critical problems and to quantify the potential benefits. Among the relevant elements we can list:

- *Hardware technology.* For example, SAN-based storage subsystem, server choices allowing scalability, high-availability solutions, etc.

- *Software technology.* For example, automated operating procedures, administration solutions, component-based approach for the applications, a rationalized choice of suppliers, etc.

- Restructuring the organization in charge of the system

- User training

- Reengineering business procedures

The process we have just described is similar in spirit to processes that have been implemented for other aspects of information technology. As an example, estimating software development costs with the use of COCOMO (*Constructive Cost Model*), or function points, or a model of the test process.

As with all processes of this nature, the old adage must never be forgotten: the secret of success is to never give up.

11.5 Endnotes

1. The real issue—much larger than list price comparisons—is how much a system costs to acquire and run over its lifetime. As we saw in Chapter 7, covering performance, the TPC benchmarks make an attempt at this, requiring the cost of purchase and three years of maintenance to be included in the notional cost of the system. But the costs of ownership include more factors than these; these factors are combined in the notion of Total Cost of Ownership (TCO), which is discussed in the next section.

2. Imagine a company that adopted Windows as a software platform, but chose Alpha or PowerPC as the processor architecture for their systems. If the processor choice ceased development (as

seems to be the case for Alpha), the company would have all the expense of moving its entire family to an Intel architecture—whether IA-32 or IA-64—and, presumably, would also find any architecture-specific advantages annulled by the move.

3. In our opinion, implementing the methodology, identifying the elements of cost, analyzing the possible remedies, and, above all, doing this as an ongoing part of business will produce the most tangible results. Continual measuring provides a great deal of information and education. In particular, it makes it possible to identify bad habits and stop doing them and to identify the most important factors behind cost.

12

Conclusions and Prospects

12.1   Part 1: Architectures

In the first part of this chapter, we conclude our examination of server and server-related architecture by systematically revisiting the major conclusions of this work and then considering possible evolutionary paths. The first part complements the conclusions of the first three chapters, which performed a similar role for server-relevant technologies; here, we look at how these technology projections could be exploited in possible future systems architectures.

The second part of this chapter is a general conclusion.

12.2   Application Architecture

Looking at the semiconductor technology trends, in which increased densities allow the integration of multiple systems elements—processors, caches, controllers, and so on—onto a single chip, it is clear that low-end and mid-range servers (say four- to eight-processor SMPs) will become commodity items. As a result, only vendors with huge volumes will be able to continue to play in these markets. Although multiprocessor workstations are emerging, we should note that server-level requirements for reliability, availability, and maintainability mean that workstations will remain very different from servers.

As we have emphasized several times, the major interesting aspect of clusters is their high intrinsic availability. The key problem with clusters is the lack of a standard programming model to make parallel programming straightforward. Although UNIX cluster products are functionally very similar, they all build on different interfaces to provide that functionality, in particular continuity of service and performance growth. Windows, having just one maker and just one set of interfaces, has no such problem.

Clusters fit naturally into three-tier architectures, in which they support the database portion and provide continuity of service and scalability. Figure 12.1 illustrates the four-tier architecture and the role of each level.

Figure 12.1
Four-tier architecture.

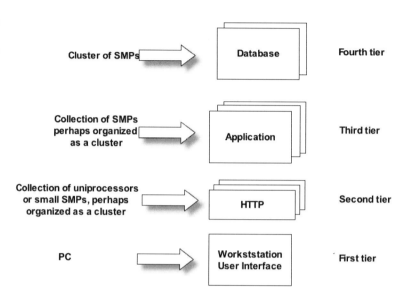

The advantages of a four-tier architecture over (particularly) two- or three-tier architectures were covered in Chapter 3, and here we will summarize them:

- The architecture is well-suited to a software component approach

- Good security because data is well-insulated

- Easy scalability, bringing needed performance to database and/or application

- Simpler Internet integration, with application servers handling applet downloads to the clients

- The ability to be interconnected with other database servers, and in particular to mainframes

- Hardware configuration flexibility

To ensure data integrity and consistent data state after a recovery, applications must be built on transactional logic [GRA92]. When this is done, partially completed transactions can be cancelled transparently by the data manager, typically the DBMS. The client must then re-run the transactions, although this can be automated, given appropriate programming of the client part of the application.

Massively parallel machines (MPPs) have specific niches, such as decision support with extremely large databases or tight response time constraints, and in scientific computing (for areas where the problem is parallelizable). We should reiterate that solutions based on very high-bandwidth, low-latency interconnects can be a practical alternative to an MPP, at least for configurations of a few tens of nodes, with the limiting factor generally being the problems of managing the configuration both physically and logically.

There has long been a sterile debate between SMP and cluster components—sterile because a combination of the two approaches provides the most benefits. Choosing a flexible large multiprocessor architecture—that is, an architecture that allows the components to be configured either as a large SMP, or as a collection of SMPs of various sizes able to operate either as autonomous machines or as elements of cluster(s)—seems a promising approach. A key proviso for the success of such an approach would be its cost relative to less flexible arrangements. The need to be able to handle partitioning large SMPs constitutes a useful step in the direction suggested.

Having quickly reviewed application architectures and their fit with server architectures in this section, we will look at possible evolutionary developments in

- Microprocessors
- Multiprocessors
- Clusters
- MPPs
- High-availability systems

We will conclude by assembling a possible future systems architecture incorporating the points discussed.

12.3 Microprocessor Architecture

We looked at various architecture options in Chapters 4 and 5 and can now comment on the possible directions for microprocessor implementations discussed in Chapter 1. We briefly recap the processor architecture approaches discussed in Chapter 1:

- *High-degree superscalar.* Increases the number of functional units in a processor, along with the ability to execute many instructions simultaneously

- *EPIC.* A large number of functional units whose proper usage is left to the compiler, which must discover available parallelism

- *Trace scheduling.* An implementation in which a number of paths of execution (*traces*) are cached and executed in parallel, with the appropriate path being chosen dynamically; the choice of cached traces is done through "learning"—the most frequently used traces are retained

- *Simultaneous multithreading.* A processor implementation is provided with extra resources, so that it can hold the state of several threads or processes simultaneously. The processor attempts to execute as many of the processes simultaneously as possible (using an appropriate priority scheme), choosing instructions to execute in each process on a clock-by-clock basis, so that all possible functional units are busy most of the time; this provides increased throughput

- *Chip multiprocessors.* Implement several processors on a single chip

- *Intelligent memory (IRAM).* Add some processing capability to each memory chip

- *Reconfigurable processors.* A collection of interconnects and very simple processing units, configurable by software both in shape and instruction set architecture

[KOZ98] presents evaluation criteria for and comments on the applicability of these approaches in the context of workstations and information appliances. Our analysis is inspired by that work, but is extended to be applicable to servers through the use of extra criteria. We apply the extended criteria not just to servers but also, in a spirit of generality, to workstations and information appliances as well.

Table 12.1 *Architectural options: evaluation criteria.* *

Criterion	Workstations and information appliances	Servers
Binary compatibility	***/**	***
Multimedia support	***	*
Fine and/or coarse grain parallelism	**	**
Program size	**/***	*
Memory bandwidth and latency	***	***
I/O band-width and latency	**	***
Power consumption	**	*
Design complexity	**	**
Design scalability	**	**

*   More asterisks indicate increased importance

We now provide some commentary on these criteria and how they apply to servers and workstations.

For an innovative architecture, high-performance support for existing binaries is both a strong constraint (on architectural possibilities) and a major requirement, giving access to an existing application base. Lack of binary compatibility can be a blocking factor for architectures; similarly, an architecture that offers binary compatibility but requires recompilation for acceptable performance may also fail.

While there are ways of providing compatibility in new architectures, it is generally at the dual price of complexity and reduced overall performance. Seeing how well IA-64's implementation of IA-32 succeeds will be interesting. Compatibility is a key issue for workstations and servers; it can be less of an issue for multimedia information appliances, since the latter may need the optimization of just one application of moderate complexity to provide competitive performance.

For multimedia appliances and workstations, the key capability is the processors' ability to provide real-time response (that is, the ability to keep up with the rate of data input and output); parallel operations on data

(SIMD); pipelined processing for collections of data; high memory bandwidth to support the display; and sufficient I/O bandwidth to support real-time acquisition of data.

For servers, these characteristics are generally of no relevance, except for "on-demand" video servers, which (at the time this is written) do not form a significant market. The appearance of low-cost, high-speed networks (WANs and MANs) could change this picture.

Supporting parallelism—whether fine- or coarse-grain—is important for both servers and workstations/appliances.

Program size is a matter of little importance for servers, since any application is shared between a large number of clients. However, code size does affect the effectiveness of caches, and so particularly large code can have a negative effect on performance. For workstations, however, extremely large programs can be a problem, since they may demand more memory than would normally be supplied. And code size may be even more important for information appliances, since they—being very high-volume products—are very cost-sensitive.

A server's memory bandwidth and latency set its ability to handle processor and I/O demands. As we have seen in Chapter 7, we need to keep the processors busy all the time to get maximum system performance; if they are waiting on memory, this will not be possible. The requirements for I/O bandwidth and latency are generally higher for servers, and as is the case for memory, a server whose performance is limited by low I/O bandwidth and latency will be far from optimal.

Power consumption is an important issue for workstations, since higher power mandates more aggressive cooling, with increases in cost and noise. Power is a key criterion for portable computers, since the machine's autonomy is dependent on battery operation and larger batteries are heavy and expensive. Power *per se* is less of an issue for small- and medium-sized servers, where the effect of higher power is mostly a requirement for larger-capacity power backup systems. However, for large servers, power density is an important issue, because their packing densities place an upper limit on how many watts per square inch of board they can cool.

Development schedule risks and the impact of R&D costs on the product cost are both increased when processor design complexity is greater. These two areas are key to success - timely introduction alongside (or, better, ahead of) the competition, and at a reasonable price. The industry is awash with examples of processors which suffered substantial introductory delays, and even of microprocessors which were never really born. Frequently, these occur when the designs are too complex and the project teams lack the ability to manage the situation.

In this context, when we refer to scalability of the design, we mean the ability to port the design, little changed, to successive generations of semi-conductor technology (which offer, in general, higher clock rates and smaller geometries). Designs which have long interconnects are unlikely to be very scalable, since the propagation time down the interconnect will quickly act as a limit to improved clock frequency; to cure this, a redesign is needed. The more redesign is needed, the greater the introduction delay and the higher the fixed costs of development (and, therefore, the risks).

Now that we have established the relevant criteria, we show in Table 12.2 a matrix of architectural options against the criteria, for both servers and workstations.

Table 12.2 *Comparison of various architectural approaches for servers.*

Criterion	Superscalar	EPIC	Trace scheduling	Simultaneous Multithreading	Chip multiproce ssor	Intellig ent Memor y	Reconfigura ble processor
Binary compatibility	=	-	=	=	=	-	-
Support of the multimedia one	-	=	-	–	=	+	+
Parallelism with fine grain and/or coarse grain	=	=	=	=	=	+/=	+
Obstruction of the programs	=	-	=	=	=	+	=
Bandwidth and latency memory	=	=	=	=	=	+	+
Bandwidth and latency E/S	=	=	=	=	=	=	=

Table 12.2   *Comparison of various architectural approaches for servers. (continued)*

Criterion	Superscalar	EPIC	Trace scheduling	Simultaneous Multithreading	Chip multiproce ssor	Intellig ent Memor y	Reconfigura ble processor
Power consumption	-	=	-	-	=	+	-
Complexity of the design	-	-	-	-	=	=	+
Scalability of the design	-	=	=	-	=	=	-

We now comment quickly on the comparisons in the table, after noting that no approach shows obvious superiority.

For **binary compatibility**, the EPIC, IRAM and reconfigurable processor approaches all imply a change in the instruction set architecture, and IRAM and reconfigurable processors also offer a radical change in computing paradigm that is unlikely to facilitate the support of existing architectures.

EPIC has no such radical architectural change, so support of an existing architecture is not an issue in principle although it will, most likely, increase complexity one way or another. The current instances of EPIC architectures, all variants of IA-64, do support IA-32 execution. It will be interesting to watch the penetration of 64-bit architecture extensions of the IA-32 architecture introduced by AMD and Intel.

There are no major differences between the other approaches as regards binary compatibility, although recompilation (with a new compiler) may be needed to get best performance out of the new architecture.

For **multimedia support**, the superscalar and trace approaches suffer somewhat because their execution model is more non-deterministic[1] (out-of-order execution, branch prediction, cache effects, etc.) The characteristics of IRAM and reconfigurable computing should make them a good match for multimedia.

In the area of **parallelism** there are few significant differences between the architectures, with the exception of IRAM and reconfigurable processing. IRAM, whose initial studies at the University of California at Berkeley centered on an array processor that exploited parallelism, has appropriate characteristics for fine-grain concurrency. A reconfigurable processor should, in principle, be suitable for defining a machine able to exploit various forms of parallelism. The approaches are all neutral as regards coarse-grain parallelism.

EPIC observably produces much larger **program sizes**, especially if compilers are required to generate no-op instructions to meet instruction-scheduling constraints. However, we must note that to get the best performance from any modern microprocessor, it is generally necessary to "unroll loops" (convert loops which iterate N times to be a loop with M times as many statements per iteration and N/M iterations) and "inline procedures" (copy the code of a called procedure into the call site, rather than calling it), operations which increase code size noticeably. Nonetheless, these operations must also be done for EPIC architectures, which will suffer more code bloat than more traditional architectures. For vector applications, IRAM offers the possibility of smaller code size, since the ability to specify vector operations reduces the need for loops.

IRAM and reconfigurable processors have an advantage over the others in **memory bandwidth and latency**, since most memory access can be internal to a chip.

I/O architecture is essentially independent of processor architectural choices, being an issue for system architecture rather than processor architecture.

IRAM offers the possibility of reduced **power consumption**; the other options tend to need increased power.

IRAM and reconfigurable processors offer the lowest **design complexity**. IRAM is mostly memory, leaving little space for a processor and thereby keeping its complexity low. A chip multiprocessor also has reasonably low complexity, since multiple copies of a processor design are integrated. However, the approach does provide challenges in the design of an efficient, cost-effective shared cache hierarchy. Reconfigurable processors are again a repetitive structure, and thus of low hardware design complexity. The other designs are all rather complex.

Looking at the table, we can see that IRAM and reconfigurable computing seem to have advantages over other approaches in many areas. This, however, cannot be taken as an indication that they will triumph over and eclipse the other approaches, since they both suffer from two probably fatal drawbacks: the lack of binary compatibility and the need for a very different programming model. Even with the development of new tool suites allowing application development for these approaches, the burden of redesigning and rewriting and requalifying major complex applications seems unbearable. Nonetheless, these approaches may find success in specialized applications.

Superscalar, simultaneous multithreading and reconfigurable computers are all shown as not being very **scalable** in the table. This is a result of their relatively long interconnects, which generally means that they would need to be reimplemented for new technologies.

In reading these comments, it should be understood that the statements made are general, intended to give the reader a flavor of the differences between architectures and a sense of how to choose between them.

12.4   SMP Server Architecture

As we saw when looking at SMPs, technological factors limit the size of feasible machines, making it necessary to resort to approaches such as CC-NUMA. Technology trends support such a direction, allowing us, for example, to integrate several processors (as seen by software) and appropriate interfaces to support an interconnect network that can provide distributed cache coherence.

Whether these choices are made, or others, technology is making it possible to integrate more and more of a system architecture onto a single chip.

Microprocessors introduced since 2000 follow this trend, as do the chip sets which accompany them. We can expect that as time goes by, the processors will increasingly integrate the chipsets, too.

In the following sections, we will discuss these new implementation possibilities and extrapolate further in several directions.

12.4.1   Extensible base SMP

A significant trend has been the integration of what used to be system architecture within microprocessors, with a key example being the trend to integrate interprocessor interconnects, which can support cache coherence into the processor. With such integration, the implementation of a low-end system with perhaps four to eight processors requires substantially fewer chips (and therefore lower cost, area and, in general, power), while the implementation of a larger system of 16 to 32 processors is much facilitated. This trend also has an interesting effect on the computer industry, since what was once a humble microprocessor vendor is transformed into a system designer and implementer, making it very difficult for a computer company with an average sales volume to develop its own systems. That is, the opportunity for hardware value-add for computer manufacturers is disappearing, and going instead to the chip vendors, who also benefit from building an OEM business.

In Chapter 4, when discussing SMPs, we showed solutions that allowed the construction of moderately-sized systems, and showed that their potential for growth (in terms of the number of processors supported) was rather limited.

Before solutions allowing this sort of growth were available from the commodity vendors, systems manufacturers developed their own solutions. Figure 12.2 shows the approach that IBM developed for its systems based on Intel microprocessors.

Figure 12.2
X-Architecture
(source: IBM).

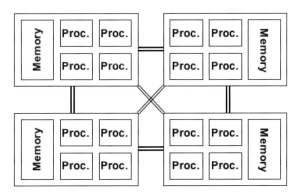

The components developed by IBM make it possible to interconnect four-processor modules to create SMPs of up to 16 processors. The key components are:

- A memory and I/O controller, providing the ability for a four-processor module to effect I/O operations on non-local PCI adapters

- A three-port (the ports are called *scalability ports*) L4 cache controller giving access by a module to other modules

Obviously, the scalability ports support the cache coherence protocol.

This architecture, along with the associated components (called XA-32 and XA-64), was developed for IA-32 and IA-64. This approach has value for systems manufacturers for only a limited time, since it will be overtaken by the continual integration of systems features into commodity silicon (discussed more later).

If a microprocessor vendor can supply basic SMP modules which integrate four to eight powerful processors along with a memory controller, interfaces for I/O, and coherency-supporting intermodule connections, the cost (both developmental and per unit) of a large SMP built from the modules will be rather low. This allows a computer vendor to concentrate expenditures on areas of added value—that is, all the elements (in general, these will be software) that make the system usable, highly available, partitionable, and so on.

To the extent that one can build, on top of the protocols provided by such modules, information access mechanisms that provide appropriate protections, the architecture just sketched can be looked upon as the basis of a flexible systems architecture based on combining SMPs and SMP clusters. For simplicity, the atomic unit (the smallest element which can be clustered) in such a system is the module.

The following example, taken from AMD's Opteron family, demonstrates the integration of the SMP dimension within microprocessors. Figure 1.3 shows the internal architecture of the Opteron microprocessor.

Figure 12.3
Internal architecture of the Opteron microprocessor (source: AMD).

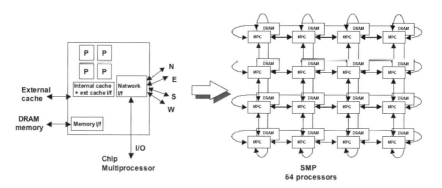

While the internal details of this processor, which extends the IA-32 architecture to 64 bits in a manner proprietary to AMD, is interesting, we will not delve into it further. The memory controller is integrated into the processor, thereby removing the bottleneck presented by a bus shared by a number of processors and avoiding the complexity of a crossbar.

We will concentrate our attention on the HyperTransport interconnect, which allows an SMP to be constructed along with I/O connections.

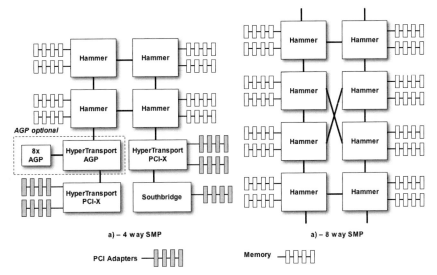

Figure 12.4
Opteron-based SMP system.

Figure 12.4 illustrates the construction of an SMP with four to eight processors.

Figure 12.4 a shows a configuration with four processors integrating a graphic interface (which is not typical of a server), connections to per-processor memory, and connections to I/Os.

With three HyperTransport links, it is possible to create a "glueless" (i.e., not requiring extra silicon) eight-processor system (Figure 12.4 b). Four Hypertransport links are left available for I/O connections. Each processor has access to all the memory, the links implementing a cache coherence protocol. The NUMA factor (the ratio between the access time for local and distant memory) is small, since the distance between a processor and a distant memory is just two (i.e., there are at most just two processors to cross to access the most remote memory). While AMD has not provided complete information, it is reasonable to suppose that this system is nearer to a UMA than a NUMA; that is, little or no software modifications will be necessary for this system to work well.

12.4.2 Single-chip multiprocessor

At the Microprocessor Forum in October 1998, IBM presented the Power4, a PowerPC architecture chip which integrates two processors, Level-1 and Level-2 caches, an interface to a Level-3 cache, and an interprocessor interconnect, allowing multiple such chips to be used to construct an SMP of more than two processors. We showed in Chapter 4 a high-end system built around the Power4. This type of architecture will grow, both in the number of processors on a chip and in the richness of interprocessor interconnect.

IBM has introduced Power5, the successor to Power4. Power5 again integrates two processors, but in the Power5 the processors support simultaneous multithreading. Systems with 32 to 64 processors can be constructed around the Power5. Since the processors are two-way multithreaded, these configurations look to software to be 64- to 128-processor systems. We show in Figure 12.5 a hypothetical architecture of a Power4 flavor, combining a chip multiprocessor; a coherency-supporting interchip network; and interfaces to external memory, an external cache, and I/O.

Figure 12.5
A chip multiprocessor architecture, and a system based on it.

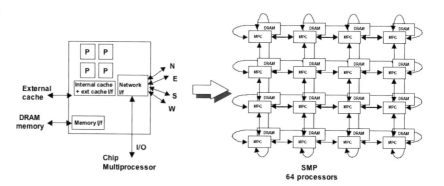

The chip integrates four processors, each with private L1 caches and a shared internal L2 and external L3 cache. An integrated memory controller substantially reduces latency to memory, compared to a solution in which memory was connected via an external bus and controller. The chip also has an I/O interface.

Integrated into the chip are four communications ports (North, East, West, and South) to connect to similar chips. These ports carry coherence information, and allow the construction of a CC-NUMA system. Such ports are generally point-to-point, or at least limited in connectivity.

Alongside the chip, we show a 64-processor system (16 chips, each with 4 processors); for simplicity we omit from the diagram the external caches and I/O.

Larger systems can be built, although for best effect they should be constructed hierarchically; for example, a subsystem like the one shown could be connected via specialist interconnect chip to form a portion of a larger system.

12.4.3 Cluster and MPP architectures

We reviewed the characteristics and properties of both cluster and MPP systems in the earlier part of this work, along with two further architectural options for high-performance systems—vector machines and networks of workstations.

As we have noted above, the combination of SMP and clusters seems the most promising, as its configuration can be parameterized to meet the needs of an application (rather than adapting an application to the needs of the server architecture). Such configuration flexibility is dynamic, and the more possibilities it offers (such as the ability to move processor, memory, and I/O resources from one system domain to another), the more effort must be put into studying systems needs and how to map the system to the application's behaviors. The limitation to any configuration flexibility likely lies in the operating system; if the OS is supplied by an independent source, then it is likely that its flexibility will be lower. Only integrated systems vendors who offer both hardware and software will be able to properly exploit such flexibility.

Independent OS Support

Roughly speaking, the support from an independent OS is likely to aim at standard industry capabilities—that is, it will be able to handle the configuration flexibility most frequently encountered across the industry. This limits the costs of development and validation. However, driven by competition, such an OS supplier could well be encouraged to work closely with a small number of system vendors to make progress in the area of flexibility management, and any advances made would eventually be picked up by other systems vendors.

As regards performance growth, clusters suffer from the lack of a standard programming model, so very few applications have been redesigned and implemented to take advantage of cluster performance capability. In fact, just about the only examples of importance are the major DBMS vendors, who were attracted initially by the high-availability capabilities of the platform, and then took advantage of their scalable performance. As we have seen in Chapter 7, there are significant efficiency differences for software between an SMP and a cluster architecture.[2]

The increasing use of Windows-based clusters, or indeed of the MPI programming model, could result in the establishment of a standard programming model that could in turn drive the creation of many more cluster-adapted applications. Success in this field will clearly be driven in part by the available market for such applications, and could spread to the UNIX-based marketplace as well, if clustering software becomes more standardized across the segment.

The emergence of high-bandwidth, low latency-interconnect will narrow the gap between clusters and MPPs, at least for reasonable-sized collections of machines. Indeed, a trend is to deliver clusters as configurable rackmount systems; if such systems use the new interconnects, they have (within the limits of their configuration) many of the properties of an MPP.

Systems that make use of standard components and interconnects can compete well against MPPs, in configurations of a few tens of processors; such solutions will have a substantial cost advantage over true MPPs.

MPPs, because of their packaging and tuned interconnect, will remain most attractive for systems with a very large number of nodes.

An OS convergence between clusters and MPPs should occur, albeit with two optimization points: high availability for clusters and high performance for MPPs.

12.5 High-Availability Systems Architecture

As we saw at the end of Chapter 10, which covered high-availability hardware and software solutions, the demand for systems that can provide continuous service is constantly growing. This is driven by the trend for business, government, and other bodies to depend more and more on information systems.

We can observe that improvements in hardware technology are producing ever more reliable components and systems, due to a number of factors, including:

- A reduction in the number of components and interconnects needed because of the increase in density

- The integration of error detecting and correcting hardware

- Improvements in design and manufacturing quality

Further, the integration of more and more system functionality into microprocessors and their associated chip sets makes it simpler to ensure quality of operation and error management. The maintainability of a system contributes greatly to its availability. We see, increasingly, that the hooks necessary to allow the replacement of hardware components (processors, memory, I/O) without stopping the system are integrated into midrange and high-end servers.

These changes in technology mean that hardware-based high-availability solutions are becoming increasingly unnecessary, and—given the costs of such an approach—unattractive. Still, hardware-based solutions will be able to find a niche in ultracritical systems.

Software-based solutions to high availability are likely to become widespread, especially solutions based on the cluster approach. Such solutions may provide reasonably-priced continuity of service for transactional applications.

Although the software contribution to systems keeps growing, there has been only modest progress of software technology in the field of service continuity. The development of software is very expensive, especially the testing phase. We offered a number of directions in which solutions could be sought. It seems to us that an approach which marries an error-handling framework with an architecture based on software components (COTS, for *Components Off The Shelf*) holds promise.

12.6 A General System Architecture

We knit together the preceding analysis and commentary, and offer a general systems architecture in Figure 12.6. Our goal in presenting this model is not to provide a precise system specification, but to crystallize the various concepts presented in the book.

This system model comprises a collection of M modules. Each module contains a number of processors, p, each processor itself being an n-way chip multiprocessor. Each module, then, contains n times p processors, tightly coupled. The system itself with M modules, has M times p times n processors. The interconnect, which we will not define precisely here, provides two classes of intercommunication between the modules

- Tight coupling with memory coherence
- Loosely coupled for message-passing, without coherence

On top of this base hardware, the system is defined as a collection of *domains*. A domain is both an SMP and a protection unit; that is, within a

Figure 12.6
General systems architecture.

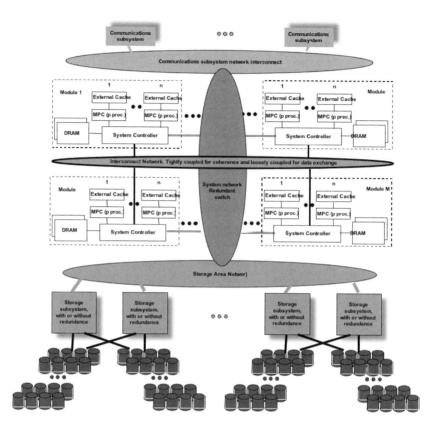

domain, the interconnect provides tight coupling. Separate domains may or may not be loosely-coupled—that is, a number of domains may be loosely coupled to form a cluster, but will have no communication with domains outside that cluster. This form of clustering—of domains within the system—is *internal clustering*; domains can also be clustered with compute resources in an entirely different system (but one built from the same elements: processors, OS, and cluster software).

The configuration and reconfiguration flexibility of this system is directly related to the ability to dynamically specify domains.

The system has three I/O networks:

- A system network, to which each module is connected (the connection can be redundant to provide high availability). The system network itself is generally redundant. Infiniband is a network aimed at this use.

■ A SAN-type storage network, connecting the storage subsystems to the system network. One of the objectives of Infiniband is to replace the Fibre Channel interconnects in use for this application. Redundancy is provided at several levels in the SAN.

■ A network to communicate with the communications subsystems. The split between this network and the SAN is purely functional - there is no reason, if the SAN latency is good enough, not to use the SAN technology for this interconnect too; or even—if bandwidth allows it—to share a single network for storage and communications.

The SAN network and the communications network can obviously be shared with other systems (whether of the same type or not). The interface with peripheral storage systems is of the "intelligent I/O" type, such as Infiniband.

Each domain runs under the control of an operating system. Within a cluster, each domain runs under the control of its own copy of the OS and identical clustering software.

Continuity of service relies upon the clustering capability of the system. For transactional applications, the correct resumption of the DBMS relies on journalizing mechanisms. In recovery, applications and the DBMS are launched using appropriate scripts. It is important to automate, as much as possible, all recovery actions since the probability of human error by operators is particularly high in anomalous situations.

It is possible to implement the top two layers (application and data) of the client/server model on this system, with the DBMS running on a cluster, and applications running on appropriately-sized SMP domains.

While we will not delve further, we should mention the importance of the operating system and of system administration: the latter must hide the underlying system complexity from the users.

12.7 Data Storage

In our discussion of storage in Chapter 6, we stressed the constantly-growing importance of this aspect of server systems. Already, according to industry analysts, the majority of expenditure on information processing systems (at least for business systems) is devoted to storage.

Key areas for future attention are: latency reduction, bandwidth increase, generalizing sharing solutions (with the SAN being the first step, albeit only at the physical level), improvements in file system performance (e.g., via the use of log-structured file systems), and improvements in backup and restore techniques.

Given the ever-increasing gap between semiconductor performance and disk performance, the performance of storage subsystems will remain a critical problem. This will open the way to almost *any* solution that can fill the gap.

12.8 Virtualization

The concept of virtualization is encountered over and over again within both architectures in general and specific solutions. This concept first became widespread in the latter half of the 60s, with virtual memory and virtual machines (first introduced by IBM with the 360/67 and then generalized with the 370 range at the beginning of the 70s).

As we discussed in Chapter 3, the concept of virtual memory frees the programmer from the constraints of physical memory capacity, while the virtual machine concept gave several users or groups of users the illusion that they had a dedicated machine, despite the fact that they were sharing a single real machine with others. At the time, the goal of the virtual machine concept was primarily economic, since it made it possible to multiplex a single expensive resource—the computer system—between several groups.

Technology has moved on, and because of changes like the increases in DRAM capacity and magnetic disk capacity in network bandwidths and latencies, it is now necessary to abstract software from the physical characteristics of storage hardware. Had this not been done, the unit of disk storage would still be the physical volume; then, for example, using a RAID 5 would set the smallest allocatable unit to be N times the size of a single disk.

The various virtualization levels that have been introduced—abstracting from the users the characteristics of the underlying processors, disks and so on—still have an economic goal, but one different from the economics behind the original virtual machine. No longer is the goal to share an expensive resource transparently, but to provide applications with an extended life without any need of modification, despite massive technological changes occurring in the platform. As examples:

- Virtual machines allow the continued use of collections of existing applications running under the control of different operating systems on a new platform. Available processing power makes it straightforward to support several systems simultaneously (as does IBM's VM), each completely isolated from the others—if one virtual machine fails, the others are unaffected.

- Localization independence is also a form of virtualization; clustered or distributed file systems (such as DFS) and the concept of a URL or of Directory Services allow an application to continue unmodified, even when the resources they need to access change or move.

- Java's JVM (Java Virtual Machine) technology and the use of XML can provide independence respectively from the details of execution and data representation.

- Along these lines, it is reasonable to look upon interpretive techniques in general as forms of virtualization.

And, in closing, we should note that to the extent that technology changes drive the need to virtualize, they also—through the increased capacity, performance, and cost reductions they bring—provide the means to do so.

12.9   Part 2: Final Word

In this book we have looked at the technologies are used in servers, how servers have evolved over time, how their uses have changed, and the impact of all of this on the architecture of servers. In this chapter, we revisit the question of how servers are used and what future changes might be, and will look at possible consequences.

First, a few comments and conclusions on servers in general.

The reliance of business and government operations on data processing continues to grow. The constant search for cost reduction, both in manufacturing (for example, just-in-time or JIT manufacturing) and in information management (for example, the introduction of workflow techniques), has been a major driver in the spread of information processing. More recently, to cost reduction has been added the need for greater reactivity.

The need to couple business activities with information systems multiplies the number of objects allowing user interaction, that is, all the devices used to capture or interrogate data. This multiplication is made possible by technological progress (particularly in software) and by the economies of scale.

Gordon Bell has proposed a price-based classification of data-processing products. He identifies seven classes:

- $10 for a system offering some integrated digital functionality; a digital watch is an example

- $100 for a hand-held computer, with personal organizers being prime examples

- $1,000 for a portable computer

- $10,000 for a workstation-class personal computer

- $100,000 for a departmental server

- $1,000,000 for a super-server, serving a complete establishment or business site

- $10,000,000 for an extremely large computer serving a complete region.

The quantities of devices deployed varies as the inverse of their price.

We would add to this computation-centric list a second type of device—the *Information Appliance*, which allows access to data stored on servers (using a network interconnect). Such devices will likely exist in very large numbers and will strongly influence data-processing infrastructure. The very number of such devices makes it essential that their management be extremely simple, and that they have extremely high availability and robustness (since they will be in the hands of the general public, which—by definition—has received no specialist training).

Such devices can be characterized by the phrase "plug and forget." From a technical point of view, this means that such devices will have means for configuration and update that require no human intervention.[3]

Ignoring devices providing a substitutional technology, Bell further claims that there are two distinct rationales for product evolution:

- Reducing price while keeping performance constant
- Increasing performance while keeping price constant

The two rationales can both be active simultaneously. As an example, in the first phase of a product's life, one may seek to attract customers by lowering price while keeping the performance more or less the same. Once the product has grown to have a respectable market share, one moves into the second phase, which involves improving performance while keeping price more or less the same. This dichotomy is somewhat unrealistic; in the real world, both effects can often be seen simultaneously rather than sequentially.

We will move on to discuss the field of **data storage**.

As we have seen earlier, data storage is a key area for servers, dominating the information system budget.

The key trends are the combination of the effects of the continual cost reduction of storage (in dollars per gigabyte) and the increasing availability of digital content: more and more information is now available in digital form, either naturally (word-processing and spreadsheet files; HTML/XML format files), or digitized through a process of scanning and OCR operations to provide text documents. A simple calculation shows that it is cheaper to keep information in some digital form (disk, tape or (for immutable data) CD-ROM or DVD-ROM), in terms of the number of square feet of office space need to store the data. The business gain offered by this cost reduction is further enhanced by the productivity improvement arising from the data being online and therefore searchable and indexable (as opposed to the older human-centric methods involving physical visits to libraries or filing cabinets).

This brings us to some predictions made by Jim Gray [GRA98]:

- All the information you need to have access to will be found in an online database (whose physical location is unimportant).

- You will be able to record everything you read, hear and see.[4]

- Recording everything you read is about 10 MB per day, for a total of 274 GB if you read at that rate for 75 years. Today, this is just six high-end helical-recording tapes, at a cost of around $360, or one consumer hard disk, at less than $250 retail.

- Recording everything you hear amounts to about 400 MB per day, for a total of 13 TB over your lifetime of 90 years (three of those high-end tapes per year, or a fraction of that disk)

- Recording everything you see is about a megabyte per second, for 86.4 GB per day and 32 TB a year

- Actually implementing technology that does all these things implies that there will be good-enough solutions in the areas of storage management and information organization, and that there will be tools for searching and analyzing the data. This, of course, is exactly what traditional databases have done, albeit only for structured information

- What is at stake is the creation of a new generation of database management able to handle unstructured data—text, sound, images. Such new databases will make strong demands on processing power and I/O capacity.

It should be apparent that if the prophecies are true, even if only in part, there are sunny days ahead indeed for the server market.

A second key issue for servers is **software**, whose constantly growing complexity must be hidden from users and system administrators with the dual goals of improving user productivity and reactivity and reducing the total cost of ownership of the systems.

As we have seen in Chapter 3 when discussing software perspectives, there are no miracle cures available.

As soon as the importance of software development sank in, the profession has been researching techniques to (better) control the situation. While the results often had substantive merit, the claims made for the techniques were vastly greater, and in any case any gains from better techniques seemed to be drowned almost immediately by an even greater growth in software complexity.

It seems unlikely that software development will become a simple matter any time soon. Continued research into all the techniques and methodologies which might help must be maintained.

With regard to **servers** themselves, more changes are in store. The internet explosion, with its associated new use patterns (such as electronic trade), will increase the demand for servers that are simple to install and operate, since in many cases they will be sold to companies with little experience in traditional data processing. Such companies will likely start by buying entry-level SMP systems, with two-, four- or eight-processor capabilities. Such systems will become as much commodity items as mainstream PCs are today.

Server architectures will face change due to a number of trends:

- The commoditization of smaller SMP systems, and the growth in the number of processors supported in such systems

- The trend to server consolidation

- The movement to consolidate storage in shared specialized sub-systems

- The integration of voice and data

- The needs of scalability

- And more

We will take a closer look at these trends.

As we have seen, the combination of improving technology and the desire for systems manufacturers to concentrate on areas of added value leads to **the commoditization of SMP architectures**. This trend is also driven by the call for increased processing power from users, resulting in SMP workstations. The number of processors supported by these systems tends to grow over the years, helped by technology and user demand. Thus, we expect that the high point of these systems—eight processors, today—will evolve towards a 16-processor configuration a few years from now, not least through the use of chips each containing multiple processors. This commoditization has an impact on server vendors, with only the large volume of these systems allowing the vendors to remain players in the entry-level and mid-range arenas.

Server consolidation is a current trend allowing cost reduction through reduction in square footage needed; simplified administration; lower-cost operation, since all system changes occur on one site; the opportunity for higher availability and load-sharing when an installation is mostly populated with a homogeneous selection of systems; lower-cost and simpler physical security; and more.

The effect on server architecture is straightforward—it favors rackmount packaging, simplified cluster installation and simplicity of use of the administration software.

Storage consolidation is an emerging trend; it provides an answer to the increasing percentage of costs for storage solutions, most notably through the SAN (Storage Area Network) concept. As we have seen, compared to the prior practices of having each server own its own storage, this approach simplifies the administration of the storage (letting it be done globally) and also allows optimization of the space needed for storage.

The effect on server architecture is that new low-cost, high-bandwidth I/O interfaces will become prevalent, and new server packaging is likely, since storage will be separate and shared.

Integration of voice and data will have repercussions beyond direct impact on networks, affecting applications as well. Call centers (CTI, or *Computer/Telephone Integration*) constitute a first stage of these effects. For servers, there will be pressure to provide increased functional integration between computation and communication.

As to **scalability**, designers of mid-range to high-end servers face the following alternatives:

- Develop a high-end SMP server, which requires development of custom components

- Integrate a number of nodes that leverage commodity technologies to form a cluster or MPP (depending on the nature of the interconnect)

- Or even adopt grid computing

Although it is true that there has been progress in the scalability of clusters and SMP for database applications (as we saw in Chapter 7), the SMP remains the most efficient processing solution up to the limits of its configuration. When this efficiency is coupled with a notion of price/performance, the economies of scale of commoditized SMPs and the costs and time-to-market issues involved in the design of new high-end SMPs that require custom components could well lead to a change in the situation.

12.10 Endnotes

1. We should note than any architecture implementing a cache is effectively non-deterministic (technically, it is deterministic, but the behavior is sufficiently complex that considering it to be non-deterministic is a sensible approach).

2. The efficiency of a system can be expressed as the ratio of the work actually done by an application to the inherent capability of the system (expressed as the product of the number of processors and the computational power of each processor).

3. As example, Bluetooth wireless connectivity to local semi-intelligent nodes, coupled with a version of Apple's "Rendezvous" technology (aka ZeroConfig).

4. The calculations in this section do not take account of the effects of compression, which generally provides substantial reduction in needed storage for audio and video. We should also note that not everything should be recorded; it should not be necessary to provide examples.

Bibliography

[ADV96]   Sarita V. Adve, Kourosh Gharachorloo. "Shared Memory Consistency Models: A Tutorial." IEEE Computer, Vol. 29, N° 12, December 1996, pp. 66-76.

[ARL96]   Martin F Arlitt, Carrey L Williamson. "Web Server Workload Characterization : The Search for Invariants." Department of Computer Science, University of Saskatchewan, March 1996

[ART01]   The Art of Lossless Data Compression
            http://www.geocities.com/eri21/texts22.html

[BED01]   T. Bedford, R. Cooke. "Probabilistic Risk Analysis: Foundations and Methods." Cambridge University Press, 2001

[BER97]   Philip A. Bernstein, Eric Newcomer. Transaction Processing. Morgan Kaufmann, San Mateo, 1997.

[BER98]   T. Berg, W Kirwin, B Redman. "Managing Distributed Computing (MDC)." Gartner Group, October 12, 1998.

[BMC01]   BMC Software. "The Case for Host Processor Compression." White Paper, www.bmc.com, February 2001.

[BOS03]   William Boswell. "Inside Windows Server 2003."
            Addison-Wesley Publishing. April 14, 2003 (second edition).

[BUL99]   Bull. "Le stockage d'entreprise à l'ère du réseau."
            Livre blanc Bull, available on www.bull.com, 1999.

[BUZ76]   J.P. Buzen. "Fundamental Laws of Computer System Perfor-
            mance." Proc. SIGMETRICS'76, Cambridge, MA, pp200-
            210.

[CAR00]   Jeffrey Carter, et al. "DAFS-Enabling Data Center Applica-
            tions."White Paper, www.dafscollaborative.org, December
            2000.

[CAR03]   CART Project from the Texas University at Austin
            www.cs.utexas.edu/users/cart

[CAP98]   Franck Cappello, Olivier Richard. "Architectures parallèles à
            partir de réseaux de stations de travail: réalités, opportunités et
            enjeux." Calculateurs parallèles, réseaux et systèmes répartis,
            Vol. 10, N° 1, February 1998, pp. 9-34.

[CAP02]   Franck Cappello, et al. "Calcul Global et Pair à Pair."
            www.lri.fr

[CHE94]   Peter M. Chen, et al. "RAID: High-Performance, Reliable Sec-
            ondary Storage." ACM Computing Surveys, Vol. 26, N° 2,
            June 1994.

[CHU97]   P.E. Chung, et al. "DCOM and CORBA Side by Side, Step by
            Step and Layer by Layer."
            www.research.microsoft.com/~ymwang/papers

[COM97]   Special Issue of IEEE Computer devoted to future processors. IEEE Computer, September 1997.

[CRI91]   Flaviu Cristian. "Understanding Fault Tolerant Distributed Systems." CACM, Vol. 34, N° 2, February 1991, pp. 56-78.

[CUL97]   D. E. Culler, et al. "Parallel Computing on the Berkeley NOW." Proceedings of Join Symposium on Parallel Processing, JSPP'97, 1997.

[CUP99]   Vinodh Cuppu, et al. "A Performance Comparison of Contemporary DRAM Architectures." Proceedings of the 26th International Symposium on Computer Architecture, May 2-4 1999, Atlanta, GA.

[CUL98]   David Culler, J.P. Singh, Anoop Gupta. "Parallel Computer Architecture: A Hardware/Software Approach." Morgan Kaufmann, August 1998

[CZE00]   Christian Czezatke, M. Anton Ertl. "LinLog FS – A Log-Structured Filesystem for Linux." Usenix 2000 Freenix Track, pp. 77-88.

[DEN78]   P.J. Denning, J.P. Buzen. "The Operational Analysis of Queuing Network Analysis." ACM Computing Surveys, Vol. 10, N° 3, September 1978, pp 225-261.

[DEW92]   David DeWitt, Jim Gray. "Parallel Data Base Systems: The Future of High Performance Data Base Systems." CACM, Vol. 35, N° 6, June 1992, pp. 85-98.

[DUL98]   Carole Dulong. "The IA-64 Architecture at Work." IEEE Computer, July 1998, pp. 24-32.

[DUN02]   William R. Dunn. "Practical Design of Safety-Critical Systems." Reliability Press, 2002.

[DYA00]   GIE DYADE (Bull/INRIA) http://www.dyade.fr

[EDW99]   Jeri Edwards. "3-Tier Client/Server At Work." John Wiley, 1999.

[ESG02]   Enterprise Storage Group. "Reference Information: The Next Wave—The Summary of: A "Snapshot" Research Study by The Enterprise Storage Group." www.enterprisestoragcgroup.com

[FLY72]   Michael Flynn. "Some Computer Organization, their Effectiveness." IEEE Transactions on Computers, Vol. 21, N° 9, September 1972.

[FOS03]   Ian Foster (Ed.), Carl Kesselman (Ed.). "The Grid 2—Blue Print for a New Computing Infrastructure." 2nd Edition, Morgan Kaufmann, Publisher, December 2003.

[GAL97]   Mike Galles. "Spider: A High Speed Network Interconnect." IEEE Micro, January/February 1997, pp. 34-39.

[GEP03]   Linda Geppert. "The New Indelible Memories." IEEE Spectrum, March 2003, pp. 49-54.

[GIL97]   Richard Gillet, Richard Kaufmann. "Using the Memory Channel Network." IEEE Micro, January/February 1997, pp. 19-25.

[GOB98]   W. Goble. "Control Systems Safety Evaluation and Reliability." ISA, 1998.

[GOT02]   K. Gottschalk, S. Graham, H Kreger, J Snell. "Introduction to Web Services Architecture." IBM Systems Journal, Vol.41, No. 2, 2002, pp. 170-177.

[GRA85]   Jim Gray. "Why do computers stop and what can be done about it?" Tandem TR85.7, June 1985. Also published in Proceedings 5th Symposium on Reliablility in Distributed Software and Database Systems." Los Angeles, January 1986, pp. 3-12.

[GRA90]   Jim Gray. "A Census of Tandem System Availability Between 1985 and 1990." IEEE Transaction on Reliability. Vol 39., No 4., October 1990, pp. 409-418.

[GRA91]   Jim Gray, Daniel Siewiorek. "High Availability Computer Systems." IEEE Computer, Vol. 24, N° 9, September 1991, pp. 39-48.

[GRA92]   Jim Gray, Andreas Reuter. "Transaction Processing: Concepts, Techniques." Morgan Kaufmann, San Mateo, 1992.

[GRA96]   Jim Gray, Andreas Reuter. "Dependable Computing Systems." http://research.microsoft.com/~Gray/WICS_96_TP.

[GRA98]   Jim Gray. "The Laws of Cyber Space." http://research.microsoft.com/~Gray.

[GRA00]   Jim Gray, Prashant Shenoy. "Rules of Thumb in Data Engineering." IEEE International Conference on Data Engineering San Diego, April 2000

[GRA03]   Jim Gray. "Distributed Computing Economics." Microsoft Research Technical Report, MSR-TR-2003-24, March 2003.

[HAM02]   Tom Hammond-Doel. "Changing from shared bandwidth to SBOD." Storage Networking World Online, www.snwonline.com, April 29th, 2002.

[HEG01]   Dominique Heger, Gautam Shah. "General Parallel File System (GPFS) 1.4 for AIX—Architecture and Performance." www.ibm.com

[HEN02]   John L. Hennessy, David A. Patterson. "Computer Architecture: A Quantitative Approach." Morgan Kaufmann, San Mateo, May 2002 (third edition).

[HAN98]   Jim Handy. "The Cache Memory Book" Morgan Kaufmann, January 1998 (second edition).

[HEN99]   John L. Hennessy. "The Future of Systems Research." Computer, Vol. 32, N° 8, August 1999, pp. 27-33.

[HEN00]   John L Henning. "SPEC CPU2000: Measuring CPU Performance in the New Millenium." IEEE Computer, July 2000, pp. 28-35.

[HIT00]   Dave Hitz. "A Storage Networking Appliance." TR3001, www.netapp.com, updated by Michael Marchi, October 2000.

[HOO97]   Raymond J. Hookway, Mark A. Herdeg. "Digital FX!32: Combining Emulation, Binary Translation." Digital Technical Journal, Vol. 9, N° 1, 1997.

[HOP87]   M. Hopkins. "A Perspective on the 801/Reduced Instruction Set Computer." IBM Systems Journal, Vol. 26, N° 1, 1987, pp. 107-121.

[IBM00]   IBM. "z/Architecture Principles of Operation." IBM SA22-7832

[IBM01]   IBM. "Web Services Conceptual Architecture (WSCA 1.0)." White Paper, www.ibm.com/software/solutions/webservices/documentation.html.

[IBM02]   Double issue of IBM Journal of Research and Development, devoted to IBM eServer z900 Vol. 46, N°s 4/5, 2002.

[IBM03]   IBM Report. "IBM eserver pSeries SP Switch and SP Switch2 Performance." www.ibm.com, February 2003.

[IEE98]   Special Issue of the IEEE Computer dedicated to COTS. IEEE Computer, June 1998.

[ITR03]   International Roadmap for Semiconductor 2003 update. http://public.itrs.net.

[JAC02]   Bruce Jacob, David Wang. "DRAM, Architectures, Interfaces, and Systems—A Tutorial." ISCA 2002, www.ee.umd.edu/~blj/talks/DRAM-Tutorial-isca2002-2.pdf

[JAI91]   Raj Jain. The Art of Computer Systems Performance Analysis. John Wiley & Sons, 1991.

[JAY]   Jay. "Compression Tutorial." www.emulationzone.org/sections/wakdhacks/docs/compress-doc.doc.

[JOH96]   James E. Johnson, William A. Laing. "Overview of the Spiralog File System." Digital Technical Journal, Vol. 8, N° 2, 1996, pp. 5-14.

[JOU89]   Norman P. Jouppi, D. W. Wall. "Available Instruction-Level
            Parallelism for Superscalar, Superpipelined Machines." ACM
            Proceedings, ASPLOS III, Boston, April 3-6, 1989, pp. 272-
            282.

[KEE98]   Kimberley Keeton, David A. Patterson, Joseph M. Hellerstein.
            "A Case for Intelligent Disks (IDISKs)."
            ACM SIGMOD record, Vol. 27, N° 3, August 1998.

[KER99]   Georges Kéryvel (Bull) Private communication

[KLE00]   Steve Kleiman, Jeffrey Katcher "An Introduction to the Direct
            Access File System" White Paper,
            www.dafscollaborative.org, July 20, 2000.

[KOZ97]   Christoforos E. Kozyrakis et al. "Scalable Processors in the Bil-
            lion-Transistor Era: IRAM." IEEE Computer, September
            1997, pp. 75-78.

[KOZ98]   Christoforos E. Kozyrakis, David A Patterson. "A New Direc-
            tion for Computer Architecture Research." IEEE Computer,
            November 1998, pp. 24-32.

[KRO86]   Nancy P. Kronenberg, Henry M. Levy, William D. Strecker.
            "Vaxclusters: A Closely-Coupled Distributed System." ACM
            Transactions on Computer Systems, Vol. 4, N° 2, May 1986.

[LAP90]   Jean-Claude Laprie. "Dependability: Basic Concepts, Associ-
            ated Terminology." Rapport LAAS, N° 90.055, www.laas.fr,
            Toulouse, 1990.

[LEL]   Debra A. Lelewer, Daniel S. Hirschberg. "Data Compression."
            www.ics.uci.edu./~dan/pubs/DataCompression.html.

[LEN95]   Daniel E. Lenoski, Wolf-Dietrich Weber. Scalable Shared-Memory Multiprocessing.
Morgan Kaufmann, San Mateo, 1995.

[LOO97]   Chris Loosey, Frank Douglas, "High Performance Client/Server." John Wiley & Sons, 1997

[LYM03]   Peter Lyman and Hal R.Varian. "How Much Information 2003." Retrieved from www.sims.berkeley.edu/how-much-info-2003 on June 2004.

[MAT97]   Jeanna Neefe, Matthews, et al. "Improving the Performance of Log-Structured File Systems with Adaptive Methods." Proceedings 16th Symposium on Operating System Principles (SOSP'97), pp. 238-251.

[MAY98]   Franck May. "SP Switch Performance."
White Paper, www.ibm.com, June 1998.

[MCK99]   Nick McKeown. "An Overview of Techniques for Network Interface Design." Course EE384c, High Performance Network Systems, Stanford University, www.cs.stanford.edu.

[MIC03]   Microsoft. "Server Clusters : Architecture Overview For Windows Server 2003."
www.microsoft.com, March 2003.

[MEI98]   Jean-Pierre Meinadier. Ingénierie et intégration des systèmes. Hermès, 1998.

[MEI99]   Jean-Pierre Meinadier. "Cours d'intégration des systèmes client-serveur."
CNAM, 1998-1999.

[MEN00]   Daniel A Menascé, et al. "In Search of Invariants for E-Business Workloads." Proc. Second ACM Conference on Electronic Commerce, Minneapolis MN, October 17-20, 2000.

[MEN02]   Daniel A Menascé, Virgilio A.F. Almeida. "Capacity Planning for Web Services—Metrics, Models, and Methods." Prentice Hall PTR, 2002.

[MET00]   Meta Group. "IT Performance Engineering & Measurement Strategies: Quantifying Performance Loss."
Meta Group, October 2000.

[MOH94]   C. Mohan, H. Pirahesh, W. G. Tang, Y. Wang. "Parallelism in Relational Database Management Systems."
IBM Systems Journal, Vol. 33, N° 2, 1994, pp. 349-371.

[MOO99]   Fred Moore. Storage Panorama 2000.
StorageTech, www.storagetech.com.

[MUE99]   M. Mueller, L.C. Alves, W. Fischer, M.L. Fair, and I. Modi. "RAS Strategy for IBM S/390 G5 and G6."
IBM Journal of Research and Development 43, No. 5/6, 1999, pp. 661-670.

[NAR98]   Bonnie A. Nardi, James R. Miller, David J. Wright. "Collaborative, Programmable Intelligent Agents." CACM, Vol. 41, N° 3., March 1998, pp. 96-104.

[NAS02]   NASA. "NASA Software Safety Guidebook." Draft of a NASA Technical Standard,
www.hq.nasa.gov/office/codeq/doctree/871913.htm, February 2002.

[NIV00]   Bernard Nivelet (Bull)
Private communication

[NT00]   Issues of Windows 2000 Magazine.
           www.ntmag.com/Articles.

[NRC81]   US Nuclear Regulatory Commission. "Fault Tree Handbook."
           www.nrc.gov/reading-rm/doc-collections/nuregs/staff/sr0492/
           sr0492.pdf, 1981.

[OCT99]   OCTO Technology. "Le livre blanc de l'EAI—Intégration des
           applications d'entreprise."
           www.octo.fr.

[ORA02a]   Oracle. "Database Architecture: Federated vs. Clustered."
           White Paper, www.oracle.com, March 2002.

[ORA02b]   Oracle. "Technical Comparison of Oracle 9i RAC vs. IBM
           UDB EEE V7.2."
           White Paper, www.oracle.com, November 2002

[ORF99]   Robert Orfali, Dan Harkey, Jeri Edwards. Client/Server Sur-
           vival Guide.
           John Wiley & Sons, 1999 (third edition).

[ORG72]   Elliot I Organick. "The Multics System—An Examination of
           Its Structure."
           The MIT Press, 1972.

[OUS89]   John Ousterhout, Fred Douglis. "Beating the I/O Bottleneck :
           A Case for Log-Structured File Systems."
           ACM SIGOPS, January 23, 1989.

[PAI98]   Jean-Jacques Pairault (Bull)
           Private Communication

[PAP98]   Jean Papadopoulo (Bull)
            Private Communication

[PAT97]   David A. Patterson. "A Case for Intelligent RAM."
            IEEE Micro, March/April 1997.

[PAT04]   David A. Patterson, John L. Hennessy. Computer Organiza-
            tion & Design: The Hardware/Software Interface.
            Morgan Kaufmann, San Mateo, 2004 (third edition).

[PFI95]   Gregory F. Pfister. In Search of Clusters The Coming Battle in
            Lowly Parallel Computing.
            Prentice Hall PTR, New Jersey, 1995.

[PIT98]   James E. Pitkow. "Summary of WWW Characterizations."
            www.parc.xerox.com, Xerox Palo Alto Research Center, 1998

[PPC94]   IBM Microelectronics, Motorola. "Power PC Microprocessor
            Family: The Programming Environments."
            Motorola, 1994.

[PUJ99]   Guy Pujolle. Les Réseaux.
            Eyrolles, 1999.

[QUA03]   Qualstar 2003. "New Tape Technologies Offer More Data on
            Less Tape."
            White Paper, www.qualstar.com.

[ROS92]   Mendel Rosenblum, John K. Ousterhout. "The design and
            implementation of a log-structured file system."
            ACM Transactions on Computer Systems (TOCS), Vol. 10,
            Issue 1, February 1992.

[RUD98]   Ken Rudin. "When Parallel Lines Meet."
            Byte, May 1998, pp. 81-88.

[RUS00]   Mark E. Russinovich, David A. Solomon. Inside Microsoft
            Windows 2000.
            Microsoft Press, September 16, 2000 (third edition).

[SAY00]   Khalid Sayood. "Introduction to Data Compression."
            Morgan Kaufmann, San Mateo, 2000 (second edition).

[SHR99]   Bruce Shriver, Peter Capek. "Just Curious: An Interview with
            John Cocke."
            IEEE Computer, November 1999, pp. 34-41.

[SIE92]   Daniel P. Siewiorek, Robert S. Swarz. Reliable Computer Sys-
            tems—Design and Evaluation.
            Digital Press, 1992 (second edition).

[SIL01]   Abraham Silberchatz, Peter Baer Galvin, Greg Gagne. Operat-
            ing System Concepts.
            John Wiley & Sons, June 26, 2001 (sixth edition).

[SIT92]   Richard L. Sites et al. "Binary Translation."
            Digital Technical Journal, Vol. 4, N° 4, Special Issue, 1992.

[SLE99]   Timothy J. Slegel, et al. "IBM's S/390 G5 Microprocessor
            Design."
            IEEE Micro, March-April 1999, pp. 12-23.

[SOL95]   Franck G. Soltis. "Inside the AS/400: An In-depth Look at the
            AS/400's Design, Architecture and History."
            Duke Press, 1995.

[SNI96]   M. Snir, S. Otto, Walter D. Hess-Lederman, J. Dongarra. MPI:
          The Compete Reference.
          MIT Press, Cambridge Mass., 1996.

[SNI01]   SNIA. "Shared Storage Model: A framework for describing
          storage architectures."
          Storage Networking Industry Association
          Draft, SNIA Technical Council Proposal, 2001.

[SWE02]   Mark Sweiger. "Scalable Computer Architectures for Data
          Warehousing."
          www.clickstreamconsulting.com.

[TAL95]   Jacques Talbot. "Turning the AIX Operating System into a
          Multiprocessing Capable OS."
          USENIX 1995 Technical Conference Proceedings, New
          Orleans, Louisiana, January 16-20, 1995.

[THO74]   Ken Thompson, Dennis M. Ritchie, «The UNIX Time-Shar-
          ing System», Communications of the ACM, Vol. 17, N° 7, July
          1974, pp. 365-375.

[UNW93]   Michael Uwalla. "A Mixed Transaction Cost Model for Coarse
          Grained Multi-column Partitionning in a Share-nothing Data-
          base Machine." Ph.D. Dissertation, www.syol.com/~munw,
          University of Sheffield, Department of Computer Science, July
          1993.

[VER00]   VERITAS. "RAID for Enterprise Computing." White Paper,
          www.veritas.com, 2000.

[VER01]   VERITAS. "Storage Virtualization."
          White Paper, www.veritas.com, 2001.

[WER99]   Ben Werther. "Distributed Systems Security."
            Computer Science course CS244B, Spring 1999.

[WHI96]   Christopher Whitaker, J. Stuart Bayley, Rod D. W. Widdow-
            son. "Design of the Server for the Spiralog File System."
            Digital Technical Journal, Vol. 8 N° 2, 1996, pp. 15-31.

[ZAM99]   Paul Zamansky (Bull)
            Private Communication

Index